THE MENTALLY DISORDERED INMATE AND THE LAW

By
Fred Cohen, LL.B., LL.M.

Civic Research Institute
4490 U.S. Route 27 • P.O. Box 585 • Kingston, NJ 08528

Printed in the United States of America

Library of Congress Cataloging in Publication Data
The Mentally Disordered Inmate and the Law/Fred Cohen, LL.B., LL.M.

ISBN 1-887554-06-8

Library of Congress Catalog Card Number 98-72903

Publisher's Foreword

HOW TO USE THIS BOOK

This book addresses the legal issues that affect the mentally disordered inmate. Chapters 1 and 2 set out the boundaries of the problem and an overview of the legal issues generally. Chapter 3 provides a broad review of the law of prisoners' rights. Subsequent chapters address in greater detail specific legal holdings and problems in this area, providing extensive citations to leading cases and specific guidance on the legal obligations and duties of those who supervise or treat mentally disordered inmates, the rights of the incarcerated mentally ill, and the best policies and practices. The text provides specific examples from case law and consent decrees that put into clear operational context the issues discussed.

There are several ways to find the specific guidance you need. Both a summary and a detailed table of contents immediately follow the Preface, to give the reader a broad overview of the scope of the book, and help to locate general areas of particular interest. Each chapter also begins with a detailed synopsis, to help pinpoint where a given concept is discussed. Chapter subheadings are numbered to enable easy cross-referencing, and both text paragraphs and appendixes are cross-referenced wherever this will help readers access related discussion elsewhere in the book.

In addition, the Table of Cases, which follows the appendixes, points readers to commentary relating to a particular case. For reference to a specific topic, use the subject index, which follows the case table. These "finding aids" are keyed to chapter paragraph numbers (and, where relevant, footnote numbers). To aid in locating the referenced text, the first (for left-hand pages) or last (for right-hand pages) numbered paragraph included on the page is noted at the top outside corner of the page.

The Mentally Disordered Inmate and the Law will be supplemented periodically, to keep you current in this constantly evolving area of the law, corrections management, and treatment of those with mental disorders. Supplements, which will be keyed to main volume chapters and paragraph numbers, will reflect all significant changes in the law and how it affects institutional practice in this area, as well as references to new studies and important new literature.

ABOUT THE AUTHOR

Fred Cohen, LL.B., LL.M., is one of America's foremost experts on correctional law and is generally recognized as the leading scholar and practitioner in the area of correctional mental health care law. He has published, lectured, and consulted widely, and is currently the federal court monitor for prison mental health in Ohio and chairman of the American Correctional Association's Mental Health Committee. He is Co-Editor of *Correctional Law Reporter* and author of "Legal Issues in the Treatment of Sex Offenders," eight chapters in *The Sex Offender: Corrections, Treatment and Legal Practice* (Civic Research Institute, 1995) and numerous articles on criminal procedure and mental health topics.

Preface

Sometime in early 1984 Donald McDonald, a former student of mine and then heading up the research unit within the New York State Department of Corrections, called me about a research initiative. He was seeking funding from the National Institute of Corrections (NIC) for some sort of study of mentally disordered prisoners. Would I lend my name to the proposal and, if successful, do a brief section on the legal issues involved?

The project was to be primarily concerned with a national survey of departments of corrections and mental health to determine their procedures for identifying and treating mentally disordered prisoners. Legal issues would be adjunctive at best.

My first surprise came months later when Donald told me that NIC had funded the project—and that now I actually would have to do something. My second surprise came when I did a self-inventory and discovered how little I knew about the topic. Ah, the stuff of expertise!

Shortly after the project was funded, I noted that NIC was holding a seminar in Boulder on the mentally disordered prisoner with a slot reserved for legal issues. Time was short and I called John Moore of NIC and asked if I might be allowed to attend. Those who know John will acknowledge his courtliness and tenacity. John quickly agreed to my request and immediately followed with, "Ah, Fred, would you be good enough to be our presenter on legal issues?" Ah, the stuff of expertise.

I accepted and began to furiously research the topic. I suppose I made an acceptable presentation, since John saw to it that I was similarly invited on numerous occasions. And now, an expert is truly born.

In 1985, NIC published *The Sourcebook on the Mentally Disordered Prisoner*. The monograph was 145 pages long, including some pages of forms, and legal issues took up 90 of those pages. For a variety of reasons best left in the historical dust, the secondary topic had swallowed the primary topic, although the title *Sourcebook* hardly told the story.

The *Sourcebook* was an extremely popular NIC publication and a couple of years later John Moore funded me to do *Legal Issues and the Mentally Disordered Prisoner*. This 256-page monograph was published in 1988 and, according to John, became NIC's most requested publication. After several printings, with NIC then sending out photocopies of the text, I decided to do, in effect, a third edition. With John Moore's blessing I was able to take the project to Civic Research Institute, and that is what you will find between these hard covers.

So many people help with a project like this and especially in its several incarnations. I will not repeat the earlier acknowledgements. For this effort Paula M. Cook, an Arizona attorney, was extraordinarily helpful as my research assistant. Julie Sheehan, poor dear, word processed the entire manuscript and patiently guided me through several deadly viruses (i.e., computer-style) and bore the brunt of my impatience with, well, things—just things!

There are many people I have recently had the privilege of working with who in their own way have made huge, yet indirect, contributions to this book. They include Jane Haddad, Jeffrey Metzner, Greg Trout, Mike Perlin and David Wexler. In addition, there are dozens of people working in Ohio's Department of Rehabilitation and Correction from whom I constantly learn about how to make a correctional mental health delivery system work. They include Sharon Aungst and her staff, Dr. Kathy Burns, and so many others working their butts off in the field; the Paul Goodwins, Gary Mohrs, Mark Saunders, Tony Briganos and Betty Mitchells. Let me add that these names are also stand-ins for the hundreds of others ranging from C.O.'s to Reginald Wilkinson who make my work in Ohio as Court Monitor meaningful and productive.

Ohio attorneys Robert Newman and Al Gerhardstein, who represent the plaintiff class in *Dunn v. Voinovich*, of which you will learn a good deal, simply represent the best in the legal profession. I thank them for their support and wisdom.

Deborah Launer, Arthur Rosenfeld, and Mark Peel of CRI are the best. I thank them and hope the book warrants the confidence they have shown in this project.

Finally, to those inmates who are doing double time, enduring prison and the pain of mental illness, I dedicate this book. I have looked into your eyes and you into mine and we understood. If this work brings you some small measure of help and dignity I will feel rewarded.

Fred Cohen
Tucson, Arizona
January 15, 1998

Summary of Contents

Table of Contents

Chapter 1

Introduction: The Boundaries of the Problem

¶ 1.1 CONSTITUTIONAL RIGHT TO TREATMENT

This work is concerned with legal issues that affect the mentally disordered prison inmate. This seemingly straightforward, boundary-setting sentence, like the topic itself, is pregnant with definitional and conceptual problems that we must address, if not fully resolve, at the outset.

First, what is and is not a legal issue is in itself a complex and important question. Issues resolved in court are not the only ones that qualify as legal issues. The traditional legal problem may have important historic import, but many of the most troublesome legal problems are future-oriented. For example, this work will clearly demonstrate that prison inmates have a constitutional right to treatment, at least for serious mental illness.[1] This establishes the basic legal right often referred to as an *Estelle v. Gamble* claim, but now there is the problem of how far in the refinement of this right the issue maintains its legal identity. At what point are the unfolding issues more accurately described either as policy, clinical, or administrative issues?[2]

---

[1] *See generally* Estelle v. Gamble, 429 U.S. 97 (1976).

[2] There are, of course, other troublesome "jurisdictional" questions that arise independent of the establishment of a predicate, or basic, legal right. For the view that the judiciary has exceeded its proper role and capacity in dealing with social and clinical problems of the type discussed in this work, *see* DONALD L. HOROWITZ, THE COURTS AND SOCIAL POLICY (1977). For the view that judicial restraint is preferred philosophically but judicial intervention has had a net positive effect, *see* John J. DiIulio, Jr.,

The answers to these questions have a major impact on judicial power and institutional-professional autonomy. While it may be difficult to draw a bright line separating legal from non-legal issues, I will establish some reasonably clear answers in specific areas, including the right to treatment.

¶ 1.2 MENTAL DISORDER DEFINED

The term "mentally disordered" as discussed in this book encompasses any form of mental illness, whether it is considered a neurosis or psychosis or is viewed as organic or functional in origin.[3] I will note in the text where it seems important to make these or similar distinctions.

Mentally retarded inmates, who are developmentally disabled, are referred to as such and the reader should not generally consider them included in the term "mentally disordered." There are obvious differences between the mentally ill and the mentally retarded[4] as to the origin and nature of the condition and the appropriate treatment or habilitation program.

Even more fundamental than the semantic or definitional problems, however, is the conclusion reached here that the constitutional right to treatment arises from a medical model of disease or injury and that the right to treatment does not extend to inmates who are only mentally retarded. This is not to argue that the mentally retarded inmate is without a constitutional basis for claims of right, but only that the analysis, the right itself and the constitutional source are different than for the mentally ill.

¶ 1.3 CONSTITUTIONAL RIGHT VS. GOOD PRACTICE

The reader should be alerted early to the critical distinction between a constitutional claim or right and what may be desirable or good practice. We encounter claims to legally required minima in dealing with such matters as Eighth Amendment claims of cruel and unusual punishment, due process claims to certain procedural safeguards, First Amendment claims to preserve one's thinking and expressive powers or to resist certain treatments as violative of religious beliefs, and right to privacy claims said to be located in penumbras emanating from specific sections of the Constitution.

The claim to a constitutional right is the loftiest claim known to our legal system, while judicial recognition of the claim for inmates is often in the right's most diluted form. For example, a constitutional right to treatment might be fashioned as a right to

---

Conclusion: What Judges Can Do to Improve Prisons and Jails, in COURTS, CORRECTIONS, AND THE CONSTITUTION: THE IMPACT OF JUDICIAL INTERVENTION ON PRISONS AND JAILS (1990), pp. 287, 290.

[3] "Mentally disordered inmate" is often used as an umbrella term to include those found incompetent to be tried, not guilty by reason of insanity, or in a special offender category such as "sex psychopath" or "defective delinquent," or those transferred from prison to a mental health facility. *See* Eliot Hartstone, et al., *Vitek and Beyond: The Empirical Context of Prison-to-Hospital Transfers*, 45 LAW & CONTEMP. PROB's 125, 126 n.5, (1982). *See* Chapter 4 for an extended discussion of "serious medical needs."

[4] The term "treatment" typically is used for illness; "rehabilitation" refers to so-called normal prisoners or persons otherwise under correctional supervision; and the terms "habilitation" and "training" refer to programs for the mentally retarded.

the most thorough diagnosis and the most skillful treatment currently available for the particular condition. Mentally retarded inmates might be entitled to such habilitative efforts that will maximize their human potential. On the other hand, the right to treatment could be construed to require only that some medical or professional judgment be brought to bear first to identify and then to provide minimally acceptable care in order to avoid death or needless pain and suffering.

As the text will make clear, the constitutional right to treatment is much closer to the second construction than the first. The more important point here is that constitutional minima in this (or any other) area must not be confused with desirable governmental policy, desirable professional practices or standards, or desirable penal practices or standards.[5] This error is easily made and, at times, in the heat of advocacy for a certain outcome, plaintiffs will conflate the desired with the required.

Although this work will include numerous references to claims of federal constitutional rights, it must be established at the outset that the source of inmate claims and rights also may be located in the various state constitutions, state and federal statutes, administrative regulations or directives, and until recently, long-followed practices.[6]

¶ 1.4 AMERICANS WITH DISABILITIES ACT

Title II of the Americans With Disabilities Act (ADA), 42 U.S. Sections 12131–12165, and Section 504 of the Rehabilitation Act of 1973, 29 U.S.C. 794, are potential federal statutory sources for claims brought by inmates with mental disorders. To date, neither statute has had any discernible impact in this area.[7]

Title II of the ADA prohibits "public entities" from discriminating against disabled individuals: "[N]o qualified individual with a disability shall, by reason of such disability, be excluded from participation in or be denied the benefits of the services, programs, or activities of a public entity, or be subjected to discrimination by any such entity."[8] A "public entity" is broadly defined under the statute to be "any State or local government" and "any department, agency, special purpose district, or other instrumentality of a State or States or local government."[9] Similarly, the Rehabilitation Act prohibits discrimination against disabled individuals "under any program or activity receiving Federal financial assistance"[10] and defines "program or activity" to include

---

[5] The term "desirable," as an unflinching normative term, is not free from ambiguity and reasonable debate. In contrasting minimum requirements with desirable practices, what is clear is that the desirable will always exceed the minimum on whatever scale is used.

[6] *See* Alan Meisel, *The Rights of the Mentally Ill Under State Constitutions*, 45 LAW & CONTEMP. PROB'S 7, 9 (1982), for the view that state constitutional and statutory grounds may be more fruitful than federal grounds for development of patient's rights, in view of the Supreme Court's unwillingness to go very far or fast in this area. That projection, or hope, has not materialized. *See* Connecticut Bd. Pardons v. Dumschat, 452 U.S. 458 (1981), which gravely impairs the doctrine that practices long engaged in create liberty interests.

[7] *See* Ira P. Robbins, *George Bush's America Meets Dante's Inferno: The Americans With Disabilities Act in Prison*, 15 YALE L. & POL'Y REV. 49 (1996), which reviews possible claims by prisoners who are elderly, mentally disabled, HIV and AIDS infected, and hearing impaired.

[8] 42 U.S.C.A. § 12132 (West 1995).

[9] 42 U.S.C.A. § 12131 (1) (West 1995).

[10] 29 U.S.C.A. § 794 (a) (West Supp. 1997).

"all of the operations of . . . a department, agency, special purpose district, or other instrumentality of a State or of a local government."[11]

This, of course, is extremely broad statutory language and in the absence of specific legislative history, the courts have had to determine initially whether the ADA even applies to state prisoners. *Amos v. Maryland Dept. of Public Safety and Correctional Services*[12] is the leading decision holding that the ADA does not apply to state prisons. Amos is based on a rather esoteric approach to statutory interpretation—the clear statement rule—and on a thinly disguised policy position that disfavors inmate claims even in the face of legislative action.

The Third,[13] Seventh,[14] Ninth,[15] and Tenth[16] Circuits have held to the contrary, finding the ADA applicable to state prisoners.[17] At this writing, however, there simply is no *substantial* body of ADA-based case law descriptive or determinative of the rights of mentally disordered prisoners.[18]

Federal constitutional rights, then, should be seen as both the loftiest and most available claim to minimal rights, with other sources of federal and state law representing an additional and considerable body of specific "do's" and "don'ts" and rights and remedies.[19] Within the broad outline of constitutional requirements there are many acceptable variations on the same theme. Those variations are the stuff of local policy and practice. As often as possible, this work will attempt to distinguish minimal mandates from allowable and perhaps desirable policy and practice.

¶ 1.5 INMATES VS. THE NON-INCARCERATED MENTALLY ILL OFFENDER

Our central concern is with the person who is convicted of a crime, sentenced to prison for that crime, and subsequently identified as mentally disordered or mentally

---

[11] 29 U.S.C.A. § 794 (b)(1)(A). Congress has directed that Title II of the ADA be interpreted in a manner consistent with Section 504 of the Rehabilitation Act. *See* 42 U.S.C. §§ 12134(b), 12201(a) (West 1995).

[12] 126 F.3d 589 (4th Cir. 1997).

[13] Yeskey v. Pennsylvania Dept. of Corrections, 118 F.3d 168 (3d Cir. 1997).

[14] Crawford v. Indiana Dept. of Corrections, 115 F.3d 481 (7th Cir. 1997).

[15] Gates v. Rowland, 39 F.3d 1439 (9th Cir. 1994), while also holding that constitutional standards of interpretation apply, thus eviscerating the Act; *see also* Clark v. California, 123 F.3d 1267 (9th Cir. 1997).

[16] White v. Colorado, 82 F.3d 364 (10th Cir. 1996).

[17] In IX CORR. L. RPTR. 65–66 (1998), it was reported that California and Pennsylvania are seeking review in the Supreme Court as to whether the ADA applies to prisons. The author regards this as a question hanging heavily over the heads of prisons and prisoners.

[18] In Ohio, a consent decree borrows from the ADA and insists that no inmate be precluded from any activity or program without an individual determination. This opens, for example, boot camp enrollment, work in the kitchen, assignment to a minimum security camp, and so on. In Helen L. v. DiDavio, 46 F.3d 325 (3d Cir. 1995), the court held that a civilly committed patient had the right under the ADA not to be needlessly segregated, which easily translates into a right to treatment in the least restrictive environment. I hasten to add that the decision is limited to civil patients, although its spirit could reach in to the confines of prisons. In Raines v. Florida, 983 F. Supp. 1362 (N.D. Fla. 1997), the court determined that a gain time provision which, in effect, discriminated against mentally ill prisoners would likely violate the ADA. *Raines* has a full discussion of the leading decision on point.

[19] The reference to specific "do's" and "don'ts" is to statutory law other than the ADA, since we still await its possible application to mentally disordered prisoners.

retarded. We will refer more than occasionally to the pretrial detainee's and the unconvicted person's special claims to care.[20] The legal principles governing detainees, if not the source of legal claims, are virtually identical to those governing the convicted prisoner. Most important, the nature and duration of a detainee's confinement dictates the remedy *vis a vis* the legal principle involved.

I will also have occasion to refer to civilly committed patients and residents, but almost always by way of analogy or by way of contrast to prisoners. Problems of consent to various forms of intrusive psychiatric intervention represent an area where it is especially useful to refer to legal developments regarding the civilly committed.

[1] The Civilly Committed

One of the most interesting points of contrast between the prisoner and the civilly committed is that the prison inmate's claim to care is not based on a "treat me or release me" type of argument—that is, the right to liberty versus the right to some needed care or service. The prison inmate or detainee presumably is lawfully deprived of liberty and his claim to services or treatment must be fashioned within that narrow framework. While I do not propose to deal in detail with the treacherous ground of right to treatment claims by the civilly committed, the contrast is stark.

Whatever the rationale or legal source relied upon, ultimately a civil patient's legal claim to treatment faces outward from the institution:

Treat me or release me.

I'm here without benefit of full criminal procedures and without the moral opprobrium of having committed a crime, or even being accused of a crime. Therefore, you cannot punish me, and if you fail to treat me, you are punishing me and this place becomes a prison, whatever you may choose to call it.

I'm here because you (or the court) said I need treatment. You, therefore, owe me treatment and if you will not or cannot deliver, then you must let me go.[21]

There is no ready analogue for prison inmates' or detainees' claims to psychiatric or psychological care. Their presence in prison does not rest on any explicit or implicit diagnosis or on promises of restorative care or rehabilitation; there is no procedural quid pro quo argument available; there is no "treat or release" argument reasonably available; and it is axiomatic in our constitutional system that the lawful conviction of a crime empowers the state to impose punishment, although not cruelly or unusually.[22]

---

[20] The American Medical Association has issued a series of useful pamphlets dealing with the medical and psychiatric needs of prisoners and detainees in jail. *See,* e.g., *The Recognition of Jail Inmates with Mental Illness, Their Special Problems and Needs for Care* (undated monograph) and William P. Isele, *Health Care in Jails: Inmate's Medical Records & Jail Inmates Right to Refuse Medical Treatment* (undated monograph).

[21] *See* ALAN STONE, MENTAL HEALTH LAW: A SYSTEM IN TRANSITION (N.I.M.H., 1975), Ch. 5. For the total rejection of these claims made on behalf of confined juvenile offenders, *see* Santana v. Collazo, 714 F.2d 1172 (1st Cir. 1983), *cert. denied*, 466 U.S. 974 (1984).

[22] *See* Bell v. Wolfish, 441 U.S 520 (1979), where the Court made it clear that a pretrial detainee may

Another comparative curiosity exists in the realm of homelessness. A prisoner simply cannot be homeless in the sense of having no shelter, irregular or inadequate food, or tattered clothing. As Chapter 3 makes plain, inmates have the constitutional right to at least the minimal conditions of survival. On the other hand, the homeless, mentally ill person is a prime candidate for civil commitment, particularly where there is proof of a life-threatening inability to care for oneself.[23]

In the realm of treatment itself, inmates will not be granted the option of care in non-institutional environments. Passes and off-ground privileges so readily available to non-sentenced patients will find no ready analogue in our prisons and jails. What may be characterized as "acting out" in a hospital may well be characterized as a serious assault, depending on the victim, in prison and lead to substantial time in segregation.

[2] Profoundly Retarded Persons

People who are profoundly mentally retarded and institutionalized occupy a sort of middle ground between the prison inmate and the civilly committed. Although a state is not constitutionally bound to provide services for the mentally retarded, once a service is provided, and especially in a custodial setting, a set of rights and reciprocal obligations arises. In *Youngberg v. Romeo*,[24] a decision to which I will frequently return, the Supreme Court dealt with a profoundly retarded, institutionalized adult whose representatives conceded that no amount of training could make possible his release. In this case, the Court gave its first decision regarding the substantive rights of involuntarily committed, mentally retarded persons. The Court determined that such persons—along with convicted persons—possess constitutionally protected liberty interests in personal safety and freedom from undue restraint.[25] Justice Powell, for the Court, concluded that those "liberty interests require the state to provide minimally adequate or reasonable training to ensure safety and freedom from undue restraint."[26]

Thus, a rather grudging and narrow right to minimal training was established in *Romeo*, and this right is not related to a claim—or perhaps even the possibility—of preparation for release from confinement. In reaching this result, the Court made reference to the rights of convicted criminals, rights that include freedom from unsafe conditions and from undue bodily restraint, and concluded that if such rights survive penal confinement, they must also survive civil confinement.[27]

---

not be punished at all, but that a person duly convicted of a crime is clearly eligible for punishment so long as it is not cruel and unusual.

[23] See MICHAEL L. PERLIN, LAW AND MENTAL DISABILITY (1994), Sec. 2.52, for an excellent discussion of deinstitutionalization, homelessness, and hospitalization.

[24] 457 U.S. 307 (1982).

[25] Romeo, 457 U.S. at 324. Liberty interests are individual rights traceable to the word "liberty" contained in the Due Process Clause of the Fourteenth Amendment to the U.S. Constitution. It is by no means an inmate's right to freedom from restraint.

[26] Romeo, 457 U.S. at 319.

[27] Romeo, 457 U.S. at 316.

¶ 1.6 HIGH INCIDENCE OF MENTAL ILLNESS IN PRISON POPULATIONS

The pretrial detainee and the civilly committed have been placed at the outer edges of this work's central concern: the seriously mentally disordered or dual-diagnosed prison inmate. This focus eliminates, or gives secondary importance to, other special categories of accused or convicted offenders, including those found incompetent to be tried and under treatment in a mental hospital, those acquitted by reason of insanity, those found guilty but mentally ill, and various abnormal offenders categorized as sexual psychopaths, sexual predators, sociopaths, or defective delinquents.[28]

But while this focus reduces the number of arguably relevant categories, it does not importantly reduce the number of people. One earlier study concluded that "more prisoners serving active sentences are admitted to mental health hospitals each year than the combined number of persons hospitalized after having been adjudicated incompetent to stand trial, found not guilty by reason of insanity, or adjudged mentally disordered sex offenders."[29] This study found that 10,895 prisoners were admitted to health facilities in 1978, and that on any given day in that year, 5,158 inmates resided in mental health facilities.[30]

We must view these numbers as quite conservative if we wish to use them as a measure of the real incidence of mental disorder among prison inmates. There clearly are many inmates who are disturbed and who, for a variety of reasons, are not transferred to a mental hospital. Indeed, hospitalization is a rare event in a prison, while care in a residential treatment unit is far more common. There are generally acceptable epidemiological data available on the incidence of mental disorder, or serious mental disorder, among prison and jail populations. Studies and clinical observation suggest that a low of 8 percent to a high of 19 percent of prisoners will have severe psychiatric or functional disabilities and that another 15 to 20 percent will need some psychiatric intervention during confinement.[31] The Correctional Association of New York conceded that no data was kept on the incidence of mental illness in New York's 274 jails and lockups. They estimated that perhaps 20 percent of the jail population suffers significant mental illness.[32] Professor Pallone, while conceding the absence of good data, argues that with 19 percent of the general population sufficiently mentally ill to warrant professional attention, it is reasonable to assume that the preva-

---

[28] We deal with those offenders who were determined, or assumed, to be sufficiently mentally intact as to be conventionally blameworthy, but who now are found to be so seriously mentally ill as to be the recipients of mandated treatment. The other categories noted in the text involve the "untriables" and those eligible for what some term "criminal interstialit." *See* Eric Janus, *Sex Offender Commitments: Debunking the Official Narrative and Revealing the Rules in Use*, 82 STAN. L. & P. REV. 71, 76 (1997), for a useful discussion of the reach of criminal law and varieties of civil commitment law.

[29] *See* Hartstone, *supra* note 3, at 135, referring to the full study in John Monahan, et al., *Mentally Disordered Offenders: A National Survey of Patients and Facilities*, 6 L. & HUM. BEHAV. 31 (1982).

[30] *See* Hartstone, *supra* note 3, at 126.

[31] Jeffrey L. Metzner, *Guidelines for Psychiatric Services*, in PRISON, CRIMINAL BEHAVIOR AND MENTAL HEALTH 3, 252–267 (1993).

[32] Insane and in Jail: The Need for Treatment Options for the Mentally Ill in New York's County Jails, p. 5 (Correctional Ass'n of N.Y., 1989).

lence of mental disorder among incarcerated offenders (mainly male, of color, and poor) is about 74 percent![33] That is an astounding estimate and the highest yet encountered.

Even more important than having a completely accurate picture of the incidence of mental disorder or mental retardation among prison inmates, however, is the knowledge that there is a large, and apparently growing, number of mentally ill prisoners, that exceeds by far the number in the other related forensic categories.

¶ 1.7 "GUILTY BUT MENTALLY ILL" VERDICT

In addition to time and space factors, there are a number of substantive reasons for making the mentally ill imprisoned the focus of this work. The deceptively reformist verdict of "guilty but mentally ill" (G.B.M.I.), first enacted in Michigan in 1975, has since gained acceptance in twelve other jurisdictions.[34] Although G.B.M.I. procedures vary from state to state, typically the judge must impose a criminal sentence. The defendant is then examined to determine suitability for treatment, and if treatment seems called for, the defendant is hospitalized subject to imprisonment to complete the remainder of the criminal sentence.

This novel verdict of G.B.M.I. does not so far involve significant numbers of inmates. Since the verdict does not exculpate the defendant and the defendant constitutionally may be punished, inmates in this category are not in a very different legal position than other inmates claiming a right to treatment. The only significant difference occurs under a statute such as the one Michigan has adopted, which requires that "the defendant . . . shall undergo further evaluation and be given such treatment as is psychiatrically indicated."[35]

This language may be—and in Michigan has been—read as creating a statutory right to treatment.[36] But in Illinois, a jurisdiction that vests vast discretion under its G.B.M.I. law in correction officials, some 60 defendants found guilty but mentally ill were all confined at Menard Correctional Facility where, it is reported, they receive the same type of treatment afforded all other inmates.[37] While the Illinois statute gives the Department of Corrections the discretion to "provide such . . . treatment for the defendant as it determines necessary,"[38] its approach has resulted in no special treatment for mentally ill inmates, making the G.B.M.I. verdict a fairly meaningless ritual.

People who are incompetent to be tried or who are acquitted by reason of insanity often present the criminal justice system with difficult problems. Such problems,

---

[33] NATHANIEL J. PALLONE, MENTAL DISORDER AMONG PRISONERS: TOWARDS AN EPIDEMIOLOGICAL INVENTORY 147 (1991).

[34] See Perlin, *supra* note 23, Sec. 4.41 for a description and critical analysis of conceptually and operationally flawed law.

[35] Mich. Comp. Laws § 768.36 (1976).

[36] See People v. McLeod, 407 Mich. 632, 288 N.W. 2d 909 (1980).

[37] Plaut, *Punishment Versus Treatment of the Guilty but Mentally Ill,* 74 J. CRIM. L. & CRIM. 428, 436 (1983). The "law reform" in Illinois was not accompanied by any appropriation for treatment resources.

[38] Ill. Rev. Stat. ch. 38 § 1005-2-6(b) (1981).

however, are not typically manifested in the prison setting. Insanity acquittees and incompetents are found in mental hospitals[39] awaiting either restoration to competence[40] or remission of their mental illness and a finding of nondangerousness.[41]

¶ 1.8 SEX OFFENDER LAWS

Until very recently, sexual psychopath and defective delinquency-type laws were either being repealed or simply not invoked.[42] In 1990, the State of Washington enacted the Sexually Violent Predator Act (SVPA). The SVPA provides for a special commitment center and allows for possible lifetime commitment for "predators" with a mental abnormality or personality disorder.

These terms are used very consciously to avoid the traditional mental illness requirement basic to civil commitment law and to allow long periods of confinement even after service of a prison term and without proof of a recent overt act.[43] A small number of states followed Washington, and the legal storm created by these controversial laws led the Supreme Court to review the decision of the Kansas Supreme Court which held its version of the SVPA unconstitutional.[44]

On June 23, 1997 the Supreme Court issued its eagerly awaited holding in *Hendricks*.[45] In a five-to-four holding, the Court validated Kansas' Sexually Violent Predator Act (SVPA) and thereby also validated the virtually identical laws in other states.

---

[39] This was not always the case. Early laws mandating that insanity acquittees be hospitalized, including New York State's, often were ignored, and prisons were used for secure confinement. *See* MENTALLY ILL OFFENDERS AND THE CRIMINAL JUSTICE SYSTEM: ISSUES IN FORENSIC SERVICES 17 (N. Beran & B. Toomey, eds. 1979).

[40] Under Jackson v. Indiana, 406 U.S. 715 (1972), persons found incompetent to be tried can no longer be hospitalized indefinitely. The state is obligated to demonstrate some progress, after a reasonable period of time (six months may be the outside limit), toward the goal of "triability." *See* Stone, *supra* note 21, Ch. 12.

[41] In Jones v. United States, 463 U.S. 354 (1983), the Court decided in a five-to-four decision that an insanity acquittee who successfully invokes the defense may be automatically committed to a mental hospital and detained there for a longer period than the maximum term of imprisonment available on conviction, and that it is constitutionally acceptable at a post-commitment hearing to require the acquitted person to prove he or she is no longer mentally ill or dangerous by a preponderance of the evidence. The most troublesome aspects of this decision are first that the Court's casual acceptance of the proposition that a conviction of a crime (here, attempted petty larceny) allows an inference to be drawn that the defendant was and remains dangerous, and second, that a finding of insanity allows a conclusion that the underlying mental illness continues post-verdict, thus obviating the need for a civil commitment hearing. *See generally Note, Commitment Following an Insanity Acquittal*, 94 HARV. L. REV. 605 (1981), for a pre-*Jones* summary of various post-acquittal laws. For an interesting study of offenders who are formally designated as mentally disordered, *see* Seymour Halleck, *The Mentally Disordered Offender* (U.S. Dept. Of Health and Human Services, 1986).

[42] George Dix, *Special Dispositional Alternatives for Abnormal Offenders*, in MENTALLY DISORDERED OFFENDERS (John Monahan & Henry Steadman, eds. 1983), 136–157.

[43] See Fred Cohen, *Washington's Sexually Violent Predator Act*, in THE SEX OFFFENDER: CORRECTIONS, TREATMENT AND LEGAL PRACTICE (B.K. Schwartz & H.R. Cellini, eds. 1995), Ch. 23.

[44] Kansas v. Hendricks, 117 S. Ct. 2072 (1997).

[45] Id.

Many commentators, including this one, believed that the SVPA would be upheld but thought the battle would be the rather esoteric one over whether the statutory terms "mental abnormality or personality disorder," when coupled with sexually violent propensities, would be constitutionally acceptable. More specifically, the thinking was that *Foucha v. Louisiana*[46] might be read as constitutionally mandating a finding of mental disease (or mental illness) and dangerousness to support civil commitment, and that the seemingly broader terms "mental disorder," "anti-social personality," and "mental abnormality" would not suffice.

In fact, the murky majority opinion authored by Justice Thomas barely touches on *Foucha* and the mental illness-disorder debate. The same is true of the dissent which focuses on the ex post facto aspects of the SVPA, finding that it reaches back and punishes conduct that already has been the subject of punishment. Only Justice Ginsburg had reservations on the substantive basis of the law and she expressed those simply by not joining in all of Justice Breyer's dissent.

Clearly, *Hendricks* gives the green light to those states waiting to enact laws similar to those found in Washington, Kansas, New Jersey, Wisconsin, Arizona, California, and Minnesota. There were perhaps 250 sex offenders committed under these laws in June of 1997, but the numbers are certain to grow. One may confidently predict a legislative stampede, along the lines of the various Megan's Laws, to "crack down" on certain sex offenders.

In fact, however, nothing in *Hendricks* would seem to limit such law to sexual predators. Some states are only now considering simple "violent predator laws" that would allow post-prison commitment for recidivists who might otherwise have been the subject of front-end habitual offender laws.

Does *Hendricks* in any direct fashion appear to impact on the subject of this book? Since predators are to be civilly committed, states will use mental or security hospitals or create distinct treatment-type facilities within their prisons. Thus, it is unlikely that even the predictable legislative stampede and the consequent rise in commitments will impact the seriously mentally ill penal captive.

There is however, at least one interesting possibility created by Justice Thomas' majority opinion. In a rather casual aside, the Justice told readers in effect not to get too worked-up about the mental illness-disorder debate because Hendricks is diagnosed as a pedophile and pedophilia is a recognized and serious mental disorder.[47] As we shall see, claims to sex offender treatment raised by convicted prisoners generally fail because courts find that the label sex offender does not itself establish, or even imply, the requisite serious mental disorder. Certainly, convicted sex offenders who are pedophiles will now cite Justice Thomas and argue for an Eighth Amendment based claim to treatment for that disorder. Unless there is some retreat from his seemingly off-hand remark, the claim should prevail.

One empirical study sheds some light on the factors that go into prosecutorial decisions to use either the mental health or the criminal justice system when presented with an accused who is possibly eligible for either system. Ellen Hochstedler looked at 379 cases of defendants identified as mentally disordered by a mental health

---

[46] 504 U.S. 71 (1992).

[47] *See* Bailey v. Gardebring, 940 F.2d 1150 (8th Cir. 1991); *see* Cohen, *supra* note 43, Ch. 24.

screening unit within a prosecutor's office.[48] Her data show that the court used its criminal authority in a significant number of cases to mandate a treatment-only disposition. Criminal justice officials tended to view misdemeanants with a verified history of mental health problems as inappropriate for criminal sanctions.[49] Thus, only the felons who are arguably mentally disordered are likely to be brought into the conviction-imprisonment process and then serve as the human subjects of the present work.

¶ 1.9 MAJOR OBSERVATIONS AND TRENDS

In concluding this aspect of the introductory section, I would like to offer a few observations that took shape as I studied the literature, talked with corrections and mental health personnel, observed treatment programs, and participated in litigation in a number of states. These observations also continue in my present service as court appointed monitor in Ohio.[50] Front-line personnel, whether they are in security or treatment, almost all agree that the number of seriously mentally disordered inmates in prison has increased dramatically in the last few years. They offer two explanations for this perceived change. First, overcrowding increases tension in prison and causes more mental illness than previously existed.[51] Second, the increasingly narrow criteria for civil commitment of the mentally ill and the general policy of deinstitutionalization have resulted in higher rates of conviction and imprisonment of persons who earlier would have entered the mental health system.[52]

---

[48] Ellen Hochstedler, *Criminal Prosecution of the Mentally Disordered*, 20 LAW & SOCIETY REV. 279 (1986).

[49] Hochstedler, at 291.

[50] Since July of 1995, I have served as a federal court monitor in the case of *Dunn v. Voinovich* with the mandate of overseeing mental health services in Ohio's prisons in accordance with the Dunn consent decree.

[51] "Studies examining [overcrowding] have varied in design but all have found a positive relationship between overcrowding and illness of communicable diseases, including tuberculosis, with elevated rates of illness complaints and with higher rates of psychiatric commitments." Terrence Thornberry, et. al., *Overcrowding in American Prisons: Policy Implications of Double-Bunking Single Cells XI* (Univ. of Ga., July 1982).

[52] This perception is thinly supported but widely held. The 1983 NIC program reported that "during recent National Institute of Corrections Advisory Board meetings, the increase in the number of mentally ill and retarded inmates was identified as a major concern for practitioners." *NIC Annual Program Plan for Fiscal Year 1983*, 15 (NIC, July 1982); *see also* Hardy, *Dealing with the Mentally and Emotionally Disturbed*, 46 CORRECTIONS TODAY 16, 17 (1984).

Although there is little data on point, Steadman's work in New York State found that the percentage of inmates statewide with prior mental hospitalizations *decreased* from 13.4 percent in 1968 to 9.5 percent in 1978. In contrast, the percentage of patients admitted to state mental hospitals with prior arrests increased from 38.2 percent to 51.8 percent. Henry Steadman, *From Bedlam to Bastille? The Confinement of the Mentally Ill in U.S. Prisons* (presented at the Annual Meeting, American Sociological Association, Aug. 1981, Toronto, Canada). *See also* George Dix, *Major Current Issues Concerning Civil Commitment Criteria*, 45 LAW & CONTEMP. PROB's 137, 154–159 (1982) for an analysis of other studies dealing with the involvement of the mentally ill in the criminal justice system. In assessing the numerous problems female inmates face in New York's Bedford Hills prison, Jean Harris writes, "Were I to be

For the moment, we may treat this perception of increase and the explanations put forward as having perceptual, although not necessarily empirical, validity. As a widely held belief, these notions take on their own identity; deviant behavior is filtered through these beliefs and explanations and solutions are framed accordingly.

Commentators and courts, as suggested earlier, offer very differing numbers and percentages of the mentally disordered and mentally retarded inmates in particular facilities or systems.[53] My impression is that this is one of those areas where the available solutions dictate the nature of the problem. To illustrate that point in a highly exaggerated fashion, I would suggest that a system oriented toward seeing certain inmate behavior as "crazy" (for example, eating one's own feces or forcefully banging one's head against the cell wall) and that has "clinical" space to deal with such inmates will react with a therapeutic-type response. The very same behavior in an intensely security-conscious system or facility that has little or no space available for any type of therapy may easily be viewed as evidence of the basic "badness" of the inmate.

[1] Role of Corrections Personnel

With diagnostic categories and labels of mental illness ambiguous under the best circumstances, it is conceivable that what is viewed as "mad" or "bad" will be colored as much by available solutions as by relatively objective diagnostic factors. This point is central, because neither courts nor legislatures perform diagnostic or clinical services. Each might insist on treatment for the disturbed inmate and there may even be funds provided for certain services, but ultimately it is corrections and clinical personnel who perform as gatekeepers. Unlike family or police officers on the outside, correction personnel cannot ignore the individual or his behavior. They must and will respond, although how they do so is not easily predictable.

It is possible to reject, or seriously question, my formulation that the available solutions greatly influence the nature of the problem and still accept the proposition that those who control prison security and clinical services ultimately determine the major dimensions of the problem. Indeed, even the most casual observations will reveal the tension between security and treatment staff in virtually any prison setting where they coexist. Clinical personnel will complain about having disciplinary problems foisted on them and security staff will be angry or bewildered at how quickly some inmates believed to be "out of it" are returned from a treatment unit or a mental hospital. In New York, this is known as "bus therapy."

The new emphasis on educating and training security staff about mental illness and medication is premised on the wholesale increase in the number of mentally ill

---

asked to choose, I would put mental illness at the top of the list." JEAN HARRIS, THEY ALWAYS CALL US LADIES (1988), p. 70. Ms. Harris also wonders whether "we are not reaching the point where treatment, however expensive, will be less expensive than the cost of neglect." Harris at 75.

[53] The trial judge in an important case challenging overcrowding at Ohio's Lucasville prison determined that 75 to 85 percent of the inmates were mentally disordered. Quoted in PHILLIP COOPER, HARD JUDICIAL CHOICES: FEDERAL DISTRICT COURT JUDGES AND STATE AND LOCAL OFFICIALS (1988), p. 253.

inmates. In some jurisdictions the officers are taught that a transmigration of mental hospital patients to prisons changes their function, especially when working in a treatment or segregation unit. Accurate or not, officers now learn about the signs and symptoms of mental illness, psychotropic medication, side-effects, non-compliance, and the like. They often take part in treatment team meetings and their daily contact with the inmate often is the basis of valuable diagnostic and treatment input.

[2] Need for Legal Clarity

Finally, it is my impression that correction and clinical personnel know and understand precious little relevant law and much of what is "known" is misunderstood. That, by itself, is not surprising. What is surprising, if only slightly, is that whenever the law—typically an appellate decision, not legislation—is misunderstood, it is almost always in the direction of appearing to be more burdensome than it is and calling for more substantive and procedural adjustments than it actually did.

On the other hand, one does not find the same sense of urgency, or even panic, engendered by such police-oriented decisions as *Miranda v. Arizona*,[54] *Mapp v. Ohio*,[55] or even *Wolff v. McDonnell*[56] and its minimal procedural requirements for prison disciplinary proceedings. There is, however, an increasing hunger to know what is and is not required by the law[57] and in many instances to simply "do the right thing" whether or not clearly legally mandated.

Security and program staff, in my experience, have come to believe that decent mental health care contributes to the security of the facility and enhances the work environment as it eases the suffering of the mentally ill. I hope this work helps to enhance understanding of the plight of the mentally ill who are incarcerated as it establishes the legal norms that must guide treatment.

---

[54] 384 U.S. 436 (1966).

[55] 367 U.S. 643 (1961).

[56] 418 U.S. 539 (1974).

[57] An excellent reference work for virtually all legal problems associated with the mentally disabled and the law is SAMUEL BRAKEL, ET AL., THE MENTALLY DISABLED AND THE LAW (A.B.F., 3d ed. 1985).

Chapter 2
Overview of Legal Issues

¶ 2.1 THE OBLIGATION OF BASIC CARE

In this chapter, the reader is taken over the general territory of this work and given sufficient detail to illustrate the particular topic. Subsequent chapters provide additional detail, extended analysis, and extended quotations from original sources. Various appendices provide even more basic source material. A prison or jail administrator, for example, who reads only this chapter should have a reasonably complete overview of the law and the mentally disordered inmate. We might describe the approach in this chapter as a map of the United States that is limited to state boundaries and interstate highways. What follows in subsequent chapters is a rather detailed network of major and minor highways along with explanatory "legends."

Having physical custody of another person invariably creates a legal duty to care for that person, while the legal basis for the actual custody determines the particular care required. And one wonders how it could be otherwise in a civilized society that adheres to a rule of law. Custody in penal confinement is sufficiently complete that prisoners must depend on their keepers for food, water, clothing, and medical care, the basic stuff of survival. There are very few shopping opportunities and even fewer private clinicians available for prison or jail housecalls. Parenthetically, officials would deny them entry should they appear at the gates.

Phrased somewhat differently, the most fundamental obligation of a prison system to those in its charge, indeed, of any system that confines people, is to maintain their life and health. This obligation of basic care now clearly includes the physical and psychological dimensions of the person and has moved from the exclusive domain of private (or tort) law to include the public domain of constitutional law. That is, we are in an era where an inmate's right to basic decency and protection as well as to medical and psychological care has moved from private legal actions to constitutionally based legal actions. This is not the era of origin nor is it an era where inmates' rights are viewed expansively.

[1] Preservation of Life and Health

At the outset, a major distinction must be established as to the type of care owed an inmate. When the law insists, as it does, that an inmate be provided with basic shelter, food, water, clothing, and insulation from known inmate predators, the objective is to preserve physical integrity, health, and life. All inmates (or penal captives) are entitled to the minimal conditions necessary to sustain life and to avoid needless suffering.

This duty—the preservation of life and health—resembles the duty to provide medical and psychological care, but it is also more expansive. Prison officials, for example, must take preventive measures against predators to protect prospective victims. The duty to the victim is not to provide relief from a physical or psychological malady, it is to prevent the infliction of harm. Keeping inmates adequately warm, clothed, and fed are similarly protective rather than regenerative.

As we shall see, both the affirmative duty to provide medical or psychological care and the duty to protect inmates (more likely an insulating function) flow from the Eighth Amendment's ban on cruel and unusual punishment. Indeed, in *Farmer v. Brennan*,[1] the Supreme Court recently clarified the meaning of "deliberate indifference" in the context of a failure to prevent a rape as claimed by an inmate. Deliberate indifference is central to the duty to provide care as well, and *Farmer*, then, will apply to both duties. In the ensuing discussions of custodial suicide and the use of physical restraints, we will encounter judicial confusion over the duty of care and the duty of protection.

---

[1] 511 U.S. 825 (1994).

[2] Medical and Psychological Care

The duty to provide medical or psychological care most clearly arises at the point where an inmate is known to be ill or injured. When that condition is a recognizable and serious psychiatric disorder, the Eighth Amendment's ban on cruel and unusual punishment kicks in and the basic coverage of this book begins. As we shall see, the duty to provide medical or psychological care is preventive and ameliorative, and emphatically includes an obligation to relieve pain, prolong life, and stabilize (if not cure) the malady. Indeed, the avoidance of gratuitous suffering is at the core of the constitutional obligation.

The Eighth Amendment's proscription of cruel and unusual punishment has been interpreted to require that state and federal prison officials must avoid deliberate indifference to the serious medical and psychological needs of inmates.[2] This less-than-demanding duty places the constitutional obligation of care a notch below the general standards of reasonableness for determining medical malpractice. What must be stressed, however, is that while constitutional minima may be met, state officials may still be liable civilly for what is the equivalent of malpractice in the omission or provision of medical or psychological care. In other words, meeting minimal federal requirements is no guarantee that officials responsible for medical and psychiatric care may not be liable under state law. Since existing state law varies greatly on standards of liability, it is incumbent on mental health workers and correctional officials to ascertain the law of their jurisdiction.

The essence of the Eighth Amendment is an obligation of government to avoid the needless infliction or prolongation of pain and suffering. Courts well understand that prisons are not likely to be models of comfort or free from damaging stress and conflict. Psychological stress and possible deterioration often are accepted as an inherent aspect of imprisonment and thus beyond the realm of legal protection. Whatever the cause—self-inflicted, inflicted by others, or "natural"—there exists the legal duty to identify and treat inmates with serious mental disorders.

There are two critical phrases in the statement of the legal obligation of care owed a mentally disordered inmate: "deliberate indifference" and "serious medical needs." Unfortunately, there is no single, authoritative definition for what constitutes a serious medical condition or mental health condition, but it is possible to distill a workable understanding from a number of leading decisions. As noted earlier, *Farmer v. Brennan* (discussed below and in more detail in Chapter 4) now provides us with an authoritative, reasonably clear definition of deliberate indifference.

¶ 2.2 DELIBERATE INDIFFERENCE

"Deliberate indifference" is an awkwardly phrased mental state in the same general category as "intention," "reckless," or "negligence." From its earliest use in 1976,

---

[2] This chapter does not document all specific statements such as the one to which this footnote is attached. The reader will find citations to the cases noted here and complete documentation in the succeeding chapters.

it was clear that it required more than poor judgment and less than intentional acts or omissions calculated to cause needless suffering. After letting the lower courts grapple with its meaning for some 18 years, in *Farmer v. Brennan* the Supreme Court engaged in its first effort to define the seemingly oxymoronic term.

Justice Souter stated, "With deliberate indifference lying somewhere between the poles of negligence at one end and purpose or knowledge at the other, the Courts of Appeals have routinely equated deliberate indifference with recklessness."[3] Recklessness, however, does not have a single meaning in law. Once the Court decided on recklessness as the functional equivalent of deliberate indifference, it then had to choose between the civil standard and the criminal standard.

[1] Civil vs. Criminal Recklessness

Under civil, most often tort, law, a person is reckless when he or she acts, or fails to act when there is a duty to do so, in the face of a high risk of harm that is known or should have been known. Under criminal law, however, recklessness exists only where the accused is found to have acted or failed to act with actual knowledge of the particular risk. Obviously, the major difference here is whether there is a duty to inquire and ascertain facts relevant to actual risks.

For example, in the area of custodial suicide, a credible threat to commit suicide coupled with knowledge of a recent attempt would establish actual knowledge of the risk. On the other hand, a general awareness of risk factors might qualify for "should have known" but would likely flunk the actual knowledge test.

The Court opted for the criminal law version of recklessness but softened the potentially harsh impact on prisoners by noting that a claimant need not show that an official actually believed that some harm actually would occur, only that there was knowledge of a substantial risk of harm. Thus, the first question on liability is what was known (in *Farmer*, that the rape victim was obviously homosexual). One then asks, what risks flow from that knowledge (here, sexual assault), what duty is thereby established (protection), and whether that duty was breached (possibly).

[2] Effect on Intake Screening

While this entire concept is more fully explored in Chapter 5, here we should at least summarize *Farmer's* possible impact on the mentally ill. The most crucial question is whether *Farmer's* actual knowledge requirement obviates the need to do intake screening and evaluation. We could theoretically ask why correctional officials should seek out the knowledge (e.g., prior suicide attempts, hospitalizations, use of psychotropic medication) that will create the duty to do more; officials should deal only with clear manifestations of mental illness as inmates "come in the door" or where the illness plainly erupts later.

First, I know of no jurisdiction that has adopted such an approach. Indeed, more

---

[3] *Farmer, supra* note 1, at 835.

and more correctional systems are using refined multi-level techniques for screening and evaluating persons in need of mental health care or at special risk of committing suicide.

Second, the approach may be said to beg the question: suppose a system did abandon intake screening. The argument that likely would be made is that given the high percentage of inmates known to be experiencing serious mental illness, there is actual knowledge of high risk among the entire population. Just as not all feminine-appearing inmates will be sexually assaulted, the risks to that group are such that a special duty of care arises. Where the risks of a large number of seriously mentally ill persons arriving at any given prison are high, the duty then is to engage in individual detection, diagnosis, and appropriate care.[4]

Third, at a policy level a "see no evil" approach is inhumane and ultimately more expensive when preventable deterioration leads to a more serious condition which, in turn, may lead to injury or hospitalization, by far the most expensive arena for treatment.

Fourth, the courts recently seem more intent on constitutionalizing a duty to do intake classification for housing-security purposes. To condemn random double-celling assignments, for example, is also to condemn a "blinkers on" approach to screening for mental illness.

¶ 2.3 SERIOUS NEEDS

Setting a standard for what is or is not a "serious" medical or psychological need suffers from the same lack of precision as the deliberate indifference standard. However, the seriousness component has not received an authoritative Supreme Court decision. To understand seriousness, we are required to sift through the leading decisions to arrive at a distillation. The test for seriousness begins with a clinical or medical necessity, not simply with what may be desired. Because the constitutional basis for the right to treatment is in the Eighth Amendment's ban against cruel and unusual punishment, courts tend to equate seriousness with the needless infliction of pain and suffering. Clearly, then, such minor ailments as anxiety, depression, or headaches are not within the judicial parameters for seriousness. Insisting on care for mild depression becomes the constitutional equivalent of demanding cosmetic surgery; both are rejected by the courts.

On the other hand, a debilitating, clinical depression where an inmate is virtually immobilized and is not attendant to even basic hygienic needs almost certainly would qualify. In the wake of a major law suit, the Michigan Department of Corrections adopted a definition that may commend itself to other jurisdictions and that clearly meets legal criteria:

Serious mental illness (or severe mental disorder) means a substantial disorder of thought or mood which significantly impairs judgment, behavior,

---

[4] The analogy is far from perfect. Feminine appearing inmates are, of course, a discrete class. Those with mental illness do not similarly display "class membership" and, thus, must be sought and identified. Knowing that 1 or 2 of every 10 inmates will be entitled to care, it may be argued, creates the duty.

capacity to recognize reality, or ability to cope with the ordinary demands of life.

A serious/severe mental state or condition (1) manifested by substantial discomfort, pain, and/or disability that cannot be legitimately ignored by appropriate clinical staff, (2) requires a mental health assessment, diagnostic evaluation, treatment planning and disposition planning, and (3) is generally associated with (a) the inability to attend to and effectively perform the usual/necessary activities of daily living, (b) extreme impairment of coping skills, rendering the patient exceptionally vulnerable to unintentional or intentional victimization and possible mismanagement and/or (c) behaviors that are dangerous to self and others.

Serious mental illness/severe mental disorder includes psychiatric conditions/states that span the entire diagnostic spectrum of DSM-III and is not limited to specific diagnosis.[5]

¶ 2.4 DUTY TO DIAGNOSE

However minimal the constitutional duty of treatment, important ancillary (or supportive) rights and duties are thereby created. The right to treatment, at least for serious disorders, would be meaningless without an additional, and anterior, duty to provide diagnosis, and this duty to diagnose sweeps more broadly than the underlying right to care. More inmates necessarily must be examined than treated unless one makes the absurd assumption that all inmates eligible for diagnosis (or screening and evaluation) somehow are also seriously mentally ill.

Despite *Farmer,* I have no doubt that all jail and prison systems must have some screening, evaluation, and classification or diagnostic system. This is a duty also owed the healthy inmate who has a right not to be disturbed or injured, let us say, by a vio-

---

[5] This definition appears in the "Comprehensive Mental Health Plan" of June 6, 1986, submitted to Judge Enslen in USA v. Michigan, No. G84-63CA (W.D. Mich.). The Plan's pages are not numbered, thus making more precise citation impossible. The first paragraph of the definition is drawn from ABA Criminal Justice Mental Health Standards, Standard 7-10.1(b). The DSM-III reference is to the DIAGNOSTIC AND STATISTICAL MANUAL OF MENTAL DISORDERS, 3d ed. (American Psychiatric Ass'n). A somewhat different approach was taken in Dunn v. Voinovich, Case No. C1-93-0166 (S.D. Ohio 1993). Section VIII of the Consent Decree in *Dunn* includes the following definition:

a) Serious mental illness means a substantial disorder of thought or mood which significantly impairs judgment, behavior, capacity to recognize reality or cope with the ordinary demands of life within the prison environment and is manifested by substantial pain or disability. Serious mental illness requires a mental diagnosis, prognosis and treatment, as appropriate, by mental health staff.

It is expressly understood that this definition does not include inmates who are substance abusers, substance dependent, including alcoholics and narcotic addicts, or persons convicted of any sex offense, who are not otherwise diagnosed as seriously mentally ill.

This particular section was the subject of more pre-Decree negotiation than any other provision in the 33-page Decree. The definition section also describes the class in *Dunn* and, thus, actually establishes who is eligible for mandatory treatment.

lent, psychotic inmate. The seriously disturbed inmate, in turn, has a right to be identified for treatment so that the needless continuation of pain and suffering—and that should include preventable deterioration—is avoided.

Every prison system should have in place a regular screening and evaluation process, adequately staffed with qualified personnel, where the information and conclusions developed are used and periodically reviewed. Any system that can be evaluated on these factors and pass need not worry about a successful legal challenge to this aspect of their mental health care. However, the cases reveal that the more glaringly deficient the classification-diagnostic system, the more sweeping the judicially mandated relief. Indeed, where a system seems utterly primitive in treatment and classification resources, judges have been inclined to mandate diagnostic information more clearly related to rehabilitation and education than the more restrictive right to treatment.

A number of federal courts have insisted that prisons deficient in classification or diagnostic systems prepare plans to learn about the inmates' skills, background, or psychological difficulties. They have ordered large scale and expensive epidemiological studies and insisted that mental health specialists be involved in this process and that certain standardized tests be used.

Thus, glaringly deficient prison systems have invited some federal judges to require programs and penal objectives they would not likely impose if the particular claim (rehabilitation, for instance) was made in isolation or if the overall prison conditions were minimally acceptable. The point is: the greater the deficiency, the more extensive the likely relief. It is difficult to imagine a constitutionally acceptable correctional mental health care system that breaks down at the front door.

¶ 2.5 RECORDS

The basic right to treatment for serious disorders has spawned a right not only to diagnosis and classification, but also to minimally adequate clinical records. Records are necessary for continuity of care, for review of the efficacy of care, for future diagnosis, and certainly for responding to questions raised about the legal obligation to provide care. Courts that have decided challenges to a facility's recordkeeping have looked for a written plan for future treatment, how well the files are organized, notations as to physical and mental examinations, progress notes, medical history, and, certainly, medication records.

Mental health professionals, and especially psychiatrists, move in and out of correctional systems. Inmates are subject to frequent transfers. Where records are incomplete, inconsistent, or simply barren, continuity of care is severely compromised. Indeed, in my own experience in monitoring correctional mental health care systems, we spend considerable time reviewing patient charts and quite often they are in shambles. Individual treatment plans are missing, progress notes absent, reasons for medication omitted, and even where laboratory tests involve life-threatening situations (e.g., lithium levels), test results are absent. Where records are so deficient, one's overall doubts about the efficacy of treatment are enhanced.

Where a clinician's notes are lucid and reasonably comprehensive and the course of future treatment clear, the legal demands noted here likely will be met. Clearly, if any administrator has doubts about the medical records system, the time to have a professional evaluation is now and not with the plaintiffs' lawyers looking over your shoulders.

Curiously, courts are divided on whether access by fellow inmates to such records is legally permissible. As a matter of policy, one should condemn the practice on the grounds of privacy and the potential for corrupt usage.

¶ 2.6 COMPONENTS OF A TREATMENT PROGRAM

[1] Minimal Components

It is difficult, although not impossible, to predict what may be constitutionally acceptable for inmate mental health care, diagnosis, and recordkeeping. Six legally acceptable components, as articulated first in *Ruiz v. Estelle*[6] involving the Texas Department of Corrections, provide a very useful initial guide to a solution:

1. First, there must be *a systematic program for screening and evaluating inmates* in order to identify those who require mental health treatment;

2. Second, as was underscored in other cases, *treatment must entail more than segregation and close supervision of the inmate patients;*

3. Third, treatment requires the *participation of trained mental health professionals*, who must be employed in sufficient numbers to identify and treat in an individualized manner those treatable inmates suffering from serious mental disorders;

4. Fourth, *accurate, complete, and confidential records* of the mental health treatment process must be maintained;

5. Fifth, *prescription and administration of behavior-altering medications in dangerous amounts, by dangerous methods, or without appropriate supervision and periodic evaluations, is an unacceptable method of treatment*;

6. Sixth, *a basic program for the identification, treatment, and supervision of inmates with suicidal tendencies is a necessary component* of any mental health treatment program.

[2] Desirable Components

It is useful to compare this guide to what may be minimally acceptable with a set of factors I recently prepared that can be described as ideal, or at least comprehensive:

---

[6] 503 F. Supp. 1265 (S.D. Tex. 1980).

1. *Diversion of selected offenders with mental illness.* There is a virtual unanimity in the literature, and among experts, that too many prisoners with serious mental illness are swept into jail and prison and often for minor offenses. A progressive system would provide legal authorization for pre-trial examinations and diversion to treatment where appropriate.[7]

2. *Identification of inmates with mental illness entering the system.* Unless the system has in place mechanisms to identify those needing care, either at reception or after confinement, it simply cannot meet its treatment obligations. Better systems will have a computerized classification and tracking system.

3. *Identification for appropriate care of inmates suffering from alcoholism, drug addiction, sexual dysfunction, or problems associated with the "Battered Woman Syndrome."* These conditions generally fall outside of legally mandated care. However, a correctional system that is a "full service" system is responsive to these impaired individuals, and that in itself is deemed desirable.

Compliance with basic legal requirements, as noted, would encompass only the seriously mentally ill. However, a comprehensive system would have a fully integrated system and not draw artificial distinctions between "special needs" categories.

4. *Training of staff on the signs and symptoms of mental disorder and inmates with "special needs."* The identification of those who need care does not end at the front door, nor is it limited to mental health specialists. Security staff, especially those assigned to mental health special care units and to segregation units, must be able to identify those who need care and understand the behavior associated with the condition or any medications involved. Such training should be subjected to rigorous evaluation of the information conveyed, attitudes changed, and behavior changed.

5. *Adequate (in quantity and quality) human resources available for the various tasks associated with mental health treatment.* Mental health staff should be appropriately licensed, multi-disciplined, and function administratively in an integrated fashion. Staffing ratios for psychiatrists, psychologists, social workers, and others should be established at least as a rough guide for judging the objective quality of a system. Opportunities will exist for staff development and enrichment. "Burn out" and "dry out" seem endemic to staff members in this highly charged work area, and comprehensive programs will provide opportunities for growth and respite.

6. *Adequate (in quantity and quality) physical resources available.* Obviously, a certain amount of physical space designed for various treatment or program objectives must be made available. The available space should be designed to meet the needs for hospitalization, long-term care that does not require hospitalization, crisis care (e.g.,

---

[7] See Brian D. Shannon, *Diversion of Offenders with Mental Illness: Recent Legislative Reforms—Texas Style*, 20 MPRLR 431 (1996).

suicide-watch placements), transitional care, and perhaps special needs (e.g., housing the dual-diagnosed inmate). A "least restrictive environment" approach suggests enhanced concern for the inmates' needs.

7. *Access to care.* Without ready access to diagnosis and care, human and physical resources become virtually meaningless. This calls for a study of waiting lists, response to "kites," knowledge by security staff and inmates on how to gain access, appropriate training, and instructing inmates how to gain access.

From the standpoint of actually auditing a system, access must be evaluated on site. Cells, beds, and staff may be counted, but access is a dynamic concept and must be observed. A model system would perform regular audits, question inmates and staff, assess the orientation process, and even do emergency "trial runs." In evaluating access to care, one necessarily also evaluates the relationship between security and mental health staff. Without a collaborative approach, no system will function very well.

8. *Contents of records.* Records are crucial to the legal requirement of continuity of care. They are evidence of the care and are instrumental in assuring its quality. As a barometer of quality, the use of regular progress notes and a comprehensible individual treatment plan will show whether appropriate care is given and will make the personnel changes that are endemic to corrections less interruptive of the care process. The legal concern here is with continuity of care. The mental health record is a necessary, although not sufficient, factor in meeting that obligation.

9. *Medication management.* Without necessarily endorsing the practice, we must recognize that medication is the treatment of choice for the mentally ill inmate. This means that there should be reasonable access to the psychiatrist, a formulary that allows access to the newer psychopharmacological agents that are emerging at a rapid pace, and regular monitoring and testing. In systems with rapid turnover, or that use locum tenens psychiatrists, special attention must be paid to medication practices, especially changes in medication.

10. *Restorative opportunities.* For the seriously mentally ill medication may well be the treatment of choice, but it should not be the only treatment or programming available. For those not taking medication it is even more important to have a full-range of activities, along with individual and group therapy. Comprehensive programs offer work opportunities along with structured physical activities, horticultural programs, guide-dog training, vocational training, and the like. Programs dealing with anger management, social skills development, educational opportunities and the like often enhance restorative opportunities.

11. *Management information system (MIS).* A model MIS should be computerized and used for needs assessment, quality assurance (CQI) and tracking. Model programs will produce concrete examples of how MIS is used in the system.

12. *Data/research on treatment outcomes.* Comprehensive programs will not be

content to simply "build, hire, and provide access." They will be concerned with the articulation of treatment objectives and will be engaged in acceptable research on outcomes. Articles in peer reviewed publications would provide extremely good evidence on this point.

13. *Economy of scale.* The administrative and organizational structures should be designed to provide the maximum care for the funds allocated. Are services regionalized (or clustered)? Are services shared and accessible? Are actual costs actually known?

14. *Policy procedure: contemporary, comprehensive, accessible.* In the interest of uniformity and consistency of practice, a system must have contemporary policy and procedures that are readily available and understandable. Special attention should be paid to transfers from correctional settings to mental hospitals, forced medication, restraints and isolation, disciplinary proceedings, confidentiality, consent, and suicide. These areas generate the most legal concern and have the clearest legal mandates.

15. *Discharge planning.* A comprehensive care system should not end at the institution's walls. Inmates needing care inside are not magically going to be free of that need on their release. Discharge planning begins inside, and appropriate community care, including medication and housing arrangements, will be the hallmark of a comprehensive system.

To reiterate, the above 15 factors are a combination of what is legally required and what is professionally desired. Anyone wishing to evaluate a correctional mental health program might well use these factors as their guide.

¶ 2.7 EVALUATION OF TREATMENT

There are essentially two approaches to evaluating the adequacy of treatment: the objective and the subjective. An objective approach focuses on such empirical items as inmate-to-staff ratios, available beds, the number of clinician-patient contacts, and so on. A subjective approach is primarily evaluative. It asks about the quality of the services provided and expresses some concern for outcomes. This approach may be, and often is, used in conjunction with the objective approach.

Courts seem to prefer the objective approach, probably because it is easier to work with. It is empirically demonstrable, standards are available, and expert witnesses can speak authoritatively as to needed numbers of personnel, clinician-inmate contact, beds, and so on. Of course, experts will also be relied on for their subjective or qualitative judgments.

The term "treatment" here and in the ensuing chapters of this book most often refers to efforts to provide short-term relief from acute psychic distress. Treatment in the sense of forward-looking, future-oriented improvement in, say, coping and social skills is not the type of treatment referred to (or likely offered) here. Perhaps the most widely espoused correctional treatment objective is preparation for life in the prison's general population.

Needless to say, much more is said in the ensuing chapters about the definition and concept of "treatment," and treatment is also contrasted with other helping terms such as "rehabilitation," "habilitation," and "training."

¶ 2.8 SUBSTANCE ABUSERS

The question of whether to treat substance abusers, and if so how, often arises in the prison and jail setting. Indeed, we should pose the most fundamental question at this early stage and attempt to answer it squarely: do prison inmates have a constitutional right to treatment for their alcoholism or drug addiction? Although there are some caveats to the answer, the basic answer is perhaps a surprising no.

This again is not a question that asks whether it would be good policy to treat such persons or whether it would be humane, effective, and so on. The question is asked only in terms of legal obligation and the answer is—no. The key to understanding this answer lies in the fact that courts generally have not characterized alcoholism or drug addition as serious medical/mental health conditions. Parenthetically, a drug reaction withdrawal may well be "serious" and require an appropriate clinical intervention.

In rejecting a claim for alcohol treatment programs at New Jersey's Rahway Prison, the federal judge indicated that not every illness or injury is "serious." He appeared to leave room for a claim that some substance abusers were seriously ill, but like many of his judicial colleagues, he ultimately viewed the claim as one for non-mandated rehabilitation.[8]

There simply is no constitutional right to rehabilitation. If alcoholism and drug addiction are viewed as a kind of status or condition, as opposed to disease, then the claim is translated as one to rehabilitation and it is lost. In many judicial proceedings a trial judge will order, or the parties may enter into an agreement for, a substance abuse program. And among my 15 desirable factors listed at ¶ 2.6[2] is the treatment of such conditions in an integrated system.

A prison system may be found so deficient that the judge requires things that are otherwise viewed as desirable and the government sees no point in challenging the requirement. This may help explain consent decrees that sweep more broadly than constitutional minima. Thus, while there are examples of judicially-mandated substance abuse programs, they result from unusual aspects of the litigation or from agreement, and not from strict adherence to legal norms.

¶ 2.9 ISOLATION

Returning now to some specific problems jail and prisons encounter in dealing with their mentally disturbed inmates, the use of isolation often creates legal entanglements. No case has been found that totally forbids isolation of the mentally ill, even though some experts find its use, especially with suicidal inmates, counterproductive.

---

[8] Pace v. Fauver, 479 F. Supp. 456 (D.N.J. 1979), aff'd, 649 F.2d 860 (3rd Cir. 1981). See supra note 5 for the Ohio approach to this matter.

The inmate's mental condition is—and should be—a crucial factor in determining whether the overall conditions of isolation are cruel and unusual.

Prison officials must be especially judicious in their use of isolation (or other forms of temporary restraint) and be certain to follow local rules closely on such items as duration, authorization, and monitoring. A "sentence" of some form of isolation by a disciplinary committee should take into account the likely impact on an inmate known to be suffering with mental illness.

¶ 2.10 RESTRAINT

Restraint and seclusion are often joined for discussion and analysis in the literature and in various standards. By restraint I refer to the use of a mechanical immobilizing device, typically and preferably leather padded wristlets and anklets, used during a crisis period to prevent injury to the individual and others. Such restraints may never be used for punishment whether or not an inmate is on a mental health caseload.

On the other hand, isolation is an acceptable form of punishment, as well as a device to prevent injury, for the mentally ill and for those who are not mentally ill. When disciplinary segregation, or isolation, is imposed on a mentally ill inmate, there are special considerations involving the projected impact on the inmate. There also is caselaw to support the notion that marginally acceptable conditions for those not mentally ill are marginally unacceptable in light of the known mental condition of certain inmates.

[1] During Civil Confinement

In referring to the civilly confined, one expert has written, "Typically, state laws and/or regulations require as a condition for application of restraints: a diagnosis of mental illness, imminent danger to self or others, and determination that less restrictive measures would be ineffective."[9] An American Psychiatric Association report actually appears to go a bit further and states:

> Indications for seclusion . . . are 1) to prevent imminent harm to the patient or other persons when other means of control are not effective or appropriate, 2) to prevent serious disruption of the treatment program or significant damage to the physical environment, and 3) for treatment as part of an ongoing plan of behavior therapy.[10]

You will note that I have not addressed the use of restraints in connection with a behavior modification program, as does the APA Report. That approach is discussed within the context of treatment modalities.

---

[9] KENNETH L. FAIVER, HEALTH CARE MANAGEMENT ISSUES IN CORRECTIONS (1988), p. 152 n.18.

[10] SECLUSION AND RESTRAINT: THE PSYCHIATRIC USE 45 (Am. Psychiatric Ass'n Task Force, 1984).

[2] Challenges to Restraint

When the use of restraints is challenged, it is often analyzed as an alleged application of excessive force. Looked at in this way, the problem falls within the contours of *Hudson v. McMillian*,[11] which holds that in order to constitute cruel and unusual punishment the application of official force must involve the unnecessary and wanton infliction of pain. There is no "significant injury" requirement, but the mental element requirement is very difficult to prove. One must show that force, here in the form of restraints, was applied for the very purpose of causing pain or other harm. Thus, even a misguided or gratuitous strapping down might not amount to constitutional injury.

The use of restraints on an inmate who is on the mental health caseload may also be challenged as a variety of deliberate indifference to the treatment needs of one who is seriously mentally ill. This approach then becomes an *Estelle v. Gamble*-type claim (see Chapter 4) and the deliberate indifference test is not as difficult for the inmate to meet. At this juncture we need only note the possibility of parallel claims and the need to approach restraints in a judicious manner with early medical involvement and close monitoring.

¶ 2.11 PRETRIAL DETAINEES

The primary focus of this book is mentally disordered prisoners, but pretrial detainees have at least the same right to diagnosis, adequate records, treatment, and other cognate rights as persons convicted of a crime. Indeed, in the hierarchy of legal rights retained by those in some form of penal confinement, convicted prisoners occupy the lowest rung. It is safe to assume that the unconvicted detainee possesses whatever rights the convicted possess and is entitled to at least the same level of care.

The source of the right to care for pretrail detainees, however, is not the Eighth Amendment, but the Due Process Clause of the Fourteenth Amendment. The distinction creates some interesting constitutional issues, but for present purposes the bottom line is the nature, rather than the specific source, of the right. To repeat the point made earlier: detainees are entitled to at least the same level of care as the convicted.

Pretrial detainees clearly present a different package of mental health problems than convicted prisoners. Their stay is relatively brief, alcohol and drug abuse problems abound, suicide is far more prevalent, examinations for trial may be performed, and the initial shock of jailing is itself traumatic for many. Many observers find that local jails may indeed be the only mental health resource available to them. As mental hospitals close and community mental health facilities fail to keep pace, the jail seems always to be there. The question is whether the resources are there or available, and too often the answer is no.

Suffice it to say that the right to care (and protection) is there: it is at least as demanding as the "deliberate indifference" standard that applies to the convicted, and jails must have ready access to diagnostic and treatment resources and personnel. Long-term care will not be an issue, but short-term care, acute care, detoxification issues, and the threat of suicide are dramatically involved.

---

[11] 503 U.S. 1 (1992).

¶ 2.12 SUICIDE

Suicide, of course, is not a problem confined to jails, although about four times as many suicides occur in jails as in prisons. The risk of suicide is sufficiently greater in a jail setting that every jailer must immediately confront that phenomenon as a problem of appropriate care, surveillance, and custody. In reviewing lawsuits that have resulted from custodial suicide, the following questions emerge:

1. Did the facility have the basic capacity to respond to the problem?

2. How many staff were in place and how were they trained?

3. Is the structure of the facility itself a contributory factor?

4. How well did staff respond to the threat posed, for example, by a highly intoxicated or highly agitated detainee?

5. How closely was the person monitored?

6. Exactly what steps, in compliance with what suicide protocols, were taken to prevent the suicide?

7. Were clinical personnel involved? If not, why not; and, if so, when and how?

These questions are not exhaustive, but they are highly representative. Jails confine a highly diverse population and often receive people who are in an extreme, albeit temporary, emotional condition. It is incumbent on jailers to initially screen and provide humane and protective care for the potential suicide. This, of course, is crisis intervention in its most basic form and not a commitment of resources to long-term care.

It would be misleading, even in a brief summary, to leave the impression that custodial suicide cases pose major liability questions for custodians. Deliberate indifference, with the *Farmer* standard of criminal recklessness as the mental requirement for constitutional liability, is difficult, indeed, to establish. Even where an inmate was known to be suicidal but was placed in an inpatient psychiatric unit where he suffocated himself with a plastic bag, the reviewing court found no deliberate indifference.[12] Why? The clinical judgment of low risk was within professional judgment norms and, thus, there was not a strong likelihood that a suicide would occur or would occur with that instrumentality.

¶ 2.13 THE MENTALLY RETARDED

The mentally retarded inmate presents a special package of problems that can confound correctional administrators. Some mental health professionals believe that the plight of the retarded inmate is even worse than that of a mentally ill inmate. Retarded inmates often are gullible, vulnerable, and too often victimized and manipulated by fellow inmates.

---

[12] *See* Estate of Max G. Cole v. Fromm, 94 F.3d 254 (7th Cir. 1996), *cert. denied,* 117 S. Ct. 945 (1997).

At the outset, there is a serious question concerning just how a severely retarded person is able to negotiate the criminal justice system and end up in prison. Persons who are severely retarded are likely to be incompetent to be tried or enter a plea since they may not understand the criminal charges or be able to assist counsel. Therefore, an inmate who is functionally impaired to the point where a conviction is improper should not be in prison. But they are, and they often are dual diagnosed.

One recent study estimated that about 2 percent of our prison population is retarded. On the other hand, some courts have found 10 to 15 percent of the prison population to be retarded. Persons who are severely or profoundly retarded simply should not be in prison and if they are, there is a failure somewhere along the way in the system. Only the mildly retarded should ever be found in prison.

With problems ranging from exploitation to the serving of longer terms, no one seems to deny the plight of this group of people. Do the mentally retarded have a constitutional right to treatment in prison? Unfortunately, the answer is no. Do the mentally retarded have any special claims to help while imprisoned? The answer is a guarded yes, grounded on a due process claim to physical safety and freedom from undue restraints.

The right-to-treatment concepts are more fully developed in Chapter 4. It is enough to say here that the right to treatment in prison exists within a disease or illness model. However mental retardation is classified, it is not a disease and inmates do not become retarded in prison. Their learning or developmental disability may contribute to problems of adjustment in prison, but that, of course, is different than acquiring a condition in prison.

The mentally retarded are prime candidates for diversion from prison and, once in prison, for programs designed to enhance their social and educational skills, and to allow them to maximize their human potential. The claim to positive help, however, as opposed to special protective concerns, is not of the same legal stature as that of the seriously mentally ill inmate.

¶ 2.14 TRANSFERS FOR TREATMENT

While all prisons and jails must provide basic treatment at least for the seriously disordered inmate, the choice as to the type of treatment *and where* it is provided raises few, if any, legal questions. Discretion clearly exists as to the mix of on-site and off-site medical and psychological services. However, when a prisoner appears to need care in a mental hospital and a transfer is contemplated, then the Supreme Court's decision in *Vitek v. Jones*[13] applies.

A *Vitek*-like situation arises when a decision is made that a particular prison does not have the treatment resources or security appropriate to a seriously mentally disordered inmate. Correctional officials will seek a transfer to a mental hospital and the inmate may seek to resist. This creates an adversary situation and one in which the inmate has important procedural rights.

Quite simply, *Vitek* decided that the combination of additional stigma, a drastic alteration in the conditions of confinement, and being subjected to a mandatory

---

[13] 445 U.S. 480 (1980).

behavior-modification program created a protected liberty interest traceable to the Fourteenth Amendment Due Process Clause.

The following minimal due process safeguards are now constitutionally required by *Vitek* before such a transfer:

1. Written notice to the prisoner that a transfer to a mental hospital is being considered.

2. A hearing sufficiently after the notice to permit the prisoner to prepare, at which disclosure to the prisoner is made of the evidence being relied on for the transfer and at which an opportunity to be heard in person and to present documentary evidence is given.

3. An opportunity at the hearing to present testimony of witnesses by the defense and to confront and cross-examine witnesses called by the state, except on a finding, not arbitrarily made, of good cause for not permitting such presentation, confrontation, or cross-examination.

4. An independent decisionmaker who need not come from outside the prison or hospital administration.

5. A written statement by the fact-finder as to the evidence relied on and the reasons for transferring the inmate.

6. Availability of "qualified and independent assistance," furnished by the state, if the inmate is financially unable to furnish his own.

7. Effective and timely notice of all the foregoing rights.

There are a number of interesting questions surrounding *Vitek* that are raised and discussed in Chapter 17. Perhaps the most basic question relates to whether *Vitek*-mandated procedures apply where a transfer is to a treatment facility administratively within the prison system. The answer suggested here is that when a finding of mental illness is a predicate for admission to a treatment facility, then the physical location and administrative responsibility should be irrelevant to *Vitek*'s applicability. Indeed, as more and more mental health services are provided by corrections—a clear movement since *Vitek* was decided—such a result is necessary to give meaning to the procedural safeguards the Court sought to provide.

Parenthetically, when such a transfer is for a relatively brief period of observation, then *Vitek* does not apply. In my experience, such transfers actually are made because a diagnosis and "need to treat" decision will have been made at the sending facility. It is also somewhat ironic that in practice the problem is not an overreliance on hospitalization or the procedural accommodation of protesting inmates. Protests are extremely rare and the more likely problem is gaining rapid access to desperately needed care.

Finally, in *Sandin v. Conner*[14] the Supreme Court recently adopted a radically different approach to establishing the liberty interest it requires before procedural due

---

[14] 115 S. Ct. 2293 (1995). Even in its relatively brief life, *Sandin* has been discussed in perhaps 800 appellate decisions.

process is mandated. Whatever impact *Sandin* will have on prison discipline, the Court specifically exempted *Vitek* transfers from its reach. Thus, *Vitek* and its progeny remain "good law."

¶ 2.15 THE TREATMENT RELATIONSHIP

[1] Confidentiality vs. Institutional Security

The treatment relationship in the institutional setting presents recurring and profound legal questions regarding confidentiality and privilege, the duty to disclose when a clinician learns about a particular kind of danger, and the problems of consent to treatment. The need for confidentiality and privilege, as a matter of law and professional ethics, rests on the individual's expectations of privacy and nondisclosure, and on the recognition that the need for information to provide necessary treatment generally outweighs even compelling demands for disclosure. Where the relationship with the inmate is for diagnosis-evaluation-classification (or something similar), then the full impact of privilege and confidentiality does not apply.

In *Jaffe v. Redmond*[15] the Supreme Court determined that Rule 501 of the Federal Rules of Evidence, which creates a psychotherapist-patient privilege rule, was broad enough to encompass psychiatrists, psychologists, and licensed social workers. The ruling preserved the confidentiality of a female police officer who participated in some 50 counseling sessions with a licensed clinical social worker who, in turn, refused to turn over notes on the demand of plaintiff's counsel in a wrongful death action.

While this is a surprisingly liberal view about the scope of the privilege, it must be emphasized that the ruling applies only in the federal courts, although it is likely to have persuasive value in other jurisdictions. Justice Scalia wrote a scathing, indeed mocking, dissent expressing doubt about whether the privilege enhances treatment, and he wondered why we do not also have a mother-child privilege.

Before proceeding with an inmate, the mental health professional in a prison or mental hospital setting is well advised to disclose his or her agency, the purpose of the meeting, and the uses to which the information will or may be put. The professional should also indicate a willingness to answer as concretely as possible all questions concerning the risks of disclosure.

The really difficult problems for the clinician are to balance the generally applicable principle of confidentiality in a treatment relationship with the countervailing demands of security—the security of specific individuals who may be in jeopardy and the general security of the institution. The treatment-security issue has become blurred as correctional officers increasingly become a part of the treatment team.

[2] When Confidentiality Does Not Apply

Every jurisdiction should adopt a clear set of rules as to when confidentiality is inapplicable. One solution is to require mental health personnel to report to correctional personnel when they identify an inmate as on of the following:

---

[15] 116 S. Ct. 1923 (1996).

- Suicidal

- Homicidal

- Presenting a reasonably clear danger of injury to self or to others either by virtue of conduct or oral statements

- Presenting a reasonably clear danger of escape or the creation of internal disorder or riot

- Receiving psychotropic medication

- Requiring movement to a special unit for observation valuation, or treatment of acute episodes

- Requiring transfer to a treatment facility outside the prison or jail

When a mental health professional has reason to believe that an inmate-patient presents a danger of violence to persons who are readily identifiable, a duty arises to use reasonable care to protect the intended victim. This often is referred to as a *Tarasoff*[16] problem and the safest response would be for the clinician to alert appropriate security personnel and allow them to implement security as needed.

An even more difficult *Tarasoff* problem arises when an inmate with mental illness is to be discharged having received the full criminal sentence, and there is a belief that the person is dangerous. What action, if any, is required, and does this vary with the specificity of the person or persons who are endangered?

¶ 2.16 CONSENT

On the question of the need to obtain consent for various types of treatment, there is a general formula that may be useful in developing an answer: the more intrusive the treatment, the more likely the risk of permanent side effects, and the more experimental the procedure, the more likely the need to obtain consent.

Where informed consent is required, the legal minima include a competent adult, the absence of duress or coercion, the disclosure of information on risks, and the likely consequences of not accepting the preferred care. Inmates and detainees have gained considerable ground in the effort to require consent to various forms of psychotherapy or drug therapy. Drugs that are intended to cause paralysis or vomiting as a part of a behavioral modification program have been characterized as cruel punishment unless there is consent.

The Constitution does not forbid "cruel treatment," only cruel punishment. Occasionally, there will be a threshold argument concerning whether a particular intervention is punishment or treatment. However, characterizing an intervention as treatment does not wholly insulate it from legal challenge. If a due process "liberty" interest or a First Amendment interest in religious freedom or expression is implicated, then a constitutional barrier to the intended treatment may be found.

---

[16] Tarasoff v. Regents of Univ. of Cal., 551 P.2d 334 (Ca. 1976).

Again, the *Sandin* decision alluded to at ¶ 2.14 does not impact existing decisions on the constitutional necessity for consent.

¶ 2.17 THE FUTURE

Looking into the future, it would appear that the conservative tone established by the present Supreme Court will prevail for some time. Among other things, this means that an inmate's basic constitutional right to minimal physical and psychological care is not likely to be enriched or expanded. It also means continued, and perhaps enhanced, deference to mental health professionals as to what is or is not appropriate diagnosis and care. And it surely seems unlikely that more in the way of inmate consent to care will be required.

The basic legal framework for a mentally disordered inmate's claim to care and services has been established and is not likely to be undone. However, it is also unlikely that the Supreme Court will further cultivate those rights, although some of the more liberal and activist federal district courts may continue to expand and enrich prisoners' rights. The substance and the direction of care for the mentally disordered and mentally retarded inmate and detainee more likely will be determined by state and federal officials and by professionals seeking to expand and improve prison and jail care.

Some legislative developments, particularly the Prison Litigation Reform Act (PLRA), will likely have an impact on the availability of certain remedial measures now widely used in the federal courts.[17] Under PLRA, consent decrees and injunctive measures must rest on a finding of unconstitutional conditions, any such remedies are severely remedially and time-limited, and fees for counsel and Masters are quite limited, along with a host of other restraints.

I must emphasize that PLRA does not—and, indeed, under the restraints of separation of powers could not—affect any of the substantive rights and duties that are the subject of this book. Beyond that, where the Court has found a liberty interest, for example, in the avoidance of the supposed stigma of mental illness or unwanted psychotropic drugs, and where it has also mandated procedures ancillary to the right, the PLRA does not, and could not, alter such problems.

Failure to accommodate the special needs of physically and mentally disabled inmates may give rise to a statutory claim under the as yet largely unexploited Americans with Disabilities Act (ADA).[18] Most important is the ADA's prohibition against discrimination in services, programs, or activities. Inmates with a variety of physical disabilities are entitled to reasonable access or accommodation, and this has led to major architectural changes in prisons and the relocation of certain activities from, for example, an upper floor to a ground level floor. There is, however, no caselaw of any consequence dealing with the ADA and mentally disordered inmates.

I have personally encountered instances where mental illness alone purportedly disqualified an inmate from a "boot camp" program or a particularly desirable hous-

---

[17] 18 U.S.C.A. § 3626.

[18] 42 U.S.C. §§ 12101–12213. *See* discussion in Chapter 1, ¶ 1.4.

ing or work situation. In each instance, when the matter was brought to the attention of authorities, the policy was changed to require an individual decision on the program, job, or housing and that appeared to satisfy the intent of the ADA.[19]

With prison and jail populations continuing to rise and bringing with it a tide of additional inmates who are mentally ill, the problems addressed here will only grow more severe. Ultimately, a policy of selective diversion from the criminal justice system and of carefully coordinated reintegration into the community after a prison or jail term is far more desirable than what we presently have.

The boundaries of constitutional obligation are the boundaries of actual physical custody. This will be discussed under the rubric of the *DeShaney*[20] principle. In a work devoted to the law those boundaries apply here as well, although I will offer opinions from time to time outside those parameters.

I am acutely aware of the practical artificiality of this boundary setting at the front and back door of the prison or jail. In the same way, I am aware of the intellectual and practical limitations of linking care to a serious mental disorder. An integrated approach to mental health care would begin with workable diversion programs at the front end; the integration of all "special needs" services within the prison walls (substance abuse, sex offender treatment, all manner of mental disorder wherever placed on the DSM[21] scale); and then follow the offender into the community with support, medication, and necessary care.

---

[19] *See also* The Rehabilitation Act of 1973, 29 U.S.C. §§ 504, 794.

[20] DeShaney v. Winnebago Dept. of Social Servs., 489 U.S. 189 (1989). *See* Chapter 4, ¶ 4.2[2].

[21] DIAGNOSTIC AND STATISTICAL MANUAL OF MENTAL DISORDERS (American Psychiatric Association, 1994).

Chapter 3

The Prison Inmate's Legal Identity

¶ 3.1 GOVERNING LAW

A prison inmate exists generally in a world of constricted legal rights. An understanding of that world will further our grasp of an inmate's rights and obligations in the area of mental disorder. This chapter provides a broad review of the law of prisoners' rights as well as a legal framework for the detailed material in subsequent chapters.

It is clear beyond argument that on conviction and sentence of imprisonment a radical change occurs in a person's legal status. The Thirteenth Amendment to the U.S. Constitution reads in part, "Neither slavery nor involuntary servitude, except as a punishment for crime whereof the party shall have been duly convicted, shall exist in the United States . . . ." The duly convicted prisoner, then, may be punished and also expect that many freedoms enjoyed as a free person have been relinquished.[1] Indeed, the Supreme Court has stated, "[p]rison brutality . . . is 'part of the total punishment to which the individual is being subjected for his crime and, as such, is a proper subject for Eighth Amendment scrutiny.'"[2] Both the inmate's punishment and his claim to psychiatric or psychological care are rooted in the Eighth Amendment. Pretrial detainees, on the other hand, may not be punished at all, and they must fashion their claims under the Due Process Clause of the Fourteenth Amendment.[3]

¶ 3.2 BASIC RIGHTS—DELINEATING THEIR SCOPE

Lawful conviction of a crime and imprisonment, although working a radical change in the legal identity of the inmate, does not strip the person of all rights. This was never the case, although some earlier observers concluded that prisoners simply have no rights.[4] Indeed, from the earliest times under English law, prisoners have had a right to the minimal conditions necessary for human survival. Nothing fancy here, just the right to such food, clothing, shelter, and medical care as was necessary to sustain life. The right to the minimal conditions for human survival may accurately be viewed as the irreducible minimum for prisoners' rights.[5]

An inmate's right to a non-life-threatening environment, in fact, goes beyond the provisions of life's necessities. Prison officials are under a general duty to protect inmates from other inmates and from themselves.[6] In a decision involving the suicide of a jail inmate, Connecticut claimed that in the absence of a clear holding that there is a constitutional right to be protected from suicide, the claim should be dismissed.[7] The district court held that "protecting inmates from themselves [is] an aspect of the broader constitutional duty to provide medical care for inmates."[8]

---

[1] *See* JOHN BOSTON & DANIEL E. MANVILLE, PRISONER'S SELF-HELP LITIGATION MANUAL (3d ed. 1995), for perhaps the best summary and analysis of the right lost or impaired.

[2] Ingraham v. Wright, 430 U.S. 651, 669 (1977), *quoting* Ingraham v. Wright, 525 F.2d 909, 915 (5th Cir. 1976).

[3] *See* Bell v. Wolfish, 441 U.S. 520, 535 n.16 (1979). Whether or not this doctrinal difference makes a difference in the detail of what care actually is required is not at all clear. My best speculation is that there is no practical difference.

[4] *See, e.g.,* Ruffin v. Commonwealth, 52 Va. (21 Gratt.) 790 (1871).

[5] H. KERPER & J. KERPER, LEGAL RIGHTS OF THE CONVICTED (1974), p. 285. The Court clearly has endorsed the statement in the text, but the more disturbing problem may be the extent to which the Eighth Amendment is interpreted to require more.

[6] *See* B. Knight & S. Early, Jr., PRISONERS' RIGHTS IN AMERICA (1986), Ch. 8. *See also* Hudson v. Palmer, 468 U.S. 512, 526–527 (1984) ("[Prisons] are under an obligation to take reasonable measures to guarantee the safety of the inmates themselves").

[7] Guglielmoni v. Alexander, 583 F. Supp. 821, 826 (D. Conn. 1984). The decedent had attempted suicide at least twice before succeeding.

[8] Guglielmoni, 583 F. Supp. at 827.

If there were any lingering doubts about a custodian's duty to protect inmates from other inmates, *Farmer v. Brennan*[9] put them to rest. Justice Souter wrote that "prison officials have a duty to protect prisoners from violence at the hands of other prisoners."[10] The rationale offered is simple: having confined persons with antisocial, often violent, propensities and then removed virtually every means of self-defense and foreclosed access to outside aid, government may not just let nature take its course. Being assaulted, then, is not part of the price of a sentence of imprisonment.

In many instances, the duty to protect inmates is unrelated to a medical or psychiatric issue. But in cases of custodial suicide, two normally independent duties—to protect and to provide medical or psychiatric care—may converge.

There are some other general statements or principles that will aid in the further development of this topic. Given the continuing lack of certainty as to precisely what specific rights are lost or retained on conviction and imprisonment, one aid to understanding is to identify the competing conceptual positions and then to select the one that most nearly points in the correct direction.[11]

[1] Variant Approaches

One position is the frequently cited view announced in *Coffin v. Reichard*[12] that a prisoner retains all the rights of an ordinary citizen except those expressly or by necessary implication taken by law. The Coffin opinion does not further explicate the matter and is open to the criticism of "glittering generality." However, there is a "rights are preferred" position inherent in this formulation, and while this will not in itself resolve any specific problem, it may provide direction for decision making.

One author has challenged the widely held view that prisoners necessarily lose rights by virtue of imprisonment itself. The necessity doctrine, he argues, is not as sweeping nor as categorical as one might first suppose. Putting aside political and empirical grounds, there is no reason in theory why the differences in social and material conditions between the inside and outside worlds cannot be diminished to the point where inmate rights, while confined, are not necessarily lost.[13]

Diametrically opposed to the Coffin position is one that views the prisoner as wholly without rights except those either expressly conferred or necessarily implied by law. Again, no particular issue can be resolved by this formula, but it is clear that fewer rights will be afforded the inmate under this formulation. Indeed, in the present climate inmates are losing access to free weights and educational programs, being forced to wear stripes, working on chain gangs, and paying for medication and access to the courts.

---

[9] 511 U.S. 825 (1994).

[10] Farmer, 511 U.S. at 833, *quoting* Cortes-Quinones v. Jiminez-Nettleship, 842 F.2d 556, 558, *cert. denied* , 488 U.S. 823 (1988).

[11] In New York State Ass'n for Retarded Children, Inc. v. Rockefeller, 357 F. Supp. 752 (E.D.N.Y. 1973) (popularly known as the Willowbrook Case), Judge Judd, after denying the existence of a constitutional right to treatment or rehabilitation for these profoundly retarded residents, determined that such residents had at least the same rights as prison inmates. At bottom; this was determined to be a tolerable living environment, including protection from assaults by fellow inmates or staff.

[12] 142 F. 2d 443, 445 (6th Cir. 1944), *cert. denied*, 325 U.S. 887 (1945).

[13] *See* Gochnaver, *Necessity and Prisoners' Rights*, 10 N. ENG. ON CRIM. & CIVIL CONFINEMENT 276 (1984).

Neither of these positions, even in their generality, is completely descriptive of an agreed-upon approach to the legal status of prisoners. The second, more grudging formula does, however, come close to describing the approach to a prisoner's claim now employed by the Supreme Court. *Meachum v. Fano*[14] is a good example of this dichotomy. Justice White, writing for a majority in denying inmates a constitutional right to procedural safeguards before a "punitive transfer," takes the view that not all "grievous losses" suffered by inmates are constitutionally protected; the state may with impunity imprison an inmate in any prison it maintains, regardless of the varying degrees of security in state prisons and in general. A state may confine and subject to its rules a convicted person so long as the conditions of confinement do not otherwise violate the Constitution. Justice Stevens, in dissent, argued "that even the inmate retains an unalienable interest in liberty—at the very minimum the right to be treated with dignity—which the Constitution may never ignore." This posture allowed Justice Stevens and two other Justices to conclude that despite the content of state law a prisoner whose transfer results in a grievous loss is entitled to some due process safeguards.[15]

Lower federal courts have appeared more generous toward prisoners than the Supreme Court and have been especially responsive to inmate claims regarding overall prison or jail conditions. In *Rhodes v. Chapman*,[16] Justice Brennan, in dissent, pointed out that there were over 8,000 pending cases filed by inmates challenging prison conditions and that individual prisons or entire prison systems in at least 24 states have been declared unconstitutional. More recently, an ACLU survey found that there were major court orders in prisons and jails in 40 states.[17]

By 1992, there were 26,824 such lawsuits filed in the federal courts, about one lawsuit for every 30 state prison inmates.[18] Of course, in the overwhelming majority of these lawsuits (94 percent) inmates won nothing, with 75 percent dismissed by the court and 20 percent resolved against the inmates on motion by the defendants. Complaints about medical care, which appear to include mental health care, were the second most common (17 percent) cause of action, following physical activity (21 percent) in this 9-state study conducted by The Bureau of Justice Statistics.[19]

One authoritative work states, "[I]n summary, prisoner status lies in the gray area between slaves and citizens."[20] Three general principles descriptive of prisoners' claims support their "slave/citizen" dichotomy. First, prisoners do not forfeit all con-

---

[14] 427 U.S. 215 (1976).

[15] Meachum, 427 U.S. at 234 (Stevens, J., dissenting). *See also* ¶ 3.7[6].

[16] 452 U.S. 337 (1981); *see also* Terrence Thornberry, et al., *Overcrowding in American Prisons: Policy Implications of Double-Bunking Single Cells XI* (Univ. of Ga., July 1982) in which the authors uncovered litigation concerning overcrowding in 37 states, the District of Columbia, Puerto Rico, and the Virgin Islands; *see also* Rod Smolla, *Prison Overcrowding and the Courts: A Roadmap for the 1980's*, 1984 U. Ill. L. Rev. 389, for a study of post-*Rhodes* litigation showing a surprising number of inmate victories.

[17] ACLU, The National Prison Project Status Report: The Courts and Prisons (Washington, D.C., 1988).

[18] Roger A. Hanson & Henry W. K. Daley, U.S. Dep't of Justice, Challenging the Conditions of Prisons and Jails: A Report on Section 1983 Litigation 3-4 (1995) [hereinafter BJS Challenging Conditions].

[19] BJS Challenging Conditions at 36, 8. Parenthetically, only 19 percent of the dismissals were found to be frivolous by the BJS study.

[20] James Gobert & Neil Cohen, Rights of Prisoners (1981), p. 12.

stitutional rights. Second, the rights they retain are not necessarily or generally coextensive with those enjoyed by free people. Third, prisoners' rights are tempered by the fact of confinement and the needs of the administration, including order, security, and discipline.[21]

[2] Hands-Off Doctrine

These principles seem accurate as far as they go, but with all deference, it is possible to go quite a bit further. The Supreme Court appears to have passionately reembraced the older doctrine of judicial "hands off."[22] That is, the Court favors a situation of minimal and nominal judicial involvement in the internal affairs of prisons. This view may be discerned in the large number of losses for inmate claims that have reached the Court, which has generated a discouragement of further suits in that area of law and excessive deference to correctional expertise, real or imagined.[23] The former Chief Justice has made repeated public pronouncements of the need to cleanse the federal courts of prison litigation,[24] and the actual holdings rendered in the most recent decisions (along with PLRA filing requirements) make it increasingly difficult even to bring a lawsuit.[25]

¶ 3.3 PRISONERS' RIGHTS VS. PRISON SECURITY

Prison security is perhaps the most frequently cited rationale for denying inmates' claims. While security concerns are authentic and compelling, it does appear that the Supreme Court too easily accepts such claims. For example, in *Jones v. North Carolina Prisoners' Union,*[26] the inmates claimed a First Amendment right to organize as a Prisoners' Labor Union, to pursue the goal of improved working conditions, to work for change in prison policies, and to serve as a conduit for prisoners' grievances. Needless to say, prison officials viewed the union as a threat and took steps to effectively ban it.

The prisoners actually won broad relief in the lower court, which found that there was not a scintilla of evidence that the union had been used to disrupt the prisons. The lower courts were also unable to perceive how soliciting union membership would disrupt prison order and discipline.[27]

In reversing, the Supreme Court took a completely different approach to the claims surrounding security. Prison officials had testified that the presence, perhaps

---

[21] Gobert & Cohen at 12, 13.

[22] The "hands-off" doctrine is not so much a doctrine as a description of judicial reluctance to accept and decide prison cases. *See* Lewis v. Casey, 116 S. Ct. 2174 (1996), an access to the courts case in which the Court established an "actual injury-standing" requirement that appears to require a preliminary showing of the merits of the legal claim as a jurisdictional prerequisite. *See* discussion of *Lewis infra* at ¶ 3.4[1] and detailed discussion in Ch. 7, ¶ 7.3[1].

[23] *See, e.g.,* Houchins v. KQED, Inc., 438 U.S. 1 (1978).

[24] Annual Report on the State of the Judiciary (transcript), by Chief Justice Warren E. Burger, 69 A.B.A.J. 442 (1983).

[25] *See* Lewis, *supra* note 22.

[26] 433 U.S. 119 (1977).

[27] Jones, 433 U.S. at 123, 124.

even the objectives, of a prisoners' labor union would be detrimental to order and security in the prisons. Such testimony could only have been impressionistic and speculative since there had been no experience in North Carolina, or anywhere else, with similar inmate organizations. Justice Rehnquist, writing for the majority, stated: "It is enough to say that they [prison officials] have not been conclusively shown to be wrong in this view. The interest in preserving order and authority in the prisons is self-evident."[28]

This quotation illustrates how the allocation of the burden of proof determines the outcome when neither side has a factual advantage. The inmates could not possibly show conclusively that prison officials were wrong in their views about a possible threat to prison security. If prison officials had been required to substantiate their impressions concerning safety—as they were in the lower court—then the inmates would have prevailed.

Jones is a powerful illustration of judicial deference to claims of threats to prison security, and it is by no means the only case that could be cited.[29] We repeatedly encounter security claims made on behalf of corrections throughout this work. In dealing with behavioral problems associated with the mentally disordered inmate, we must grapple with maintenance-of-order claims on the one hand and issues of inmate accountability and treatment on the other hand. Parenthetically, some jurisdictions are adopting procedure and policy in the disciplinary context that takes into account an inmate's mental condition. This is quite a concession from security.[30]

The specific legal claims and rights of prisoners can be arranged into different categories. First, the unconvicted possess a significant number of important legal rights that are entirely lost to prisoners: for example, freedom from punishment, the right to move about freely, freedom of association, and the right to cohabit with one's mate. Second, some rights possessed by free people are retained by inmates but in a diluted fashion. Inmates have some First Amendment rights, especially in the area of religious beliefs and practices, that resemble the same rights possessed by free persons. However, an inmate's First Amendment right to freedom of expression is subject to inspection and censorship that would be unthinkable in the free world. As *Jones* made clear, inmate claims to freedom of association carry virtually no weight.

[1] Reasonableness Test

In two fairly recent Supreme Court decisions, the already attenuated First Amendment rights of prisoners were further reduced. In addition, *Turner v. Safely*[31] and *O'Lone v. Shabazz*[32] appear to have brought virtually all inmate First Amendment and so-called "fundamental rights" claims within the so-called reasonableness test—that is, rules are considered valid if reasonably related to legitimate penological interests. As a consequence, it is now even easier for prison officials to legally justify a broad array of prison regulations.

---

[28] Jones, 433 U.S. at 132.

[29] *See, e.g.,* Procunier v. Martinez, 416 U.S. 396, 413–414 (1974).

[30] Note that in deciding a challenge to the availability of, or access to, mental health care, security is not a countervailing balancing factor.

[31] 482 U.S. 78 (1987).

[32] 482 U.S. 342 (1987).

This rule of reasonableness is actually another means of expressing the extraordinary deference to prison officials being extended by the Court. This analysis received unexpected support in *Lewis v. Casey*,[33] an access to the courts case, where Justice Scalia astonished correctional experts by wedding the reasonableness test of Turner to the "reasonable access" test independently governing access to the courts. Justice Scalia, with no hint of breaking new analytic ground, simply wrote that Turner's deferential standard must be read together with prior case law on access.

Turner involved challenges lodged against two Missouri prison regulations, one relating to inmate marriages and the other relating to inmate-to-inmate correspondence. *O'Lone* dealt with New Jersey prison policies that resulted in Muslim inmates' inability to attend a weekly congregate service known as Jumu'ah, a service viewed as central to the observance of the Muslim faith.

Both the correspondence issue in Turner and the religious service issue in O'Lone are plainly grounded in the First Amendment. The Missouri marriage rule was characterized by the Court as a fundamental right that does accompany any inmate to prison.[34] Such a right will usually be traced to the Due Process Clause and characterized as substantive due process in contrast to the procedural due process (e.g., notice, hearing, burden of proof, etc.) we normally associate with that clause. The right to marry also might be grounded in the First Amendment as an aspect of the "free exercise clause." The Court did not further expand on the constitutional basis for its view of marriage as a fundamental right. Since *Turner* applied the same analysis to inmate-inmate correspondence and marriage, we may safely assume that the Court did not view either of these rights as weightier than the other.

The Court did elaborate on the analytical framework to be used in measuring "reasonableness." A four-prong test was announced:

(1) Is there a valid, rational connection between the prison regulation and the government's legitimate interest?

(2) Are there alternative means open to the inmate to exercise that right?

(3) What impact will accommodation of the asserted right have on other inmates and prison personnel?

(4) The absence of ready alternatives will be taken as evidence of reasonableness.[35]

The Court's decision in *Turner* to uphold the inmate-to-inmate correspondence ban sets the tone for the other inmates claims. Subject to a couple of narrow exceptions, Missouri inmates could correspond with other inmates only when prison personnel deemed it in the best interest of the parties involved.[36] According to the trial court, the practice was that inmates simply did not write to nonfamily inmates.[37]

---

[33] *Supra* note 22.

[34] Turner, 482 U.S. at 94.

[35] Turner, 482 U.S. at 89–90.

[36] The exceptions allowed inmates to correspond with other inmates who are also relatives and to correspond over legal matters. *See* Turner, 482 U.S. at 91–93.

[37] Safely v. Turner, 586 F. Supp. 589, 591 (W.D. Mo. 1984).

[2] Strict Scrutiny/Least Intrusive Test

The most critical aspect in resolving any First Amendment claim, whether for a prisoner or a nonprisoner, is to decide first on the standard to be used in reaching a decision. In finding the Turner mail ban unconstitutional, both lower federal courts applied a strict scrutiny/least intrusive standard. That is, these courts read an earlier Supreme Court decision, *Procunier v. Martinez*,[38] as supporting the proposition that the correspondence restriction could be justified only if it furthered an important or substantial governmental interest unrelated to suppression of expression and the limitation was no greater than necessary to protect that interest.[39]

Justice O'Connor, writing for a slim five-to-four majority, rejected the lower court's reliance on *Procunier* and stated: "When a prison regulation impinges on inmates' constitutional rights, the regulation is valid if it is reasonably related to legitimate penological interests."[40] This standard of review (i.e., the reasonableness test) is obviously less demanding on government than the strict scrutiny/least intrusive means test that the Court rejected.

Two points bear emphasis. Under the reasonableness test as adopted in *Turner*, the governmental interest need only be legitimate (as opposed to important or substantial), and the regulation need only be reasonably related to that legitimate interest (as opposed to the least intrusive means available).

Turning to the actual decision in *Turner*, we can demonstrate how the competing tests produce quite difference outcomes. The inmates claimed, and the lower courts accepted, that the monitoring of inmate correspondence was sufficient to satisfy the prison's undoubtedly valid security interests. A majority of the Court, however, found that monitoring was an unduly burdensome alternative not required by the Constitution, and that it would tax limited prison resources and still not be wholly effective. Thus, a total prohibition of all correspondence with a limited class of persons (other Missouri prisoners) was upheld as reasonable.[41]

The Missouri marriage rule also at issue in *Turner* prohibited inmates from marrying inmates or civilians unless the prison superintendent found "compelling reasons" for allowing the marriage. Generally, only pregnancy or the birth of a child were considered to be "compelling reasons."[42] After determining that marriage is a fundamental constitutional right that inmates do not fully surrender, the Court next determined that the Missouri rule swept too broadly for rehabilitative purposes and was an exaggerated response to valid security objectives.

---

[38] *Supra* note 29.

[39] Safely v. Turner, 777 F.2d. 1307, 1310 (8th Cir. 1985).

[40] Turner, 482 U.S. at 89.

[41] Turner, 482 U.S. at 93–94. Given the limited purposes of this section of this work, a detailed analysis of the reasonable test is not warranted. However, deep-rooted problems are immediately apparent. For example, if the Court's first point simply means a *logical* connection between the end (security) and the means, then—as Justice Stevens argues in a separate opinion—imaginative wardens and deferential courts will nearly always find that connection. Experience proves Justice Stevens to be correct.

[42] Turner, 482 U.S. at 96. Justice O'Connor added a cryptic note that the "strict scrutiny" standard of review might apply if the interest of nonprisoners was directly involved in the decision. That issue was not reached because the regulation fell under the less demanding reasonableness test.

Although the Missouri marriage rule was found constitutionally infirm, the majority made it very clear that a rule requiring a finding of a threat to security or to public safety would be constitutionally satisfactory.[43] A moment's reflection reveals just how undemanding that would be especially in light of the Court's capitulation to prison officials' conclusions about security interests.

[3] Summary of *Turner* Issues

Although much more could be written about Turner, for our purposes enough has been articulated. The primary points to be made may be summarized as follows. Until *Turner* (and *O'Lone*), there was good reason to believe that even for prisoners there was a hierarchy of constitutional rights and that hierarchy would importantly include First Amendment rights to expression. Therefore, when a prison rule or practice impinged on such a lofty right, courts were mandated to look very closely at the objective sought and to decide whether less drastic means were available to achieve that objective. This is simply another way of phrasing the strict scrutiny test. It must be emphasized, of course, that this discussion does not relate to the First Amendment rights of noninmates, namely publishers or free world correspondents. There is good reason to believe that the *Martinez* test survives for nonprisoners.[44]

The Supreme Court very plainly intended to substitute the easily complied with reasonableness test for strict scrutiny and thereby lend instant constitutional credibility to a number of restrictive rules and practices. The policy of deference to prison officials and the purging of the federal courts of a number of inmate legal claims received additional impetus in *Turner* and *O'Lone*. More recent decisions would only expand that judicial deference.

In *O'Lone,* Chief Justice Rehnquist employed an interesting analysis to reach the end result. Muslim inmates at New Jersey's Leesburg State Prison challenged policies that resulted in their inability to attend a religious service every Friday afternoon. The service, known as Jumu'ah, was accepted by the Court as central to the faith and no question was raised as to the legitimacy of the religion or the sincerity of the inmate claimants.

Muslim inmates who were given a work assignment outside the prison's main building were required to spend all day outside and were thereby effectively precluded from attending the congregate religious service. The inmates asked to be placed on inside work details or to be given substitute weekend tasks. These alternatives were rejected by prison officials based on an assertion of scarce prison personnel.

Prison officials also raised the ubiquitous security factor and Chief Justice Rehnquist found a logical connection between security and the prohibition against the return to the prison.[45] We should note that the Chief Justice used the word "logical" whereas in *Turner* Justice O'Connor had used "reasonable." But the most interesting maneuver in *O'Lone* relates to the issue of alternative means of exercising the claimed

---

[43] Turner, 482 U.S. at 97–98. The Court cited with approval the relevant federal prison rules; *see* 28 CFR § 551.10 (1986).

[44] *See, e.g.,* Abbot v. Meese, 824 F.2d 1166 (D.C. Cir. 1987), *cert. granted,* 108 S. Ct. 1572 (1988).

[45] O'Lone, *supra* note 32.

right. As indicated earlier,[46] the critical factor here is how the absence or presence of alternatives is analyzed. In this case, there was no alternative offered to Jumu'ah and one would think this would strengthen the inmate claim. However, the Chief Justice found that the availability of a number of other avenues for religious observance created reasonable alternatives.[47] In other words, the more expansive the universe of alternatives, the easier it is to uphold as reasonable the denial of one aspect of that universe.

One might add somewhat facetiously that *O'Lone* is the first important legal decision where inmates sued to gain entry to prison and the Court is so anti-inmate that they cannot prevail even on this claim. More seriously, the reasonableness test destroys any hierarchy of constitutional rights possessed by inmates and puts increasing responsibility on correctional officials to use wisdom and a sense of humanity in dealing with their captives.

O'Lone and *Turner* together represent a serious dilution of inmate claims to free expression and the free exercise of religion, both encompassed by the First Amendment. The extent to which this development may ultimately have direct or indirect effects on the constitutional obligation to provide medical and psychological care to inmates remains speculative although seemingly remote.

[4] Effect on Mental Disorder Claims

These developments should not cause any significant impact on medical and psychiatric claims. The Court appears reluctant to dilute inmates' health care rights beyond the "serious" and "deliberate indifference" standards.[48] A claim to medical or mental health care does not evoke competing claims to security. There is nothing to balance, then, against a claim to physical or psychological survival.

When we broach other areas of prisoners' rights, however, the Court is not so reluctant. In *Whitley v. Albers*,[49] for example, the Court had the problem of determining which standard governs an inmate's claim that prison officials subjected him to cruel and unusual punishment by shooting him during their attempt to quell a prison uprising. In the process of adopting a standard requiring that the force be used maliciously and sadistically to cause harm, Justice O'Connor also wrote:

> The deliberate indifference standard articulated in Estelle was appropriate in the context presented in that case because the State's responsibility to attend to the medical needs of prisoners does not ordinarily clash with other equally important governmental responsibilities. Consequently, "deliberate indifference to a prisoner's serious illness or injury" can typically be established or disproved without the necessity of balancing competing institutional concerns for the safety of prison staff or other inmates.[50]

---

[46] *See* court's analysis at ¶ 3.3[1].
[47] O'Lone, *supra* note 32, at 351–352.
[48] *See* detailed discussion of these standards in Chapter 4.
[49] 475 U.S. 312 (1986).
[50] Whitley, 475 U.S. at 320 (citation omitted).

Six years after adopting the "malicious and sadistic" standard for use of force claims directed against officials in a riot situation, the Court had to decide on the requisite mental element when such force was used on an inmate outside the demands of a riot. Faced with allegations by an inmate that he was beaten by staff while shackled and suffered bruises, facial swelling, loosened teeth and a cracked denture, the Court adopted the same "malicious and sadistic" standard it had fashioned for the turmoil of a riot.

Interestingly, a majority rejected the need to find significant injury as an aspect of liability, leaving the extent of the harm for damage determinations. Justices Thomas and Scalia, in dissent, argued that a constitutional use of force claim requires serious harm, otherwise there would not be the punishment required by the Eighth Amendment. On the other hand, they believe that the less onerous standard of deliberate indifference is the proper mental element, and that *Whitley's* "malicious and sadistic" standard is properly confined to the riot situation and all of its competing considerations.

[5] Civil Confinement

Inmates have a right to be free of cruel and unusual punishment, a right which for those in official confinement now may be reserved exclusively for convicted prisoners.[51] Persons who are civilly confined, such as the mentally ill or retarded, are protected from cruelty, but that protection is expressed as a liberty interest traceable to the Due Process Clause or as a form of impermissibly intrusive treatment also safeguarded by the Fourteenth Amendment. Detainees, as noted earlier, have the right not to be punished at all, a right residing in the Due Process Clause of the Fourteenth Amendment.

¶ 3.4 RIGHT OF ACCESS TO COURTS

One of the most fundamental rights possessed by inmates is the right of access to the courts.[52] In *Johnson v. Avery,*[53] the Supreme Court struck down a state prison regulation that allowed inmates to be punished for assisting other inmates in the preparation of habeas corpus applications and other legal documents. Johnson was decided in the context of a prison which provided inmates with no apparent alternatives to the so-called jailhouse lawyers.[54]

Johnson should be understood as an analogue to the injunction that "thou shalt not discriminate." It is a constitutional ruling that only goes so far as to require that prison officials not prevent access, or erect barriers to access, to the courts. The decision stops short of requiring "affirmative action." In *Bounds v. Smith,*[55] the Court decided

---

[51] Ingraham v. Wright, *supra* note 2, held that public school students who are subjected to corporal punishment are not protected by the Eighth Amendment's prohibition against cruel and unusual punishment; *see also* Bell v. Wolfish, *supra* note 3.

[52] *See* Ex parte Hull, 312 U.S. 546 (1941).

[53] 393 U.S. 483 (1969).

[54] Discussed in Wolff v. McDonnell, 418 U.S. 539, 577–580 (1974). The Court extended the *Johnson* rationale to civil rights actions.

[55] 430 U.S. 817 (1977).

that a prisoner's right of access to the courts required either an adequate law library or assistance from persons trained in the law, although not necessarily lawyers. Bounds, then, added "affirmative action" to the right of access to the courts.[56]

Once again, as we shall see in the area of treatment, the establishment of a predicate right—here, access to the court—necessarily spawns important ancillary rights. If there is a right to seek redress of grievances through the courts, then inmates must have paper, writing implements, envelopes, stamps, and so on. And courts have so decided.[57] Does an inmate require a typewriter? Probably not unless a particular court will accept only typed documents.

The rationale or policy behind the establishment of a right of access to the courts is plain enough. The walls that keep prisoners in, keep the community out. Prisons ought not to be allowed to function as hermetically sealed places of confinement subject to no outside scrutiny or challenge. Inmates are not so legally naked as to be without access to legal redress. Prisoners may seek access to the courts because of a legal matter that preceded their confinement (e.g., a contract dispute or a tort action); they may wish to challenge their conviction or confinement; or they may wish to bring a tort action arising from a claim of intentional or negligent injury related to a breach of duty to provide care on the part of the defendant.

[1] Procedural Hurdles to Access

All of this remains true, even the primary-ancillary rights analysis, except that after June 24, 1996 and the decision in *Lewis v. Casey*,[58] a series of procedural hurdles have been enacted to make access to the courts terribly difficult. We need to remind ourselves that we are dealing with an essentially functionally illiterate population, who are often destitute and find it near impossible to obtain counsel for the vast majority of their legal claims. Indeed, the problems created by *Lewis* were predictable given what I view as a fatal flaw in *Bounds* itself.

That is, to endorse a constitutional right of access to the courts with one hand and then give government the option of providing either books for the illiterate or trained legal assistance is to provide a cynical choice. Law books represent the less expensive, and of course less efficient, option, and most systems have chosen books for a population that in fact cannot really use them. *Bounds,* however, invited this.

Lewis, while conceding that inmates are mainly uneducated or illiterate, now imposes an actual injury, or what is technically known as a standing, requirement on inmates who complain of inadequate access to the courts. This means that a complaining inmate, whether or not illiterate or non-English speaking, must show that an

---

[56] A correction system that opted for providing access to adequate law libraries might have been required to provide assistance to those inmates not able to comprehend legal material. In Hooks v. Wainright, 536 F. Supp. 1330 (M.D. Fla. 1982), a federal district court sensibly found that given the high rate of illiteracy among Florida's inmates, it would be dishonest to conclude that meaningful access to the courts would be provided only with law libraries. This federal court ruling required some access to attorneys in addition to the availability of libraries. The district court's decision in *Hooks* was reversed at 775 F.2d 1422 (11th Cir. 1985), *cert. denied*, 479 U.S. 913 (1986); Lewis v. Casey, *supra* note 22, now forecloses any imaginative constitutional imperitives to provide meaningful access.

[57] *See* O'Bryan v. County of Saginaw, Mich., 43 F. Supp. 582 (E.D. Mich. 1977).

[58] *Supra* note 22.

actionable (or meritorious) claim was lost or rejected or that such a claim is now being impeded. This injury, in turn, must relate to government's failure to assist with access.

Before *Lewis,* courts might decide such cases on the basis of a claim that "I wanted to sue over lack of exercise, or filthy living conditions, or failure to protect me, but the law books were so inadequate and dated and no other help was available that I could not really frame my complaint." No more. Such an inmate or class of inmates must initially show a meritorious claim, but they have no independent right to books or people to help decide whether a grievance has legal merit.

Lewis goes further and holds that where a law library is provided it need not be comprehensive; it need only deal with attacks on the sentence or challenges to conditions of confinement. What happens to a lawyerless pretrial detainee who seeks to prepare pro se for trial is not clear.

Suppose a given state simply has no law books or legal assistance available to prisoners? Justice Scalia suggests that this is not a constitutional violation per se, unless and until someone can show impairment of a meritorious claim. Justices Stevens and Souter strongly disagree on this point. Justice Scalia does suggest that this is more hypothetical than real in that an inmate with standing is likely to exist somewhere in the rubble of such a system.

Justice Scalia does use an analogy that has some ominous undertones for inmates' rights to medical and mental health care. He argues that a healthy inmate who has suffered no deprivation of needed medical care cannot claim a constitutional violation simply because prison medical facilities are inadequate. That seems reasonable until one asks: Suppose a given system had no contract with a hospital for surgery and no operating rooms within the system. Is it inevitable that some inmate will need emergency surgery? Immediate access to a mental hospital? Prescription of certain medications?

Obviously it is inevitable, just as inevitable that illiterate inmates will have putatively meritorious lawsuits. Justice Scalia's approach for the Court seems to be that federal courts somehow interfere with state sovereignty and autonomy when they act preventively. And what he terms premature (or without standing) is in fact a type of preventive law approach. Insistence on actual (or imminent) injury is yet another hurdle for inmates seeking legal redress and appears to be an excessive reaction to the real problem of "frequent filers" and frivolous litigation. We must watch with caution to see if *Lewis* spills over into the mental health arena.[59]

[2] Tort Actions

In *Estelle v. Gamble,*[60] the Supreme Court denied relief to a Texas inmate who claimed that he received inadequate diagnosis and treatment for a back injury and thus

---

[59] In Reynolds v. Wagner, 128 F.3d 166 (3d Cir. 1997), inmates and detainees unsuccessfully challenged a fee for the medical care system; mental health was exempt here as it usually is; and the defendants did claim there was no standing because no plaintiff alleged serious harm due to delay or denial of care. The court simply finessed the question but suggested that Helling v. McKinney, 509 U.S. 25 (1993), allowing suit for future harm related to exposure to second-hand smoke, is inconsistent with the *Lewis* argument.

[60] 429 U.S. 97 (1976).

had been subjected to cruel and unusual punishment. The Court did say of the inmate's claim that "At most it is medical malpractice, and as such the proper forum is the state court under the Texas Tort Claims Act."[61]

As one authoritative work puts it, "Tort remedies may be critically important to the prisoner who sustains an injury in prison."[62] This is not the appropriate occasion to review tort remedies available to inmates. Suffice it so say that prisoners generally have a right to seek damages for injuries they claim have been intentionally or negligently inflicted on them.[63]

Tort actions may be brought in state courts and in the federal courts. State prisoners favor the use of federal courts and a variety of damage suits are brought under the Federal Civil Rights Act.[64] Apart from problems of proof and access to counsel, the major hurdle to success in such suits is the doctrine of immunity.

Prison officials have a qualified (or good faith) immunity when sued under Section 1983 of title 42 of the U.S. Code.[65] In *Cleavinger v. Saxner,*[66] federal prisoners gained a modest victory when a divided Court refused to extend absolute immunity to members of a prison discipline committee. Justice Blackmun reasoned that unlike judges, committee members are not truly independent. As employees of the prison system they are under obvious pressure to favor their colleagues, and the procedural safeguards afforded inmates are rather nominal.[67] Finding that qualified immunity was appropriate in this situation, the Court did offer balm by noting, "All the committee members need to do is follow the clear and simple constitutional requirements of *Wolff v. McDonnell*, and they then should have no reason to fear substantial harassment and liability."[68]

In practical effect, qualified immunity means that the law controlling the matter complained about was known and clearly established and that the violation was malicious. As a matter of practical consequence, this means that winning damages often will be difficult and that inmate law suits often must look to more injunctive remedies.

[a] Negligence

Although prison officials remain open to suits for money damages under Section 1983, post-*Cleavinger* Supreme Court decisions have severely limited the acts or omissions that could create liability. In *Daniels v. Williams,*[69] an inmate at a city jail slipped and fell on a pillow negligently left on the stairs by a deputy. The inmate

---

[61] Estelle, 429 U.S. at 107.

[62] Gobert & Cohen, *supra* note 20, p. 63.

[63] *See* Carey v. Piphus, 435 U.S. 247 (1978), finding a right to at least nominal damages for a denial of procedural due process regardless of the merits of the substantive aspects of the case.

[64] *See* 42 U.S.C. § 1983; *see also* William Turner, *When Prisoners Sue: A Study of Prisoner Section 1983 Suits in the Federal Courts*, 92 HARV. L. REV. 610 (1979).

[65] Procunier v. Navarette, 434 U.S. 555 (1978); *see also* Ward v. Johnson, 690 F.2d 1098 (4th Cir. 1982), extending judicial-type immunity to prison officials when serving on a disciplinary tribunal.

[66] 474 U.S. 193 (1985).

[67] Cleavinger, 474 U.S. at 203–204.

[68] Cleavinger, 474 U.S. at 207 (citation omitted).

[69] 748 F.2d 229 (4th Cir. 1984), *aff'd,* 474 U.S. 327 (1986). There were several concurring opinions in this case.

claimed that his resultant injuries deprived him of his constitutionally protected liberty interest in freedom from bodily injury.[70] The Court rejected the claim and announced that injuries inflicted by governmental negligence simply are not encompassed by the Constitution.[71]

Negligence involves a lack of due care on the part of the person who causes the injury. In *Daniels,* the Court indicated that the intentional infliction of harm by prison officials would likely suffice in a Section 1983 claim but found no occasion to decide whether recklessness or gross negligence could trigger the protections of due process.[72]

In a case decided the same day as *Daniels,* the Court dealt with a similar problem but on facts that were sufficiently different to attract three dissenters. *Davidson v. Cannon*[73] involved a New Jersey prison inmate who sought damages for serious injured inflicted on him by a fellow inmate. Davidson had been threatened by another inmate and he sent a note reporting the threats to the assistant superintendent. This official read the note and passed it along to a corrections sergeant. The sergeant forgot about the note and a day or two later—no on-duty staff having been properly advised—the threat was made good and Davidson was seriously injured.

The Court reiterated its position from *Daniels* and found that mere negligence was not a basis for a Section 1983 claim. But there is an obvious difference between a slip and fall due to the careless placement of a pillow and the failure to take some action, if only to alert on-duty personnel, in the face of an apparently authentic threat. Justice Blackmun's dissenting opinion captures that difference:

> [W]here the State renders a person vulnerable and strips him of his ability to defend himself, an injury that results from a state official's negligence in performing his duty is peculiarly related to the governmental function. . . . The deliberate decision not to protect Davidson from a known threat was directly related to the often violent life of prisoners. And protecting inmates from attack is central to one of the State's primary missions in running a prison—the maintenance of internal security.[74]

What is even more compelling about *Davidson* is that New Jersey law provided that neither a public entity nor a public employee is liable for any injury caused by a prisoner to another prisoner.[75] Thus, an inmate in Davidson's position either has a federal claim for damages or his injuries go uncompensated.

[b] Role of State Courts

Daniels and *Davidson* suggest one of two different avenues of approach by inmate litigants. Where the state courts are open (unlike New Jersey), and especially if negli-

---

[70] Recall that it is necessary to ground a Section 1983 claim either in the U.S. Constitution or in federal law. Without an available federal statute, the inmate sought to shoe-horn his claim into the Due Process Clause.
[71] Daniels, *supra* note 69, 474 U.S. at 328.
[72] Daniels, *supra* note 69, 474 U.S. at 334.
[73] 474 U.S. 344 (1986).
[74] Davidson, 474 U.S. at 355 (Blackmun, J., dissenting) (citations omitted).
[75] N.J. Stat. Ann. § 59:5-2(b)(4).

gence will suffice as a basis for recovery, we would expect more actions for damages to be brought in state courts. Where the state courts are not open or not particularly friendly to inmate claims, facts such as those in *Davidson* will be relatively easy to plead the case as involving "deliberate indifference" or "gross negligence."[76]

Plainly, if prison officials know that some powerful and violent inmate has threatened to dismember a weak and passive inmate and officials place the two in the same cell, the resulting violence approximates the intentional infliction of harm. Presumably this hypothetical case remains within the coverage of a Section 1983 suit.[77] Injured inmates and their counsel will therefore increasingly attempt to array the facts and construct their legal theory to resemble the above type of problem. Proving this claim, of course, is another matter.

¶ 3.5 CONDITIONS OF CONFINEMENT

Prison and jail populations have risen to a point that would have been unimaginable even a few short years ago. At the end of 1995 there were 1,078,357 inmates in our nation's prisons. This is more than double the prison population in 1985.[78] Our jail population also doubled in this same period, from 258,615 inmates to 507,044.[79] We confine 600 of every 100,000 residents.

New prisons seemingly rise overnight (realistically, within three months) and at a cost of $80,000 per bed for maximum security, $54,000 for medium security, and $32,346 for minimum security.[80] Billions of dollars are being spent for new construction with corrections budgets now looming higher than many states' education budgets. Adding capacity and personnel has not relieved overcrowding, as witnessed by some 39 or 40 jurisdictions operating under some type of court order relating to conditions of confinement.

General conditions lawsuits began to emerge in the 1970's and met with a certain amount of success. So-called structural injunctions were issued, or consent decrees having the same effect entered into, on the basis of broad challenges to systemic conditions in a prison, prison system, or jail. A general conditions law suit would claim a violation of cruel and unusual punishment under the Eighth Amendment in such areas of prison life as heating and cooling, noise, food, showers and other aspects of personal hygiene, exercise, sanitation, fire safety, and similar items.[81]

---

[76] In a case involving a fight in the District of Columbia Jail, an injured inmate received a $75,000 jury verdict. On appeal, the reviewing court held that the "deliberate indifference" standard—as opposed to "wanton and malicious" standard—was properly invoked. Morgan v. District of Columbia, No. 85-5331, 85-5709, slip op. (D.C. Cir. July 21, 1987).

[77] This example should qualify as deliberate indifference in *Farmer v. Brennan*, *supra* note 9.

[78] BUREAU OF JUSTICE STATISTICS, U.S. DEPT. OF JUSTICE, PRISON AND JAIL INMATES (1996).

[79] Id.

[80] CAMILLE G. CAMP & GEORGE M. CAMP, THE CORRECTIONS YEARBOOK—ADULT 45 (1995). The so-called "maxi-maxi" prisons may cost as much as $135,000 per bed to construct.

[81] *National Prison Project, Status Report: State Prisons and the Courts* 1 (Jan. 1996). The impact of the Prison Litigation Reform Act, 18 U.S.C. §§ 3, 26 et seq. is as yet unknown. The act does make it much easier for a state to seek termination of injunctions, whether by consent or not. Consent decrees may be terminated immediately where there is no finding of unconstitutionality on record (and there never is) and as this is written, a few jurisdictions are moving to escape long-standing decrees.

[1] Overcrowding

In *Rhodes v. Chapman*[82] the Supreme Court decided a general conditions lawsuit involving Ohio's then recently opened maximum security prison known as Southern Ohio Correction Facility (SOCF), or simply Lucasville, its location near the Kentucky border. SOCF was constructed for single-celling with cells measuring 63 square feet. Built for 1,620 inmates, 2,300 inmates quickly filled SOCF, with 1,400 double celled.

The double-celling led to what was characterized as an overcrowding lawsuit. More accurately, the claim was that overcrowding led to an increase in violence, mental deterioration, limits on movement, and access to reformative and recreational opportunities. The plaintiff-inmates prevailed in the trial court and in the Sixth Circuit but were soundly defeated in the Supreme Court. Justice Powell, for the Court, stated that the Eighth Amendment question is whether evolving standards of decency are violated, whether there is the wanton and needless infliction of pain. Conditions that are harsh and restrictive are part of the penalty flowing from conviction and sentence.[83]

Thus, the overcrowding inquiry is not only into how many inmates are housed in a cell designed for one; it also must encompass access to day rooms, the yard, work and educational opportunities, meals, visits, and the like. The evidence did not show inordinate reductions in those areas or even a disproportionate increase in violence. Design capacity is seen as relevant, as are recommendations in various Model Rules and Standards, but neither is determinative. With only Justice Marshall dissenting, the Court reversed.

In 1994, a terrible riot erupted at Lucasville and one officer and 11 inmates died. Ironically, part of the terms of the negotiated settlement was that inmates will not be double celled. This solution allowed officials to avoid the racially charged aspects of mixed-race double celling, something vigorously opposed by Aryan Brotherhood prisoners who exist in large numbers at SOCF.

[2] Objective Severity

Rhodes established what is known as the objective component of a prison conditions case, the nature and extent of the harm required by the Eighth Amendment.[84] In *Wilson v. Seiter* the Court dealt with yet another Ohio prison, Hocking Correctional Facility, which is a rather benign and relaxed prison used to house Ohio's older, male prisoners.[85] *Wilson* held that even if prison conditions deprive inmates of a basic human need—inadequate heat, for example, in a cold climate—this will not reach the

---

[82] 452 U.S. 337 (1981).

[83] Id.

[84] In Bell v. Wolfish, *supra* note 3, the Supreme Court rejected a challenge to double-celling at a new federal jail in New York City. These cells were 75 feet square and held two detainees. Justice Rehnquist foreshadowed *Rhodes* in stating that there is no "one man, one cell" principle lurking in the Fourteenth Amendment. Detainees spent only their sleeping hours in their cells and only an average of 60 days at the jail. The extended terms—often life—at SOCF did not sway the Court.

[85] 501 U.S. 294 (1991). I have toured Hocking three times in a two-year period and have found one of the best libraries and vocational programs I have seen, a terrific gym, and inmates consistently content with their dormitory living, unlike younger inmates who often rebel at congregate living space.

level of cruel and unusual punishment unless prison officials are shown to be deliberately indifferent in maintaining, or not alleviating, such a condition.

Four Justices found it hard to believe that there was any state of mind requirement where prison conditions could be shown to inflict needless pain or suffering. These Justices believed that objective severity, not subjective mental states, should govern constitutional liability.

Of course, the Court could have stated plainly that damages are not available where there is no subjective culpability but that an injunctive remedy is available when conditions objectively are below constitutional minima. With deliberate indifference the requisite mental state and with that now equated with criminal recklessness, inmates again have been dealt a severe blow to their legal identity by an increasingly conservative Supreme Court.

¶ 3.6 RIGHT TO PRIVACY

Does a prison inmate retain any legal rights to privacy? The very asking of the question may strike some readers as frivolous. The answer may be no, but the inquiry is not frivolous. The meaning of the term "privacy" is quite relative. In prison or jail it relates to freedom from the most intrusive searches or surveillance, but not much more.[86] Indeed, the Oregon Supreme Court has relied on privacy concepts to decide a case brought by male inmates of the Oregon State Penitentiary who sought to enjoin the assignment of female guards from duties that involved frisking them.[87]

The lower court decided the case on the theory that male prisoners have a federal constitutional right of privacy against searches by female guards involving the genital and anal areas. The Oregon Supreme Court upheld the injunction, as modified, and while the court appeared to agree that inmates possessed a federal constitutional right to privacy, it was of the view that the state constitution provided a more solid legal footing. Article I, Section 13 of the Oregon Constitution guarantees that no person arrested or confined in jail shall be treated with unnecessary rigor. This guarantee was treated as the functional equivalent of privacy.

This rather unusual decision should not be taken as representative of the treatment given inmate claims to privacy. The Fourth Amendment, which provides protection from illegal searches and seizures, and which is applied with special vigor to searches conducted in a person's home, is virtually nonexistent in prison. Cell searches, body searches, including strip and body cavity searches, and intensive surveillance, with or without any specific reason or probable cause, are regular occurrences in prison. Restriction of such activities is at the core of the privacy protections afforded by the Fourth Amendment, a virtual stranger to prison life.

The Oregon decision is unusual in that the court relied on the state constitution as a source for prisoners' rights and in its recognition of inmate privacy. A more repre-

---

[86] An expansive view of privacy would include solitude, autonomy, freedom of choice, the desire for control over what is known about you, freedom to say or do things with people you love that you would not say or do with others present, the preservation of secret pockets in the mind to allow the imagination a fertile field—and more. *See* JANA M. SMITH, PRIVATE MATTERS: IN DEFENSE OF THE PERSONAL LIFE (1997). The very listing of these notions is to establish a checklist of what is unavailable in prison or jail.
[87] Sterling v. Cupp, 290 Ore. 611, 625 P.2d 123 (1981).

sentative and more recent decision is *Johnson v. Phelan*,[88] which was decided by the Seventh Circuit Court of Appeals with that Circuit's two heavyweight judges—Easterbrook and Posner—squaring off against each other.

Female guards at the Cook County Jail monitor inmate activities and see men naked in the shower, their cells, and at the toilet. Johnson argued that such cross-gender monitoring of him violated his due process rights. Judge Easterbrook conceded that observation is a form of search, so the question became whether it is an unreasonable search.

After reviewing a number of court decisions and legal claims that might exist under various constitutional provisions, Judge Easterbrook wrote:

> Where does this leave us? The fourth amendment does not protect privacy interests within prisons. Moving to other amendments does not change the outcome. Cross-sex monitoring is not a senseless imposition. As a reconciliation of conflicting entitlements and desires, it satisfies the Turner standard. It cannot be called "inhumane" and therefore does not fall below the floor set by the objective component of the eighth amendment. And Johnson does not contend that his captor adopted their monitoring patterns because of, rather than in spite of, the embarrassment it causes some prisoners. He does not submit that the warden ignored his sensibilities; he argues only that they received too little weight in the felicific calculus. Like the district court, therefore, we conclude that the complaint fails to state a claim on which relief may be granted.[89]

Judge Posner, uncomfortably on the side of an inmate claim, used this decision as a vehicle to express his deepest beliefs about the legal identity of inmates. They seem worthy of extensive coverage here, especially since the goal of this chapter is to present a composite picture of the legal identity of inmates.

> There are different ways to look upon the inmates of prisons and jails in the United States in 1995. One way is to look upon them as members of a different species, indeed as a type of vermin, devoid of human dignity and entitled to no respect; and then no issue concerning the degrading or brutalizing treatment of prisoners would arise. In particular there would be inhibitions about using prisoners as the subject of experiments, including social experiments such as the experiment of seeing whether the sexes can be made interchangeable. The parading of naked male inmates in front of female guards, or of naked female inmates in front of male guards, would be no more problematic than "cross-sex surveillance" in a kennel.
>
> I do not myself consider the 1.5 million inmates of American prisons and jails in that light. This is a non-negligible fraction of the American population. And it is only the current inmate population. The fraction of the total population that has spent time in a prison or jail is larger, although I do not know

---

[88] 69 F. 3d 144 (7th Cir. 1995).

[89] Johnson, 69 F.3d at 150–151.

how large. A substantial number of these prison and jail inmates, including the plaintiff in this case, have not been convicted of a crime. They are merely charged with crime, awaiting trial. Some of them may actually be innocent. Of the guilty, many are guilty of sumptuary offenses, or of other victimless crimes uncannily similar to lawful activity (gambling offenses are an example), or of esoteric financial and regulatory offenses (such as violation of the migratory game laws) some of which do not even require a guilty intent. It is wrong to break foolish laws, or wise laws that should carry only civil penalties. It is wrongful to break the law even when the lawbreaker is flawed, weak, retarded, unstable, ignorant, brutalized, or profoundly disadvantaged, rather than violent, vicious, or evil to the core. But we should have a realistic conception of the composition of the prison and jail population before deciding that they are a scum entitled to nothing better than what a vengeful populace and a resource-starved penal system choose to give them. We must not exaggerate the distance between "us," the lawful ones, the respectable ones, and the prison and jail population for such exaggeration will make it too easy for us to deny that population the rudiments of humane consideration.

The nudity taboo retains great strength in the United States. It should not be confused with prudery. It is a taboo against being seen in the nude by strangers, not by one's intimates. Ours is a morally diverse populace and the nudity taboo is not of uniform strength across it. It is the strongest among professing Christians, because of the historical antipathy of the Church to nudity; and as it happens the plaintiff alleges that his right "to practice Christian modesty is being violated." The taboo is particularly strong when the stranger belongs to the opposite sex. There are radical feminists who regard "sex" as a social construction and the very concept of "opposite sex," implying as it does the dichotomization of the "sexes" (the "genders," as we are being taught to say), as a sign of patriarchy. For these feminists the surveillance of naked male prisoners by female guards and naked female prisoners by male guards are way stations on the road to sexual equality. If prisoners have no rights, the reconceptualization of the prison as a site of progressive social engineering should give us no qualms. Animals have no right to wear clothing. Why prisoners, if they are no better than animals? There is no answer, if the premise is accepted. But it should be rejected, and if it is rejected, and the duty of a society that would like to think of itself as civilized to treat its prisoners humanely therefore acknowledged, then I think that the interest of a prisoner in being free from unnecessary cross-sex surveillance has priority over the unisex-bathroom movement and requires us to reverse the judgment of the district court throwing out this lawsuit.[90]

This is powerful stuff and it is the type of judicial dialogue rarely encountered in prisoners' cases. Judge Posner ultimately concluded that the Eighth Amendment requires that reasonable efforts be made to prevent the frequent, deliberate, gratuitous physical exposure of one gender to guards of another. This is hardly the stuff of revolution, and many prisons actually do this without a second thought.

---

[90] Johnson, 69 F.3d at 151–152.

What is important here is the judicial battle over the very concept of prisoner and person. For Judge Easterbrook, the label "prisoner" appears to reduce people to mere objects who may be acted upon for convenience, economy, security, and career enhancement. Judge Posner, on the other hand, is somewhat more circumspect, although his version of an inmate's legal and human identity is hardly expansive. And it is a testament to these conservative times that Judge Posner appears here in the "liberal" corner.

The overwhelming weight of legal authority simply refuses to apply the Fourth Amendment, or apply it favorably, to prison inmates. In *Bell v. Wolfish*,[91] the Supreme Court was asked to determine a broad array of claims brought by pretrial detainees housed at the Federal Metropolitan Correctional Center in New York City. Concerning the challenge to routine strip and body cavity searches, Justice Rehnquist wrote:

> Admittedly, this practice instinctively gives us the most pause. However, assuming for present purposes that inmates, both convicted prisoners and pretrial detainees, retain some Fourth Amendment rights upon commitment to a corrections facility, we nonetheless conclude that these searches do not violate that Amendment. The Fourth Amendment prohibits only unreasonable searches, and under the circumstances, we do not believe that these searches are unreasonable.[92]

Justice Rehnquist did not bind himself or the Court to the acceptance of any Fourth Amendment safeguards in jail or prison. The Justice simply accepted that position in stipulative (or *arguendo*) fashion.[93] More important, however, is the allowance of the second most intrusive of searches[94]—the body cavity inspection—on pretrial detainees and without regard to articulable facts suggesting a security problem. One might safely infer then that searches conducted in prison are inherently reasonable, according to the Rehnquist view.

In general, prisoners have no expectation of privacy as to their place or possessions. An inmate's body, at least for the most highly intrusive searches, may be subject to nominal safeguards. Prison officials may have to show at least reasonable suspicion to justify, for example, a body cavity probe for drugs.[95]

The prisoner's body, his few possessions, and his "home" (cell or dormitory space) are subject to surveillance and inspection with no anterior safeguards (in the form of a requirement of cause or a warrant) and with no realistic opportunity for subsequent challenge.[96]

---

[91] *Supra* note 3, at 520.

[92] *Supra* note 3, at 558 (citations omitted).

[93] *See also* Lanza v. New York, 370 U.S. 139 (1962), for *dicta* supportive of the inapplicability of the Fourth Amendment to prison cells.

[94] I would regard the body cavity probe as the most intrusive of such searches.

[95] *See* Fred Cohen & Kate King, *Drug Testing and Corrections*, 23 CRIM. L. BULL. 151 (1987), for a review of the Fourth Amendment and drug testing of inmates, visitors, and employees; *see also* Hayes v. Marriott, 70 F.3d 1144 (10th Cir. 1995), reinstating a law suit alleging a highly intrusive, videotaped, cross-gender search.

[96] Hudson v. Palmer, 468 U.S. 517 (1984), and Block v. Rutherford, 468 U.S. 576 1984), made it

An inmate may, however, have significant protections in the area of custodial interrogation[97] or when incriminating statements are deliberately elicited after the right to have an attorney has become operative. For example, when an informer, planted in a jail cell, manages to elicit damaging statements later used to help convict the duped inmate, a violation of the Sixth Amendment right to the effective assistance of counsel may be found.[98] This is *not* a recognition of an inmate's right to privacy. Rather, it is the continuation of an extensive set of pretrial safeguards designed to protect an accused's privilege against self-incrimination and right to counsel. Thus, it is a right safeguarded in the present but designed for the future when an inmate's legal identity is transferred from inmate to defendant.

¶ 3.7 RIGHTS IN DISCIPLINARY PROCEEDINGS, TRANSFERS, AND ADMINISTRATIVE SEGREGATION

The maintenance of order and security and the use of prison disciplinary proceedings go hand-in-glove. Do prison inmates have any procedural or substantive legal rights when accused of a violation of prison rules? Suppose a prisoner is simply transferred from one prison to another as opposed to being placed in solitary confinement, and the underlying motivation for the transfer is punitive? Does a prisoner entering the prison system have any rights during what I view as the mandated classification-diagnostic process?

These problems may seem quite different from each other, and indeed the Supreme Court has given answers that are at variance. However, the issues involved here are quite similar and provide important background for understanding the Court's decision in *Vitek v. Jones*,[99] which involves the transfer of a prison inmate to either a mental hospital or mental health facility.

[1] Procedural Due Process

Until quite recently, the most significant decision involving prison discipline was *Wolff v. McDonnell*.[100] *Sandin v. Conner*,[101] while it did not alter the requirements of a Wolff hearing, dramatically altered the circumstances of just when *Wolff* must be applied. We turn first to a discussion of the still viable *Wolff* decision.

---

absolutely clear that inmates simply have no Fourth Amendment rights in connection with their possessions or their cell. In Griffin v. Wisconsin, 463 U.S. 868 (1987), the Court went so far as to uphold a warrantless search on less than probable cause of a probationer's *home*. The product of the search, a weapon, was used to support a new conviction and not simply a revocation where more relaxed procedures generally apply. There is an interesting question concerning an inmate's claim to privacy surrounding the content of his medical records when those records are maintained by fellow inmates. *See* Ruiz v. Estelle, 503 F. Supp. 1265, 1323 (S.D. Texas 1980), *mot. to stay granted in part and denied in part*, 650 F.2d 555 (5th Cir. 1981), *aff'd in part and rev'd in part*, 679, F.2d 1115 (5th Cir. 1982), *op. amended in part and vacated in part, and reh'g denied*, 688 F.2d 266 (5th Cir. 1982), *cert. denied*, 460 U.S. 1042. *See also* Ruiz v. Estelle, 553 F. Supp. 567 (S.D. Texas 1982) on the award of attorney fees.

[97] Custodial interrogation, of course, is the essential condition for the application of *Miranda* rights.
[98] This is exactly what was found in United States v. Henry, 447 U.S. 264 (1980).
[99] 45 U.S. 480 (1980).
[100] *Supra* note 54.
[101] 515 U.S. 472 (1995).

Wolff involved a challenge to the procedures used in Nebraska state prisons for the imposition of disciplinary sanctions[102] as a result of flagrant or serious misconduct. Loss of good-time credits was clearly at issue, with confinement in a disciplinary cell less obviously at issue. *Wolff* procedures were generally understood to apply to charges of "serious misconduct." Serious misconduct, in turn, is determined by the nature of the sanction.

Nebraska's position was that the procedure for imposing prison discipline is a matter of policy that raises no constitutional issues. A majority of even this highly conservative Supreme Court strenuously objected to that argument, stating:

> If the position implies that prisoners in state institutions are wholly without the protections of the Constitution and the Due Process Clause, it is plainly untenable. Lawful imprisonment necessarily makes unavailable many rights and privileges of the ordinary citizen, a "retraction justified by the considerations underlying our penal system." But though his rights may be diminished by the needs and exigencies of the institutional environment, a prisoner is not wholly stripped of constitutional protections when he is imprisoned for crime. There is no iron curtain drawn between the Constitution and prisons of this country.[103]

The Due Process Clause of the Fourteenth Amendment contains whatever procedural rights inmates may be afforded at disciplinary proceedings. However, before the procedural safeguards of due process may be unraveled and put to work, constitutional analysis requires first that you identify a constitutionally recognized and protected interest. In other words, it is not enough to claim some loss, even a serious loss. The loss, or harm, complained of must be either (1) an interest located within the flexible boundaries of life, liberty, or property as stated in the Fourteenth Amendment, or (2) an interest created by the state. This analytical approach is of relatively recent origin. In the very recent past, where government activity caused a serious or grievous harm, it was assumed that due process applied, leaving only the question of what process was due.[104]

No state is required to create a good-time credit system or is prohibited from deciding that such credits may be forfeited for major infractions of the rules. However, Nebraska having awarded good time, the prisoner's state-created liberty interest had real substance. Since the forfeiture invariably effected the duration of confinement, it was embraced within the procedural safeguards of the Fourteenth Amendment. At a minimum, this assured that the right was not arbitrarily abolished.

Once it is decided that due process applies, as the Court did in *Wolff,* the second task is to determine what process is due. The fact that this task remains tells us that the procedural safeguards required by due process are not invariable. Indeed, the

---

[102] In New York, "keeplock" was considered a sufficiently onerous sanction to trigger *Wolff*-like procedures, and keeplock is simply confinement in one's own cell even for a day. *See* Powell v. Ward, 487 F. Supp. 917 (S.D.N.Y. 1980). *Sandin,* of course, makes *Powell* read like a fairy tale now.

[103] Wolff, *supra* note 54, at 555–556 (citation omitted).

[104] *See, e.g.,* Bell v. Burson, 402 U.S. 535 (1971).

importance, or weight, assigned to the right and the setting in which it operates are then major factors in reaching this decision.[105]

[2] Hearings

At the core of procedural due process is the requirement of some kind of hearing before an impartial tribunal.[106] In *Wolff*, the Court held that inmates facing serious disciplinary charges are entitled to written notice of the claimed violation at least 24 hours in advance of the hearing. In addition, the fact-finders must provide a written statement of the evidence relied on and reasons for the disciplinary action.[107] These are the only unconditional procedural rights in disciplinary proceedings extended to inmates.

The Court also determined that inmates have certain additional conditional rights, including the right to call witnesses or present documentary evidence when permitting them to do so will not be unduly hazardous to institutional safety or correctional goals.[108] Illiterate inmates or inmates facing complex charges have a right to seek aid from a fellow inmate, or if this is forbidden, to seek help from staff or a sufficiently competent inmate designated by staff.[109]

The Court rather casually rejected the inmate's claim that the hearing tribunal composed entirely of correction officials was not sufficiently impartial to satisfy due process.[110] Apparently the only constitutional basis for preclusion is whether or not a decision-maker was actually involved in the incident or in bringing the charge. Confrontation and cross-examination were found to present grave hazards to institutional interests. Allowing an inmate to hear the evidence against him and to examine his accusers, said the Court, creates the potential for havoc and for making these proceedings unmanageable and longer than need be.[111]

Taking a step away from the details of *Wolff*, we note that the Supreme Court recognized a liberty interest both in an inmate's good-time credits and, less clearly, in the avoidance of solitary confinement. However, it held that those liberty interests required a rather undemanding procedural format before they may be taken away. Prison officials remain in charge of the investigating, charging, adjudicating, and sentencing phases of these disciplinary proceedings.

[3] What Creates a Liberty Interest

In *Sandin v. Conner*[112] the Court reaffirmed its earlier view that the actual loss of good-time credits is a liberty (or constitutionally protected) interest calling for due process, but it disavowed the position that disciplinary segregation per se required *Wolff*'s due process. It also disavowed the very confusing approach it was using to determine whether any liberty interests called for due process.

---

[105] *See* JOHN NOWAK, et al., CONSTITUTIONAL LAW (1978), p. 449.
[106] Wolff, *supra* note 54, 418 U.S. at 557.
[107] Wolff, 418 U.S. at 563.
[108] Wolff, 418 U.S. at 566.
[109] Wolff, 418 U.S. at 570.
[110] Wolff, 418 U.S. at 570–571.
[111] Wolff, 418 U.S. at 567.
[112] *Supra* note 101.

Before *Sandin,* a state might create a liberty interest by the semantic accident of using certain verbal combinations in statutes or even policy and procedure. For example, if a rule stated that "no inmate shall be transferred to a prison with higher security than the sending facility unless it is determined that security is inadequate at the sending facility," then a state-created liberty interest would have been found in the "shall-unless" verbal combination. An inmate would be said to have a right to challenge the transfer given the need for the factual predicate—inadequate security—created by the rule. Without the rule, there would be no right to a hearing.

Sandin avoided this type of semantic due process in favor of an analysis concentrating on the nature of the loss. In *Sandin,* the Court substituted a requirement that a deprivation be "significant and atypical" before a protected liberty interest is created, and held that 30 days in disciplinary segregation is not atypical or significant. As it so often does, and particularly when Chief Justice Rehnquist writes in his infuriatingly obfuscatory manner, the Court left the definition of "significant and atypical" for another day. This, of course, harkens back to the 18 years in the wilderness before the Court deigned to define deliberate indifference.

As this is written, there are perhaps 800 post-*Sandin* decisions struggling with the meaning of this phrase. One thing is clear: not very much that is punitive is also an atypical or significant hardship. Confinement for a year, for example, has been upheld without a *Wolff* hearing. It seems likely that the Court, without realizing it, has fused liberty interest analysis with Eight Amendment analysis. That is, if the conditions of segregated confinement are so harsh or prolonged as to be an atypical and significant hardship, they will also likely violate the cruel and unusual punishment laws.[113] Once again, a major Supreme Court decision detracts from the already diminished legal identity of prisoners.[114]

[4] Limitations of the *Wolff* Decision

Returning to *Wolff* itself, it must be said that the decision does not reallocate any important power between prison officials and inmates. At best, it creates some paperwork requirements (the notice and reasons) and requires the assignment of some personnel to the hearing tribunal. If the Court had decided, for example, that due process required that inmates had a right to full representation before a tribunal composed of outside hearing officers, there is a real possibility that the appearance and reality of impartiality might have been obtained.[115] This may help explain why no jurisdiction of which I am aware has as yet accepted *Sandin*'s invitation to limit the scope of *Wolff* procedures.

Eleven years after the decision in *Wolff,* the Court answered two of the many pro-

---

[113] In Wagner v. Hanks, 128 F.3d 1173 (7th Cir. 1997), Chief Judge Posner suggests that in order for a one-year term of disciplinary segregation to be "atypical," one must engage in a comparative analysis, and if there is one prison in this country as restrictive, then *Sandin*'s requirements have not been met. That is, "atypical" is a comparative term and one has the threshold problem of deciding whether to compare various segregtion units in the prison at issue, in the same state, or in the entire country. Posner suggests that it is possible that the Supreme Court meant a transnational comparative effort. Prisoners may be relieved to learn that Turkey and the Gullag seem not to be included.

[114] Some courts have held that *Sandin* does not apply to pretrial detainees. *See* discussion in Chapter 15.

[115] For an excellent overview of the *Wolff* cases, see Barbara Babcock, *Due Process in Prison Disciplinary Proceedings,* 22 BOST. C.L. REV. 1009 (1981).

cedural issues it left unresolved. In *Ponte v. Real*,[116] the question was whether the Due Process Clause requires that prison officials provide some reason for the denial of an inmate's conditional right to call witnesses at a disciplinary hearing.

The Court answered in the affirmative:

> We think the answer to that question is that prison officials may be required to explain, in a limited manner, the reason why witnesses were not allowed to testify, but that they may do so either by making the explanation a part of the "administrative record" in the disciplinary proceeding, or by presenting testimony in court if the deprivation of a "liberty" interest is challenged because of that claimed defect in the hearing. In other words, the prison officials may choose to explain this at the hearing, or they may choose to explain it "later." Explaining the decision at the hearing will of course not immunize prison officials from a subsequent court challenge to their decision, but so long as the reasons are logically related to preventing undue hazards to "institutional safety or correctional goals," the explanation should meet the Due Process requirements as outlined in *Wolff*.[117]

Thus, when the conditional right of an inmate to call witnesses at a disciplinary hearing is denied, a stated reason is required, but the reason need not be in writing nor be contemporaneous with the denial.[118]

[5] Burden of Persuasion in a Disciplinary Procedure

Superintendent v. Hill[119] raised the question of the evidentiary requirement constitutionally necessary to support a prison disciplinary proceeding, at least where a loss of good time is involved. The choices available to the Court ranged from the criminal law's "proof beyond a reasonable doubt" to a "some evidence" or "unreasonable and arbitrary" rule.

The Court opted for the featherweight requirement of "some evidence."[120] What this appears to mean is that if there is virtually any evidence in the record to support a disciplinary tribunal's conclusion, and despite what might be stronger yet countervailing evidence, the tribunal's decision is constitutionally acceptable.[121] Clearly, the Court has not been devoted to strengthening the prisoner's legal identity in the context of disciplinary proceedings.

---

[116] 471 U.S. 491 (1985).

[117] Ponte, 471 U.S. at 497.

[118] In New York, for example, the denial must be supported with a written contemporaneous reason. Curiously, the Court's decision to allow reasons to be given in a subsequent law suit seems contrary to its general policy of discouraging inmate litigation.

[119] 472 U.S. 445 (1985).

[120] Hill, 472 U.S. at 457.

[121] *See* People ex rel. Vega v. Smith, 66 N.Y.2d 130 (1985), for an elaboration of what evidence suffices under New York's self-imposed, more stringent "substantial evidence" rule.

[6] Inter-Prison Transfers

In *Meachum v. Fano*[122] and *Montanye v. Haymes,*[123] the Supreme Court dealt with the inter-prison transfer question and handed the inmates yet another damaging defeat. Justice White made it clear that not even every *grievous* loss visited on a person by the state entitles that person to procedural due process. Changes in the conditions of confinement that do not otherwise violate the Constitution are not within the ambit of constitutional protection.

The Court made it clear that the rights protected in *Wolff* were rights created by the state. Here, neither Massachusetts nor New York created any right—a hope, perhaps, but no right—to remain in any particular prison. Transfers occur for a variety of reasons, and in many jurisdictions they occur on a frequent basis. The Court was unable to locate any state-created rights and was unwilling to create a federal right deserving of procedural due process safeguards. After *Sandin,* even if a state uses the "shall-unless" verbal combination described at ¶ 3.7[3], there is no right to any hearing challenging the transfer.[124]

Parenthetically, the significant and atypical deprivation now required by *Sandin* for establishing a liberty interest is very much like the "grievous loss" requirement addressed in *Meachum.* The loss now, however, must be grievous in the extreme, so grievous that it is likely the equivalent of cruel and unusual punishment.

Whether a transfer is for punitive, security, or program purposes, there are no constitutionally required procedural rights, not even to a hearing. Only if the inmate is able to show a retaliatory transfer, one done, for example, because of the exercise of a First Amendment right, is there any chance of challenging a prison-to-prison transfer.

¶ 3.8 RELIGIOUS FREEDOM

The First Amendment to the Constitution protects the free exercise of religion and prohibits the official establishment of any religion. Virtually all prisoner claims in this area relate to interference with various religious practices deemed important or fundamental to the prisoners' faith. Only recently have some Establishment Clause claims made their way into the courts, and with surprising results.

In *Kerr v. Farrey,*[125] the Seventh Circuit held that requiring offenders to participate in Alcoholics Anonymous (AA) or Narcotics Anonymous (NA) violates the Establishment Clause because these programs rely on a belief in God. Where no secular alternative exists and some penalty is imposed or loss is incurred, the First Amendment is now being found to have been violated.

---

[122] *Supra* note 14.

[123] 427 U.S. 236 (1976), *cert. denied,* 431 U.S. 967 (1977).

[124] Inmates may still bring suit claiming a retaliatory transfer and they may prevail on this issue. Baraldini v. Thornbrush, 884 F.2d 615, 620 (D.C. Cir. 1989).

[125] 95 F.3d 472 (7th Cir. 1996). The New York Court of Appeals previously ruled to the same effect in Griffin v. Coughlin, 743 F. Supp. 1006 (N.D.N.Y. 1990). *See* discussion at VIII CORR. L. RPTR. 1 (1997).

Free exercise claims require first that the beliefs be religious (which leads to some interesting questions regarding nonmainstream religions) and second that the beliefs be sincerely held. Courts have heard claims involving the right to congregate for worship, access to religious advisors, special diets, hair, beards and special garment requirements, religious objects (e.g., crosses, stars, rosary beads), religious names, sweat lodges, and more.

Of course, after the *O'Lone* decision discussed earlier, it is relatively easy for prison officials to prevail in their denial of a religious practice. You will recall that *O'Lone* required only a showing of reasonableness, and the mere mention of security appeared to establish reasonableness.

In 1993, Congress passed the Religious Freedom Restoration Act (RFRA)[126] which was designed, in part, to overrule *O'Lone*. The RFRA basically enacted pre-*O'Lone* law and provided that government may not substantially burden a person's exercise of religion unless it is to further a compelling government interest and unless it uses the least restrictive means available to further that compelling interest. The RFRA held prison officials to a much higher standard than *O'Lone,* and various religious practices should have been much more available.

In *City of Boerne v. Flores,*[127] the Supreme Court struck down the RFRA, finding that Congress exceeded its legislative authority under Section 5 of the Fourteenth Amendment in enacting it. Section 5 is an enforcement section, and basically the Court was telling Congress it lacked the constitutional authority to legislatively overrule a Supreme Court decision dealing with the formula by which to resolve constitutional issues.

Prison officials are now back on the religious roller coaster and must make some difficult decisions on such items as beards and hair length, religious objects, sweat lodge ceremonials, and the like. Those decisions, again, may be much more deprivational than during the short life of the RFRA.

¶ 3.9 RIGHTS IN CLASSIFICATION DECISIONS

All correctional systems have some form of a security classification system, and properly so. Classification decisions have a major impact on the immediate security status of an inmate, and thus prison placement and the longer-term question of parole. Classification decisions rely not only on professional judgment and intuition, they rely heavily on factual data—data that may be wrong, incomplete, or in need of clarification.[128] Although the Supreme Court seems not to have spoken directly to the issue, its reasoning in *Meachum* and *Moody v. Daggett*[129] strongly suggests that the Court recognizes no inmate legal rights in the ordinary classification process.

In *Meachum,* the Court stated:

---

[126] 42 U.S.C. § 2000b. Congress also took aim at Employment Div. v. Smith, 494 U.S. 872 (1990), a decision applicable to free world persons.

[127] 117 S. Ct. 2157 (1997). Since *Boerne,* there is no question that the RFRA is unconstitutional.

[128] *See* SHELDON KRANZ, MODEL RULES AND REGULATIONS ON PRISONERS' RIGHTS AND RESPONSIBILITIES 96–100 (1973).

[129] 429 U.S. 78 (1976).

[G]iven a valid conviction, the criminal defendant has been constitutionally deprived of his liberty to the extent that the State may confine him and subject him to the rules of its prison system so long as the conditions of confinement do not otherwise violate the Constitution. The Constitution does not require that the State have more than one prison for convicted felons; nor does it guarantee that the convicted prisoner will be placed in any particular prison, if, as is likely, the State has more than one correctional institution. The initial decision to assign the convict to a particular institution is not subject to audit under the Due Process Clause, although the degree of confinement in one prison may be quite different from that in another. The conviction has sufficiently extinguished the defendant's liberty interest to empower the State to confine him in any of its prisons.[130]

The Court was even more explicit, although in *dicta*, in *Moody,* stating:

[N]o due process protections [are] required upon the discretionary transfer of state prisoners to a substantially less agreeable prison, even where the transfer visit[s] a "grievous loss" upon the inmate. *The same is true of prisoner classification and eligibility for rehabilitative programs in the federal system.*[131]

Whatever the practical importance of the classification decision, it is reasonably clear that the Court is not likely to decide that inmates have a right of access and input into the decision. However, not all legal questions surrounding classification are thereby laid to rest. An inmate's constitutional right to medical and psychological care necessarily mandates that a reckless failure to identify serious physical or mental problems constitutes a cruel and unusual punishment where, for example, such failure results in confining aggressive psychotics with passive and physically vulnerable inmates. Resultant attacks may well be violations of the Eighth Amendment duty to protect inmates.[132]

¶ 3.10 SUMMARY

This Chapter provides a broad framework for understanding the law regarding prisoners' rights. Much of that law is derived from the U.S. Constitution and is pronounced by the Supreme Court. Therefore, much of this discussion necessarily focused on the development and status of federal constitutional rights.

This material is representative, but hardly exhaustive, of the entire body of prisoners' legal rights and responsibilities. For example, the Supreme Court has condemned racial discrimination in prisons[133] and has dealt with questions involving lim-

---

[130] Meachum, *supra* note 14, 427 U.S. at 244 (emphasis in original).

[131] Moody, *supra* note 129, 429 U.S. at 88 n.9 (emphasis added).

[132] *See* Farmer v. Brennan, *supra* note 9; *cf.* Withers v. Levine, 449 F. Supp, 473 (D. Md. 1978), *aff'd,* 615 F.2d 158 (4th Cir. 1980), *cert. denied,* 449 U.S. 849 (1980), involving the homosexual assault of an inmate by his cellmate when his cell assignment was made without regard to known or available information on point.

[133] Lee v. Washington, 390 U.S. 333 (1968).

itations on visits.[134] Other important matters, including access to literature and problems of media access and coverage, are merely noted in passing. The mechanics of litigation are hardly mentioned at all.

My objective for this Chapter is to present enough law for the reader to generally grasp the less-than-clear picture of the inmate as a legal entity. Among the more important points to take from this Chapter are:

1. The Supreme Court now repeatedly decides cases against the inmate position and has adopted a non-activist (or "hands-off") approach to prisons. Recent decisions on the use of force, access to the courts, inmate privacy, procedural requirements incident to disciplinary matters, and the analytical approach to liberty interests, all serve to reinforce this proposition.

2. The Court has repeatedly deferred to the real or presumed expertise of prison officials. Inmates need a powerful case to overcome the opinions of correctional authorities and their concerns about order and security.

3. There is no longer any remaining hierarchy of constitutional rights held by inmates. After *Turner* and *O'Lone,* reasonableness may be the exclusive test for prison conditions not plainly encompassed by specific constitutional provisions.

4. Earlier thinking by correction officials to the effect that "no rules make good rules" should now be tempered by the Court's ruling in *Sandin.* That is, written policy and procedure will not likely create a liberty interest calling for procedural due process.

5. Correctional authorities may not always realize that at times their interests actually coincide with the legal claims put forward by inmates. For example, if the corrections establishment "loses" a general conditions-overcrowding case, then the "loss" means fewer inmates, more programs, more personnel (typically professionals or specialists), and less tension.

6. On the legislative front, the Prison Litigation Reform Act (PLRA) may have a more far reaching effect on inmates' legal claims than even the most restrictive of the Court's opinions. For example, inmates now face filing fees and penalties for frivolous litigation; fees for attorneys and Masters are reduced; consent decrees require an (unthinkable) confession of constitutional violation, and so on.[135]

7. Just as the state courts have begun to reassert themselves in the area of criminal procedure, they likely will see more prison litigation and contracts arising from consent decrees enforceable only in state courts.

---

[134] *See* Pell v. Procunier, 417 U.S. 817 (1974).

[135] *See* discussion in Lynn S. Branham, LIMITING THE BURDENS OF *PRO SE* INMATE LITIGATION: A Technical Assistance Manual for the Courts, Corrections Officials, and Attorneys General, p.19 where Attorneys General are admitted to abandon any no-settlement policy and to problem-solve with Corrections. The PLRA changes dangerous inducements to "fight on," and Branham counsels settlement. This work in general is quite valuable in dealing with inmates' legal problems.

8. As a segue into the next chapter, we will observe that courts do not show as much deference to prison officials on questions of medical and psychiatric care as they do in other areas. Typically, there is no valid security interest to balance against an inmate's claim to treatment, and it is the right to mental health treatment which is the core of this book. And it is to that right we now turn.

Chapter 4

The Right to Treatment

¶ 4.1 CONSTITUTIONAL RIGHT TO CARE

Both the concept and the parameters of treatment are central to the comprehensive coverage of the legal rights of the mentally disordered offender. The key question regarding treatment is simply whether or not a prison inmate has a legal right to it.[1] This and subsequent chapters will detail the many issues encompassed by legal claims to treatment and will rely on extended quotations from legal material. The quoted material provides specific facts and details of judicial decisions, decrees, and orders to help the reader assess the legal health of the challenged individual prisons or prison systems.

Statements made earlier in this work should leave no doubt that *Estelle v. Gamble*[2] established that prisoners have an Eighth Amendment right to treatment for physical ailments. Subsequent federal court decisions, *Bowring v. Godwin*[3] being an early, important example, find no reason to distinguish physical illnesses from mental illnesses on the question of mandated care. Indeed, no case has been found distinguishing such illnesses when the issue is the constitutional right to care, although there are obvious differences related to the diagnosis and nature of such care. We turn now to a detailed consideration of *Estelle v. Gamble*, which provides the genesis of correctional health care.

[1] *Estelle v. Gamble*

J.W. Gamble, while an inmate in the Texas prison system, was injured while performing a prison work assignment. He complained of back pains after a heavy bale of cotton fell on him. Gamble was seen by doctors and medical assistants, examined, and given some medication. His complaint was not that his medical needs were wholly ignored, but that he received inadequate or inappropriate care, that some medical orders were not observed, and that his subsequent punishment—in effect, for malingering—was illegal.

The Court was asked to find that Texas's allegedly inadequate medical care violated the Eighth Amendment. The Court refused to so hold on these facts, but it did decide that the *deliberate indifference to the serious medical needs of prisoners constitutes unnecessary and wanton infliction of pain*. This is true whether the indifference is manifested by doctors in their response to the prisoner's needs or by prison guards intentionally denying or delaying access to medical care.[4]

[2] "Deliberate Indifference"

Elaborating on this constitutional obligation to provide medical care, Justice Marshall attempted to explain the meaning of "deliberate indifference":

---

[1] This question includes the similar right of pretrial detainees and the claim to habilitation made by mentally retarded inmates. Specific attention is given to the mentally retarded in Chapter 16.

[2] 429 U.S. 97 (1976).

[3] 551 F.2d 44 (4th Cir. 1977).

[4] Estelle, *supra* note 2, at 104–105.

[A]n inadvertent failure to provide adequate medical care cannot be said to constitute "an unnecessary and wanton infliction of pain" or to be "repugnant to the conscience of mankind." Thus, a complaint that a physician has been negligent in diagnosing or treating a medical condition does not state a valid claim of medical mistreatment under the Eighth Amendment. Medical malpractice does not become a constitutional violation merely because the victim is a prisoner. In order to state a cognizable claim, a prisoner must allege acts or omissions sufficiently harmful to evidence deliberate indifference to serious medical needs. It is only such indifference that can offend "evolving standards of decency" in violation of the Eighth Amendment.[5]

While *Estelle* clearly establishes the inmate's constitutional right to medical care, along with "deliberate indifference" as the requisite mental state, it left several crucial questions unanswered. It was unclear what the Court meant by "serious medical needs," whether mental disorders were intended to be included, and what specific acts or omissions might meet the deliberate indifference standard.[6] Indeed, it is fair to say that Justice Marshall said more about what deliberate indifference is not than what it is. Not until *Farmer v. Brennan*,[7] in 1994, did we obtain an authoritative definition of this exceedingly slippery term.

[3] Medical and Mental Health Conditions

In *Bowring v. Godwin,* a federal court of appeals confidently asserted that "we see no underlying distinction between the right to medical care for physical ills and its psychological or psychiatric counterpart."[8] The court went on to state:

We therefore hold that Bowring (or any other prison inmate) is entitled to psychological or psychiatric treatment if a physician or other health care provider, exercising skill and care at the time of the observation, concludes with reasonable medical certainty (1) that the prisoner's symptoms evidence a serious disease or injury; (2) that such disease or injury is curable or may be substantially alleviated; and (3) that the potential for harm to the prisoner by reason of delay or the denial of care would be substantial.[9]

---

[5] Estelle, *supra* note 2, at 105–106. Justice Marshall stated that the various courts of appeal were in essential agreement with this standard. On remand, the Fifth Circuit concluded that no claim was stated against supervisors for the doctor's conduct. Gamble v. Estelle, 554 F.2 653 (5th Cir. 1977). Despite a broadly shared fear of malpractice litigation, psychiatrists actually are quite safe. Indeed, it is reported that "[n]o reported decision by an American court has been found that deals with a psychiatrist's liability for purely verbal therapy." Dennis Horan & Robert Milligan, *Recent Developments in Psychiatric Malpractice*, 1 BEHAV. SCI. & L. 23, 27 (1983).

[6] Justice Marshall's own examples of constitutional abuse are fairly gross: refusing to administer a prescribed pain killer during surgery, choosing to throw away an ear and stitching the stump instead of attempting to reattach the ear, and administering penicillin knowing that an inmate is allergic and then refusing to treat the allergic reaction. Some 20 years later, these examples retain their vitality.

[7] 511 U.S. 825 (1994).

[8] Bowring, *supra* note 3, at 47. No post-*Estelle* decision to the contrary has been found.

[9] Id. *See also* Cody v. Hillard, 599 F. Supp. 1025, 1058 (D.S.D. 1984), *aff'd,* 799 F.2d 447 (8th Cir. 1986), *cert. denied*, 485 U.S. 906 (1988), fully supportive of *Bowring*.

Bowring arose in a somewhat unusual fashion. The inmate argued that he had been denied parole by the Virginia Parole Board in part because a psychological evaluation indicated he might not successfully complete a parole period. Bowring, not surprisingly, then argued that if that was the reason for denial of parole, the state must provide him psychological diagnosis and treatment so that ultimately he might qualify for parole. The court did not decide that inmates have a right to rehabilitation—a claim consistently rejected by the judiciary—although it did express the belief that failure to attend to an inmate's psychological illness thwarts the purported goal of rehabilitation and jeopardizes an inmate's ability to assimilate into society.[10]

The case was remanded for a hearing to determine whether the inmate was suffering from a qualified mental illness. At the hearing, the trial judge found that the inmate did not suffer from such an illness. The Virginia Parole Board has since been advised not to use psychological impairment as a reason to deny parole.[11] This, indeed, seems to be a general practice now and this calculated silence makes it difficult to fully comprehend the relationship between an inmate's mental illness and parole decision-making.

¶ 4.2 LEGAL BASIS FOR THE OBLIGATION OF TREATMENT

In Chapter 2,[12] we delineated how the official exercise of physical custody predicates the constitutional obligation of treatment. Some elaboration on that point is called for as we now delve into the subject in greater detail. When government deprives a person of the freedom to move about, to select associates, to select a place to live; when government deprives a person of access to care or a means of self-defense, the deprivation creates parallel obligations. A person in penal captivity has no right of self-determined access to required or desired medical or mental health care. While we as free persons remain free to define a need as medical and to select a caregiver, prisoners have no such freedom. However, where a serious medical or mental health need is established, prisoners, oddly enough, have available the only socialized medicine in this country.

[1] Seriousness Requirement

Given a medical or psychological condition of sufficient seriousness, unless government officials provide access to appropriate diagnosis and care, the captive will experience needless suffering, possible deterioration or permanent harm, even death. Without the seriousness requirement, captives, like free persons, would have a right to define for themselves when to obtain ameliorative medical or mental health care.[13]

---

[10] Bowring, *supra* note 3, at 48 n.2. This approach does depend on accepting rehabilitation and rejecting punishment as objectives of imprisonment. Rehabilitation is viewed as one possible goal and is at times considered to be an objective that an inmate has a right to pursue, although not necessarily with aid from the state. *See* Chapter 8 for further discussion of rehabilitation.

[11] Letter to Fred Cohen from Donald C. Gehring, Deputy Attorney General, Commonwealth of Va., Aug. 25, 1983.

[12] *See* Chapter 2, ¶¶ 2.1–2.2[2] regarding the obligation of basic care.

[13] Inmates have asked me to explain why prison officials will not let them have access to care for

Seriousness, linked with an avoidable pain requirement, is the bridge from discretionary to mandated care; it is the bridge that must be crossed before deliberate indifference is at issue. This requirement is analyzed in more detail at ¶ 4.5.

[2] Custody Question

DeShaney v. Winnebago Department of Social Services[14] establishes the constitutional proposition that it is official custody which creates affirmative governmental obligations under the Due Process Clause.[15] In a grudging and mean-spirited decision involving permanent brain damage inflicted on a young boy by his father, after early but passive involvement by child welfare officials, the Supreme Court held that prior cases, when taken together,

> stand only for the proposition that when the State takes a person into its custody and holds him there against his will, the Constitution imposes upon it a corresponding duty to assume some responsibility for his safety and general well-being. The rationale for this principle is simple enough: when the State by the affirmative exercise of its power so restrains an individual's liberty that it renders him unable to care for himself, and at the same time fails to provide for his basic human needs—e.g., food, clothing, shelter, *medical care*, and reasonable safety—it transgresses the substantive limits on state action set by the Eight Amendment and the Due Process Clause.[16]

Narrowly read, *DeShaney,* speaks to the state's duty to prevent harm. However, it is clear from the opinion that the Court also is addressing such affirmative obligations as medical care. In the actual decision, recovery was denied to the child's representative because the battering by the father occurred at home and the State was not held to any obligation to intervene or otherwise protect the victim. The Court in *DeShaney* did not define custody more generally as to encompass a social agency's knowledge of a dangerous situation involving a minor and the agency's legal authority to intervene. Custody in our context has come to mean actual physical possession of the body, not some form of constructive possession, and that being the case, the custody question simply is not a troublesome issue within the contours of this work.[17]

Thus, even conviction and penal confinement does not wholly denude a person of

---

which they are willing and able to pay. Prison officials respond by citing the need to avoid favoritism. They tend to rely on Turner v. Safely, 482 U.S. 78 (1987), and its "reasonableness test" to support them. *See also* Flanagan v. Shively, 783 F. Supp. 922, 932–933 (M.D. Pa. 1992) (upholding denial of access to outside medical advice).

[14] 489 U.S. 189 (1989).

[15] Id. This is not to say that the duty of care described in *DeShaney* originates with the decision. Indeed, there is a common law obligation of a similar sort that is now constitutionalized. *See* Spicer v. Williams, 132 S.E. 291 (N.C. 1926); Ex parte Jenkins, 58 N.E. 560 (Ind. App. 1900).

[16] DeShaney, *supra* note 14, at 199–200 (emphasis added).

[17] *But see* Miracle v. Spooner, 978 F. Supp 1161 (N.D. Ga. 1997), in which the court ruled that involuntary placement in a foster home is sufficiently analagous to confinement in a prison or mental health facility to create the requisite custody for *DeShaney* purposes; *see also* Walker v. Ledbetter, 818 F.2d 791 (11th Cir. 1987), to the same effect.

legal rights; it is custody *simpliciter* that creates a constitutional obligation of medical care. Medical care has been consistently interpreted to encompass mental health care, although the Supreme Court has yet to specifically so hold.[18] Medical and mental health care are so intertwined in legal principle that this work relies on cases from both areas to make common doctrinal points.[19]

¶ 4.3 HOW THE "DELIBERATE INDIFFERENCE" STANDARD IS APPLIED

Since the decisions in *Estelle* and *Bowring,* many courts have grappled with the precise meaning of "deliberate indifference."[20] *Estelle* itself marked out the general territory; deliberate indifference requires something more than poor judgment, inadvertence, or failure to follow the acceptable norms for practice in a particular geographic area. On the other hand, it was understood early on that deliberate indifference is not coextensive with the intentional infliction of needless pain and suffering.

In 1994, the Supreme Court decided *Farmer v. Brennan* and provided an authoritative and reasonably clear answer to the question of just how to define deliberate indifference. Like so many legal formulae, however, the real problems are in the application. Three years prior to *Farmer,* in *Wilson v. Seiter,*[21] the Court gave us something of a preview to *Farmer.*

Wilson determined that the deliberate indifference standard applied to all prison-condition cases—those involving crowding, exercise, ventilation, sanitation, food, and so on. The decision expanded the reach of deliberate indifference, and while it added nothing to the search for a definition, Justice Scalia gave added emphasis to the punishment component of the Eighth Amendment. That is, the Justice made it clear that deliberate indifference is semantically and umbilically tied to the Eighth Amendment and that the amendment itself does not use the term "punishment" as some sort of metaphor for unpleasantness. Punishment, in turn, in any of its several definitions necessarily includes some reference to pain.[22] Some familiarity with the meaning and subtleties associated with pain will facilitate our further excursion into *Farmer.*

[1] "Pain" Requirement

Pain, of course, is essentially a subjective matter. Indeed, like the mental state of deliberate indifference, pain is known when it is reported by the sufferer or through inferences drawn from observation of the individual. Ascertaining the presence of

---

[18] See Bowring, *supra* note 3, at 47, generally regarded as the first important decision to equate medical and psychiatric conditions for the purpose of an Eighth Amendment claim to treatment.

[19] *See* Fred Cohen, *Captives' Legal Right to Mental Health Care,* 17 LAW & PSYCHOLOGY REV. 1, 2–3 (1993), for coverage of the same points.

[20] The continued validity of the deliberate indifference standard for adult prison inmates' claims to medical and psychiatric care is not open to serious doubt.

[21] 501 U.S. 294 (1991).

[22] In Bell v. Wolfish, 441 U.S. 520 (1979), the Court determined that under the Due Process Clause, pretrial detainees could not be punished. However, while the Court indicated that not every disability

pain—whether needless or unavoidable—is not a problem limited to Eighth Amendment jurisprudence. Chronic pain with no discernible physical cause is the most common reason for lost workdays in this country, yet doctors remain uncertain of causation, treatment, or even the validity of the complaint. Recent studies have failed to link chronic pain to physical injury or x-ray findings, but they have found that it correlates with such factors as job satisfaction, depression, and the resolution of lawsuits.[23] This, of course, closely resembles the kind of secondary gains (e.g., housing changes, hospital admission) attributed to prisoners whose behavior patterns create the disciplinary/need-for-care dichotomy.

A football player in a championship game may redouble his efforts after a bloody gash to the forehead; a factory worker may go home with a minor scratch to the finger. An inmate acts out, and a clinician may eventually have to make the call on the etiology of the behavior and perhaps invoke either a disciplinary process or a mental health process responsive to the pain of mental illness. If the illness and pain are serious, care is mandatory; if not, it is discretionary. The avoidance of needless pain, however, is the link between the trigger of a serious disorder and the mental state of deliberate indifference.[24] Deliberate indifference always must articulate with a serious disorder for constitutional liability; if both factors are shown, then constitutionally adequate pain necessarily must be present. We return, then, to the *Farmer* formulation of deliberate indifference.

[2] Recklessness

Farmer v. Brennan[25] dealt with a transsexual federal prisoner who alleged that he was raped while in confinement and that prison officials violated his Eighth Amendment right to personal security in being deliberately indifferent to the risks associated with the inmate's rather obvious condition. Justice Souter, writing for the Court, reaffirmed that prison officials have a clear duty to protect prisoners from violence at the hands of other prisoners and that the challenged act or omission is to be

---

imposed during detention was punishment, the closest it came to a definition was a reference to the earlier decision in Kennedy v. Mendoza-Martinez, 372 U.S. 144 (1963). Punishment in the simple form of restraint, banishment, or public humiliation ceremonies may involve more generalized suffering than actual pain. In medical and mental health cases the claimed deprivation–as–punishment and punishment-as-pain is not as difficult to ascertain, as above examples show. *See* FRED COHEN, THE LAW OF DEPRIVATION OF LIBERTY: CASES AND MATERIAL (1990), for a collection of material on point. For interesting discussions on various forms of punishment, *see* Dan. M. Kahan, *What Do Alternative Sanctions Mean?*, 63 U. CHI. L. REV. 591 (1996), arguing for the uniqueness and the expressive value of imprisonment; Toni M. Massaro, *Shame, Culture, and American Criminal Law*, 89 MICH. L. REV. 1880 (1991), arguing against increasingly popular shaming techniques.

[23] E. Rosenthal, "Chronic Pain Fells Many But Lacks Clear Cause," *N.Y. Times* (Dec. 29, 1992), pp. C1–C3. *See* Stickler v. Waters, 989 F.2d 1375, 1381, n.6 (4th Cir. 1993), regarding serious "pain" as basis for liability.

[24] *See* Fred Cohen, *Offenders with Mental Disorders in the Criminal Justice-Correctional Process* 397, 405 in LAW, MENTAL HEALTH, AND MENTAL DISORDER (Bruce Sales & Daniel W. Shuman, eds. 1996). In Cooper v. Casey, 97 F.3d 914, 916–917 (7th Cir. 1996), Chief Judge Posner wrote at length on the centrality of pain, noting that it is subjective and nonverifiable, but at times the only symptom of a serious medical condition.

[25] *Supra* note 7, 511 U.S. at 825.

governed by the deliberate indifference standard that first arose in the area of health care obligations.[26] Deliberate indifference is described by Justice Souter as a mental state positioned somewhere between negligence at one end and purpose or intent at the other. The mental state between these two extremes is recklessness—that is, a high degree of risk creation followed by conduct that seemingly ignores the risk.

Having settled on recklessness as the closest analogue to deliberate indifference, the Court still had to choose between a "mild" and a "hot" version of recklessness. The essential difference between these two extremes is the extent to which a corrections official must actually know and disregard a risk or whether recklessness might be based on a more objective standard, which in turn places a certain duty of inquiry on the official.

In opting for the "hot" version of recklessness—criminal recklessness—the Court endorsed the subjective or "actually knew" approach. The *Farmer* definition of deliberate indifference clearly applies to medical and mental health cases. Perhaps more intriguing is to ask what difference might this approach make for inmate claims to unconstitutional mental health care? Minimally, the rhetoric will change somewhat, and within the federal judicial system the courts should now be at least more linguistically consistent. It also appears to me that all of the major class actions in this area won by plaintiffs pre-*Farmer* likely would be won (or settled) in similar fashion post-*Farmer*.

While *Farmer* plainly states that corrections officials have no particular duty of inquiry, it also states that knowledge of a risk is to be determined from the facts, including inferences to be drawn from circumstantial evidence. Thus in a *Farmer* situation, officials know they have in their custody in a male prison, a full-breasted, rouged, off-the-shoulder-dressing inmate. What are the risks that must be inferred from these facts by even a remotely competent corrections official? The possibility of sexual attack or exploitation is too obvious for further comment.

[3] Duty

After a particular risk is identified and knowledge thereof attributed to a prison official or agent, the inquiry then turns to duty; that is, what conduct is required to eliminate or materially reduce the risk? With a situation like *Farmer*, some type of protective action or way of reasonably insulating the prospective victim is the duty. With a seriously mentally ill person, there must be a treatment plan that includes the exercise of professional judgment as to an appropriate diagnosis, a treatment plan, and responsive treatment interventions.

Two experts in correctional law are of the view that *Farmer* is not as tough on inmate claims as it might have been. They point out that earlier courts had decided that deliberate indifference required actual knowledge of impending harm easily preventable.[27] They argue that now the requisite harm need not be impending and that

---

[26] Farmer, *supra* note 7, 511 U.S. at 831–833.

[27] *See* JOHN BOSTON & DANIEL E. MANVILLE, PRISONERS' SELF-HELP LITIGATION MANUAL (3d ed. 1995), 15–18 [hereinafter Litigation Manual], citing to Jackson v. Duckworth, 955 F.2d 21, 22 (7th Cir. 1992). The Seventh Circuit consistently interpreted deliberate indifference in the most demanding fashion possible for inmate claims.

Farmer permits liability where serious damage to prisoners' future health is shown.[28] In addition, the harm does not have to be easily preventable.[29] *Farmer* requires that prison officials do what is reasonable and not simply what is easy. *Farmer* also holds that it is enough to show that an official acted, or failed to act, despite his knowledge of a substantial risk of serious harm and that there is no need to show the official acted because of the known risk.[30]

[4] Actual Knowledge

The actual knowledge requirement, of course, is the central feature of *Farmer,* but even this requirement may not be as onerous as may first appear. As noted, *Farmer* itself is a textbook example of how the actual knowledge of risk may be inferred from the facts known, given the inmate's physical appearance and manner of dressing. A knowledge requirement, like any legally required mental state and somewhat like pain as addressed earlier, is almost always a matter of inference. How often will a defendant "confess" to knowing facts, sensing danger, and then doing nothing to prevent the harm anticipated from the danger? Not often, one would wager.[31]

Boston and *Manville* use two pre-*Farmer* examples to make their point. In *Cortes-Quinones v. Jiminez-Nettleship,*[32] the court found that a jury could infer deliberate indifference from the conduct of prison officials who transferred a psychotic prisoner to a general population facility with no mental health care and then failed to segregate him. The psychotic prisoner was murdered by fellow inmates. Would *Cortes-Quinones* be decided the same way today? The answer is almost certainly yes. However, one would want to know a bit more about the particular psychosis and its behavioral implications because not every serious mental disorder creates homicide victim status.

The conservative Seventh Circuit recently stated that any injury to the head unless obviously superficial should be considered serious and merits medical attention.[33] An injury to the cranial cavity calls for rather immediate medical attention rather than telling the detainee to stop being a baby after a slip and fall in the shower.[34]

At the risk of being somewhat redundant, I must emphasize the need to separate the known facts from the known risk or risks. Knowledge of relevant facts is just the threshold requirement; it is the risk known or inferred from the facts that is the determinative factor in deliberate indifference. For example, where an inmate's knee was damaged in an altercation with guards and surgery was delayed for two years, prison

---

[28] Citing to Helling v. McKinney, 113 S. Ct. 2475, 2480 (1993), finding the possibility of an Eighth Amendment claim involving anticipated harm from second-hand tobacco smoke.

[29] Litigation Manual, *supra* note 27, at 17.

[30] Id.

[31] The plaintiffs probably came to believe in an evidentiary God when a C.O. charged with deliberate indifference testified that he knew he was reckless, but did not strive to intentionally harm an inmate. *See* Street v. Corrections Corp. of Am., 102 F.3d 810, 816 (6th Cir. 1996).

[32] 842 F.2d 556, 559–560 (1st Cir.), *cert. denied,* 488 U.S. 823 (1988).

[33] Murphy v. Walker, 51 F.3d 714, 717–718 (7th Cir. 1995).

[34] Id.

officials could hardly deny knowledge of the injury and at least the generalized risks of deterioration and needless pain when surgery was delayed for two years.[35]

Suicide cases, discussed in detail in Chapter 14, provide morbid but excellent examples of the need to dichotomize facts and risks. Where the decedent hung himself with leg irons casually left on the bars of his cell and the offending officer had responded to a "domestic" where he learned the decedent was drunk and trying to cut his wrists, the known facts clearly join with the obvious risk of suicide.[36] Failing to take the normal precautionary measures (e.g., observation, removal of belts, shoelaces, and the like) is one thing; here the officers virtually handed the decedent the means to take his life.

In the situation just described, the nature of the risk—suicide—is as plain as its instrumentality—access to the leg irons. However, there are fact situations in which a similar risk is obvious but the argument is over the instrumentality. For example, in *Estate of Max G. Cole v. Fromm,*[37] a pretrial detainee was hospitalized and then placed on "suicide precaution," but not a close watch. The detainee committed suicide by placing a plastic bag used as a hamper liner over his head and suffocating to death. Clearly, there was knowledge of some risk of suicide and some precautions were taken; the question is whether the defendants can be held to knowledge of the risk related to the use of the particular type of bag as the instrumentality. Summary judgment for the defendants actually was upheld here on a combination of the remoteness of the risk, no prior suicidal experience with the liners, and a finding that knowledge of "some risk" does not require use of all preventative measures.[38]

[5] Discovering the Existence of Mental Illness

Mental disorder need not be, and often is not, worn as a badge, so there need not always or even regularly be actual knowledge that an inmate falls into the general class of those with a mental disorder, to say nothing of having a serious disorder. How do prison and jail officials learn of the "fact" of mental illness?

One obvious way to establish actual knowledge is where an inmate is housed in a mental health unit. For example, in a case arising from confinement in a mental health unit in New York City's Riker's Island, an inmate on the unit was attacked by another inmate, resulting in the loss of an eye.[39] The plaintiff alleged, in effect, that there was inadequate supervision and especially so in light of the heightened need for security on a mental health unit.

The court found that due to his particular placement on the unit, the plaintiff belonged to a group of prisoners who were at risk of substantial harm. "Psychiatric

---

[35] Lowrance v. Coughlin, 862 F. Supp. 1090 (S.D.N.Y. 1994). The plaintiff was awarded $20,000 as compensation for the pain suffered during the needless delay, but there was no further compensation because no permanent damage to the meniscus was shown. *See also* Gonsalves v. City of New Bedford, 939 F. Supp. 921 (D. Mass. 1996), where police beat a suspect who died two hours later and knowledge of the harm and risks were found to be obvious.

[36] Olivas v. Denver, 929 F. Supp. 1329, 1333 (D. Colo. 1996).

[37] 94 F.3d 254 (7th Cir. 1996).

[38] Estate of Max G. Cole, 94 F.3d at 260.

[39] Byrd v. Abate, 1998 U.S. Dist. LEXIS 1761 (S.D.N.Y. Feb. 18, 1998).

evaluations confirm that (plaintiff), like all Lower 3 inmates, posed a clear danger of injury to himself or others."[40]

This is an interesting and unusual finding. If the judge had made the sweeping finding of danger related to an entire mental health unit, the empirical premise would have been doubtful. The judge, however, apparently based his dangerousness conclusion on the characteristics of those assigned to the mental health observation unit of the jail. As a predicate for the actual knowledge requirement of *Farmer,* that is more acceptable than to generalize dangerousness to an entire mental health unit.

There are, of course, a variety of other ways in which this occurs. An inmate's prior record of hospitalization or other mental health care, awareness of suicide ideation or attempts, or recent behavior suggestive of illness may come to the attention of officers. In my experience, very few relevant records are available early (if ever) at the reception process. A transport officer may report strange conduct—indeed, in at least one jurisdiction the officer is specifically questioned on this. Or, an inmate may display the signs and symptoms of paralyzing fear, clinical depression, auditory hallucinations, and the like. Again, such reporting or discovery is not very common.

[a] Reception Screening and Evaluations

The most common means by which to detect illness is to engage in reception mental health screening, followed as needed by more detailed clinical evaluation. Metzner reports that at least 42 Departments of Correction provide this combination.[41] As discussed in Chapter 2, *Farmer* does raise the question of whether intake screening for mental illness is required or merely elective, and whether prison officials invite liability by acquiring information as to previously unknown illnesses or even nonobvious dangers. This is analyzed in detail in Chapter 5.

As a matter of policy, there simply can be no doubt that reception screening and evaluation must be done. With perhaps 10 percent of the population likely to be seriously mentally ill, and with female inmates consistently showing even higher rates, corrections officials are on notice of the general nature of the problem. Good policy, however, is not always coextensive with legal mandates. A case involving the women prisoners in the District of Columbia is instructive on the legal mandate to screen.[42] Judge June Green found that women prisoners experience a higher rate of illnesses than the general population and, thus, that doctors should examine people in a "high risk" health category much more frequently and also anticipate complications.[43] Failure to screen and test can shorten a female inmate's life and result in infertility or preventable diseases in newborns. Failure to perform intake screening for serious

---

[40] Id.

[41] Jeffrey Metzner, et al., *Mental Health Screening and Evaluating in Prison*, 32 BULL. AM. ACAD. PSYCHIATRY & L. 451, 455 (1994).

[42] Women Prisoners of the D.C. Dept. of Corrections v. District of Columbia, 877 F. Supp. 634 (D.C. 1994) [hereinafter Women Prisoners]; *modified,* 899 F.Supp 659 (D.C. 1995); *vacated in part and remanded,* 93 F.3d 910 (D.C. Cir. 1996), *cert. denied,* 117 S. Ct. 1552 (1997); *on remand,* 968 F. Supp 744 (D.C. 1997). No issue was taken, however, with the validity of the point used here.

[43] Women Prisoners, 877 F. Supp. at 642.

mental illness invites further deterioration, especially when the illness is of the "quiet and passive" variety and allows certain preventable violence to staff and other inmates.[44]

[b] Cell Assignment Risks

In a much broader and far reaching decision, the Eighth Circuit Court of Appeals upheld a lower court ruling which basically found that random cell assignments created a pervasive risk of violence.[45] Without finding unconstitutional overcrowding but

---

[44] Fred Cohen, Linda S. Grossman & Robert M. Wettstein, *Treatment In Jails and Prisons,* in TREATMENT OF THE MENTALLY DISORDERED OFFENDER (Robert M. Wettstein, ed. 1998), Ch. 5, pp. 211, 230–231, report the following on prevalence rates:

Less research has been conducted in prisons than jails. James and colleagues (1980) interviewed mostly male, Oklahoma prisoners, and diagnosed 5% with schizophrenia, 35% with a personality disorder, and 25% with a primary diagnosis of substance abuse. Steadman and colleagues (1987) found that 8% of the New York State prison population had severe psychiatric and/or functional disability, and 16% had significant psychiatric and/or functional disability. A study in a Maryland, all-male, prison found that 19.5% had "definite psychiatric problems" excluding personality disorders and substance abuse, with 9.5% diagnosed as having a "major thought or schizophrenic disorder" (Swetz, Salive, Stough & Brewer, 1989). Of this sample, 24% had received inpatient psychiatric treatment prior to their present incarceration. Using the Diagnostic Interview Schedule (DIS) for males in the Quebec, Canada prison system, Cote and Hodging (1990) found lifetime rates of serious mental disorders which far exceeded those in the general population: schizophrenia seven times higher, bipolar disorder six times higher, and major depression twice as high. Substantial comorbidity was also detected, with many coexisting diagnoses of substance abuse/dependence and personality disorders. In a randomized sample of male prisoners in two prisons in Edmonton (Alberta, Canada), Bland and colleagues (1990) found overall lifetime prevalence rates for any mental disorder to be twice that of a community sample; while mood and substance use disorders were found at two times expected rates, antisocial personality disorders were found at nearly seven times expected rates.

Regarding jails, a nationwide mail survey of 1391 jails in the United States found that 7.2% of inmates were thought to have serious mental illness by the jail officials who provided the data (Torrey et al., 1992). Serious mental illness was defined as "schizophrenia, manic-depressive illness and related symptoms." A well-regarded, large-scale study of male urban jail detainees using the DIS found that 9% had schizophrenia or major depression during their lifetimes, while 6% had an episode within two weeks of their arrest (Teplin, 1990). The prevalence rates of schizophrenia, mania, and major depression were two to three times higher than in the general community population. Nearly 35% had a current mental disorder other than antisocial personality disorder (Teplin, 1994).

The references in the above quoted material are, in order of their usage, as follows: JAMES, J.F., et al., HOSP. & COMMUNITY PSYCHIATRY 31, 674–677 (1980); STEADMAN, H.J., et al., HOSP. & COMMUNITY PSYCHIATRY 38, 1086–1090 (1987); SWETZ, A., et al., J. PRISON & JAIL HEALTH 8, 3–15 (1989); COTE, G. & HODGINS, S., BULL. AM. ACAD. PSYCHIATRY & L. 18, 271–281 (1990); BLAND, R.C., et al., CANADIAN J. PSYCHIATRY 35, 407–413 (1990); Torrey, E.F. et al., *Criminalizing the Seriously Mentally Ill: The Abuse of Jails as Mental Hospitals* (Public Citizen's Health Research Group, Washington, D.C., 1992); TEPLIN, L.A., AM. J. PUB. HEALTH 80, 663–669 (1990); and TEPLIN, L.A., AM. J. PUB. HEALTH 84, 290–293 (1994).

[45] Jensen v. Clarke, 94 F.3d 1191 (8th Cir. 1996). *See* McMurray v. Sheehan, 927 F. Supp. 1082 (N.D. Ill. 1996), in which the plaintiff-detainee was raped while in jail on a quashed warrant and officials would

relying on an increase in violence related to increased use of double-celling, the court was led to insist on the use of a classification system. Classification for security is, of course, a direct analogy to reception-intake screening and evaluation for mental disorder. While classification as such is clearly related to security, and reception-intake screening to a need to provide care, with security implications also present, the processes are more alike than different.

The important point, of course, is that the routinized screening-classification process is not responsive to knowledge of any individuals' propensity for violence or need for mental health care. It is responsive to the generalized knowledge of the magnitude of both sets of problems.[46] Moving past the screening-generalized knowledge discussion, there are post-*Farmer* decisions that clearly illustrate the actual knowledge requirement. In *Haley v. Gros,*[47] the plaintiff was double-celled with an inmate widely believed to be seriously and dangerously mentally ill. The plaintiff repeatedly asked to be moved because of conflicts with the cellmate and his bizarre behavior.

During one argument, known to staff, the cellmates were actually "deadlocked"—requiring a key instead of the gang unlocking device—and the cellmate set a fire, killing himself and seriously burning the plaintiff. A lieutenant who witnessed the argument, a superintendent with whom plaintiff spoke at least four times prior to the fire, and a sergeant who was reportedly told about the dangers all were held liable on a "failure to protect" theory.

A jury awarded the plaintiff $1.65 million in compensatory damages, a very large damage award in a prison case. In the process of upholding the award, the Seventh Circuit made it clear that after *Farmer* there is no requirement that the officials actually intend the harm.[48] Knowledge of the risk is logically derived from knowledge of the facts as shown. The duty to separate the men, and thus protect the plaintiff, clearly is the basis of liability. The decedent's possible legal claim would have been to allege deliberate indifference to his obvious and serious mental illness, along with failure to adequately treat him in a safer environment.

[6] Evidentiary Issues

In an important Seventh Circuit Court of Appeals case,[49] Chief Judge Posner wrote at length on deliberate indifference in the context of an eight-hour delay in obtaining medical aid after the defendants physically beat the plaintiffs. An extended quotation is in order here:

---

not be heard to say "we didn't know" in face of a readily available police data base on warrant, quashed or alive; *see also* El Tabech v. Gunter, 922 F. Supp. 244 (D. Neb.), *aff'd*, 94 F.3d 1191 (8th Cir. 1996) (failure to use classification information for housing assignment is an unreasonable response to a known, substantial risk).

[46] In Delgado-Burnet v. Clark, 93 F.3d 339 (7th Cir. 1996), the plaintiff lost an eye when attacked by a known gang member, which by itself did not create sufficient knowledge of the risk. However, if the plaintiff and defendant were known to be rival gang members there would likely be a different result.

[47] 86 F.3d 630 (7th Cir. 1996).

[48] Haley, 86 F.3d at 641.

[49] Cooper v. Casey, 97 F. 3d 914 (7th Cir. 1996)

Deliberately to ignore a request for medical assistance has long been held to be a form of cruel and unusual punishment, e.g., Estelle v. Gamble, 429 U.S. 97, (1976), but this is provided that the illness or injury for which assistance is sought is sufficiently serious or painful to make the refusal of assistance uncivilized. A prison's medical staff that refuses to dispense bromides for the sniffles or minor aches and pains or a tiny scratch or a mild headache or minor fatigue—the sorts of ailments for which many people who are not in prison do not seek medical attention-- does not by its refusal violate the Constitution. The Constitution is not a charter of protection for hypochondriacs. But the fact that a condition does not produce "objective" symptoms does not entitle the medical staff to ignore it. A similar point is familiar from social security disability cases. Pain, fatigue, and other subjective, nonverifiable complaints are in some cases the only symptoms of a serious medical condition. To insist in such a case, as the social security disability law does not, that the subjective complaint, even if believed by the trier of fact, is insufficient to warrant an award of benefits would place a whole class of disabled people outside the protection of that law.

The issue here is not disability. It is whether the plaintiffs were in sufficient pain to entitle them to pain medication within the first 48 hours after the beating. That was an issue for the jury. See Murphy v. Walker, 51 F.3d 714, 719 (7th Cir. 1995) (per curiam). To require a threshold showing of an "objective" injury, the sort of thing that might reveal itself on an x-ray, or in missing teeth, or in a bruised and battered appearance, would confer immunity from claims of deliberate indifference on sadistic guards, since it is possible to inflict substantial and prolonged pain without leaving any "objective" traces on the body of the victim. So the plaintiffs were not required to call a medical expert as a witness; and the defendants' medical witness helped the plaintiffs' case as much as he helped the defendants'. He acknowledged on cross-examination that he would not have ordered x-rays had he not had some reason to believe that the plaintiffs might be injured. And notwithstanding the negative result of the x-rays he prescribed a prescription painkiller, even though for minor pain nonprescription painkillers are adequate. It would be a different case if, as in Goffman v. Gross, 59 F.3d 668 (7th Cir. 1995), the existence or gravity of the particular medical harm were outside a layperson's, and hence the jury's, understanding. That was a case about the effects on human health of ambient smoke; this is a case about pain—which students of philosophy will recognize as the textbook example of a uniquely subjective experience.

As to whether the defendants knew that the plaintiffs needed pain medication—a prerequisite to liability for deliberate indifference to a prisoner's medical needs, Farmer v. Brennan, 511 U.S. 825, (1994); Billman v. Indiana Dept. of Corrections, 56 F.3d 785, 788 (7th Cir.1995)—we do not think that the fact that the plaintiffs directed their request to the world at large, as it were, by screaming from their cells, rather than directing the request to a specific guard, entitled the defendants to judgment as a matter of law. The defendants were all stationed in the plaintiffs' wing of the prison. It was a permissible though not inevitable inference that all of them would have heard the plaintiffs" cries during the period of almost 48 hours before medical assistance was offered, especially since all had participated in the beating of the plaintiffs and would therefore have no basis for believing them simply noisy malingerers. When guards use excessive force on prisoners, the requirements for proving deliberate indifference to the medical needs of the beaten prisoners ought to be relaxed somewhat. Beating a person in violation of the Constitution should impose on the assailant a duty of prompt attention to any medical need to which the beating might give rise, by analogy to the duty in ordinary tort law to provide assistance to a person whom one has injured, even if without fault. And here it was not without fault.[50]

Perhaps the key point for us in this extended quotation is that there is no need for so-called objective proof of serious medical or mental health conditions. In addition, when knowledge of a need for care is established, the unreasonable period of delay is the time line for damages. Here, the needless suffering may be limited to the 48-hour delay. Parenthetically, Judge Posner is wrong to imply that only unconstitutional force causing injury is the base for authenticating a need for care. Obviously, even the use of lawful force which causes serious injury also calls for a prompt clinical response.

Another evidentiary issue concerning deliberate indifference that has plagued the courts is whether repeated acts of negligence may cumulate to establish deliberate indifference. The Sixth Circuit recently grappled with the problem post-*Farmer* and produced an opinion that despite its flaws, is worth reproducing in some detail.[51]

Prior to Farmer, some courts of appeals decisions might be read to hold that repeated acts of negligence by themselves might constitute deliberate indifference. See *DeGidio v. Pung*, 920 F.2d 525 (8th Cir. 1990); *White v. Napoleon*, 897 F.2d 103 (3d. Cir. 1990); [**8] *Rogers v. Evans*, 792 F.2d 1052 (11th Cir. 1986); *Wellman v. Faulkner*, 715 F.2d 269 (7th Cir. 1983), cert. denied, 468 U.S. 1217, 82 L.Ed. 2d 885, 104 S.Ct. 3587 (1984); *Ramos v. Lamm*, 639 F.2d 559 (10th Cir. 1980), *cert. denied*, 450 U.S. 1041, 68 L.Ed. 2d 239, 101 S.Ct. 1759 (1981); *Todaro v. Ward*, 565 F.2d 48 (2d Cir. 1977).

However, these cases really establish that one way to prove that an official acted with deliberate indifference is to show that he repeatedly acted in a certain manner. In such cases, the repeated acts, viewed singly and in isolation, would appear to be mere negligence; however, viewed together and as a pattern, the acts show deliberate indifference. Thus, when the courts referred to "repeated acts of negligence," the language was simply unfortunate—the

---

[50] Cooper, 97 F.3d at 916–917. Where staff incite a known mentally ill inmate into harm, producing bad conduct or a self-destructive episode (a not uncommon experience), a similar analysis should apply. Indeed, where staff mock mentally ill inmates at the pill line (again, not uncommon) and an inmate simply becomes noncompliant, the officers should be liable for the consequences of the noncompliance.

[51] Brooks v. Celeste, 39 F.3d 125 (6th Cir. 1994) (some citations omitted or abbreviated).

pattern of the acts actually helps prove that each act was committed with deliberate indifference.

For example, in *Wellman*, the Seventh Circuit stated that "as a practical matter", "deliberate indifference" can be *evidenced* by "repeated examples of negligent acts which disclose a pattern of conduct by the prison medical staff . . . " 715 F.2d at 272 (emphasis added) (quoting *Ramos*, 639 F.2d at 575). Thus, the court in *Wellman* seemed to describe a method of proof, not a per se equating of negligent acts to deliberate indifference. Similarly, in *Todaro*, the case most heavily relied upon by other courts, see *Wellman*, 715 F.2d at 272; *Ramos*, 639 F.2d at 575, the Second Circuit explained: "And while a single instance of medical care denied or delayed, viewed in isolation, may appear to be the product of mere negligence, repeated examples of such treatment bespeak a deliberate indifference by prison authorities . . ." 565 F.2d at 52. Again, the court in *Todaro* merely described a method of proving deliberate indifference that involved proving a repetition of misconduct that would appear to be negligence when viewed alone.[1]

We should note that *Farmer* recognizes the legitimacy of showing deliberate indifference by circumstantial proof. The Court in *Farmer* reminded courts that "whether a prison official had the requisite knowledge of a substantial risk is a question of fact subject to demonstration in the usual ways, including inference from circumstantial evidence . . ." 114 S. Ct. at 1981. In *Farmer*, the prisoner wished to equate the obviousness of the risk—placing a transsexual prisoner into the general male prisoner population—with deliberate indifference. Although the Court rejected this purely subjective approach, it noted that "a factfinder may conclude that a prison official knew of a substantial risk from the very fact that the risk was obvious." Id. Similarly, the courts in *Wellman* and *Todaro* merely sought to approve using repeated acts as circumstantial evidence of deliberate indifference; *Farmer* suggests that this use is proper.

To the extent that some cases in fact hold that repeated acts of negligence could by themselves constitute deliberate indifference, *Farmer* teaches otherwise. The Supreme Court in *Farmer* reiterated that the Eighth Amendment requires that the inflicting official act or fail to act with subjective awareness of the deprivation. Lack of objective reasonableness, i.e., a failure to act as a reasonable person would have acted, does not by itself equal deliberate indifference. Repeatedly violating an objective standard of reasonableness does not necessarily mean that the official acted with "deliberate indifference" as defined in *Farmer*. The official may be incompetent, but he is not acting wantonly, and thus is not inflicting "punishment."

Neither the special master nor the district court had the benefit of *Farmer*'s holding. Given the ambiguity in the special master's report, *Farmer*'s importance is now clear. If, as the district court read the report, Dr. Martinez was merely repeatedly negligent, then *Farmer* dictates that he did not act with deliberate indifference. However, if Dr. Martinez was subjectively aware of a substantial risk of serious harm, then he acted with deliberate indifference as indicated in *Farmer*. Also, no specific findings of fact were made regarding the deliberate indifference of the defendants who are Dr. Martinez's supervisors. Therefore, we remand to the district court with instructions to supplement the factual findings and conclusions of law in order to clarify whether deliberate indifference was proven.

> *(1) Similarly, the court in* White *explained that the plaintiff alleged more than mere isolated episodes of inadvertence; from the persistently painful conduct "one reasonably may infer that the doctor is either intentionally inflicting pain . . . or is deliberately indifferent." 897 F.2d at 109. Likewise, the court in* Rogers *explained that medical care can be "so inappropriate as to evidence intentional maltreatment." 792 F.2d at 1058.*[52]

Essentially, the Sixth Circuit is saying that a fifth act of negligence, for example, is not going to relate back and either elevate any of the four prior negligent acts to deliberate indifference or become deliberate indifference because of the earlier conduct. On the other hand, and more importantly, this is actually an evidentiary problem. Evidence of repeated acts or omissions in light of knowledge that they have caused past harm or needless pain is an important window to the present, subjective disregard of known risks required by *Farmer.*

For example, where a psychiatrist continuously changes medications over time and the inmate-patient deteriorates, and where it is shown that the psychiatrist acted on little or no clinical information, deliberate indifference is quite likely to be found.[53] The early discountenances may be characterized as negligent, but after a certain point the term "negligence" can be discarded in favor of "prior misconduct."

[7] Negligence Defined

To this point I have written a good deal about deliberate indifference, while the reader has been given little detail on the legal concept of negligence, which regularly is referred to as a distinguishing touchstone. Negligence is conduct that falls below the standard established by law for the protection of people against unreasonable risks.[54] A prima facie case of negligence requires a showing of (1) the existence of a duty owed by defendant to plaintiff, (2) a breach of this duty, (3) and an injury to plaintiff caused by the breach.

This, of course, sounds very much like deliberate indifference until we note that the latter requires a highly culpable subjective finding along with an objective component and that the alleged deprivation must be "sufficiently serious." Deliberate indifference describes a mental state more blameworthy than negligence and insists on actual knowledge of relevant facts, whereas negligence does not.

Negligence may be shown where a defendant knew the facts and risks involved or *should have known them.* On the breach of duty, courts ask whether the injury was reasonably foreseeable and proximately caused by the breach. Negligent actions allow courts to perform case-by-case analyses and bring to bear logical, policy, and moral considerations.[55] Deliberate indifference, on the other hand, is coupled with constitu-

---

[52] Brooks, 39 F.3d at 128–129.

[53] *See, e.g.,* Steele v. Shah, 87 F.3d 1266 (11th Cir. 1996), where a detainee went without previously prescribed medication for 182 days when the doctor discontinued medication without explanation and after only a brief and superficial encounter.

[54] W. PAGE KEETON, et al., PROSSER AND KEETON ON THE LAW OF TORTS (5th ed. 1984), § 43 at 280.

[55] For an interesting analysis of these terms, *see* Burke v. Warren County Sheriff's Dept., 890 F. Supp. 133, 138–139 (N.D.N.Y. 1995).

tional standards, and courts are far less likely to engage in policy and moral debates or to refer to cost-sharing or risk reduction as legitimate outcome objectives.

If negligence may be seen as inadvertence, deliberate indifference should be seen as rash, intemperate conduct, quite the opposite of being inattentive. Indeed, the risks associated with deliberate indifference are to be so plain and known, and their disregard so callous, that it is but a small step away from actually intending the harm.

[8] Malpractice

Malpractice is simply a form of negligence. It is usually defined as unskillful practice that results in injury to the patient or as a failure to exercise the requisite skill, care, and diligence demanded by the undertaking.[56] While malpractice alone is not the equivalent of deliberate indifference, obviously not every instance of malpractice is precluded from constituting deliberate indifference. Indeed, in one case a federal judge erroneously charged the jury that a finding of medical malpractice precludes a finding of deliberate indifference.[57] This led to reversal, although it seems that the judge meant to say that malpractice alone cannot establish deliberate indifference.

In *Guglielmoni v. Alexander*,[58] in the context of a suit for damages based on the suicide of the plaintiff-mother's son, the court wrote:

> The "deliberate indifference" standard implicitly requires assessment of states of mind in order to determine the constitutional adequacy of inmate medical care. Isolated negligence or malpractice is insufficient to state an *Estelle* claim. Deliberate indifference exists when action is not taken in the face of a "strong likelihood, rather than a mere possibility," that failure to provide care would result in harm to the prisoner.[59]

Guglielmoni elaborated on a problem faced earlier in the Second Circuit: the relationship between a single incident of denied, delayed, or improper care and a series of such incidents closely related in time.[60] There is little doubt that even under *Farmer* a single dramatic incident as well as a series of less dramatic, but cumulatively painful, incidents may meet the "deliberate indifference" standard. The key for plaintiffs is to avoid characterizing the prior acts as negligence or "mere malpractice." The earlier incident either stands on its own or is evidence of knowledge as it relates to the conduct presently at issue.

Wellman v. Faulkner,[61] an early and important decision involving the Indiana State Prison at Michigan City, recites an increasingly popular litany for understanding "deliberate indifference":

---

[56] BARRY R. FURROR, et al., HEALTH LAW (1995), p. 359.

[57] Hathaway v. Coughlin, 99 F.3d 520, 554 (2d Cir. 1996).

[58] 583 F. Supp. 821 (D. Conn. 1984).

[59] Guglielmoni, 583 F. Supp. at 826 (citations omitted).

[60] Todaro v. Ward, 565 F.2d 48 (2d Cir. 1977).

[61] 715 F.2d 269 (7th Cir. 1983), *cert. denied*, 468 U.S. 1217 (1984). Denial of access to needed care is one of the more likely successful claims made by inmates, as discussed at ¶ 4.3[9].

As a practical matter, "deliberate indifference" can be evidenced . . . by "proving there are such systemic and gross deficiencies in staffing, facilities, equipment, or procedures that the inmate population is effectively denied access to adequate medical care."[62]

In dealing with a successful challenge to the South Dakota prison system, a federal district court judge went a step beyond the quotation from *Faulkner*, adding: "A court need not wait "until an inmate bleeds to death" or until institutional health care deficiencies reach catastrophic proportions in order to exercise its declaratory or injunctive powers to cure an otherwise inadequate health care system."[63]

[9] Access to Care

This issue of the maturation of harm surfaced in a recent Supreme Court decision involving inmate claims of access to the courts. In *Lewis v. Casey*,[64] a majority of the Court found, in effect, that abstract claims of deficiencies in the prison law library or legal assistance program did not present an "actual injury," and without such injury or harm the inmates could not litigate their claims.[65] This is not the occasion to again review the law of access to the courts, but on the way to reaching the ultimate result of "no jurisdiction" Justice Scalia laced his pithy opinion with analogies drawn from the health care area. For example, in arguing that an inmate cannot show actual injury by showing that the library or legal assistant is sub-par he states: "That would be the precise analogue of the healthy inmate claiming constitutional violation because of the inadequacy of the prison infirmary."[66]

In discussing an earlier Supreme Court decision,[67] Justice Scalia notes that it did not establish a right to library or legal assistance, "any more than *Estelle* established a right to a prison hospital."[68] The point he is attempting to make is that the right at issue is access to the courts and not the precise manner in which it is provided. His final analogy is most instructive:

> If . . . a healthy inmate who had suffered no deprivation of needed medical treatment were able to claim violation of his constitutional right to medical care, simply on the ground that the prison medical facilities were inadequate, the essential distinction between judge and executive would have disap-

---

[62] Wellman, 715 F.2d at 272.

[63] Cody v. Hillard, *supra* note 9.

[64] Lewis v. Casey, 518 U.S. 343 (1996). In Helling v. McKinney, 509 U.S. 25 (1993), the Court rejected the argument that inmates must already have suffered from the injuries or illnesses of the condition complained about, in this case exposure to second-hand tobacco smoke.

[65] Technically, this is characterized as a lack of standing and without standing there is no "case or controversy," which is an Article III constitutional requirement. Never before had the Court dealt with a prisoner's claim on the basis of standing.

[66] Lewis, *supra* note 64.

[67] Bounds v. Smith, 430 U.S. 817 (1977).

[68] Lewis, *supra* note 64.

peared: it would have become the function of the courts to assure adequate medical care in prisons.[69]

With all due respect, Justice Scalia is simply pursuing false and empty analogies that do not advance the struggle to comprehend the law in this area. Let us approach the same set of problems from a different angle: is it a 100 percent certainty that not a small percentage of inmates during their confinement will suffer some form of serious physical and mental illness? The answer, obviously, is yes, and for our purposes it is not important to have a precise number for either category.[70]

If that is the case—and it most assuredly is—then we must first address the resource question and then the access question. Access to an empty room is meaningful only if one seeks solitude. Access to mental or physical health care can make sense only if there are appropriately trained staff and physically appropriate setups for diagnosis and care. It is an absolute certainty that there are and will be inmates who experience the pain of injury and disease, which means there will always be inmates available with legal standing to challenge inadequate resources or access. There will also always be inmates who feel aggrieved about their conviction, their confinement, food, visits, and so on. Whether those grievances translate into legally congnizable claims is another matter. That requires another step, of course, as does the translation of a reported pain into a diagnosis followed by appropriate care.

The legal claim translation, so to speak, comes from access to books or persons trained in law, or both. What Justice Scalia sought to accomplish in *Lewis* was to deny inmates the right to the resources needed to determine whether their grievances had a legal basis. In the world of medicine, the pain of certain illness in a given captive population requires adequate resources.

In my own writing I have used the term "primary right" to describe inmates' rights to physical survival, access to the courts, and to mental health care. I then use the term "ancillary rights" to describe that which is absolutely required to effectuate the primary right. The analysis has several uses, but its main focus is to anticipate what courts would mandate; it also gives agencies an opportunity to act proactively. For example, if the primary right is to physical survival and the prison is in a cold climate, the secondary right would be to heat and the various ways in which heat is provided: clothing, blankets, indoor heating systems and the like.

Justice Scalia's effort with regard to "access" clearly is aimed at curtailing what he views as excessive frivolous litigation. By not requiring a library, I suppose he

---

[69] Id.

[70] CURTIS PROUT & ROBERT N. ROSS, CARE AND PUNISHMENT: THE DILEMMAS OF PRISON MEDICINE (1988), Ch. 6, discusses the relationship of pre-prison lifestyles and prison medical disorders. Conceding that there are few accurate studies of the diseases found among inmates, the authors analyze the cases of AIDS, tuberculosis, liver disease (common), ulcers (common), heart disease, diseases associated with an aging prison population, and the like. While they suggest that the incidence of serious illness is lower than expected, it obviously exists in sufficient numbers to require substantial medical resources. *See* GAO, Report to the Chairman, Subcommittee on Intellectual Property and Judicial Administration, Committee on the Judiciary, House of Representatives, "Inmates' Access to Health Care Is Limited by Lack of Clinical Staff" (Feb. 10, 1994). On mental illness, *see* NATHANIEL J. PALLONE, MENTAL DISORDER AMONG PRISONERS: TOWARD AN EPIDEMIOLOGICAL INVENTORY (1991). On female inmates experiencing a higher rate of illness than the general population, *see* Women Prisoners, *supra* note 42.

hopes to reduce the opportunity for inmates searching for ways to give legal expression to grievances.[71]

Make no mistake, in the real world there must be in place adequate human and physical resources along with ready access to meet the short- and long-term physical and mental health requirements of inmates. Justice Scalia was writing in the rarified air of intellectual speculation and from an extremely negative ideology about inmates. Many readers of this work deal with the reality of pain and suffering in prison and understand the need for physical and human resources responsive to the certainty of illness.[72]

¶ 4.4 LEADING RECENT CASES: DELIBERATE INDIFFERENCE AND SYSTEMIC FAILURE

Here we review four fairly recent cases—two from California, one from Arizona, and one from Ohio. Three of the cases involved bitter and expensive legal proceedings with the inmates ultimately prevailing, while the Ohio case was settled rather quickly, amicably, and inexpensively.[73]

[1] *Coleman v. Wilson*

In *Coleman v. Wilson*,[74] the plaintiff class was composed of all inmates in the California prison system, now or in the future, who suffered a serious mental illness. It is difficult to imagine either a more comprehensive legal attack or a more comprehensive set of findings and recommendations made initially by Magistrate Judge Moulds and then upheld on appeal by the redoubtable Chief Judge Emeritus, Lawrence K. Karlton.

Coleman challenged California's lack of screening, inadequate staffing, personnel qualifications, access to care, supervision of psychotropic medication, use of restraints, medical records, and suicide prevention efforts. While each of the items will reappear for closer study, for now they are offered only as a broad factual mosaic to further our grasp of deliberate indifference.

After establishing a record rife with examples of the defendant's delay, recalcitrant refusals to act, attitudes and conduct suggestive of obfuscation and reckless denials, the court turned to application of the standard of deliberate indifference:

The magistrate judge found that the defendants were deliberately indifferent

---

[71] *See* Fred Cohen, *supra* note 19.

[72] *See* Hans Toch, CORRECTIONS: A HUMANISTIC APPROACH (1997), for a valuable collection of his previously published material dealing with many aspects of the subject matter of this book. Toch's work on prison violence and the disturbed, disruptive prisoner is especially valuable.

[73] Dunn v. Voinovich, C1-93-0166 (S.D. Ohio July 10, 1995) (reference is to filing number and date of consent decree). The author helped resolve *Dunn* and currently serves as the court-appointed Monitor. For a full discussion of this case, *see* Fred Cohen & Sharon Aungst, *Prison Mental Health Care: Dispute Resolution and Monitoring in Ohio*, 33 CRIM. L. BULL. 299 (1997) [hereinafter Prison Mental Health Care, Ohio]. See Appendix D for an extensive excerpt from the Decree itself.

[74] 912 F. Supp. 1282 (E.D. Cal. 1995).

within the meaning of Eighth Amendment jurisprudence.[1] Defendants challenge that finding.

The court acknowledges the caution which both the law and propriety enjoin upon an inquiry as to whether high officials of state government are deliberately indifferent to the rights of persons within their charge. With due regard for the defendants and the difficult task that is theirs, but with equal regard for the duty that is the court's by virtue of its office, the court turns to that task. In doing so, the court stresses that the issue is not whether as to some particular deficiency the defendants have exhibited deliberate indifference. Rather, given the overwhelming evidence of the systemic failure to deliver necessary care to mentally ill inmates, the issue is whether the defendants have demonstrated deliberate indifference to that condition.

In order to find that defendants have acted with deliberate indifference to the needs of the plaintiff class, the court must find (1) that defendants knew that inmates face a substantial risk of harm as a result of the systemic deficiencies noted above and (2) that defendants have disregarded that risk by "failing to take reasonable measures to abate it." *Farmer,* 114 S. Ct. at 1984.

(1) He specifically found that the evidence bearing on the issue "was not seriously contested," and that "defendants have known [about and repeatedly acknowledged] the serious problem with understaffing at least since . . . 1985." He further found that "defendants have known that there were thousands of mentally ill inmates . . . who were not even identified as needing care, let alone being provided necessary care, at least since . . . July, 1989." Moreover he found that "the inadequacies in the mental health care delivery system . . . remain today." In like manner he noted that "defendants repeatedly acknowledged that . . . their medical record keeping system . . . was woefully outdated and inadequate, and that they did not have a mechanism in place for screening and identifying mentally ill inmates." He concluded that "the fact that defendants have known about these deficiencies for over eight years without taking any significant steps to correct them is additional evidence of deliberate indifference."

Plaintiffs seek prospective injunctive relief. Under such circumstances, deliberate indifference is examined "in light of the prison authorities current attitudes and conduct," *Helling,* 113 S. Ct. at 2477, i.e., the defendants attitudes and conduct "at the time suit is brought and persisting thereafter." *Farmer,* 114 S.Ct. at 1983.[2]

The question of whether a defendant charged with violating rights protected by the Eighth Amendment has the requisite knowledge is "a question of fact subject to demonstration in the usual ways, including inferences from circumstantial evidence [citation omitted], and a factfinder may conclude that a prison official knew of a substantial risk from the very fact that the risk was obvious." Id. at 1981. The inference of knowledge from an obvious risk has been described by the Supreme Court as a rebuttable presumption, and thus prison officials bear the burden of proving ignorance of an obvious risk. Id. at 1982. It is also established that defendants cannot escape liability by virtue of their having turned a blind eye to facts or inferences "strongly suspected to be true." Id. at 1982 n.8, and that "if . . . the evidence before the district court established that an inmate faces an objectively intolerable risk of serious injury, the defendants could not plausibly persist in claiming lack of awareness." Id. at 1984 n.9.

(2) Farmer addressed suit by an inmate seeking "injunctive relief to prevent a substantial risk of serious injury from ripening into actual harm." Farmer v. Brennan, 128 L. Ed. 2d 811, 114 S. Ct. 1970, 1983 (1994). In the matter at bar members of the plaintiff class are not only facing substantial risks of serious injury, they are experiencing actual harm as a result of the systemic deficiencies identified in this order.

As the court concluded above, the evidence demonstrates that seriously mentally ill inmates in the California Department of Corrections daily face an objectively intolerable risk of harm as a result of the gross systemic deficiencies that obtain throughout that Department. The evidence also demonstrates that inmates have in fact suffered significant harm as a result of those deficiencies; seriously mentally ill inmates have languished for months, or even years, without access to necessary care, they suffer from severe hallucinations, they decompensate into catatonic states, and they suffer the other sequela to untreated mental disease.

Defendant's knowledge of the risk of harm to these inmates is evident throughout this record. (See e.g., Defendants' Exhibit D880)[3] It is equally apparent that defendants have known about these gross deficiencies in their system for years. The risk of harm from these deficiencies is obvious to plaintiffs' experts, to defendants' experts, to defendants' consultants, to individual employees of the Department of Corrections in the field, and to this court. The actual harm suffered by mentally ill inmates incarcerated in the California Department of Corrections is also manifest in this record.

(3) The exhibit, an internal Department of Corrections memorandum, reads in pertinent part, "the need to assess [inmates backlogged awaiting transfer to mental health services] is urgent." Seriously mentally ill inmates who do not receive needed treatment can worsen severely, losing most or all of their ability to function. Such inmates can also become suicidal or can pose significant risks to others or to the safety of the institution. In addition, the litigation facing the Department in this area, especially the Department-wide Coleman case, puts the Department at extreme liability risk if these inmates go untreated.[75]

This, of course, is powerful medicine and it seems written with an air of both resignation and outrage. Elsewhere, Judge Karlton states that when the defendants were confronted with uncomfortable facts, they (1) questioned the experts who brought the message, (2) commissioned other studies, (3) worked on a new administrative approach to an obviously dry-rotted system, and (4) litigated vigorously and in exquisite detail.[76] Later, high ranking officials were heard to say, in effect, "we didn't know how bad it was or we would have . . .."

In a systemic challenge of this sort, deliberate indifference emerges from the complex array of facts presented: what was and was not done and in what fashion, what was known and when, and what individual and collective suffering finds its way into the record. The *Coleman* litigation legacy of "fight or flight" left in its wake a very difficult post-litigation environment in California that even today has not healed.

---

[75] Coleman, 912 F. Supp. at 1315–1316.
[76] Coleman, 912 F. Supp. at 1317–1318.

[2] *"Pelican Bay"*

Madrid v. Gomez,[77] also comes to us from California but is cut from somewhat different cloth than *Coleman*. *Madrid* involves only the Pelican Bay State Prison, located 363 miles north of San Francisco. It also involves findings of brutality not disclosed in judicial opinions since the 30-odd-year-old prison cases from the deep South. These first generation brutality cases arose in a mixed medium of racism, older facilities, and a plantation mentality as to the use of force. The *Pelican Bay* case, as it is known, arose in a five-year-old, state of the art maximum security facility, in a jurisdiction formerly known for enlightened penal policies and the cosmopolitan tolerance of a San Francisco or Los Angeles.

Experts like Vince Nathan and Steve Martin were awed by the general level of force used at Pelican Bay. One of the most revolting episodes involved a mentally ill prisoner who bit an officer. The inmate suffered second- and third-degree burns when he was "bathed" by officers in scalding water in the infirmary. Five or six officers drew the water, then placed the inmate in the blistering hot water and then scrubbed him with a hard bristle brush announcing that the African-American is going to be a white boy since his rotten skin had fallen off.

Judge Henderson's findings of fact, with incidents such as these in the record, made his conclusion as to deliberate indifference almost redundant. California decided to house its more disruptive inmates in the Special Housing Unit (SHU) at Pelican Bay, knowing that this group contained significant numbers of inmates with serious mental illness. Armed with this knowledge, the facility bravely opened with only one or two psychologists for a SHU population that would reach 1,500.[78]

In concluding that there was *Farmer*-style, systemic deliberate indifference, the judge identified the following as critical factors:

- Inadequate screening
- Inadequate staff training
- Sketchy psychiatric records
- Delayed transfers for psychiatric care (up to three months)
- No involuntary treatment protocols
- No input from mental health staff on housing
- No suicide prevention program, and
- No quality assurance program.[79]

---

[77] 889 F. Supp. 1146 (N.D. Calif. 1995). *See* Fred Cohen, *"Pelican Bay:" Excessive Force; Mental and General Health Care So Deficient as to Show Deliberate Indifference,* VI Correctional L. Rep. 81, 82 (1995); much of the recounting of this decision is taken from this article.

[78] Justice Scalia, one would assume, also would have been content to await the actual breakdown of inmates, whereas I have argued that it is inevitable and requires "people and places" in advance.

[79] Madrid (Pelican Bay), 889 F. Supp. at 1256. This case is discussed in further detail in Chapter 7, ¶¶ 7.3[2]–7.3[2][d]; see also the extensive excerpt from this case reproduced in Appendix B of this book.

The plaintiffs showed that the defendants actually knew of this shockingly low level of care and consciously disregarded the substantial risk of harm posed thereby. Would knowledge of these conditions—essentially a high number of seriously mentally ill inmates placed in a SHU with virtually no care and affirmative evidence of mindless brutality—pre-*Farmer* have been a basis for finding deliberate indifference? Of course. Indeed, if *Farmer* had adopted the more lax "should have known" approach, deliberate indifference would scream even more loudly at us.

[3] *Casey v. Lewis*

In *Casey v. Lewis*,[80] a pre-*Farmer* decision, we encounter a systemic claim on the order of *Coleman*, whereas *Pelican Bay* is systemic as to one facility in the vast California system. Casey lacks the brutality overlay of *Pelican Bay*, although a Special Program Unit (SPU) was reported to have recently stopped placing seriously ill inmates into unshaded pens in the torrid Arizona heat without water or bathroom facilities.[81]

Judge Muecke found constitutionally adequate care in three facilities and that with adequate staff the Special Program Unit (SPU) would meet the needs of the male inmates incarcerated there. Thereafter, he found:

> However, the overwhelming evidence establishes that the defendants are deliberately indifferent to the serious mental health care needs of the inmates in other institutions throughout the state. Seriously mentally ill inmates are housed in most of the other facilities. Such inmates tend to be concentrated in the lockdown facilities of SMU, CB6 and Santa Maria in Perryville. Those facilities have inadequate mental health staff and programming for inmates. Rather than providing mental health care for these inmates, security staff lock inmates down for prolonged periods of time because of the behavior that is the result of their mental illnesses. During lock down the inmates are provided little or no mental health care by psychiatrists or psychologists.
>
> Because of the lack of staff and programming, inmates do not have "ready access" to mental health care. Severely mentally ill inmates cannot make their needs known to mental health staff. Untrained security staff assess inmates' mental health. Further, referrals to B ward, Flamenco, and ASH are not "reasonably speedy." Inmates remain in lockdown for days to months waiting for transfer to these facilities. Although psychological staff request transfers, they are not consistently carried out by security staff. All of these problems result in deliberate indifference to inmates' serious mental health needs such that the inmates' constitutional rights to be free from cruel and unusual punishment are violated by the defendants.
>
> The fact that the lack of staff and programming is partially a result of lack of funding from the Legislature is not a defense to these constitutional violations.

---

[80] 834 F. Supp. 1477 (D. Ariz. 1993).

[81] Casey, 834 F. Supp. at 1549 n.11; this occurred after suit was filed and plaintiff's expert psychiatrist visited the facility.

The system for female inmates is even worse than for male inmates because female inmates have no SPU or transitional facility. Rather, female inmates are returned to general population and are generally locked down for behavior caused by their mental illness. Sometimes, the lockdown reoccurs within 24 to 72 hours of return to general population. Seriously mentally ill female inmates are limited to the G Ward with its 15 to 17 beds or transferred outside ADOC [Arizona Department of Corrections] to ASH [Arizona State Hospital]. Even at G Ward, female inmates receive less programming than that provided to males.

The Court finds the treatment of seriously mentally ill inmates to be appalling. Rather than providing treatment for serious mental illnesses, ADOC punishes these inmates by locking them down in small, bare segregation cells for their actions that are the result of their mental illnesses. These inmates are left in segregation without mental health care. Many times the inmates, such as H.B., are in a highly psychotic state, terrified because of hallucinations, such as monsters, gorillas or the devil in her cell.[(1)] Nor does it appear that H.B. is the exceptional case as seven to eight mentally ill women may be locked down at the Santa Maria Unit in Perryville at any one time and may remain there for months without care. In addition, such treatment is common for male inmates in other lockdown facilities or units in the state including SMU and CB6. The Court considers this treatment of any human being to be inexcusable and cruel and unusual punishment in violation of the eighth amendment of the Constitution.

> *(1) In fact, one psychiatrist expert stated he wouldn't treat his dog the way the defendants treated H.B.* [82]

Earlier in his detailed opinion, Judge Muecke established his understanding of pre-*Farmer* deliberate indifference. There are some now questionable statements along the way (e.g., that repeated negligence may establish deliberate indifference), but ultimately he relies on proof of systemic and gross deficiencies in staffing, facilities, equipment, or procedures to conclude that the inmate population is effectively denied access to adequate care.

The defendants' awareness and their failure or inability to act are implicit in this opinion, which post-*Farmer* simply would have been written slightly differently. The pattern of knowingly tolerating avoidable pain, which satisfies *Farmer,* is clearly established in this record.

[4] *Dunn v. Voinovich*

The Ohio case, *Dunn v. Voinovich,*[83] has certain features shared by the three cases discussed above, but is completely different in its resolution. California and Arizona have spent millions of dollars fighting lawsuits where the readily available facts dictated a losing result. In Ohio, after suit was filed, counsel for the class of seriously mentally ill inmates and for the state suspended time-consuming and expensive dis-

---

[82] Casey, 834 F. Supp. at 1549–1550. *See also* the discussion of *Casey* in Chapter 7, ¶ 7.3[3].

[83] *Supra* note 73. *See* discussion of *Dunn* at Chapter 7, ¶¶ 7.3[5]–7.3[5][b].

covery and named an expert team to study the system and to make findings and recommendations.[84]

The study concluded that Ohio had an unconstitutional system, albeit without the brutality noted elsewhere; that officials were likely aware of this, if only because of several prior reports on point, and a plan for increasing human and physical resources and facilitating access to mandated care was outlined.[85] The parties basically accepted the report emanating from the study and when entering into a Consent Decree followed the usual practice of no admission of constitutional violation while agreeing to perform wholesale systemic changes. The poisoned post-judgment environment in California and Arizona was avoided and an environment conducive to positive change exists at this writing.

To summarize the discussion on deliberate indifference to this point, we have learned that not until 1994 did the Supreme Court, in *Farmer v. Brennan*, provide us with an authoritative definition although the term had been in use since 1976. Deliberate indifference, a mental state, lies somewhere between intentionality and "ordinary" (or civil) recklessness. The crucial feature is actual knowledge of the facts that create the risk that those with serious mental illness will go undetected or untreated.

The actual knowledge requirement may not be as onerous as it first appears, since knowledge may be inferred from known facts and conditions. Prison officials cannot easily claim expertise on the one hand and then also disclaim awareness of risks when obvious and relevant facts are parading through their door.

Cases of individual inmate grievances or class action challenges to an entire facility or correctional facility will focus on a range of similar items to establish the objective failure to provide care and the mental state of deliberate indifference. Those factors are:

- Screening and evaluation to detect serious mental illness

- Adequate staff in terms of training and numbers

- Adequate physical facilities, expressed often as bed/treatment space, to meet varying treatment needs

- Adequate records to assure continuity of care

- Proper administration and follow-up of psychotropic medications

- A program to deal with suicidal inmates

- A humane and clinically sound (e.g., medical monitoring) approach to mechanical restraints

- Staff training

- The absence of brutality toward inmates with mental illness

---

[84] I was fortunate enough to have headed the team and drafted the 800-page report. At the further invitation of the parties, I served as the facilitator in the negotiation of the Consent Decree and was then appointed as the Monitor.

[85] *See* Prison Mental Health Care, Ohio, *supra* note 73.

- Presence of a quality assurance program and management information system

- Reasonable post-admission access to adequate care

These are the significant and recurring items in the case law while, other conceptually important factors in a health care system (e.g., confidentiality) are rarely encountered. Deliberate indifference will not require known deficits in all these areas, but this is a handy checklist of the factors that enter into the calculus of the culpable mental state of deliberate indifference.

We turn next to the second *Estelle* prong, which requires that the physical, and now mental, illness be serious. Deliberate indifference to minor aches and pains, mild depression, ordinary headaches and the like invokes no constitutional issues. What is or is not serious, however, can be a very difficult question both in the abstract and in practice.

¶ 4.5 "SERIOUS MEDICAL NEEDS" STANDARD

Writing in 1986 about civil commitment, one author stated, "there has been remarkably little consideration given to the kind and degree of illness that should be required before one is committed."[86] Where civil commitment law is importantly legislative in character, correctional mental health law is essentially judicially created. Until quite recently, the courts have been almost as reticent as the legislatures in addressing the threshold question of what is a serious medical or psychiatric need.[87] Even where the courts have spoken, nagging uncertainty remains.

In *Ramos v. Lamm*, a 1980 decision, the court provided more of a description than a definition in stating that "A medical need is serious if it is 'one that has been diagnosed by a physician as mandating treatment or one that is so obvious that even a lay person would easily recognize the necessity for a doctor's attention.' "[88]

The initial reference to a physician's diagnosis simply transfers the actual decision-making process, while the reference to that which is "obvious" merely evades the

---

[86] Mark Mills, *Civil Commitment of the Mentally Ill: An Overview*, 484 Annals Am. Acad. Pol. & Soc. Sci. 28, 33 (1986).

[87] Judges may well feel a sense of institutional constraint or a sense of institutional incompetence in this murky area.

[88] Ramos v. Lamm, 639 F.2d 559, 575 (10th Cir. 1980) (citation omitted), *cert. denied*, 450 U.S. 1041 (1981). Downs v. Andrews and Liberty Co. Comm'rs, LEXIS 15815 (S.D. Ga. 1986), used the *Ramos* formulation in dealing with an inmate's claim of deliberate indifference to his acne:

> The Court is unaware of any decision that has found acne to be a serious medical need or the failure to treat the condition a constitutional violation. Nevertheless, is must be acknowledged that such a skin disease can be painful and extensive, and that the Court has before it sufficient evidence concerning the scope or severity of the Plaintiff's acne infection to determine whether it was so serious that even a lay person would have seen the necessity of a doctor's attention. Whether the plaintiff's acne represented a "serious medical need" is a question of fact that must be addressed at trial. If the plaintiff can prove that the need was serious, he will also bear the burden of showing that the defendant was deliberately indifferent. In this regard, it might be relevant that the defendant Andrews allegedly refused to allow the plaintiff to receive treatment from his wife for his skin condition, and that defendant Andrews prescribed the allegedly inad-

problem.[89] In partial defense of the court, it should be noted that Ramos dealt with the Colorado State Penitentiary, which then housed 1,350 inmates. Experts estimated that 5 to 10 percent of those inmates were seriously ill and another 10 to 25 percent needed treatment.[90] At the time of the trial, the regular mental health staff consisted of three civilians and two inmates, all five of whom were occupied more with clerical than clinical work.[91] Given the expert testimony on the number of seriously ill inmates and the stark testimony on the absence of clinical assistance, perhaps unconstitutionality was so clear that no more precise definition was needed.

[1] Serious Mental Illness

What is or is not a serious mental illness is likely to be fought out before or at trial in a battle of experts.[92] The trial court will use the term "serious" as a line-drawing norm, offer some general guidance, and then require the experts to maintain a position on either side of the line.

Courts also properly focus on the functional aspect of the *Estelle* formulation, the unnecessary and wanton infliction of pain.[93] As discussed earlier, pain as a consequence of illness is known essentially through self-reporting or inference. Whatever the abstract merits of including pain in the formulation of "serious medical needs," *Estelle* is fastened to the Eighth Amendment and its punishment-pain combination. Pain or suffering must be a critical part of every administrator's and every court's consideration of when clinical services are required.

Beyond the basic-line drawing and the functional emphasis on pain, courts frequently state that the *seriousness test is one of medical necessity and not simply what is desirable*.[94] An inmate's statement that he was depressed was held not to require that the prison official to whom the statement was made schedule him for an appointment

---

equate remedy of hot soap and water. On this latter issue, it also should be borne in mind that "[a]lthough [a] plaintiff has been provided aspirin, this may not constitute adequate medical care. If 'deliberate indifference caused an easier and less efficacious treatment' to be provided, the defendants have violated the plaintiff's Eight Amendment rights by failing to provide adequate medical care." *Ancata v. Prison Health Services, Inc.* 769 F.2d 700, 704 (11th Cir. 1985), quoting *West v. Keve*, 571 F.2d 158, 162 (3d Cir. 1978) (citations omitted).

[89] The "obvious" reference is a somewhat unusual use of a tort doctrine known as *res ipsa loquitur*, or "the thing speaks for itself." If, for example, a surgeon sews up a patient leaving an instrument or a sponge inside, then we may say that the need for expert testimony is obviated since the negligent act "speaks for itself."

[90] Ramos, 639 F.2d at 575, 577. Other experts testified to a great gulf between psychiatric needs and available services.

[91] Ramos, 639 F.2d at 578. A psychiatrist visited once every two months.

[92] Judges are not alone with the definitional dilemma. In one of the best and most comprehensive articles on health care for incarcerated juveniles, not a word is spent on what is or is not serious. *See* Jan Costello & Elizabeth Jameson, *Legal and Ethical Duties of Health Care Professional to Incarcerated Children*, 8 J. LEGAL MED. 191 (1987). *See* Amos v. Maryland Dept. of Pub. Safety & Correctional Serv., 126 F.3d 589, n.15 (4th Cir. 1997), in which the defendants conceded "serious medical need" and defended successfully on the deliberate indifference component. Amos also rejected the applicability of ADA to prisons. 126 F.3d at 591.

[93] *See, e.g.,* Cody v. Hillard, *supra* note 9, 599 F. Supp. at 1055.

[94] Bowring v. Godwin, *supra* note 3, at 47.

with a psychologist. Mere depression, said the court, is not a serious medical need.[95] In yet another case, the court held that inmates with behavioral and emotional problems did not necessarily suffer from serious mental illness.[96]

On the other hand, acute depression, paranoid schizophrenia and "nervous collapse" have been identified as disorders sufficiently dramatic and painful to qualify as serious medical needs.[97] After stating that psychiatric intervention clearly is necessary where an inmate is contemplating suicide or displays psychiatric symptoms to such a degree that he presents a risk of harm to himself or others, the court stated: "An inmate experiencing significant personality distress in the form of depression or psychotic symptoms to the degree that he has lost contact with reality not only require(s) but is amenable to psychiatric intervention and treatment."[98]

The few authors who have addressed the definitional problems have not been able to advance the matter much beyond the typically descriptive efforts of the courts. One ambitious writer lists five categories of medical needs which he believed qualify for care under the Eighth Amendment:

1. Highly contagious or dangerous conditions or illnesses which a statute clearly mandates that prison officials treat,

2. Injuries which are both severe and obvious,

3. Professionally diagnosed mental or physical illnesses or injuries which are either curable or relievable, and threaten substantial harm when left untreated,

4. Chronic disabilities and afflictions, and

5. Conditions or illnesses which result in serious injury when requests for their treatment are denied.[99]

[a] Competing "Seriousness" Tests Used by Courts

In recent years, two competing legal tests for "seriousness" have emerged: the "obvious to a layman" test described above and the more recent emphasis on a doctor's judgment plus "pain" and "impairment." The latter test is exemplified in *McGuckin v. Smith,*[100] which held:

---

[95] Partee v. Lane, 528 F. Supp. 1254, 1261 (N.D. Ill. 1981). Depression, of course, may be mild or debilitatingly severe. One can only conclude that the court was speaking to mild depression and equating that with discomfort rather than constitutionally significant pain.

[96] Capps v. Atiyeh, 559 F. Supp. 894, 920 (D. Ore. 1983).

[97] Robert E. v. Lane, 530 F. Supp. 930, 939 (N.D. Ill. (1981).

[98] Cody v. Hillard, *supra* note 9, 599 F. Supp. at 1043. In considering the "serious" problem outside the mental health area, the court held that a toothache and a cut were not serious medical needs in Tyler v. Rapone, 603 F. Supp. 268, 272 (E.D. Pa. 1985); the court held that reasonable minds could differ as to whether injuries that caused bleeding from the nose, mouth, and back of the head created a serious medical need in Lewis v. Cooper, 771 F.2d 334, 337 (7th Cir. 1985).

[99] Comment, *State Prisoners' Rights to Medical Treatment: Merely Elusive or Wholly Illusory?*, 8 BLACK L.J. 427, 441 (1983).

[100] 974 F.2d 1050 (9th Cir. 1992).

A "serious medical need" exists if the failure to treat a prisoner's condition could result in further significant injury or the "unnecessary and wanton infliction of pain". . . . Either result is not the type of routine discomfort [that] is "part of the penalty that criminal offenders pay for their offenses against society." . . . The existence of an injury that a doctor or patient would find important and worthy of comment or treatment; the presence of a medical condition that significantly affects an individual's daily activities; or the existence of chronic and substantial pain are examples of indications that a prisoner has a "serious" need for medical treatment.[101]

Even more recently, several courts have compressed a part of the *McGuckin* formula into a requirement that seriousness equates with conditions that can produce death, degeneration, or extreme pain.[102]

In my opinion, the "obviousness" test is seriously flawed in several respects. First, doctors frequently diagnose minor ailments as calling for minimal care. Thus, medical involvement by itself does not determine seriousness. Second, in the exercise of professional judgment clinicians often disagree, and a correctional decision maker is entitled to select from among such differing opinions. Third, the obviousness test does not mention pain and avoidable, gratuitous suffering as a key ingredient of the *Estelle v. Gamble* Eighth Amendment formulation. Fourth, the obvious-to-a-layperson factor has not become clearer by virtue of its repetition. A broken bone protruding through the skin is one type of obvious-to-a-layperson's call, but serious mental illness is another matter. Are the acts of inmates in a prison disciplinary unit—climbing the bars, disrobing and displaying their genitals, and letting loose a string of profanities—mental illness or rebellion?

In arriving at a judgment of "seriousness" or disease, the possibility of secondary gain in the jail and prison setting appears to color the perceptions and reactions of mental health professionals as well as security staff. Inmates may be seeking any of the following things:

- Hospitalization and a chance to earn more money there,

- Greater freedom,

- An excuse not to work,

- A chance to establish mental illness as a basis for an incompetence finding or an insanity defense (obviously more critical in jail), or simply

- Being locked down to avoid something bothersome or threatening in the general population.

The appearance of objectivity, of cold clinical judgment in the world of captives, often masks a basic distrust for the captive.

Both tests for seriousness refer to the consequences of a failure to treat as evi-

---

[101] McGuckin, 974 F.2d at 1059–1060.

[102] *See, e.g.,* Davidson v. Scully, 914 F. Supp. 1011, 1015 (S.D.N.Y 1996); Abdush-Shahid v. Coughlin, 933 F. Supp. 168, 181 (N.D.N.Y. 1996).

dence of the seriousness of the condition. The obviousness test refers to the consequences of delay, but improper care, no matter how quickly provided, must also be a
part of the formulation. The Ninth Circuit test refers to further significant injury or
"needless" pain, and while the reference to "significant injury" is flawed and actually
contradicted by the holding, overall this is a somewhat more desirable approach.[103]

[b] "Seriousness": Liability vs. Damages

An interesting medical care case from a federal district court in New York illustrates a certain confusion as to the seriousness standard and also provides an instructive list of physical ailments that qualified. First, the court took the position that the
Second Circuit requires a deprivation of medical care to be objectively "sufficiently
serious."[104] From there the court properly focused on causing or needlessly prolonging
pain. However, the fundamental error is in suggesting that after an ailment is characterized as serious there must be a second inquiry on seriousness as an aspect of liability. In other types of prison condition cases, it is true that the *Wilson v. Seiter* analysis requires an objective component—extent of harm, and a subjective component—
deliberate indifference.

However, since *Estelle* requires a serious disorder at the liability threshold, the
only concern for seriousness thereafter should be the measure of damages or the
extent of future-oriented relief. The district court's litany of medical cases that qualify as serious is a useful checklist and is reproduced in a footnote.[105]

---

[103] Fred Cohen, *supra* note 19, pp. 17–25.

[104] Citing, inter alia, Wilson v. Seiter, *supra* note 21.

[105] Koehl v. Dalsheim, 85 F.3d 86, 88 (2d Cir. 1996) (deprivation of prescriptive eye glasses constitutes denial of serious medical need; although deprivation did not cause pain, it prolonged plaintiff's suffering); Hathaway v. Coughlin, 37 F.3d 63, at 67 (2d Cir. 1994) (finding plaintiff with degenerative hip
condition who experienced great pain over an extended period of time and had difficulty walking had
"serious medical needs"); Davidson v. Flynn, 32 F.3d 27, 31 (2d Cir. 1994) (denying defendant's motion
to dismiss plaintiff's Eighth Amendment claim based on wrist and ankle injuries caused by shackles); Gill
v. Gilder, 1996 U.S. Dist. LEXIS 2757, No. 95 Civ. 7933, 1996 WL 103837 (S.D.N.Y. Mar. 8, 1996)
(Sweet, J.) (denying defendants' motion to dismiss where plaintiff had alleged that a back problem caused
him "severe pain"); Candelaria v. Coughlin, 1996 U.S. Dist. LEXIS 2298, No. 91 Civ. 2978, 1996 WL
88555, at 7–8 (S.D.N.Y. Mar. 1, 1996) (Sand, J.) (denying cross-motions for summary judgment because
the parties disputed whether plaintiff's medical claims based on failure to provide proper wheelchair, failure to provide doctor-ordered heating pad, and refusal to treat blood in his urine were "serious" medical
conditions); Orr v. Hoke, 1995 U.S. Dist. LEXIS 4789, No. 91 Civ. 1256, 1995 WL 217541 (S.D.N.Y.
Apr. 12, 1995) (Preska, J.) (rejecting defendants' argument on summary judgment motion that delay of
treatment for a severed finger did not cause plaintiff sufficient pain; Davidson v. Kalonick, No. 984 Civ.
6985, 1986 WL 3775 (S.D.N.Y. March 21, 1986) (holding that plaintiff who alleged he was in pain and
discomfort after a bilateral otoplasty sufficiently showed a serious medical need; noting that "pain,
although subjective and difficult to measure, may well be serious"). The fact that the plaintiff's surgery
was elective "does not abrogate the prison's duty, or power, to promptly provide necessary medical treatment for prisoners." Johnson v. Bowers, 884 F.2d 1053, 1056 (8th Cir. 1989); *see also* Hathaway v.
Coughlin, 37 F.3d 63, at 64–69 (2d Cir. 1994) (upholding a jury verdict on Eighth Amendment claim in
favor of plaintiff where defendants delayed plaintiff's elective hip surgery for two years).

[c] "Seriousness": Clinical Uncertainty

In *Coleman v. Wilson,*[106] the district court was asked to reject the Magistrate Judge's findings, in part, because his failure to define "serious mental illness" allegedly undermined his findings. Judge Karlton noted that the Department of Corrections had been studying this not-so-amorphous group of inmates for many years; they were certified as a class; and the expert witnesses at trial had no trouble dealing with the term.[107] Thus, any definitional omissions did not impair a shared understanding on who was seriously ill.

In Ohio, the term "serious mental illness" was defined as a substantial disorder of thought or mood that (1) significantly impairs judgment, behavior, or the capacity to recognize reality or cope with the ordinary demands of life within the prison environment and (2) is manifested by substantial pain or disability. Serious mental illness requires a mental health diagnosis, prognosis and treatment, as appropriate, by mental health staff. It is expressly understood that this definition does not include inmates who are substance abusers or substance dependent (including alcoholics and narcotic addicts), or inmates convicted of a sex offense who are not otherwise diagnosed as seriously mentally ill.[108]

In turn, there simply is not one clear definition or predictive certainty as to what is or is not a serious mental disorder. Schizophrenia, bipolar disorders, and clinically significant depression that causes relative inability to function will all clearly qualify as serious. But even these diagnoses are often in the eye of the beholder.

On many occasions I have observed an inmate with a long history of schizophrenia suddenly rediagnosed as merely anti-social and malingering. "Malingering" is a common term used to express disagreement with prior diagnoses and a belief that the inmate is pursuing some sort of secondary gain. Some clinicians become known for using this approach on a regular basis. Others, often the locum tenens psychiatrists, use it on an ad hoc basis while appearing to test the prison waters. That is, they do not wish to appear gullible, so they demonstrate their independence by displaying distrust for the inmate.

[d] Disease Vel Non: Sexual Disorders

At times, a legal battle overtly fought over seriousness actually is a more fundamental battle over whether the condition at issue is a disease. For example, there are conflicting views on whether a dysthymic disorder, or transsexualism, is a mental disorder. In *Long v. Nix,*[109] the inmate was found not to be a transsexual and, thus, his gender disorder was determined not to be a serious medical need.

Transsexualism is at unspecified times considered a recognized medical disorder;

---

[106] *Supra* note 74.

[107] Coleman, *supra* note 74, 912 F. Supp. at 1300.

[108] This definition, taken from Section VIIIa. of the *Dunn v. Voinovich* Consent Decree, is a somewhat condensed version of the Michigan definition provided at ¶ 4.6.

[109] 86 F.3d 761 (8th Cir. 1996).

the Sixth Circuit has agreed that a transexual person often has a serious need for treatment.[110] A complete refusal of treatment could constitute a claim for deliberate indifference, but when the argument is over actual estrogen dosage levels arrived at by the professional judgment of physicians, courts are quite reluctant to second guess that opinion.[111]

Chief Judge Posner of the Seventh Circuit Court of Appeals, in his inimitable way, recently addressed the question of mandated care for gender dysphoria (transsexualism). The judge accepted gender dysphoria, on the basis of what the afflicted will do to cure it, as a serious (alternative profound) mental disorder.[112]

The cure for this disorder, he states, is not simply psychiatric treatment to accommodate sexual identity, but it includes estrogen therapy followed by surgical removal of the genitals and the construction of a vagina-substitute from the penile tissue.[113]

Having accepted the condition as a serious mental disorder and having described the only treatment which appears to be effective, one would think that the necessary conclusion is that the Eighth Amendment would mandate treatment. Not in this case. Referring to Minnesota as the only state im which Medicaid currently pays for sex-change operations costing about $100,000, this is said to put such treatment out of the reach of ordinary, free persons.

Thus, it is neither cruel nor unusual to withhold from prisoners what is generally not available in the free world. The perceived danger is a line of transsexuals snaked around the prison walls clamoring for entrance as a ticket to otherwise unavailable care.

Judge Posner is stating in effect that if a prisoner's mental illness is authentic and serious but the treatment is terribly expensive, then the constitutional right succumbs to economics. While we may sympathize with the awkward policy choices available here, and we may even smile at the paradox, the conclusion reached here is profoundly at odds with the current state of the law.

In another recent case[114] in which the plaintiff inmates complained about the unavailability of treatment for their "sex addiction disorders," the court stated:

> While they have alleged that each has a mental disorder—sex addiction—the critical issue is whether they have adequately alleged that they suffer from a serious mental disorder. Each has alleged that he is driven by sexually compulsive drives that are deviant; and that his condition erodes his self-esteem to the point of apathy, reinforcing fear and feelings of differentness, inter alia.

---

[110] Murray v. United States Bureau of Prisons, 1997 U.S. App. LEXIS 1716 (6th Cir. Feb. 28, 1997) (unpublished).

[111] Murray, LEXIS 1716 at 4; *see also* White v. Farrier, 849 F.2d 322, 325 (8th Cir. 1988); Phillips v. Michigan Dept. of Corrections, 731 F. Supp. 792, 799–800 (W.D. Mich. 1990), *aff'd,* 932 F.2d 969 (6th Cir. 1991).

[112] Maggert v. Hanks, 131 F.3d 670, 671 (7th Cir. 1997).

[113] Judge Posner discusses other, additional treatment protocols that need not detain us here.

[114] Riddle v. Mondragon, 83 F.3d 1197(10th Cir. 1996). Using the term "sexual addiction disorder" was an interesting play to escape earlier case law that a sex offender does not per se also suffer with a mental disorder. Recall that Justice Thomas in Kansas v. Hendricks, 117 S. Ct. 2072 (1997), casually suggested that pedophilia is a recognized mental illness.

We feel that these averments do not meet the test of *Estelle* so as to demonstrate an Eighth Amendment violation. "The mere fact that the plaintiffs are convicted sexual offenders does not mean that they have psychological disorders or that they are in need of . . . psychiatric treatment." *Patterson v. Webster*, 760 F. Supp. 150, 154 (E.D. Mo. 1991). There are no averments of diagnosis by a physician of a medical need mandating treatment, nor of a condition which a lay person would easily recognize as necessitating a doctor's attention. "Because society does not expect that prisoners will have unqualified access to health care, deliberate indifference to medical needs amounts to an Eighth Amendment violation only if those needs are "serious." See *Estelle v. Gamble, supra*, 429 U.S. at 103-104; *Hudson v. McMillian*, 503 U.S. 1, 9, (1992). Vague allegations of eroded self-esteem, apathy, fear and feeling of differentness, keeping a plaintiff in the "addictive cycle," do not amount to the basis for a constitutional claim.[115]

[e] The Retarded; Professional Judgment

Youngberg v. Romeo,[116] a major decision involving the claims of institutionalized, retarded persons, decided that this class of persons had at least the same rights as inmates as well as a narrow right to training. In determining whether adequate training was provided, courts were admonished to accord due deference to the judgment of the professional decision maker. Indeed, a decision by a professional is presumptively valid and liability exists only when such judgment is such a substantial departure from accepted professional judgment, practice, or standards as to amount to no judgment at all.[117] The Court indicated that:

> By professional decisionmaker, we mean a person competent, whether by education, training or experience, to make the particular decision at issue. Long-term treatment decisions normally should be made by persons with degrees in medicine or nursing, or with appropriate training in areas such as psychology, physical therapy, or the care and training of the retarded. Of course, day-to-day decisions regarding care—including decisions that must be made without delay—necessarily will be made in many instances by employees without formal training but who are subject to the supervision of qualified persons.[118]

In a contested case, the battle over seriousness will be waged by the experts; where there are conflicting views by qualified experts then the problem is not one of *Romeo* deference but deciding among the experts. *Romeo* deference will play a key role when defendants act or fail to act in a particular way relying on the professional

---

[115] Riddle, 83 F.3d at 1203.

[116] 457 U.S. 307 (1982).

[117] Romeo, 457 U.S. at 307, 323.

[118] Romeo, 457 U.S. at 323 n.30. *See* Susan Stefan, *Leaving Civil Rights to the "Experts": From Deference to Abdication Under the Professional Judgment Standard*, 102 YALE L.J. 639 (1992), for a highly critical reading of *Romeo*, and especially so in the correctional setting.

judgment of their employee or agent. Even if the result is disastrous, professional judgment is a powerful liability insulating mechanism.

[2] Distillation of Case Law Analysis

While professional judgment is perhaps the key factor in the "seriousness" inquiry, some generalities in assessing seriousness may be distilled from the case law:

1. The diagnostic test is one of medical or psychiatric necessity.

2. Minor aches, pains, or distress will not establish such necessity.

3. A desire to achieve rehabilitation from alcohol or drug abuse, or to lose weight to simply look or feel better, will not suffice.

4. A diagnosis based on professional judgment and resting on some acceptable diagnostic tool (e.g., DSM-IV) is presumptively valid.

5. By the same token, a decision by a mental health professional that mental illness is not present also is presumptively valid.

6. While "mere depression" or behavioral and emotional problems alone do not qualify as serious mental illness, acute depression, paranoid schizophrenia, "nervous collapse" and suicidal tendencies do qualify.

With regard to the sixth point, it is actually the clinician's choice of the diagnostic terminology that will move these cases from no care to discretionary care or to mandated care. Regretfully, as suggested earlier, diagnosis in a custodial setting is likely to say as much about the availability of resources, security concerns, and a judgment about the captive's possible pursuit of secondary gain as about an objective diagnosis based on signs and symptoms. Indeed, even the available epidemiological data may be significantly influenced by the availability of solutions. The number of captives identified as having serious mental illness may be more responsive to the space and personnel available to deal with them, than to clinically sound assessments.

In accepting or rejecting various diagnostic categories, courts are strongly influenced by accounts of the inmate's behavior. For example, in *Torraco v. Maloney*,[119] a Massachusetts prison suicide case, a federal court of appeals held that "the record contains sufficient evidence that Torraco had a serious mental health need." In support of this conclusion, the court referred to an earlier suicide attempt while in confinement, an assault on a prison official later attributed to impaired mental health, and an overdose of THC (an active component of marijuana) pills somewhat later.[120] Thus, clinical diagnoses supported by incidents supportive of those judgments are likely to be important factors in determining serious disorders.

The same court suggested that the prisoner least likely to have an illness that is constitutionally acceptable as "serious" is a prisoner with a temporary, latent illness that goes undiagnosed and will not result in any significant lasting injury if left

---

[119] 923 F.2d 231, 236 n.5 (1st Cir. 1991).
[120] Torraco, 923 F.2d at 236 n.5, 237 n.4.

untreated.[121] By failing to focus on the pain component of *Estelle,* the court did not closely adhere to the *Estelle* mandate.

[3] Passivity, Withdrawal—Undetected Illness

Based on my own observations and discussions, it does appear that the inmate whose mental illness is characterized by passivity and withdrawal is the one most likely to be overlooked. This illness may indeed be a severe psychosis which causes much pain and suffering and yet the equally ill inmate who is aggressive and acting out is likely to be viewed as more "eligible" for care. Returning to a point made earlier, the law of the mentally ill prisoner is essentially judicially made. The courts, in turn, remain strongly influenced by the opinions of mental health care professionals in determining whether an inmate has a "serious" need. In trying to describe what is "serious mental illness" for constitutional purposes, I have found myself using an analogy of a prisoner suffering the psychiatric equivalent of a compound leg fracture that even a layman would insist needs care. "Broken psyches" and broken legs both require care. More subtle "breaks" are more subject to debate.

Other writers construct a somewhat different description, arguing that only "blatant, abnormal behavior" qualifies for constitutionally mandated care.[122]

Whatever else is meant by a serious mental illness or disorder, it is clear that the Court in *Estelle* meant to eliminate the minor ailments and the mild depressions and anxieties many of us experience. The focus is on pain, and most clearly on such factors as agitation, manifest psychopathology (hallucinations or delusions), deep depression, personal neatness, social interaction, and disorientation.

¶ 4.6 DILEMMA EXACERBATED BY PRISON MILIEU

Even with the apparent "broken psyche" or "blatant, abnormal behavior," we face a dilemma exacerbated by the prison milieu. Take a hypothetical male prisoner who is observed hoarding his own feces, talking to himself, asking to wear lipstick for the first time, and so on. This is obviously strange behavior, but does it manifest mental illness? Is this inmate challenging the system in his own way? Is he a "wise guy" looking for a transfer? For discipline leading to a safe haven?

At a minimum, this is the type of behavior that calls for a professional diagnosis. It should not be assumed that this inmate is "mad" or "bad." There could be no obvious challenge to a professional diagnosis of serious mental illness (especially if the history was supportive) and the prescription of treatment. By the same token, a contrary diagnosis would not be a priori unreasonable.

In dealing with an incarcerated child molester diagnosed as a pedophiliac who was claiming deliberate indifference to his serious medical needs, the Fifth Circuit stated:

---

[121] Torraco, 923 F.2d at 235 n.4.

[122] Susan Brenner & David Galanti, *Prisoners' Rights to Psychiatric Care,* 21 IDAHO L. REV. 29–30 (1985). These writers realize that this standard qualifies relatively few inmates for mandated care.

The complaint must allege enough facts of prior psychiatric illness or treatment, of expert medical opinion, or of behavior clearly evincing some psychiatric ill to create a reasonable ground to believe that psychiatric treatment is necessary for his continued health and well-being. Woodall's allegations meet this initial burden. He has alleged prior hospitalization and treatment, a medical diagnosis and prescribed manner of treatment, and confirmation by the Parish Prison's Staff psychiatrist. With this [sic] kind of allegation, the district court should not have dismissed Woodall's complaint.[123]

The court of appeals tended to view this claim, at least in part, as a failure to continue previously prescribed treatment. When that claim is made and proved, then the inmate claimant invariably establishes deliberate indifference.

When the heat of the courtroom battle has cooled and the experts have returned to their respective corners, an interesting new encounter often begins. If the inmate's successful legal attack was focused on the mental health care system, as opposed to an individual complaint of inadequate care or a deliberately indifferent omission, the trial judge is likely to request the parties to prepare a mental health service plan. Such a plan must include reasonable estimates of the target population—the seriously mentally ill—as well as a service delivery plan and schedule. Obviously, the target population cannot be estimated without some working definition of "seriously mentally ill."

The State of Michigan, for example, has been involved in protracted litigation over general conditions in its prisons.[124] One of the more perplexing areas of the litigation has been the issue of improving mental health services to the then over 20,000 inmates in that system. The Michigan Department of Corrections adopted the following definition of serious mental illness:

> Serious mental illness (or severe mental disorder) means a substantial disorder of thought or mood which significantly impairs judgment, behavior, capacity to recognize reality, or ability to cope with the ordinary demands of life.
>
> A serious/severe mental state or condition (1) is manifested by substantial discomfort, pain, and/or disability that cannot be legitimately ignored by appropriate clinical staff, (2) requires a mental health assessment, diagnostic evaluation, treatment planning and disposition planning; and (3) is generally associated with (a) the inability to attend to and effectively perform the usual/necessary activities of daily living, (b) extreme impairment of coping skills, rendering the patient exceptionally vulnerable to unintentional or intentional victimization and possible mismanagement and/or (c) behaviors that are dangerous to self or others.

---

[123] Woodall v. Foti, 648 F.2d 268, 273 (5th Cir. 1981).

[124] The primary case is USA v. Michigan, No. G84-63CA (W.D. Mich.), which is before the Honorable Richard A. Enslen, an exceptionally able federal district court judge, *aff'd in part, rev'd in part* in an unpublished disposition. The Sixth Circuit denied defendant's motion to terminate the Consent Decree and remanded the appeal to the district court. U.S. v. Engler, 1996 WL 382243 (6th Cir. 1996) (unpublished).

> Serious mental illness/severe mental disorder includes psychiatric conditions/states that span the entire diagnostic spectrum of DSM-III and is not limited to specific diagnosis.[125]

The proponents of this definition note that it is drawn from the American Psychiatric Association's DSM-III as modified by language from the Michigan Mental Health Code. Further, they note that the diagnosis is only one factor in a treatment decision. Other factors would include the severity of the symptomatology, the inmate's mental state, and the availability of external resources.

In Paragraph VIII(a) of the Consent Decree entered into in *Dunn v. Voinovich*, the Ohio case noted earlier, the following more compressed definition was adopted:

> Serious mental illness means a substantial disorder of thought or mood which significantly impairs judgment, behavior, capacity to recognize reality or cope with the ordinary demands of life within the prison environment and is manifested by substantial pain or disability. Serious mental illness requires a mental health diagnosis, prognosis and treatment, as appropriate, by mental health staff.
>
> It is expressly understood that this definition does not include inmates who are substance abusers, substance dependent, including alcoholics and narcotic addicts, or persons convicted of any sex offense, who are not otherwise diagnosed as seriously mentally ill.[126]

It is not my intent to wholly endorse either of the above definitions. They are, however, among the more comprehensive and manageable definitions yet encountered and for those who must continue to deal with the issues dealt with in this book, they are at least worthwhile points of departure.

---

[125] This definition appears in the "Comprehensive Mental Health Plan" of June 6, 1986, submitted to Judge Enslen in the matter cited at note 119, supra. The Plan's pages are not numbered, thus making more precise citation impossible.

[126] *See* Appendix D, in which the *Dunn v. Voinovich* Consent Decree is reproduced.

Chapter 5

Intake Screening/Classification Requirements

¶ 5.1 BASIC OBLIGATIONS AND RIGHTS

On entering a prison, every inmate undergoes some kind of "sorting out," or classification, process, ranging from highly sophisticated multi-factor security and health screening to rather uncomplicated prison assignments based on the instant crime, age of the inmate, and prior record.[1] (In fact, some prison assignments are made simply on the basis of the availability of space.) As discussed in Chapter 3, the Supreme Court has made it clear that prison inmates have no constitutionally based procedural rights in the reception-classification process. That is, there is no right to participate in or challenge the process as it relates to security decisions or prison assignments.

On the other hand, an inmate's undoubted right to a non-life-threatening environment and to treatment for at least serious mental disorders does create some obligations and rights. For example, there is little doubt that a prison system that repeatedly exposes inmates to contagious diseases through failure to detect and treat the diseased person would be open to tort liability and cruel and unusual punishment charges. The duty to protect and isolate, if not cure, is owed the exposed, nondiseased inmate at least as clearly as the duty of care is owed the ill inmate. These issues are

---

[1] *See, e.g.,* Nat'l Adv'y Comm'n on Criminal Standards and Goals Standards Secs. 6.1, 6.2, emphasizing classification based on risk and program factors.

analogous to the risk of exposure to violence and disruption that arises when mentally ill and violent inmates are not so identified.

Putting aside classification decisions based primarily on security factors and putting aside ambiguities in the legal mandate for mental health screening, there are urgent policy reasons for multi-level, mental health screening and evaluation. All of the major intake screening standards call for this process. It is difficult to comprehend why any prison system would not want to quickly identify for needed care inmates with mental illness.

The rate of mental illness in jail appears to be even higher than for inmates in prison, although the shorter jail stays raise very different treatment issues.[2] Jails tend to concentrate on suicide prevention and short-term crisis. Prisons house many impaired people for the long-haul, making it legally and penologically urgent to know who among this widely impaired group is seriously mentally ill.

¶ 5.2 RECOMMENDED PROCESSES

Several entities have recognized the urgency of mental health screening. The American Correctional Association's policy to screen inmates on arrival at a facility includes queries about mental health problems, past and present treatment, or hospitalization(s). The American Psychiatric Association calls for immediate screening on a person's arrival at a prison, including a review of all pertinent records. Its screening process calls for inquiries about past treatment, with the questions designed to identify the signs of severe emotional, intellectual, and/or behavioral problems. The American Public Health standards call for every individual entering custody to undergo an initial medical assessment, with specific determinations made that the inmate may be safely kept at the facility. These standards also require that each inmate be screened for withdrawal from alcohol and drugs as part of the intake screening. The National Commission on Correctional Health Care defines initial screening as an essential function, to be performed by qualified health care personnel on all persons immediately on arrival. A person who is deemed mentally unstable or otherwise in need of care must be transferred immediately for emergency care. These standards are set forth in detail in Appendix A of this book.

A distillation of these various standards and important writings clarifies the processes recommended for adequate screening and evaluation:

1. *Receiving mental health screening*—Done immediately on admission through brief observation and structured interview. This is a "wide mesh" point in the process, and any suicide ideation or history of hospitalization, for example, leads to further assessment.

2. *Intake screening*—Trained staff make further inquiry into relevant factors, usually as part of the obligatory comprehensive medical evaluation. This is more extensive than the receiving stage but does not approximate the intensity and professionalism required in the next stage.

---

[2] *See e.g.,* Linda A. Teplin, *The Prevalence of Severe Mental Disorder Among Urban Jail Detainees: Comparison With the Epidemiological Catchment Area*, 80 AM. J. PUB. HEALTH 663 (1990). Teplin is the important scholar of mental illness rates for those in jail.

3. *Evaluation*—A comprehensive examination by a mental health professional, using histories, testing and clinical judgment. Usually conducted only if there is a "positive hit" at stage 1 or 2 or if the inmate presents clearly with a major illness and the first two steps are omitted.

Prisons have enormous discretion in just how the screening-evaluation is done, and virtually anything clearly within the realm of professional judgment will pass legal muster. A prison system without any such system simply breaks down at the front door and invites disastrous consequences for staff, other inmates, and the inmate in need who deteriorates and suffers needlessly.

¶ 5.3 CONSTITUTIONALLY DEFICIENT SYSTEMS

We will approach this topic first by looking at the major cases in which a prison's classification system was deemed constitutionally deficient. We will then examine the cases upholding the challenged system and conclude with an overview of the area.

[1] *Ruiz v. Estelle*: Texas

Ruiz v. Estelle,[3] a landmark overall prison-conditions case, is also one of the more significant early judicial decisions on classification. Judge Justice found that nearly all of the conditions and practices of the Texas Department of Corrections (TDC) were constitutionally defective. He described the TDC classification system as follows:

A variety of tests are administered to incoming inmates to determine intelligence, educational achievement, and psychological stability. Nonetheless, these tests have not been adequate to screen or diagnose mentally disturbed inmates. The Minnesota Multi-phasic Personality Inventory (MMPI) is the sole test administered to measure personality abnormalities; however, it cannot be understood by persons with less than a sixth grade reading ability, and it is, therefore, useless in evaluating the large number of TDC inmates who read at lower levels. Other tests are administered which measure general employment aptitudes and educational achievement levels, but they are not designed for use by persons whose dominant language is other than English. It follows that those inmates who primarily speak Spanish cannot be effectively tested. Furthermore, Dr. Jose Garcia, Chief of Mental Health Services at TDC, testified that all of the tests were culturally and racially biased.[4]

To make matters worse for Texas, a member of the TDC Classification Committee

---

[3] Ruiz v. Estelle, 503 F. Supp. 1265, 1323 (S.D. Tex. 1980), *mot. to stay granted in part and denied in part*, 650 F.2d 555 (5th Cir. 1981), *aff'd in part and rev'd in part*, 679 F.2d 1115 (5th Cir. 1982), *op. amended in part and vacated in part, and reh'g denied*, 688 F.2d 266 (5th Cir. 1982), *cert. denied*, 460 U.S. 1042 (1983); *see also* Ruiz v. Estelle, 553 F. Supp. 567 (S.D. Tex. 1982) on the award of attorney fees. For an excellent discussion of the litigation in Texas, *see* STEVEN MARTIN & SHELDON EKLAND-OLSON, TEXAS PRISONS: THE WALLS CAME TUMBLING DOWN (1987).

[4] Ruiz, 503 F. Supp. at 1332 (footnote omitted).

admitted that the Committee did not consider MMPI test results because only a handful of their personnel knew how to analyze them. As a consequence the results were merely "filed."[5] The court determined that in order to meet basic minimum standards for mental health treatment, among other things, "There must be a systematic program for screening and evaluating inmates in order to identify those who require mental health treatment."[6]

[2] *Pugh v. Locke*: Alabama

Pugh v. Locke[7] involved a major challenge to the then constitutionally vulnerable Alabama prison system. The classification system (or more accurately, the lack thereof) was described as follows:

> There is no working classification system in the Alabama penal system . . . Although classification personnel throughout the state prisons have been attempting to implement a wholly new classification process established in January, 1975, understaffing and overcrowding have produced a total breakdown of that process . . . Prison officials do not dispute the evidence that most inmates are assigned to the various institutions, to particular dormitories, and to work assignments almost entirely on the basis of available space. Consequently the appreciable percentage of inmates suffering from some mental disorder is unidentified, and the mentally disturbed are dispersed throughout the prison population without receiving treatment.[8]

The court then ordered the state to prepare a classification plan for all inmates incarcerated in the Alabama penal system, as follows:

> 2. The plan to be submitted to the Court shall include:
> (a) due consideration to the age; offense; prior criminal record; vocational; educational and work needs; and physical and mental health care requirements of each inmate;
> (b) methods of identifying aged, infirm, and psychologically disturbed or mentally retarded inmates who require transfer to a more appropriate facility; or who require special treatment within the institution; and
> (c) methods of identifying those inmates for whom transfer to a pre-release, work-release, or other community-based facility would be appropriate.

---

[5] Ruiz, 503 F. Supp. at 1333. Inadequate training or education is a recurrent problem throughout this area. Subsequently we shall note how low levels of training contribute to the legal deficiency of various prisons and prison systems.

[6] Ruiz, 503 F. Supp. at 1339.

[7] 406 F. Supp. 318 (M.D. Ala. 1976), *aff'd in part and modified in part sub nom.* Newman v. Alabama, 559 F.2d 283, (5th Cir. 1977), *rev'd in part sub nom.* Alabama v. Pugh, 438 U.S. 781 (1978), *cert. denied sub nom.* Newman v. Alabama, 438 U.S. 915 (1978).

[8] Pugh, 406 F. Supp. at 324. In Newman v. Alabama, 349 F. Supp., 278 (M.D. Ala. 1972), *aff'd in part,* 503 F.2d 1320 (5th Cir. 1974), *cert. denied,* 421 U.S. 948 (1975), the court had found that approximately 10 percent of the inmates in the Alabama penal system were psychotic and that an astounding 60 percent were sufficiently disturbed to require treatment.

3. The classification of each inmate shall be reviewed at least annually.[9]

[3] *Barnes v. Government of Virgin Islands*

Barnes v. Government of Virgin Islands[10] involved a constitutional challenge to the archaic prison system of the Virgin Islands. Calling the classification system a "glaring deficiency," the court found that the lack of pertinent data about the inmate made it impossible to develop a rational penal program.[11] To remedy the situation, the court ordered that:

> A mental status examination should be given as part of the intake and classification procedure. If at that time or any time subsequent thereto, the psychiatrist believes that proper mental health care cannot be provided for the inmate at the facility, the inmate shall be transferred to an institution which is adequate to deal with his problems.[12]

[4] *Feliciano v. Barcelo*: Puerto Rico

The Puerto Rican prison system was the subject of a devastating legal attack in *Feliciano v. Barcelo*.[13] In condemning the prison system, the court was urgently concerned with the unknown, but believed to be large, number of psychotic inmates. It attributed much of the blame for this chaos on an inadequate screening or classification system in which guards, who had no training in the area, carried out what evaluations there were.[14]

In addition to finding many aspects of the Puerto Rican prison system unconsti-

---

[9] Pugh, 406 F. Supp. at 333. On appeal, the order was modified only slightly, placing primary responsibility for the classification system on the Board of Corrections. Newman v. Alabama, 559 F.2d 283, 290 (5th Cir. 1977), *rev'd in part sub nom.* Alabama v. Pugh, 438 U.S. 781 (1978), *cert. denied sub nom.* Newman v. Alabama, 438 U.S. 915.

[10] 415 F. Supp. 1218 (D.V.I. 1976).

[11] Barnes, 415 F. Supp. at 1229. In 1997, the situation had hardly improved. A federal judge found that newly admitted inmates were not consistently screened for mental illness and that when mental illness was detected, there was terribly inadequate care. Carty v. Farrelly, 957 F. Supp. 727 (D.V.I. 1997).

[12] Barnes, 415 F. Supp. at 1235. In this case, the court specified a psychiatrist as a part of the classification system. In Hines v. Anderson, 439 F. Supp. 12, 17 (D. Minn. 1977), a consent decree was entered and, with regard to classification, the court ordered that "a psychological test and/or examination as determined by a certified psychologist shall be administered to each inmate who entered the Minnesota State Prison."

[13] 497 F. Supp. 14 (D. P.R. 1979).

[14] The subsequent judicial history of the prison litigation in Puerto Rico is virtually unparalleled. In Feliciano v. Hernandez Colon, 775 F. Supp. 488–489 (D.P.R. 1991), the court indicated that the Commonwealth had paid, to date, $68,240,910 in contempt fines. The fines, of course, are not limited to unconstitutional care of the mentally ill and relate primarily to overcrowding. Interested readers will gain a complete understanding of the Puerto Rico prison litigation by consulting the following cases in chronological order: Feliciano v. Barcelo, 605 F. Supp. 967 (D.P.R. 1985); Morales Feliciano v. Romero Barcelo, 672 F. Supp. 591 (D.P.R. 1986); Morales Feliciano v. Hernandez Colon, 697 F. Supp. 37 (D.P.R. 1988); Morales Feliciano v. Hernandez Colon, 704 F. Supp. 16 (D.P.R. 1988); Morales Feliciano v. Parole Bd. of the Commw. of P.R., 887 F.2d 1 (1st Cir. 1989); and Morales Feliciano v. Hernandez Colon, 775 F. Supp. 477 (D.P.R. 1991).

tutional, the district judge entered a detailed order concerning classification, which includes:

> ORDERED, that from the commencement of the screening of all incoming inmates, each inmate shall be screened medically and psychologically within one week from the date of his entry into the custody of the Administration of Correction of the Commonwealth of Puerto Rico; and it is further
>
> ORDERED, that among the persons to be employed by the medical director shall be one in charge of the psychiatric care for emotionally and mentally disturbed inmates; and it is further
>
> ORDERED, that the psychiatrist in charge employed by the medical director shall forthwith establish procedures for the psychiatric screening of all incoming inmates into the facilities operated by the Administration of Correction; and is further
>
> ORDERED, that those incoming inmates who require hospital treatment in a psychiatric institution shall be transferred thereto and that those incoming inmates who require intensive psychiatric treatment shall have such treatment provided as is necessary; and it is further
>
> ORDERED, that the psychiatric screening of all incoming inmates shall commence within one week from the appointment of the psychiatrist in charge, whose appointment shall be made within one week of the appointment of the medical director; and it is further
>
> ORDERED, that within two months from the date of this Order the medical director shall cause the entire existing population in the custody of the Administration of Correction to be screened with a complete physical examination and psychiatric examination for the detection of any chronic disorder or any communicable disease; and it is further
>
> ORDERED, that the screening of the entire population of the facilities operated by the Administration of Correction shall be completed within three months of the date it is commenced . . ."[15]

[5] *Laaman v. Helgemoe*: New Hampshire

Laaman v. Helgemoe[16] involved yet another constitutional challenge to overall prison conditions, this time aimed at the New Hampshire State Prison (NHSP). At NHSP, a new inmate passes through "quarantine," a 14-day period during which he is supposed to undergo, among other things, an initial classification interview, a complete psychological evaluation, and a social work-up. Although most of the inmates who testified before the court had been visited and interviewed by personnel from the Mental Health Division, only three had actually been tested. Only one had actually seen the psychiatrist.[17] Mentally ill inmates could receive treatment at NHSP only after screening and acceptance by the treatment unit.

---

[15] Feliciano, 497 F. Supp. at 40.

[16] 437 F. Supp. 269 (D.N.H. 1977).

[17] Laaman, 437 F. Supp. at 283.

The court thought that the difficulty in gaining access to appropriate mental health care presented one of the most distressing aspects of NHSP.[18] To remedy this situation, the court entered the following orders, which are even more detailed than the orders entered in the *Feliciano* decision involving Puerto Rico. These orders obviously go beyond the mentally disordered inmate. Inclusion of references to the infirm, aged, and physically disabled is to illustrate the commonality of legal concerns for "special needs" inmate categories.

VIII. Mental Health Care

1. Defendants shall immediately establish, by means of psychiatric and psychological testing and interviews, the actual mental health care needs of the prison population. Defendants shall file with plaintiffs and this court, within six months, the results of said testing, and shall, at the same time, submit a plan as to how to satisfy the needs established by the study. Defendants shall immediately hire a psychiatrist or Ph.D. psychologist and sufficiently qualified support staff to conduct said survey.

2. Defendants shall establish an ongoing procedure to identify those prisoners who, by reason of psychological disturbance or mental retardation, require care in facilities designed for such persons. Such persons shall be transferred as soon as the necessary arrangements can be made.

3. Defendants shall establish ongoing procedures, including, but no limited to, a psychiatric interview during the quarantine period to identify those prisoners who require mental health care within the institution and shall make arrangements for the implementation of the provision of care.

4. The mental health care unit shall be administered by a psychiatrist or Ph.D. psychologist in coordination with the Chief of Medical Services.

IX. Classification

1. Defendants shall establish within ninety days of this order a classification system which shall include:
   a. Due consideration to the age; offense; prior criminal record; vocational, educational and work needs; and physical and mental health care requirements of each prisoner;
   b. Methods of identifying aged, infirm, and psychologically handicapped or physically disabled prisoners who require transfer to a more appropriate facility, or who require special treatment within the institution;
   c. Educational, vocational, rehabilitative, training, religious, recreational and work programs specifically designed to meet the needs of the classification system;
   d. Methods of identifying those prisoners for whom pre-release, work release or school release are appropriate;
2. All persons currently incarcerated at the NHSP shall be classified pursuant to the classification plan mandated by this order within six months. The classification of each prisoner shall be reviewed every six months thereafter.

---

[18] Laaman, 437 F. Supp. at 290.

3. Quarantine status for the purpose of admission, orientation, and classification shall not exceed fourteen days, and, while in each status, each prisoner shall receive adequate exercise, recreation, food, health and hygiene services.

4. Defendants shall establish reasonable entrance requirements and rational objective criteria for selecting prisoners to participate in work, vocational training or educational or recreational programs; such criteria may be a part of the general classification system;

5. Defendants shall hire an outside expert in classification to aid in the planning of and the implementation of a classification system.[19]

[6] *Palmigiano v. Garrahy*: Rhode Island

In *Palmigiano v. Garrahy*,[20] prisoners and pretrial detainees challenged conditions at the Rhode Island Adult Correctional Institutions (ACI). After a recitation of problems caused by a deficient classification system whose shortcomings parallel the problems described in the previous cases, this court took a somewhat different approach. Chief Judge Pettine found it clear that prison officials had never given heed to the authoritative expressions of the Rhode Island legislature as embodied in two statutes. The first expresses the policy that "efforts to rehabilitate and restore criminal offenders as law-abiding and productive members of society are essential to the reduction of crime."[21] The second requires prison officials "to furnish the means as shall be best designed to effect . . . rehabilitation,"[22] a requirement that they failed to fulfill.

It was also determined that the classification system failed to comply with yet another statute requiring that each inmate be evaluated as to his proper security status and for such medical or rehabilitative care as may be proper.[23] Parenthetically, we may note that the heavy reliance on state law is unusual in a federal decision.

Nine years after the first decision in *Palmigiano*, Judge Pettine, by now Senior District Judge, lamented, "[I]t is discouraging to find that virtually the same conditions still exist nine years later."[24] The judge severely criticized the lack of mental health protocols, suicide prevention practices, and the tracking of psychotic patients, and concluded that "there is no smoothly functioning health delivery system."[25]

---

[19] Laaman, 437 F. Supp. at 328–329.

[20] 443 F. Supp. 956 (D.R.I. 1977), remanded on issue of deadlines, 599 F.2d 17 (1st Cir. 1979); defendants found in contempt of court, 737 F. Supp. 1257 (D.R.I. 1990).

[21] R.I.G.L. § 42-56-1 (Supp. 1976).

[22] Palmigiano, 443 F. Supp. at 980; R.I.G.L. § 42-56-19 (Supp. 1976).

[23] *See* R.I.G.L. § 42-56-29 (Supp. 1976). As the Supreme Court becomes more conservative in the creation of federal liberty interests, we may expect to see more reliance on state constitutional and statutory law. The complete order includes program mandates that are not limited to classification matters and that look suspiciously like rehabilitation-type activities without a clear label to that effect. Note, however, that the program mandates are included to "implement the classification process." The point is that some courts, while denying a right to rehabilitation, actually grant it within the context of an order in the form of implementing another right. The link between classification and "help," however named, is not inescapable, but it is close. Palmigiano, 443 F. Supp. at 987–988.

[24] Palmigiano v. Garrahy, 639 F. Supp. 244, 249 (D.R.I. 1986).

[25] Palmigiano, 639 F. Supp. at 254.

Showing remarkable restraint given the 9-year hiatus, the judge merely ordered the state to develop a compliance plan within 60 days.[26]

A more recent case involving the District of Columbia's Lorton Correctional Complex emphasized the importance of classification and screening from the dual aspects of security and services.[27] Judge Green wrote:

Classification of inmates is essential for prison security. One critical function of classification is the efficient identification of violent, aggressive inmates and those in need of psychiatric care so they can be separated from the rest of the population . . . Mental health screening of all inmates should be performed by a trained mental health professional and appropriate psychological tests administered in order to identify those in need of psychological care. The experts at the D.C. Jail [the point of entry to the Lorton Complex] are not successful in identifying all those suffering with serious mental disturbances. This is not surprising given that no formal mental health screening performed by trained mental health professionals is conducted there. At the same time, in place at Occoquan is only an informal system for screening inmates for psychological problems. The system, or lack thereof, is entirely inadequate.[28]

Even more recently, Judge Green granted substantial relief to female prisoners in the custody of the District of Columbia.[29] Characterizing these women as in a high-risk category, Judge Green held that doctors should examine them much more frequently and anticipate complications, especially with prenatal patients.[30] She also required routine testing for sexually transmitted diseases.[31]

[7] *Coleman v. Wilson*: California

The broad based, successful attack on California's correctional mental health system in *Coleman v. Wilson*[32] resulted in a finding of a fundamentally flawed screening system. An extensive quotation from Judge Karlton is in order:

---

[26] Palmigiano, 639 F. Supp. at 259. For a complete history of this case, please refer to the following: Palmigiano v. Garrahy, 443 F. Supp 956 (D.R.I. 1977); Palmigiano v. Garray, 599 F.2d 17 (1st Cir. 1979); Palmigiano v. Garrahy, 639 F. Supp 244 (D.R.I. 1986); Palmigiano v. DiPrete, 700 F.Supp. 1180 (D.R.I. 1988); Palmigiano v. DiPrete, 710 F.Supp. 875 (D.R.I. 1989); Palmigiano v. DiPrete, 887 F.2d 258 (1st Cir. 1989); and Palmigiano v. DiPrete, 737 F. Supp. 1257 (D.R.I. 1990).

[27] Inmates of Occoquan v. Barry, 650 F. Supp. 619 (D.C. Cir. 1986), *vacated,* 844 F.2d 828 (D.C. Cir. 1988).

[28] Inmates of Occoquan, 650 F. Supp. at 623, 630 (citation omitted). Judge Green also emphasized the special need for adequate classification in a prison system relying on dormitory housing and where the inmate population is mixed.

[29] Women Prisoners of D.C., Dept. of Corrections v. District of Columbia, 877 F. Supp. 634 (D.D.C. 1994), *modified* 899 F. Supp. 659 (D.D.C. 1995); *vacated in part and remanded*, 93 F.3d 910 (D.C. Cir. 1996), *cert. denied*, 117 S. Ct. 1552 (1997); *on remand*, 968 F. Supp. 744 (D.D.C. 1997).

[30] Women Prisoners, 877 F. Supp. at 642.

[31] Women Prisoners, 877 F. Supp. at 643. The same high-risk rationale, I believe, applies to mental illness.

[32] 912 F. Supp. 1282 (E.D. Cal. 1995).

The magistrate judge found that "in order to provide necessary mental health care to prisoners with serious mental disorders, there must be a system in place to identify those individuals, both at the time they are admitted to the Department of Corrections and during their incarceration." He further found that the "CDC lacks an adequate mechanism for screening for mental illness, either at the time of reception or during incarceration, and has lacked adequate screening since at least 1987." Judge Moulds concluded that "only those inmates who self-report or present with medical records demonstrating a prior psychiatric history, those who exhibit bizarre behavior, or those who ask to be seen by a psychiatrist will be identified as needing psychiatric care."

Defendants object to the factual finding that the ODC does not have adequate procedures for screening for mental illness. Defendants also object to the legal conclusion that the Constitution requires defendants to do more to screen for mental illness than they presently do. Those objections must be rejected.

The evidence cited by defendants depicts precisely the type of screening described by the magistrate judge. It is screening based on self-reporting, use of records of prior hospitalization and/or past or current use of psychotropic medications, exhibition of bizarre behavior and requests for care. Certainly each of those means of identifying ill inmates is appropriate. The question, however, is whether the Eighth Amendment requires more.

Under the Eighth Amendment the defendants are required to maintain a system in which inmates are able to make their need for mental health care known to staff competent to provide such care before inmates suffer unnecessary and wanton infliction of pain. The evidence demonstrates that some inmates with serious mental disorders are, by virtue of their condition, incapable of making their needs for mental health care known to staff. Delivery of adequate mental health care to such inmates requires their identification. For that reason, it has been held that correctional systems are required by the Constitution to put in place a "systematic program for screening and evaluating inmates in order to identify those who require mental health treatment."

Defendants do not have a systematic program for screening and evaluating inmates for mental illness. Plaintiffs' Exhibit 440 at 4 ("There is a lack of comprehensive, standardized screening for mental illness and suicidality" in the CDC). The mechanisms on which they rely are either used haphazardly, or depend for efficacy on incomplete or nonexistent medical records, self-reporting, or the observations of custodial staff inadequately trained in the signs and symptoms of mental illness. The evidence before the court plainly shows that thousands of inmates suffering from mental illness are either undetected, untreated, or both.

The consultants found that "[a] large number of unidentified individuals in the general population, were they to be screened, would be diagnosable with the same serious disorders and exhibit related symptoms. Given the size of the unidentified population (over 57,000 at the time of the survey), even the small base-rate of 7 percent for the four serious disorders amounts to over 4,000 undetected SMD individuals."[33]

---

[33] Coleman, 912 F. Supp. at 1304–1305 (citations and references omitted).

In preparing this aspect of a lawsuit there are two fundamental approaches available to a plaintiff's counsel:

- An evaluation of the intake process, the instruments and techniques used, followed by a clinical assessment of those inmates not flagged for care or further evaluation, and

- A clinical assessment of inmates recently entering prison, emphasizing the segregation population, and who were not diagnosed as mentally ill.

In my own experience, and as a clinical layman, some misses are so obvious that the particular prison, or prison system, is simply not exercising any judgment. One encounters inmates who are hallucinatory, who obviously are suffering some sort of organic brain damage, or whose records indicate a recent and serious suicide attempt. And yet these inmates have gone undetected, and thus untreated. I must emphasize that the failure to treat is the primary problem, and that screening and evaluation provide the best way to identify the truly mentally ill.

The cases discussed above do not implicate reasonable disagreement over a particular diagnosis or diagnostic categories. These types of misses are blatant omissions and evidence of systemic failure. When evaluating an overall correctional mental health system, after one encounters such a breakdown at the front door one becomes quite cynical about staffing, treatment space, and ready access to care.

In *Casey v. Lewis*,[34] Judge Muecke carefully weighed the evidence on Arizona's efforts to identify and then to treat their mentally ill prisoners. He stated flatly, "Defendants fail to identify seriously mentally ill prisoners in their custody."[35] In addition, "ADOC lacks a system and the psychiatric staff to identify and evaluate female inmates with serious mental illnesses when those inmates come into the system. Thus, at the Perryville Santa Maria Unit, unqualified security staff must identify seriously mentally ill inmates . . ."[36]

Judge Muecke also reviewed a set of post-admission screening problems on a facility-by-facility basis. That is, after an inmate enters the system it is quite likely that he or she will be transferred. Where an inmate is transferred to a treatment facility we may have a *Vitek*[37] issue, but if the transfer is to another prison, uncontested and routine, the question arises whether a form of intake screening or evaluation should be repeated. If an inmate has just come through the reception process and has been adequately screened or evaluated, then most systems will not, and probably need not, duplicate the effort. However, after a lapse of time—six months, a year, two years—a strong argument arises that the screening-evaluation process should be repeated. In Ohio, for example, this is routinely done. In *Casey*, the record is rife with examples of delays in further assessments, and thus consequent delays in providing necessary care.[38]

The cases reviewed to this point make it abundantly clear that many federal courts

---

[34] 834 F. Supp. 1477 (D. Ariz. 1993)
[35] Casey, 834 F. Supp. at 1513.
[36] Casey, 834 F. Supp. at 1547.
[37] Vitek v. Jones, 445 U.S. 480 (1980).
[38] Casey, 834 F. Supp. at 1526–1529.

are willing to scrutinize prison intake screening/classification systems and to accept challenges to the most glaringly deficient. In fact, the more glaringly deficient the system, the more detailed the corrective solution likely to be judicially imposed on the system. Some judges also go beyond the strict confines of classification with facility, on occasion, to order programs that more nearly resemble rehabilitative efforts than classification systems. This excessive zeal also seems to be directly related to the magnitude of a system's failure to identify and care for the seriously mentally ill.

The detail provided in this chapter is important, but we should not let it obscure the fact that that legal issues involved here are inmates' constitutional right to treatment for serious mental disorders and the concomitant need for some reasonably accurate, regular way of spotting mental disorders as inmates enter the prison system, and as they are moved about thereafter.

¶ 5.4 CONSTITUTIONALLY VALID SYSTEMS

Not all prison systems challenged on screening or classification fared as badly as those described above. Where a regular screening and evaluation process is in place, adequately staffed with presumptively qualified personnel, and where the information and conclusions are in fact used and then periodically reviewed, the courts are not likely to impose additional requirements.

Hendrix v. Faulkner[39] considered and rejected a constitutional challenge to the Indiana State Prison. The court described the acceptable conditions and practices as follows:

> Screening and assessment is first done at the RDC [Reception and Diagnostic Center] when inmates are first admitted to the Department of Correction. Psychological evaluations, histories and physical evaluations are performed on each inmate and compiled in a report. The packets randomly inspected had surprisingly thorough psychological or psychiatric reports. Some packets had both. Once an inmate arrives at the I.S.P., the Director of Classification reviews these reports and notifies the psychologist and counselors of past or present mental problems. Dr. DeBerry also receives a copy of the RDC report for his review. Mental health problems that surface during incarceration are observed and reported by all types of staff, other inmates, or the inmate himself. This screening and referral system was quite adequate.[40]

In *Johnson v. Levine*[41] the Maryland House of Corrections was found to be unconstitutionally overcrowded, but classification procedures were upheld. The classification system was briefly described as follows:

---

[39] 525 F. Supp. 435 (N.D. Ind. 1981), *aff'd in part, vacated in part sub nom.* Wellman v. Faulkner, 715 F.2d 269 (7th Cir. 1983), *cert. denied*, 468 U.S. 1217 (1984).

[40] Hendrix, 525 F. Supp. at 493. Interestingly, the court did find that the overcrowding in the prison system violated the Eighth Amendment and a reduction was ordered.

[41] 450 F. Supp. 648 (D. Md. 1978), *aff'd*, 588 F.2d 1378 (4th Cir. 1978). Parole and release procedures also were upheld.

Classification activities and offices are located in a building which adjoins the South Wing. The classification staff includes two supervisors, fourteen counselors and two full-time psychologists. These figures result in an average caseload per counselor of 120.[42]

¶ 5.5 SUMMARY

In conclusion, there is little doubt that a prison system's initial intake screening and evaluation system implicates an inmate's right to treatment for serious mental and physical disorders as well as the right of all inmates to a non-life-threatening environment.[43] There must be acceptable tests and other evaluative devices that are racially unbiased and effective given the characteristics of the inmate population. Where psychologists, psychiatrists or nurses are involved in the process, as opposed to wholly untrained, unqualified personnel, courts are more inclined to validate the system. On the other hand, the initial broad-screen stage often is handled quite well by persons with minimal academic credentials who are trained in the process.

A disorganized system that cannot show consistent development, use, and review of intake and evaluation information and conclusions is extremely vulnerable to legal challenge.[44] Where a facility or system is found constitutionally deficient at this stage, it is not likely to fare well on post-admission treatment issues.

---

[42] Johnson, 450 F. Supp. at 652.

[43] Nathan Glazer, who is generally critical of activist courts, especially in their creation and implementation of rights for those who are incarcerated, incorrectly writes, "[O]ne would think that a classification system for prisoners is a matter of prison policy . . . rather than a matter of right." He is, of course, just wrong. Nathan Glazer, *The Judiciary and Social Policy,* in The Judiciary in a Democratic Society (L. Theberge, ed. 1979), pp. 67, 73.

[44] *See* Gary A. DeLand, *Classification: A Tool for Safely and Securely Managing Prisoners,* 2 Corrections Managers' Rpt. 1 (1997). The author makes a strong case for the importance of a security classification system, but (incorrectly in my view) does not believe it is legally mandated. One must not confuse the fact that inmates have no constitutional, or due process, right to participate in the process with a constitutional obligation to engage in the process. *See, e.g.,* Jensen v. Clarke, 73 F.3d 808 (8th Cir. 1996). In Clark v. McMillin, 932 F. Supp. 789 (S.D. Miss. 1996), an inmate was killed by a jail cell inmate with a violent history and facing murder charges; and while the plaintiff did not prevail, this was due to a failure to produce evidence of the failure to classify and separately house violent detainees.

Chapter 6
Defining Treatment

¶ 6.1 TREATMENT AND OTHER "HELPING" TERMS

Earlier chapters have established that inmates have a basic constitutional right to treatment, and that this right is in turn supported by an ancillary right to some form of initial screening, evaluation, and classification. We will now turn to a more detailed review of treatment as distilled from the leading cases on point. Before undertaking this exercise, however, some cautionary words concerning treatment are in order along with a brief excursion into other legally relevant "helping" terms.

There are fundamental conceptual, definitional, and empirical questions about treatment that rarely are addressed by the courts. For example, is there treatment if there simply is some regular "professional" exchange between a person labeled "client" or "patient" and another person labeled "mental health professional"? Is there treatment in the absence of one or both of these persons? Is the term "treatment" descriptive of the process or is it an end product? If it is more process than result—which seems generally agreed—then what are acceptable aims of treatment? Cure? Relief of suffering? Amelioration? Prevention of deterioration? And to what extent are treatment objectives to be correlated with the environment in which it occurs? Is it acceptable to view treatment in prison or jail as basically aimed at making a prisoner functional in the general population, or does it include the prisoner's ultimate ability to function in the community?

It is perhaps easiest to agree with the assertion that treatment generally is a process of intervention within a model that seeks to heal, to relieve pain and suffering, and to prolong and enhance life. The involvement of a mental health professional implies, but certainly does not guarantee, that there is treatment. A generic definition of treatment is difficult enough, but additional complexity is added when legal context is part of the inquiry.

The *Diagnostic and Statistical Manual of Mental Disorders* (DSM-IV) is the diagnostic Bible for mental health specialists. Even this manual concedes that while it "provides a classification of mental disorders, it must be admitted that no definition adequately specifies precise boundaries of the concept of 'mental disorder'."[1] The DSM-IV goes on to indicate that various concepts—distress, disability, dyscontrol, for example—are useful, but different contexts call for different definitions.[2]

[1] Contingency Definition

While not wholly embracing its own work, the DSM-IV goes on to offer a contingent-type of definition of mental disorder. It is

> a clinically significant behavioral or psychological syndrome or pattern that occurs in an individual and that is associated with present distress (e.g., a painful symptom) or disability (e.g., impairment in one or more important areas of functioning) or with a significantly increased risk of suffering death, pain, disability, or an important loss of freedom. In addition, this syndrome or pattern must not be merely an expectable and culturally sanctioned response to a particular event, for example, the death of a loved one. Whatever its original cause, it must currently be considered a manifestation of a behavioral, psychological, or biological dysfunction in the individual. Neither deviant behavior (e.g., political, religious, or sexual) nor conflicts that are primarily between the individual and society are mental disorders unless the deviance or conflict is a symptom of a dysfunction in the individual, as described above.[3]

Despite advances in neurobiology, the "brain sciences," and pharmacology, it remains true that "the definition of mental illness is left largely to the user and is dependent upon the norms of adjustment that he employs."[4] With definitional elasticity the norm, it is easy to understand how the diagnosis and application of mental illness will vary importantly with context and the desired outcome.

Civil commitment statutes vary greatly in their definition of mental illness. A legal term like "insanity" is incorrectly used as a synonym for psychosis; mental illness when linked with the search for "dangerousness" further complicates the matter; and diagnostic consistency among psychiatrists is woefully lacking.[5]

---

[1] DIAGNOSTIC AND STATISTICAL MANUAL OF MENTAL DISORDERS, 4th ed. (American Psychiatric Association, 1994), Intro., p. XXI [hereinafter DSM-IV]. The DSM is also a wildly financially successful publication issuing new editions with minor changes with alacrity. *See* HERB KUTCHIN & STUART R. KIRK, MAKING US CRAZY: THE PSYCHIATRIC BIBLE AND THE CREATION OF MENTAL DISORDERS (1997), for a broad based critique of the DSM.

[2] DSM-IV, Intro., p. XXI. Note that the authors say different definitions and not different applications.

[3] DSM-IV, Intro., pp. XXI–XXII.

[4] Joseph Livermore, et al., *On the Justifications for Civil Commitment*, 117 U. PA. L.REV. 75, 80 (1968). This is one of the most influential articles ever written in this area of law.

[5] MICHAEL L. PERLIN, LAW AND MENTAL DISABILITY (1994), pp. 10–25. This is an exceptionally well

Fortunately, I need not attempt to grapple with, let alone try to unravel, all of this, given the relatively narrow confines of this work. However, it is important to at least establish the definitional and conceptual uncertainty about mental illness and to articulate my perspective that its presence often is determined by context and the outcome desired. Our context is the jail and prison, and certainly even within that limited context there are numerous questions.

[2] Definition Within Prison Setting

Dunn v. Voinovich,[6] the Ohio prison case often referred to in this work, adopted the following definition:

> Serious mental illness means a substantial disorder of thought or mood which significantly impairs judgment, behavior, capacity to recognize reality or cope with the ordinary demands of life within the prison environment and is manifested by substantial pain or disability. Serious mental illness requires a mental health diagnosis, prognosis and treatment, as appropriate, by mental health staff.
> It is expressly understood that this definition does not include inmates who are substance abusers, substance dependent, including alcoholics and narcotic addicts, or persons convicted of any sex offense, who are not otherwise diagnosed as seriously mentally ill.[7]

This definition sought to accomplish the following objectives:

1. Limit the class eligible for mandated prison mental health care to those generally made eligible by the Supreme Court in *Estelle v. Gamble*;[8]

2. Use the prison environment as the diagnostic and treatment context; and

3. Specifically exclude a variety of persons who arguably might be characterized as mentally ill, or certainly in need of some care, but who are not clearly eligible for mandated care under existing case law—namely, the alcoholic and drug addict.

Having stated all of that, I concede that only the most general boundary setting is accomplished. Part of this relates to the inherent tyranny and limitations of language and a recognition that even if one adopted an IRS-detailed "regs" approach, the need for interstitial interpretation would still be required. Ultimately, but within limits, "seriously mentally ill" will be in the eyes of the beholder. There are, indeed, many beholders and, thus, many different visions.

---

researched and written book on the general area of mental health law. *See also* FRANCIS A. ALLEN, THE DECLINE OF THE REHABILITATIVE IDEAL (1981).

   [6] C1-93-0166 (S.D. Ohio 1995). *See* discussion in Chapter 4, ¶ 4.4[4].

   [7] *Dunn v. Voinovich* Consent Decree, Section VIII(a), Definitions. This Decree is reproduced in Appendix D of this book.

   [8] 429 U.S. 97 (1976). *See* facts of case in Chapter 4, ¶ 4.1[1].

¶ 6.2 TREATMENT VS. REHABILITATION AND TRAINING

The right at issue in this work is the right to treatment, and not to rehabilitation, habilitation, or training. The latter three "helping" terms have a distinct legal identity and have their own meaning and vitality in their separate domains. Let me provide my own definition and commentary for each of these terms.[9]

[1] Treatment

Treatment generally refers to a process of diagnosis, intervention, and prognosis designed to relieve pain or suffering or to effect a cure. In law, the concept of treatment is superimposed on a disease (or medical) model. Whether the claim to treatment is made on behalf of a civilly committed mental patient, a convicted prisoner suffering with a psychiatric diagnosis, or a civilly committed sex offender, the required treatment need never be the state of the art available for the particular illness. More important, not every ailment will be recognized as a disease for the purpose of a legal right to treatment.

Within this medical model, terms such as "sex psychopathy," "sexual predator," and "sexually dangerous" are not clinically valid terms. Thus, to the extent the Constitution requires a disease as a predicate for a duty to treat, and most certainly when it requires a serious disease as in *Estelle v. Gamble*, people in one of these categories do not qualify per se.

[2] Rehabilitation

One authority views the rehabilitative ideal as concerned with changing the offender both as a means of social defense and to contribute to the welfare and satisfaction of offenders. According to Santamour, inmates have no federal constitutional claim to rehabilitation, which:

> refers to the process of restoring the individual to behaviors and values which fall within the social definition of what is acceptable. Socially acceptable behavior and values are by definition not "illegal." Thus, it is assumed in the rehabilitative process that the individual formerly held socially acceptable values with appropriate behavior . . ..[10]

The absence of any reference to a disease or illness as the predicate for rehabilitative efforts in this definition is conspicuous. Rehabilitation also is aimed at such conditions as alcoholism, drug addition, and sex psychopathy. Whether or not these conditions are viewed as medical problems for other purposes (e.g., medical insurance or contracted-for medical services), they are not per se within the constitutional law of the disease-medical care model.

---

[9] The material on these four "helping" terms is adapted from Fred Cohen, *Right to Treatment*, in The Sex Offender: Corrections, Treatment and Legal Practice (Barbara K. Schwartz & Henry R. Cellini, eds. 1995), Ch. 24.

[10] Miles Santamour & Bernadette West, Retardation and Criminal Justice: A Training Manual for Criminal Justice Personnel 25 (President's Commission on Mental Retardation, 1979).

The implicit causal assumptions associated with rehabilitation seem to be that an absence of adequate socialization has somehow created a poorly socialized person who requires "restoration." The rehabilitation model carries with it at least mild implications of culpability, of a kind of personal blight that needs restoration to some former, likely imaginary, luster. Unfortunately, too many offenders are not like once glittering neighborhoods that need only gentrification. The concept of treatment requires the presence of a disease or a serious medical disorder. For reasons best left unexplored here, persons are not held responsible for the mental diseases which overtake or "invade" them.

Parenthetically, rehabilitation seems to be used both in the sense of a process and as a desired outcome. Treatment, however, should be used only to refer to a process. Cure or relief, for example, are among the desired outcomes of treatment.[11]

[3] Habilitation vs. Rehabilitation

"Habilitation" may now be contrasted with "rehabilitation." A Wisconsin court dealt with this definitional task in a succinct fashion by stating: "Habilitation means the maximizing of an individual's functioning and the maintenance of the individual at such level. Rehabilitation, in turn, means returning an individual to a previous level of functioning."[12]

Habilitation tends to be used primarily with retarded or developmentally disabled individuals. The term focuses on the use of a variety of activities and programs designed to achieve the maximum human potential of the impaired individual.

[4] Training

The term "training" also has crept into the legal lexicon of helping terms. The Supreme Court dealt with the question of training in *Youngberg v. Romeo*.[13] The case involved a 33-year-old, profoundly retarded (IQ between 8 and 10), institutionalized person who was claiming the constitutional right to a safe environment, to freedom from undue restraint, and to training or habilitation. Justice Powell, for the Court, almost casually recognized the claimant's right to safe conditions, reasoning that if persons convicted of crimes enjoy that right (as they do), then surely it extends as well to wholly innocent persons confined in government-operated institutions. Similarly, the right to avoid what this author believes is meant to mean "undue" restraint, also applies to the civilly confined.[14]

---

[11] Robert A. Burt, *Cruelty, Hypocrisy, and the Rehabilitative Ideal in Corrections*, 16 I<small>NT'L</small> J. L. & P<small>SYCHIATRY</small> 359 (1993), indicates that by 1980 the rehabilitative ideal for prisoners had been thoroughly discredited and banished from the objectives of imprisonment. Thus, whatever help may be extended in prison is via a disease (or condition) model, which rarely focuses on the crime or release. Adjustment to prison becomes the goal.

[12] Matter of Athans, 320 N.W. 2d 30, 32 (Wis. Ct. App. 1982). Additionally, in the monitoring process associated with the *Dunn* decree, my team and I reviewed records and performed clinical assessments as a means to assure at least a shared understanding of who is mentally ill.

[13] 457 U.S. 307 (1982).

[14] Romeo, 475 U.S. at 315.

Justice Powell then grappled with the claims to habilitation or training, concluding that if all Romeo demanded was the sort of minimal training related to safety or restraint, the Court would have no trouble in providing a constitutional basis for the claim. Thus, the state is obliged to provide minimal help, or "training," to enhance a resident's safety and minimize additional restraint. As an aside, it would be interesting to know whether the Court intended to carve training out of the larger concept of habilitation or, given Romeo's extremely low IQ and then conceded inability to live at large, whether training and habilitation were meant to be functional as well as conceptual equivalents.[15]

[5] Who Fits the Disease Model in Case Law

To recapitulate, this book is concerned with the constitutional right to treatment for inmates and detainees with serious mental illness. The retarded person, the substance abuser, and the sex offender simply do not fit the disease model constructed by the Court. Without a separate medical diagnosis—and dual diagnoses in prison are not uncommon—members of these groups, however needy, cannot enforce the *Estelle v. Gamble*-based claim to treatment.[16]

¶ 6.3 SUBJECTIVE VS. OBJECTIVE APPROACHES TO TREATMENT

We turn now to the relevant case law for an exposition on the meaning of treatment and, initially, within the legal demand for treatment on behalf of the civilly confined. *Rouse v. Cameron*,[17] the landmark right-to-treatment case, although involving an insanity acquittee, fashioned a three-factor, qualitative approach to the treatment question:

1. Whether the hospital (we might substitute prison) has made a bonafide effort to cure or improve the patient;

2. Whether the treatment given the patient was adequate in the light of present knowledge; and

3. Whether an individual treatment plan was established initially and updated periodically thereafter.

Another landmark case, *Wyatt v. Stickney*,[18] sought to avoid the essential subjectivity of *Rouse* by employing the objective standards approach. These standards, often

---

[15] Ironically, it is reported that Romeo is out of the institution and living in a community group home.

[16] However, recall that Justice Thomas in Kansas v. Hendricks, 117 S. Ct. 2072 (1997), upheld sexual predator laws and remarked that pedophilia is a serious disease. Thus, the stage is set for at least some sex offenders to claim a right to treatment under the Eighth Amendment. Also, a number of studies show that persons with chronic mental impairments also have an alarmingly high rate of undiagnosed medical problems. An analysis appears in Charles E. Schwartz, *Medical Decision-Making for People with Chronic Mental Impairments*, in CHOICE & RESPONSIBILITY: LEGAL AND ETHICAL DILEMMAS IN SERVICES FOR PERSONS WITH MENTAL DISABILITIES, CH. 13 (Clarence Sundram, ed. 1994).

[17] 373 F.2d 451 (D.C. Cir. 1966).

[18] 325 F. Supp. 781 (M.D. Ala. 1971).

expressed primarily in terms of staff-patient (or staff-inmate) ratios, seek to guarantee access to adequate levels of humane and professional care.[19]

Neither the subjective nor the objective approach fastens on "cure" as the sole objective of treatment, neither articulates a preference for a particular modality of treatment, and neither expresses a requirement for where the care is provided. Perhaps the reader has noted the ease with which this text has moved from the basic question of what is treatment to the question of assessing the adequacy of treatment within the legal context of a right to treatment. That type of unannounced transition characterizes a very common approach used as well by the courts. The independent questions of what treatment is, whether proposed treatment is adequate, and what the required treatment modality may be too often are dealt with as though they were a single question.

We should be grateful that courts do not express binding preferences for one type of treatment over another.[20] However, courts do, and in my judgment should, express skepticism when presented with fact situations in which, for example, a simple regimen of room or ward confinement is described as milieu-therapy, in which housekeeping chores are described as work-therapy, or in which a kick in the pants is termed physical-therapy. I strongly suggest that readers beware of such hyphens and adopt a healthy skepticism about the manipulative potential of clinically oriented terms.

As the ensuing material unfolds it will become clear that courts favor an objective approach in measuring the adequacy of treatment. It will also become painfully evident that as deficient as many of the available treatment programs for the mentally ill are, the mentally retarded inmate seems almost totally ignored. When this issue is recognized, it often is simply submerged in the judicial orders issued to improve various state facilities.

[1] Expansive vs. Narrow Claims to Treatment

We also should be able to distinguish the type of treatment rights spawned by *Estelle* from the earlier, more expansive type of treatment claims that equated treatment with efforts to achieve personal growth, a satisfactory life, happiness, and so on.[21] Legally mandated treatment often is aimed at short-term relief from acute psychic distress, for which the DSM-IV provides a ready diagnostic category. In the prison setting the most frequently articulated goal of treatment is preparation for life in the general population.[22]

---

[19] See Hoffman & Dunn, *Guaranteeing the Right to Treatment*, in Psychiatrists and the Legal Process: Diagnosis and Debate 298 (R. Bonnie, ed. 1977).

[20] One distinguished lawyer-psychologist examined hundreds of "outcome" studies, of differing methodological vigor, which have analyzed various therapies. The overall conclusions, he states, are remarkable: all therapies conducted under all types of conditions seem to offer a greater chance of improvement in short-term emotional feelings than spontaneous remissions. With the exception of success with behaviorally oriented therapies for certain phobias and habituation, no one dynamic therapy seems more successful than any other. Stephen Morse, *Failed Explanations and Criminal Responsibility: Experts and the Unconscious*, 68 Va. L. Rev. 971, 1000–1001 (1982).

[21] See Joint Comm'n on Mental Illness and Health, Action for Mental Health, Ch. II (1963).

[22] Rudolph Alexander, Jr., *Determining Appropriate Criteria in the Evaluation of Correctional Mental Health Treatment for Inmates*, 18 J. Offender Rehab. 119, 124–128 (1992).

The expansive version of treatment is forward looking and includes what some refer to as cultivation of functioning.[23] On the other hand, treatment, as in right to treatment, may be narrowly limited to a serious mental disorder and far less oriented to the future. Indeed, whereas expansive treatment focuses on the person—and at times seems indistinguishable from rehabilitation in concept—treatment needs as used here often arise from a provocative incident that raises immediate questions about an inmate's mental health. The correctional response is likely to be as concerned with "curing" the incident as with "curing" the inmate.

[2] Issues Regarding Termination of Care

Before turning to Chapter 7 for a review and analysis of the leading cases, a final introductory question must be addressed here: When does a mentally ill inmate's right to treatment end? Does it end when the absence of "deliberate indifference" may be shown? When the inmate's pain and suffering is diminished or is in remission? When the inmate is deemed able to function in the general population? When the clinician believes that the inmate will not further benefit from the available therapy?

If an inmate's enforceable claim to care ends at the point when the prison has met its minimal constitutional obligation, then the right to continued care will indeed terminate early. Preparing an inmate for return to the general population is the most frequently adopted, although often unarticulated, goal. In truth, this treatment objective masks more problems than it solves. On the affirmative side, it does give treatment staff an operational objective—they believe they can visualize what it takes to simply survive in the pressure-packed world of prison. On the other hand, it poses the ethical dilemma of ending care before substantial progress is made and the attendant risk that, in many cases, the marginally adjusted inmate will quickly deteriorate in the general population, even if seen on an out-patient basis. The policy dilemma goes even deeper, as it concerns the relationship between early termination and inadequate preparation for, and follow-up after, release or discharge.

As case after case makes clear, correctional treatment staff range from being seriously limited in numbers to being virtually nonexistent. In some instances, treatment staff perform case management or even security functions making their presence illusory for treatment goals. Understaffing clearly forces staff to engage in triage-like decisions. This, again, creates often unbearable ethical dilemmas.

¶ 6.4 DILEMMAS PRISON PROFESSIONALS FACE

There are six problem situations that frequently occur and that must be faced by mental health care professionals:[24]

---

[23] In a seminal article, Professor Lewis Swartz described cultivation of functioning as the pursuit of value goals, in therapy, beyond the prolongation of life and the avoidance of pain. The latter goals are quite consistent with the *Estelle* constitutional minima for treatment. *See* Lewis Swartz, *"Mental Disease": The Groundwork for Legal Analysis and Legislative Action*, 111 U. PA. L. REV. 389 (1963).

[24] Most of these problems are drawn from an excellent article, Jan Costello & Elizabeth Jameson, *Legal and Ethical Duties of Health Care Professional to Incarcerated Children,* 8 J. OF LEGAL MED. 191,

1. The health care professional can give adequate care to a few inmates, but clearly not to all who are in need in the prison.

2. The professional can do adequate evaluation, diagnosis, and prescription, but prisons do not have adequate follow-up systems.

3. The professional believes that a disciplinary measure taken in the name of security is likely to be injurious to the inmates' physical or mental health.

4. The professional is asked to use seeming therapeutic methods or procedures, in a way that is inconsistent with their curative or ameliorative purpose, in order to advance institutional goals.[25]

5. The professional believes that good progress is being made by a particular inmate, and with continued care long-lasting relief seems likely, yet the pressure to treat others requires disengaging from the inmate.

6. The professional is asked to perform evaluations for a parole authority and is thus placed in a conflict of interest situation if he is also performing treatment.

These problems are quite complex and require prison mental health professionals to first resolve a very difficult question: to what extent will they act as advocates for inmates' needs? The advocate's role may create sufficient conflict with security staff that the advocate's tenure could be cut short.

202–207 (1987). I have modified the issues these authors present to reflect this work's concern with incarcerated adults.

[25] The answer to problem 4 is the easiest: no medication or isolation, for example, should ever be "prescribed" in the name of care where the real objective is to cause pain. Costello & Jameson, *supra* note 24, at 207, mention a doctor in a juvenile facility who injected juveniles with vitamin B in solution for the express purpose of causing pain, as a disciplinary measure.

Chapter 7

Case Law on Treatment Obligations

¶ 7.1 INTRODUCTION—*CAMERON*'S DUAL STATUS RESOLUTION

We begin with a review of an important case, *Cameron v. Tomes*,[1] decided in 1993, and then turn to some of the earlier major cases. This may seem to be a strange case with which to begin this section; it is out of chronological sequence and is compounded by Cameron's status as a convicted felon and his concurrent civil commitment under Massachusetts's sexual psychopath law. But Cameron's dual status and the claims related to treatment (1) in the curative sense and (2) in the incidents-of-security sense should serve as an excellent introduction to the cases that follow. In some ways, *Cameron* is a more complex case than those in which the claimant has a single legal status as arrestee, detainee, patient, or prison inmate.

In 1978, Cameron was convicted of sexual assault in Vermont and sentenced to a term of 6 to 20 years. He was then extradited to Massachusetts, convicted of other sex offenses, and received another sentence of 10 to 20 years commencing after the Vermont sentence. Vermont paroled Cameron in 1982 to Massachusetts, and the saga began. After serving a few years in prison, officials initiated successful sexual psychopath proceedings and Cameron was committed to the Treatment Center at the Massachusetts Correctional Institution (MCI) at Bridgewater. The civil commitment is for a day to life, while the criminal sentence is due to expire in 2002.[2]

The district court ruled that Cameron had a constitutional right to minimally adequate treatment for his mental disorders based on the exercise of professional judgment. The court also ruled in Cameron's favor on such matters as access to outside medical care, excessive use of shackles and an armed guard during transport, his housing, searches, and similar matters.[3]

Thus, we encounter two lines of rights, and judicial oversight, at the outset: (1) the right to curative treatment, not as a convicted prisoner under the Eighth Amendment, but as a committed patient under the Fourteenth Amendment, and (2) the trumping of professional judgment by security over the judgment exercised by mental health staff.

The right to treatment claim is rebuffed on appeal with the following rationale:

> Although the parties seek to litigate the abstract issue of a right to treatment, we prefer to plow a furrow no wider than the case demands. Cameron's claims for the most part are not really "right to treatment" claims at all: he is receiving substantial psychological treatment for his condition, and most of the

---

[1] 900 F.2d 14 (1st Cir. 1993).

[2] Id. This portion of the case contains all of the history noted in the text and alludes as well to Bridgewaters' troubled history and constant litigation. Bridgewater is where the famous "Titicut Follies" was filmed. There was an outstanding Consent Decree governing treatment at the Treatment Center which is also a source of rights for Cameron.

[3] Cameron, 900 F.2d at 16. Cameron is disabled and uses a wheelchair. His leg was amputated while under state care.

arguments he is making concern housing, mobility, transportation, and security. Further, under existing state law, there is already a regulation-based right to treatment at the Treatment Center that equals or exceeds anything that the Supreme Court would likely impose under the Due Process Clause. It is also unclear whether, if the Supreme Court did provide a general "right to treatment" for civilly committed persons, it would apply that right to those held as well under criminal sentence. At the very least, the Court's approach in *Youngberg* suggests hewing to the case-by-case approach.[4]

The First Circuit then chose to use a Due Process approach, asking if Cameron's claims fell below the minimum standards of civilized decency.[5] If the claims had been judged under the Eighth Amendment, there would have to be an objective decision on seriousness and a subjective decision on whether the "harm" was imposed with deliberate indifference. It would seem, however, that any claim won by Cameron on a "civilized decency" analysis likely would also be won on a deliberate indifference analysis.

The relief ordered by the district court actually was fairly modest, most of it in the nature of a reconsideration of Cameron's case and some interim, injunctive relief. The First Circuit then characterized the Treatment Center as a pretty dangerous place. "Any professional judgment that decides an issue involving conditions of confinement must embrace security and administration, and not merely medical judgments."[6]

I would suggest that exactly the same analysis would be applied in a prison-mental health situation. That is, treatment decisions by professionals are presumptively correct as to the treatment but not necessarily so when the treatment relates directly to security concerns. The court stated:

> Thus, when it comes to appraising the judgments of the administrators, it does not follow that they are bound to do what the doctors say is best for Cameron even if the doctors are unanimous. The administrators are responsible to the state and to the public for making professional judgments of their own, encompassing institutional concerns as well as individual welfare. Nothing in the Constitution mechanically gives controlling weight to one set of professional judgments. Indeed, when it comes to constitutional rights, none of the professionals has the last word. Professional judgment, as the Supreme Court has explained, creates only a "presumption" of correctness; welcome or not, the final responsibility belongs to the courts.[7]

Reviewing specific provisions of the district court's requirements, the First Circuit held:

---

[4] Cameron, 900 F.2d at 18.

[5] Cameron, 900 F.2d at 19. The court cited Rochin v. California, 342 U.S. 165 (1952), where the Supreme Court used this standard to measure the constitutionality of a particularly outrageous search and seizure conducted and reviewed before the Fourth Amendment was held to apply to the states.

[6] Cameron, 900 F.2d at 19.

[7] Id.

With this clarification as to the role of "professional judgment," we sustain the first injunctive relief provision ordered by the district court directing the general reappraisal of Cameron's personal dangerousness and of his general conditions of confinement. The findings . . . and the evidence portrayed in this district court's decision support this fairly modest directive. In framing equitable relief, a district court has substantial latitude, and we think its "remand" to the Treatment Center administration is well within its authority.

We also conclude that, on the same basis and with the same clarification as to the role of professional judgment, the district court's findings support several other conditioned decree provisions: that administrators consider requests by Cameron for treatment outside the Treatment Center; that the ten-minute movement restriction and oral-cavity searches be suspended as to Cameron unless and until a qualified decision-maker concludes that they are appropriate for Cameron; and that the "Extraction Team" searches of Cameron be barred unless there is prior consultation with a Treatment Center clinician.

Second, we similarly modify the district court's general injunction preventing the Treatment Center from enforcing the current disciplinary system, run by Department of Correction personnel, against Cameron until a new system suitable to his needs is constructed. We have no problem with the decree's requirement that the administrators consider whether changes are warranted in the current system as applied to Cameron and that medical judgments be weighed in this process. But we think that a generally phrased suspension of "the current disciplinary system" in the meantime cuts too broadly and may raise security issues as well.

On two other decree provisions, we believe modifications are required. First, the district court ordered that an armed guard and shackles no longer be used when transporting Cameron outside the facility unless and until a qualified decision-maker determines this to be necessary. In matters of security, as opposed to administrative convenience, the administrators' discretion is at its zenith and Cameron is still under criminal sentence. An armed guard and shackles may seem needless precautions for an amputee, but we think that the Treatment Center should not be obliged to suspend its specific security measures for outside visits while Cameron's case is being reexamined. If the district court wished to require this armed-guard-and-shackles requirement to be re-examined on an expedited basis, that is within its province.[8]

Let us underscore that *Cameron* is not a class action but involves an individual seeking change as it relates to his individual condition and alleged requirements. A win for *Cameron* is far more limited in its impact on the system than the major cases that follow.

One would think that a person who is civilly committed would have a stronger claim to adequate treatment than the Eighth Amendment claims available to those in penal confinement. For the civil committee, curiously enough, there usually is no

---

[8] Cameron, 900 F.2d at 20.

threshold debate on whether there is a serious illness. Typically, the mental illness and dangerousness that support the commitment establish whatever treatment claims are available. Cameron's dual status set the stage for some interesting analysis on the above points, but the court simply elected to conclude that the inmate/patient is getting all of the psychological care he can hope for, pray for, or litigate for.

Does an inmate or detainee also have the arguable right to a legally mandated environment with rules governing transportation, use of force, shackles and the like? As a general proposition, and as Chapter 3 makes clear, inmates do have a complex, although not powerful, legal identity. And whatever the dimensions of that identity, it is not lost by suffering with mental illness. Indeed, the reverse should be true. Needless shackling that exacerbates a mental condition should be forbidden; segregation conditions that are marginally acceptable for the non-mentally ill may be unacceptable for the mentally ill and their non-mentally ill neighbors; disciplinary hearings should not go forward when an inmate's illness impairs comprehension; and routine searches that feed an inmate's paranoia should be forbidden.

¶ 7.2 EARLIER CASES GRANTING RELIEF

As we now begin our excursion into the earlier, significant cases, ask yourself whether they likely would be decided the same way with the advent of *Farmer v. Brennan*[9] and the actual knowledge aspect of deliberate indifference. I will offer my own conclusions as we move forward.

[1] Inadequate Care—*Ruiz v. Estelle*

We begin with Judge Justice's 1980 assessment of the Texas Department of Corrections, where it was found that:

> "Treatment" there consists almost exclusively of the administration of medications, usually psychotropic drugs, to establish control over disturbed inmates. Other options, such as counseling, group therapy, individual psychotherapy, or assignment to constructive, therapeutic activities are rarely, if ever, available on the units. Essentially, an inmate with a mental disorder is ignored by unit officers until his condition becomes serious. When this occurs, he is medicated excessively. If his condition becomes acute, he is deposited at TDC's Treatment Center, a facility exclusively for inmates with mental disorders. Located at the Huntsville Unit, the Treatment Center only has limited professional staffing, and inmates who are sent there are the recipients of little more than medication and what amounts to warehousing.[10]

At the prison-unit level, it was found that the part-time psychiatrists:

---

[9] 511 U.S. 825 (1994). *See* the review of *Farmer* in Chapter 4, ¶ 4.3[2].

[10] Ruiz v. Estelle, 503 F. Supp. 1265, 1332 (S.D. Tex. 1980), *aff'd in part*, 679 F.2d 1115 (5th Cir. 1982), *cert. denied*, 460 U.S. 1042 (1983).

have little time to supervise the psychologists technically under their supervision or to provide treatment to the inmates with mental disorders. Instead, their primary activities consist of approving and renewing prescriptions of psychotropic medications for these inmates.[11]

Psychologists were found to provide the bulk of the treatment at the TDC units. The usual result of a psychological interview was the prescription of psychotropic medication for the inmate or the relegation of the inmate to administrative segregation, hospital lock-up, or solitary confinement. No facilities for more sophisticated treatment existed on the units.[12]

Inmates diagnosed as schizophrenic or as having an acute psychosis spent long periods of time (as long as five months) in segregation without receiving treatment or seeing a member of the psychiatric staff. Inmates displaying suicidal tendencies were either ignored or punished (TDC officials felt that these inmates were attempting to manipulate the system).[13]

As noted earlier, problems associated with manipulation, malingering, or secondary gain, are deeply rooted and widespread in correctional mental health. Interviews with numerous uninformed prison staff and clinical personnel reveal that no small part of the tension between them consists of (1) security personnel believing that some inmates "fake it" and manipulate gullible treaters and (2) treaters (gullible or not) believing that security staff often foist behavioral problems on them regardless of actual mental illness.[14] Additionally, even today where adequate treatment does not exist, seriously mentally ill inmates will be found—as in Texas—locked away in segregation.

Recent developments in some jurisdictions (e.g., Ohio), where correctional officers actually serve on treatment teams and receive extensive training on the signs and symptoms of mental illness tend to alleviate this problem. Indeed, as prisons become the depository of larger numbers of persons with mental illness and thus increasingly serve some of the clientele and objectives of mental hospitals, these new roles and enhanced training become almost obligatory.

Returning to *Ruiz*, Judge Justice moved from TDC's generally inadequate care for the mentally disordered inmate to an evaluation of the Treatment Center that housed the most seriously disturbed inmates. The Center was described as an overcrowded warehouse virtually identical to administrative segregation, with very strict confinement and virtually no treatment the rule. Security staff were plentiful, while mental health professionals were hardly in evidence. Psychotropic medication and unadorned confinement constituted TDC's inadequate response to inmates' serious mental disorders.[15]

---

[11] Ruiz, 503 F. Supp. at 1333.

[12] Ruiz, 503 F. Supp. at 1333–1334.

[13] Ruiz, 503 F. Supp. at 1334. That, of course, is precisely what TDC officials believed about Mr. Gamble and his back pains. This is a recurrent theme in correctional mental health.

[14] Interview with Ken Adams, then a doctoral student at S.U.N.Y. at Albany, Graduate School of Criminal Justice, Aug. 10, 1983, Albany, N.Y. Mr. Adams completed his doctoral thesis on prison decision-making and the mentally disordered inmate.

[15] Ruiz, 503 F. Supp. at 1334–1336. These pages are rich in detail and should be consulted by those needing such detail.

Finding the level of mental health care in TDC to be constitutionally inadequate, the court held that "treatment must entail more than segregation and close supervision of the inmate patients . . . [and the] . . . prescription and administration of behavior-altering medications in dangerous amounts, by dangerous methods, or without appropriate supervision and periodic evaluation is an unacceptable method of treatment."[16] The court went on to find that "a basic program for the identification, treatment, and supervision of inmates with suicidal tendencies is a necessary component of any mental health treatment program."[17]

[2] Early Guidelines Toward Legally Adequate Care

Judge Justice's six components for a minimally adequate mental health treatment program may continue to serve as the basic outline to assess the constitutional adequacy of any prison system's mental health services:

First, there must be a systematic program for screening and evaluating inmates in order to identify those who require mental health treatment . . . Second, as was underscored in both Newman and Bowring, treatment must entail more than segregation and close supervision of the inmate patients . . . Third, treatment requires the participation of trained mental health professionals, who must be employed in sufficient numbers to identify and treat in an individualized manner those treatable inmates suffering from serious mental disorders . . . Fourth, accurate, complete, and confidential records of the mental health treatment process must be maintained. Fifth, prescription and administration of behavior-altering medications in dangerous amounts, by dangerous methods, or without appropriate supervision and periodic evaluations, is an unacceptable method of treatment. Sixth, a basic program for the identification, treatment, and supervision of inmates with suicidal tendencies is a necessary component of any mental health treatment program . . . TDC's mental health care program falls short of minimal adequacy in terms of each of these components and is, therefore, in violation of the eighth amendment.[18]

Since the *Ruiz* decision, additional caselaw on point suggests that I add at least two additional components to the above listing: access and physical resources. By access I mean nothing more sophisticated than the process by which an inmate may gain entry to the human and physical resources necessary to diagnose a mental illness and, if needed, to provide treatment. By physical resources I refer to treatment environments matched to the inmates' treatment needs. Thus, one looks to hospital beds, other types of residential care, special needs units, and crisis management areas.

Access, of course, is the crucial dynamic in this process. Its adequacy is assessed by studying a prison's orientation materials and practices, its response time to emergencies and other treatment needs, including its waiting list, and whether it conducts

---

[16] Ruiz, 503 F. Supp. at 1339.

[17] Id.

[18] Id. The six criteria in the text may serve as the most basic outline assessing the legal adequacy of any prison system's mental health program. With the addition of the other factors discussed in the text, a comprehensive outline is provided.

"rounds" in segregation where untreated mentally ill inmates are not likely to be found. A corrections system might have the best physical resources known to man; each inmate might have a personal mental health professional; yet without timely access, the system would be unconstitutional. Obviously, this is a hypothetical situation, but hopefully it makes the point.

In *Langley v. Coughlin,*[19] New York inmates presented a long list of grievances regarding the identification and treatment of severe mental illnesses. In deciding on behalf of the inmates, the court developed an even more extensive checklist than *Ruiz.* These items, together with the items previously noted, provide a fairly comprehensive inventory of legally relevant assessment factors:

1. Failure to take a complete medical (or psychiatric) record.

2. Failure to keep adequate records.

3. Failure to respond to inmates' prior psychiatric history.

4. Failure to at least place under observation inmates suffering a mental health crisis.

5. Failure to properly diagnose mental conditions.

6. Failure to properly prescribe medications.

7. Failure to provide meaningful treatment other than drugs.

8. Failure to explain treatment refusals, diagnosis, and ending of treatment.

9. Seemingly cavalier refusals to consider bizarre behavior as mental illness even when a prior diagnosis existed.

10. Personnel doing things for which they are not trained.

To the *Langley* list I would add:

11. Abrupt termination of medication, especially without prior records.

12. Refusal by security staff to implement medical orders.[20]

In *Finney v. Hutto,*[21] another of the important early wave of cases, the court found that mental health care for mentally or emotionally ill prisoners in the Arkansas system consisted of nothing more than the administration of drugs or, for violent inmates, transfer to the state hospital for a temporary hold. A form of group therapy had recent-

---

[19] 715 F. Supp. 522, 540–541 (S.D.N.Y. 1989), *aff'd,* 888 F.2d 252 (2d Cir. 1989).

[20] *See* Arnold ex rel. H.B. v. Lewis, 803 F. Supp. 245 (D. Ariz. 1992), discussing a 10-year failure to provide psychiatric care to a schizophrenic female inmate. *Arnold* became a part of the judicial findings that terminated in broad-based relief being granted to Arizona prisoners. *See* discussion of Casey v. Lewis at ¶ 7.3[3].

[21] 410 F. Supp. 251, 259 (E.D. Ark. 1976), *aff'd,* 548 F.2d 740 (8th Cir. 1977), *aff'd,* 437 U.S. 678 (1978).

ly been introduced by corrections, and while the court viewed this favorably, it did not accept this minimal effort as a total substitute for the unavailable, conventional methods of psychotherapy.[22]

[3] Isolation Practices and Conditions

The challenge to the Maryland House of Corrections in *Johnson v. Levine*[23] resulted in a finding that the overall mental health care was constitutionally acceptable except for the Special Confinement Area (SCA). Inmates judged to have "psychological or psychiatric" problems were housed there in conditions found elsewhere only in punitive segregation. One more difference, moreover, was that disciplinary confinement tended to be of relatively short duration, while SCA confinement lasted an average of six to eight months and for some, even longer.[24]

Johnson combines the absence of treatment—mentally ill inmates are warehoused—with uncivilized overall conditions, to find a failure of the SCA to meet minimum constitutional standards. The court forces the remedy issue by requiring that the actively psychotic inmates be transferred to a mental hospital, threatening to join any recalcitrant agencies as defendants.[25]

Newman v. Alabama,[26] a well-known early decision, involved a similar situation, a combination of no treatment and dubious isolation practices and conditions.

> Severe, and sometimes dangerous, psychotics are regularly placed in the general population. If they become violent, they are removed to lockup cells which are not equipped with restraints or padding and where they are unattended. While some do obtain interviews with qualified medical personnel and a few are eventually transferred for treatment to a state mental hospital, the large majority of mentally disturbed prisoners receive no treatment whatsoever. It is tautological that such care is constitutionally inadequate.[27]

Living conditions for mentally disordered prisoners in the Puerto Rican system[28] were at least as unacceptable as the Maryland House of Correction and the Alabama systems. Psychiatric treatment, or rather the lack of it, was described as disgraceful. Psychotics were confined in dungeons or isolation cells known as "calabozos," where they received no treatment. Others who were mentally ill were generally kept in their

---

[22] Finney, 410 F. Supp. at 260.

[23] 450 F. Supp. 648 (D. Md. 1978), *aff'd*, 588 F.2d 1378 (4th Cir 1978).

[24] Johnson, 450 F. Supp. at 657. It is difficult to resist the comparison between indefinite confinement of the mentally ill and determinate confinement for criminal offenders.

[25] Johnson, 450 F. Supp. at 657–658 (citations omitted).

[26] 349 F. Supp. 278 (M.D. Ala. 1972), *aff'd in part*, 503 F.2d 1320 (5th Cir. 1974), *cert. denied*, 421 U.S. 948 (1975).

[27] Newman, 349 F. Supp. at 284 (footnote omitted). The court pointed out in Footnote 5 that "The inadequacy of the treatment available at the mental hospitals within the state was the subject of this Court's opinion in Wyatt v. Stickney, 325 F. Supp. 781 (1971), and subsequent orders in that case, 344 F. Supp. 373, 344 F. Supp. 387 (1972)."

[28] Feliciano v. Barcelo, 497 F. Supp. 14 (D.P.R. 1979).

own dormitory ward and also received no treatment. Even at the Bayamon prison, which did have a psychiatric unit, the inmates were merely confined and otherwise neglected. A few inmates received treatment only because one of them tampered with the records and ordered medication.[29] The court held that the above conditions violated the inmates' constitutional rights.[30]

[4] Existent Care System Deficiencies

The problems of adequate treatment were a little more sophisticated in the New Hampshire prison system.[31] A semblance of mental health care existed. Indeed, the *Laaman* court even reviewed a debate concerning the relative amount of time to be spent on diagnosis and on treatment, and a discussion of manageable caseloads. What was actually available, however, was constitutionally deficient.

> In the face of the professed orientation of the program and the severe understaffing, it is not surprising that plaintiffs' experts found mental health treatment at NHSP basically nonexistent. The program is reactive and crisis oriented, and, while there is some diagnostic work done, there is little or no capacity to follow through with treatment. There are no therapy groups run by the mental health unit. Less than 20% of the inmate population is seen at all, and most of those are counseled only irregularly. Defendants themselves recognize that they do not have the facilities, staff or expertise to deal with seriously disturbed persons.[32]

The court did not order any specific type of care, but did order that the NHSP establish procedures to identify those inmates who require mental health care within the institution and make arrangements to implement the provision of such care.[33]

The Menard Correctional Center in Illinois succumbed to a broad-based attack on its health care delivery system.[34] The court did not prescribe what would constitute an adequate number of health care professionals, but it plainly found the following conditions and available resources inadequate:

- Inmates were not properly assessed.

- Potential suicides were not given professional care.

[29] Feliciano, 497 F. Supp. at 30. *See* Chapter 5, ¶ 5.3[5] n.14 for a listing of cases in this matter.

[30] Feliciano, 497 F. Supp. at 34. *See* Santana v. Collazo, 714 F.2d 1172 (1st Cir. 1983), *cert. denied*, 466 U.S. 974 (1984), in which conditions at a Puerto Rico industrial school and juvenile camp were reviewed, with special attention given to isolation units. The court took the view that acceptable conditions for the isolation of adults and juveniles are inherently different and that adults could be constitutionally subjected to a generally harsher environment than juveniles.

[31] Laaman v. Helgemoe, 437 F. Supp. 269 (D.N.H. 1977). This is actually a fairly sophisticated issue for the cases on point in the 1970s.

[32] Laaman, 437 F. Supp. at 290.

[33] Laaman, 437 F. Supp. at 328.

[34] Lightfoot v. Walker, 486 F. Supp. 504 (S.D. Ill. 1980).

- No clinical psychologist was employed for ongoing therapy.

- No psychiatrist was employed for psychotherapy.

- Recordkeeping was inadequate.

- Of 18 employees available for counseling, eight had no formal training. The counselors' duties were primarily administrative and the ratio of counselor to convicts was 1:155, well above the 1:100 ratio recommended in trial testimony. Consequently little, if any, actual counseling occurred.

- Psychotropic medication was overprescribed and inadequately monitored. Of 80,000 doses of medication dispensed, 50 percent was psychotropic medication.

- Delays were routine in transferring those in need of psychiatric care.

- Psychiatric care was available for only 15 hours per week.[35]

In *Hoptowit v. Ray*[36] the Ninth Circuit upheld the district court's finding that health care was inadequate at the Washington State Penitentiary. The penitentiary lacked basic psychiatric services and had deficiencies in staff and programs. The Court of Appeals, however, did reject the trial judge's reliance on the standards promulgated by the American Medical Association and the American Public Health Association as constitutional minima. Following a recurring pattern in resolving this question, the court stated, "A higher standard may be desirable but that responsibility is properly left to the executive and legislative branches. The remedy of the court could go no further than to bring the medical services up to the constitutional minima."[37]

[5] Judicial Responses to Deficient Care

In *Cody v. Hillard*,[38] inmates successfully challenged almost every aspect of the South Dakota State Penitentiary. Of the 538 inmates at the time of the suit, 20 to 25 percent were estimated to be psychotic.[39] A volunteer psychiatrist visited the prison once a week for about five hours, which he devoted primarily to parole board workups.[40]

The prison employed one full-time psychologist who spent most of his time on testing, seven full-time counselors, and the equivalent of two and one half full-time drug and alcohol counselors. In its decision, the court emphasized the need for an adequate counseling staff:

---

[35] Lightfoot, 486 F. Supp. at 521–522.

[36] 682 F.2d 1237 (9th Cir. 1982).

[37] Hoptowit, 682 F.2d at 1253. Standards clearly are relevant to, but not determinative of, constitutional norms. *See* the various standards reproduced in Appendix A of this book.

[38] 599 F. Supp. 1025 (D.S.D. 1984) *aff'd*, 799 F.2d 447 (8th Cir. 1986), *cert. denied*, 108 S. Ct. 1078 (1988).

[39] Cody, 599 F. Supp. at 1042.

[40] Id.

Adequate counseling staff reduces the number of instances in which individuals in the general population deteriorate both physically and mentally, thus reducing the number of inmates who must be referred to a mental hospital for psychiatric treatment. Adequate counseling services aid in the treatment and prevention of mental health problems among the inmate population by enabling qualified personnel to intervene at an early stage in the diagnosis, care and treatment of these problems. Adequate counseling services also assist, for example, in the continued monitoring of inmates who have returned to the general population after having been removed from the general population for psychiatric treatment. At present, the counseling staff at the SDSP does not have time to adequately perform psychotherapy or psychological treatment on inmates.[41]

This court's emphasis on the need for mental health services to alleviate mental deterioration is interesting and important. Where a court emphasizes this concern as a constitutional duty—and many do not—it creates a predicate for earlier intervention and a broader base for mandated services.[42] As a matter of policy, preventive measures clearly make sense. As a matter of constitutional law, with increasing judicial support for actual harm, the matter may be in some doubt.[43]

To further highlight the systemic failure of the South Dakota State Penitentiary, the court discussed the case of one inmate for whom the sentencing judge urged that psychiatric care be given. This inmate met with the volunteer psychiatrist for, at most, 12 minutes and received no other psychiatric or psychological attention during his entire prison stay.[44] The court also found instances in which certain inmates interfered with other inmates' treatment plans, which led in at least one case to a suicide.[45]

In devising a mandated plan for South Dakota, the *Cody* decision went into considerably more detail than most other decisions:

> b. There are three levels of care which are essential in providing an adequate system of psychiatric and psychological care. Absent such a system, the probability is strong that inmates requiring psychiatric and psychological treatment will not be cared for adequately and will experience unnecessary mental and/or physical deterioration in the general inmate population.
>
> c. The first necessary level of care consists of in-patient hospitalization care to treat acutely psychotic individuals, individuals experiencing suicidal

---

[41] Id. Notice the court's reference to the merits of prevention and reduction of deterioration. While it is obviously good practice to engage in preventive efforts, on closer analysis, one runs into the seriousness component of the *Estelle* formula (see discussion in Chapter 4, ¶¶ 4.1, 4.2). There are various degrees of, and stages for, seriousness allowing for a claim, then, at the earliest stage.

[42] The *Cody* decision called for services before an inmate bleeds to death or the facility reaches catastrophic proportions. Cody v. Hillard, *supra* note 38, 599 F. Supp. at 1056, using Palmigiano v. Garrahy, 413 F. Supp. 956, 973 (D.R.I. 1977).

[43] *See, e.g.,* Lewis v. Casey, 518 U.S. 343 (1996).

[44] Cody, *supra* note 38, 599 F. Supp. at 1043. A sentencing judge's recommendation as to psychiatric care normally is not binding on correctional authorities. The recommendation, however, was used in the *Cody* decision to compound the system's failure to deliver care.

[45] Id.

tendencies, and those other individuals most significantly impaired by psychiatric illness.

d. The second necessary level of care consists of intermediate care and treatment for those individuals who have been stabilized by medication and supportive psychotherapy but who cannot return immediately to the general inmate population. This level of care is designed to provide a transition for inmates coming from an inpatient psychiatric hospital environment back into the general inmate population. An intermediate level care facility would provide the inmates an environment less intensive than the first level psychiatric hospital, but more supportive than that provided by the general population facility. An intermediate level care facility requires appropriate nursing staff, support staff, and psychiatric and psychological staff.

e. The third necessary level of care consists of out-patient care for inmate-patients who have received psychiatric treatment and who have returned to the general population so that these inmates can have prescribed medications monitored and can receive supportive group or individual psychotherapy as indicated.

f. The mental health needs of inmates at the SDSP require that the SDSP maintain an acute (first level) care and an intermediate (second level) care facility equipped with approximately twenty to twenty-five beds. Of these number, approximately eight to ten beds would be devoted to psychiatric care—requiring twenty-four hour nursing coverage and adequate support staff. The remaining beds would be devoted to intermediate care.

g. Staffing for this facility would require a full-time psychiatrist, two full-time psychologists, approximately six full-time equivalent nurses in order to provide twenty-four hour coverage, at least four full-time equivalent counselors or psychiatric social workers to provide support to the psychiatric and psychology staff, and the necessary correctional staff to provide twenty-four hour security over the facility.

h. The mental health needs of inmates at SDSP also require that the SDSP provide outpatient (third level) care.

i. In addition to the staff necessary to provide acute and intermediate care, adequate outpatient care would require approximately two days per week of on-site psychiatric coverage, a full-time psychologist whose work is devoted exclusively to the treatment component of mental health care, and increased counseling staff. The full-time psychologist position would be in addition to the present full-time psychologist who performs primarily administrative functions involving the evaluation and assessment of newly admitted inmates. While it is preferable that every counselor have a master's degree, a counselor holding a bachelor's degree accompanied by sufficient experience and appropriate supervision is acceptable.[46]

The three levels of care approach mandated in *Cody* is rapidly becoming the con-

---

[46] Cody, 599 F. Supp. at 1043–1044.

temporary model for prison mental health services.[47] It is within the range of legally acceptable options for long-term, acute or chronic patient care to be provided "off campus." So long as emergency care exists within the facility (or at a moment's call), then prison systems presumably continue to have the right to choose the preferred place for care.[48]

Decisions like *Ruiz* and *Cody* exert a powerful and long-term influence on correctional mental health care. The findings of fact and the detailed injunctive requirements become a model for legal analysis in subsequent cases. As noted earlier, most law suits that escape dismissal or summary judgment are not ultimately tried, they are settled.[49] *Ruiz* and *Cody* have been extremely important in shaping settlements as the more recent decisions discussed in the next section will influence the future.

Settlement discussions involve exchanges of the various parties' view of the law, of both its doctrinal and its empirical components. Thus, as these first wave correctional mental health decisions took hold and were promulgated, they exerted an influence well beyond the parties involved and the geographical reach of a district court or circuit court of appeals. In the continued absence of authoritative Supreme Court case law on point, these early decisions—and the leading contemporary decisions—are the persuasive precedents.

[a] Separate Facility Requirement

In *Finney v. Mabry*,[50] a federal court took an approach similar to *Cody*'s but also insisted on a separate facility for the most severely disturbed:

> [P]rovision of a separate facility and treatment for the most severely mentally disturbed is constitutionally required. Persons who are severely sick simply cannot be held in custody unless they are provided with necessary medical services. Mental health treatment is clearly a necessary medical service in certain cases. Many inmates who have mental and emotional problems, and need temporary or "outpatient" type of treatment or counseling by psychiatrists or other mental health personnel, may, of course, remain in the general population; but there must be some manner of dealing with them while in the population . . . However, in addition, there must be a permanent, separate facility so that those people who are most severely mentally disturbed may be removed, for their own protection and for the safety of others, from the cor-

---

[47] *See* Herbert A. Makra, David A. Shively & Jerry Minaker, *Community Mental Health and Prisons: A Model for Constitutionally Adequate Care in Correctional Mental Health*, 17 J. CRIM. J. 501 (1989), outlining changes made in the state of Washington based on a community mental health services model.

[48] *See* Wardlaw, *Models for the Custody of Mentally Disordered Offenders*, 6 INT'L J. L. & PSYCHIATRY 159, 164–165 (1983), for an analysis of six competing models for inmate mental health services. The author favors a mix of prison psychiatric units, including at least one that is secure, along with links to regional forensic centers. Wardlaw at 166.

[49] *See* Austin v. Pennsylvania Dept. Corrections, 877 F. Supp. 1437, 1454 (E.D. Pa. 1995), in which Judge Du Bois indicated that in traditional two-party litigation there is a general policy favoring settlements. In class action litigation this general policy is elevated to an overriding public interest, citing to Armstrong v. Board of School Directors, 616 F.2d 305, 313 (7th Cir. 1980).

[50] 534 F. Supp. 1026 (E.D. Ark. 1982).

rectional environment of the general population and provided with the treatment and services they need.[51]

[b] Staff Reductions Creating Unconstitutional System

In *Duran v. Anaya*,[52] Federal District Judge Burciaga was confronted with the New Mexico prison system, which was still recovering from the 1980 prison riot considered "the bloodiest in the history of American corrections." This case was confounded by a political struggle within the state that came to a head, for our purposes, when the legislature actually reduced the budget for prison medical and mental health care.[53]

The proposed budget would have eliminated 36 percent of the psychologists and mental health support personnel, thus causing even greater harm to mentally ill prisoners in the form of added mental and emotional stress. The reductions would have impacted greatly on outpatient, intermediate, and acute treatment.[54] In a word, the court adopted the views of the then Secretary of the New Mexico Corrections Department. The reductions, he said, "will devastate our . . . mental health system."[55]

In responding favorably to the plaintiff's request for an injunction prohibiting staff reductions and to require that vacant mental health positions be filled, the court stated:

> As a result of the reductions projected to occur on July 1, 1986, defendants will be unable to meet their constitutional obligation to provide a level of medical care that is reasonably designed to meet the routine and emergency health care needs of prisoners. This will be true with respect to medical care, dental care and psychiatric care. By implementing drastic reductions in the number of medical and mental health professionals available to treat prisoners, defendants will deny prisoners access to medical personnel capable of evaluating the need for treatment and providing necessary medical care. By reducing the level of security staffing below the minimal safety level recommended by the Court's expert consultant on security staffing, and below the level found by the Special Master and approved as necessary by the Court without objection from either party, defendants are significantly increasing the risk of violence and assaults and thus are evidencing deliberate indifference to the legitimate safety needs of prisoners.

> It is apparent that the medical and psychiatric needs of prisoners that will

---

[51] Finney, 534 F. Supp. at 1037. Discussed in Susan Brenner & David Galanti, *Prisoners' Rights to Psychiatric Care*, 21 IDAHO L. REV. 1, 26 (1985). It is important to note that inmates may be characterized as seriously mentally ill while on an outpatient caseload.

[52] 642 F. Supp. 510 (D.N.M. 1986).

[53] The Corrections Department Director of Administrative Services testified that the budget was cast as a punitive response to the consent decree entered in the case and as a way to make it virtually impossible for the Department to comply. Duran, 642 F. Supp. at 527, 527 n.2.

[54] Duran, 642 F. Supp. at 519.

[55] Duran, 642 F. Supp. at 521. The court made detailed findings of fact as to the system's inadequacies which need not be fully repeated here.

go unmet if proposed staffing reductions are implemented are serious ones. Unnecessary deaths, physical traumas, suicides and self-mutilation are virtually inevitable. Both plaintiffs' and defendants' experts have testified that the impact of the proposed staffing reductions will make the delivery of satisfactory routine and emergency medical care impossible. As a result, prisoners will endure an unnecessary level of pain and suffering and will be the victims of irreparable physical and mental injury. In summary, the proposed staffing reductions in the medical and mental health areas reflect deliberate indifference to serious medical needs of prisoners in the four institutions under the Court's jurisdiction in this case. *Estelle v. Gamble*, 429 U.S. 97 (1976).

The evidence before the Court makes it abundantly clear that the Secretary of Corrections has attempted to persuade both the New Mexico Legislature and the Governor of New Mexico (the latter being the defendant in this action) to make sufficient funds available to avoid the dangerous and life threatening reductions in medical, mental health and security staff that are imminent. These efforts thus far have been to no avail. Nonetheless, defendants' constitutional obligations may not be avoided for lack of financing. Moreover, this Court's exercise of its equitable powers is not limited by the fact that needed equitable remedies implicate state funds.

Turning to the criteria that must be met for the issuance of a preliminary injunction, the Court finds that there is a substantial likelihood that plaintiffs eventually will prevail on the merits in upcoming hearings on plaintiffs' contempt motion and the parties' cross motions for modification insofar as those motions relate to medical, mental health and security staffing. There is no evidence before the Court that staffing reductions of the magnitude contemplated in the medical and mental health areas will permit the maintenance of minimal constitutional standards in these areas. Indeed, the Court's expert, plaintiffs expert, defendants' expert and the New Mexico Secretary of State of Corrections all have testified to the contrary. Particularly in view of the steady increase in the penal population that will occur in New Mexico's incarcerated population, deficiencies outlined in earlier reports of the Special Master and in testimony before the Court in connection with the pending motion for preliminary injunction no doubt will be exacerbated. Likewise, the consistent evidence before the Court is that the level of psychiatric care being provided at this time, particularly to prisoners in need of acute care, is unacceptable by any conceivable measure or standard. All expert testimony is in agreement that the magnitude of mental health staffing reductions contemplated will eliminate essential mental health services.[56]

It should be emphasized that the *Duran* case involved a previously "settled" dispute about the unconstitutional level of mental health services and a mutually acceptable way to remedy the deficiencies. The court was dragged into the matter when there was an attempt to veto the consent decree with the "power of the purse." Consent decrees can be modified—although with great difficulty[57]—but that was not the strat-

---

[56] Duran, 642 F. Supp. at 525–526 (citations omitted).

egy employed by New Mexico. Where a consent decree is unmodified, then the law of the case is derived from the terms of the decree. These face-offs between state legislatures and federal judges are wrenching exercises of judicial authority and federal constitutional supremacy versus state power.[58]

With the horrors of the 1980 prison riot still relatively fresh, and with the prospect of an increasing number of violently mentally ill prisoners going untreated, Judge Burciaga had little choice except to act as he did.[59] As recently as February 1997, the *Duran* decree remained operative although the parties seemed to be close to agreeing that substantial compliance had been achieved.

[c] Qualified Physicians

Wellman v. Faulkner[60] is an interesting and useful decision involving yet another successful inmate challenge to medical and psychiatric care, this time against the Indiana State Prison at Michigan City. In finding that there was deliberate indifference to serious medical needs, the reviewing court cited the fact that two physicians at the prison were recent immigrants from Vietnam who could not communicate with their patients. It also found that the position of staff psychiatrist had gone unfilled for two years, leaving no one qualified to evaluate suicidal or homicidal candidates or to monitor patients on psychotropic medication.

Before remanding the case for further orders concerning specific relief, the court observed that "the policy of deferring to the judgment of prison officials in matters of prison discipline and security does not usually apply in the context of medical care to the same degree as in other contexts."[61] This point is interesting in several aspects. First, in *Youngberg v. Romeo*,[62] the Supreme Court held that a profoundly retarded resident of a state school had a due process right to minimally adequate training in order to maximize his right to be free of harm and minimize undue restraint. In evaluating what training was reasonable, the Court stated that courts should show deference to the judgment exercised by a qualified professional.[63]

Romeo raised the possibility that courts might defer to the opinions of experts who find that the state's mental health system, or design for care in an individual case,

---

[57] *See* Rufo v. Inmates of the Suffolk County Jail, 502 U.S. 367 (1992), on modification. Relying subsequently on the Prison Litigation Reform Act (PLRA), 18 U.S.C. § 3626, the defendants managed to have this 1979 consent decree terminated. Inmates of Suffolk County Jail v. Rouse, 1997 U.S. App. LEXIS 3088 (1st Cir. Nov. 7, 1997).

[58] 18 U.S.C. § 3626(b), pre-PLRA consent decrees may be vacated unless there are findings of unconstitutionality and narrowly drawn relief that is the least intrusive available. *See* Benjamin v. Jacobson, 124 F.3d 162 (2nd Cir. 1997), in which the Court upheld the constitutionality of this provision, but only if the contractual aspects of the decree were fully enforceable in state court. In other words, only the federal judicial remedy was annulled, and not the binding nature of the agreement itself.

[59] *See* Palmigiano v. Garrahy, 639 F. Supp. 244 (D.R.I. 1986), in which Rhode Island was not in compliance with medical and mental health care mandates nine years after the initial judgment. The judge gave the state 60 days to prepare an acceptable compliance plan.

[60] 715 F.2d 269 (7th Cir. 1983), *cert. denied,* 468 U.S. 1217 (1984).

[61] Wellman, 715 F.2d at 272. Again, this differential deference statement is now widely accepted.

[62] 457 U.S. 307 (1982); see discussion of *Romeo* in Chapter 1, ¶ 1.5[3], and Chapter 6, ¶ 6.2[4].

[63] Romeo, 457 U.S. at 322–323.

is appropriate and adequate.[64] In other words, the argument is that prison officials who are security experts should receive deference in their areas of expertise and prison employees who provide health care should receive deference in their area of expertise. However, I do not believe that this is what the Court had in mind in *Romeo*. Under the present state of the law, where an inmate is given medical or psychiatric care and the inmate either disagrees with the treatment methodology or argues that good medical or psychiatric care would have provided him with more or different treatment, the inmate is very likely to lose.[65]

Second, in reiterating the "deliberate indifference" standard as appropriate for prison medical care issues in *Whitley v. Albers*,[66] the Court showed no inclination to further facilitate a prison system's defense of arguably unconstitutional mental health care systems. Indeed, the Court has maintained its position that where lifesaving and pain reducing care are at issue, then it is not necessary to weigh competing concerns about security.

In sum, the *Whitley* Court's position of less deference to prison officials in matters of physical and mental health is well taken. While it is not a position often made explicit by other courts, one anticipates that if confronted with this proposition, most courts would accept it.

¶ 7.3 MORE RECENT DECISIONS GRANTING RELIEF

[1] Deliberate Indifference—*Coleman v. Wilson*

Coleman v. Wilson[67] is perhaps the blockbuster decision of the last decade; it is to the 90's what *Ruiz* in Texas was for the 70's. It is a case that reportedly could have settled much earlier and for much less than what resulted from the fiercely litigated approach actually taken. Magistrate Judge John Moulds conducted the extensive hearings involved and is the principle author of the opinion adopted, in effect, by Lawrence E. Karlton, Chief Judge Emeritus of the United States District Court in Sacramento.[68]

Coleman involved eight critical findings of fact, findings that are vital to the ultimate victory for the plaintiff class:

> First, Judge Moulds found that defendants do not have an adequate mechanism for screening inmates for mental illness, either at the time of reception or during incarceration. He further found that the CDC [California Department of Corrections] has lacked adequate screening since at least 1987.

---

[64] In many cases there is no expert available for such testimony. *See* Susan Stefan, *Leaving Civil Rights to the "Experts": From Deference to Abdication Under the Professional Judgment Standard*, 102 YALE L.J. 639 (1992), for a blistering attack on this standard and especially so in the medical-correctional arena.

[65] *See, e.g.,* Ferola v. Moran, 622 F. Supp. 814 (D.R.I. 1985), on an inmate's disagreement with the therapeutic regimen.

[66] 475 U.S. 512 (1986). *See* Chapter 3, ¶ 3.3[4].

[67] 912 F. Supp. 1282 (E.D. Cal. 1995).

[68] If I may be permitted a bit of hyperbole, Judge Karlin is to the California Department of Corrections what Judge Morris Lasker has been to the New York City Department of Corrections.

Second, he found that the CDC is seriously and chronically understaffed in the area of mental health care. Indeed, he found that there was no dispute in this regard.

Third, he found that defendants have no effective method for insuring the competence of their mental health staff and, therefore, for insuring that inmates have access to competent care.

Fourth, he found that "there are significant delays in and sometimes complete denial of, access to necessary medical attention, multiple problems with use and management of medication, and inappropriate use of involuntary medications."

Fifth, he found that the mental health status of class members is adversely impacted by inappropriate use of punitive measures without regard to the impact of such measures on their medical condition.

Sixth, the magistrate judge found that the medical records system maintained by defendants is extremely deficient.

Seventh, the magistrate judge found that defendants have designed an adequate prevention program and have taken many of the steps necessary to implement that program. He also found, however, that the program has not yet been fully implemented at least in part because of the severe understaffing in mental health care.

Finally, the magistrate judge found substantial evidence of defendants' deliberate indifference to the deficiencies in their system.[69]

Judge Moulds recommended a series of steps to correct constitutional deficiencies, including (1) the development of certain forms and protocols, (2) the appointment of a Special Master, and (3) the use of experts, as well as other remedial matters.

The crucial legal threshold, of course, is establishing post-*Farmer*[70] deliberate indifference.[71] After reviewing in some detail the eight points noted above, the district court stated:

[T]he evidence demonstrates that seriously mentally ill inmates in the California Department of Corrections daily face an objectively intolerable risk of harm as a result of the gross systemic deficiencies that obtain throughout the Department. The evidence also demonstrates that inmates have in fact suffered significant harm as a result of those deficiencies; seriously mentally ill inmates have languished for months, or even years, without access to necessary care. They suffer from severe hallucinations, they decompensate into catatonic states, and they suffer the other sequela to untreated mental disease.

Defendants' knowledge of the risk of harm to these inmates is evident throughout this record. It is equally apparent that defendants have known about these gross deficiencies in their system for years. The risk of harm from

---

[69] Coleman, 912 F. Supp. at 1295–1297 (citations and references omitted).

[70] Farmer v. Brennan, *supra* note 9. *See* discussion of deliberate indifference in Chapter 4.

[71] Judge Karlton strongly disagreed with the requirement of a subjective component here, believing that the application of cruel and unusual punishment is all that should be required. He does, however, apply the law as it is. Coleman, 912 F. Supp. at 1298 n.11.

these deficiencies is obvious to plaintiffs' experts, to defendants' experts, to defendants' consultants, to individual employees of the Department of Corrections in the field, and to this court. The actual harm suffered by mentally ill inmates incarcerated in the California Department of Corrections is also manifest in this record.[72]

In a touch of irony, the defendants' claim of lack of knowledge of the gross deficiencies in the system is found to be not plausible after five years of rigorous litigation, numerous reports to that effect, and even their own experts' conclusions.[73] Thus, one of the consequences of an unwillingness to settle in the face of powerful evidence is the accumulation of inferences of knowledge of facts and risks, which then contributes to a finding of deliberate indifference.

The findings quoted above stress the required harm (or pain) component, now and into the future, as well as the knowledge component as manifest, although usually inferred, in the record.[74] The state raised a number of objections to the findings, some of which Judge Karlton found bordering on unethical, none of which were persuasive. For example, defendants actually sought to exclude the deposition testimony of their own experts, raising it for the first time on appeal from the Magistrate to the District Court;[75] they argued that an injunction dealing with heat plans for inmates on psychotropic medication was improper; they wished to delay matters (perhaps three to four years) pending yet another study; and so on. Judge Karlton, writing about the heat plan, stated:

> The history of defendants' response to this issue demonstrates a recalcitrant refusal to address the serious issues underlying the preliminary injunction until forced to do so under pressure of this litigation. Sadly, the response in that specific context echoes throughout the record. Defendants have been confronted repeatedly with plain evidence of real suffering caused by systemic deficiencies of a constitutional magnitude. Their responses have frequently occurred only under the pressure of this and other litigation. Given that history, the court not only has no confidence that defendants will continue to adequately monitor inmates on psychotropic medication for risks from heat exposure, it regretfully concludes that without an order defendants are

---

[72] Coleman, 912 F. Supp. at 1315. The Court was impressed with an internal CDC memorandum which reads in pertinent part, "[T]the need to assess [inmates backlogged awaiting transfer for mental health services] is urgent. Seriously mentally ill inmates who do not receive needed treatment can worsen severely, losing most or all of their ability to function. Such inmates can also become suicidal or can pose significant risks to others or to the safety of the institution. In addition, the litigation facing the Department in this area, especially the Department-wide Coleman case, puts the Department at extreme liability risk if these inmates go untreated." One might describe this as a "killer memo" from the defendant's perspective.

[73] Coleman, 912 F. Supp. at 1317.

[74] The "seriousness" component of deliberate indifference is derived from McGuckin v. Smith, 974 F.2d 1050, 1059 (9th Cir. 1992). Judge Moulds used the six components in *Ruiz* for an acceptable prison mental health program, but referred to the *Balla* decisions recital thereof. *See* Balla v. Idaho, 595 F. Supp. 1558, 1577 (D. Idaho, 1984).

[75] Coleman, 912 F. Supp. at 1294. This is improper practice.

likely not to do so. The preliminary injunction presently in place will be made permanent for a period of three years.[76]

[a] Systemic Deficiencies—Chronic Understaffing

The judge's exasperation with the defendants is plain throughout the *Coleman* opinion. At another point he wrote that while he feels obliged to review the state's numerous objections, he does not want to obscure the real issue, a finding of systemic deficiency in the mental health care delivery system.[77] We will now review some of the specific factors and leave others (such as poor records and forced mediation) for discussion in later chapters of this book.

The size and competence of mental health staff is, of course, crucial. Relying on an earlier consultants' report, there was evidence that 732 mental health staff would be needed for an inmate population of 119,000, while the budget for 1992–1993 authorized only about one-half that number. The Department was running about a 25 percent staff vacancy rate as well.[78] Earlier studies on workload and expert testimony focusing on inordinate delays on access to care led to the conclusion that the defendants were "significantly and chronically understaffed in the area of mental health care services."[79]

The competence question is always a bit more difficult to handle than raw numbers and the opinion does not review the training, certification, and educational attainments of existing staff along with hiring criteria. As an aside, anyone litigating in this area, or an agency wishing to take stock of itself, would have to engage in such a review and analysis preferably as part of a broad quality assurance program.[80]

Whether a correctional system legally must have a quality assurance or management information system in place is a topic now hotly debated in the field. *Coleman* simply states that staff must be competent to provide adequate care and a system must be in place to remedy constitutional deficiencies. As I understand it, that is a quality assurance program.

[b] Inordinate Delays in Access

The California system is rife with inordinate delays in access to care, beginning with an unacceptable intake screening program and continuing with the assignment of inmates to various prisons in the system. There is evidence of some 400 inmates waiting up to three months to see a psychiatrist after initial screening, with wrist-cutting adopted as a means to expedite medication. There are backlogs of 300 to 400 inmates awaiting transfer to enhanced psychiatric facilities and hospital care, and similar evidence. Delays, of course, lead to exacerbation of the existing symptoms and needless suffering, both of which are at the very heart of Eighth Amendment concerns.

---

[76] Coleman, 912 F. Supp. at 1311. Persons taking psychotropic medication are very susceptible to heat, and in a warm climate especially there must be a heat plan in force.

[77] Coleman, 912 F. Supp. at 1304 n.28.

[78] Coleman, 912 F. Supp. at 1305 n.30.

[79] Coleman, 912 F. Supp. at 1306–1307.

[80] Coleman, 912 F. Supp. at 1307. The precise features of a management information system and quality assurance program are the types of things the Master undoubtedly is working out.

Curiously, I find no specific findings in the judge's opinion about the adequacy of available (or projected) bed/treatment space. There are asides regarding too much reliance, perhaps, on hospitalization, but no close analysis of the number and variety of treatment units required for adequate care. In my judgment, access, staff, and bed/treatment space are the "holy trinity" of the basic criteria when considering mandated mental health care in correctional settings.[81]

There are many more findings in *Coleman* that are addressed in other chapters. Here we have reviewed the factors showing deliberate indifference in this lengthy, bitterly contested case, which has cost millions to litigate, and which was litigated in the face of the defendants' experts actually aiding the plaintiffs' cause and studies that pilloried the system. Needless to say, *Coleman* resulted in a poisoned, post-litigation environment.

As this is written, battles are being waged over fees for the Master; implementation of "the plan," I am told, is perhaps 10 years away; and this all could have been settled, and peace reigned, long ago and for a great deal less money and personal costs. Obviously, there are occasions when a system appropriately may rigorously resist demands upon it and there are other times when the need to settle, to get on with the business at hand, is so obvious that resistance is terribly counter-productive.

[2] Unparalleled Excessive Force to Cause Harm—*Pelican Bay*

The second case in this sequence is *Madrid v. Gomez*.[82] Referred to now simply as the *Pelican Bay* case, it involved challenges to such a broad range of conditions that it encompassed virtually every facet of daily life in this remote, highly secure, supposedly state-of-the-art prison. In this instance I have opted to provide a summary of the findings on use of force, medical care, and mental health care. The situation at Pelican Bay was so extreme that to isolate mental health from the overall legally relevant environment would be to abandon the malodorous for the merely unacceptable.

The name Pelican Bay itself evokes images of birds wheeling overhead, romantic weekends by the sea, and the rugged beauty of a rocky shoreline. Pelican Bay, the prison complex, is indeed located on the seashore 363 miles north of San Francisco, but anyone familiar with the place, and surely anyone who reads the full opinion in *Pelican Bay* will quickly be disabused of anything resembling romance or beauty.

I have been studying prison and jail cases for a long time, and not since the now 30-odd-year-old cases from Arkansas, Alabama, and Mississippi have I read anything that compares with the practices found at Pelican Bay.[83] The Pelican Bay facility, which was constructed in 1989, does not present the horrifying and deteriorated physical conditions present in some older prisons involved in the first generation of prison litigation. However, it presents its own special brand of horrors.

Pelican Bay actually consists of three separate facilities. One houses about 2,000 general population, but maximum security, inmates; another is a small minimum secu-

---

[81] *See* the discussion about the Ohio litigation at ¶ 7.3[5] regarding how one large system approached this issue.

[82] 889 F. Supp. 1146 (N.D. Cal. 1995). This is a masterfully crafted, 137-page opinion.

[83] The discussion at ¶ 7.3[2] is a somewhat revised version of Fred Cohen, *"Pelican Bay": Excessive Force; Mental and General Health Care So Deficient as to Show Deliberate Indifference*, VI CORRECTIONAL L. REP. 81–91 (1995). (Reproduced with permission.)

rity prison that houses what appears to be about 200 inmates. The third facility, the "real" Pelican Bay that is the subject of this lawsuit, is actually a Special Housing Unit (SHU) for inmates described as "the worst of the worst."

Plaintiff's experts were awed by the level of force at Pelican Bay. The highly respected and experienced Vince Nathan testified that "in 18 years of involvement with a number of the most repressive and unlawful prisons in the United States, I have never observed the level of officially sanctioned unnecessary and excessive force that exists [here]."[84] Steven Martin, who with 20 years' prison experience is considered an expert and a scholar-author, testified that "the amount of force used in Pelican Bay cell extractions, as a routine practice, has been grossly excessive, utterly unbelievable, and without parallel in present-day American corrections."[85]

Medical care was described as "grossly inadequate." Mental health care was described as inadequate by the *state's expert* and the plaintiff's experts. Ultimately, the court characterized it as dramatically short of minimum standards.[86] We may recall that in *Coleman,* it also was the case that California's expert witnesses were less than helpful to the state's position.

Before specifically addressing the major areas of concern in this litigation, it should be said that California did not come away from the litigation entirely empty handed. The basic concept of a large SHU survived, and it was held that the Eighth Amendment may be violated only by the extended use of such a SHU for particularly vulnerable subgroups such as the mentally ill. The procedures for assigning prison gang members to the SHU for extended times was upheld, as was the use of force in certain inmate-to-inmate confrontations.

In an extraordinarily well crafted and balanced opinion, Federal District Judge Henderson found against the state on many instances of excessive force, the descriptions of which are crackling with pain, and he found against the state on medical and mental health care. He wrote that "the dry words on paper can not adequately capture the senseless suffering and sometimes wretched misery the defendant's unconstitutional practices leave in their wake."[87]

We turn now to an examination of the three major subjects of this litigation: excessive force, medical care, and mental health care.

[a] Excessive Force Litany

One of the more revolting episodes in the use of force litany involved staff treatment of a mentally ill inmate. The judge's description speaks for itself:

Vaughn Dortch, a mentally ill inmate, suffered second-and-third degree burns over one-third of his body when he was given a bath in scalding water in the prison infirmary. The week before the incident Dortch bit an officer. Dortch had also created a nuisance by smearing himself and his cell with his own

---

[84] Madrid, 889 F. Supp. at 1176.
[85] Madrid, 889 F. Supp. at 1214.
[86] Madrid, 889 F. Supp. at 1280.
[87] Madrid, 889 F. Supp. at 1166–1167.

fecal matter. Although there was a shower near Dortch's cell, which would have provided a more efficient method of cleaning Dortch than a bath (assuming Dortch was uncooperative), the officers instead forcibly escorted Dortch to a bathtub in the SHU infirmary, located some distance away in another complex.

According to Barbara Kuroda, the nurse on duty at the infirmary, a Medical Technical Assistant arrived shortly before Dortch, and was asked if he "want[ed] part of this bath," to which he responded, yes, he would take some of the "brush end," referring to a hard bristle brush which is wrapped in a towel and used to clean an inmate. Five or six correctional officers then arrived with Dortch. Although a nurse would normally run the water for a therapeutic bath, Dortch's bath was managed solely by correctional staff.

Kuroda later observed, from her nurse's station, that Dortch was in the bathtub with his hands cuffed behind his back, with an officer pushing down on his shoulder and holding his arms into place. Subsequently, another officer came into the nurse's station and made a call. Kuroda's unrebutted testimony is that she overheard the officer say about Dortch, who is African - American, that it "looks like we're going to have a white boy before this is through, that his skin is so dirty and rotten, it's all fallen off." Concerned by this remark, Kuroda walked over to the tub, and saw Dortch standing with his back to her. She testified that, from just below the buttocks down, his skin had peeled off and was hanging in large clumps around his legs, which had turned white with some redness. Even then, in a shocking show of indifference, the officers made no effort to seek any medical assistance or advice. Instead, it appeared to Kuroda that the officers were simply dressing Dortch to return him to his cell. When Kuroda told them they could not return him in that condition, Officer Williams responded, in a manner described by Kuroda as disparaging and challenging, that Dortch had been living in his own feces and urine for three months, and if he was going to get infected, he would have been already. Williams added, however, that if Kuroda wanted to admit him, she could do the paperwork. Dortch then either fell, or began falling, to the floor from weakness, at which point Kuroda had Dortch taken to the emergency room. Although Dortch was not evidencing any pain at this point, Kuroda testified that this did not surprise her. Because severe burns destroy the surrounding nerve endings, the victim does not experience any pain until the nerves began to mend. Dortch was ultimately transported to a hospital burn center for treatment.[88]

To convey a sense of Judge Henderson's evenhandedness, he found the record unclear as to whether the officers intended the severity of the burns or knew the precise temperature of the water. The officers, did, however, act in a punitive fashion, according to the judge.[89]

---

[88] Madrid, 889 F. Supp. at 1167.
[89] Madrid, 889 F. Supp. at 1161, 1163, 1172, 1175, 1182.

Beyond this shocking incident, the record reveals a pattern of staff assaults on inmates, punitive cagings under harsh conditions (e.g., keeping naked inmates outside in telephone booth-sized cages in freezing rain), the use of "hog-tying" restraints (fetal restraints), needless force in conducting cell extractions (tasers, gas guns, mace, etc.), and a dubious, but found to be constitutional, policy of deploying and using firearms.[90]

There are documented accounts of other horrifying incidents: an inmate cowering in his cell being first struck with a disabling high-voltage taser gun and then beaten so badly that a piece of his scalp detached; an inmate whose jaw was fractured while he was defending himself from an attack by staff; another inmate described as powerfully built, who had his upper-left arm snapped in two while putting his hands through a narrow food slot to be cuffed up; still other inmates who were beaten while restrained and lost their teeth, had their eyes cut, and so on.[91]

The record on cell extractions is equally shocking; incident after incident of needless, injury-causing cell extraction practices were described. The judge found that the pattern of extractions demonstrated that they were conducted to inflict punishment and serious pain for minor violations.[92] The critical point is that the incidents just recounted were not isolated acts by renegade officers. Instead, they were part of a general pattern that seemed countenanced by administrators who failed to monitor or correct it and who could not explain the total neglect of care. In light of this, the court had little difficulty finding a general pattern of excessive force for the very purpose of causing harm.

[b] "Stunning Indifference" to Health Care Needs

Because a regime that so brutalizes its captives is not likely to have a sophisticated and responsive medical system, it is not surprising that Pelican Bay did not have a single physician on staff when it opened. Physicians were, of course, later hired: first in a ratio of 1:1166, and then 1:780. The CDC's official policy is 1:550 inmates.

Important triage functions were performed by untrained medical personnel. Medical records were described as "nothing short of disastrous." Screening functions either were not done or were done poorly.

In addition, the key to adequate medical care—the inmate's ability to quickly access the available care—was missing. Pelican Bay's system, like California generally and Arizona, was rife with delay. In one dramatic case, a misdiagnosis by an inadequately trained aide resulted in an inmate's death. Medical testing also was subject to serious delays. There were no protocols for handling emergencies, and quality control procedures were nonexistent.

The court held that:

[D]efendants had abundant knowledge of the inadequacies of medical care at Pelican Bay. That knowledge is reflected in records of complaints by prison-

---

[90] Madrid, 889 F. Supp. at 1162–1166.
[91] Madrid, 889 F. Supp. at 1173.
[92] Madrid, 889 F. Supp. at 1214.

ers and staff, audit reports, and budget requests that allude to the risk of harm (and of litigation) if conditions are not ameliorated. We find that by failing to remedy deficiencies in health care, Pelican Bay's medical staff did not merely create a risk of harm to inmates but practically insured that inmates would endure unnecessary pain, suffering, debilitating disease, and even death. We agree with Dr. Start's opinion that "[t]he fact that a new prison with contemporary medical facilities nevertheless could be so shockingly deficient in its provision of health care is a terrible indictment of the defendants, and compellingly illustrates what is their stunning indifference to the health care needs of the prisoners at Pelican Bay."[93]

[c] Exacerbation of Existing Mental Illness

After reading about the force employed and the quality of medical care at Pelican Bay, the abysmal quality of mental health care will come as no surprise. Despite quickly becoming a repository for the violently mentally ill, Pelican Bay opened without a psychiatrist on staff. For about two years, it functioned with either one or two psychologists. After two-and-half years, a resident psychiatrist was hired. That psychiatrist lasted about a month.

Recall that inmate Dortch, who was scalded by staff, was characterized as a mentally ill inmate. One might well imagine that he annoyed the staff by smearing feces on himself. However, anyone familiar with prison mental health knows that this is not uncommon behavior. Special training and sensitivity is required to deal adequately with it. If such training ever was performed, one would surely want to review the content and techniques employed.

The plaintiffs relied on two well-regarded mental health experts who spent considerable time on the case, while the defendants inexplicably relied on a single, albeit highly regarded expert, who spent only a total of two days at the prison and reviewed a scant 11 inmate files. The defendant's expert stated that he could not represent to the court that the mental health system was adequate or met constitutional standards. And that was the best that could be said about the system.

It is vital to note that by virtue of its mission, Pelican Bay houses the most assaultive and psychiatrically disabled of California's inmates. Problematic, psychiatrically disabled inmates were transferred to the SHU, thus creating a "psychiatric ghetto." While I know of no case law that would constitutionally forbid such a policy of concentration, it surely signals the need for full mental health staffing, special training, and clear policy and procedure on access to care. Pelican Bay failed in each of these areas and perhaps dictated the very terms of its utter failure by initially adopting the highly dubious policy of concentrating the housing of seriously mentally ill inmates under seriously deficient physical conditions.

In the three basic areas required for constitutional compliance—staff, access, and treatment space—Pelican Bay received flunking grades. Indeed, the prison was found constitutionally deficient in virtually every area of concern.

Driven by *Coleman* and this lawsuit, the number of clinicians climbed to nine,

---

[93] Madrid, 889 F. Supp. at 1217–1218.

with additional positions allocated but not yet filled. With 1,000 to 1,500 high-need inmates confined in the SHU, none of the experts thought that even this litigation-driven increase was adequate.[94]

One of the more dramatic findings relates to the use of the SHU itself. The court determined that those who were seriously mentally ill deteriorated in the SHU, and that other inmates who had not previously displayed symptoms developed mental illness. Judge Henderson found that:

> While the deficiencies in defendants' system of mental health care are felt prison-wide, the problems are especially severe in the SHU. At least three factors have contributed to this result. The first stems from the very mission of the SHU, which is to house the most dangerous and disruptive inmates. Since inmates suffering from mental illness are more likely to engage in disruptive conduct, significant numbers of mentally ill inmates within the California prison system are ultimately transferred to the Pelican Bay SHU. Second, the severity of the environment and restrictions in the SHU often cause mentally ill inmates to seriously deteriorate; other inmates who are otherwise able to psychologically cope with normal prison routines may also begin decompensating in the SHU. Third, defendants chose to provide only limited psychiatric services to inmates in the SHU. Aside from the obvious limitations which ensue from lack of staffing, defendants have made no effort to provide appropriate treatment for inmates suffering from major mental disorders. The prison is not equipped to provide any inpatient or intensive outpatient treatment or involuntary medication. At the same time, delays prevent urgently needed care from being provided off-site as well. While inpatient care can be provided elsewhere, in 3 to 5 days, this does not help the inmate who needs immediate hospitalization or involuntary medication. And, it was found that transfers to institutions where inpatient care was available took 1-3 months, which effectively denies adequate treatment for seriously ill inmates needing immediate intensive outpatient treatment. In some cases, security concerns preclude any transfer at all.[95]

In short, the defendants created a prison which, given its mission, size, and nature, would inevitably result in an extensive demand for mental health services, perhaps more so than at any other California facility; yet at the same time they scarcely bothered to furnish mental health services at all, and then only at a level appropriate to a facility much smaller in size and modest in mission.[96]

[d] Other Conditions Giving Rise to Eighth Amendment Violations

Given deficient staff, inadequate treatment space (although surprisingly, as was the case in *Coleman* as well, little is made of this), and seriously impeded access to

---

[94] Madrid, 889 F. Supp. at 1223.

[95] Id.

[96] Madrid, 889 F. Supp. at 1235–1236.

the limited care that there was, these problems alone result in an Eighth Amendment violation. There is, however, much more. The problems listed below, while only briefly explored here, also arise in *Pelican Bay*.

1. *Inadequate screening.* The screening (initial identification) system either did not exist or functioned inadequately (e.g., inmates with mental illness were not identified until they had a psychiatric episode).

2. *Inadequate staff training.* The staff was not adequately trained to identify problems. The system depended on post-admission referrals that often were based on the untrained eye of uniformed staff. Whatever else these officers were trained for, their training did not include sensitivity to mental illness.

3. *Sketchy psychiatric records.* Psychiatric records were found to be sketchy. Important information was missing, maintenance was poor, the records were difficult to access, and clinical inputs were not integrated.

4. *Delayed transfers.* Without inpatient or intensive mental health care available, Pelican Bay relied on transfers to Atascadaro, Vacaville, or the California Men's Colony. By now, readers will not be shocked to learn that delays of up to three months were noted.

5. *Treatment protocol.* Involuntary psychiatric treatment protocols simply did not exist.

6. *Housing.* Mental health staff had no input into housing decisions concerning mentally ill inmates. While housing always is a delicate matter of security versus treatment concerns, this prison never overtly faced the issue.

7. *Suicide.* There was no suicide prevention program in place, although there was the omnipresent training program. (It does seem that no matter how inadequate the mental health services, every prison and jail at least nods at suicide prevention and response training.)

The court reviewed the scope of the extraordinary deprivations associated with the near total isolation imposed by the fortress-like SHU and compared Pelican Bay with such facilities as Marion, Illinois and Florence, Arizona. Accepting the social science and clinical literature on the effect of such deprivations on the marginal and mentally ill inmate, the court found that:

> [M]any, if not most, inmates in the SHU experience some degree of psychological trauma in reaction to their extreme social isolation and the severely restricted environmental stimulation in the SHU. As one court recently observed in connection with an Illinois state prison, "the record shows, what anyway seems pretty obvious, that isolating a human being from other human beings year after year or month after month can cause substantial psychological damage, even if the isolation is not total." *Davenport v. De Robertis*, 844 F.2d 1310, 1313 (7th Cir.), *cert. denied*, 488 U.S. 908 (1988). It is also equally clear that although the SHU conditions are relatively extreme, they do not have a uniform effect on all inmates. For an occasional inmate, the SHU environment may actually prove beneficial. For others, the adverse psychological

impact of the SHU will likely lead to serious mental illness or a massive exacerbation of existing mental illness. . . .

Certain inmates who are not already mentally ill are also at high risk for incurring serious psychiatric problems, including becoming psychotic, if exposed to the SHU for any significant duration. As defendants' expert conceded, there are certain people who simply can[no]t handle a place like the Pelican Bay SHU . . ..[97]

Judge Henderson stated that "federal courts are not instruments for prison reform, and federal judges are not administrators."[98] He cannot possibly mean his first thought, and by immediately appointing a Special Master in this case, he took a step toward judicially administering Pelican Bay. I suspect that the judge meant that federal courts should not consciously undertake institutional reform and certainly should not substitute a judicial preference for an administrator's allowable preference. On administration, he presumably means that even with a Special Master the court should not micro-manage any state agency, including a prison.

This judge cannot be accused of overstepping his boundaries, of being gleeful to discover a facility in need of his "reformist" efforts, of being anything other than cautious and judicious in his approach to a record that invited hyperbole of the most passionate sort. This deadly quiet opinion marches efficiently from one point to another, from one parade of horribles to the next. Indeed, it is most effective in its understatement.

Judge Henderson, of course, was required to decide the medical and mental health issues using the "deliberate indifference" test mandated in *Farmer v. Brennan*.[99] As we have learned, deliberate indifference is defined as the equivalent of criminal recklessness. That is, the defendants must have consciously disregarded a substantial risk of serious harm to the plaintiffs' health or safety. The court held that the plaintiff-inmates met this burden with respect to the treatment of both physical health needs and mental health needs.

Once again displaying an excess of caution, the judge actually measured California's culpability by the demanding *Farmer* standard and also by the even more demanding standard related to the official use of force: the "willful, wanton and malicious test."[100] Under either approach, Pelican Bay's inadequate mental health care violates the Eighth Amendment.[101]

I realize there is a certain stridency in my own tone in writing about, and in trying to analyze, the decision in *Pelican Bay*. As I stated at the outset, it has been a long time since I have been exposed to anything as systemically shocking as this. With ref-

---

[97] Madrid, 889 F. Supp. at 1279. The Human Rights Watch recently released a report entitled "Cold Storage: Super-Maximum Security in Indiana" (1997), attacking conditions in Indiana's super-maxi facilities. They were especially critical of the impact on prisoners who are mentally ill. The report urges the legislature to bar the use of extreme measures of isolation for the mentally ill and those at risk of serious injury to their mental health.

[98] Madrid, 889 F. Supp. at 1279.

[99] *Supra* note 9. *See* discussion of this test in Chapter 4.

[100] Madrid, 889 F. Supp. at 1279; *see also* Whitley v. Albers, 475 U.S. 312 1986).

[101] A colleague asked me, perhaps facetiously, "Why didn't the judge put the place in the hands of a receiver and order everyone fired?" He wonders how a code of employee silence and brutality took root so quickly and determinedly, especially when officials had a chance to establish their own culture in a

erence to Vince Nathan and Steve Martin's earlier quoted statements, I am not alone. The California prison system is in a general state of crisis. With plans for another 15 to 20 prisons unfolding, and with California's prison budget now exceeding its higher education budget, one hopes that *Pelican Bay* is a wake-up call.[102]

[3] Severe Mental Illness—Care Obligations in *Casey v. Lewis*

Casey v. Lewis[103] is the *Coleman* of Arizona. This, too, was a bitterly contested case, although it lacked some of the more sophisticated trappings of *Coleman* such as its professionally polished studies, "big name" experts, and a prior history of well-regarded research and treatment. Like *Coleman*, *Casey* is almost a textbook example of the violation of the treatment rights of inmates with serious mental illness. The court found the Arizona system deliberately indifferent with regard to staffing, screening, programming, excessive use of lock-down, medication monitoring, physical facilities, access to care, and male-female parity. Access to care, staffing, and physical resources—essentially, appropriate treatment space—are the "holy trinity" of correctional mental health care, and Arizona received failing grades in each.

After a facility-by-facility analysis and establishing the legal framework (to which I will return), District Judge Muecke made textbook findings that I will allow to speak at length for themselves:

B. Mental Health Care System

1. *Problems with the Mental Care System*

> Plaintiffs have established numerous problems with the mental health care system provided to inmates by the ADOC. Plaintiffs allege that as a result of these problems, the mental health care system is inadequate to treat the serious mental health care needs of inmates.

a. Intake Procedure

> ADOC lacks a system and the psychiatric staff to identify and evaluate female inmates with serious mental illnesses when those inmates come into the system. Thus, at the Perryville Santa Maria Unit, unqualified security staff must identify seriously mentally ill inmates so that they may receive treatment.[(1)]

> Defendants have also implemented a policy that provides for reviews of

---

new place like Pelican Bay. The answer is probably that the administrators did establish their culture—and that its fruits stain the pages of this decision. To return briefly to the scalding of inmate Dortch: how did we learn how this inmate was tortured? Only through a nurse who was on duty, Barbara Kuroda. What courage it took for this employee to speak up, and what must be her current fate.

[102] In fact, the California prison system is in a state of crisis that would have been unimaginable 20 years ago. For example, the FBI reportedly is investigating the Corcoran facility, where officers have killed seven inmates since the facility opened in 1988. California prison guards have killed 37 inmates in the past decade, which is more than three times the total of all other federal and state prisons.

[103] 834 F. Supp. 1477 (D. Ariz. 1993). This is a 106-page opinion.

inmates' medical records upon transfer to other facilities. However, such reviews are not routinely performed due to shortages of staff. Therefore, seriously mentally ill male and female inmates do not receive treatment until they request treatment or regress to the point that security staff recognize the illness or lock them down for the behavior caused by the mental illness. Thus, mentally ill inmates are unable to make their problems known to staff and their constitutional rights are violated.

(1) Defendants have established a routine intake procedure for males at Alhambra. In addition, Alhambra has the mental health staff available for the system.

b. Staffing Problems

Defendants fail to provide sufficient mental health staff to diagnose and treat the serious mental health needs of inmates. The experts agreed that shortages of mental health staff existed within the facilities. Alhambra is the only facility that has a full-time psychiatrist. The facilities also lack an adequate number of psychologists. Special Program Unit (SPU) lacks sufficient staff to consistently provide all of the programs to the inmates that need such programs. The staff shortage has also resulted in no 24-hour mental health coverage at SPU. Further, there is always a waiting list of inmates for admission to SPU.

Because of inadequate numbers of staff, the existing staff cannot adequately treat inmates and their constitutional rights are violated.

The staffing problem exists partly because the Legislature will not fund positions and partly because ADOC has vacancies in positions that have been funded. Defendants admit that they have requested further staff and could function better with those staff. However, lack of funding is not a defense to eighth amendment violations.

c. Programming for Mentally Ill Inmates

ADOC provides insufficient mental health programming at SMU (Special Management Unit). At the time of filing of this action, little or no programming existed at SMU. At the time of trial, more programming existed. However, programming for mentally ill inmates at SMU is still insufficient. The level system behavioral modification program is implemented by security officers who are untrained both in mental health care and in the program they are implementing.

d. Delays in Assessment and Treatment

Inmates with serious mental health needs experience unacceptable delays in assessment and treatment. Assessments by mental health professionals should be made within a few days of an inmate's complaint of hearing voices or feeling anxious, tense or "about to explode." Because of staffing shortages and inadequate policies, such assessments are rarely made by mental health personnel. Rather, inmates' mental health care is consistently delayed. Inmates experience delays in assessment, treatment and in commitment to mental hospitals. (Baker Ward for men or ASH [Arizona State Hospital] for women). When inmates act out because of their mental illness, they are locked down. While in lock-down, inmates generally wait months for transfer to the mental hospital. In addition, it may take several days to a week for inmates to see a psychiatrist.

e. Inappropriate Use of Lockdown

Rather than providing timely mental health care to inmates with serious mental illnesses, defendants lock down those inmates in the higher security facilities such as SMU and CB6 for men and Santa Maria detention for women. Yet, both the plaintiffs' and defendants' experts agreed that it is inappropriate to house acutely psychotic inmates in segregation facilities for more than three days. Further, psychiatrists employed by the ADOC, Drs. Pera and Fernandez, admit that lockdown damages, rather than helps, mentally ill inmates. Despite their knowledge of the harm to seriously mentally ill inmates, ADOC routinely assigns or transfers seriously ill inmates to SMU, CB6 and Santa Maria lockdown. The inmates remain in lockdown for more than three days. In most cases, the inmates are locked down because of the behavior resulting from their mental illness. In addition, the inmates are locked down on orders by security rather than medical personnel. According to Dr. Pera, economic conditions prevent this system from being changed.[2] Even when inmates are referred for transfer to mental health facilities, they remain in lock-down for more than three days awaiting a transfer. Defendants also discharge inmates with serious mental illnesses from Baker Ward and send them to SMU. Because they are assaultive or a behavior problem, they are not eligible for treatment at SPU.

(2) Budgetary constraints are not a defense to liability for deliberate indifference to inmates' serious medical care needs. Jones v. Johnson, F.2d 769, 771 (9th Cir. 1986); Harris v. Thigpen, 941 F.2d 1495, 1509 (11th Cir. 1991).

During lockdown, inmates are provided improper mental health care or no mental health care. Inmates with serious mental illnesses who have been locked down should receive almost immediate psychiatric follow-up. Further, inmates that are locked down should be seen daily by a psychiatrist. Daily checks by nurses are insufficient care and according to Dr. Garcia are "not treatment at all." Yet, while in lock-down for their mental illness prisoners are not seen by a psychiatrist either immediately for an evaluation or daily. Rather, security staff, or possibly the nurses, perform health and welfare checks. Most of the logs from the facilities indicate that security staff performs the welfare checks on most inmates.

The most egregious example of the inappropriate use of lockdown is H.B., who was locked down for approximately 11-1/2 months in Perryville Santa Maria Unit. During that time, she was seen only nine times by the psychiatrist. During her 10 years of custody, she has been locked down numerous times for her mental health condition. Yet, she has never received immediate psychiatric evaluation. During these times, she was actively psychotic and hallucinating. H.B. is not the only inmate in this condition in Santa Maria. Dr. Pera testified that at any one time there were several seriously mentally ill inmates locked down in Santa Maria.

Defendants also inappropriately house self-abusive inmates in SMU, despite their knowledge that SMU is not suitable for self-abusive inmates. Since the filing of this action, defendants have established the self-abuser pod. However, they have not established that the pod is appropriately staffed or fully operational. At the time of trial, the psychiatric nurse at SMU did not know if there was any specific programming for the unit, other than the fact that the individuals received more attention.

This use of lockdown as an alternative to mental health care for inmates with serious mental illnesses clearly rises to the level of deliberate indifference to the serious mental health needs of the inmates and violates their constitutional rights to be free from cruel and unusual punishment.

f. Medication

Defendants do not properly monitor the prescription of psychotropic medication. Despite the expert testimony that inmates on psychotropic medication should be seen on a monthly basis, ADOC prescribes, continues and discontinues psychotropic medication without face-to-face evaluations by the psychiatrists.

Defendants also have no system or method to insure that inmates take medications. The only policy presented at trial requires the nurse to talk to the inmate to convince him or her to take the medications and then note the refusal on the chart. The policy does not require that the inmate be seen by a psychiatrist.

2. Constitutionality of the Mental Care System

The mental health care provided at B Ward, Flamenco and Alhambra meets the serious mental health needs of inmates. If defendants had adequate staff to provide all of the programs at SPU,[3] the mental health care would meet with serious mental health needs of the male inmates incarcerated in that facility. Unfortunately, SPU also lacks staff and the capacity to house all of the inmates that qualify for such care.

However, the overwhelming evidence establishes that the defendants are deliberately indifferent to the serious mental health care needs of the inmates in other institutions throughout the state. Seriously mentally ill inmates are housed in most[4] of the other facilities. Such inmates tend to be concentrated in the lockdown facilities of SMU, CB6 and Santa Maria in Perryville. Those facilities have inadequate mental health staff and programming for inmates. Rather than providing mental health care for these inmates, security staff lock inmates down for prolonged periods of time because of the behavior that is the result of their mental illnesses. During lockdown the inmates are provided little or no mental health care by psychiatrists or psychologists.

(3) After the filing of this action and Dr. Newkirk's (plaintiff's expert) review of SPU, that facility eliminated the socialization chair and pens. Use of these treatments rises to the level of deliberate indifference to the serious medical/mental health care needs of inmates. Placing inmates into unshaded pens outside the Arizona heat without bathroom facilities and water is clearly cruel and unusual punishment in violation of the eighth amendment.

(4) Defendants presented evidence that seriously mentally ill inmates are not housed in the work camp type of facilities such as Yuma. The fact that the lack of staff and programming is partially a result of lack of funding from the Legislature is not a defense to these constitutional violations.

Because of the lack of staff and programming, inmates do not have "ready access" to mental health care. Severely mentally ill inmates cannot make their needs known to mental health staff. Untrained security staff assess inmates' mental health. Further, referrals to B Ward, Flamenco and ASH are not "reasonably speedy." Inmates remain in lockdown for days to months waiting for transfer to these facilities. Although psychological staff request transfers, they are not consistently carried out by security staff. All of these problems result in deliberate indifference to inmates' serious mental health needs such that the inmates' constitutional rights to be free from cruel and unusual punishment are violated by the defendants.

The system for female inmates is even worse than for male inmates because female inmates have no SPU or transitional facility. Rather, female inmates are returned to general population and are generally locked down for behavior caused by their mental illness. Sometimes, the lockdown reoccurs within 24 to 72 hours of return to general population. Seriously mentally ill female inmates are limited to the G Ward with its 15 to 17 beds or transferred outside ADOC to ASH. Even at G Ward, female inmates receive less programming than that provided to males.

The Court finds the treatment of seriously mentally ill inmates to be appalling. Rather than providing treatment for serious mental illnesses, ADOC punishes these inmates by locking them down in small, bare segregation cells for their actions that are the result of their mental illnesses. These inmates are left in segregation without mental health care. Many times the inmates, such as H.B., are in a highly psychotic state, terrified because of hallucinations, such as monsters, gorillas or the devil in her cell. Nor does it appear that H.B. is the exceptional case as seven to eight mentally ill women may be locked down at the Santa Maria Unit in Perryville at any one time and may remain there for months without care. In addition, such treatment is common for male inmates in other lockdown facilities or units in the state including SMU and CB6. The Court considers this treatment of any human being to be inexcusable and cruel and unusual punishment in violation of the eighth amendment of the Constitution.

EQUAL PROTECTION CLAIM

Plaintiffs also allege that defendants discriminate against female inmates in the delivery of mental health care in violation of the equal protection clause.

The equal protection clause states that no State shall "deny to any person within its jurisdiction the equal protection of the laws." Thus, all similarly situated persons should be treated alike. *City of Cleburne, Tex. v. Cleburne Living Center*, 473 U.S. 432 (1985). Gender based differences require a heightened standard of review. A party seeking to uphold dissimilar treatment based on gender must show an "exceedingly persuasive justification." *Kirchberg v. Feenstra*, 450 U.S. 455 (1981). To withstand constitutional challenges, classifications based on gender must serve as important governmental objectives and must be substantially related to achievement of those objectives. *Craig v. Boren*, 429 U.S. 190 (1976). Under this standard of review, female inmates must be treated "in parity" with male inmates.

Defendants clearly provide, because there are fewer women in the system, fewer mental health services for women than they provide for men within the prison system. In addition, the lack of these mental health services for women result in more egregious cases of deliberate indifference to the women's mental health needs.

For men, defendants provide a psychiatric hospital within the ADOC. Women are given access to the ASH, which is not within the ADOC. Inmates cannot remain at ASH during the period of incarceration unless they were found innocent by reason of insanity. Thus, women inmates are discharged after a short period of time, returned to general population and often again locked down. After September of 1991, women inmates can be involuntarily committed to G Ward. However, it is not a psychiatric hospital. At Flamenco, men are provided more advance programming and facilities than women. Men can progress in a phase program from the acute unit to the sub-acute unit and then into SPU or general population. Women of all levels are treated in G Ward. Men have better access to occupational therapy with more equipment and supplies. In addition, mental health activities logs indicate that men are offered more substantive programs such as computer training, communication training, stress management and anger control. However, at the same time, women are offered aerobics, board games, movies and "Women Who Love Too Much."

ADOC also has the SPU progressive unit for men, but no comparable unit for women. Thus, ADOC houses men with other men of similar functioning. However, women of all levels of functioning are housed together at G Ward. As a result, chronically ill women who are stabilized are returned to general population; act out when then are provided little or no mental health care; are locked down [sometimes within 24 to 72 hours]; remain in lockdown where they decompensate and eventually, after a serious delay, return to Flamenco or ASH. Yet, chronically ill men who are not assaultive are allowed to progress back to general population, through the SPU facility. Dr. Newkirk identified female inmates that needed long-term chronic care that could benefit from an SPU-type of unit for women.

Defendants argue that the additional units, like SPU, are necessary for men because they are more predatory, and more likely to pick on weaker male inmates. However, such considerations do not justify the unequal treatment in the provision of mental health care. The Court does not consider that the different care serves any "important governmental objectives" so that the disparity could be constitutional. Clearly, the unequal treatment results in even more egregious denials of mental health care for seriously ill female inmates violating those inmates' equal protection rights under the constitution in addition to their rights under the eighth amendment.

Defendants also argue that female inmates receive the same number of beds in mental health facilities in proportion to the number of inmates within the system. However, this argument ignores the very clear differences in care and the impact of that unequal treatment.[104]

Given the length of the opinion—106 pages—a two-page order, including medical and dental care issues, seems oddly mild. Basically, the judge gave the parties six months to work out procedures and remedies responsive to the deficiencies. To my knowledge, as of the latter part of 1997, a Master remained in place and much remained to be done.

Judge Muecke necessarily used a pre-*Farmer* test for determining deliberate indifference. Where serious medical or mental health needs are involved, then delays that cause substantial harm, denial of care, or intentional interference with medical judgment can establish deliberate indifference.[105] He is also of the view (a view now substantially in doubt)[106] that repeated acts of negligence may establish deliberate indifference.[107]

Access, he believes, is the key, and as I mentioned previously, I agree. While access is a dynamic concept, it requires at a minimum competent staff, a screening and referral system, and a plan to respond to emergencies.[108] In my view, needless delays in providing basic diagnosis and care will by definition always meet any pain/harm requirements. That is, to be seriously mentally ill (the legal threshold requirement) and

---

[104] Casey, 834 F. Supp. at 1547–1551. The ADOC is the Arizona Department of Corrections; SPU is its Special Program Unit and SMU is its Special Management Unit.

[105] Casey, 834 F. Supp. at 1543.

[106] *See* Brooks v. Celeste, 39 F.3d 125 (6th Cir. 1994).

[107] It would be more accurate now to say that repeated acts of negligence known to officials may establish the actual knowledge base required by *Farmer*.

[108] Casey, 834 F. Supp. at 1543–1544.

improperly denied care is always to suffer needlessly. The nature and extent of the suffering may be at issue, and the decision as to these factors will importantly affect the remedy.

In at least one case involving a medical problem, the court distinguished pain from suffering (conditions almost always dealt with in the conjunctive). For example, a person may have a condition, which if attended to could result in a cure or halt in progressive deterioration. However, that person may be given pain-killers instead of the medically available treatment that could cure or ameliorate the condition.[109] A mental health analogy to this is, for example, the prescription of massive doses of Thorazine, with no other care; this would "anesthetize" the inmate, relieving the pain but not the suffering.[110]

This analysis of pain and suffering is also useful to shore up some of the statements in the earlier cases (e.g., *Ruiz*) that psychotropic medication alone is not constitutionally adequate treatment. Judge Muecke is plainly of the view that programming of some sort is a required adjunct to properly monitored medication. I am certain he would accept group or individual therapy as readily as, say, an anger management group in meeting constitutional treatment requirements.

[4] Making Mental Health Care Delivery Work— *Austin v. Pennsylvania DOC*

Austin v. Pennsylvania Department of Corrections[111] (DOC) was the subject of yet another of these broad, class action lawsuits, but Pennsylvania's approach to the litigation was quite different than California's or Arizona's. The complaint was filed on November 27, 1990 and a settlement agreement was approved on January 5, 1995. The lawsuit involved constitutional claims about the use of force, medical care, AIDS, and mental health care. While the litigation ultimately was settled, it was also hotly contested—and not according to the California "scorched earth" school, but in the best tradition of advocacy.[112]

The record in *Austin* is not peppered with Pelican Bay-like incidents that appall the reader. On the other hand, the extensive discovery in this case created a record that made it expedient to settle and move on to the demanding task of making the mental health care delivery system work. And that is what the parties did in *Austin*.

What follows is Judge Du Bois' summary of the mental health provisions of the Stipulated Agreement, which is the product of this settlement:

---

[109] Logan v. Clarke, 119 F.3d 647 (8th Cir. 1997).

[110] Indeed, this was a fairly common practice in prisons and, among other things, Thorazine could mask the symptoms of tardive dyskinesia, which is largely irreversible (see description of this disease in Chapter 9, ¶ 9.3[2]. Today, doctors do the AIMS testing (Abnormal Involuntary Movement Scale) to check for involuntary movement while a person is medicated.

[111] 876 F. Supp 1437 (E.D. Pa. 1995). I served as a litigation consultant to the DOC for part of this litigation, although I took no part in settlement negotiations. I did visit all of the prisons subject to the lawsuit and its resolution.

[112] Linda Barrett, Francis Fillipi, and Pia Taggart represented that the DOC acted superbly on behalf of this client and that the local plaintiffs were represented by the best of the National Prison Project and outstanding legal counsel. The attorney fee awarded here was $1.4 million, half the fee they might have claimed.

In the area of mental health care, the Settlement Agreement is intended to provide substantive improvements in the availability and types of services for inmates and to increase quality control over mental health treatment decisions. To achieve this goal, the DOC has agreed not only to increase the number of beds available for on-site, therapeutic treatment but also to establish specific treatment standards which will be reviewed by an independent peer review committee. Plaintiffs' counsel will have the right to monitor the DOC's performance to ensure compliance with the mental health provisions of the Settlement Agreement.

Inmates in need of mental health care are currently assigned to Special Needs Units ("SNUs") and Mental Health Units ("MHUs"). These units are intended to provide on-site therapeutic bed space for inmates who are seriously mentally ill or who require short term commitment to a forensic facility. Placement in either unit requires the development of a treatment plan with specific criteria to address an inmate's particular mental health problem. Inmate access to the SNU is governed by DOC policy; MHUs are licensed and admission to such units is governed by state law.

The DOC has agreed nearly to double the number of beds in the SNUs from 450 to 800 and not to reduce the number of SNU beds unless the correctional institution population decreases. This expansion will alleviate the problem of placing inmates in Restricted Housing Units where treatment and other programs are far less accessible. Inmates placed on psychotropic medications will be evaluated at least once every six months for signs of tardive dyskinesia and, if such signs are detected, the inmate will receive necessary medical treatment. Individuals who refuse to take prescribed psychotropic medications will not be placed in administrative custody solely on the basis of a mental health diagnosis and refusal to be medicated with psychotropic drugs. The Agreement will also strengthen the programming provided to inmates in the SNUs.[113]

Resolution of the *Austin* case was done by a Stipulation of Dismissal without prejudice, which explicitly does not become a consent decree or other order of the court. With the dismissal, the federal court relinquished its authority over the case, so the plaintiff's recourse in the event of default appears to be limited to reinstituting the lawsuit.

The plaintiff's counsel were given certain monitoring authority and Dr. Jeffrey Metzner, their expert, was given permission to interview staff and review case files beginning June 30, 1995. In a sense, the matter ended with a light judicial touch, with the plaintiffs betting heavily on (1) the DOC's good will, (2) legislative appropriations adequate for the job, and (3) monitoring to provide sufficient compliance information.[114]

---

[113] Austin, 876 F. Supp. at 1450–1451. While class members objected to a perceived lack of confidentiality as to their mental health reports, insufficient mental health beds, and double celling, the judge rejected their objections, relying on subsequent review and monitoring.

[114] My personal view is that the agreed-upon monitoring should have been far more extensive and intensive, especially in the first two or three years.

[5] *Dunn v. Voinovich*: The Ohio Approach

Dunn v. Voinovich involved mental health care in the Ohio Department of Rehabilitation and Correction (ODRC).[115] The complaint was filed on October 6, 1993, and a 33-page Consent Decree approved by the Court in Cincinnati was filed on July 10, 1995. The time frame for this entire process was less than two years, and when compared with the cases just discussed, this is mercurial.

Soon after the lawsuit was filed, counsel for the plaintiff-class of inmates and for ODRC agreed to place *Dunn* on the inactive trial docket and thus suspend formal discovery proceedings.[116] The parties agreed to the appointment of an Expert Team to study ODRC's mental health delivery system, and after eight months the team delivered a highly critical report. Using a standard of "minimally adequate" rather than the legal conclusionary term of deliberate indifference, the Expert Team concluded that the defendants were seriously deficient in the following three basic areas of legally mandated prison mental health care:

- *Appropriate personnel*—Sheer numbers and appropriate training
- *Treatment/bed space*—Hospital, crisis, and chronic care
- *Access to care*—The dynamics of reaching available staff and appropriate treatment settings

Having found these deficiencies, and at the invitation of the defendants with the concurrence of plaintiffs' counsel, solutions were proposed. With regard to staffing, the report found that between 1990 and 1994 the prison population increased from about 31,500 inmates to 40,253 (about a 28 percent increase), while the ODRC clinical staff went from 59.3 full-time equivalent positions (FTEs) to 61.21 (a slight decrease in the ratio of inmates to treatment providers).

There were only 9.35 FTE psychiatrists in place. The Expert Team proposed that 25.5 FTEs would be minimally adequate, and this was eventually accepted by the parties. There were 65.49 FTE clinical positions filled on June 15, 1994, with a total of 246.4 clinical positions recommended and ultimately agreed on as needed. All of these projections were based on a prison population of 40,253.[117]

In summary, the Expert Team's other basic findings, none of which were challenged formally or informally by the plaintiffs or the defendants, were as follows:

1. Inadequate intake screening for mental illness, which allowed many inmates with serious mental illness to enter the system undetected and unevaluated, and to remain untreated.

---

[115] No. C1-93-0166 (S.D. Ohio July 10, 1995). This Decree is not published nor have there been any post-Decree matters creating a judicial history.

[116] In *Austin*, the DOC hired extra staff just to coordinate the plaintiffs' extensive discovery demands, amounting to millions of pages of documents and requiring a large room in the central office just to store the material.

[117] In addition to mandating the hiring of this number of additional staff, the decree provides for further increases in staffing and bed space proportionate to increases in the inmate population, based on a "precise formula by which to operationalize the . . . adjustments." *See* Consent Decree, §§ XV(b), XV(c).

2. An inadequate referral system that regularly resulted in behavior symptomatic of mental illness being treated as misconduct. This, in turn, led to inmates with serious mental illness being placed in control (or, segregated) settings where virtually no mental health care was available. These inmates found themselves in a cycle of clinical deterioration and disciplinary actions from which it was difficult to escape.

3. The paucity of residential care and crisis beds, and the underuse of psychiatric hospital beds at Oakwood Correctional Facility, the only psychiatric hospital beds available to inmates, also contributed to the use of disciplinary confinement settings for the housing of inmates with serious mental illness.

4. A shortage of clinical staff along with highly restrictive criteria and conservative decision making served to create daunting obstacles in gaining access to psychiatric care.

5. Psychiatric care, when available, was frequently limited to psychotropic medication. In this connection, the Expert Team found that monitoring of inmates receiving medications was dangerously inadequate and in certain instances— for example, the lack of monitoring of lithium blood levels—could be life threatening.

6. In addition to a lack of treatment staff and space, the system was lacking in appropriate space for mental health care providers and support staff. This compromised safety, confidentiality, and appropriate care.

7. Inmates with serious mental illness were often found to be simply locked down with no care, no activities, and no opportunity to simply walk about, exercise, or breathe fresh air.

8. Training of personnel, especially security staff, concerning the signs and symptoms of mental illness, the side-effects of medication, and the like, was essentially lacking. Because security staff so often serve as gatekeepers to mental health care, this deficiency was viewed as highly significant in limiting access to mandated mental health care.

9. Mental health records were found to be seriously deficient, compromising efforts at continuity of care. Individual treatment plans, progress notes, and comprehensible diagnoses were systematically absent.

10. Guidelines on the most basic aspects of mental health care were not followed. This was traced to ongoing friction and role confusion between the Ohio Department of Mental Health, which provided psychiatric care, and the prison system, which provided psychological services.

11. All the earlier studies, which pointed out similar problems and solutions, had not spurred remedial action.[118]

---

[118] Many other issues were addressed as well, including suicide prevention, involuntary medication, use of restraints, and the probate process.

In sum, the Expert Team found a prison system whose population had expanded dramatically and that included a large and growing number of inmates with serious mental illness. In the absence of hard, epidemiological data, the parties agreed to use an estimate of 10 percent of the overall population as seriously mentally ill, acknowledging also that female inmates (usually with clinical depression) might exceed that estimate, perhaps by 50 percent.

[a] Omission vs. Commission

The exploding prison population and the decrease in resources led to the situation where minimally adequate care for inmates with serious mental illness was not being provided. The team reported many instances of needless deterioration, compromises to institutional security, and some life-threatening situations for inmates with serious mental illness. Unlike some findings made in the California litigation, these findings did not emanate from evidence of intentional infliction of harm.

Indeed, the report emphasized that a number of mental health specialists and security staff were utterly frustrated by their inability to systematically recognize and provide care even for those inmates whose bizarre behavior was plainly indicative of mental illness. Dunn, then, resolved itself into a case of systemic inability to meet minimal conditions of acceptable mental health care. In a legal sense, inability translates into omission rather than commission. The omission is culpable if it is violation of a duty, and here the duty was clearly established.[119]

Certainly by now, readers have detected recurring themes in this type of litigation, although the intensity and manner of resolution vary. The Expert Team in *Dunn* uncovered systemic problems but no brutality and, perhaps most surprising, no organizational denial or blame shifting.

One review of correctional law litigation has described the various litigation eras as moving from the "brutal practices" model of the 1950's and 1960's (although plainly not having Pelican Bay available) to a doctrinal, collaborative, implementation model.[120] Naturally, when a lawsuit is settled the opportunity for doctrinal innovation or development is lost with the settlement. The Expert Team's Report provided the basis for resolution once the defendants agreed to accept it, which they quickly did. The groundwork was laid for a collaborative, implementation model and this is precisely what has occurred.

Negotiations on the Decree went quickly and even as they were ongoing, Ohio officials were meeting to lay the groundwork for political acceptance, budgetary assurances, and institutional support for what promised to be a very different delivery system. ODRC would move to take over mental health cases from a sister agency and with Director Reginald Wilkinson's leadership, ODRC was poised to deliver.

---

[119] The description of the Expert Team report is drawn largely from an even more complete discussion in Fred Cohen and Sharon Aungst, *Prison Mental Health Care: Dispute Resolution and Monitoring in Ohio*, CRIM. L. BULL. 299, 303–306 (1997). Reproduced with permission of Warren, Gorham and Lamont.

[120] Susan P. Sturm, *The Legacy and Future of Corrections Litigation*, 142 U. PA. L. REV. 639, 735–738 (1993).

[b] Highlights of Consent Decree

The *Dunn* Consent Decree tracks the findings of the Expert Team Report and it is quite detailed.[121] The list below simply highlights the Decree and offers some commentary.

1. One objective is to reduce the disabling effects of serious mental illness and enhance the inmate's ability to function in the general population.

2. Mental health care must be provided in the least restrictive environment, by the least intrusive measure professionally prescribed, and within a community mental health model. This has resulted in the creation of 13 clusters (or catchment areas), each with a single Residential Treatment Unit (RTU), a director, outpatient and crisis care.[122] One of the clusters is the mental hospital (Oakwood) used for inmate-patients.

3. Mandated care (e.g., beds and staff) may be adjusted upward or downward in response to population changes. A formula for doing so has been agreed to by the parties.

4. Intake screening and evaluation is mandated.

5. Inmate orientation to mental health services is mandated.

6. 246 FTE mental health staff have been agreed to (and defined) based on a prison population of about 40,000 inmates.

7. There are now about 5,000 more inmates, and adjustments have been made.

8. Some 25 psychiatrists, compared with 4.35 when the Expert Team conducted its study, are to be hired.

9. A specific number of hospital, RTU, and crisis beds was agreed to (830 beds).

10. Some 11 policies and procedures were to be developed and implemented with participation of the Monitor and plaintiffs' counsel.

11. Disciplinary proceedings must take into account an inmates' mental health status.

12. Extensive staff training was agreed to along with an evaluation of the results.

13. A monitor was appointed for the presumptive 5-year life of the Decree. The monitor has been provided with adequate staff as well as total access to staff and facilities.[123]

---

[121] Substantive provisions of the Decree are reproduced in Appendix D of this book.

[122] ODRC and the Monitor's office prepared a description of an RTU; given the dearth of literature on point, this description is reproduced in Appendix C of this book.

[123] For a complete description of monitoring and implementation, *see* Cohen & Aungst, *supra* note 119, at 313–319.

[6] *Carty v. Farrelly*: Systemic Failure

The Virgin Islands' correctional system has been under judicial siege for many years. In its latest incarnation, *Carty v. Farrelly*,[124] the government was found in contempt for failure to adhere to a number of undertakings expressed in a 1994 Consent Decree.

With regard to mental health services, Federal District Judge Brotman found that the intake screening for mental illness was not consistently done and that inmates who showed signs of mental illness were simply locked down instead of being hospitalized.

Speaking more broadly, Judge Brotman found:

> Failure to house mentally ill inmates apart from the general prison population also violates the constitutional rights of both groups. See *Tillery v. Owens*, 719 F. Supp. 1256, 1303-04 (1989), *aff'd*, 907 F.2d 418 (1990). Commingling the two populations increases the level of tension among all prisoners and endangers the well-being of the mentally ill who suffer from retaliation. Id. Moreover, prisoners with psychiatric conditions are entitled to treatment by qualified, professional mental health staff. *Id. at 1302-03*. Indeed, lack of a mental health facility can support a court's decision to close the jail. *Inmates of Allegheny County Jail v. Wecht*, 874 F.2d at 153.
>
> Mental health services at CJC do not exist. The facility does not have on-site mental health staff to identify systematically and regularly those prisoners with mental illness. As a result, prison staff, otherwise unqualified to assess properly mental illness, identify inmates who require mental health services. Even then, however, these inmates do not receive proper care. The Bureau of Corrections medical director works in St. Croix, is available only for telephone consultations, and prescribes medication for the prisoners via telephone without first examining the patient or reviewing the medical chart. Inmates are not transferred to local hospitals in emergency situations.[20] Generally, logbooks cataloguing the status of mental health referrals are not maintained. (Id.)
>
> Instead of segregating the mentally ill inmates from the general population, the CJC attempts to house the mentally ill together in clusters, often four to five inmates per cell.[21] Cluster 3, the formally designated holding cell for mentally ill pretrial detainees, is filthy and overcrowded.[22] Acutely psychotic inmates, housed in inhumanly close quarters, are extremely aggressive and dangerous, both to themselves and others, and engage in extreme violence. Between March and November 1996, two inmates were beaten into comas and suffered severe, permanent neurological damage as a result of inmate-to-inmate[23] violence. Indeed, the majority of inmate assaults occurs in Cluster 3, where inmates frequently beat each other and, in turn, are beaten by correctional staff. Moreover, correctional staff taunt the mentally ill inmates in

---

[124] 957 F. Supp. 727 (D. V.I. 1997).

Cluster 3, "rewarding" inmates by throwing cigarettes at them after instructing them to pull down their pants and hold their crotch, crawl across the floor, and do push-ups.

> *(20) Mental health beds at the local hospital are unavailable for the sole use of inmates.*

> *(21) Approximately 10% of the CJC population is maintained on psychotropic drugs, while an even greater number of prisoners requires mental health care.*

> *(22) Mentally ill prisoners are not always segregated from the general population. (Court Exh. 3, at 63, App. 1 at 10; Tr. at 81.) Some are commingled with other, non-mentally ill inmates in other cells and clusters.*

> *(23) The court notes that there is an equally prevalent phenomenon of violence inflicted on prisoners by CJC correctional officers.*

The CJC also lacks segregation cells for inmates who require restraints, seclusion, or close observation. To control disruptive mentally ill inmates, the defendants either lock down the prisoners with as many as four cellmates, or lock individual inmates into the "attorney visiting room," sometimes for time periods of three to six days. The attorney visiting room, however, is isolated completely from the staff and central patrol area, and does not have a toilet. Mentally ill inmates impounded in the attorney visiting room are given a plastic container in which to urinate. One inmate who was locked in the room for six days had to urinate and defecate on the floor.

The abominable treatment of the mentally ill inmates shows overwhelmingly that defendants subject inmates to dehumanizing conditions punishable under the Eighth Amendment.[125]

Obviously, the remedy called for in the face of such devastating findings will be expansive and expensive. The National Prison Project represents the plaintiffs and will be certain to pursue broad remediation.

¶ 7.4 INTERFERENCE WITH TREATMENT

[1] "Interference" vs. Deliberate Indifference

Deliberate indifference may be manifested in a variety of ways, such as treatment staff's negative reaction to a prisoner's needs, a staff's needless denial or delay in providing access to diagnosis or help, resources that are wholly inadequate to meet basic needs, a staff's interference with prescribed care, or even a staff's general attitude and conduct. When an inmate establishes that staff intentionally interfered with treatment already prescribed, the inmate almost certainly will prevail. The only substantial question likely remaining would be the nature and extent of the relief.[126]

On the other hand, where a record shows repeated medically acceptable interven-

---

[125] Carty, 957 F. Supp. at 738–739.

[126] *See, e.g.,* Tooley v. Boyd, 936 F. Supp. 685, 690 (E.D. Mo. 1996), on "attitudes"; Mandala v. Coughlin, 920 F. Supp. 342, 353 (E.D.N.Y. 1996), on denying a medically prescribed diet; and Pugliese v. Cuomo, 911 F. Supp. 58 (N.D.N.Y. 1996), on routine disregard of medical recommendations in the record.

tions and an inmate's repeated refusal of treatment, it is impossible (pre- or post-*Farmer*) to show deliberate indifference.[127] Where a course of treatment was recommended (e.g., surgery for a hernia) and where there were regular evaluations, even a two-month delay in performing the surgery was not viewed as inordinate.[128] This type of delay is not characterized as the type of interference with prescribed care that is central to this section.

Where interference or neglect is alleged, the defendant's best proof consists of "[m]edical records of sick calls, examinations, diagnoses, and medications [which] . . . rebut an inmate's allegations of deliberate indifference."[129] Those who view accurate and timely records as "something to get to" should reassess their views on this.

[2] Classic Case of Interference—*Jones v. Evans*

Jones v. Evans,[130] while not a mental illness case, is almost a textbook classic on how to plead and prove a case of "interference." Jones had undergone back surgery and wore a prescribed back brace before he entered the Georgia Prison System. On entry, an officer took away the brace and allegedly stated, "[T]he doctor . . . isn't running this place."[131] Jones was given a substitute brace that he claimed was inadequate, and was also provided with heat and whirlpool treatments after completing required work that his physician prescribed.[132]

Federal District Judge Hall provided the following analysis for the resolution of a defendant's motion for a directed verdict:

> In cases alleging a denial of care, or inadequate, negligently provided care, such as *Estelle*, assessment of deliberate indifference weighs equally with assessment of the plaintiff's serious medical needs. A defendant in such cases may show a lack of deliberate indifference by establishing he was generally attentive to the prisoner's needs. By contrast, *in cases alleging interference with prescribed care, a defendant has a more difficult task in showing the absence of deliberate indifference.* First, in some sense, a non-medical, prison employee's refusal to follow a doctor's instructions regarding a prisoner's care can almost never be characterized as other than deliberate and indifferent. Second, one episode of gross misconduct is not excused by general attentiveness to a prisoner's medical needs. Where a prisoner, as in this case, alleges that a guard disregarded written instructions and interfered with prescribed care, a question of gross misconduct is raised.
>
> A guard's interference with prescribed care does not establish a *per se* case of unnecessary and wanton infliction of pain violative of the Eighth Amendment. A plaintiff prisoner must still show that the interference was

---

[127] *See* Neville v. Irve, 990 F. Supp. 972 (N.D. Ill. 1995).

[128] Bellazerious v. Booker, 99 F.3d 1149 (10th Cir. 1996) (unpublished except for docket information).

[129] Banvelos v. McFarland. 41 F. 3d 232, 234 (5th Cir. 1995).

[130] 544 F. Supp. 769 (N.D. Ga. 1982). As noted, medical and mental health decisions are doctrinally interchangeable.

[131] Jones, 544 F. Supp. at 772.

[132] Jones, 544 F. Supp. at 774.

unjustified, and that serious medical needs were affected. Moreover, where a plaintiff makes a mixed allegation that interference with prescribed care marked the start of a course of inadequate treatment, *Estelle* leaves the door open to the argument by personnel not involved with the interference with prescribed care, that the extent and timing of care given subsequent to isolated incidents of interference can establish that those personnel were not indifferent to the prisoner's serious needs.

Nonetheless, in the context of a defendant's motion for summary judgment in a case alleging interference with prescribed care, or episodes of gross misconduct, a showing of general attentiveness is not sufficient to establish an absence of deliberate indifference in the conduct complained of. Assuming for purposes of the summary judgment motion that the alleged interference occurred, a court's primary attention must be on the second element of the *Estelle* test, the seriousness of the plaintiffs' medical needs. In such cases, whether interference with prescribed medical care rises to the level of cruel and unusual punishment depends upon the degree of pain or harm suffered by the prisoner as a result of the interference with prescribed care, the adequacy of alternative care if and when it begins, and whether the interference with care is an isolated event or one incident in a pattern.

Instead of addressing the issue of the plaintiff's serious medical needs during the period he was without his back brace and offering evidence on the factors listed above, the defendants treated this case as directly analogous to *Estelle,* and simply sought to show that the prison system was generally attentive to the plaintiff's needs. To this end, the defendants attempted to demonstrate that the plaintiff made numerous visits to the prison infirmary, and that along with other care, he received Motrin and other drugs, was on a program of whirlpool and heat treatments throughout his two-year incarceration, and eventually received a new back brace. As discussed, this approach is inadequate.

In order to counter the plaintiff's allegations in a case such as this, the defendants must demonstrate in their affidavits that even assuming misconduct for which they were responsible led to interference with prescribed care, the misconduct was not gross. In other words, the defendants must show that the interference with prescribed care was not only a temporary aberration in a pattern of attentive care, but also that it was *de minimis*. To make this showing, the defendants, in line with the second prong of the *Estelle* test, must give evidence that the plaintiff's medical needs were not serious, given the duration of the interference with prescribed care.[133]

Thus, *Jones v. Evans* establishes very clearly that prison officials should not lightly disregard an inmate's previously prescribed treatment. What is especially interesting here is that it is no defense to show that on other occasions care and attention were provided if the omission complained of caused needless pain and the underlying condition was serious. Of course, if there is an intervening medical or psychiatric diag-

---

[133] Jones, 544 F. Supp. at 775–776 (citations omitted) (emphasis added). The extended quote is provided in the belief that it is an exceptionally accurate and complete guide to the preparation and defense of this type of case; one need only substitute "medication" for the brace and a "psychosis" for the back problem.

nosis, then we do not likely face an interference question. Rather, we would have a new diagnosis and treatment that may face an independent test of constitutional acceptability. Where intervening professional judgment has been exercised, correctional officials normally should be comfortable in their reliance on it.

On facts similar to *Jones v. Evans* in the post-*Farmer* world of deliberate indifference, would a similar result be reached? Most assuredly, yes. The factual knowledge base in *Jones* could not have been more clearly established. While the extent of risk to be drawn from this knowledge might be arguable, recent back surgery and a medically prescribed brace certainly strongly suggests, at the least, a risk of needless pain and a delay in healing. In my view, one of the clearest cases for showing deliberate indifference is the willful interference with clinical orders by non-clinical personnel.

[3] Prescribed Medications Discontinued

Willful interference with clinical orders was also the complaint in *Steele v. Shah*.[134] The plaintiff had been provided with Prozac and Tofranil while confined in Florida's Polk Correctional Institution. He was described as labile and potentially suicidal, but when he was transferred to the Orange County Jail, awaiting trial, only his rudimentary treatment plan accompanied him.

After an extremely brief encounter with the plaintiff and with no apparent explanation or effort to obtain relevant records, Dr. Shah, the defendant-psychiatrist, discontinued the prescribed medication. The plaintiff went without his medication for about six months. While he was able to show "suffering," he did not attempt suicide or have a major breakdown.

In reversing summary judgment for Dr. Shah, the circuit court held:

In this circuit, it is established that psychiatric needs can constitute serious medical needs and that the quality of psychiatric care one received can be so substantial a deviation from accepted standards as to evidence deliberate indifference to those serious psychiatric needs. See Greason v. Kemp, 891 F.2d (11th Cir. 1990). In Greason, reviewing the denial of summary judgment on qualified immunity grounds, we held that there exists a "clearly established right to have [one's] psychotropic medication continued if discontinuance would amount to grossly inadequate psychiatric care." Id. at 834 n.10. In that case, the evidence as forecast in the summary judgment record would have supported a jury finding that a prison psychiatrist had abruptly discontinued a prisoner's psychotropic drugs on the basis of a visit of a "few minutes" and without reviewing the prisoner's medical file or doing a "mental status examination" and that had he reviewed the file, he would have seen that the prisoner was a serious suicide risk. We concluded that on those facts, a jury would have been entitled to find that the private doctor afforded the prisoner grossly inadequate care and "that he realized he was doing so at the time," thus exhibiting deliberate indifference to the prisoner's needs. Greason, 891 F.2d at 835. See also Waldrop v. Evans, 871 F.2d 1030, 1034-35 (11th Cir.

---

[134] 87 F.3d 1266 (11th Cir. 1996).

1989) [FN2] (holding, where a prisoner was deprived of lithium, that summary judgment was precluded by a genuine dispute between experts on the question whether the doctor's acts constituted legitimate medical practice or either gross incompetence or the deliberate choice of an easier but less effective course of treatment).[135]

Parenthetically, the *Greason* and *Waldrop* cases referenced in this opinion are pre-*Farmer* decisions, and in analyzing their continued vitality, the court here reasoned that there surely was subjective awareness in *Greason* and almost as surely in *Waldrop*.[136] Thus, their specific holdings remain intact and are very important precedential decisions in this area.

To the extent that *Steele v. Shah* might have been decided or analyzed differently, we would have encountered such language as that used in *Williams v. Kearne*:[137] "[M]ere disagreements in professional judgment, over a course of treatment, are not the basis for deliberate indifference."[138] On *Steele's* record, however, showing no authentic clinical interview, diagnosis, or review of relevant records, this type of care is, in fact, interference with continuing treatment, albeit by a professional who did not act professionally.

Steele includes an interesting point not touched on by the court but explored in more detail in Chapter 10: the extent of Dr. Shah's deliberate indifference in failing to request the plaintiff's records. Steele had no medical records at the jail, but the rudimentary treatment plan accompanying his transfer did outline the course of drugs prescribed at Polk. The initial jail screening was perfunctory. Under *Farmer v. Brennan,* did Dr. Shah have a duty to inquire further?

Again, although it was not addressed, this is not a situation in which Orange County Jail officials had no relevant knowledge about the detainee. They knew he was undergoing treatment for a mental disorder. In my view, this fact alone should be a trigger for acquiring further information, and most certainly before prescribing a dramatic change in care. Dr. Shah's action, then, was the equivalent of "turning one's back," which is very different from the problem of determining what mental health information should be obtained. We will have occasion to further explore this knotty problem in Chapter 14 on suicide.

¶ 7.5 DELAY IN/DENIAL OF ACCESS TO TREATMENT

In addition to the willful interference problem just discussed, denying or willfully impeding access to medical and psychiatric services is looked on with extreme disfavor by the courts. In *Balla v. Idaho State Board of Corrections,*[139] the federal district court was sharply critical of Idaho's access procedures. Idaho inmates were required to file a written request for medical services, which in turn would initiate medical staff review. The court was skeptical about this procedure and the attendant practices and

---

[135] Steele, 87 F.3d at 1269.
[136] Steele, 87 F.3d at 1269 n.2.
[137] 940 F. Supp. 566 (S.D.N.Y. 1996) (one of the numerous decisions to so hold).
[138] Id.
[139] 595 F. Supp. 1558 (D. Idaho 1984).

stated: "A system which does not respond to written requests for medical attention cannot possibly be construed as affording access to, nor being responsive to, complaints about the health care system."[140]

The court found that a combination of inadequate staff, poor training, insufficient hours, and the absence of written procedures amounted to considerable evidence of deliberate indifference.[141] We have seen many instances in which a failure of resources may be viewed as a form of denial of access to required care. *Balla,* however, is a case in which one might stipulate to the presence of adequate human and physical resources, but also determine that the dynamic of access—the only point that really matters here—is impeded.

In other cases, the courts have condemned a pharmacists' refusal to fill prescriptions written by a doctor[142] and a nurse's refusal to give pain medication and to change drugs as ordered by a doctor.[143] Even where medically or psychiatrically indicated care is not available in-house, concerns about security, staff availability, or transportation cannot impede access to such care, especially when an emergency exists.[144] That is, while correction agencies are free to elect where they will provide for mandated care, once a decision is made to "go off campus," the same officials cannot say "we don't have a bus." One authoritative work states, "Courts have long recognized that denial of access to a physician for diagnosis of a serious ailment or one causing persistent pain, or an unreasonable delay in affording access, constitutes an unconstitutional denial of medical [and mental health] care."[145]

[1] Access Components

Unlike the concrete quality of physical and human resources, access is a process that at times consists of a number of seemingly disconnected components. In a very real sense, access begins with intake screening and evaluation; it proceeds to some reasonable form of inmate orientation on how to access available care; it involves training the staff to recognize symptoms of mental illness and to know the availability of resources; it involves rounds in segregation for the safety of ill inmates and others; and it includes a written and/or oral mechanism by which inmates may gain ready access to care.

Certainly any correctional system that has the above components in place and sees to it that they are coordinated and actually work, will never have to be concerned about deliberate indifference in the systemic sense of access denials. Individuals, of course, may perform in renegade fashion and block access, but the system will be insulated from liability.

---

[140] Balla, 595 F. Supp. at 1567.

[141] Balla, 595 F. Supp. at 1568. The court ordered the preparation of an "access" plan within 90 days.

[142] Johnson v. Hay, 931 F.2d 456, 461 (8th Cir. 1991).

[143] Boretti v. Wiscomb, 930 F.2d 1150, 1154–1155 (6th Cir. 1981).

[144] *See* Arnold ex rel. H.B. v. Lewis, 803 F. Supp. 246, 257 (D. Ariz. 1992) (H.B. is the same inmate referred to in Lewis v. Casey, *supra* note 43); Kaminsky v. Rosenblum, 929 F.2d 922, 927 (2d Cir. 1991) (failure to follow-up on need for emergency hospitalization).

[145] B. JAYE ANNO, PRISON HEALTH CARE: GUIDELINES FOR THE MANAGEMENT OF AN ADEQUATE DELIVERY SYSTEM 36 (N.I.C. 1991) [hereinafter Prison Health Care]. This is an excellent and comprehensive reference work.

The *Coleman* decision discussed earlier in this chapter is representative of the recent, major decisions on access to mental health care. The *Coleman* court stated:

> The magistrate judge found that "there are significant and unacceptable delays" in inmate access to mental health care at each level of the mental health care delivery system as it exists in the CDC. Defendants object to these findings insofar as they are based on the opinion testimony of experts and contradicted by "percipient witness caregivers." Defendants also argue that there was no finding by the magistrate judge that the delays caused harm to any individual inmate. Finally, defendants argue that there was no finding by the magistrate judge as to whether the delays are a result of deliberate indifference by the defendant.
>
> The constitutional requirement that defendants provide inmates with "a system of ready access to adequate medical care" means simply either ready access to physicians at each prison or "reasonably speedy access" to outside physicians or facilities. In addition, there must be an "adequate system for responding to emergencies."
>
> At the outset, the court notes that the previous findings with respect to the inadequacies in screening and staffing, standing alone, render inescapable the conclusion that mentally ill inmates' access to care within the CDC is unconstitutionally delayed. Additionally, the evidence before the court plainly demonstrates substantial delays in access to mental health care for inmates housed in the California Department of Corrections.
>
> The Scarlett Carp Final Report highlighted delays in access to necessary care as a deficiency in the present mental health care system. It identified a "major problem" with access to acute inpatient hospitalization, and a "backlog of cases awaiting transfer to Enhanced Outpatient Program due to the limited number of beds available in designated institutions."
>
> Beyond the 1993 report there was extensive testimony concerning delays in access to necessary care at every level. (In February 1992, the waiting list to see a psychiatrist after initial screening was over 400 inmates at the reception center at Wasco State Prison; delays lasted up to three months and had "escalated to the point where inmates were cutting their wrists just to receive medication"); (In 1991 and again in 1992, there were backlogs of 300–400 inmates awaiting transfer to enhanced outpatient psychiatric programs at California Men's Colony or California Medical facility); (delays of up to several months in transfer to Atascadero State Hospital for inpatient hospitalization.).
>
> Defendants' objections to the magistrate judge's findings in this regard are without merit. Because the evidence demonstrates that there are delays everywhere within the system and that those delays result in exacerbation of illness and patient suffering, a violation of the objective facet of the test for violation of the Eighth Amendment has been demonstrated.[146]

It is of interest that Judge Karlton first indicates that the deficient screening prac-

---

[146] Coleman v. Wilson, *supra* note 67, at 1307–1309 (E.D. Cal. 1995) (citations omitted).

tices alone would support a finding of a denial of access. It seems likely that he would agree with my earlier description of the component parts of access and quite possibly find that a major deficiency in any component, and obviously a systemic breakdown, would be denial of access.

Corrections officials who have any doubts about their system of access to mental health care should act to allay those doubts. Doing so before the lawyers come calling to ask the same questions after filing a complaint is a far less expensive undertaking.

[2] Co-Pay and Access

Ken Faiver, in his excellent new work on correctional health care,[147] has a subsection entitled "Co-payment—A Strategy to Limit Access: Charging Inmates for Health Care." The title is both descriptive and evaluative. That is, co-pay is hardly likely to be a revenue enhancer for jails or prisons, and indeed the costs of accounting and collecting likely will exceed the revenue produced.[148] Co-pay is, however, likely to impede or even deny access to care, especially self-referred early clinical evaluation and interventions.

Is co-pay defensible as a technique to purge medical and mental health caseloads of malingerers? Is co-pay a handy teaching device to instill responsibility, to force inmates and detainees to make the same cost-benefit analysis required of free persons?

With regard to charging for health care services in general, no ready answers to these, or to other vital questions, are available. In one sense the problem is a bit easier with mental health care, since only Florida[149] appears to have mental health co-pay in its prison system. In an interview with a Florida official, I learned that inmates are charged only for self-initiated, nonemergency referrals. On gaining access to a mental health treatment program, on-going treatment is not subject to co-pay.[150] Interestingly, about 10 percent of all Florida inmate grievances are said to be related to such co-pay.

Fifteen states were found to allow for medical co-pay; while Louisiana allows for co-payment[151] for services rendered by a psychiatrist, no state other than Florida appears to have any provision allowing for mental health co-pay. The official position of the National Commission on Correctional Health Care (NCCHC) is that no charges should be made for mental health care, including any for drug abuse and addiction.[152]

---

[147] Kenneth L. Faiver, Health Care Management Issues in Corrections (1998), p.114.

[148] Faiver, *supra*, p. 120. I questioned one corrections official about plans for co-pay and indicated my position on its seeming futility. He said, "Well, Fred, it's like boot camps. Just because we all know it doesn't work, doesn't mean we won't do it." And so it goes.

[149] Fla. Crim. Pro. & Corrections, Title XLVII, Ch. 945-6037(d)(7), allowing for waiver of the fee when an inmate is referred by a designated employee.

[150] The official asked not to be named, but I have no doubt of his or her veracity and knowledge. The waiver provision is said to be liberally employed.

[151] La. Rev. Stat. 15, §705(3)(b) (1997). There is no reference to mental health services as such.

[152] N.C.C.H.C., Position Statement: Charging Inmates a Fee for Health Care Services (adopted March 31, 1996).

At the moment, co-payment for medical care appears to be gaining momentum, while co-payment for mental health services has barely emerged. We might ask whether it is inherently unconstitutional for a prison, or jail for that matter, to initiate a fee for access to a mental health care program. The answer would have to be this: while it may be exceedingly poor policy and counterproductive, the policy and practice are not inherently unconstitutional. The only significant question is whether mentally ill inmates or detainees are substantially impeded from, or denied access to, required mental health care. The scattering of cases on point support this analysis.[153]

I personally suggest that jurisdictions think long and hard about the adoption of co-pay for mental health care. The first issue to face is: just exactly what will co-pay accomplish? If it is to purge existing caseloads and remove at least some secondary gain from malingering, there are other methods which do not carry the seeds of interfering with those who have genuine needs.

Mental health staff surely can systematically reassess in-patient populations and participate in the transfer decisions possibly thereby generated. In facilities with dormitory housing for the general population, being "mad" or "bad" are the two handiest ways to obtain privacy or safety. This is a structurally driven problem that co-pay will not cure.

Staff should be encouraged to make the early referral, and members of this inherently poor population rife with multiple disabilities should be encouraged to seek help. Malingering and secondary gain exists in the free world and co-pay will not likely eliminate self-serving attitudes and behaviors in prison. Prisoners need not be asked to choose between deodorant or stationary and a mental health assessment and possible co-pay.

¶ 7.6 A SAMPLING OF CASES UPHOLDING AVAILABLE CARE

I must again emphasize that defendants prevail in far more lawsuits than they lose. One recent study categorized prisoners' lawsuits as either "win nothing," "win little," or "win big."[154] The overwhelming majority of prisoners have won nothing (94 percent); in 4 percent of the cases prisoners have won little, through stipulated dismissals or undetailed settlements; and 2 percent of cases have resulted in trial verdicts, with less than half of the verdicts (i.e., under one-half of one percent) resulting favorably for the plaintiffs.[155] After reading the above discussions on *Coleman, Pelican Bay,*

---

[153] In Reynolds v. Wagner, 128 F.3d 166 (3rd Cir. 1997), the inmates brought several consitutional challenges to the fee-for-services program initiated in Pennsylvania. Among them were violation of the 8th and 14th Amendments and of the Due Process Clause. The court found none of the arguments persuasive. The inmates had not shown that the facility was deliberately indifferent to their serious medical needs. Scott v. Angelone, 980 F.2d 738, 1992 WL 354598 (9th Cir. 1992, unpub.), involved an assertion that the inmate had been denied due process because the Nevada Department of Corrections had not provided him a hearing before deducting funds from his inmate trust account. The court stated that "[d]ue process requires only 'such procedural protections as the particular situation demands.'" Id. at 4. The court held that Scott had enough notice of the billing procedure. *See also* Gardner v. Wilson, 959 F. Supp. 1224 (C.D. Ca. 1997); Woods v. Graves, 1997 WL 298458 (D. Kan. 1997, unpub.); Mourning v. Correctional Medical Services of St. Louis, 692 A.2d 529 (N.J. 1997).

[154] ROGER A. HANSON & HENRY W.K. DALE, CHALLENGING THE CONDITIONS OF PRISONS AND JAILS: A REPORT OF SECTION 1983 LITIGATION (B.J.S., 1995).

[155] Hanson & Dale, *supra* note 147, at 36.

Austin, Dunn and the other cases, readers may well have the impression that prisoners simply file such lawsuits and await a settlement or verdict. Obviously, this is not true.

It is true that plaintiffs have won a fair number of medical and mental health care cases, especially the all-encompassing class action variety.[156] When plaintiffs have prevailed, the pre-resolution record was so damning, the harm so pervasive and obvious that it was no surprise. Here, we review a sampling of reported cases in which the defendants prevailed.

[1] *Hendrix v. Faulkner*

In an important decision from the early 1980's, the Indiana State Prison (ISP) was found to provide adequate levels of on-site and off-site psychological care for that prison's mentally disordered inmates.[157] According to the chief psychologist, he personally saw about 150 inmates per month and spent 80 percent of his time counseling. He testified that there were group therapy sessions for sex offenders and inmates with special adjustment problems.

A grant provided therapeutic services for inmates on self-lockup, and an outside consultant conducted a stress and relaxation therapy group two days per week. In addition, psychotherapy groups were run by a consulting psychiatrist.[158] Mentally ill inmates were transferred to Westville Correctional Institution, which had a program consisting of psychotropic drugs, group and individual therapy, milieu therapy, and recreational therapy.[159]

Although the troubling theme of desirable (not attained) versus constitutional (easily attained) runs through this extensive opinion, ultimately the existing level of mental health care was upheld. The availability and use of an acceptable off-site treatment facility may have tipped the balance in favor of the state.

The cases generally do not reflect a strong judicial preference for on-site or off-site services, although some of the decisions divide the analysis along those lines. And there is good reason for doing so. Suppose that a hypothetical jurisdiction—one not yet encountered—decides that all psychological or psychiatric services will be provided away from the site of the prison.[160] A question would then arise concerning the emergency case, the inmate with a sudden, acute, and perhaps life-threatening episode. There should be no doubt that such an inmate has a right to immediate, and perhaps life-sustaining, care and that such a right almost certainly calls for some kind of on-site care.[161]

---

[156] No precise figures are available, but text statement is based on conversations with leading attorneys in this field.

[157] Hendrix v. Faulkner, 525 F. Supp. 435 (N.D. Ind. 1981), *aff'd in part, vacated and remanded on the issue of costs*, 715 F.2d 277 (7th Cir. 1983), *cert. denied*, 468 U.S. 1217 (1984).

[158] Hendrix, 525 F. Supp. at 495–496.

[159] Lock-up and use of the yard have been known to receive the "hyphen approach" as in the recreation-therapy.

[160] For a description of five service patterns prevailing in correctional mental health care, *see* Ingrid D. Goldstein, et al., *Mental Health Services in State Adult Correctional Facilities* 231, 232, in MENTAL HEALTH, UNITED STATES, 1992 (Ronald W. Manderscheid & Nancy Anne Sonnerscheim, eds. 1992).

[161] Cf. Schmidt v. Wingo, 499 F.2d 70, 75–76 (6th Cir. 1974).

In *Grubbs v. Bradley*,[162] inmates successfully challenged many of the conditions in 12 of Tennessee's penal institutions, but the court upheld the state's provision of mental health care.[163] It was determined that while on-site care was not extensive, most inmates suffering with serious mental disorders were identified and transferred to the DeBerry Correctional Institute for Special Needs Offenders, a maximum care facility housing about 275 inmates.[164] The full-time mental health staff at DeBerry consisted of two clinical psychologists, two psychological examiners, six psychiatric social workers, five counselors, and one nurse clinician. Another 90 hours of professional services were obtained from outside professionals.[165]

Although the court lamented the paucity of on-site care and believed that there was room for improvement, it felt constrained to find that the care provided met minimum constitutional standards. In other words, the "deliberate indifference" standard had not been breached.

[2] *Canterino v. Bland*

The plaintiffs in *Canterino v. Bland*,[166] involving inmates at the Kentucky Correctional Institute for Women (KCIW), won a significant overall victory in court by demonstrating unconstitutional disparities between the male and female prisons on such matters as (1) overall restrictions, (2) vocational, educational, and job opportunities, and (3) the general allocation of resources and benefits. The inmates did not prevail, however, on their claim concerning inadequate medical and psychological care.[167]

A report prepared by the Kentucky Department of Education had earlier concluded that out of 189 female inmates, 144 should be classified as "emotionally disturbed" for the purpose of planning the vocational education program.[168] A consulting physician testified that depression and anxiety were major problems and that he prescribed psychotropic medication for 33 to 50 percent of the female population.[169] Other treatment at KCIW consisted of a visit once a week by a mental health team from a newly opened Psychiatric Center, psychiatric evaluations for parole purposes by a consultant, some counseling by a psychologist and the chaplain, and a self-help program called rational behavior counseling.[170] Although the court indicated a concern about

---

[162] 552 F. Supp. 1052, 1130 (M.D. Tenn. 1982).

[163] Grubb, 552 F. Supp. at 1130.

[164] Id.

[165] Id.

[166] 546 F. Supp. 174 (W.D. Ky. 1982).

[167] For a complete view of subsequent actions in this matter, *see* Canterino v. Wilson, 562 F. Supp. 106 (W.D. Ky. 1983); Canterino v. Barber, 564 F. Supp. 711 (W.D. Ky. 1983) (gender based discrimination); Canterino v. Wilson, 644 F. Supp. 738 (W.D. Ky. 1986) (holding no liberty interest in work/study releases); Canterino v. Wilson, 689 F.2d 948 (6th Cir. 1989) (issues of court and library access); Canterino v. Wilson, 1989 WL 40131 (6th Cir. 1989) (unpublished, on the issues of court and law library access); and Wilson v. Canterino, 491 U.S. 991 (1989) (certiorari denied).

[168] Canterino, 546 F. Supp. at 200 n.22.

[169] Canterino, 546 F. Supp. at 200.

[170] Id.

the seriousness and extent of the psychological problems and the rather minimal care provided at KCIW, it nonetheless held that constitutional minima were obtained.[171]

[3] *Toussaint, Ferola,* and *Taylor*

In *Toussaint v. McCarthy,*[172] California's Folsom Prison escaped a constitutional challenge, but just barely. The plaintiffs were able to show isolated instances of neglect, but on the whole the circuit court upheld the district court's determination that Folsom provided almost all of the strictly necessary treatment, and on a timely basis.[173]

The circuit court clarified the difference between a good system and a constitutionally acceptable one:

> In sum, Folsom's health care conditions fall below medical standards. The fact that a given condition might constitute medical malpractice, however, does not necessarily mean that the condition constitutes cruel and unusual punishment . . . It is only deliberate indifference to serious medical needs that can offend "evolving standards of decency" in violation of the eighth amendment. However, the district court's failure to render the specific factual findings regarding the level of reliance on unqualified personnel requires a remand for entry of such findings.[174]

Ferola v. Moran[175] is an interesting example of how a system that is not in compliance with an order entered nine years previously on mental health care can successfully defend an individual complainant's suit for money damages. *Ferola* involves the Adult Correctional Institutions of Rhode Island which had been under the supervision of a court appointed Master since 1977.[176]

The 25-year-old inmate who filed suit had repeatedly manifested bizarre and aberrant behavior. He injured himself some 60 times and set fire to his cell. He also saw a prison psychiatrist about once a week for a couple of years and took prescribed drugs. The court found that the doctor did all that was possible to administer to Ferola's anti-social personality.[177] In short, "Ferola was not ignored however; in fact, there was almost solicitous concern for him."[178]

---

[171] Canterino, 546 F. Supp. at 215.

[172] 801 F.2d at 1080 (9th Cir. 1986), *cert. denied,* 107 S. Ct. 2462 (1987).

[173] Toussaint, 801 F.2d at 1111.

[174] Toussaint, 801 F.2d at 1113 (citations omitted). Rest assured that if a challenge to a system is upheld pre-*Farmer v. Brennan*, it would also be upheld thereafter. In *Toussaint*, the result may have turned as much on the state of the record as on findings supportive of the care.

[175] 622 F. Supp. 814 (D.R.I. 1985).

[176] *See* Palmigiano v. Garrahy, 639 F. Supp. 244 (D.R.I. 1986), in which Judge Pettine, who is also the judge in *Ferola*, finds the state out of compliance with the nine-year-old order.

[177] Ferola, 622 F. Supp. at 816.

[178] Ferola, 622 F. Supp. at 817. Ferola was successful on his claim relating to physical abuse as a result of being shackled to his bed for 20 hours, where he was denied use of toilet facilities for 14 hours. He was awarded $1,000 in damages.

In *Taylor v. Wolff,*[179] the Nevada Department of Corrections asked the court to find it in full compliance with a stipulated Agreement entered into in 1984. Judge Burns, while awkwardly amusing himself by reciting quaint parables, found that while Nevada had completed the steps necessary to create a state of the art mental health system, it was still not in full compliance because mental health unit patients were strip searched whenever they left their housing unit, which was two to four times a day, and this was expected to cause adverse psychological effects.[180] In addition, these inmates were locked down whenever staff entered the cell block, which also was viewed as anti-therapeutic.

Nevada was found to have a superb staff, new state of the art facilities, a state of the art computer tracking system, and to have adopted the appropriate revisions in rules, practices, and documentation. Judge Burns wondered aloud if 99 44/100 percent pure, as in Ivory Soap, was enough and he "set-up" Chief Justice Rehnquist, who once wrote that nobody ever promised inmates a rose garden. It is also true, of course, that nobody is entitled to promise them a jungle.[181]

Judge Burns rebuffed the idea that full compliance meant oversight concerning precisely how well various systems (e.g., tracking) were working. He did, however, continue the monitoring for at least a year to evaluate how security and mental health staff could avoid the negative psychological impact from the tight security described above.[182]

[4] Summary

This brief review and analysis of decisions finding adequate treatment for mentally disordered inmates highlights several distinct conclusions. First, the constitutional floor is relatively easy to meet. The cases echo the theme of generally unsatisfactory yet constitutionally acceptable levels of care—care that is below professional standards but constitutionally acceptable. Second, even with a minimally demanding standard for assessing mental health services, many jurisdictions failed either the federal constitutional test or, less frequently, a similar state law test. Reliance on psychotropic drugs alone, simple confinement or minimal group therapy alone, reacting only to crises believed to stem from mental disorders, heavy reliance on untrained or nonprofessional personnel, and obstacles to access to care are all lethal factors in a finding of unconstitutionality.

Each jurisdiction has a number of options available in formulating its mental health care policy. The distribution of on-site and off-site care, the ratio of various mental health professionals employed, and the reliance on various types of recognized treatment all are important examples of, shall we say, local option. There is, of course, no option to simply do nothing, to view all inmate requests as frivolous or manipula-

---

[179] 158 F.R.D. 671 (D. Nev. 1994); *see also* Crain v. Bordenkircher, 342 S.E.2d 422 (W.Va. 1986).

[180] Taylor, 158 F.R.D. at 673.

[181] Taylor, 158 F.R.D. at 674 n.4, using Atiyeh v. Capps, 449 U.S. 1312, 1315–1316 (1981). Why is it that judges seem at their worst when attempting to be humorous?

[182] Taylor, 158 F.R.D. at 674. Defendants' motion to terminate jurisdiction, vacate Consent Decree and dismiss was granted November 10, 1994. 158 F.R.D. 675 (D. Nev. 1994).

tive. The more that is done in advance of the maturation of a problem, the more insulated a facility or system is from successful legal challenge.

Available statistical and anecdotal data would have us believe that the number of mentally disordered inmates in any given system varies greatly. One suspects that the variance is more a result of research methods and individual perceptions than objective diagnoses or testing. It would be interesting for a court to be confronted by a claim of "no mental health care" to which the answer was "no mentally disturbed inmates." One envisions a subsequent battle of experts with one side finding all "bad guys" and the other finding only "mad guys."

Neither side would be correct and neither side could prevail. The parties would be remitted to do what should have been done earlier: clinical assessments and/or epidemiological surveys. Have no doubt, the seriously ill are there and must be treated.

Systems that wait for the lawyers to call before doing some self-examination and change are simply courting disaster. Corrections' typical reactive approach to problems is particularly unwise where inmate claims tend to receive a fair hearing, where there may be much needless suffering, and where badly handled litigation poisons the post-litigation environment.

Chapter 8

Substance Abuse Programs and Rehabilitation

¶ 8.1 SUBSTANCE ABUSER STATUS VS. CRIMINAL CULPABILITY

In *Marshall v. United States*,[1] the Supreme Court considered a challenge to the Narcotic Addict Rehabilitation Act of 1966[2] insofar as the act excluded from discretionary rehabilitative commitment, in lieu of penal confinement, addicts with two or more prior felony convictions. Possibly the most persuasive argument for the excluded class of inmates was that the statutory classification had little or no relevance to the purpose for which it was made, and that the two-felony exclusion rule would irrationally exclude some addicts most in need of, and most likely to profit from, treatment.

The Supreme Court agreed with the court of appeals that there was no fundamental right to rehabilitation from drug addiction at public expense after conviction of a crime and that there was no suspect classification in the statutory scheme.[3] This meant that the act had to pass only a rationality test, and the majority thought it rational for Congress to exclude those with two prior felonies on the strained rationale that they might be more disruptive and less amenable to treatment.[4]

Marshall stands as a major barrier, then, to any constitutional claims brought by narcotic addicts or alcoholics to rehabilitative care after conviction and confinement. It is appropriate to pause here and ask why a drug addict or an alcoholic does not have at least the same constitutional claim to treatment extended to the mentally ill?

---

[1] 414 U.S. 417 (1974).
[2] 18 U.S.C. §§ 4251–4255.
[3] Marshall, 414 U.S. at 421–422.
[4] Marshall, 414 U.S. at 428–429.

In *Robinson v. California*,[5] the Supreme Court determined that it was cruel and unusual punishment to convict and criminally punish a person for his status as narcotic addict. Counsel for the state conceded that narcotic addiction was an illness, citing *Linder v. United States* to support this view.[6]

Five years later, in *Powell v. Texas*,[7] the Court dealt with the question of whether it was constitutionally permissible to punish a chronic alcoholic for being drunk in a public place. The Justices apparently saw the potentially explosive implications of the expansion of the disease concept and elected to halt the logical push outward from *Robinson*. A plurality of the Court refused to concede that alcoholism was a disease and distinguished *Robinson* on the basis that in *Powell* there was conduct (being drunk in public) whereas in *Robinson* there was none.[8]

This is not the occasion for any detailed analysis of these decisions. *Robinson* and *Powell* may be read as deciding that it is unconstitutional to punish a person for having a disease, at least where the state concedes the existence of a disease, but it is permissible to punish for criminal conduct a person who has a disease. *Robinson* does seem to turn on the Court's acceptance of narcotic addiction as a disease, while *Powell* is extremely cautious about characterizing alcoholism as a disease. Justice White, in concurring and providing the swing vote, stated that, "the alcoholic is like a person with smallpox, who could be convicted for being on the street but not for being ill, or, like the epileptic, who could be punished for driving a car but not for his disease."[9] Justice White upheld the conviction based on the state of the record and not an express or tacit rejection of alcoholism as a disease.

¶ 8.2 CONCEPT OF SUBSTANCE ABUSE AS DISEASE

[1] High Prevalence Among Inmates

However these complex decisions ultimately are read, the problems they deal with arise in the shadowy world of criminal responsibility. The concept of disease surely is not clarified. Thus, while *Robinson and Powell* cannot be ignored in this work, neither are they central, especially since the *Estelle v. Gamble*[10] standard for medical care requires a serious disorder and, at least for some individuals, there remains room to debate alcoholism and addiction on the seriousness scale.[11]

---

[5] 370 U.S. 660 (1962).

[6] Robinson, 370 U.S. at 667 n.8 (*citing* Linder v. United States, 268 U.S. 5 (1925)), which recognized addicts as diseased for the purpose of receiving treatment).

[7] 392 U.S. 514 (1968).

[8] Powell, 392 U.S. at 532.

[9] Powell, 392 U.S. at 550. In Traynor v. Turnage, 485 U.S. 535 (1988), the Court dealt with the question of whether certain types of alcoholism could be treated as "willful misconduct," which thereby meant that certain alcoholic veterans would not be able to claim educational benefits. The case did not directly decide whether alcoholism is a disease and, indeed, Justice White wrote, "This litigation does not require the Court to decide whether alcoholism is a disease whose course its victims cannot control." For an interesting analysis of the above case, *see* Andrea Neal, *Is Alcoholism a Disease?*, A.B.A.J. 58 (Feb. 1988).

[10] 429 U.S. 97 (1976); *see* discussion of the seriousness standard in Chapter 4, especially ¶ 4.5.

[11] *See* Charles Winick, "The Alcohol Offender" & "The Drug Offender" in Psychology of Crime

Substance abuse problems appear to abound among prisoners. A study of inmates admitted to the North Carolina prison system between March and May of 1983 revealed that half of the sample were (or had been) alcohol abusers and 19 percent were dependent on drugs.[12] The data, and general impressions, support the view that alcohol and drug abuse are major factors in the criminal behavior of a very high percentage of inmates.[13] The National Institute of Justice's (NIJ) Drug Use Forecasting Reports (DUF) regularly report astonishingly high percentages of positive tests for drugs at the time of arrest—53 to 83 percent for males and 45 to 83 percent for females, while perhaps 20 percent of both sexes tested positive for more than one drug.[14]

In a series of NIJ reports, Marcia Chaikin found some 62 percent of prisoners reported regular use of illicit drugs, and 35 percent used either heroin, cocaine, LSD or PCP.[15] Anyone familiar with correctional settings will not be surprised at this data. Indeed, in my efforts to gather anecdotal data, I regularly ask prison employees how many of the inmates are, or have been, substance abusers. "Do you mean where the drug or alcohol was, like, involved in the criminal behavior somehow?" "Yes." And the answer invariably is 80 percent—whether in Utah, Michigan, Ohio or Vermont— the magically persistent 80 percent is recounted. If unrehearsed consistency in experientially based opinions carries any weight, this area is heavily weighted.

It will likely surprise some readers to learn that alcoholism or drug addiction are not *by themselves* viewed as medical or psychiatric diseases for the purposes of a mandated right to treatment.[16] However, they often are accepted as medical problems for noncriminal purposes such as contractual medical care, medical leave, and insurance. I hasten to add that the very concept of disease is not static; it is uncertain and shifts over time and cultures, and it varies with context.[17]

AND CRIMINAL JUSTICE (H. Toch, ed. 1979), Chs. 15, 16. On the manipulative uses of the language of disease and care, *see* MURRAY EDELMAN, POLITICAL LANGUAGE: WORDS THAT SUCCEED AND POLICIES THAT FAIL (1977). *See also* THOMAS SZASZ, CEREMONIAL CHEMISTRY (1985), Ch. 1.

[12] Paper delivered by James J. Collins & William E. Schlenger at the American Society of Criminology Meeting, Denver, CO, Nov. 9–13 (1983). *See also* James, Gregory & Jones, *Psychiatric Morbidity in Prisons*, 31 HOSP. & COMM'Y PSYCH'Y 674 (1980); Robert Hare, *Diagnosis on Antisocial Personality Disorder in Two Prison Populations*, 140 AM. J. PSYCHIATRY 887 (1983).

[13] One court took judicial notice of the magnitude of the problem, terming it serious, Pace v. Fauver, 479 F. Supp. 456, 459 (D.N.J. 1979), *aff'd*, 649 F.2d 860 (3d Cir. 1981). *See* NATHANIEL J. PALLONE, MENTAL DISORDER AMONG PRISONERS: TOWARD AN EPIDEMIOLOGICAL INVENTORY (1991), Ch. 3, for a valuable collection of arrest data and data related to those in confinement.

[14] Drug Use Forecasting Annual Report 2 (N.I.J. 1989).

[15] *See* MARCIA R. CHAIKEN, IN-PRISON PROGRAMS FOR DRUG-INVOLVED OFFENDERS (N.I.J. 1989).

[16] Bailey v. Gardebring, 940 F.2d 1150 (8th Cir. 1991) (holding that a convicted inmate then civilly committed as a "dangerous psychopath" had no constitutional right to treatment, and further that the failure of prison officials to establish sex offender treatment programs did not constitute deliberate indifference to serious medical needs). *See* HERBERT FINGARETTE, HEAVY DRINKING: THE MYTH OF ALCOHOLISM AS A DISEASE (1988); *see also* Fingarette, *We Should Reject the Disease Concept of Alcoholism*, 8 HARV. MED. SCH. MENTAL HEALTH LETTER 4, 6 (1990). The text material on alcoholism and the disease concept is drawn largely from Fred Cohen, *Captives' Right to Mental Health Care*, 17 LAW & PSYCHOLOGY REV. 1, 15–17 (1993).

[17] In the context of the insanity defense, much has been written about the Model Penal Code's exclusion of repeated antisocial behavior from the predicate mental disease or defect. *See e.g.,* Emily

There is no medical unanimity concerning whether alcoholism *per se* is a disease, although perhaps the leading authority in the field argues that at a certain point in the loss of control over alcohol consumption, a "drinking problem" qualifies as the disease of alcoholism.[18] Anthropologists inform us that ideas about types of disease and their signs are astonishingly diverse and profoundly shaped by culture. Indeed, the cultural specificity of psychiatric illness has itself spawned a vast and controversial literature.[19]

For example, currently there is debate about whether compulsive gambling should be recognized as a disease. There are organizations like Gamblers Anonymous and the National Council on Problem Gambling, and since 1980, the authoritative *Diagnostic and Statistical Manual of Mental Disorders*[20] (DSM) has listed pathological gambling as an impulsive control disorder.[21] One possible method for dealing with compulsive gambling as a disease is for at-risk individuals to obtain insurance coverage and persuade health care providers that at least some gambling is a disease. I have never encountered evidence of a compulsive gambler who consistently won. Therefore, poor impulsive control and either poor skill or bad luck must presumably combine for the disease to be present.[22]

A compulsive gambler (with opportunities to gamble) in prison or jail is not likely to be diagnosed as having a disease, much less a serious disease. There is no good reason for the system to stretch already thin resources to recognize a highly dubious candidate for disease status. This point is instructive not only in recognizing a particular disease status but also in diagnosing an inmate as seriously mentally ill and thereby triggering the medical model and the *Estelle* claim to mandatory treatment.

Given a moment's reflection, I suppose one could find a condition, status, ailment, syndrome or psychiatric symptom in virtually every inmate's background. When used as a basis for understanding and hopefully preventing repetition of harmful behavior, reliance on such information is not a problem. Used as a basis for claiming constitutionally mandated treatment involves a policy shift, a shift in outlook and in resources of major dimensions. In our present climate of just deserts and severe punishment,

---

Campbell, *The Psychopath and the Definition of Mental Disease or Defect Under the Model Penal Code Test of Insanity,* in LAW AND PSYCHOLOGY: THE BROADENING OF THE DISCIPLINE (James R., P. Ogloff, eds. 1992), p. 139.

[18] *See* GEORGE E. VAILLANT, THE NATIONAL HISTORY OF ALCOHOLISM: CAUSES, PATTERNS, AND PATHS TO RECOVERY (Harvard Univ. Press 1988), pp. 15–23, 43–44. Alcohol abuse does not conform to Koch's postulates—the rule that four conditions must be met before there is biological acceptance that a given organism causes a disease. *See* II INTERNATIONAL DICTIONARY OF MEDICINE AND BIOLOGY (1986).

[19] *See* Michael MacDonald, *Anthropological Perspectives on the History of Science and Medicine*, in INFORMATION SOURCES IN THE HISTORY OF SCIENCE AND MEDICINE (Pietro Corsi & Paul Weindling, eds. 1983), pp. 71–79.

[20] The DSM is published by the American Psychiatric Association.

[21] Michel Marriott, *Fervid Debate on Gambling: Disease or Moral Weakness?* N.Y. TIMES, Nov. 21, 1992 Section 1, p.1, col.5.

[22] One possible consequence of recognizing compulsive gambling as a disease (likely to be called "Pete Rose's disease") is the enactment of civil commitment laws for compulsive gamblers. A distressed family could be viewed as harmed and the gambler as in need of enforced therapy, and an entire group of treatment experts would be spawned. One wonders if cure would equate with improvement of one's skills or some means to improve one's luck!

such a shift simply will not happen regardless of the merits. It is difficult enough to obtain mental health care for the authentically and seriously mentally ill.

[2] Constitutional Claim to Treatment vs. Substance Abuse Care

When directly confronted with a constitutional claim to treatment for problems of substance abuse, courts consistently reject it. On the other hand, there have been many instances in which drug and alcohol treatment programs were ordered (or agreed to) when substance abuse was presented in the larger framework of an overall failure to provide adequate medical or psychological care. Thus, the legal obligation to provide substance abuse programs is almost totally dependent on how the claim is presented and resolved.

Pace v. Fauver[23] presented a New Jersey district court directly with the question "whether failure to provide treatment for alcoholic prisoners constitutes cruel and unusual punishment, in violation of the Eighth Amendment . . . ."[24] The court recognized the constitutional obligation of government to provide medical care to those it confines, and it correctly pointed out that any alleged failures were measured by the less-than-demanding standard of deliberate indifference.[25] The court went on to state:

Nor may it be assumed that every debilitation or addiction cognizable as medically-related requires that the government establish a treatment facility or program in order not to violate a prisoner's Eighth Amendment rights. Rather, in order to state a sufficient Eighth Amendment claim a plaintiff must show such deliberate indifference on the part of prison officials to his serious medical needs as to offend evolving standards of decency. As the Third Circuit has stated, "not every injury or illness evokes the constitutional protection—only those that are 'serious' have that effect." A "serious" medical need may fairly be regarded as one that has been diagnosed by a physician as requiring treatment or one that is so obvious that a lay person would easily recognize the necessity for a doctor's attention.

The Court does not regard plaintiffs' desire to establish and operate an alcoholic rehabilitation program within Rahway State Prison as a serious medical need for purposes of Eighth Amendment and Sec. 1983 analysis. As the Supreme Court has stated in the context of drug addiction, "there is no 'fundamental right' to rehabilitation . . . at public expense after conviction of a crime." [citing Marshall v. United States] . . . [T]his Circuit has held that there is no constitutional right to methadone maintenance facilities for the treatment of drug addiction, although under certain emergent circumstances failure to provide a prisoner with methadone treatment may constitute an Eighth Amendment violation.

The Court takes judicial notice that alcohol and narcotics abuse is a serious problem in the United States. Moreover, the Court recognizes that in

---

[23] 479 F. Supp. 456 (D.N.J. 1979).

[24] Pace, 479 F. Supp. at 458. The court also dealt with a similar claim based on state law.

[25] *See* discussion of the deliberate indifference standard in Chapter 4.

deciding whether the Eighth Amendment requires that State prison and health officials allow the establishment of rehabilitation programs, that Amendment "must draw its meaning from the evolving standards of decency that mark the progress of a maturing society." However, whatever may be our hopes for the standards of the future, the Court cannot at this time hold that failure or refusal to provide opportunities to establish and operate alcoholism rehabilitation facilities in state prisons rises to the magnitude of cruel and unusual punishment.[26]

The *Pace* court did not anguish about the complexities of the disease concept and quietly slipped in references to rehabilitation *vis a vis* treatment, thus making it easier to deny the inmate claim. As has been discussed, claims to rehabilitation generally lose while claims to treatment for serious diseases may win. Thus, rehabilitation is a lethal term in the context of demanding correctional mental health treatment.

Norris v. Frame[27] confronted the Third Circuit with a pretrial detainee who was denied access to a methadone maintenance program he was participating in at the time of his arrest and subsequent detention. Finding that a detainee's legal status exceeded that of a convict, the court concluded that Norris had made out a claim to an interference with a protected liberty interest in the continuation of his drug treatment program. On remand, the state was invited to show whether a countervailing security interest could be shown to outweigh the detainee's interest in the continuation of his treatment.[28] The key here is the detainee's claim to the *continuation* of his program. The court did *not* decide there was a right to the establishment of a drug treatment program or of access to methadone.[29]

In *Palmigiano v. Garrahy*,[30] the court found a variety of conditions at the Rhode Island Adult Correctional Institutions (ACI) to be below constitutional minima. Among its findings, the court linked the prison system's failure to identify drug users as a contributing factor in the increased drug traffic, increased risk of suicide, and overall deterioration in the prison.[31]

The chief physician at ACI testified that between 70 and 80 percent of inmates enter as drug abusers and remain drug abusers while confined. The court found no written or unwritten protocols or policies despite the powerful dimensions of the problem.[32] The court ordered that:

> (a) Defendants shall within thirty days from the entry of this order establish a program for the treatment of inmates physiologically addicted to drugs or alcohol that does not require withdrawal by means of an abrupt denial or "cold turkey" approach.

---

[26] Pace, 479 F. Supp. at 458–459 (citations omitted).

[27] 585 F.2d 1183 (3d Cir. 1978).

[28] Norris, 585 F.2d at 1189.

[29] Id. The court's reasoning here is pre-Bell v. Wolfish, 441 U.S. 520 (1979), which among other things has served to discredit the notion that detainees have more rights than the convicted.

[30] 443 F. Supp. 956 (D.R.I. 1977).

[31] Palmigiano, 443 F. Supp. at 972.

[32] Id.

(b) Defendants shall within three months from the entry of this order establish a program for the treatment of drug abuse that is in compliance with the minimum standards of the American Public Health Association, the United States Public Health Service, and the Department of Health, State of Rhode Island.

(c) Defendants shall within thirty days from the entry of this order place the responsibility for the treatment of drug abuse under a physician able and willing to treat prison addicts.[33]

In *Palmigiano,* the trial judge was far more willing than his fellow judges to characterize drug and alcohol abuse as medical problems requiring a treatment response. There is no extended analysis of the disease concept, and those searching for doctrinal purity would insist on a more vigorous analysis of "serious disease" and the "deliberate indifference" standard. This court, when shown a problem of crippling dimensions with an insidious effect on prison life, elected to press the constitutional treatment button.[34]

In *Alberti v. Sheriff of Harris County, Texas,*[35] a challenge to jail conditions, the court ordered that a medical screening program be designed to include detection of alcohol and drug problems. In addition, the court ordered the creation of a program where afflicted inmates would be housed in a separate treatment unit.[36] The court decided that the totality of the conditions at the Harris County Jail were unconstitutional. The more serious problems involved inmates with substantial abuse histories who were not properly cared for or treated. Testimony indicated that failure to properly care for these inmates contributed to overall medical and security problems.[37] Other courts may simply nudge the parties in the constitutional treatment direction as part of settlement negotiations. Still others are content to encourage but not require treatment programs. Most will simply not recognize the claim.

Claims of a constitutional right to treatment for the substance abuse problem must be distinguished from the often serious medical problems associated with the condition and especially so during withdrawal. Here, the case law consistently recognizes a right to medical treatment, with the major stumbling block being the "serious medical need" requirement.

A refusal to provide standard treatment for the pain and threat to life associated with withdrawal for 4 days[38] in one case, and 10 days in another,[39] could establish

---

[33] Palmigiano, 443 F. Supp. at 989.

[34] The same is true in Barnes v. Government of Virgin Islands, 415 F. Supp. 1218 (D.V.I. 1976), in which it was ordered that: "Arrangements shall be made to introduce an alcohol and drug rehabilitation program. Otherwise, inmates who are in need of such treatment, in the opinion of the psychiatrist, shall be transferred to an appropriate institution." 415 F. Supp. at 1235.

[35] 406 F. Supp. 649 (S.D. Tex. 1975).

[36] Alberti, 406 F. Supp. at 667.

[37] Alberti, 406 F. Supp. at 658; *see also* Ramos v. Lamm, 485 F. Supp. 122, 146 (D. Colo. 1980), *aff'd in part, vacated on other grounds*, 639 F.2d 559 (10th Cir. 1980), *cert. denied* , 450 U.S. 1041 (1981) (failure to address substance abuse contributes to overall deterioration and hinders self improvement).

[38] Pedraza v. Meyer, 919 F.2d 317, 318–319 (5th Cir. 1990).

[39] United States ex rel. Walker v. Fayette County, Pa. 599 F.2d 573, 575–576 (3d Cir. 1979).

deliberate indifference. Even where a detainee or inmate was on a methadone program on the outside, most courts will not require its continuance while insisting on medical care for the symptoms of withdrawal.[40]

In Chapter 2, I listed 15 components as basic to a correctional mental health program, although not all were legally mandated.[41] A substance abuse program integrated with the basic mental health program was one such factor. One need only cite to the dimensions of the problem to see the need. And one need pause but a moment to realize that where the law makes artificial distinctions for one set of reasons, that surely does not mean that a prison or jail system need perpetuate the distinction.

Prisons, of course, generally see the substance abusing inmate after the detoxification experience that transpired at the local jail. Obviously, the problem has not gone away, it is just sleeping. This quiescent period, however does allow prison officials to see the problem as someone else's.[42]

¶ 8.3 OBJECTION TO TREATMENTS HAVING A RELIGIOUS BASIS

In the last few years, a new line of cases has emerged dealing with corrections programs that require participation in Alcoholics Anonymous (AA) or Narcotics Anonymous (NA) as a condition to maintaining or acquiring a desirable security classification or privilege. The New York Court of Appeals decision in *Griffin v. Coughlin*[43] is representative of such a challenge brought under the Establishment Clause of the First Amendment to the United States Constitution.

Griffin, confined in New York's highly secure Shawangunk facility, has a long history of having declared himself to be atheist or agnostic. The inmate was able to participate in the highly prized Family Reunion Program—a euphemism for private, conjugal visits—so long as he participated in the prison's AA-type program. Being nonreligious, Griffin argued that to condition his participation in the visiting program on his attendance at AA meeting is to require his conformance with a state-sponsored religion. This respected state court found that the writings of AA have a "dominant theme [that] is unequivocally religious . . . ."[44] In addition, the court found that participation was coercive, although over a strong dissent, in part because there were no secular alternatives.

Thus, the court of appeals found AA essentially religious and Griffin's participation in it coercive although, curiously, the inmate had no enforceable right to otherwise participate in the conjugal visit program.

In *Kerr v. Farrey*,[45] a Wisconsin inmate was required to participate in Narcotics Anonymous (NA) as part of his rehabilitation; nonparticipation would result in a higher security classification and have a negative impact on parole eligibility. Kerr object-

---

[40] *See, e.g.,* Holly v. Rapone, 476 F. Supp. 226, 231 (E.D. Pa. 1979); Cudnik v. Krieger, 392 F. Supp. 305, 312–313 (N.D. Ohio, 1974), is the rare decision to the contrary.

[41] *See* Chapter 2, ¶ 2.6[2] and attendant discussion.

[42] *See* B. JAYE ANNO, PRISON HEALTH CARE 152, for a similar analysis and point of view along with a description of some programs.

[43] 673 N.E. 2d 98 (N.Y. 1996).

[44] Griffin, 673 N.E. 2d at 102.

[45] 95 F.3d 472 (7th Cir. 1996).

ed to the theistic views of NA and regarded them as in conflict with his own beliefs. The Seventh Circuit summarized its views by stating, "When a plaintiff claims that the state is coercing him or her to subscribe to religion generally or to a particular religion, only three points are crucial: first, has the state acted; second, does the action amount to coercion; third, is the object of coercion religious or secular?"[46]

The court found that the program favors religion over non-religion, which violates the Establishment Clause.[47] And, if you can win that one in the extraordinarily conservative Seventh Circuit, I dare say, it will be won by inmates virtually anywhere.[48]

Parenthetically, until this line of decisions, religious claims by inmates were essentially of the "free exercise" variety, involving hair or beard lengths, sweat lodges, congregate worship, and the like. Thus, invocation of the Establishment Clause has been rare.

Correctional authorities need not fret too long over these AA and NA decisions, since it is the coercion and absence of secular alternatives that are the determinative factors. Remove the coercion or incorporate easily available non-religious alternatives, and substance abuse program coordinators need not worry about this Establishment Clause issue.

In conclusion, it seems plain enough that substance abuse problems are fairly common in our prisons and jails, and that the cases on point are inconsistent and often poorly reasoned in dealing with alcoholism or drug addiction as "disease," or if seen as a disease, in recognizing that it is sufficiently serious to evoke constitutional recognition. Although the constitutional mandate may be murky or lacking, programs for substance abusers are among the most common in our prison systems and even without the whip of constitutional mandate, should be encouraged.

¶ 8.4 REHABILITATION VS. TREATMENT CONCEPTS

In more than a few cases, issues involving treatment and rehabilitation are confounded and dealt with in overlapping fashion.[49] Rehabilitation:

> refers to the process of restoring the individual to behavior and values which fall within the social definition of what is acceptable. Socially acceptable behaviors and values are by definition not "illegal." Thus, it is assumed in the rehabilitative process that the individual formerly held socially acceptable values with appropriate behavior and temporarily laid it [sic] aside.[50]

---

[46] Kern, 95 F.3d at 480.

[47] Id.

[48] To the contrary is Boyd v. Coughlin, 914 F. Supp. 828 (N.D.N.Y. 1996), which, in effect, is superseded by the New York Court of Appeals decision. *See* O'Conner v. California, 855 F. Supp. 303 (C.D. Cal. 1994), where AA was one among several treatment options available to a probationer, thus the coercion was absent.

[49] It is also the case that mentally retarded inmates may present claims to habilitation adding further semantic and conceptual complexity to the area.

[50] MILES B. SANTAMOUR & BERNADETTE WEST, RETARDATION AND CRIMINAL JUSTICE: A TRAINING MANUAL FOR CRIMINAL JUSTICE PERSONNEL 25 (President's Committee on Mental Retardation, 1979). Two authorities suggest that "rehabilitation" is simply the wrong word, since inmates arrive at prison

The supposed differences between treatment, to which there now is a clear but narrow constitutional right, and rehabilitation, to which there is no clear right, may be more formal than real. In our context, we view treatment as a mental health response to a disease process, while we see rehabilitation as a forward looking response to inadequate or improper socialization. Thus, in addition to the distinctions noted earlier, another difference between treatment and rehabilitation may be in the causal assumptions about the individuals' problem.[51]

A further difference relates to professional and occupational claims over the particular territory. Mental health professionals, with psychiatrists and psychologists as the elite, provide treatment services. Efforts at rehabilitation certainly may, but need not, include mental health professionals. Indeed, what constitutes rehabilitative activity is so amorphous, and earlier claims to success analyzed as so dubious, that the definition of rehabilitation founders at its conceptual and empirical core.[52]

[1] Rehabilitative Ideal

While the rehabilitative ideal was thoroughly discredited by 1980 and the just deserts-punishment model triumphed, lately there have been longings expressed for that "old friend."[53] In this context, our reference is to the policy that underpins both sentencing structures and practices and the attitude and climate within correctional facilities. That climate is harsh, retributive, and pessimistic.

The longing expressed for the rehabilitative ideal appears to be for its sense of hope for human redemption, for reconciliation, and for a softening of the me/them chasm along racial, economic, and offender lines.

Persons who want help or relief of some sort, especially in such extreme situations as prisons and jails, will try to shoe horn themselves into whatever behavior or expression of need will likely result in the desired payoff. It is what you and I would do but perhaps with different tools. Inmates "cut up" to avoid paying debts or to get out of something; inmates "hear voices" to get into a hospital; inmates act out to be placed in the safety of lock-down and avoid any negative stigma of appearing to be "crazy" or suicidal. Inmates, in other words, exchange the only commodities they have for desirable "goods" and services.

The absence of rehabilitative activities has a tendency to push behavior toward

---

without ever having acquired educational, vocational, or social skills adequate for success in the free world. *See* DeWolfe & DeWolfe, *Impact of Prison Conditions on the Mental Health of Inmates*, 1979 S. ILL. UNIV. L. J. 497, 521 (1979).

[51] *See* Chapter 6 for an earlier discussion. The concepts of rehabilitation and treatment as cultivation of functioning have much in common.

[52] *See* R. Martinson, *California Research at the Crossroads*, in REHABILITATION, RECIDIVISM, AND RESEARCH (R. Martinson, et. al., eds., N.C.C.D. 1976), p.63. *See generally* MURRAY EDELMAN, POLITICAL LANGUAGE: WORDS THAT SUCCEED AND POLICIES THAT FAIL (1977).

[53] Robert A. Burt, *Cruelty, Hypocrisy, and the Rehabilitative Ideal in Corrections*, 16 INT'L J. L. & PSYCHOLOGY 359 (1993), is the most eloquent voice for that nostalgia, and he adds a contemporary framework to his beliefs. *See generally* FRANCIS A. ALLEN, THE DECLINE OF THE REHABILITATIVE IDEAL: PENAL POLICY AND SOCIAL PURPOSE (1981). Today we witness the taking of exercise equipment, loss of Pell Grants and other educational opportunities, and the reemergence of chain gangs. These and similar practices hardly promote an environment in which any version of rehabilitation may flourish.

badness or madness, depending on what the captive seeks. The courts are clear, however, that no prisoner has a right to rehabilitation—to redemptive or restorative programs.

[2] Merger of Rehab/Treatment Concepts

Ohlinger v. Watson,[54] a fascinating decision that will be discussed at some length, contains the following sentence: "Lack of funds, staff or facilities cannot justify the State's failure to provide appellants *with that treatment necessary for rehabilitation*."[55] The italicized phrase should be digested slowly—treatment-for-rehabilitation. Does this indicate some unpublicized marriage of the two concepts? Is it just loose usage and perhaps attributable to the context of the case? Is this an example of a conceptual dilemma posed by treatment and rehabilitation? Is this an example of an author spending one day too many reading small print?

Ohlinger, in fact, is a special case. It involves a situation in which the inmates had been convicted under a sodomy statute carrying a maximum term of 15 years, but were confined under indeterminate life sentences on a finding that they possessed a mental disturbance predisposing them to the commission of sex offenses.[56]

In analyzing what ultimately is recognized as a statutory right to treatment, the court stated:

> Having chosen to incarcerate appellants on the basis of their mental illness, the State has determined that it no longer has an interest in punishing appellants, but rather in attempting to rehabilitate them.
>
> The rehabilitative rationale is not only desirable, but it is constitutionally required. *Robinson v. California* strongly suggests that the State may not justify appellants' extended sentence on the basis of mental illness without affording appropriate treatment. The Supreme Court of California has so interpreted Robinson. Indeed the State concedes that appellants are constitutionally entitled to treatment. The disagreement between the parties is solely over the level of treatment which is constitutionally required.
>
> The district court held that "[a]ll that is required is that [appellants] be provided a reasonable level of treatment based upon a reasonable cost and time basis." We do not agree.
>
> Constitutionally adequate treatment is not that which must be provided to the general prison population, but that which must be provided to those committed for mental incapacity.[57]

The opinion in *Ohlinger* uses the terms "rehabilitation" and "treatment" interchangeably. This appears to be more careless than considered. For example, in review-

---

[54] 652 F.2d 775 (9th Cir. 1980).

[55] Ohlinger, 652 F.2d at 779 (emphasis added).

[56] Ohlinger, 652 F.2d at 777. Today, they would likely be dealt with as Sexually Violent Predators.

[57] Ohlinger, 652 F.2d at 777, 778 (citations and footnote omitted). The California case referred to is People v. Feagley, 14 Cal. 3d 338, 359, 535 P.2d 373, 386, (1975), where the court determined that:

ing the appellants' individual needs, the court emphasized the inadequacy of the limited group therapy available and held: "The treatment provided appellants, therefore, does not give them a reasonable opportunity to be cured or to improve their mental conditions."[58]

The *Ohlinger* court considered the relevance of *Bowring v. Godwin*,[59] but found it inapplicable precisely because *Bowring* involved inmates confined for their offenses, while the instant decision involved inmates confined at least in part because of their mental condition. In the *Bowring* situation, then, an "ordinary" inmate would have no constitutionally recognized claim to rehabilitation or treatment, since treatment was reserved for those with serious mental disorders. In *Ohlinger,* the special findings and extended term of confinement created a hybrid constitutional and statutory claim to psychiatric care.[60]

[3] No Constitutional Right to Rehabilitation

Despite the implications of *Ohlinger,* the widely followed general rule is that there is no constitutional right to rehabilitation, rehabilitation being the operative term applied to claims for affirmative programs by ordinary inmates, those with problems of substance abuse, and "ordinary" sex offenders. Rehabilitation, in the sense of efforts to socialize or resocialize inmates where a disease model is not imposed, does slip into some decisions and does so in various ways.[61]

Some courts will assess the general unavailability of rehabilitative programs as an aspect of a broader claim that the overall conditions of prison or jail are unconstitutional. Another approach is to view the unavailability as a factor that militates against self-help and reform and that contributes to the emotional deterioration of inmates. One article put it this way:

> Under the current case law of most jurisdictions, prisons have no constitutional duty to provide rehabilitative programs designed to prevent the

---

A person committed as a mentally disordered sex offender is not confined for the criminal offense but because of his status as a mentally disordered sex offender.

[I]nvoluntary confinement for the "status" of having a mental or physical illness or disorder constitutes a violation of the cruel and unusual punishment clauses of both the state and federal constitutions . . . unless it is accompanied by adequate treatment.

In Kansas v. Hendricks, 117 S. Ct. 2072 (1997), the Court upheld Kansas' sexual predator law, with no clear mandate for requiring treatment. Indeed, the Court appeared to accept treatment as an ancillary goal on its way to upholding indefinite civil confinement.

[58] Ohlinger, 652 F.2d at 780.

[59] 551 F. 2d 44 (4th Cir. 1977).

[60] For an excellent analysis of abnormal offenders and special sentencing options, *see* George Dix, *Special Dispositional Alternatives for Abnormal Offenders: Developments in the Law*, in MENTALLY DISORDERED OFFENDERS: PERSPECTIVES FROM LAW AND SOCIAL SCIENCE (John Monahan & Henry Steadman, eds. 1983), p.133.

[61] *See* Grubbs v. Bradley, 552 F. Supp. 1052, 1123 (M.D. Tenn. 1982) (court held squarely that there is no federal constitutional right to rehabilitation); Cameron v. Tomes, 990 F.2d 14 (1st Cir. 1993) (involved a dual prisoner-patient legal status, but the court focused more on conditions of confinement than a general right to treatment). *See* Chapter 7, ¶ 7.1 for a discussion of *Cameron.*

inevitable "mental, physical, and emotional deterioration" of inmates which is part of the general human condition. Prisons must, however, avoid unconstitutional conditions which would produce such deterioration or which prevent inmates from pursuing self-rehabilitation. In other words, only where the failure to provide rehabilitation services is found to be a part of an overall prison situation which "militate[s] against reform and rehabilitation" is such failure of constitutional proportions.[62]

Where a court is focusing in on the familiar "psychotropic drugs alone are not adequate treatment" theme, a variety of counseling-type programs or simply supervised activity will be debated as an aspect of treatment. Programs like "anger management" or "building self-esteem," once candidates for the rehabilitation label, become adjuncts to mandated treatment but only for the seriously mentally ill.

Justice Stevens, still alone among his Supreme Court colleagues, has yet another view of rehabilitation in prison. In dealing with the problem of whether procedural due process should apply to interprison transfers, Justice Stevens, in dissent, writes:

> Imprisonment is intended to accomplish more than the temporary removal of the offender from society in order to prevent him from committing like offenses during the period of his incarceration. While custody denies the inmate the opportunity to offend, it also gives him an opportunity to improve himself and to acquire skills and habits that will help him to participate in an open society after his release. Within the prison community, if my basic hypothesis is correct, he has a protected right to pursue his limited rehabilitative goals, or at the minimum, to maintain whatever attributes of dignity are associated with his status in a tightly controlled society. It is unquestionably within the power of the State to change that status, abruptly and adversely; but if the change is sufficiently grievous, it may not be imposed arbitrarily. In such cases due process must be afforded.[63]

Again, it should be emphasized that even this limited version of rehabilitation rights is exotic. The rather cursory rejection of a right to rehabilitation in *Marshall v. United States*[64] is much more representative of judicial thinking. Justice Stevens' position seems aligned with the "militating against self-help and reform" position noted above.

Holt v. Sarver,[65] a landmark prison case, is often cited for the following proposition:

> Given an otherwise unexceptional penal institution, the Court is not willing to hold that the confinement unit is unconstitutional simply because the institu-

---

[62] DeWolfe & DeWolfe, *Impact of Prison Conditions on Mental Health of Inmates*, 1979 S. Ill. Univ. L. J. 497, 522.

[63] Meachum v. Fano, 427 U.S. 215, 234 (1976) (Stevens, J., dissenting).

[64] *Supra* note 1.

[65] 309 F. Supp. 362 (E.D. Ark. 1970), *aff'd*, 442 F.2d 304 (8th Cir. 1971).

tion does not operate a school, or provide vocational training, or other rehabilitative facilities and services which many institutions now offer.[66]

That, however, is not quite the end of the matter. The absence of an affirmative
program of training and rehabilitation may have constitutional significance where in
the absence of such a program conditions and practices exist that actually militate
against reform and rehabilitation. In *Rhodes v. Chapman*[67] the Court refused to equate
prison overcrowding with cruel and unusual punishment. Diminished job and education opportunities due to overcrowding were found not to violate the Eighth
Amendment, even when viewed as "desirable aids to rehabilitation."[68]

[4] Right to Avoid Deterioration

The right to avoid deterioration has been explicitly recognized by some courts.[69]
In *Battle v. Anderson,*[70] the Tenth Circuit said: "[W]hile an inmate does not have a federal constitutional right to rehabilitation, he is entitled to be confined in an environment which does not result in his degeneration or which threatens his mental and
physical well-being."[71] The nature of this emergent duty to prevent degeneration was
synthesized by the court in *Laaman v. Helgemoe.*[72] The court said the conditions of
incarceration should not threaten the inmates' sanity or mental well-being, should not
be contrary to the inmates' efforts to rehabilitate themselves, and should not increase
the probability of the inmates' future incarceration.

The *Laaman* court included the scarcity of rehabilitation, recreation, and skills
training as part of its balance sheet demonstrating that prison life in New Hampshire
causes prisoners to degenerate and lose whatever social conscience and skills they
may have had.[73] In its expansive order, the court required vocational programs and
meaningful access to services and programs that are offered, and it also mandated certain programs with an emphasis on pre-release inmates.[74]

---

[66] Holt, 309 F. Supp. at 379. *See also* McCray v. Sullivan, 509 F.2d 1332, 1335 (5th Cir. 1975);
Newman v. Alabama, 559 F.2d 283, 291 (5th Cir. 1977); Madyun v. Thompson. 657 F.2d 868, 874 (8th
Cir. 1981).

[67] 452 U.S. 337 (1981).

[68] Rhodes, 452 U.S. at 348. There is also the (by now) trite rhetoric about the Constitution not mandating comfortable prisons. Rehabilitation and comfort clearly need not be viewed as synonymous, but
the philosophy favoring rejection of minimal comfort is consistent with the rejection of minimal rehabilitation.

[69] Concerning the English system, Margaret Brazier writes: "Although no English court has determined the issue, I would suggest that those authorities owe to each prisoner a duty not only to take reasonable steps to preserve him in good physical health but also as far as is practicable to ensure that he
does not sink into such a state of anxiety, depression, or emotional stress that it becomes likely that he
will inflict injuries upon himself. Margaret Brazier, *Prison Doctors and Their Involuntary Patients*, 1982
PUBLIC L. 282, 286.

[70] 564 F.2d 388 (10th Cir. 1977).

[71] Battle, 564 F.2d at 403.

[72] 437 F. Supp. 269, 316 (D.N.H. 1977). *See also* James v. Wallace, 564 F.2d 97 (5th Cir. 1977).

[73] Laaman, 437 F. Supp. at 325.

[74] Laaman, 437 F. Supp. at 329–330.

In *Pugh v. Locke,*[75] the Alabama prisons were subjected to very much the same analysis as the New Hampshire prisons. Conditions in those prisons were found to be generally deficient, with failure to provide rehabilitation opportunities listed among the system's many liabilities. Among other things, the court ordered that inmates be provided with the opportunity to participate in job and educational programs.[76]

Canterino v. Wilson[77] is a somewhat unusual decision resting on equal protection grounds when comparing the programs available to female inmates with those available to men. Equal protection analysis does not lead to the creation of rights.[78] Rather, the problem is the fairness or rationality with which desirable items—here rehabilitative programs—are distributed, along with the rationale used to support the challenged misallocation.

Where gender is the basis for unequal distribution, "The State must show that the disparate treatment of females is substantially related to an important government objective."[79] Judge Johnson found that equal protection was violated in the unequal distribution of resources and in the more onerous conditions imposed in the exercise of privileges. The assumption underlying the gender-based disparities appeared to be the innate inferiority of women, a proposition that was rejected out of hand.[80]

Thus, it should be kept in mind that while a system may not be legally obliged to provide rehabilitative opportunities, when it does, gender-based (and, obviously, race-based) discrimination may well violate the Equal Protection Clause of the Fourteenth Amendment.

¶ 8.5 SUMMARY

To conclude this topic, it may appear odd to analyze inmate claims to rehabilitation at a time when sentencing policy is so strongly committed to just deserts and punishment, and when prison systems are engaged in removing amenities and imposing humiliation. But our concern with rehabilitation is not directly related to judicial sentencing goals. It is related more to the conceptual and factual overlaps between rehabilitation and treatment and to the minimal obligations of constitutionally mandated care imposed on our penal systems.

This is an area where it is relatively easy to identify and state the general rules—yes, there is a limited right to treatment, and no, there is no general right to rehabilitation. If you dig a bit, however, you will uncover a line of decisions that consider the lack of rehabilitative opportunities as a factor in the overall assessment of conditions in prison. Where the overall conditions in a prison, or prison system, are so primitive

---

[75] 406 F. Supp. 318 (M.D. Ala. 1976), *aff'd in part and mod. in part sub nom.* Newman v. Alabama, 559 F.2d 283 (5th Cir. 1977), *remanded on other grounds sub nom.* Alabama v. Pugh, 438 U.S. 781 (1978).

[76] Pugh, 406 F. Supp. at 330, 335. *See also* Barnes v. Government of V.I., 415 F. Supp. 1218 (D.V.I. 1976), for a similar view on rehabilitative programs and the duty to avoid (or reduce) inmate degeneration.

[77] 546 F. Supp. 174 (W.D. Ky. 1982).

[78] Id.

[79] Canterino, 546 F. Supp. at 211.

[80] Canterino, 546 F. Supp. at 207.

as to contribute importantly to inmates' mental or physical debilitation, then a finding of an Eighth Amendment violation may result in an order where no practical distinctions may be drawn between treatment and rehabilitation. Again, however, this is a far cry from an explicit and affirmative duty to provide opportunities for self-improvement.

Finally, although unadorned claims to rehabilitation are rejected when urged straightforwardly as demands for substance abuse programs, such programs do slip into judicial orders and consent decrees when the problems in a given prison are massive and the remedy encompassing.

Chapter 9

The Treatment Relationship

¶ 9.1 CONFIDENTIALITY AND PRIVILEGE

[1] Divided Loyalties

Questions concerning confidentiality and privilege, or when information a mental health professional gains from an inmate-patient/client may or must be shared, are among the most frequently asked in the field, and they rank with the most difficult to clearly answer.[1] The prison or secure mental hospital setting creates often-conflicting

---

[1] Confidentiality in the treatment relationship is generally in decline and seemingly accepted by some and decreed by others. In their devastating critique of DSM-IV, the authors state:

demands on the mental health specialist that give rise to much of the difficulty. There are questions of "split agency" (e.g., court ordered evaluation, jail, or prison screening) and of confusion of agency.[2] For example, one of the most frequently occurring "divided loyalty" problems, in my experience, involves psychologists who offer therapy or counseling and who then are also asked to perform evaluations for parole boards. This is such a clear conflict of interest, and so potentially destructive of a treatment relationship, that it simply should never be done.

There are also questions related to duties owed to identifiable others who may be in danger from an imate-patient[3] and questions related to the general security and order of the facility.

Concerns about the confidentiality of medical and mental health records are not limited to the self-contained world of corrections. With the managed care industry developing sophisticated technology and seeking quality reviews, research, and economic analyses, we may have slipped into a new era where a patients' consent is presumed and confidentiality succumbs to technology.[4]

This chapter broaches these complex issues, and more. However, let me propose at the outset a general solution to a great many (but certainly not all) of these problems. The need for confidentiality and privilege, as a matter of professional ethics and law, rests on assumptions about an individual's expectations of privacy and nondisclosure.[5] It posits that the need for information to provide needed treatment generally

---

> Certainly, one element of our concern is the decline of confidentiality in psychotherapy. State laws and court decisions have altered the therapist-client relationship, making the relationship less a sanctuary for the emotionally distressed than a new arena for state surveillance. There is an expanding list of third parties (state legislatures, regulatory agencies, courts, licensing boards, insurance companies, child welfare authorities, police, etc.) demanding information about the private details of the therapeutic relationship. Therapists are mandated to report a presumed instance of child abuse, to warn a possible victim of a violent crime, to protect the innocent lover of an HIV positive client, and so on. Although each of these breaches of confidentiality has a compelling justification, the trend of requiring reporting to third parties erodes therapists' primary responsibility to the individual client and redirects them toward serving the needs of the state and the health care industry.

HERB KUTCHINS & STUART A. KIRK, MAKING US CRAZY: DSM: THE PSYCHIATRIC BIBLE AND THE CREATION OF MENTAL DISORDERS (1997), p. 261. The DSM-IV is, of course, the DIAGNOSTIC AND STATISTICAL MANUAL OF MENTAL DISORDERS, 4th ed. (American Psychiatric Association, 1994).

[2] These insights are taken from THOMAS GUTHEIL & PAUL APPLEBAUM, CLINICAL HANDBOOK OF PSYCHIATRY AND THE LAW (1982), p.15. In general, this is an excellent source for mental health professionals involved with the criminal justice system. *See also* Vanessa Merton, *Confidentiality and the "Dangerous" Patient: Implications of* Tarasoff *for Psychiatrists and Lawyers*, 31 EMORY L.J. 263, 273 (1982), who writes, "Those who have expressed concern about the divided loyalties of psychiatrists intimate that clarification and differentiation of the psychiatrist's professional role is most urgently required in institutional settings such as hospitals, prisons, schools, and the armed services."

[3] This refers to the duty arising from the landmark decision in Tarasoff v. Regents of the University of California, 17 Cal. 3d 425, 551 P.2d 334 (1976). *See* discussion of *Tarasoff* at ¶ 9.2[1].

[4] *See* discussion growing out of the 13th Annual Rosalynn Carter Symposium on Mental Health Policy, held November 19-20, 1997, at the Carter Center in Atlanta, Georgia, in 7 MENTAL HEALTH WEEKLY 1, 5 (Dec. 22, 1997).

[5] The purpose of ordinary rules of evidence is to promote ascertainment of the truth. Another group of rules, however, permits the exclusion of evidence for reasons wholly unconnected with ascertaining the truth. These reasons are found in the desire to protect an interest or relationship. The term "privilege" is used broadly to describe such rules of exclusion. Michael Graham, in *Evidence and Trial Advocacy*

outweighs even compelling demands for disclosure. Where the interaction with the inmate is for diagnosis, evaluation, or classification (or something similar), the full impact of privilege and confidentiality does not apply, if at all. Privilege, more accurately termed testimonial privilege, is narrower than the right of confidentiality and applies in judicial or jurisdiction-like settings.

While the matter is not free from doubt, recent empirical studies certainly raise questions about the significance of a psychotherapist-patient privilege as a factor in a person's seeking, or remaining in, treatment. The Shuman-Weiner studies are the best known and are aptly summarized by Professor Jeffrey A. Klotz:

1. Patients are probably not deterred from seeking psychiatric help to any significant degree by the absence of the privilege, partly because they are generally unaware of the privilege when deciding to seek therapy.

2. The absence of privilege does not typically delay potential patients from seeking treatment.

3. Patients often withhold information from their therapist, but this bears little relationship to fear of disclosure. The basic reason patients withhold information is because they fear the judgment of their therapists; the ethics of the therapist and confidentiality are most important for therapeutic trust. Interestingly, psychologically sensitive information was withheld more often than legally sensitive information, and patients avoid withholding or discussing acts or thoughts of violence. The presence of the privilege, then, does not greatly increase a patient's willingness to convey private thoughts.

4. A threat to disclose or actual disclosure by a therapist causes a small number of premature terminations from therapy and probably deters a large percentage of these people from seeking further help. However, the incidence of actual disclosure may be minimal.

5. Although actual disclosure can lead to premature termination in a few cases, there is no convincing evidence that psychological harm comes to those patients whose confidences have been revealed in judicial proceedings.

6. The impact that the lack of privilege has on the accuracy of judicial proceedings is, at most, minimal.[6]

Workshop: Privileges—Their Nature and Operation, 19 CRIM L. BULL. 442 (1983), quotes Professor Wigmore regarding the exclusion of relevant communications by operation of a privilege:

(1) The communications must originate in a *confidence* that they will not be disclosed; (2) This element of *confidentiality must be essential* to the full and satisfactory maintenance of the relation between the parties; (3) The relation must be one which in the opinion of the community ought to be sedulously *fostered*; (4) The *injury* that would inure to the relation must be *greater than the benefit* thereby gained for the correct disposal of litigation. 8 WIGMORE, EVIDENCE (1961), § 2285. (Emphasis in original.)

For an excellent discussion of privilege and confidentiality *see* M.C. MACDONALD & K.C. MEYER, HEALTH CARE LAW: A PRACTICAL GUIDE (1987), § 19.00 et seq.

[6] Jeffrey A. Klotz, *Limiting the Psychotherapist-Patient Privilege: The Therapeutic Potential*, 27 CRIM. L. BULL. 416, 421–422 (1991). Klotz's therapeutic jurisprudence speculation is that fear of disclosure of criminal inclinations may retard their being acted out.

Professor Bruce Winick, one of the founding fathers of therapeutic jurisprudence, speculating on the outcome and possible impact of *Jaffe v. Redmond*,[7] believed that the Supreme Court's imprimatur on a broad privilege "would provide an important signal to those considering whether to enter therapy that the confidentiality of their disclosures will generally be protected."[8] *Jaffe,* of course, did bring the Court's endorsement to a strong privilege and we must now await some evidence of its positive impact on persons entering therapy.[9]

Mental health treatment in prisons and jails is such a precious commodity, and prisoners' sophistication about legal rights in such short supply, that I doubt whether this debate, certainly as to deterring inmates from seeking treatment, has very much (if any) application. On the other hand, disadvantaging a prisoner by trading on ignorance or fear is hardly consonant with professional norms or ethics.

The mental health professional in a prison or mental hospital setting is well advised to make certain disclosures to an individual before proceeding. The professional should disclose his or her agency, the purpose of the encounter, and the uses to which information may or will be put. He or she should indicate a willingness to answer questions as clearly as possible concerning the risks of disclosure. For example:

"Mr. Jones, I am Mr. Smith, a psychologist employed by the Department of Corrections. I have been asked to meet with you and evaluate your present mental condition in order to help decide whether you should or should not be transferred to a mental hospital. Do you have any questions about who I am and what use may be made of what you say to me?"

If the therapist is fairly certain that uses other than the ones explained will be made of this information, that too should be volunteered. This approach to disclosure is perhaps most appropriate when the inmate-clinician contact is *not* for treatment. However, it also has application during the course of treatment where certain categories of information, to be discussed shortly, are likely to be disclosed.[10]

Certainly, the general principle of confidentiality of information obtained in the course of treatment applies in the prison or jail setting.[11] While recognizing the prin-

---

[7] 116 S. Ct. 1923 (1996).

[8] Bruce J. Winick, *The Psychotherapist-Patient Privilege: A Therapeutic Jurisprudence View*, in LAW IN A THERAPEUTIC KEY 483, 495 (David B. Wexler & Bruce J. Winick, eds. 1996).

[9] Jaffe, *supra* note 7, was decided in the broadest possible fashion as to the meaning of Fed. R. Evid. 501, and as to those who are included within the privilege.

[10] In Estelle v. Smith, 451 U.S. 454 (1981), the Supreme Court imported the Fifth Amendment's privilege against self-incrimination to the pretrial psychiatric evaluation of a person accused of capital murder, who was later convicted and sentenced to death, and who presented no psychiatric testimony on his own behalf. Dr. Grigson gave lethal testimony on dangerousness at the penalty phase, and his failure to provide a *Miranda*-type warning resulted in a denial of the condemned inmate's constitutional rights. The *Estelle* decision strives to limit itself to the unique penalty of death, although the same factors on the fairness of the type of disclosure here seem to apply. In Eng v. Kelly, No. 80-285-T (W.D.N.Y. Jan. 27, 1987), the court expressed the view that all psychiatric problems of inmates should be considered confidential except for those related to security matters.

[11] *See* Barbara A. Weiner & Robert M. Wettstein, LEGAL ISSUES IN MENTAL HEALTH CARE (1993), Chs. 7 and 8, for a valuable discussion of confidentiality and *Tarasoff*-like issues.

ciple, we must also note that maintaining confidentiality is quite another matter. Prison and jails may be closed societies, but information is a valued commodity and "the wire" always seems open. A prisoner's HIV status, even when accorded confidentiality, is signaled to staff and inmates in a variety of ways, including obvious gestures in taking the recommended precautions.

[2] Governing Law

The common law did not recognize the doctor-patient privilege in a prison setting, and not until 1828 did New York pass the first statute granting doctors the right to refuse to testify.[12] The late-arriving and narrowly expressed medical doctor-patient privilege has not always been extended to psychotherapists and other mental health professionals.[13]

In the federal courts, Rule 501 of the Federal Rules of Evidence applies. It provides:

RULE 501—GENERAL RULE

Except as otherwise required by the Constitution of the United States or provided by an Act of Congress or in rules prescribed by the Supreme Court pursuant to statutory authority, the privilege of a witness, person, government, State, or political subdivision thereof shall be governed by the principles of the common law as they may be interpreted by the courts of the United Sates in light of reason and experience. However, in civil actions and proceedings, with respect to an element of a claim or defense as to which State law supplies the rule of decision, the privilege of a witness, person, government, State or political subdivision thereof shall be determined in accordance with State law.[14]

[3] Rejected Law of Privilege

The general rule quoted above, which defers to the privilege laws of the various states, should be contrasted with the highly specific rule that had been proposed and

---

[12] Gutheil & Applebaum, *supra* note 2, at 10. The authors state that nearly three-quarters of the states now have such statutes. For an interesting general discussion of privileges, *see* Saltzburg, *Privileges and Professionals: Lawyers and Psychiatrists*, 66 VA. L. REV. 597 (1980).

[13] For consideration of the privilege as applied to social workers, *see* Annot., 50 A.L.R. 3d 563 (1997); Jaffe v. Redmond, *supra* note 7. In New York, psychologists are granted the privilege as follows: "The confidential relations and communications between a psychologist . . . and his client are placed on the same basis as those provided by law between attorney and client, and nothing in such article shall be construed to require any such privileged communications to be disclosed." N.Y. CIV. PRAC. LAW § 4507 (McKinney Supp. 1983–1984).

[14] Jaffe, *supra* note 7, interpreted this rule to include a psychotherapist-patient relationship and to include in the term "psychotherapist" psychiatrists, psychologists, and licensed social workers. *Jaffe* also noted that there is to be no post-therapy determination of the relative importance of the privilege versus the evidentiary need for disclosure. The Court did state, however, that the privilege must give way where

was rejected. This rejected rule, while not law, is an excellent guide to the more expansive thinking of this area.

PSYCHOTHERAPIST-PATIENT PRIVILEGE

(1) A "patient" is a person who consults or is examined or interviewed by a psychotherapist.

(2) A "psychotherapist" is (A) a person authorized to practice medicine in any state or nation, or reasonably believed by the patient so to be, while engaged in the diagnosis or treatment of a mental or emotional condition, including drug addiction, or (B) a person licensed or certified as a psychologist under the laws of any state or nation, while similarly engaged.

(3) A communication is "confidential" if not intended to be disclosed to third persons other than those present to further the interest of the patient in the consultation, examination, or interview, or persons reasonably necessary for the transmission of the communication, or persons who are participating in the diagnosis and treatment under the direction of the psychotherapist, including members of the patient's family.

(b) General rule of privilege.

A patient has a privilege to refuse to disclose and to prevent any other person from disclosing confidential communications, made for the purposes of diagnosis or treatment of his mental or emotional condition, including drug addiction, among himself, his psychotherapist, or persons who are participating in the diagnosis or treatment under the direction of the psychotherapist, including members of the patient's family.

(c) Who may claim the privilege.

The privilege may be claimed by the patient, by his guardian or conservator, or by the personal representative of a deceased patient. The person who was the psychotherapist may claim the privilege but only on behalf of the patient. His authority so to do is presumed in the absence of evidence to the contrary.

(d) Exceptions.

(1) *Proceedings for hospitalization.* There is no privilege under this rule for communications relevant to an issue in proceedings to hospitalize the patient for mental illness, if the psychotherapist in the course of diagnosis or treatment has determined that the patient is in need of hospitalization.

(2) *Examination by order of judge.* If the judge orders an examination of the mental or emotional condition of the patient, communications made in the course thereof are not privileged under this rule with respect to the particular purpose for which the examination is ordered unless the judge orders otherwise.

---

there is a serious threat of harm to the patient or others and disclosure is the only means to avert the harm. Jaffe, *supra* note 7, 116 S. Ct. at 1923 n.3.

(3) *Condition an element of claim or defense.* There is no privilege under this rule as to communications relevant to an issue of the mental or emotional condition of the patient in any proceeding in which he relies upon the condition as an element of his claim or defense, or, after the patient's death, in any proceeding in which any party relies upon the condition as an element of his claim or defense.[15]

Recognizing that privilege and confidentiality generally apply in institutional settings, and that these privacy safeguards are most clearly implicated during a treatment relationship, author Christine Boyle points out:

> It is suggested that there is a basic conflict here between the authoritative or controlling aspect of imprisonment, represented, in a very general way, by the custodial and administrative staff, and the need to rehabilitate, which is largely seen as the responsibility of the professional personnel. Because of this conflict, organization problems are bound to arise in an institution which must perform custodial as well as rehabilitative functions, since confidentiality may be seen as vital to the latter, but dysfunctional to the former.[16]

The difficult problem for the clinician, then, is to balance the generally applicable principle of confidentiality in a treatment relationship with the countervailing demands of security, both for specific individuals who may be in jeopardy and for the general security of the institution.

Legally safeguarded expectations of privacy in jail or prison are virtually nonexistent. Prisoners may hope for a modicum of privacy, but it is a hope that does not often translate into legal protection. In the context of freedom from unreasonable searches and seizures, claims that an inmate's cell is "home" and thus subject to some protections simply are not recognized.[17] Parenthetically, while the attorney-client relationship is vital to detainees and inmates, there is often little choice as to where to meet with counsel. Clearly, the attorney-client privilege and the need for privacy attach during attorney-client contacts in the facility.

[4] Delineating Boundaries on Access to Information

Privacy and privilege issues are further complicated by the growing trend to include correctional officers on institutional mental health treatment teams. Once this step is taken, it seems inherently impossible to draw occupation- or profession-based boundaries on access to sensitive mental health information. One might argue that officers and others who are not health care specialists properly may be exposed to conclusions (e.g., "he was sexually abused as a child") but not to underlying details.[18] But

---

[15] Fed. R. Evid., Rejected R. 504, Patient's Privilege. *See* Jaffe, *supra* note 7, 116 S. Ct. at 1081.

[16] Christine Boyle, *Confidentiality in Corrections Institutions*, 26 CANADIAN J. CRIM. & CORRECTIONS 26, 27 (1976).

[17] Id.

[18] An approach similar to this is recommended in B. JAYE ANNO, PRISON HEALTH CARE: GUIDELINES FOR THE MANAGEMENT OF AN ADEQUATE DELIVERY SYSTEM 65 (N.I.C. 1991), in the discussion of medical records and their proposed limited availability to classification committees.

clinical experts with whom I have spoken suggest that such partial disclosure is not feasible if decisions are to be authentically based in the entire treatment team. They suggest that the real problem concerns how an inmate's otherwise confidential or privileged material is used. The solution is rather uncomplicated: it does not leave the room, and at a minimum severe employment-related sanctions will result from such breach.[19] The possibility of sanctions under a licensing or certification of professions law is, of course, absent in the case of security staff.[20]

The rules of nondisclosure and sanctions for breach should be a part of the employment contract and clearly explained. For mental health professionals—psychiatrists, psychologists, nurses, and social workers—there are professional norms of conduct as well as tort suits for damages lurking for breaches of confidentiality.

In *Peterkin v. Jeffes*,[21] inmates under sentence of death in Pennsylvania complained generally about their conditions of confinement. One rather unusual claim was that inmates felt constrained to reveal their innermost feelings or the more than occasional thoughts of suicide that sweep over persons on death row. The inmates, for good reason, feared disclosure.

The Commonwealth's psychiatrists testified that they would disclose confidences, even if such disclosure engenders mistrust, but only under circumstances that create necessity and are in accord with standard psychiatric practice:

> Thus, Dr. Wawrose testified that he would disclose confidentially revealed plans to escape, intentions to injure, and possession of contraband, even though revealed to him in confidence. He would not disclose, however, confidentially revealed sexual or emotional problems. Moreover, even though the Commonwealth's policy of reacting sternly to an inmate ostensibly contemplating suicide may deter inmates from discussing suicidal inclinations, both sides agree that the overriding concern for the welfare of the inmate necessitates this practice.[22]

There is so much uncertainty among practitioners concerning confidentiality and privilege that a clear policy and procedure should exist in the form of an administrative regulation having the force of law. A mere policy directive is not enough. The rationale for this suggestion is that each state likely has enacted some confidentiality and disclosure laws, and administrative regulations should not conflict with such laws but serve as more explicit legislative-type enactments.

---

[19] A tort action by an aggrieved party is possible, and recovery may be for the disclosure itself, for economic loss, or for mental anguish. RALPH REISNER & CHRISTOPHER SLOBOGIN, LAW AND THE MENTAL HEALTH SYSTEM: CIVIL AND CRIMINAL ASPECTS (2d ed. 1990), p. 236.

[20] In Morra v. State Board of Examiners, 510 F.2d 614 (Kan. 1973), the court held that the obligation to adhere to professional ethical standards was implied by the state's licensing statute. The American Medical Association, the American Psychiatric Association, and the American Psychological Association all have codes of ethics protective of patient/client confidentiality.

[21] 661 F. Supp 895 (E.D. Pa. 1987), *aff'd in part, vacated in part*, 855 F.2d 1021 (3d Cir. 1988), *on remand*, 1989 WL 140489 (E.D. Pa. 1989); *enforcement denied*, 1991 WL 137122 (E.D. Pa. 1991); *decision aff'd*, 953 F.3d 1380 (E.D. Pa. 1992).

[22] Peterkin, 661 F. Supp. at 919.

¶ 9.2 WHEN CONFIDENTIALITY DOES NOT APPLY

Every jurisdiction should adopt a clear set of rules as to when confidentiality in the correctional setting is inapplicable. I suggest that mental health personnel be required to report to appropriate correctional personnel when an inmate is identified as one of the following:

- Suicidal

- Homicidal

- Presenting a reasonably clear danger of injury to himself or to others, either by virtue of conduct or oral statements

- Presenting a reasonably clear risk of escape or the creation of internal disorder or riot

- Receiving psychotropic medication, or is noncompliant with medication

- Requiring movement to a special unit for observation, evaluation, or treatment of acute episodes

- Requiring transfer to a treatment facility outside the prison or jail

This is essentially a "need to know" approach. Readers may agree or disagree with some of the categories listed above, or believe I have overlooked one or more. However, "need to know" should serve as the guiding principle.

Not according confidentiality to these various categories serves a variety of purposes. The duty to preserve the life and health of inmates underpins the need to breach putative confidences in order to prevent suicide, homicide, or self-inflicted harm and harm to others. Prisons and jails are under a constitutional duty to provide a non-life-threatening environment, and these proposals are consistent with activating that duty. Riot or escape from prison is a crime, and as a general proposition, no privilege attaches to discussions of future criminality.[23] Given the alterations in behavior that occur as a result of psychotropic medication, or even more so when an inmate is non-compliant in taking such medication, it is in the inmate's best interests that correction staff are informed of the use or noncompliance and that they receive training as to the effects. Finally, if there is a need for any type of restraint or transfer, then it is perfectly obvious that correction staff must know and likely assist.[24]

[1] Duty to Warn Identifiable Third Party—*Tarasoff*

The *Tarasoff* situation alluded to at the outset calls for some elaboration. In *Tarasoff*, a mental health outpatient carried out his intention to kill his former fiancée, having previously confided his plan to his therapist. The decedent's parents sued for damages and the Supreme Court of California held that a psychotherapist owes a duty

---

[23] *Tarasoff, supra* note 3, 551 P.2d at 431.
[24] *Vitek v. Jones*, 445 U.S. 480, 489–490 (1980).

of reasonable care to identifiable third parties endangered by the therapist's patient. The court held:

> When a therapist determines, or pursuant to standards of his profession should determine, that his patient presents a serious danger of violence to another, he incurs an obligation to use reasonable care to protect the intended victim against such danger. The discharge of this duty may require the therapist to take one or more various steps, depending upon the nature of the case. Thus it may call for him to warn the intended victim of the danger, to notify the police, or to take whatever other steps are reasonably necessary under the circumstances.[25]

Professor David Wexler raises the question of just how the therapist may discharge the duty to warn, suggesting that alerting the intended victim would be the standardized safe response.[26] In a prison or jail the standardized safe response for mental health staff would seem to call for alerting the appropriate security personnel and allowing them to take the steps required to protect the intended victim. This may be in the form of a separation order, use of protective custody, or transfer.

A *Tarasoff* situation does not arise unless there is an identifiable victim. If a patient (or client) during treatment talks generally about murderous thoughts or hostility against authority, then clearly this is not a *Tarasoff* situation because there is no enforceable duty to an identifiable victim. Here, it seems, the world of professional ethics and individual judgment prevails.[27]

A study of psychiatrists, psychologists, and social workers in the eight largest metropolitan areas of the country disclosed widespread awareness of *Tarasoff* and a substantial increase in willingness to warn potential victims.[28] As of 1980, according to the study, there was a widespread endorsement of the *Tarasoff* obligation to protect potential victims as a personal and professional norm.[29]

In a survey of practicing psychiatrists, Beck found that about 40 percent had been involved in a case in which a *Tarasoff* warning had been provided to a potential victim. The only harmful effects to the psychiatric relationship appeared to occur where the patient had believed that all communications were absolutely confidential.[30] This,

---

[25] Tarasoff, *supra* note 3, 551 P.2d at 431.

[26] DAVID WEXLER, MENTAL HEALTH LAW: MAJOR ISSUES (1981), p.158. The reference, of course, is outside the prison or jail setting. *See* McIntosh v. Milano, 168 N.J. Super. 466, 403 A.2d 500 (1979), for elaboration on the duty to warn.

[27] In Shaw v. Glickman, 415 A.2d 625 (Md. App. 1980), a therapist revealed to a person in group therapy that the person's wife, who was also a part of the group, was having an extramarital affair with yet a third group member. The enraged husband shot his wife's lover, but *Tarasoff* was held inapplicable because the husband did not disclose his lethal plans. In addition, the court opined that under Maryland law, no member of the psychiatric team could have revealed to the intended victim a propensity to "invoke Solon's law."

[28] William J. Bowers, et al., *How Did Tarasoff Affect Clinical Practice?* ANNALS. Mar. 1986, at 70.

[29] Bowers, *supra* note 28, at 83. *See* Jaffe v. Redmond, *supra* note 7, 116 S. Ct. at 1932 n.19, in which the court, without mentioning *Tarasoff* by name, strongly endorsed its principles.

[30] James C. Beck, *When The Patient Threatens Violence: An Empirical Study of Clinical Practice After* Tarasoff, 10 BULL. AM. ACAD. PSYCHIATRY L. 189 (1982). *See also Note, Where the Public Peril*

of course, underscores my earlier admonition favoring and specifying advance disclosure.

It seems reasonable to suggest that an important tort decision from one state has by now infiltrated the professional norms of mental health workers, and that we may also expect those norms to migrate to the prison world. Indeed, with the dangers generally intensified and with a more compact world of identifiable victims, *Tarasoff* norms may actually be more compelling in prison.[31] It may also be much easier to comply with *Tarasoff* in the controlled world of prison.

[2] Other Probabilities for Harm

One authority would solve the ethical question of disclosure when *Tarasoff* is not clearly involved by treating such disclosures as generally confidential to the extent that the "public" is not imperiled. She states:

> Actually this . . . is not discrepant with the American Psychological Association's Ethical Standards of Psychologists, Principle 6, Section a (1972:3), which reads as follows: "Such information is not communicated to others unless certain important conditions are met: (a) information received in confidence is revealed only after most careful deliberation and when there is clear and imminent danger to an individual or to society, and then only to appropriate professional workers or public authorities."[32]

On the practical level, students of this problem indicate that with the exception of the probability of harm to the clinician or others, the decisions to be made are far from clear-cut. Quijano and Logsdon put it this way:

> It seems to be the general practice among correctional psychologists to inform their inmate clients—and the inmates must understand—that aside from plans to escape and/or harm themselves or others, the principle of confidentiality holds. Even in these two cases, the issue is not clear-cut. Special care must be exercised not to report just any talk about escape or violence to the security authorities. Only those threats whose probability of actual execution is reasonably high should be reported, and the only basis for that decision is historical data and the psychologist's best judgment. Unnecessary reports may harm not only the inmate client in question but also the correctional psychol-

---

Begins: A Survey of Psychotherapists to Determine the Effects of Tarasoff, 31 STAN. L. REV. 165 (1978); *Comment*, "Tarasoff v. Regents of the University of California," 22 N.Y.L. SCH. L. REV. 1011 (1977).

[31] While this book is almost exclusively concerned with the inmate-as inmate, it should be noted that *Tarasoff*-like claims arise when an inmate is furloughed, given work or education release, or paroled. For example, in Estate of Gilmore v. Buckley, 787 F.2d 714 (1st Cir. 1986), *cert. denied*, 479 U.S. 882 (1986), a furloughed jail inmate killed a woman who was easily identifiable as a prospective victim. The First Circuit Court of Appeals held that without some special relationship between the state and the plaintiff (e.g., being in custody), the Fourteenth Amendment simply provided no remedy for errors in release or failure to warn.

[32] Kaslow, *Ethical Problems in Prison Psychology*, 7 CRIM. JUST. & BEHAV. 3, 4 (1980).

ogist's credibility to both the inmate clientele and the administration. It is obvious that in the implementation of the principle of confidentiality many decisions will be "judgment calls," and prudence (whatever that means to the psychologist) is the guide.[33]

Another observer admonishes the prison counselor or therapist to consider:

1. The role conflict in seeking to balance the therapeutic needs of the patient with the security and stability of the institution.
2. Inherent problems in accurately predicting dangerousness.
3. The impact of a breach of confidentiality in the relationship with the inmate.[34]

Thus, where there is no identifiable, intended victim and the therapist encounters "threats in the air," so to speak, there is no easy answer. Confidentiality in the treatment relationship should be the norm, with therapists ultimately having to exercise their best judgment on the seriousness of the general threat. Therapists who regularly reveal their patient's every threatening word surely compromise themselves professionally and likely undermine their ability to help inmates. They also will likely lose the respect of security officers who will quickly tire of responding to false alarms.

¶ 9.3 CONSENT TO TREATMENT

The basic principle of the law concerning how treatment decisions should be made is most clearly embodied in the doctrine of informed consent.[35] We begin with a general norm of the sanctity of the body of a competent adult. This in turn implies autonomy in decision-making by the individual whose body—or life or health—is at stake.

The patient has autonomy and need, while the healer has information and expertise. Informed consent strives for some equilibrium between these two, so the patient can apply his personal value system to the alternatives presented.[36] This approach—let us call it the traditional model—applies most comfortably to physical medicine outside the area of psychological treatment.

A right to refuse treatment where mental disorder is at issue raises the question of the competency of the individual to make the decision, or even at times to absorb the

---

[33] Quijano & Logsdon, *Some Issues in the Practice of Correctional Psychology in the Context of Security*, 9 PROF. PSYCHOLOGY 228, 231 (1978).

[34] P. Lane, *Prison Counseling and the Dilemma of Confidentiality*, in CONFERENCE ON CORRECTIONS (V. Fox, ed. 1978). The author concludes, unremarkably, that each decision is an individual one.

[35] *See generally* FAY ROZOVSKY, CONSENT TO TREATMENT: A PRACTICAL GUIDE (1984); Symposium, *Informed Consent*, 1 BEHAV. SCI. & L. (Fall 1983). For an extensive review of consent issues, with an emphasis on physical (nonpsychotropic) medicine, *see* Steven E. Deardoff, *Informed Consent, Termination of Medical Treatment, and the Federal Tort Claims Act; A New Proposal for the Military Health Care System*, 115 MIL. L. REV. 1 (1987).

[36] *See* II MAKING HEALTH CARE DECISIONS: THE ETHICAL AND LEGAL IMPLICATIONS OF INFORMED CONSENT IN THE PATIENT-PRACTITIONER RELATIONSHIP 397 (President's Commission for the Study of Ethical Problems in Medicine and Behavioral Research, 1982).

proferred information. The content of the information appears to have received far more critical attention than the issues related to reception and comprehension. Obviously, this elevates the formal over the operational. Another curiosity of this area of concern is the manner in which we define the basic problem. That is, we tend to speak of a right to resist unwanted treatment and not of the need to obtain consent. Consent seems to be presumed in the absence of resistance.

[1] Situational Coercion: Limits on Free Choice

When an individual is in penal confinement, all of these issues are even more complicated, given a conceivably legitimate constitutional right to treatment on the one hand, and the inherent coercion of the institutional setting on the other. The legally impaired status of the prisoner combines with the inherent coercion of the facility to require an approach especially tailored to these circumstances.

Al Bronstein, one of the country's foremost litigators and activists on behalf of prisoners, is quoted as saying, "You cannot create [a prison] institution in which informed consent without coercion is feasible."[37] If informed consent, then, is to be a legal requirement for the more intrusive types of treatment (e.g., electric convulsion therapy or psychotropic medications), Mr. Bronstein's approach rules out the treatment.[38]

Prisons and jails do create what I will term situational (or structural) coercion. Situational coercion arises when the characteristics inherent in the particular environment impinge on, but do not necessarily vanquish, free choice. If coercion is defined as an environment, or as efforts intended (or likely) to influence another by severe and credible threats that appear to be irresistible, then the prison-jail environment clearly must be factored into the coercion calculation. This environment of distrust should place a heavy burden on the person seeking consent.

Although situational coercion creates hurdles, it need not create barriers. As a matter of policy and law this seems an eminently reasonable approach because it allows for informed consent and possibly valuable treatment while it accommodates obvious environmental pressures.

In one rather early federal case, a prisoner confined in Leavenworth complained that prison clinicians authorized the injection of psychotropic medication over his general and religious objections.[39] The inmate had been diagnosed as paranoid-schizophrenic and exhibited hostile and destructive behavior (self-mutilation, destruction of a prison cell, unprovoked fights with other inmates, and so on). The medication was authorized on the basis of a clinical judgment that the inmate posed a substantial threat to his own safety and the safety of other inmates.

The essence of the court's reasoning in rejecting the inmate's claim was that the

---

[37] Bronstein, quoted in RUTH FADEN & TOM BEACHAMP, A HISTORY AND THEORY OF INFORMED CONSENT (1986), p. 344.

[38] In at least one case, this is precisely what the court decided concerning psychosurgery. Kaimowitz v. Department of Mental Health, No. 73-1934-AW (Cir. Ct. Wayne Co., Mich. July 10, 1973), published in 13 CRIM. L. RPTR. 2452 (1973). *Kaimowitz* was as concerned about risks and knowledge as with institutional coercion.

[39] Sconiers v. Jarvis, 458 F. Supp. 37 (D. Kan. 1978).

prison officials were under a duty to provide medical care for an inmate's serious medical needs, and that the inmate's disagreement with the nature and type of care provided presented no legally recognized claim.[40] The court dismissed the inmate's religious objections because he had not expressed them and because he failed to show that he was a sincere adherent of an established religion that prohibited psychotropic medication. Thus, the right to care was judicially converted into a duty to accept the case with no intermediate concerns expressed about competency and consent.[41]

If this decision had been factually characterized as presenting an emergency situation, with forced medication as the clinically preferred choice to achieve temporary control, then other issues would arise. That is not the case, however, so the rule that emerges is that where clinical judgment is brought to bear on the choice of treatment, a combination of the need to control penal institutions and to provide care for the seriously disordered inmate allows for the forcible administration of psychotropic medication.

[2] Harmful Effects; Severity of Treatment

An inmate's *right* to care, however, may not be so easily converted to a duty of uninformed and unquestioning obligation to accept the proferred care. Let me assume that there are two competing purposes that might be served by the doctrine of informed consent: protection from potential harm and/or respect for personal autonomy.[42] Prolonged injection of psychotropic medication over an inmate's or an inmate-patient's objection may actually violate both purposes. On the other hand, if a balancing approach is taken and the prison's ubiquitous claim to safety and security is factored in, then inmates' dignitarian health concerns begin to fade.

Even those who generally favor the use of psychotropic medication for in-patients are careful to point out the side effects. Gutheil and Applebaum state:

> The anticholinergic effects include dry mouth, blurred vision, constipation, and urinary retention, each of which can be variably disturbing. Some patients find visual blurring particularly disturbing; others are more distressed by alteration in bowel irregularity.
>
> The autonomic side effects include postural hypotension, leading to dizziness on abrupt rising to a standing posture.
>
> The extrapyramidal side effects are often the most subjectively disturbing. These include dystonias and dyskinesias (spasms and abnormalities of movement); alathisia (motor restlessness, occasionally experienced as dis-

---

[40] Sconiers, 458 F. Supp. at 40.

[41] The later decision in Youngberg v. Romeo, 457 U.S. 307 (1982), with its emphasis on professional judgment, closely resembles *Sconiers*.

[42] Ruth Mackin, *Some Problems in Gaining Informed Consent from Psychiatric Patients*, 31 EMORY L.J. 345, 371 (1982). *See also* GEORGE ANNAS, et al., INFORMED CONSENT TO HUMAN EXPERIMENTATION: THE SUBJECT'S DILEMMA (1977). The authors argue that the primary functions of informed consent are to promote individual autonomy and to encourage rational decision-making. It appears to this observer that rational decision-making and autonomy go hand-in-glove and that the avoidance or acceptance of harm (or pain) needs separate mention as a qualitatively different phenomenon.

comfort without a movement component); akinesia or stiffness; or tremor and incoordination. When these movement disturbances affect eye muscles, tongue or pharynx musculature, they can be especially upsetting, as the eyes may roll upward, and speech and swallowing may be interfered with.[43]

The authors go on to define tardive dyskinesia and the problems it presents to both professionals and inmates:

> *Tardive dyskinesia* (TD). This side effect is the most problematic for the psychiatric profession and is the one most seized upon by legal and other opponents of pharmacotherapy. The term refers to lasting (tardive) effects of medication that may involve movement disorders (dyskinesias) of face and tongue musculature, as well as muscles of the extremities. Fear of, or the appearance of, this effect may lead to medication refusal, although patients are not often conscious of the existence of the abnormal movements.
>
> This relatively recently discovered deleterious effect of antipsychotic medication use poses several problems. First, in terms of diagnosis, a careful reading of Kraeplin's observations of schizophrenics, in the century before phenothiazines were first synthesized, reveals descriptions of movement disorders appearing in late life and strikingly resembling TD. Second, concerning prevention, this affect appears at times to occur even following relatively brief exposure to medication at low doses. Third, treatment response for TD has been variable but generally poor; at present, research in treating TD, though extremely active, is in an embryonic stage.
>
> Given the current irreplaceable importance of medications in the treatment of major illness and in facilitating the return of patients to the community, tardive dyskinesia must be viewed as a risk to be carefully weighed against the benefits, as with all treatments.[44]

Accepting all of the above as accurate, and accepting further the potential benefits of such medication, when it comes to weighing the risk, the authors suggest that the inmate-patient should be involved and consent generally required.[45] The general practice now in American prisons is to obtain written consent for such medication, although mental health records and files are often in such disarray that consent forms believed to have been signed cannot be located.

Whether informed consent is required (or desirable) for treatment of a mentally disordered inmate should not turn on whether the proposed treatment will be admin-

---

[43] Gutheil & Applebaum, *supra* note 2, at 118–119.

[44] Id.

[45] Other writers are not so reserved or sanguine about the problems. Margaret Brazier, in *Prison Doctors and Their Involuntary Patients*, 1982 PUB. LAW 282, describes similar problems in English prisons. She argues that the Prison Medical Service overuses drugs because it saves time and possible violence, and estimates that up to 40 percent of those treated with powerful psychotropic drugs will suffer some degree of side effects: "Apparently the view of the Home Office is that drugs will be administered without consent only if life is endangered without it, serious harm to the inmate or others is likely, or there would be an irreversible deterioration in the inmate's condition."

istered in a prison or a mental health facility. The identity of the agency administering the treatment facility seems equally irrelevant. The objectives of autonomy and protection from harm simply are not related to the place of care or administrative arrangements. Obviously, it may be more professionally appropriate to medicate in a clinical setting, but just as obviously this is not determinative of the need for consent.

Does an inmate's legal status dilute his claims to autonomy or protection from harm to the point where consent to treatment is not generally required, but rather is applied in some diluted form? Where does the person convicted of a crime fit on the chart where the two extreme positions are: (a) that a clinician always knows best and acts in the best interests of the individual, and (b) that a person, no matter how disturbed, always has the right to resist therapy? Do the same considerations apply to all forms of psychiatric care?

It may be recalled that in *Vitek v. Jones*,[46] the Supreme Court imposed procedural due process on prison-to-mental-hospital transfers because the requisite finding of mental illness is qualitatively different from conviction and punishment for crime, and because the transferee was subject to a mandatory behavior modification program.[47] In *Vitek,* although the challenge was not to the enforced participation in any particular treatment program, the Court did inferentially accept involuntary treatment. The due process requirements were imposed to reduce the risk of error in fact finding and to provide an adjudicative format for those inmates seeking to resist the move, and thus the treatment. *Vitek,* then, is early Supreme Court acceptance of some types of enforced treatment. And depending on the treatment, such a position is not remarkable.[48]

In Mental Health and the Law, an NIMH publication, Dr. Alan Stone ranks various psychiatric treatments "according to criteria or severity, such as the gravity and duration of intended effects and likely side-effects, the extent to which a reneging patient can avoid these effects, and the sheer physical intrusiveness of the therapy. Presumably, as one moved from the more to the less severe treatments, the patient's consent would be less consequential."[49]

In the context of requiring a full judicial hearing in the face of a protesting patient, Dr. Stone ranks more to less severe treatments as follows:

1. Ablation or destruction of histologically normal brain cells by any medical or surgical procedure (there is a growing consensus that such psychosurgery is experimental and should be subject to stricter regulations governing experimentation on humans).

---

[46] *Supra* note 24.

[47] Vitek, *supra* note 24, 445 U.S. at 494. In Jones v. United States, 463 U.S. 354 n.19, Justice Powell wrote, "The Court has held that a convicted prisoner may be treated involuntarily for particular psychiatric problems . . ." The treatment at issue was the powerful drug Thorazine.

[48] In Lappe v. Loeffelholz, 815 F.2d 1173, 1176–1177 (8th Cir. 1987), the court uncritically found that once a Vitek hearing was held, and while the inmate remained at the treatment facility, intramuscular injections of psychotropic medication could be prescribed and administered without consent. This position was taken in the context of resolving another issue—whether such injections could continue without a new hearing after the inmate was returned to the prison. Since a *Vitek* hearing does not necessarily address competence or the specific need for psychotropic medication, *Lappe's* uncritical acceptance of the right to forcibly medicate based on a *Vitek* hearing is suspect.

[49] ALAN STONE, MENTAL HEALTH AND LAW: A SYSTEM IN TRANSITION (N.I.M.H. 1975), p.103.

2. Electroshock therapy or any other convulsive therapy.
3. Coma or subcoma insulin therapy.
4. Behavior modification utilizing aversive therapy.
5. Medically prescribed, highly addictive substances (e.g., methadone).[50]

Professor Bruce Winick takes a similar approach:

Two conclusions may be reached . . . . First, because the verbal and many of the behavioral techniques are not seriously intrusive, do not result in long-lasting effects, and are readily capable of being resisted even when the subject is nonconsenting, these techniques do not so infringe on fundamental rights as to create a constitutional right to refuse the treatments. Second, the therapeutic interventions in the higher range of the continuum do present significant, pervasive invasions of the subjects' minds and bodies with effects that are often long-lasting and always incapable of being resisted when the subject is nonconsenting. When applied involuntarily, these techniques invade such fundamental constitutional rights as the first amendment right to be free from interference with mental processes, the due process right of privacy and the fundamental liberty interest associated with bodily integrity.[51]

[3] Autonomy: Issues of Competency and Voluntariness

Where informed consent is required, at a minimum there must be a competent adult, the absence of duress or coercion (i.e., voluntariness), and the disclosure of information on risks, alternatives, and the likely consequences of refusing the proffered care.[52] The term "informed consent" may appear to be redundant. Consent, it would be argued, necessarily must be informed. However, informed consent in law needs to be distinguished from voluntary consent (i.e., a merely voluntary assent but not necessarily with awareness of options).[53] The mere listing of such factors should not serve to camouflage inherent difficulties in each factor and the lively debate surrounding this area.

For example, by what standards shall we measure competency? Too often an inmate's or patient's competence is questioned primarily when his treatment decision varies from that of the clinician's.[54] The circularity of this approach is apparent, but its use may be unavoidable, especially in the institutional setting.

We must emphasize that informed consent, then, is a two-way street. One lane involves the provision of relevant information, while the other requires some compre-

---

[50] Stone, *supra* note 49, at 105.

[51] Bruce Winnick, *Legal Limitations on Correctional Therapy and Research*, 65 MINN. L. REV. 331, 373 (1981).

[52] *See* WEXLER, *supra* note 26.

[53] *See* Schneckloth v. Bustamonte, 412 U.S. 218 (1973), validating "consent" searches so long as there is no coercion.

[54] *See* Loren Roth, et al., *Tests of Competency to Consent to Treatment*, 134 AM. J. PSYCHIATRY 279, 281 (1977).

hension. With psychiatric patients, and certainly the mentally retarded, it is the second lane that is most problematic.

As indicated earlier, some will argue that any informed consent, and especially the notion of voluntariness, is an illusion in an institutional setting.[55] Voluntariness, however, seems to be more of a problem with *research* on prisoners than it is with traditional treatment techniques. One important study concluded *"that more detailed disclosures and no therapeutic privileges should be the rule in the experimental setting."*[56]

The possibility of secondary gain from participation in prison experiments— money, better living conditions, early release—all contribute to problems of voluntariness that are not likely to be present in a treatment situation. Indeed, the inmates themselves may "fake it" in order to obtain what is seen as the benefits of being labeled mentally ill. For truly mentally disturbed prisoners, the key element in consent would seem to be the richness of the information concerning risks, alternatives, possible consequences, and—too often neglected—the prisoner's comprehension.

One critical point requires absolute clarity: neither the impaired legal status of the prisoner nor the loss of liberty inherently associated with confinement reaches into the inmate's physical or psychic interior. Obviously, imprisonment per se will have a profound physical and emotional impact on inmates. What I mean, however, is that the inmate's autonomy is not sufficiently breached so that the basic legal norm of autonomy mentioned earlier is vitiated.

[4] Suggested Norm for Informed Consent

While rarely explicit, the more recent judicial decisions involving prisoners do draw the line between the exterior and the interior of a person. Although the line is rudimentary and may appear to be obvious, it is nonetheless useful. Where official activity requires penetration of the body, whether by scalpel, needle, or pill, the inmate's legal and human autonomy should make informed consent the norm.[57]

This observation is based on a distillation of many legal decisions and the thoughts of many scholars. I do not, however, rely on any single or sharply defined authority for my points. But while this may read like a personal position, which it is, it is also a fair distillation of the law on point.

Professor Norvall Morris directly faced the issue of inmate informed consent, and did so in the context of a debate on highly experimental and dangerous treatments. Morris states:

> I adhere to the view that it is possible to protect the inmate's freedom to consent or not; that we must be highly skeptical of consent in captivity, particu-

---

[55] *See, e.g.,* Annas, *supra* note 42, at 104; *see also* Bronstein, *supra* note 37.

[56] Annas, *supra* note 42, at 44 (emphasis in original). Ruth Macklin, on the other hand, reaches the general conclusion that the same standards should be used in the research and treatment contexts. Indeed, because of our tendency to put so much trust in doctors we may accept risks we might otherwise be unwilling to accept, with shock therapy used as a primary example. Macklin, *Some Problems in Gaining Informed Consent from Psychiatric Patients,* 31 EMORY L.J. 345, 352–353 (1982).

[57] For an excellent discussion of the autonomy concept, *see* Marjorie Maguire Schultz, *From Informed Consent to Patient Choice: A New Protected Interest,* 95 YALE L.J. 219 (1985).

larly to any risky and not well-established procedures; but there seems little value in arbitrarily excluding all prisoners from any treatment, experimental or not. Like free citizens they may consent, under precisely circumscribed conditions to any medical, psychological, psychiatric, and neurosurgical interventions which are professionally indicated; their protection must be more adequate than that surrounding the free citizen's consent, since they are more vulnerable. It is better directly to confront the potentialities of abuse of power over prisoners than to rely on the temporary exclusion of prisoners from "experimental" programs.[58]

Many judicial decisions in this area, and especially the more recent ones, are supportive of Professor Morris' views, often without being as direct or thoughtful.

¶ 9.4 EARLIER CONSENT DECISIONS

In the relatively early case of *Haynes v. Harris*,[59] a federal prisoner, confined at the Medical Center in Springfield, Missouri, unsuccessfully challenged his forced medical care. He claimed that he was being subjected to corporal punishment, which was outside the scope of permissible punishment, and that as a citizen he had a right to decide for himself whether to receive treatment.

The court summarily rejected both claims, without any analysis of the nature of the challenged treatment or the possible need for the inmate's consent. In an institution designed for treatment, the court assumed that the complaint here was really about the enforcement of rules and regulations, an area deemed the exclusive prerogative of administrative authorities.[60]

A little later, in the case of *Ramsey v. Ciccone*,[61] a similar approach resulted in a similar ruling. The prisoner did not raise the issue of consent, but the court found that:

Having custody of the prisoner's body and control of the prisoner's access to medical treatment, the prison authorities have a duty to provide needed medical attention . . .. Even though the treatment is unusually painful, or causes unusual mental suffering, it may be administered to a prisoner without his consent if it is recognized as appropriate by recognized medical authority or authorities.[62]

In *Peek v. Ciccone*,[63] a federal prisoner also confined at Springfield challenged his forced medication. After refusing to take a tranquilizer ordered by a physician, the prisoner was forcibly given an injection of Thorazine by prison guards. The court held that the prisoner did not have a valid Eighth Amendment claim because "[t]he officers

---

[58] Norval Morris, The Future of Imprisonment (1974), pp. 25–26 (citation omitted).

[59] 344 F. 2d 463 (8th Cir. 1965).

[60] Haynes, 344 F. 2d at 465. This decision also is a good example of the then prevailing "hands-off" doctrine.

[61] 310 F. Supp. 600 (W.D. Mo. 1970).

[62] Ramsey, 310 F. Supp. at 605 (emphasis added) (citations omitted).

[63] 288 F. Supp. 329 (W.D. Mo. 1968).

of the Medical Center [Subordinates of the Attorney General] were not attempting to punish or harm the petitioner by forcibly administering under medical direction the intramuscular injection . . . ."[64]

The *Peck* court gave weight to the following factors in reaching its decision:[65]

- The prisoner was given a chance to take the drug orally and refused;

- The prison guard had received sufficient training at the medical center to administer an intramuscular injection; and

- Although the Thorazine did cause the prisoner to become dizzy and faint on occasion, the drug is non-narcotic and not habit forming.

The court also indicated its general deference to the discretion of institutional administrators. Of course, whether or not Thorazine is habit forming is the least of one's worries about this powerful drug. There are many side effects, including tardive dyskinesia, which is defined and described at ¶ 9.3[2].

In *Smith v. Baker*,[66] a prisoner confined in the Missouri State Penitentiary claimed that his federal rights were violated when he was injected with prolixin against his will and against his religious beliefs. The Court dismissed the Eighth Amendment claim of improper and inadequate medical care by following *Ramsey v. Ciccone*. Surprisingly, the court casually dismissed the First Amendment claim by simply stating, "[I]t is well established that medical care which is administered over the objections of a prisoner does not constitute the denial of any federal right."[67]

Clearly, these early decisions left prisoners with very little voice in the medical or psychiatric care they received. It should be noted, however, that the cases all are from the Federal District Court of the Western District of Missouri and the Eighth Circuit Court of Appeal. The reason for this is that the United States Medical Center for Federal Prisoners is located in Missouri. Thus, little diversity of opinion will be found or is to be expected.[68]

Mackey v. Procunier[69] involved a challenge to a type of experimental behavior modification program used at the California Medical Facility at Vacaville in which the drug succinylchloride (Anectine) was used.[70] The protesting inmate conceded that he had consented to ECT but not to the succinylchloride. The inmate (one of 64 involved)

---

[64] Peck, 288 F. Supp. at 337.

[65] Id.

[66] 326 F. Supp. 787 (W.D. Mo. 1970), *aff'd*, 442 F.2d 928 (8th Cir. 1971).

[67] Smith, 326 F. Supp. at 788. Oddly, the court relied on *Ramsey* and *Haynes*, neither of which dealt with a religious objection.

[68] *See* Annas, *supra* note 42, at 121. The authors also suggest that the cases were inartfully presented due to the lack of counsel.

[69] 477 F.2d 877 (9th Cir. 1973).

[70] *See* Note, *Aversion Therapy: Punishment as Treatment and Treatment as Cruel and Unusual Punishment*, 49 S. CAL. L.R. 880, 959–981 (1976). The Physician's Desk Reference 748 (1994) issues urgent warnings about this drug's use; it states the need for a person skilled in artificial respiration and tracheal intubation to be on hand and warns that severe hyperklamia is possible, among other cautions.

had described the drug as a "breath-stopping and paralyzing 'fright drug.'"[71] This program caught the eye of the late Jessica Mitford, who wrote:

> According to Dr. Arthur Nugent, chief psychiatrist at Vacaville and an enthusiast for the drug, it induces "sensations of suffocation and drowning." The subject experiences feelings of deep horror and terror, "as though he were on the brink of death." While he is in this condition a therapist scolds him for his misdeeds and tells him to shape up or expect more of the same. Candidates for Anectine treatment were selected for a range of offenses: "frequent fights, verbal threatening, deviant sexual behavior, stealing, unresponsiveness to the group therapy programs." Dr. Nugent told the San Francisco Chronicle, "Even the toughest inmates have come to fear and hate the drug. I don't blame them, I wouldn't have one treatment myself for the world." Declaring he was anxious to continue the experiment, he added, "I'm at a loss as to why everybody's upset over this."[72]

Although the district court dismissed the complaint, the court of appeals held that "[p]roof of such matters could, in our judgment, raise constitutional questions respecting cruel and unusual punishment or impermissible tinkering with the mental process."[73]

Clonce v. Richardson[74] involved a challenge to the Special Treatment and Rehabilitative Training (START) behavior modification proposed for federal prisoners at Missouri's Springfield facility. The program was designed for highly aggressive and destructive inmates whose behavior the government sought to alter by a type of token economy. As Professor David Wexler described it:

> The inmate plaintiffs contended that the deprivations which they were involuntarily required to endure at the first level of the program (such as visitation rights, exercise opportunities, and reading materials) amounted to a constitutional violation. In response, the government argued that it was necessary, at the initial stage, to deprive the inmates of those rights so that those items and events might be used as reinforcers. Moreover, the government continued, the fact that the inmates deemed the denial of rights sufficient enough to challenge actually established the psychological effectiveness of those reinforcers as behavioral motivators. Note that the government's argument comes close to creating a legal Catch 22: If you complain of the denial of certain rights, you are not entitled to them; you are entitled only to those rights the denial of which you do not challenge.

While the lawsuit was pending, the Bureau of Prisoners decided to terminate the START program, though the Bureau's director testified that such

---

[71] Mackey, *supra* note 69.

[72] JESSICA MITTFORD, KIND AND UNUSUAL TREATMENT: THE PRISON BUSINESS (1973), p.128.

[73] Mackey, *supra* note 69, 477 F.2d at 878. After the reversal and remand, no further judicial history appears. The writer has been told that the use of the drug "anectine" has long since been discontinued.

[74] 379 F. Supp. 338 (W.D. Mo. 1974).

"positive-reinforcement" approaches would in all likelihood be employed in future correctional efforts. Because of the START termination, however, the federal court found the suit to be moot, except with respect to certain procedural aspects, and accordingly did not address the merits of the deprivation issue.[75]

Souder v. McGuire[76] involved a former inmate at Pennsylvania's Farview State Hospital for the criminally insane who claimed that a violation of his constitutional rights occurred when he and other inmates were forcibly treated with psychotropic drugs. The court denied a motion to dismiss, stating that the administration of drugs that have a painful or frightening effect can amount to cruel and unusual punishment.[77]

One of the most decisive of the first generation cases in this area, *Knecht v. Gillman*,[78] involved the Iowa State Medical Facility (ISMF), to which an Iowa prisoner could be transferred for diagnosis, evaluation, and treatment. Inmates challenged the forcible injection of apomorphine, a drug that caused vomiting for 15 minutes to an hour and also caused a temporary increase in blood pressure. The drug was used as an aversive stimulus when inmates were caught swearing, lying, or getting up late. These rule infractions were reported to a nurse, who would administer the injection in a room containing only a water closet.

The court refused to accept as final the characterization of this program as treatment and thereby insulate it from scrutiny under the Eighth Amendment. The court concluded that:

> Whether it is called "aversive stimuli" or punishment, the act of forcing someone to vomit for a fifteen minute period for committing some minor breach of the rules can only be regarded as cruel and unusual unless the treatment is being administered to a patient who knowingly and intelligently has consented to it . . . The use of this unproven drug for this purpose on an involuntary basis, is, in our opinion, cruel and unusual punishment prohibited by the eighth amendment.[79]

To remedy the situation at ISMF, the court ordered that before apomorphine treatments can be used, the following conditions must be met:[80]

---

[75] Wexler, *supra* note 26, at 247. The court's procedural concerns about transfer would now be resolved with reference either to Meachum v. Fano, 427 U.S. 215 (1976), or Vitek v. Jones, *supra* note 24.

[76] 423 F. Supp. 830 (M.D. Pa. 1976).

[77] Souder, 423 F. Supp. at 832. Farview patients apparently included transferees from the corrections system. No further reported proceedings were found. Farview is now used exclusively for Pennsylvania's seriously mentally ill inmates. It is richly staffed and nicely appointed, a far cry from its earlier "snake pit" days. For an interesting case involving medical experimentation at the Maryland House of Correction, *see* Bailey v. Lally, 481 F. Supp. 203 (D. Md. 1979).

[78] 588 F.2d 1136 (8th Cir. 1973).

[79] Knecht, 588 F.2d at 1139–1140.

[80] Knecht, 588 F.2d at 1140–1141.

- A written consent must be obtained with the patient being fully informed of the nature, purpose, risks, and effects of treatment;
- The consent is revocable at any time, even orally; and
- Each injection must be authorized by a physician.

Knecht is important in several aspects. First, it did not insulate aversive therapy from the strictures of cruel and unusual punishment. The simple expedient of labeling an intervention as treatment will not prevent a court from engaging in a type of functional analysis to arrive at an independent judgment concerning the accuracy of the label. So long as the courts are unwilling to apply the concept of cruel and unusual punishment to treatment, the intellectual task is to analyze the complained about activity on a treatment versus punishment scale. Second, *Knecht* established that consent was the essential element of the treatment program, and that it must be informed and is revocable.

Thus, the treatment community must be on notice that while many of these earlier judicial decisions are rather permissive and deferential to clinical judgments as to proper treatment, in instances where the direct effects of treatment are physically or emotionally painful, at a minimum, informed consent is the norm.[81]

The well-known *Kaimowitz*[82] case represents the outer limits of intrusive therapy and consent issues. A three-judge trial court held that as a matter of law, involuntarily confined patients cannot give consent to experimental psychosurgery. The court reasoned that institutionalization created a type of impaired competency, that confinement itself dramatically affected voluntariness, and that the risks, known and unknown, of psychosurgery made it impossible to impart an adequate information base.[83]

¶ 9.5 DOCTRINE OF LEAST DRASTIC ALTERNATIVES

[1] Mental Patients—*Rennie v. Klein*

Of the several second generation decisions dealing with the constitutional right of involuntarily committed mental patients to refuse antipsychotics, the decision in *Rennie v. Klein*[84] ranks among the more important. The suit originally was filed in 1977, after Rennie's twelfth hospitalization. The initial evidentiary hearing took about a year, and the case has gone as far as the Supreme Court,[85] which remanded the case

---

[81] *See Annot., Civil Liability for Physical Measures Undertaken in Connection with Treatment of Mentally Disordered Patients*, 8 A.L.R. (4th ed.) 464 (1981).

[82] Kaimowitz, *supra* note 38, in 13 CRIM. L. RPTR. 2452 (1973).

[83] Id. *See* David Wexler, *supra* note 26, at Ch. 8 for a view of *Kaimowitz* that is supportive of the result but critical of the court's reasoning.

[84] 720 F.2d 266 (3d Cir. 1983), *mod. and remanded*, 653 F.2d 836 (1981), *vacated and remanded*, 458 U.S. 1119 (1982).

[85] Rennie, 458 U.S. at 1119.

for reconsideration in light of *Youngberg v. Romeo*.[86] On remand, the Third Circuit Court of Appeals held:

> that antipsychotic drugs may be constitutionally administered to an involuntarily committed mentally ill patient whenever, in the exercise of professional judgment, such an action is deemed necessary to prevent the patient from endangering himself or others. Once that determination is made, professional judgment must also be exercised in the resulting decision to administer medication.[87]

This standard for the forcible (or nonconsensual) administration of drugs eliminates this court's earlier additional requirement of applying the "least intrusive means" concept. That is, other options to control the danger short of drugs, such as temporary isolation and soft restraints, need not be expressly eliminated in the clinical decision to use forced medication.

On the other hand, the *Rennie* standard assumes that the exercise of professional judgment so heavily relied on in *Romeo* includes whether, and to what extent, the patients will suffer harmful side effects. Those side effects are not controlling or necessarily determinative and, most important, they are not part of any need for consent.[88] Rather, these considerations simply play a role in the clinical judgment to forcibly medicate, and it is impossible to imagine a clinician stating: "No, come to think of it, I never considered the side effects. We just went ahead and injected ole Jones."

Only 3 of the 10 judges deciding the *Rennie* case joined in the opinion of the court. Six others concurred in the result and one dissented. Much of the debate centered on the vitality or emphasis to be given to the "least intrusive means" concept. Judge Adams, for example, agreed that while the least-intrusive-means test did not survive *Romeo*, with "forcible use of antipsychotic drugs, a state-employed physician must, at the very least, consider the side effects of the drugs, consult with other professionals and investigate other options available before that physician can be said to have discharged full professional judgment."[89]

Chief Judge Seitz wrote, "The State is not restricted to helping the patient only if he wishes to be helped."[90] Judge Seitz is even more restrictive of patients' rights than the opinion for the court in that he seems to eliminate the need for a threshold judgment on dangerousness. His view is "that the Due Process Clause at a minimum requires the authorities to administer antipsychotic drugs to an unwilling patient only where the decision is the product of the authority's professional judgment."[91]

---

[86] *Supra* note 41. *See* discussion of *Romeo* in Chapter 4, ¶ 4.5[1][e], and Chapter 16, ¶ 16.2[1].

[87] Rennie, 720 F.2d at 269–270.

[88] Rennie, 720 F.2d at 269.

[89] Rennie, 720 F.2d at 272.

[90] Rennie, 720 F.2d at 273.

[91] Rennie, 720 F.2d at 274. The chief judge went on, however, to state that as a general matter, the physician must consider both harmful side effects *and* possible alternatives to the drug, as well as whether the prescription is in response to or in anticipation of violent outbreaks. Economic or administrative convenience as part of a simple "warehousing" scheme is not justified. Thus, Judge Seitz would seem to desire to provide "binding guidance" rather than binding rules. The result seems the same.

Judge Weis, joined by two colleagues, strongly believes that *Romeo* does not govern the standard for long-term forcible administration of antipsychotic drugs.[92] *Romeo* dealt with physical restraints that are unlikely to have permanent effects.

> By contrast, the long-term administration of antipsychotic drugs may result in permanent physical and mental impairment. As our earlier opinion noted, all antipsychotic drugs affect the central nervous system and induce a variety of side effects. . . . The permanency of these effects [description omitted] is analogous to that resulting from such radical surgical procedures as pre-frontal lobotomy.[93]

It appears as though all of the judges in *Rennie* believed the Constitution supports the forcible administration of antipsychotic drugs to involuntarily committed mental patients.[94] They agreed most clearly where the patient is determined to be dangerous to himself or others and the drugs are administered on a short-term basis, although none of the judges addressed the vital issues of nature, degree, and imminence of harm. The rather mild disagreements in the Third Circuit relate to the emphasis to be given the consideration of less drastic alternatives and the analysis to be used for long-term treatment, which raises issues of long-term consequences.

While *Rennie* does not directly address the mentally disordered prisoner, we may unhesitatingly assume that the prisoner is legally entitled to no more protection and may well receive less. On the other hand, the standards charted here consistently focus on consent to treatment as the norm, with emergencies and present danger to self or to others as the most compelling exceptions.

A 1983 study of patient violence attributed much of the blame for an increasing rate of violence to the decision in *Rennie*. The authors write:

> After *Rennie v. Klein* the pattern of drug prescription changed dramatically at our hospital. Medication was no longer prescribed unless the patient consented to take it, or unless the patient had already become intolerably aggressive or combative. Paranoid and litigious patients were especially reluctant to take psychotropic medication. Many patients aggressively asserted their right to go unmedicated, and some flaunted their control over staff to the point of invoking other patients into aggressive reactions. A nine-month sampling of persistent medication refusers who were considered potentially dangerous showed that 40 percent eventually injured either themselves or someone else.[95]

---

[92] Rennie, 720 F.2d at 275.

[93] Rennie, 720 F.2d at 275–276 (citations omitted).

[94] *See* Rogers v. Okin, 634 F.2d 650 (1st Cir. 1980) *vacated and remanded sub nom.* Mills v. Rogers, 457 U.S. 291 (1982) (court had identical issue as in *Rennie* and in the remand did not specifically comment on the "least intrusive means" concept).

[95] JOHN ADLER, et al., *Patient Violence in a Private Psychiatric Hospital*, in ASSAULTS WITHIN PSYCHIATRIC FACILITIES 81, 87–88 (J. Lion & W. Reid, eds. 1983).

[2] Pretrial Detainees—*Bee v. Greaves*

Bee v. Greaves[96] was decided a year after *Rennie,* and the Tenth Circuit Court of Appeals expressed some different views about forcibly medicating pretrial detainees. The precise issue was whether a presumptively competent pretrial detainee may initially be forcibly injected with Thorazine and then forced to submit to further injections based on the continuing threat of force. Bee, who was hallucinating, was booked into the Salt Lake County Jail and first insisted on receiving Thorazine. After medical evaluation, the drug was prescribed and Bee voluntarily took it. He did so for about 60 days and then complained about drug-related problems.[97]

A judge determined that Bee was competent to stand trial and also ordered that Bee be medicated with Thorazine each evening. Parenthetically, the decision that Bee was competent to be tried involved an affirmative finding that he understood the charges and could assist counsel in his defense.[98] The jail staff conceded that they forcibly injected Bee when he refused to take the medicine orally. A jail medic testified this was for the purpose of "intimidating him so he wouldn't refuse the oral medication anymore."[99]

The defendants did not dispute Bee's claim that the side effects of Thorazine were extremely disabling and, at worse, can cause serious, permanent injury.[100] The defendants asserted that detainees have no right to refuse medical care while confined, but if there was a narrow right to refuse, the government's interests in security and maintaining a defendant's trial competence outweighed the defendant's interests.[101]

The trial judge accepted the government's position and granted summary judgment. In an expansive decision, the court of appeals reversed and remanded. The court found broad, legal support for Bee's argument that detainees have constitutional rights, grounded in the concept of liberty as expressed in the Fourteenth Amendment Due Process Clause, to refuse treatment with antipsychotic drugs. The court relied on (1) the general applicability of the doctrine of informed consent as to a course of treatment, (2) a constitutionally protected right of privacy, which includes bodily integrity, and (3) a liberty interest in the avoidance of needless bodily restraints.[102]

---

[96] 744 F. 2d 1387 (10th Cir. 1984), *cert. denied,* 469 U.S. 1214 (1985). Thoughtful decisions involving civilly committed patients distinguish the type of treatment interventions permitted, based in part on the rationale for intervention. For example, emergency commitments provide no predicate for highly intrusive, or certainly long-term, treatments. *See, e.g.,* Bell v. Wayne Co. General Hospital, 384 F. Supp, 1085 (E.D. Mich. 1974).

[97] Bee, 744 F.2d at 1389.

[98] Even if Bee had been found incompetent to be tried, there is no a priori connection between that finding of incompetence and incompetence to decide on a course of medical treatment. Granted, the decision to forcibly medicate an incompetent detainee carries with it greater indicia of propriety. Nonetheless, a specific determination of incompetency should accompany forcible medication, especially when the person already is experiencing and complaining of deleterious side-effects.

[99] Bee, 744 F. 2d at 1390. Bee submitted to the threat and took the drug for about three more weeks.

[100] Id.

[101] Bee, 744 F. 2d at 1391, 1394.

[102] The court relied heavily on the following cases: Davis v. Hubbard, 506 F. Supp. 915 (1980); Whalen v. Roe, 429 U.S. 589 (1977); Youngberg v. Romeo, *supra* note 41; and Vitek v. Jones, *supra* note 24.

Bee also claimed that the enforced medication impinged on his First Amendment right to the communication of ideas, a right that required protection of the capacity to produce ideas.[103] The court again agreed, based on Thorazine's capacity to severely and permanently affect thinking and communication.[104]

Finding that Bee, and thus pretrial detainees generally, have a protected liberty interest and a First Amendment interest in avoiding forcible medication is only the beginning of this analysis. The court next had to determine if the competing governmental interests were sufficiently compelling to override the detainee's rights.

First, the court noted that the government's duty is to provide medical care *when it is desired by the detainee.*[105] "Absent legitimate government objectives, . . ." stated the court, "we believe that involuntary medication may itself amount to unconstitutional punishment."[106] Second, in responding to the government's claim of a need to keep Bee competent for trial, the court stated:

> Generally speaking, a decision to administer antipsychotics should be based on the legitimate treatment needs of the individual, in accordance with accepted medical practice. A state interest unrelated to the well-being of the individual or those around him simply has no relevance to such a determination.[107]

The third and final asserted governmental interest—protection of staff and others—gave the court more problems:

> The third interest asserted by defendants is the jail's duty to protect the jail staff and others from a violent detainee. Admittedly, this is a serious concern. Bee does not dispute that forcible medication with antipsychotic drugs may be required in an emergency. *Absent an emergency, however, we do not believe forcible medication with antipsychotic drugs is "reasonably related," to the concededly legitimate goals of jail safety and security."*
>
> Determining that an emergency exists sufficient to warrant involuntary medication with this type of drug requires a professional judgment-call that includes a balancing of the jail's concerns for the safety of its occupants against a detainee's interest in freedom from unwanted antipsychotics. Any decision to administer antipsychotic drugs forcibly must be the product of professional judgment by appropriate medical authorities applying accepted medical standards. It requires an evaluation in each case of the gravity of the

---

[103] Bee, 744 F. 2d at 1394.

[104] Id. Some years ago it was reported that a Bethesda, Maryland psychiatrist was under investigation by the State's Commission on Medical Discipline for comments he made on the Oprah Winfrey television show. The accused doctor spoke out against anti-psychotic drugs and now stood accused of precipitating patients' wholesale refusals of their medication. Not surprisingly, the doctor argued that his First Amendment rights were being trampled on. Albany Times Union, Sept. 20, 1987, at 2.

[105] Bee, 744 F.2d at 1395 (emphasis in original). The court's point is essentially accurate. However, there are life-threatening situations in which the custodian's duty is to preserve life even if the inmate wishes to expire or continue to suffer in a life-endangering situation. Prison officials routinely force life-saving dialysis on nonconsenting inmates, for example.

[106] Id.

[107] Id.

safety threat, the characteristics of the individual involved, and the likely effects of particular drugs.

The availability of alternative, less restrictive courses of action should also be considered. In view of the severe effects of antipsychotic drugs, forcible medication cannot be viewed as a reasonable response to a safety or security threat if there exist "less dramatic means for achieving the same basic purpose." Our constitutional jurisprudence long has held that where a state interest conflicts with fundamental personal liberties, the means by which that interest is promoted must be carefully selected so as to result in the minimum possible infringement of protected rights. . . . Thus, less restrictive alternatives, such as segregation or the use of less controversial drugs like tranquilizers or sedatives, should be ruled out before resorting to antipsychotic drugs.[108]

One aspect of the court's treatment of the third interest—the use of less restrictive alternatives—appears to contradict part of its earlier analysis. Previously the court seemed to hold that only the treatment needs of the individual could serve as a legitimate basis for forced medication. Under the third interest, and in accordance with the court's carefully formulated norms, forced medication would seem an available course to quell an emergency if no less restrictive options exist. This would amount to use of the drug for control, and not treatment, purposes.

In addition, the *Bee* decision is plainly at odds with *Rennie* on the mandate of least drastic alternative analysis. The court stated:

We recognize that the Supreme Court has declined to apply a "less intrusive means" analysis to a decision regarding treatment of an involuntarily committed mental patient. See *Romeo,* 457 U.S. at 322–24. *Romeo* is distinguishable both because it involved temporary physical restraints rather than mental restraints with potentially long term effects, see *Rennie v. Klein*, 720 F. 2d 266, 274–77 (3d Cir. 1983) (Weis, J., concurring), and because Romeo had been certified as severely retarded and unable to care for himself, see *Romeo*, 457 U.S. at 309–10. In this case, the question is whether an emergency exists sufficient to justify the state injecting a pretrial detainee, who has not been declared mentally incompetent under appropriate state procedures, with a potentially dangerous drug. Under these circumstances, we believe the state is required to consider less restrictive alternatives. Cf. *Wolfish,* 441 U.S. at 575 (Marshall, J., dissenting) ("There is no basis for relaxing when the rights of presumptively innocent detainees are implicated."). Indeed, the jail regulations suggest segregation as the appropriate measure when mentally ill patients "upset or provoke" other inmates. The jail regulations also contemplate that commitment "shall be considered for inmates with moderate to severe mental problems."[109]

---

[108] Bee, 744 F. 2d at 1395-96 (citation omitted) (emphasis added).
[109] Bee, 744 F. 2d at 1396 n.7.

In the Fourth Circuit case *United States v. Charters*,[110] involving a federal prisoner held at Butner Federal Correctional Institution who had been found incompetent to be tried, the reviewing court correctly held that deciding such incompetency is distinct from the ability to make medication decisions. The court held that if the detainee was found competent, he could refuse psychotropic medication, but if he was found medically incompetent, then the court must also decide whether the detainee might have consented if able to or, in the alternative, whether the medication was in the detainee's best interests.

Thereafter, *Charters* was reviewed by the en banc court and the panel decision reversed.[111] The court held that due process is satisfied if the decision to medicate is left to prison doctors without an adversary hearing. The patient is entitled only to the exercise of "professional judgment," and if challenged the standard for review is whether the decision was arbitrary. This is a substantial departure from acceptable judgment or practice.[112]

In *Riggins v. Nevada*,[113] the Supreme Court dealt with a pretrial detainee who was awaiting trial for murder. Based on his own complaint, Riggins was prescribed the antipsychotic drug Mellaril. After he was found competent to stand trial, the detainee unsuccessfully moved to terminate the administration of Mellaril, arguing that its unwanted use infringed on his freedom and his ability to show the jurors his "real self" during presentation of an insanity defense.[114]

Postulating that administration of the drug was involuntary from the point of the detainee's unsuccessful motion to terminate, the Court found a violation of due process here. Referring to *Washington v. Harper*,[115] (discussed later in this chapter), the Court held that due process requires at least as much protection for detainees as for the convicted. Nevada need only have found the enforced treatment medically appropriate, which it did not, and have considered less intrusive measures essential for the safety of Riggins and others.[116] The Court also stated that Nevada might have justified forcible medication if it had shown there was no other way to obtain an adjudication of guilt or innocence using less intrusive means.[117]

Essentially, *Riggins* is a denial of a fair trial decision, and while clearly relevant to our concerns, it is not central. The relevant point for us is the requirement of a consideration of least drastic alternatives and whether that doctrine may now apply in jail and prison cases.

Returning to *Bee* and *Rennie,* readers may be puzzled about the appropriate course

---

[110] 829 F.2d 479 (4th Cir. 1987).

[111] 863 F.2d 302 (4th Cir.1988) (en banc), *cert denied*, 494 U.S. 1016 (1990).

[112] Charters, 863 F.2d at 313. The American Psychiatric Association joined as amicus for the victorious government position, while the American Psychological Association served as amicus to the losing inmate. This decision is a rather obvious setback to inmate and patient autonomy and a major victory for institutional psychiatrists who wish to avoid judicial oversight.

[113] 504 U.S. 127 (1992).

[114] Riggins, 504 U.S. at 130.

[115] 494 U.S. 210 (1990).

[116] Riggins, 504 U.S. at 135.

[117] Id.

of action to follow when two distinguished federal courts of appeal disagree on some-thing as fundamental as requiring a least-drastic-alternative analysis regarding forcible medication. *Riggins* compounds the matter a bit more. The most prudent legal course to follow would be to adopt the more protective procedures of *Bee*. This is *not* because *Bee*'s approach may be mandatory outside the Tenth Circuit, but because it is a more cautious approach. It can be followed with little or no additional burden on jail or prison staff, and it is more respectful of human autonomy and decency.

[3] Competency to Refuse Antipsychotics

A more recent decision by the Arizona Supreme Court dealt specifically with the rights of convicted prisoners to refuse antipsychotic medication as a matter of state constitutional law. In *Large v. Superior Court*,[118] the court decided that inmates do indeed have a right to be free from arbitrary chemical restraint, although the right to refuse is not absolute.[119] Without a true emergency—something more immediate and compelling than generalized security claims—the forced administration of dangerous medication is not permitted. Even with a specific emergency, procedural safeguards are required.[120]

Where forced medication is based on treatment needs, due process under the Arizona Constitution requires the exercise of professional judgment evidenced by a treatment plan that complies with legislative or departmental regulations governing the matter.[121] Justice Cameron dissented in the belief that an inmate's surviving right of privacy allowed a competent prisoner the right to refuse the ingestion or injection of dangerous drugs.[122]

Thus, the majority of the Arizona court leaves the state power to administer dangerous drugs against a prisoner's will in nonemergency situations if done for a treatment purpose and in accordance with the criteria and procedural safeguards written into law. *Large* stops far short of *Bee* in not requiring a finding of incompetence and in not requiring a "least intrusive alternative analysis." *Large* does rule out the reflexive use of drugs simply for control purposes, but it leaves Arizona prison inmates very much in the hands of the attending doctors when medication is solely for treatment purposes.

[a] Judicial Decision Requirement

Another decision deserves some discussion in our consideration of consent issues. In *Rivers v. Katz*,[123] the New York Court of Appeals rendered a decision extraordinarily protective of the rights of patients civilly committed to New York State Hospitals. In *Rivers*, civilly committed patients appealed various regulations and procedures that

---

[118] 714 P.2d 399 (Az. 1986).
[119] Large, 714 P.2d at 406.
[120] Large, 714 P.2d at 408.
[121] Large, 714 P.2d at 409.
[122] Large, 714 P.2d at 410 (Cameron, J., dissenting).
[123] 67 N.Y.2d 485 (1986).

permitted the state to forcibly administer antipsychotic drugs.[124] The court emphasized that none of these patients had been judicially determined to be mentally incompetent and that commitment and competency decisions were wholly distinct.[125]

The court's ultimate decision was as follows:

> We hold, therefore, that in situations where the State's police power is not implicated (i.e. no emergency exists), and the patient refuses to consent to the administration of antipsychotic drugs, there must be a judicial determination of whether the patient has the capacity to make a reasoned decision with respect to proposed treatment before the drugs may be administered pursuant to the State's parens patriae power. The determination should be made at a hearing following exhaustion of the administrative review procedures provided for in 14 NYCCR 27.8. The hearing should be de novo, and the patient should be afforded representation by counsel (Judiciary Law Sec. 35[1][a]). The State would bear the burden of demonstrating by clear and convincing evidence the patient's incapacity to make a treatment decision. If, after fully considering the State's proof, the evidence offered by the patient, and any independent psychiatric, psychological or medical evidence that the court may choose to procure, the court determines that the patient has the capability to make his own treatment decisions, the State shall be precluded from administering antipsychotic drugs. If, however, the court concludes that the patient lacks the capacity to determine the course of his own treatment, the court must determine whether the proposed treatment is narrowly tailored to give substantive effect to the patient's liberty interests, taking into consideration all relevant circumstances, including the patient's best interests, the benefits to be gained from the treatment, the adverse side effects associated with the treatment and any less intrusive alternative treatments. The State would bear the burden to establish by clear and convincing evidence that the proposed treatment meets the criteria.[126]

The court also suggested a detailed list of factors to be considered in evaluating competence to refuse treatment:

(1) the person's knowledge that he has a choice to make;
(2) the patient's ability to understand the available options, their advantages and disadvantages;
(3) the patient's cognitive capacity to consider the relevant factors;
(4) the absence of any interfering pathologic perception or belief, such as a delusion concerning the decision;
(5) the absence of any interfering emotional state, such as severe panic, depression, euphoria or emotional disability;

---

[124] Rivers, 67 N.Y.2d at 490. The medication decision, including the treating doctor's initial decision, was reviewed and upheld on four different occasions.

[125] Rivers, 67 N.Y.2d at 495.

[126] Rivers, 67 N.Y.2d at 497–498.

(6) the absence of interfering pathologic motivational pressure;

(7) the absence of any interfering pathologic relationship, such as the conviction of helpless dependency on another person; and

(8) an awareness of how others view the decision, the general social attitude toward the choices and an understanding of his reason for deviating from that attitude if he does.[127]

Interestingly, the state did not disagree with the proposition that competent mental hospital patients had a right to refuse psychotropic medication. The only real debate was whether the detailed administrative review procedures were adequately protective of that right. Clearly, the *Rivers* decision disagreed with the state and not only placed the competency decision in the courts, but gave the courts a fair involvement in the nature and the course of the prescribed treatment for those found incompetent.

Rivers v. Katz, unlike virtually all of the decisions previously noted in this section, is based exclusively on state law—on the Due Process Clause of the New York State Constitution. The most significant impact of that approach is that the state had no apparent grounds for appeal into the federal courts, since the decision was wholly grounded on independent state law.

One strategy the state indicated it would now employ is to reduce the administrative review steps presently required, in the belief that *Rivers* only mandated judicial review and not the continuation of any particular administrative format.[128]

Preliminary data and observations about the impact of this decision show that civil patients are winning very few of their court challenges. Patients report that when they refused medication, they often lost such privileges as honor cards, cigarettes, or time spent at home. Some have been harassed to the point where an emergency was precipitated.[129] Conversations with mental hygiene staff reveal that initial refusal rates are about .05 percent of recent admissions, and that even this relatively small number declines greatly after about three weeks of hospitalization. For others, the threat of being sent home—which may be the streets—produced "consent." Prisoners, one would assume, would likely reach a different conclusion.

One authority, Clarence Sundram, points out that studies from other states show that "refusniks" spend more time in the hospital, are restrained more often, and spend more time in seclusion. If patients do not act out, they may simply be sent home with no improvement in their mental condition.[130]

Obviously, the consent-forced medication issue is somewhat different in prison. Prison officials cannot simply release a nonconsenting inmate. On the other hand, the withdrawal of privileges and the use of seclusion is at least as easy to impose. However, as more courts require informed consent, the prison treatment and security community are on notice that no matter how difficult, inmate autonomy must be respected.

---

[127] Rivers, 67 N.Y.2d at 497 n.7.

[128] *See* People v. Medina, 705 P.2d 961 (Colo. 1985), for a similar approach to the question of forcibly medicating a mental patient.

[129] Talan, *When Mental Patients Say No*, Newsday Part 3, 1, 3 (Oct. 20, 1987).

[130] Clarence Sundram, Chairman of New York's Commission on Quality of Care, a watchdog agency that has oversight functions over mental hospitals.

[b] Forced Medication

The *Rivers* decision in New York should be briefly contrasted with a federal court's decision upholding Wisconsin's claim of a right to forcibly medicate patients. In *Stensvad v. Reivitz*[131] a patient claimed the right to refuse the psychotropic medication he had been taking for about 11 years. Under the Wisconsin statutory scheme, subject to a few exceptions not applicable here, civilly committed mental hospital patients were subject to forcible medication. Indeed, the law could fairly be read as creating a statutory presumption of incompetence as to medication decisions.[132] Judge Shabaz upheld the statutory scheme, finding that the prior decision to commit was also acceptable as to incompetency with respect to treatment decisions. He also determined that the exercise of professional judgment required by *Youngberg v. Romeo*[133] was present and, in effect, overrode any specific constitutional objections the patient might have.[134]

Stensvad is at odds with other judicial decisions that refuse to equate incompetency with commitability, including *Rivers v. Katz*. The Wisconsin court actually avoids the difficult competency question by upholding the statutory scheme. A statute that calls for specific decisions as to an individual's competency would be more acceptable than the present Wisconsin law and would also be more in line with current thinking on the matter.[135]

¶ 9.6 THE NEED FOR JUDICIAL SAFEGUARDS

[1] Resistance to Treatment vs. "Professional Judgment" Standard

The case *Washington v. Harper*[136] speaks directly to the involuntary medication of convicted prisoners. One may safely assume that whatever rights are afforded the convicted also apply to detainees (with the added issue of whether detainees receive more protection). *Harper* does recognize a substantial liberty interest on the part of the prisoner to resist unwanted psychotropic medication, but it undermines the inmate position in three important ways:

- It does not require a consideration of less intrusive measures;
- It does not insist that the prisoner be decisionally incompetent; and

---

[131] 601 F. Supp. 128 (W.D. Wis. 1985).

[132] *See* Alex Brooks, *The Right to Refuse Antipsychotic Medications: Law and Policy*, 39 RUTGERS L. REV. 339 (1987), for an interesting review of the consent issue. The article is an excellent source for earlier bibliographic material in this area.

[133] *Supra* note 41.

[134] Stensvad, *supra* note 131, 601 F. Supp. at 131.

[135] Persons convicted of a crime could not be placed in the same category of statutory presumptions because no judicial decision has been made as to the required anterior finding of mental illness.

[136] *Supra* note 115.

- It does not require a judicial decision before the forcible medication.[137]

Before exploring *Harper* in some detail and then analyzing some important post-*Harper* cases, I wish to make explicit some personal views and experiences in this area. First, in the jurisdictions in which I have done legal work and in others with which I am familiar, *Harper* is well understood and closely followed. Second, and without denigrating the concerns of libertarians and proceduralists, the problems I encounter are with treatment delayed and not controlling some therapeutic, mind-altering orgy. Third, over time psychiatrists have learned a great deal about psychotropic medications, and the medications themselves have improved to the point where there is a diminished concern for debilitating side effects.

In one dramatic but not isolated instance, I observed a seriously mentally ill state prisoner who would never leave his cell, who exercised endlessly but never spoke to anyone, and who refused medication for 18 months. After months of trying, a court order was finally obtained; the prisoner was forcibly medicated, and he is now in the general population and an active leader and spokesperson for inmate causes.[138]

Anecdotal? Of course. Representative of a number of cases? Yes, in my experience. And when an inmate becomes noncompliant? The results often are personally and institutionally disastrous.

As we shall see, while *Harper* is easy to accommodate, somehow its message of inmates' substantive rights appears to have gotten through to the doctors and psychiatrists. That is, I detect more professional reluctance to forcibly medicate than mere reliance on judicially created impediments.

Returning to the case, the Washington Supreme Court had determined that the inmate-patient had a liberty interest in refusing antipsychotic medication and that a competent, nonconsenting inmate was entitled to an adversarial proceeding, along with proof by "clear, cogent, and convincing evidence, measured by the state's compelling (not merely legitimate) interests."[139] In reversing, the Supreme Court cleared away all of these safeguards, requiring only an administrative-type hearing with a mental health professional and correctional officials. Its decision included no provision for legal counsel and no requirement of incompetency, judicial decision-making, or consideration of less intrusive measures.

The Court held that the decision to medicate must be made by a medical professional and that none of the hearing committee's members may be involved in the inmate's current treatment or diagnosis. The decision must be a medical decision, although institutional factors (security) may be considered. The decision also requires a finding that the mental disorder will likely cause harm.[140]

---

[137] *Harper, supra* note 115, 494 U.S. at 230.

[138] This jurisdiction was operating under a very restrictive consent decree which made it very difficult to obtain a court order to medicate.

[139] *See* Harper v. Washington, 759 P. 2d 358, 364–365 (Wash. 1988).

[140] The Court actually upheld the Washington procedure, indicating that it meets constitutional minima. It is a bit of a leap from using this approach to being certain that it alone provides constitutionally acceptable procedures. For example, where Washington used a three-person committee, would a two-person committee suffice? *See* Sullivan v. Flannigan, 8 F.3d 591, 596 (7th Cir. 1993), endorsing two-person

The court used a reasonableness (rational basis) approach that almost guaranteed a state-oriented result. If the inmate's interest in autonomy had actually been treated as fundamental, the Court would have pursued a strict approach to due process. Justice Stevens continued his lonely battle for judicial recognition of inmates' dignitarian values.[141] He believes that the substantive and procedural basis for the majority opinion were seriously flawed.

There are a number of interesting post-*Harper* decisions, but in my view the most interesting and pernicious is *Sullivan v. Flanagan*.[142] Inmate Sullivan had been forced by Illinois correctional officials to take mind-altering drugs. He had a long history of assault in prisons and mental hospitals, especially when he was taken off various antipsychotic drugs. His case included complaints of dry mouth, nervousness, blurred vision and speech, weakness, and the like as a result of Haldol.[143]

His most poignant claim was that he was an older person now and that his recent record was devoid of aggression. Based on this and on his reading of *Harper*, he argued that he was entitled to a drug-free interlude to demonstrate that he can function without being a threat to himself or others. Finding a certain common sense appeal to his argument, the Seventh Circuit still rejected his claim, fully realizing that its rejection gave doctrinal support for a life sentence to involuntary medication.[144]

In *Sullivan*, the court rebuffed the inmate's post-*Harper* arguments. He argued that the State of Washington provided a 24-hour drug-free period before a hearing. *Harper* itself observed that the inmate was not allowed any drug-free periods during his eight years of forced medication and that a single dose of antipsychotic drugs may last up to a month.[145] While *Harper* required a medical basis, an impartial tribunal, and an opportunity to argue capably before the tribunal, all of those factors were found to be in place in Illinois.[146]

Dr. Ron Shansky testified that there were dangers associated with going from the inmate's regular low doses to a very large dose that would be required should an abstinence period be tried and fail. In addition, the court was impressed by testimony that the medication did not impair the inmate's ability to function at the administrative hearing.[147]

The court also found Sullivan's reliance on *Riggins v. Nevada*[148] to be misplaced. "*Riggins* cannot be read to require Illinois to afford its inmates regular drug-free hear-

---

committees.

[141] Harper, *supra* note 115, 494 U.S. at 258. In my experience, the psychiatrist who sits on the panel is not presently treating the inmate but almost certainly has in the past and likely will have previously ordered the medication at issue. This will *not* disqualify the psychiatrist, but it speaks grandly to bias. I hasten to add that this bias is not necessarily sinister, but bespeaks firm inclination to decide in a particular fashion.

[142] *Supra*, note 140.

[143] Sullivan, *supra* note 140, 8 F.3d at 592.

[144] Sullivan, *supra* note 140, 8 F.3d at 597.

[145] Id. The 24-hour notice period in *Harper* is said to be most significant for inmates protesting an initial forced medication.

[146] Id.

[147] Sullivan, *supra* note 140, 8 F.3d at 597–598.

[148] *Supra* note 113. *See* discussion of *Riggins* at ¶ 9.5[2].

ings . . . *Riggins* requires something more than *Harper*. When the right to stand trial is at issue, the state must consider less intrusive alternatives to forcing drugs upon the accused."[149]

[2] No Normative Position on Force

The majority in *Sullivan* missed some vital points in its analysis and ultimate decision. Harper must be read as positing freedom from unwanted psychotropic drugs as the norm. Unless one is willing, in effect, to give virtually unlimited life to one acceptable decision to forcibly medicate, there should be some opportunity to return to the norm. Actually, that is all that *Sullivan* was asking.

Should the professional judgment rule be read to trump the "return to the norm" rule argued for here? Certainly not. To do so would be to return to pre-*Harper* procedures.[150] If an inmate during a drug-free trial run lapses into destructive behavior, then that should be a factor in a "drug free" hearing. Thus, the norm of freedom from unwanted drugs argues for a right to a drug-free period and a separate hearing on that very claim. This decision would, in effect, validate professional judgment as the deciding factor on a decision as vital as a lifetime of forced medication.

[3] Emergency Treatment—"As Needed"

There is no doubt that *Harper* was not intended to apply to an emergency situation. As suggested earlier, there is an overlooked parallelism between emergency-based medication and the similar application of mechanical restraints. In *Bullock v. Smith*,[151] the court upheld the single injection of an antipsychotic drug to an inmate who had a history of mental disorders and whom the medical staff found dangerous. *Harper* was correctly read as limited to longer-term treatment. However, in discussing the Eighth Amendment, this court used an irrelevant "evolving standard of decency" criterion when in fact the case must be analyzed as one of excessive force or, more likely, as deliberate indifference, within the contours of the inmate's treatment regimen.[152]

In *Walker v. Ghoudy*,[153] an Illinois prisoner who is a hemophiliac and mentally ill was pushed down onto a bed and handcuffed, and a nurse then forcibly administered Haldol. Walker had been engaged in destructive and abusive behavior and the injection apparently was based on, in my view, a dubious "standing order" (i.e., an as-needed basis without immediate consultation with the doctor issuing the order). The court found that the force was not excessive, based on the "malicious and sadistic" test, and that there was no violation of the treatment mandates outlined in *Ruiz v.*

---

[149] Sullivan, *supra* note 140, 8 F.3d at 598.

[150] *See* United States v. Charters, *supra* note 111, 863 F.2d at 307–309.

[151] 1996 U.S. App. LEXIS 9968; 1996 WL 209606 (4th Cir. 1996) (otherwise unpublished).

[152] On these facts, in either case the authorities would prevail. *See* Hogan v. Carter, 85 F.3d at 1113, (7th Cir. 1996), which also dealt with a one-time involuntary injection and found that *Harper* deals with long-term medication.

[153] 1996 U.S. App. LEXIS 5501 (7th Cir. 1996) (unpublished). This occurred in 1988, before *Harper*, but it clearly would be decided in the same fashion.

Estelle.[154] Given the accuracy of the events leading to the injection, the minimal use of force, and the single-incident status of the treatment, this would not be unconstitutional both pre- and post-*Harper*.[155]

Thus, *Washington v. Harper* does not apply when correctional authorities forcibly medicate a prisoner during an emergency, for medical reasons (i.e., not to punish), and the administration is of limited duration. The emergency should involve an imminent threat to the life or safety of the prisoner or others, or an imminent threat to the destruction of property.

Obviously, a jurisdiction that elects to allow this use of force option should have clear policy and procedure for such an intervention. Not all jurisdictions authorize it. Where permitted, there is no apparent reason to allow the force at an earlier point than should be permitted for the application of mechanical restraints.

Where a prisoner is involuntarily committed and the court also authorizes the involuntary administration of medication, courts may not require a separate *Harper* hearing. In *Washington v. Silber*,[156] the Fourth Circuit Court of Appeals upheld a state court order to commit a Virginia prisoner for 180 days, and also found the inmate incompetent to give informed consent, as a predicate for the order authorizing medication "as needed."

In invoking the professional judgment standard, the *Silber* court found *United States v. Charters*[157] viable after *Harper.* That is, given the prior judicial determination of commitability and, more importantly, incompetence, the court found that due process is satisfied in allowing medical decisions to be made as needed for the 180-day period. There was no judicial finding of dangerousness. This decision makes it clear that a new decision on incompetence and dangerousness is not required at the time medication is proposed.[158] Complaints about involuntary medication after a judicial order are to be judged by the professional judgment standard, with the patient's expressed desires merely a factor in that judgment.

[4] "Liberty Interest" Recognition

In *Cochran v. Dysart*,[159] the court dealt specifically with post-*Harper* acceptable reasons for forced medication and reached a surprisingly liberal result. The plaintiff was in the custody of the Attorney General pursuant to 18 U.S.C. Section 4246, allowing commitment after the expiration of sentence due to "mental defect." When pressed for the medical reason for the commitment, the defendants responded that Cochran suffered from schizophrenia and that the treatment was necessary to control the symptoms, to allow for transfer to less restrictive quarters, and to allow for participation in

---

[154] 503 F. Supp. 1265 (S.D. Tex. 1980), *aff'd in part*, 679 F.2d 115 (5th Cir. 1982), *cert. denied*, 460 U.S. 1042 (1983). *See* discussion of this case and the treatment mandates in Chapter 7, ¶ 7.2.

[155] *See* Walker v. Shansky, 28 F.3d 666 (7th Cir. 1994), addressing this same inmate's earlier claims.

[156] 1993 U.S. App. LEXIS 13046 (4th Cir.) (unpublished).

[157] *Supra* note 111.

[158] *See* State v. Nording, 485 N.W.2d 781 (N.D. 1992), upholding forced medication after a finding of not guilty by means of insanity along with notice that such an order would be at issue.

[159] 965 F.2d 649 (8th Cir. 1992).

more programs.[160] The court held unequivocally, however, that none of these reasons "justifies forcibly medicating Cochran with potentially fatal psychotropic drugs."[161]

While not unsympathtetic to the use of psychotropic drugs, the court was acutely sensitive to the substantive limits found in *Harper*:

> Psychotropic drugs have provided the psychiatric community with an alternative to heavy sedation, seclusion, straightjackets, electroconvulsive therapy, and frontal lobotomies, but their use is not without controversy. The purpose of psychotropics is to change a patient's cognitive processes by altering the chemical balance in the brain; the drugs can have serious, even fatal, side effects. *See Harper*, 494 U.S. at 229. In Harper, the Supreme Court held that "given the requirements of the prison environment, the Due Process Clause permits the State to treat an inmate who has a serious mental illness with *antipsychotic drugs against his [or her] will, if the inmate is dangerous to himself [or herself] or others and the treatment is in the inmate's medical interest*. Id. at 227." (Emphasis added.)
>
> Dr. Jacob's March 1 report states that "Dr. Gallinanes feels [Cochran] is dangerous to himself and others without medication." Dr. Gallinanes' medical reports, however, are not in the record; there is no indication of the basis for Dr. Gallinanes' "feeling" or what "medication" Cochran allegedly cannot do without; and there is no other record evidence of dangerousness. We are unable to review Dr. Jacobs' decision without reviewing the documents—especially the medical records—upon which Dr. Jacobs relied in authorizing Cochran's involuntary psychotropic medication."[162]

[5] Parolees and Forced Medication

In *Felce v. Fiedler*[163] the court had the interesting question of whether, and if so, to what effect, *Harper* applied to conditions of parole. As a condition of his parole, Felce has been required to have monthly injections of prolixin, and he sought damages for those forcible injections. Wisconsin argued, inter alia, that it actually had a greater interest in requiring drugs to control a parolee's behavior than it did for a more easily contained prisoner.[164] Curiously, Wisconsin had no law governing this situation.

The court did state unequivocally "that the liberty interest against involuntary use of antipsychotic drugs guaranteed for parolees is essentially the same as that recognized for those incarcerated in an institutional setting."[165]

---

[160] Cochran, 965 F.2d at 649.

[161] Cochran, 965 F.2d at 651.

[162] Cochran, 965 F.2d at 650. Judge Loken, in dissent, found ample evidence of dangerousness in the record, while Judge Wollman focused his concern on the defects in Dr. Jacob's report. 965 F.2d at 651. Thus, Judge McMillian alone endorsed the more ringing statements in the opinion.

[163] 974 F.2d at 1484 (7th Cir. 1992). This type of parole, termed mandatory release parole in Wisconsin and conditional release elsewhere, actually is a discharge from prison at the maximum minus earned good time credits. The prison and releasing authority have no discretion in the matter, although the inmate probably may elect to reject supervision on parole and remain until the full term expires.

[164] Felce, 974 F.2d at 1494.

[165] Felce, 974 F.2d at 1495.

Having found a protected liberty interest in the parolee, the next question was whether the precise due process safeguards of *Harper* could apply to this situation. The court found *Harper* to be an important guide, but not directly applicable.[166] In reviewing Wisconsin's procedure, the court held that the involvement of a decision-maker independent of the state agencies was required. Felce was not commitable, but the record was replete with fears for the future. It appears that the court would have been satisfied with an independent medical evaluation,[167] but in the maddening style of so many opinions, it left us to speculate.

We can be certain, however, that parole conditions are not immune from the *Harper* liberty interest analysis, although the precise procedures validated for prisoners in Washington may not be the only way to satisfy due process.

In concluding this chapter I would suggest that as a matter of sound policy, every jurisdiction, through legislation or administrative regulations, should adopt rules dealing with:

- Informed consent, its precise content and a standardized form

- The conditions for when consent is not required (e.g., clear and present danger of causing [serious] injury to self and/or others)

- Least restrictive measures, what they are and when they need not be used

- Authorization—who may authorize, administer, and review

- Charting requirements

- Duration of forced treatment-medication orders

- Cooperative measures between corrections and mental health offices

---

[166] Felce, 974 F.2d at 1496.
[167] Felce, 974 F.2d at 1498. The case was remanded.

Chapter 10
Recordkeeping Requirements

¶ 10.1 LEGAL DUTY

Some years ago, while visiting with the head of psychiatric services for a southern state's prison facilities, I casually asked about the medical recordkeeping system. The doctor moved things about his desk, seeming to search for something. Looking relieved, he found a paper restaurant placemat and on the back he located some record entries dealing with mentally ill prisoners.

The right to receive, and the obligation to provide, treatment creates important ancillary rights and duties. The courts regularly recognize the preparation and maintenance of adequate medical records as an integral part of providing constitutionally acceptable medical care. In *Ruiz v. Estelle*,[1] Judge Justice clearly articulated the purposes of proper medical records as:

> . . . legal documentation of treatment; audits of the quality of treatment; providing an indication of the needs of treatment of the institution; a record of major illnesses; and a record of treatment that can be followed by a doctor who is unfamiliar with the patient.[2]

In *Ruiz,* records at corrections facilities that consisted merely of the inmate's complaint and documentation of prescribed medication were found to be inadequate. The records failed to include the physician's diagnosis, test results, entries indicating the care actually provided, and admission and discharge summaries. Furthermore, inmates frequently made or transcribed the records, and many inmates had access to them. The court held that inmate involvement contributed to the inaccuracy of the records and also represented an invasion of privacy.[3]

---

[1] 503 F. Supp. 1265, 1323 (S.D. Tex. 1980), *aff'd in part*, 679 F.2d 1115 (5th Cir. 1982), *cert. denied*, 460 U.S. 1042 (1983). *See* discussion of *Ruiz* in Chapter 5, ¶ 5.3[1].

[2] Id.

[3] Ruiz, 503 F. Supp. at 1323.

The essence of the ruling is that "accurate, complete, and confidential records of the mental health treatment process must be maintained."[4] Obviously, informal methods such as using the back—or even the front—of a placemat is inherently unacceptable by every criteria used to measure the legal adequacy of mental health records. Judge Justice's statement of purposes, or objectives, for proper medical records hardly can be improved upon. To encapsulate and rephrase his several points: adequate records are prerequisite to continuity of care.

¶ 10.2 ENDEMIC DEFICIENCIES

In my own work encompassing a large number of prisons, I would say that broadly deficient mental health records is the most consistently encountered problem I uncover. A jurisdiction with a primitive correctional mental health delivery system will never have adequate records. What may be surprising is that even in relatively sophisticated systems, the mental health records are sometimes so deficient that there often is no treatment plan or only an old one that has not been changed or updated; what is there is illegible; there is no medical history or a clinically inadequate one; treatment recommendations are sparse or nonexistent; and there are no follow-up or progress notes.

Curiously, decent treatment may in fact be occurring, at least in some individual cases, but it would not be remotely evident from many of the files I scrutinize. In a case involving individual liability for alleged lack of care, testimony on the provision of actual care will be admitted and may serve as a successful defense. Where there is a legal challenge to the entire mental health delivery system, however, the abysmal records will provide strong evidence favoring the inmate-claimants' position.

On the other hand, where there are at least adequate records, they can support a defendant's motion to dismiss or for summary judgment. For example, in *Dulany v. Carrahan*,[5] female inmates confined in Missouri raised a number of seemingly compelling claims regarding their medical care, and while the medical conditions were serious, "Medical records revealed in each instance that the defendants had responded to and provided treatment."[6]

The district court's limitation on discovery and summary judgment itself was upheld. Thus, while it may be the last act performed by a health care provider, decent records may be the first thing that limits liability and the time and effort required to defend the lawsuit.

[1] Ambiguous Directives

In a very important decision involving consent to psychotropic medication, *Bee v. Greaves*,[7] the ambiguity of the attending psychiatrist's records formed an important backdrop for the decision. The plaintiff, a detainee of the Salt Lake County Jail, was

---

[4] Ruiz, 503 F. Supp. at 1339.

[5] 132 F.3d 1234 (8th Cir. 1997).

[6] Dulany, 132 F. 3d at 1239.

[7] 744 F.2d 1387 (9th Cir. 1984), *cert. denied*, 469 U.S. 1214 (1985). *See* discussion of *Bee* in Chapter 9, ¶ 9.5[2].

forcibly medicated intramuscularly and then required to continue the unwanted medication (Thorazine) orally for several weeks under the threat of forcible injection. The record notation in question read simply: "give repeat." At the doctor's deposition, he stated that this meant he would allow one more intramuscular injection if there was refusal to accept oral medication. Any further injections, said the doctor, would call for additional medical instructions.[8]

The court, however, concluded that the jail staff clearly interpreted this notation to mean that the doctor authorized them to medicate the detainee against his will any time there was a refusal of oral medication. This led to the further critical finding that all subsequent medications over roughly a three week period were taken under the continuing threat of force.[9] The point was critical to the plaintiff's victory in this case.

[2] Constitutional Necessity—Continuity of Care

In *Hendrix v. Faulkner*,[10] the court reviewed testimony indicating chaotic and disorganized medical recordkeeping, but ultimately found that this situation did not create a constitutional violation. Testimony indicated that although records were sometimes incomplete, records of intake screening were adequate, and the physician's notes were intelligible and contained sufficient information to indicate to a reviewer the manner and approach to treatment.[11] The major flaw in the recordkeeping system was the absence of a suspense file to trigger information on the need for follow-up visits. Most inmates were left to their own devices to request a follow-up visit through the normal sick call procedure. The court concluded that these problems were not in the nature of a constitutional violation and accepted testimony indicating that the medical records procedure was being reevaluated.[12]

As an important aspect of the minimal care available in a Virgin Islands case, the district court's order stated:

Complete and accurate medical records should be maintained under the physician in charge. Whenever an inmate is involved in a situation with another inmate or staff member which requires medical attention, a complete record of his physical condition shall be made at the time.[13]

In *Burks v. Teasdale*,[14] a Missouri court found that the prison's recordkeeping sys-

---

[8] Bee, 744 F.2d at 1390 n.2.

[9] Bee, 744 F.2d at 1390.

[10] 525 F. Supp. 435 (N.D. Ind. 1981), *aff'd in part, vacated in part*, Wellman v. Faulkner, 715 F.2d 269 (7th Cir. 1983), *cert. denied*, Faulkner v. Wellman, 468 U.S. 1217 (1984). *See* discussion of *Hendrix* in Chapter 5, ¶ 5.4, and Chapter 7, ¶ 7.6[1].

[11] Hendrix, 525 F. Supp. at 504.

[12] Hendrix, 525 F. Supp. at 504, 520.

[13] Barnes v. Government of Virgin Islands, 415 F. Supp. 1218, 1235 (D.V.I. 1976). *See* Carty v. Farrelly, 957 F. Supp. 727 (D.V.I. 1997), for further developments within the prison system, including a finding on contempt for failure to comply with a 1994 consent decree that covered mental health care, among other things. *Barnes* is also discussed in Chapter 5.

[14] 492 F. Supp. 650 (W.D. Mo. 1980).

tem contributed to the overall unacceptability of the medical care provided. This court emphasized the constitutional necessity of continuity of care, an objective that was impaired by the frequent rotation of clinicians, decentralized records, and the general disorganization that prevailed.[15]

Surprisingly, the court did not find anything constitutionally objectionable about the use of inmates in the medical records department. Even if there is doubt about the connection between inmate access and quality of care, the potential for blackmail and other abuse is so great as to be an independent basis for denying access to such records.[16]

The *Burks* decision, to the contrary, held:

> This Court finds that while the use of inmates in the medical records department may be in many respects an undesirable practice, the evidence does not support a finding that a deliberate indifference to the serious medical needs of the inmates has resulted thereby. It was the opinion of one of plaintiffs' experts that for confidentiality purposes, inmates should not have access to the medical records. Defendants indicated that they have not experienced any problems with the use of inmates in the medical record department. In the absence of any showing of how the use of inmates for these clerical tasks has adversely affected the prisoner patients, the use of inmates in the medical records department is not proscribed on constitutional grounds.[17]

Recordkeeping in the New Hampshire penal system fared no better than in Missouri. In *Laaman v. Helgemoe*,[18] medical records were found to be deficient on the following grounds: no basis for the medical care was noted; there were no written plans for future treatment; at times physicians used only an order sheet; and the records were disorganized.[19] Of 370 records submitted to the court for study, 75 percent contained no notation of a physical examination and 86 percent contained no medical history. Only 9 percent contained complete records, including a physical examination and a mental health diagnosis. Failure to document and record these matters, certainly including mental health diagnosis, was held to create a grave risk to the inmates because it prevented continuity of care inside and outside the prison.[20]

The court found the recordkeeping inadequate and ordered "complete and accurate records documenting all medical examinations, medical findings, and medical

---

[15] Burks, 492 F. Supp. at 676. *See* Susan Kay, The Constitutional Dimensions of an Inmates' Right to Health Care (Nat'l Comm'n on Correctional Health Care, 1991), p. 12–13, emphasizing continuity of care and detailing the minimum requirement of an adequate health care record.

[16] In Cody v. Hillard, 599 F. Supp. 1025, 1036 (D.S.D. 1984), *aff'd*, 799 F.2d 447 (8th Cir. 1986), *cert. denied*, 108 S. Ct. 1078 (1988), the court stated simply, "[I]t is inappropriate for inmate workers to have any sort of access to the medical records of other inmates."

[17] Burks, 492 F. Supp. at 681. A more recent decision came to the same debatable conclusion, Toussaint v. McCarthy, 801 F.2d 1080, 1112 (9th Cir. 1986), *cert. denied,* 107 S. Ct. 2462 (1987).

[18] 437 F. Supp. 269 (D.N.H. 1977). *See also* Chapter 5, ¶ 5.3[5].

[19] Laaman, 437 F. Supp. at 287.

[20] Id.

treatment maintained pursuant to standards established by the American Medical Association, under the supervision of the physician in charge."[21]

Review of the South Dakota State Penitentiary's medical records revealed similar glaring deficiencies. In *Cody v. Hillard*,[22] the court stated:

> The eighth amendment is implicated when "inadequate, inaccurate and unprofessionally maintained medical records" give rise to the possibility for disaster stemming from a failure to properly chart" the medical care received by inmates. Dawson v. Kendrick, 527 F. Supp. 1252, 1306-07 (S.D. W.Va. 1981) (quoting Burks v. Teasdale, 492 F. Supp. at 676). In Burks, 492 F. Supp. at 676, the court recognized "the critical importance of adequate and accurate medical records in any attempt to provide a continuity of medical care." It held that "inadequate, inaccurate and unprofessionally maintained medical records" constituted a "grave risk of unnecessary pain and suffering" in violation of the eighth amendment. Id. at 676, 678. Similarly, in Lightfoot v. Walker, 486 F. Supp. at 517, 724-25, the court found that inmate medical records were "disorganized and failed to meet minimal standards" and that the recording system was not properly coordinated to ensure that all medical information and test results were entered into an inmate's file within a reasonable time. The court held that these deficiencies contributed to an unconstitutional health care system, and it ordered prison officials to develop and maintain "complete and accurate records documenting all medical examinations, medical findings and medical treatment . . . pursuant to accepted professional standards."

> Applying these principles to the instant case, the court concludes that the inadequate organization of medical records and files at the SDP constituted a deficiency in the health care system.[23]

In *Coleman v. Wilson*,[24] Judge Karlton wrote,

> A necessary component of minimally adequate care is maintenance of complete and accurate medical records. Defendants have a constitutional obligation to take reasonable steps to obtain information necessary to the provision of adequate medical care. . . . The harm that flows . . . from inadequate or absent medical records is manifest. Eighth Amendment liability in this regard is not predicated on the failure of the counties to deliver medical records. It is predicated on the failure of defendants to take reasonable steps to implement policies that will aid in obtaining necessary medical information about class members when they are transferred from county jails to the CDC.[25]

---

[21] Laaman, 437 F. Supp. at 327.

[22] *Supra* note 16. *See also* Chapter 7, ¶ 7.2[5] for further discussion of this case.

[23] Cody, supra note 16, 599 F. Supp. at 1057–1058; *see also* Inmates of Occoquan v. Barry, 650 F. Supp. 619, 630 (D.C. Cir. 1986), *vacated*, 844 F.2d 828 (D.C. Cir. 1988) for a similar holding.

[24] 912 F. Supp. 1282 (E.D. Cal. 1995).

[25] Coleman, 912 F. Supp. at 1313–1314. *See also* Chapter 7, ¶ 7.3[1].

The defendants argued that an individual treatment plan was not constitutionally mandated for every inmate who received psychiatric care. Judge Karlton replied that the magistrate judge had not so found and did not recommend that it be required.[26]

[3] Duty to Obtain Relevant Facts

The *Coleman* concern with the transfer or request of medical and mental health records is a variation on the general legal mandate to create and maintain adequate records related to a custodian's delivery of care. There are interesting legal questions here not really dealt with in *Coleman* that relate to the actual knowledge requirement of *Farmer v. Brennan*.[27] In a tragic and factually complicated case involving the custodial suicide of a juvenile, there are fascinating *Coleman*-like questions swirling about a probation worker.[28] The worker knew that the young man had been hospitalized just before his commitment to the St. Charles Youth Correctional facility in Illinois. The youth was never given the Ritalin he was prescribed; he was never seen by a mental health professional; and he was not placed in any special observation unit.

The probation worker certainly knew of the hospitalization, and while there is a dispute here, she did know of the boy's general mental health history. In my judgment, knowing he was hospitalized and that he was taking medication for "nerves" raises the ante on "need to know." That is, the probation officer heard a general alarm and that created a rather easily complied with duty to obtain available and highly relevant, recent mental health history that likely would have led to a mental health intervention and special housing.[29]

In the discussion of *Steele v. Shah*[30] in Chapter 7, I treated the psychiatrist's precipitous and uninformed discontinuance of prescribed medication as a form of interference with treatment. When the doctor, Shah, acted without access to available records, he effectively failed in his duty to obtain facts. *Farmer v. Brennan* was not seen as dictating a contrary result.[31]

In *Reeves v. Collins*,[32] an inmate who took a nasty fall and was placed on medical restriction was told this would be noted in his file. It apparently was not, and the staff forced him to work, causing him great pain. The officers were found not to be liable—and given a barren record, there can be no fault in their not having checked it. One wonders whether a doctor might be deliberately indifferent in failing to create a record that could avoid needless pain. If asked to decide, I would so hold.

---

[26] Coleman, 912 F. Supp. at 1314 n.46.

[27] 511 U.S. 825 (1994). *See* discussion of *Farmer* in Chapter 4, ¶ 4.3[2].

[28] Viero v. Bufano, 925 F. Supp. 1374 (N.D. Ill. 1996).

[29] Viero, 925 F. Supp. at 1388. Summary judgment was denied due to a finding that the officer had some knowledge and should have obtained and/or conveyed more.

[30] 87 F.3d 1266 (11th Cir. 1996).

[31] *See* Brown v. Coughlin, 758 F. Supp. 876, 882 (S.D.N.Y. 1991) (failure to transfer medical records expeditiously could support finding of deliberate indifference). *But see* Sanderfer v. Nicholas, 62 F.3d 151, 155 (6th Cir. 1995), holding that failure to read records of inmate who eventually died was an aspect of negligence.

[32] 27 F.3d 174 (5th Cir. 1994).

In *Casey v. Lewis*,[33] the record is riddled with systemic and individual problems: records not being transferred, records not available at sick call, and a lack of required documentation. As already noted, this is symptomatic of a correctional health care system found to be unconstitutional.

¶ 10.3 POLICY GUIDELINES

The cases briefly described above indicate that constitutionally acceptable physical and mental health care is highly dependent on adequate records. Mere disorganization and occasional incomplete recordkeeping will not violate constitutional minima, although the precepts of professionally acceptable care may dictate otherwise. Where the course of treatment is apparent and the clinician's notes intelligible, then minimum standards may be met. Where the records do not trigger an automatic follow-up, the practice may be dubious although not necessarily below legal requirements.

The objectives to be achieved through proper recordkeeping are well stated in *Ruiz* and *Cody*, and they should serve as a guide for those who must review recordkeeping practices and for those facing a legal challenge. At a minimum, documentation of diagnosis and the record of treatment allowing the assessment and continuity of care seem to be the most basic considerations.

Inmates and staff move into and around a correctional system with great regularity. Without a standardized and reasonably complete medical and mental health file, the individual is in jeopardy and the system is exposed to liability. What follows is a suggested guide to mental health file documentation. The guide is an amalgam of legal and policy considerations. It was prepared by Barbara Peterson, R.N., a member of the *Dunn v. Voinovich*[34] monitoring group, with substantial contributions by Dr. Jane Haddad, also on the *Dunn* monitoring group, and myself.

MENTAL HEALTH FILE DOCUMENTATION

Goal: To ensure the ready availability of comprehensive and specific information about the mental /medical status of an inmate and the treatment provided in order to enhance staff communication and interaction, to contribute to continuity of care, and to serve as the legal record of the care.

- Organization of the mental health file is consistent throughout the system.

- Initial mental health screening is completed within 24 hours of inmate's arrival at each institution.

- Detailed mental health screening is completed within 10 days of inmate's arrival at each institution, or as otherwise indicated.

---

[33] 834 F. Supp. 1477, 1502–1503, 1513–1514 (D. Ariz. 1993). *See* discussion of *Casey* in Chapter 7, ¶ 7.3[3].

[34] No. C1-93-0166 (S.D. Ohio July 10, 1995).

- Mental health evaluation is completed by a psychiatrist or psychologist within 30 days of referral and evaluation and contains Axis 1 through 5, DSM-IV[35] diagnosis.

- If inmate is prescribed medication, informed consent with information regarding the benefits and risks of a dosage range (identified by a physician) of the prescribed medication is present. A new consent form is completed whenever there is a change in the type or range of medication.

- Treatment plan is completed or reviewed within 10 days of admission to Residential Treatment Unit (RTU) or within 30 days of arrival at institution.

- Treatment plans for inmates on the outpatient psychiatric caseload are revised whenever there is a significant clinical change and reviewed no less than once every six months.

- Treatment plans for RTU inmates are revised as based on identified need and/or as required by the inmate classification system.

- Medication orders are reviewed by the physician no less then every 60 days or as otherwise required.

- Mental health staff document in progress notes at least monthly for inmates on the psychiatric caseload to indicate current status and response to treatment interventions.

- Progress notes provide thorough, clinically relevant information and are related to the treatment plan.

- Documentation of the staff follow-up of inmate refusals or "no shows" for appointments is present and includes documentation that the potential consequences of refusing services has been explained to the inmate.

- If inmate is transferred to another institution, the sending facility provides documentation of inmate's current status, a summary of the treatments provided, and the inmate's response to treatment interventions.

- If inmate is discharged from the psychiatric caseload, the rationale for the discharge, a summary of treatment provided, the inmate's response to the treatment/discharge, and plan for monitoring within six months is documented.

---

[35] DIAGNOSTIC AND STATISTICAL MANUAL OF MENTAL DISORDERS, 4th ed. (American Psychiatric Association, 1994).

Chapter 11

Effect of Isolation on Mental Disability

¶ 11.1 CONCEPT AND LIABILITY FOUNDATIONS

After studying the supposedly therapeutic effects of solitary confinement in American prisons in the 1800s, Charles Dickens wrote:

> I believe it, in its effects, to be cruel and wrong. In its intention, I am well convinced that it is kind, humane, and meant for reformation; but I am persuaded that those who devised this system of Prison Discipline, and those benevolent gentleman who carry it into execution, do not know what it is that they are doing. I believe that very few men are capable of estimating the immense amount of torture and agony which this dreadful punishment . . . inflicts upon the sufferers . . . I hold this slow and daily tampering with the mysteries of the brain, to be immeasurably worse than any torture of the body . . . .[1]

In *Crain v. Bordenkircher,*[2] which involved the wholesale condemnation of the West Virginia Penitentiary by a state court, a cryptic footnote reads:

> Mr. Lane [Director of the Illinois Department of Corrections and an expert witness here] was particularly upset over what he observed in what was termed the psychiatric ward of the infirmary area which had to be entered by unlocking a door off a hallway. It contained a toilet area and a dark cell from which somebody stuck his hand out. Mr. Lane, who said that without a flashlight he could not see in the cell, asked if there was a toilet in the cell and the person inside said no.[3]

---

[1] CHARLES DICKENS, AMERICAN NOTES AND PICTURES FROM ITALY (1903).
[2] 342 S.E.2d 422 (W.Va. 1986).
[3] Crain, 342 S.E.2d at 427 n.5.

Isolation, of course, remains a part of prison life, and here we examine the various forms and competing objectives involved in the isolation of mentally disordered inmates. Isolation, or segregation, may be imposed in a variety of ways and for a variety of objectives. An inmate may be confined to his cell for punishment, protection, or convenience and deprived of the amenities associated with life on that cell-block. In New York, this is referred to as keep-lock. Other jurisdictions use the term "cell is" (cell isolation). Some residential mental health units will confine a resident to his cell for a period of time either for punishment or even for some clinically indicated "time out." These styles of segregation rarely raise any concerns related to our subject.

When an inmate is removed from his regular housing assignment and placed in a specially designated cell or an isolation cell in a specially designated unit, we begin to approach our area of concern. Such isolation, or segregation, may be termed punitive, clinical, administrative, protective, or observational; however denominated, these descriptions tend to be indistinguishable except in name. Inmates are likely confined in their cell for 23 hours each day. Jobs and programs are severely limited or simply unavailable; meals are eaten alone in one's cell; radio and television are limited, or more likely forbidden; exercise is severely limited; surveillance is likely intense, and so on. The frequently encountered double doors may both be closed, creating visual and auditory isolation, or an outer door may be left open providing access to sights and sounds. Physically, these cells or units are likely to be the barest and least desirable places to live in the entire prison, and that is usually the intent. Ironically, some inmates will seek out such confinement as a means of protection and regularly perform in a disruptive manner to be so confined. Inmates in a facility with dormitory housing actually may prize a brief respite in these otherwise uninviting cells.

Where a prison or prison system is believed to be providing inadequate mental health care, one of the first places to be studied is the prison's segregation (isolation or lockdown) units. This is where the untreated prisoner likely will be hidden along with all of his psychiatrically driven disturbing behavior; it is where he is likely to deteriorate as well.

When doing site visits to evaluate mental health services, I will ask the officers assigned to such units who, in their opinion, are the "really sick guys you have in here." They will invariably tell me. I will then go cell-to-cell and randomly ask the inmates the same question and they invariably will identify the same inmates. No matter what state, no matter what the unit is called, the outcome is almost always the same. And when staff tell me there are no mentally ill inmates locked-up, the inmates in residence invariably, and confidentially, will confirm that.

The cases make it clear that isolation, even prolonged isolation, of adult prisoners, by itself generally raises no constitutional problems.[4] Legal problems do arise concerning the procedures used, especially for disciplinary isolation;[5] they arise where

---

[4] *Cf.* LeReau v. MacDougall, 473 F.2d 974, 978 (2d Cir. 1972), *cert. denied*, 414 U.S. 878 (1973) (threatening an inmate's sanity and severing his contacts with reality by a lengthy confinement in a "strip cell" violates the Eighth Amendment). *See* cases cited in Thomas Benjamin & Kenneth Lux, *Constitutional and Psychological Implications of the Use of Solitary Confinement: Experience at the Maine State Prison*, 9 CLEARINGHOUSE REV. 83, 86–88 (1975).

[5] Sandin v. Conner, 115 S. Ct. 2293 (1995), dramatically expands the duration of segregated confinement permissible without a *Wolff*-hearing (i.e., a due process hearing). In Bonner v. Parke, 918 F.

the conditions of isolation involve the wanton infliction of pain, where the conditions deny basic human needs, or occasionally where conditions may be disappropriate to the crime warranting the imprisonment.[6]

On the other hand, where confinement is extraordinarily long[7] or even where isolation might cause psychiatric deterioration, courts have been extremely reluctant to interfere.[8] There is some worry in the judicial reluctance to intervene, however, as some of the earliest affirmative rulings for inmates involved punitive conditions in solitary confinement.[9]

[1] Mental Disability Itself as a Variable in Decision to Isolate

Is there a legal argument to be made that the physical isolation of a mentally disordered inmate is unconstitutional per se or that the inmate's disorder should be viewed as an important variable in determining what may be unduly harsh or damaging? The question seems to presuppose that isolation is damaging, in a way that exceeds the pain that many of us feel in being denied even minimal human interaction. Professor Hans Toch's study of prison inmates leads him to conclude that whatever the law may be, isolation for some inmates may indeed have a devastating effect.[10] Pathologically fearful inmates can regress into a panic reaction that is psychologically devastating. According to Toch, paranoid-schizophrenics often have a counter-productive reaction to isolation.[11]

At least one other authority has found that the isolation of some inmates may actually produce positive results.[12] Inmates may use the break in routine to improve themselves. Thus, from the clinical perspective there is no certain connection between isolation and psychological reactions.[13] At a minimum, results seem linked with prior psychological strengths or weaknesses. As a matter of policy and law, individual decisions seem appropriate.

Let us look at another, more specific case involving mentally disordered inmates.

Supp. 1264 (N.D. Ind. 1996), the court held that three years' disciplinary confinement is not atypical or significant under *Sandin*.

[6] *See* Rhodes v. Chapman, 452 U.S. 337, 347 (1981).

[7] Sostre v. McGinnis, 442 F.2d 178 (2d Cir. 1971), *cert. denied*, 404 U.S. 1049 (1972).

[8] Jackson v. Meachum, 699 F.2d 578, 581–583 (1st. Cir. 1983). In Hutto v. Finney, 437 U.S. 678, 686–687 (1978), the Court indicated that the duration of confinement in a filthy, overcrowded isolation cell might be determinative on the question of unconstitutional cruelty.

[9] See Wright v. McMann, 387 F.2d 519 (2d Cir. 1967), *aff'd in part and modified in part and rev'd in part,* 460 F.2d 126 (2d Cir. 1972), *cert. denied,* 409 U.S. 885 (1972); E. J. Jordan v. Fitzharriss, 257 F. Supp. 674 (N.D. Cal. 1996).

[10] *See generally* HANS TOCH, MEN IN CRISIS: HUMAN BREAKDOWN IN PRISON (1975).

[11] Interview with Hans Toch, Jan 21, 1984, Albany, N.Y. Professor Toch argues strongly for the availability of intermediate care-type facilities in prisons, space that is between isolation and general population.

[12] P. SUEDFELD, RESTRICTED ENVIRONMENTAL STIMULATION: RESEARCH AND CLINICAL APPLICATIONS (1980).

[13] Professor Toch's findings do strongly argue for a shift in certain practices that may in fact be based on folklore. Isolation of suicidal inmates is a clear example of a well-intentioned practice that may be counterproductive.

Assume that our hypothetical inmate is on a mental health case load and that he is diagnosed as a paranoid-schizophrenic who is violently claustrophobic. In his moments of wildly acting out, he is very disruptive and security staff seeks an administrative or punitive placement in a tightly run segregation unit. Assume also that security staff knows the diagnosis but that they proceed to confine him anyway, and within a short period he deteriorates badly, slams his head against the wall, screams for help, and ultimately is hospitalized.

Is there liability? Did security act with knowledge of facts that there was a reasonable degree of risk in isolating this inmate? The answer is at least a tentative yes. The proper approach would have been first to explore every option short of segregation, maintain a detailed record on point, and use a crisis holding cell. Presumably, the inmate would then have bypassed segregation and been hospitalized.

While it is reasonably well established that isolation is not unconstitutional per se, it may be exceedingly poor policy to isolate certain mentally disordered inmates, and in the example just given it may well establish liability. The inmate's mental condition, like the incarcerated juvenile's age, becomes a factor in the constitutional formula, along with duration and the overall conditions of confinement. An important federal case decided that while juveniles might be kept in isolation, their non-criminal status and youth were important factors in assessing the acceptability of the nature and duration of such isolation.[14]

In addition to questions of law and effectiveness, health care providers face serious ethical questions. Two commentators go so far as to state:

> Medical practitioner involvement in the isolation and restraint of juveniles for nonmedical purposes, for example, violates every fundamental tenet of ethical medicine . . . .. The United Nations Principles of Medical Ethics, for example, specifically condemns the active or passive participation of health personnel in any cruel, inhumane, or degrading treatment or punishment of inmates.[15]

Of course, a prison inmate has been convicted of a crime and will be punished. The inmate's mental condition, however, becomes a factor in how much pain must be inflicted. Where isolation has been found to violate an inmate's Eighth Amendment rights, the surrounding conditions have been sufficiently brutal or uncivilized that it becomes difficult to assess the specific weight accorded to the mental disorder.

[2] Rights of the Non-Mentally Ill

In one recent case, *Bracewell v. Lobmiller*,[16] the plaintiff alleged that she was held in a segregation unit along with inmates who were violently and disturbingly mental-

---

[14] Santana v. Collazo, 714 F.2d 1172 (1st Cir. 1983), cert. denied, 466 U.S. 974 (1984). *See also* Nelson v. Heyne, 355 F. Supp. 451 (N.D. Ind. 1972); Lollis v. New York Dept. Soc. Serv., 322 F. Supp. 473 (S.D.N.Y. 1970).

[15] Jan Costello & Elizabeth Jameson, *Legal and Ethical Duties of Health Care Professionals to Incarcerated Children*, 8 J. LEGAL MED., 191, 248–249 (1978).

[16] 938 F. Supp. 1571 (M.D. Ala. 1996).

ly ill. There was evidence that several inmates were housed in the unit who screamed day and night and deprived others of sleep. They cursed, threw urine and feces, causing putrid smells; they spit, threw cups, and so on. Their behavior caused the plaintiff persistent sleeplessness and psychological distress; she was the target of the behavior and lived constantly with the sight and smell of bodily waste. The court concluded that there was certainly deliberate indifference in 1995 when these problems emerged, but that since then, with only one such disruptive inmate present, the requisite culpability may not have been present.[17]

Bracewell is a very good illustration of the rights possessed by non-mentally ill inmates to be free of the harmful environment created by some inmates with mental illness. There is no doubt that the Eighth Amendment rights of the severely compromised non-mentally ill inmates are implicated under such conditions. No system should tolerate this. It is easy enough, and as a last resort, to have crisis stabilization or isolation beds that are secure and isolated. This would allow mental health staff to continue to work with the disruptive inmates while minimizing the impact on others. It would also allow correctional staff to be less severely impacted by this type of situation. In fact, correctional union representatives often address this problem as a conditions of employment matter.

¶ 11.2 WHEN ISOLATION CROSSES A CONSTITUTIONAL LINE

It will come as no surprise that *Madrid v. Gomez*,[18] referred to now simply as the *Pelican Bay* case, presents the most recent and starkest example of the impact of a highly restrictive Security Housing Unit (SHU) on the marginally mentally ill and those already diagnosed or diagnosable as mentally ill. Pelican Bay's SHU housed about 1,500 of the most disruptive, dangerous, and often unstable inmates in the California system.[19]

The plaintiffs claimed basically that the conditions in the SHU were so extreme as to inflict psychological trauma or "deprive inmates of sanity itself."[20] A detailed description of the cells and the practices in this SHU will tell its own story:

> Each cell is 80 square feet and comes equipped with two built-in bunks and a toilet-sink. Cell doors are made of heavy gauge perforated metal; this design prevents objects from being thrown through the door but also significantly blocks vision and light. A skylight in each pod does allow some natural light to enter the tier area adjacent to the cells; however, cells are primarily lit with a fluorescent light that can be operated by the inmate. Each cell block is supervised and guarded by a separate control station which is staffed by armed correctional officers and separated from the pods by an electronically controlled gate. The officers also electronically control the opening and closing of the cell doors.

---

[17] Bracewell, 938 F. Supp. at 1579.

[18] 889 F. Supp. 1146 (N.D. Cal. 1995). *See also* the discussion of *Pelican Bay* (*Madrid*) in Chapter 7, ¶ 7.3[2], focusing on excessive force to inflict harm.

[19] Madrid, 889 F. Supp. at 1227.

[20] Madrid, 889 F. Supp. at 1228.

Patterned after a "Special Management Unit" in Florence, Arizona (albeit with some modifications), the SHU interior is designed to reduce visual stimulation. The cellblocks are marked throughout by a dull sameness in design and color. The cells are windowless; the walls are white concrete. When inside the cell, all one can see through the perforated metal door is another white wall.

A small exercise pen with cement floors and walls is attached to the end of each pod. Because the walls are 20 feet high, they preclude any view of the outside world. The top of the pen is covered partly by a screen and partly by a plastic rain cover, thus providing access to some fresh air. However, given their cell-like design and physical attachment to the pod itself, the pens are more suggestive of satellite cells than areas for exercise or recreation.

The overall effect of the SHU is one of stark security and unremitting monotony. Inmates can spend years without ever seeing any aspect of the outside world except for a small patch of sky. One inmate fairly described the SHU as being "like a space capsule where one is shot into space and left in isolation."

Social Isolation

Inmates in the SHU can go weeks, months or potentially years with little or no opportunity for normal social contact with other people. Regardless of the reason for their assignment to the SHU, all SHU inmates remain confined to their cells for 22 and _ hours of each day. Food trays are passed through a narrow food port in the cell door. Inmates eat all their meals in their cells. Opportunities for social interaction with other prisoners and vocational staff are essentially precluded. Inmates are not allowed to participate in prison job opportunities or any other prison recreational or educational programs. Nor is group exercise allowed. Inmates who are single celled exercise alone. Inmates who are double celled exercise with their cellmate or alone if the cellmate chooses not to exercise. No recreational equipment is provided. As the Court observed during its tour of the SHU, some inmates spend the time simply pacing around the edges of the pen; the image created is hauntingly similar to that of caged felines pacing at the zoo. Inmates in adjoining cells can hear but not see each other.

Interaction with correctional staff is kept to an absolute minimum. According to defendants' expert, Dr. Joel Dvoskin[1], the SHU has "attempted to reduce physical contact between inmates and staff to the extent possible, as much probably [as] anyplace I've ever seen in a segregation environment." For example, when an inmate leaves his cell to go to the exercise pen, the door is opened automatically by the control booth officer. Once in the tier area, the inmate must strip naked in front of the control booth; the door to the exercise pens is controlled electronically. In addition, the contact the correctional staff do have with inmates often occurs in a routinized setting while inmates are in handcuffs and waist and ankle chains, such as during an escort from the cell to another point in prison. As previously found, there is also a pattern of correctional officers using excessive force against inmates. The resulting tension in the SHU has further limited the ability of inmates and staff to engage in normal and constructive interactions.

The social isolation, however, is not complete. Inmates may leave their pod area on certain specified occasions; however, such opportunities may be infrequent and generally provide only a limited type of interaction. For example, inmates may leave their pod periodically to go to the law library; however, they are assigned to an individual library cell and have little interaction with other inmates or library staff. Inmates may also leave their pods to receive visitors or their attorney; however, all visits are conducted by telephone through a thick glass window, precluding opportunity for human touch. Moreover, because of Pelican Bay's distance from metropolitan areas, many inmates get either few visitors or none at all. Inmates also attend periodic on-site classification committee meetings, and those who become ill may leave their pod for diagnosis or treatment by the medical or mental health staff. Inmates may also request a counseling, prayer or Bible study visit from a religious volunteer under a program operated by the Pelican Bay chaplain.

For security reasons, inmates are always restrained in handcuffs and/or waist and ankle chains any time they leave the pod area.

(1) Dr. Dvoskin spent two days at the prison, separated by nine months, toured and spoke with inmates and staff, and reviewed eleven inmate files. Plaintiffs' experts spent far more time at the prison and studied considerably more files, Dr. Dvoskin's tepid defense of the prison seemed actually to aid plaintiffs.

Roughly two-thirds of the inmates are double-celled; however, this does not compensate for the otherwise severe level of social isolation in the SHU. The combination of being in extremely close proximity with one other person, while other avenues for normal social interaction are virtually precluded, often makes any long-term, normal relationship with the cellmate impossible. Instead, two persons housed together in this type of forced, constant intimacy have an "enormously high risk of becoming paranoid, hostile, and potentially violent towards each other." The existence of a cellmate is thus unlikely to provide an opportunity for sustained positive or normal social contact.

In sum, those incarcerated in the SHU for any length of time are severely deprived of normal human contact regardless of whether they are single or double celled. As former Warden Fenton testified, conditions in the SHU amount to a "virtual total deprivation, including, insofar as possible, deprivation of human contact."

While it is difficult to assess exactly how conditions in the Pelican Bay SHU compare to other security housing units, there is little doubt that, by any measuring stick, the Pelican Bay SHU by design lies on the harsh end of the SHU spectrum. Plaintiffs' expert Craig Haney, who has toured 20 to 25 segregation units, concluded that inmates at Pelican Bay are more isolated than inmates in any other segregation unit he has experienced. . . . Defendants' expert Dvoskin testified that SHU conditions at Pelican Bay are the conditions "of segregation as they exist in American prisons." However, he acknowledged that some SHUs provide more "privileges and freedom" than others, and that "Pelican Bay has clearly, on that continuum, decided to err on the side of physical safety rather than . . . increased privileges and freedom and increased staff to inmate contact."

Impact of SHU Conditions on Mental Health

Social science and clinical literature have consistently reported that when human beings are subjected to social isolation and reduced environmental stimulation, they may deteriorate mentally and in some cases develop psychiatric disturbances. These include perceptual distortions, hallucinations, hyperresponsivity to external stimuli, aggressive fantasies, overt paranoia, inability to concentrate, and problems with impulse control. This response has been observed not only in the extreme case where a subject in a clinical setting is completely isolated in a dark soundproofed room or immersed in water, but in a variety of other contexts. For example, similar effects have been observed in hostages, prisoners of war, patients undergoing long-term immobilization in a hospital, and pilots flying long solo flights. While acute symptoms tend to subside after normal stimulation or conditions are returned, some people may sustain long-term effects. This series of symptoms has been discussed using varying technology; however, one common label is "Reduced Environmental Stimulation," or RES. According to Dr. Grassian, the complex of symptoms associated with RES is rarely, if ever, observed in other psychotic syndromes or in humans not subject to RES, a point which defendants did not refute with any specificity.

There is also an ample and growing body of evidence that this phenomenon may occur among persons in solitary or segregated confinement – persons who are, by definition, subject to a significant degree of social isolation and reduced environmental stimulation.

More recent studies have also documented the potential adverse mental health effects of solitary or segregated confinement. As the Seventh Circuit noted in *Davenport v. DeRobertis,* 844 F.2d 1310, 1316 (7th Cir. 1988), "there is plenty of medical and psychological literature concerning the ill effects of solitary confinement (of which segregation is a variant)" (citing Grassian, Psychopathological Effects of Solitary Confinement, 140 American Journal of Psychiatry 1450 (1983)).[2]

Defendants' expert Dr. Dvoskin acknowledged that it is "possible" that a "syndrome" could be associated with segregated conditions in confinement, although he does not believe there is sufficient data to support "an exact syndrome." Dr. Dvoskin has, however, used the term "AD SEG [Administrative Segregation] Syndrome" or other terms in his work to describe those people who "can't handle" segregation or find "segregation intolerable." Dr. Sheff, the former chief psychiatrist at Pelican Bay, also testified that he observed prisoners at Pelican Bay demonstrating the RES "symptom complex," although he did not observe it in a "large number" of the patients with whom he interacted.

Regardless of whether there is an "exact syndrome" associated with incarceration in solitary confinement or security housing units, the Court is well satisfied that a severe reduction in environmental stimulation and social isolation can have serious psychiatric consequences for some people, and that these consequences are typically manifested in the symptoms identified above.

(2) See also Grassian & Friedman, Effects of Sensory Deprivation in Psychiatric Seclusion and Solitary Confinement, 8 Int'l Journal of Law & Psychiatry 49 (1986); Brodsky and Scoggin, Inmates in Protective Custody: First Data on Emotional Effects, 1 Forensic Reports 267 (1988); Toch, Mosaic of Despair: Human Breakdowns in Association, 1992; Benjamin & Lux, Solitary Confinement as Psychological Punishment, 13 Cal. W.L. Rev. 265, 268-277 and citations therein. (1997).

Turning to the case at bar, it is clear that confinement in the Pelican Bay SHU severely deprives inmates of normal human contact and substantially reduces their level of environmental stimulation, as detailed above. It is also clear that there are a significant number of inmates in the Pelican Bay SHU that are suffering from serious mental illness. At least one Pelican Bay psychologist, Dr. Ruggles, also observed that there was a "psychiatric deterioration that occurred in correlation with placement . . . [in the] SHU." He did not, however, explain the nature of the deterioration or know the cause. Indeed, the critical question is whether any of the psychiatric problems being experienced by SHU inmates are attributable to conditions in the SHU as opposed to other factors, and if so, the extent and degree of such problems.

To address these issues, Dr. Grassian conducted in-depth interviews with 50 inmates in the SHU over the course of two weeks (in September 1992 and May 1993), and reviewed their medical records. Fourteen inmates were interviewed twice. The inmates were not chosen randomly but were selected because there was some basis to believe that they might be experiencing psychiatric problems.

Dr. Grassian concluded that in forty of the fifty inmates, SHU conditions had either massively exacerbated a previous psychiatric illness or precipitated psychiatric symptoms associated with RES conditions.

Dr. Grassian concluded that an inmate's symptoms were attributable to the SHU only where the inmate's records indicated that the symptoms, or the exacerbation of mental illness, surfaced after confinement in the SHU, and where the inmate was experiencing a constellation of symptoms that is rarely found outside conditions of social isolation and restricted environmental stimulation.[21]

I have omitted the detailed case studies from Pelican Bay descriptive of deterioration and psychotic episodes causally connected to the conditions of segregation. Judge Henderson concluded that the inmates most vulnerable to serious psychological harm from continued exposure to this Draconian SHU are those inmates already suffering from mental illness.[22] There are also others at high risk, such as borderline personalities, chronic depressives, and the mentally retarded, who are dubious candidates for such a placement.

---

[21] Madrid, 889 F. Supp. 1228-1232. Despite the difference in time, *Pelican Bay* and isolation bears a distressing relationship to the *Ruiz* decision and the Texas prison system, as discussed in Chapter 7.

[22] Madrid, 889 F. Supp at 1235.

Does the continued placement of the mentally ill and those "at risk" in this SHU constitute deliberate indifference? Were the facts and risks sufficiently known or obvious that the *Farmer v. Brennan*[23] "actual knowledge requirement" is met? Judge Henderson stated, "With respect to the SHU, defendants cross the constitutional line when they force certain subgroups of the prison population, including the mentally ill, to endure the conditions in the SHU, despite knowing that the likely consequence for such inmates is serious injury to their mental health . . . ."[24]

A recent report by Human Rights Watch condemns the housing of mentally ill inmates in Indiana's Maximum Control Facility and the Secured Housing Unit of the Wabash Valley Prison.[25] The Report suggests that the conditions are so harsh and the consequences to the mentally ill so severe that the practice is a form of torture. The Report offers a series of recommendations, including enhanced treatment, physical alterations, and increased human interaction.[26]

Pelican Bay may be viewed, then, as a paradigm case of what not to do with segregation/isolation and the mentally ill or mentally fragile. Some readers will think: "My facility is not like that." "But what can you do with the disordered and disruptive inmate?" Clearly some form of a controlled environment, protective of the inmate, staff, and other inmates is permissible, if not actually required. The critical factors to observe include regular interaction with mental health staff, detailed documentation, and regular efforts to use various treatment methods to avoid or ameliorate deterioration.

¶ 11.3 EARLIER CASES FINDING UNCONSTITUTIONALITY

Pelican Bay aside, and without particular regard for an inmate's mental condition, courts have repeatedly condemned segregation conditions that are unsanitary, lack bedding or clothing, and similar primitive conditions. In *Chandler v. Baird*,[27] for example, the court found that an Eighth Amendment claim was stated where the inmate was confined in shorts, without bedding, toilet paper, running water, soap and toothpaste and in a filthy, cold cell. There are a number of decisions supportive of this view.

To this point, I have examined the more recent cases on segregation-isolation and the mentally disordered inmate. There are a host of earlier decisions that also may profitably be examined. For example, *McCray v. Burrell*,[28] a 1974 case involving the Maryland Penitentiary, early raised many questions about isolation as well as the interaction between punishment and treatment. McCray initially asked to be removed

---

[23] 511 U.S. 825 (1994). *See* discussion of *Farmer* in Chapters 2 and 4, and ¶ 4.3[4] for an analysis of the actual knowledge requirement.

[24] Madrid, 889 F. Supp. at 1279.

[25] In Cold Storage: Super-Maximum Security Confinement in Indiana (Human Rights Watch, Oct. 22, 1997); the committee is a privately supported organization operating internationally and reporting on human rights.

[26] Id.

[27] 926 F.2d 1057, 1063 (11th Cir. 1991). In a similar case involving a 14-day confinement the inmate was awarded damages, Maxwell v. Mason, 668 F.2d 361, 363–365 (8th Cir. 1981).

[28] 516 F.2d 357 (4th Cir. 1975), *cert. dismissed*, 426 U.S. 471 (1976).

from his cell on the grounds that it was unsanitary. The warden issued an order that the inmate's law books be provided to him in his new cell but there was some delay and a disturbance ensued.

An officer had McCray placed in Isolated Confinement (IC), which further enraged the inmate. The officer now viewed the behavior as evidence of mental instability and directed that McCray be placed in IC without clothing or bedding. The cell was described as:

> . . . quite long and narrow with a high ceiling. The walls, ceiling and floor were all concrete and there was a one-foot high concrete slab, six to eight feet long and three feet wide, which was McCray's bed. Although, initially, McCray was furnished no blankets or other bedding, during the night a prison guard gave him a mattress. McCray testified that it was so cold that he tore open the mattress, which was old and deteriorated, and dug a channel down in the cotton so that he could sleep nestled in the mattress. Subsequently, McCray was disciplined for destroying the mattress.

The cell contained a toilet and a sink. The record does not show whether the cell had a window, but evidence was offered that there was a lightbulb recessed in the rear wall. The cell had two doors—the inner one composed of bars, and the outer one made of solid wood but not closed. McCray was given no materials with which to clean himself or the cell, and was fed in plastic cups. He was deprived of reading and writing materials.

The next morning Sergeant Smith returned to check on McCray and found that he had defecated into a cup and smeared feces over himself and the cell wall. Accordingly Smith decided not to return him to his former cell. Instead, he had McCray bathed and the cell scrubbed, and then returned McCray to I.C. cell No. 5 for another twenty-four hours. It was not until that time that Smith caused notice to be given to a psychologist or psychiatrist in accordance with the applicable written administrative directive which had become effective August 10, 1970. The directive stated that "an inmate who is displaying mentally disturbed behavior may be placed in an isolation cell for the inmate's own safety, or that of the inmate population, until the psychologist/psychiatrist is notified . . ." and directed that the *"psychologist/psychiatrist should be contacted immediately after the confinement of the inmate, and the inmate should be evaluated within a twenty-four (24) hour period."* By its terms, the directive permitted the placing of inmates displaying mentally disturbed behavior in a punitive or isolation cell when the institution lacks a mental observation cell and a psychologist or a psychiatrist approves the lodging of such an inmate in an isolation cell.

The next day, November 22, McCray according to Smith, "started acting [sic] alright." He was then returned to his regular cell on the third tier. We infer that McCray's clothes were not returned to him until this time. The record on appeal does not show that he was ever evaluated by a psychologist or psychiatrist.[29]

---

[29] McCray, 516 F.2d at 365–366 (emphasis added).

On or about January 1, 1972, McCray again was removed to another cell, where a fire soon broke out. Captain Burrell, not unreasonably according to the court, concluded that McCray set the fire and placed the inmate in a mental observation (MO) cell. Again, the inmate was denied clothing, a mattress, and any bedding.[30]

The M.O. Cell in which McCray was placed was described by Captain Burrell as a bare cell. The windows were covered with sheet metal, but the cell had an electric light. The cell had concrete walls, a concrete ceiling, and a tile floor. There was no sink, and the only sanitary facility was an "oriental toilet" —a hole in the floor, six to eight inches across, covered by a removable metal grate which was encrusted with the excrement of previous occupants. The "toilet" flushed automatically once every three to five minutes. McCray was not permitted to bathe, shave or have use of articles of personal hygiene, including toilet paper. He was not afforded reading or writing materials. He claimed that during the forty-six hours he spent in this confinement "it was impossible to sleep . . . I stood up most of that [first] night, the floor was cold."[31]

The district court found that the inmate's confinement in these cells was intended not as punishment but for mental observation and as a precaution against self-inflicted harm. The court of appeals, however, disagreed and found that while these confinements were not intended as punishment, they amounted to punishment in violation of inmate McCray's Eighth Amendment rights.[32] The court reasoned that McCray's isolation occurred within a prison context and was, in whole or in part, a reaction to his misdeeds. Characterizing this reaction as punishment, the court determined that the Eighth Amendment was applicable, and went on to decide that two separate violations had occurred.[33] First, when the initial protective measures were taken, a clinician should have been contacted immediately and an evaluation performed within 24 hours. The administrative directive calling for this procedure was held to be the constitutional minimum as well. Thus the discomforts and suffering during the period of unwarranted delay in seeking professional diagnosis and help was found to be a cruel and unusual punishment.[34] Second, the conditions of confinement in the MO cell per se fell short of the current standards of decency of present-day society. Indeed, it is probably of no legal consequence for liability that the inmate may have been mentally disordered. The previously described conditions in the MO cell should not be judged constitutionally acceptable for any inmate.

Like *Pelican Bay, McCray* is an extreme individual case, but it does invite some generalizations. There is a written directive to seek professional advice and care that the courts treated as a constitutional obligation. This aspect of the decision clearly needs to be reconsidered in light of more recent case law. Whether this approach would prevail today is another matter. Where prison officials defend a practice by

---

[30] McCray, 516 F.2d at 366.
[31] McCray, 516 F.2d at 367.
[32] Id.
[33] Id.
[34] McCray, 516 F.2d at 369.

characterizing it as treatment and not punishment, their argument will trigger an obligation to seek further help. Where officials characterize this type of practice as punishment, they then face the demands of meeting civilized standards of decency and a compelling Eighth Amendment conditions of confinement claim. The requirement of actual knowledge, per *Farmer v. Brennan*, should not be difficult to prove on facts such as these. Treating this as punishment for the mentally ill makes the abuse even more dramatic.

In an interesting Pennsylvania case involving broad-based challenges to conditions in the prisons, Judge Lord wrote, "[I]t is clear that [solitary] confinement is not *per se* violative of the Eighth Amendment."[35] After upholding the constitutionality of the isolation cells at three other prisons, he reviewed the Huntingdon Correctional Institution and found certain isolation cells intolerable.

> The maximum security area at Huntingdon contains 144 cells. The psychiatric quarters consist of seventeen cells. Three of these cells are known as the "Glass Cage" and provide the focus of the Huntingdon inmates' constitutional attack. We conclude that use of the Glass Cage constitutes treatment so inhumane and degrading as to amount to cruel and unusual punishment. Its continued use cannot be tolerated.
>
> The Glass Cage is enclosed by glass walls and a locked steel door. The cells measure approximately nine feet deep by eight feet wide by nine feet high. There is no furniture, no window, and no inside lighting. Cells are equipped with a toilet and sink and are supposed to include a mattress, two sheets, a pillow, and blankets. We saw none of these items during our visits, but the cells were not in use at that time. Outside lighting is totally inadequate for reading. In addition, despite use of a large fan, ventilation is insufficient. The cells are unclean and an unpleasant odor pervades.
>
> Our conclusion that the cells in the Glass Cage cannot remain in use is based in large part on our to visits to the institution. On each occasion we were genuinely shocked by dark, dirty, and totally isolated conditions we observed. We agree with plaintiffs that the continued existence of the Glass Cage constitutes a serious threat to the physical and mental well-being of every resident who is confined there, and thus we conclude that confinement in such conditions could serve no legitimate penological purpose.[36]

Judge Lord's reference to psychiatric cases seems almost casual and clearly is not central to his finding the Glass Cage unconstitutional. *Laaman v. Helgemoe*,[37] however, provides a much more direct reference to the special needs and problems of the mentally disordered inmate and the use of isolation. The isolation cells in New Hampshire were described as having "the potential of devastating psychic, emotional, and physical damage."[38] Judge Bownes wrote further that:

---

[35] Imprisoned Citizens' Union v. Shapp, 451 F. Supp. 893, 896 (E.D. Pa. 1978). Most of the issues had been settled by consent decree.

[36] Imprisoned Citizens, 451 F. Supp. at 898.

[37] 437 F. Supp. 269 (D.N.H. 1977).

[38] Laaman, 437 F. Supp. at 280. *Laaman* is also discussed in Chapter 5, ¶ 5.3[5].

The experts concurred that the use of isolation for disturbed inmates violates all modern treatment practice and is potentially destructive and physically dangerous. Disturbed persons need at a minimum, to be observed and not to feel isolated and abandoned. Isolation is counterproductive in terms of treatment. . ..[39]

¶ 11.4 REVIEW OF MORE RECENT CASES

In a 1983 ruling concerning isolation, and in which the inmate had been diagnosed as suicidal, the Fifth Circuit confronted the question:

> . . . whether very extended, indefinite segregated confinement in a facility that provides satisfactory shelter, clothing, food, exercise, sanitation, lighting, heat, bedding, medical and psychiatric attention, and personal safety, but virtually no communication or association with fellow inmates, which confinement results in some degree of depression, constitutes such cruel and unusual treatment, violative of the Eighth and Fourteenth Amendments, that prison authorities can be required to provide several hours' daily interaction with other inmates.[40]

The court concluded that such isolation was not unconstitutional and stated:

> We do not suggest that the district court's prescription of several hours of inmate contact a day is a mere "amenity" to use the language of *Newman*. It might very well be helpful therapy. But to accept plaintiff's proposition that there is a constitutional right to preventive therapy where psychological deterioration threatens, notwithstanding that the physical conditions of confinement clearly meet or exceed nominal standards, would make the Eighth Amendment a guarantor of a prison inmate's prior mental health. Such a view, however civilized, would go measurably beyond what today would generally be deemed "cruel and unusual."
>
> We conclude that the confinement which has taken place in this case has not been wanton, unnecessary, or disproportionate and that there has been no "deliberate indifference" to the mental health needs of plaintiff.[41]

In arriving at its decision, the court relied heavily on the landmark case of *Newman v. Alabama*,[42] and from it extracted this grim but probably accurate quotation:

> The mental, physical, and emotional status of individuals, whether in or out of custody, do deteriorate and there is no power on earth that can prevent it

---

[39] Id. Prison officials agreed that psychiatric inmates should be transferred to the state mental hospital because of the lack of proper staff at the prison.

[40] Jackson v. Meachum, *supra* note 8, at 581.

[41] Jackson, 699 F.2d at 583–584.

[42] 559 F.2d 283 (5th Cir. 1977), *rev'd in part sub nom.* Alabama v. Pugh, 438 U.S. 781, *cert. denied*, 438 U.S. 915 (1978).

. . . We decline to enter this uncharted bog. If the State furnishes its prisoners with reasonably adequate food, clothing, shelter, sanitation, medical care, and personal safety, so as to avoid the imposition of cruel and unusual punishment, that ends its obligations under the Eighth Amendment. The Constitution does not require that prisoners, as individuals or as a group, be provided with any and every amenity which some person may think is needed to avoid mental, physical, and emotional deterioration.[43]

One must keep in mind the *Pelican Bay* situation, however, where the inmates were obviously at risk and the conditions so extreme that mental crises were found to be inevitable, and in fact did occur. Thus, the First Circuit's more accommodating findings must be placed in the context of a generally less shocking record.

In *Ferola v. Moran*,[44] the inmate was awarded damages for the suffering he endured when his cell became the equivalent of an isolation unit. He lost his claim that he did not receive adequate psychiatric care while imprisoned in Rhode Island. Ferola was diagnosed as having an antisocial personality, as defined in the DSM-III. He was seen by a psychiatrist at least once a week for approximately two years. Treatment, however, did not reduce the self-injurious and antisocial behavior.

In 1980, Ferola severely cut himself and was taken to the hospital where the wound was sutured. On his return to prison Ferola said he was going to injure himself again because he wanted to be in the prison hospital. At this point, the prison psychiatrist had a dilemma and his record entry is most interesting:

He has been superficially slashing his wrists and beating his head against the wall. So far, his self-inflicted injuries have not been such that he has had to be placed in the Dispensary for medical or surgical reasons. He may very well harm himself sufficiently to receive such placement. Can this be prevented?

1. Were I to place him in observation he still could harm himself and would if his placement were not satisfactory to him. Therefore, to place him in the rear room now would be to consent to being manipulated with no reasonable end in sight.

2. Should I load him up on Thorazine, whether in BCU (Behavioral Correctional Unit) or in the Dispensary? This kind of pharmaceutical behavior control is acceptable to totalitarians but is repugnant to our culture and ethical values. There is no psychiatric ground present at this time for an invasive pharmaceutical intervention.

3. Should he be restrained physically in order to reduce the likelihood of serious self injury? This non-invasive procedure impinges less immediately on his integrity and exposes him less to personal degradation, although it appears more brutal. Physical restraint would seem to be the response of choice, however short of ideal it may be.

4. Must he be placed in the Dispensary to be restrained? No! Physical

---

[43] Jackson, 699 F.2d at 582–583, *citing to* Newman, 559 F.2d at 291.

[44] 622 F. Supp. 814, 820 (D.R.I. 1985). DSM-III, of course, refers to the *Diagnostic and Statistical Manual of Mental Disorders*, 3d ed. (American Psychiatric Association, 1980).

restraint, whether short lived or more prolonged, is a proper custodial activity. Custodial authorities, for a variety of reasons, do not like to be involved in more prolonged physical restraint. While I can sympathize with them, I can not agree that dislike for an acceptable procedure is a sufficient reason to shift the burden to the medical staff under the arbitrary and false rubric that the inmate is "crazy and belongs in the rear room." Consequently, in response to Erickson's call, I advised him to follow custodial procedure, assuring him that Ferola is not a psychiatric patient.[45]

The doctor's candid record entry reveals a thoughtful process akin to the "least intrusive alternative" approach adopted by some courts faced with similar problems. The doctor rejected use of the psychiatric observation room (the "rear room") and the use of restraint in a treatment setting. Ferola was diagnosed as antisocial and untreatable and more a disciplinary problem than a medical problem.

Ferola's own cell became, in effect, an isolation unit when it was stripped bare and Ferola shackled and handcuffed in a supine position. For 20 hours he was shackled to his bed and for 14 consecutive hours he was spread-eagled.[46] Judge Pettine first noted that prior cases:

> . . . establish that, while there is no *per se* constitutional prohibition on the use of restraints such as shackles, chains, handcuffs and the like, courts must review with great care the circumstances surrounding their use in a particular instance to determine whether the strictures of the Eighth Amendment have been satisfied. These cases are, of course, only particular applications of the general rule that no measure instituted by prison officials, whether it be denominated "punishment," "control," "treatment," or otherwise, may inflict wanton and unnecessary pain. And in these cases, as is generally true in Eighth Amendment analysis, the individual circumstances surrounding a challenged measure, including its duration and the objective sought to be served, weigh heavily.[47]

Relying both on Rhode Island prison regulations forbidding restraints that cause physical pain or discomfort and Eighth Amendment principles, Judge Pettine found:

> 1. The absence of medical monitoring, control or supervision during the shackling created health risks.
> 2. The spread-eagling and tightening of the restraints caused pain which should have been mitigated.
> 3. Denial of access to a toilet for at least 14 consecutive hours worked great and gratuitous suffering.[48]

---

[45] Ferola, 622 F. Supp. at 818–819.

[46] Ferola, 622 F. Supp. at 818.

[47] Ferola, 622 F. Supp. at 820–821. The judge rejected the state's claim that a single isolated incident of mistreatment cannot amount to cruel and unusual punishment. Indeed, he said it had no support in law or logic.

[48] Ferola, 622 F. Supp. at 822.

The plaintiff was awarded one thousand dollars compensatory damages and Judge Pettine granted relief in the form of imposing on Rhode Island the federal prison system's rules on restraint.[49]

Ferola is not an isolation case in the sense that the inmate was placed in restrictive prison housing used exclusively for segregation purposes. The inmate's cell became a functional isolation unit and the practices encountered here are often encountered in special housing units. While this topic is examined in more detail in Chapter 12, great care should be used in restraining the unruly inmate and, very clearly, medical supervision and the infliction of minimal pain are legal prerequisites.

In *Inmates of Ocoquan v. Barry*,[50] the court dealt with the prison's use of a unit for disciplinary and punitive segregation as a holding area for mentally ill prisoners awaiting transfer to a mental hospital. The court found that this confinement was inappropriate and aggravated the inmates' mental condition. While it is not clear what specific relief was granted—the court ultimately placed population limits on the prison—it appears that confinement in this unit for over 24 hours was proscribed.[51]

¶ 11.5 DEATH PENALTY INMATES

The final isolation issue dealt with here concerns prisoners facing the death penalty. Such prisoners almost always are confined in a form of lock-down or isolation. These inmates obviously have at least the same rights to medical and psychiatric care as other inmates. The interesting question is whether their status as condemned and their pro forma isolation combine to create a special set of needs.

In *Peterkin v. Jeffes*,[52] the district court judge stated: "Since I find that the capital inmates' collective medical needs are serious, I only consider whether the system of care evinces a deliberate indifference to their medical needs."[53] The court upheld the prison system's provision of psychiatric and counseling services while seemingly accepting as self-evident that condemned inmates had an Eighth Amendment right to such care.[54] If it is good practice, and perhaps legally mandated, to perform weekly mental health rounds in segregation, then death row inmates plainly should be included.

¶ 11.6 SUMMARY AND CONCLUSION

It should be emphasized that the critical legal aspects of isolation and the mentally disordered inmate relate first to the provision of the basic conditions necessary for

---

[49] Ferola, 622 F. Supp. at 824. Judge Pettine indicated that the plaintiff-inmate, in a telephone conversation, amended the complaint to include declaratory and injunctive relief.

[50] 650 F. Supp. 619, 630 (D.D.C. 1986).

[51] Inmates of Ocoquan, 650 F. Supp. at 630.

[52] 661 F. Supp. 895 (E.D. Pa. 1987), *aff'd in part and vacated in part*, 855 F.2d 1021 (3rd Cir. 1988).

[53] Id. *See* McFarland v. Scott, 512 U.S. 849 (1994) (death row inmates receive no special consideration on their right to counsel claims).

[54] *See* Groseclose v. Dutton, 829 F.2d 581, 583 (6th Cir. 1987) (discussing Grubbs v. Bradley, 552 F. Supp. 1052 (M.D. Tenn. 1984), and issues relating to the confinement and treatment of death row inmates.

survival, and next to the duration of confinement and the special needs of the mentally disordered inmate. Where clinical judgment dictates, the use of temporary isolation along with regular observation to deal with an inmate who is acting out is not likely to create any legal problems. Prison officials have a duty to preserve life and limb, and limited use of isolation may indeed be more humane and effective than the more prolonged use of body restraints or the reliance on psychotropic drugs. Housing seriously mentally ill inmates in the newly popular super-maximum facilities may well be a per se violation of such an inmate's Eighth Amendment rights. When Ohio opens its super-maximum facility, it will not knowingly house the mentally ill there; procedures and training have been put in place to identify and transfer such inmates as they may become known.[55]

Crisis cells, with nursing care on site, should be available as another option to the use of lock-down areas. Such cells may be as stark as clinical and security needs dictate; there should be good visibility to every part of the cell; and the cells should be as isolated from other inmates as is architecturally possible.

Certainly, whenever a "caseload inmate" is to be moved to any form of special housing area, there must be consultation between security and mental health staff and it is a good idea to have policy and procedure on point governing how to resolve any differences.

---

[55] Information learned personally from various Ohio officials during the course of serving as Monitor of the prison system.

Chapter 12
Use of Bodily Restraints

¶ 12.1 MECHANICAL RESTRAINT DEFINED

As recently as 1995, the Seventh Circuit Court of Appeals could state, "Whether using bodily restraints as punishment violates the Eighth Amendment is an open question in this circuit."[1] The law is reasonably clear elsewhere, however, that while mechanical restraints may be used as an aspect of the legitimate use of force to prevent violence or property destruction and as a means to temporarily restrain a mentally ill inmate who is acting out, they may not be used for punishment alone.[2]

Mechanical restraints include any means of restricting an inmate's or detainee's ability to react physically, and they usually involve the use of such devices as leather straps, cuffs, braces, and most recently, a specially designed chair to which the person is strapped. The Standards for New York City Correctional Facilities are a bit more definitionally explicit: physical restraint is the deliberate use of a device to interfere with the free movement of an inmate's arms and/or legs, or which totally immobilizes the inmate and which the inmate is unable to remove without assistance.[3]

Various forms of mechanical restraints—cuffs and leg irons are the most common—are used when transporting certain inmates, during visits, or when simply moving about the facility. This type of restraint when limited to the type of specified activity just described is not within the reach of this material.[4] Previously I noted that the

---

[1] Murphy v. Walker, 51 F.3d 714, 717 n.6 (7th Cir. 1995) *Murphy* also suggests that detainees have greater protection as to restraints than convicts.

[2] Ferola v. Moran, 622 F. Supp. 814 (D.R.I. 1985); Stewart v. Rhodes, 785 F.2d 310 (6th Cir. 1986). There is no standard on point that would permit restraints as punishment, or for the mentally ill, for "mere convenience" as well.

[3] Board of Corrections for New York City, Correctional Facilities § 6.3 (1984).

[4] Where seven inmates were chained together and their hands further immobilized with the use of a "black box," the lead inmate fell during the one-mile walk injuring the plaintiff who could not break his

shackling of one inmate-patient, who was also an amputee, during transportation, was determined to be unnecessary and also harmful to his mental health. In addition, searching him while handcuffed created moods of helplessness, anger, and despair.[5]

¶ 12.2 BASIC LEGAL RIGHTS AND DUTIES

We begin with the important legal proposition that inmates, and certainly detainees, retain a residual liberty interest in being free of mechanical restraints.[6] This interest is conditional, and in a variety of circumstances will give way to legitimate security or treatment interests. We may contrast this conditional liberty interest with the inherent power of government to house a detainee or inmate in a secured cell where free movement obviously is restricted. This, of course, is at the core of the lawful right to deprive a person of his or her liberty interest in free movement. To manacle or shackle is not an inherent part of government's undoubted right to incarcerate persons awaiting trial or convicted of a crime and to do so in a highly restrictive environment.

Being restrained on a bed or, as is now in vogue, a molded plastic lounge-like device, is a terrifying experience.[7] The constant or regular surveillance that accompanies mechanical restraint only magnifies the feeling of being vulnerable and exposed. This procedure must occasionally be used, but it should be made subject to the least drastic intrusion or least drastic alternative principle. It must be clearly and severely limited both in its objectives and in its duration, and appropriate monitoring and recording procedures must be in place beforehand.

¶ 12.3 STANDARD FOR RESTRAINING INMATES

As a template by which to gauge the material that follows, I reproduce the standard for treatment of hospitalized mental patients fashioned a quarter of a century ago in the landmark case of *Wyatt v. Stickney*:[8]

Patients have a right to be free from physical restraint and isolation. Except for emergency situations, in which it is likely that patients could harm themselves or others and in which less restrictive means of restraint are not feasi-

---

fall. In Morisette v. Godinez, 103 F. 3d 133 (7th Cir. 1996) (Table only printed), the court found that there would be deliberate indifference only if the defendant was actually aware of the extreme dangerousness of using the "black box" under these conditions. It is not clear whether the dangerousness related to the likelihood of a fall or to the harm that would likely ensue if there was a fall, or both. Where such restraints are used for nonemergency, security purposes, the most common complaints are in the application or duration.

[5] Cameron v. Tomes, 900 F.2d 14, 20 n.9 (1st Cir. 1993). See discussion in of *Cameron* in Chapter 7, notably at ¶ 7.1.

[6] Youngberg v. Romeo, 457 U.S. 307 (1982).

[7] I have had myself "strapped down" briefly in a prison setting just to get a feel for it, and even knowing release was only a moment's request away, it was one of the most abject feelings of vulnerability and helplessness that I have known. I suggest that no employee should be "certified" to restrain until that employee has himself been so restrained.

[8] 344 F. Supp. 373 (M.D. Ala. 1972).

ble, patients may be physically restrained or placed in isolation only on a Qualified Mental Health Professional's written order which explains the rationale for such action. The written order may be entered only after the Qualified Mental Health Professional has personally seen the patient concerned and evaluated whatever episode or situation is said to call for restraint or isolation. Emergency use of restraints or isolation shall be for no more than one hour, by which time a Qualified Mental Health Professional shall have consulted and shall have entered an appropriate order in writing. Such written order shall be effective for no more than 24 hours and must be renewed if restraint or isolation are to be continued. While in restraint or isolation the patient must be seen by qualified ward personnel who will chart the patient's physical condition (if it is compromised) and psychiatric condition every hour. The patient must have bathroom privileges every hour and must be bathed every 12 hours.[9]

In reading this provision and knowing that it was applied to the civilly committed who have a greater claim to personal autonomy than the convicted, does it appear to be unduly restrictive from the staff's perspective? Is the rationale for the imposition of restraints clearly stated? Sufficiently protective? How likely is "likely"? What is to be done in the absence of a mental health professional? What type of restraints are to be used? Preferred? Is there some outer time limit for a single episode? What type of observation or medical monitoring is, or should be, done? Should the individual be restrained face up or face down?

Obviously, these questions either are not answered or are answered obliquely. Just as obviously, a prison/jail restraint policy should deal with such vital questions, and more. We shall return to the matter of appropriate policy and procedure as we proceed.

¶ 12.4 CASE LAW REVIEW

[1] "Conditions of Confinement" Claim

Anderson v. County of Kern, California[10] is an interesting case with which to begin our exploration of the law on point. We will discover that the courts are less than clear or consistent on the source of the constitutional right and on the proper legal formula that governs decisions in restraint cases. *Anderson* included a Section 1983[11] action that challenged the use of so-called safety cells at five jails. The plaintiffs were a group of detainees and convicted prisoners. The prototype cell at issue was 10 feet by 10 feet. It was covered with rubberized foam paddings and had a pit toilet with a grate that was encrusted with excrement and urine. Inmates had to eat in this cell, described as dark, dirty, foreboding, and foul smelling. Clothing issue was minimal.[12]

The cell was described as one used for violent, suicidal, or mentally disturbed

---

[9] Id.

[10] 45 F.3d 1310 (9th Cir. 1995). *Anderson* also is a good example of the frequent interplay between the use of isolation and mechanical restraints.

[11] 42 U.S.C. § 1983.

[12] Anderson, 45 F.3d at 1314.

prisoners. In a 7-month period, at least 10 prisoners were recorded as shackled to the grate over the pit toilet along with "handcuffs attached to a waist chain, leg irons separated with a 12-inch chain," with the secondary chains running to the toilet grate.[13]

The district court refused to enjoin officials from placing mentally disturbed or suicidal prisoners in the cells just described. This ruling has been affirmed.[14] The reviewing court set out its understanding of the applicable constitutional standards:

> Under the Eighth Amendment, the pertinent inquiry is (1) whether placement of mentally disturbed or suicidal inmates in safety cells constitutes an infliction of pain or a deprivation of the basic human needs, such as adequate food, clothing, shelter, sanitation, and medical care, and (2) if so, whether prison officials acted with the requisite culpable intent such that the infliction of pain is "unnecessary and wanton." *Farmer v. Brennan, 114 S. Ct. 1970, 1977 (1994).* In prison condition cases, prison officials act with the requisite culpable intent when they act with deliberate indifference to the inmates' suffering. Id. Similarly, the placement of pretrial detainees in safety cells is "punishment" in violation of the Fourteenth Amendment only if prison officials act with deliberate indifference to the inmates' needs.
>
> The test for whether a prison official acts with deliberate indifference is a subjective one: the official must "know [] of and disregard [] an excessive risk to inmate health and safety; the official must both be aware of the facts from which the inference could be drawn that a substantial risk of serious harm exists, and he must also draw the inference." *Farmer, 114 S. Ct. at 1979.*[15]

The court then focused on the essential, albeit temporary, needs of the prisoners who are briefly confined; the plaintiff's failure to establish the requisite pain; and the failure to show a culpable state of mind on the part of the officials.[16] The court reasoned that in an emergency, officials must have the ability to temporarily place a prisoner where he cannot harm himself.

There is no specific mention of the shackling as a further deprivation that when added to the gruesome physical conditions may well have, and perhaps should have, taken the case in another direction. There was no discussion as to the need for further restraint in a cell already padded and denominated "safe." There was no analysis of the nature of the mechanical restraints, only a description of them. Obviously, from the writer's standpoint, there should have been close scrutiny of the interplay between the protective isolation and the primitive shackling.

[2] "Use of Force" Claim

In *Murray v. Marshall,*[17] *Pelican Bay* makes another judicial appearance, this time concerned with a blanket policy of applying mechanical restraints to all Secured

---

[13] Anderson, 45 F.3d at 1312.

[14] Anderson, 45 F.3d at 1310.

[15] Anderson, 45 F.3d at 1312–1313.

[16] Anderson, 45 F.3d at 1315.

[17] U.S. Dist. LEXIS 2419 (N.D. Calif. 1995).

Housing Unit (SHU) inmates while they were housed in the prison's medical infirmary. The plaintiff asked to be placed in a "suicide cell" after reportedly having been raped. While there, he was placed in waist chains for 24 hours, consisting of a chain that secures around the waist with a hand cuff attached at each side of the waist so that wrists are secured along each side of the hip.

The court applied the "unnecessary and wanton infliction of pain test" first announced in *Whitley v. Albers*,[18] but due to the brevity of the time in restraints, found the *Murray* claim de minimis. More interesting for our purposes is the court's firmly held view that a blanket policy of requiring mechanical restraints (since abandoned in California) would not meet constitutional muster.[19] Medical advice on the propriety of restraints is required in the case of a suicidal inmate, although the court did not require it at the outset, and individual determinations must be made on the necessity for the restraints.[20]

[3] Mechanical Restraint Use Analysis

Both *Anderson* and *Murray* invited Eighth Amendment rights. *Anderson* was a "conditions of confinement" claim, while *Murray* was a "use of force" claim. The former applied a "deliberate indifference" analysis, the latter a "willful, wanton and malicious" analysis. To confound matters even more, where the restrained prisoner is known to be mentally ill (e.g., on an active case load), then a deliberate indifference test related to treatment should apply and not the more onerous *Whitley* test governing the use of force.[21]

In other words, when mechanical restraints are used on an unruly prisoner, the legality of the application should be analyzed as a straight use of force claim. When such restraints are used on a person known to be mentally ill (or, I also believe, who is suicidal),[22] the analysis required is a combined *Estelle v. Gamble-Farmer v. Brennan* analysis. Does it matter?

Yes, I strongly believe so. Whatever the rationale for applying mechanical restraints, there must be some subsequent medical involvement due to the medical risks inherent in using any of these various devices. For a prisoner with mental illness, there must be some involvement by a mental health professional who should early assess the impact on the prisoner's course of treatment. This would not be required in the straight use of force on a disruptive prisoner.

---

[18] 475 U.S. 312 (1986). *Whitley* additionally focuses on the need to restore order, not to punish an offending inmate.

[19] LeMaire v. Maass, 12 F.3d 1444 (9th Cir. 1994); *see also* Spain v. Procunier, 600 F.2d 189 (9th Cir. 1979), to the same effect.

[20] *See* Haslar v. Megerman, 104 F.3d 128 (8th Cir. 1997), in which a blanket policy of shackling detainees while hospitalized was implicitly upheld; the plaintiff suffered permanent damage due to careless monitoring, but the court upheld the details of the written policy.

[21] *See* Wells v. Franzen, 777 F.2d 1258 (7th Cir. 1985) (freedom of bodily movement is a substantive, due process right that is breached when an allegedly suicidal inmate is restrained without an exercise of professional judgment by a mental health care professional).

[22] In Estate of Max G. Cole v. Fromm, 94 F.3d 254, 261 (7th Cir. 1996), the court stated that an inmate's right to be free from bodily restraint is breached when the person is restrained unless the decision is made by a health professional. When made, it is presumptively valid.

¶ 12.5 THERAPEUTIC RESTRAINTS AND PROPOSED POLICY

The National Commission on Correctional Health Care (NCCHC) recently amended their standard on restraints, including a revised title, as follows:

P-66 Therapeutic Restraints and Therapeutic Seclusion (essential)

Written policy and defined procedures require, and actual practice evidences, the appropriate use of *therapeutic restraints* and *therapeutic seclusion* for patients under treatment for a mental illness. They specify the type(s) of restraint that may be used and when, where, how, and for how long restraints or seclusion may be used. Use is authorized in each case by a physician, or other qualified health care professional where permitted by law, upon reaching the conclusion that no other less restrictive treatment is appropriate. For restrained or secluded patients, the treatment plan addresses the goal of removing the inmate from restraint or seclusion as soon as possible. The health care staff does not participate in the non-medical restraint of inmates except for monitoring their health status.

Discussion

Therapeutic restraints refer to measures taken as part of medical or mental health treatment, which are designed to confine a patient's bodily movements, such as the use of leather cuffs and anklets. *Therapeutic seclusion* refers to the placement (by health workers) of an inmate-patient in a bare room for the purpose of containing a clinical situation (e.g., extreme agitation, threatening behavior, assaultive behavior) that may result in a state of emergency.

This standard applies to those situations where the restraints are part of health care treatment. Generally, an order for therapeutic restraint or therapeutic seclusion should not exceed 12 hours, or should follow state health code requirements. There should be documented 15 minute checks by health-trained personnel or qualified health care professionals.

The same kinds of restraints that would be appropriate for individuals treated in the community may likewise be used for therapeutically restraining incarcerated individuals: for example, fleece-lined leather, rubber, or canvas hand and leg restraints, and 2-point and 4-point ambulatory restraints. Metal or hard plastic devices (such as handcuffs and leg shackles) should not be used for therapeutic restraint. Persons should not be restrained in an unnatural position (for instance, hog-tied, facedown, spread-eagle).

Both the health authority and the person legally responsible should receive daily reports on the frequency and use of therapeutic restraints and therapeutic seclusion.

Medical monitoring of the health of inmates held under non-medical restraint should be carried out periodically by qualified health care professionals. When health staff note what they consider to be improper use of restraints, jeopardizing the health of an inmate, they should communicate their concerns as soon as possible to the facility administrator or his/her designee."[23]

The title "Therapeutic Restraints" is actually quite felicitous in inviting a clean distinction between, let us call it, a clinical situation and one that is not. This standard would clearly be governed legally by the *Estelle v. Gamble* deliberate indifference test, not the *Whitley-McMillian* use of force test.

The above standard also addresses a recurring problem: efforts to involve clinical personnel in the initial decision to apply mechanical restraints. The standard, again right on target, rules out such participation except for the all-important regular medical monitoring.

[1] Permissible vs. Impermissible Types of Restraint

Where a restraint might be otherwise permissible, some types of applications may be constitutional violations, such as "hog-tying" for five days,[24] the use of metal restraints, except for transportation,[25] or cuffing a prisoner to fences, bars, or other such fixtures.[26] Inmates in restraints should have mattresses and clean bedding; such restraint should be accompanied by medical authorization and a log should be kept.[27]

A particularly offensive use of mechanical restraints was employed in the Iowa penal system in the late 1980's. In *Buckley v. Rogerson*,[28] a mentally ill prisoner complained that he was subjected to the repeated use of segregation and restraints without medical approval. In the district court, Buckley's principal contention against Dr. Paul Loeffelholz, the prison hospital director, was that the hospital's policies and procedures allowed correctional officers—rather than trained medical personnel—to develop and implement the treatment plans. Buckley also contended that the treatment plans that were developed lacked sufficient specificity to guide the staff in administering the treatment. Buckley argued that Loeffelholz's conduct constituted deliberate indifference to a serious medical need and violated his Eighth and Fourteenth Amendment rights.[29]

In response, the district court found:

While Buckley [was hospitalized] defendant Dr. Paul Loeffelholz was responsible for developing the policies and operating procedures of the institution. These policies allowed . . . staff to develop "treatment plans" designed to address Buckley's mental illness. At trial, Buckley introduced evidence that, rather tha[n] assign its staff doctors to his case, the prison entrusted the

---

[23] Therapeutic Restraints and Therapeutic Seclusion (NCCHC amended Standards).
[24] Jones v. Thompson, 818 F. Supp. 1263 (S.D. Ind. 1993).
[25] Gawreys v. D.C. Gen. Hosp., 480 F. Supp. 853 (D.D.C. 1979).
[26] Gates v. Collier, 349 F. Supp. 881, 890–900 (N.D. Miss. 1972), *aff'd,* 501 F.2d 1291 (5th Cir. 1974).
[27] Owens-El v. Robinson, 457 F. Supp. 984, 990–991 (W.D. Pa. 1978).
[28] 133 F.3d 1125 (8th Cir. 1998).
[29] Buckley, 133 F.3d at 1126.

responsibility of implementing and administering many of Buckley's treatment plans to correctional officers who had no medical training. Dr. Fredrickson, one of [the hospital's] medical doctors, testified that correctional officers were allowed to initiate treatment of Buckley without Dr. Fredrickson's approval.

Part of the "treatment" in these treatment plans involved stripping Buckley of his clothes and placing him in a Spartan "quiet" or "segregation" cell. Other parts of the "treatment" involved placing Buckley in restraints so that h[e] could hardly move. There was testimony at the full trial that segregation and restraints the correctional officers ordered for Buckley were more akin to punishment than treatment. The evidence further showed that Buckley was forced into the "quiet" room on seventeen occasion[s] without human necessities such as clothes, a blanket, a bed, and a mattress. Buckley testified it was "very cold" in the quiet room, that he could not hear outside noises when he was in the quiet room, and that a doctor never checked on him while he was in the quiet room. The evidence also showed that the decision to send Buckley to the quiet room was made by non-medical staff. Dr. Loeffelholz, ostensibly responsible for Buckley's treatment, checked on Buckley once every ninety days.[30]

Expert testimony established that this alleged treatment more nearly resembled punishment. There was no guidance on how to improve, and many of the so-called "violations" that culminated in restraint and isolation were violations of hospital routines and not evidence of psychiatric deficiencies.[31]

In the present posture of the case, the Eighth Circuit had to rule only on the defendant's motion for summary judgment based on a claim of qualified immunity. The court found that the case law was clear at the time of these practices, that the decision to use segregation or restraints had to be made under close medical supervision, and that Dr. Loeffelholz should have known the law on point.[32]

The upshot of the cases on point is that certain forms of restraint may be used for clinical purposes or simply to contain a mental health patient or client, but restraints should not be imposed for punishment or mere convenience. There must be clinical involvement and supervision, and it must be conducted in a humane manner.

[2] Essential Policy Guidelines

Every facility must have a policy and procedures for handling cases requiring restraints. I suggest that there are five irreducible (or essential) points that must be included:

1. *Clarity on the rationale (or criteria) for the intervention.* There are always

---

[30] Buckley, 133 F.3d at 1126–1127.

[31] Buckley, 133 F.3d at 1128.

[32] Buckley, 133 F.3d at 112631. The important, earlier decisions relied on by the Eighth Circuit include United States v. Michigan, 680 F. Supp. 927 (W.D. Mich. 1987); Burks v. Teasdale, 492 F. Supp. 650 (W.D. Mo. 1980); and Negron v. Preiser, 382 F. Supp. 535 (S.D.N.Y. 1974).

emergencies that will require the prevention or reduction of harm or damage. The nature of emergencies that trigger therapeutic restraint or seclusion must be spelled out.

2. *Authorization.* In an emergency (and these situations always are emergencies) it may not always be possible to have a doctor or a psychiatrist perform an initial authorization. However, the regulations should clarify (1) who may then authorize, (2) how soon thereafter clinical authorization is required, and (3) whether or when personal observation must precede clinical authorization.

3. *Monitoring.* The policy should specify who will do the monitoring, at what intervals monitoring will occur, and whether it is for medical, psychiatric, or comfort purposes.

4. *Bodily function factors.* The policy should provide for details on provision of food, relief of bodily wastes and fluids, water intake, nonimpairment of blood circulation, and the like.

5. *Duration.* The policy must state how long a single restraining episode will last and the time frames for monitoring, recordkeeping, and the like.

To reiterate, I suggest that these factors are essential for any acceptable policy and procedure. Many other matters should also be dealt with, including the types of restraint authorized, positioning, and so on. The use of partial releases is yet another interesting (although not essential) point to clarify, as the following case shows.

In *Williams v. Burton,*[33] a disruptive inmate with a history of assaultive behavior was placed in four-point restraints and gagged for 28 hours. He was allowed up a number of times and moved about the cell causing no problems. Each time, he was replaced in restraints and again gagged.

The majority actually had no problem with this, relying on the ubiquitous professional judgment standard. Judge Pittman, in dissent, agreed that the initial restraint was probably reasonable, but that sometime after the first hour it became excessive and, thus, punishment.[34] He pointed out that the cell used was in segregation, where all the doors were solid metal, so the danger of further disruption was nonexistent or nominal. He noted that the plaintiff had quieted down.[35]

The point I wish to make, however, is that when the inmate was released and showed no sign of further "dangerousness," the routine reapplication of restraints could only signal needless punishment. Thus, a seemingly humane provision—partial or temporary release—should be carefully analyzed and addressed in any policy covering the use of restraints.

An all-encompassing policy and procedure on point would also address:

1. The forcible administration of psychotropic medication as parallel to the application of mechanical restraints; the policies should be compatible.[36]

---

[33] 943 F.2d 1572 (11th Cir. 1991).

[34] Williams, 943 F.2d at 1578, 1581.

[35] Williams, 943 F.2d at 1578.

[36] This is a point corrections administrators often overlook. Forcible administration of medication

2. A principle of less restrictive intervention with clarification as to what steps to follow and what should be recorded (e.g., talking to inmate) before the escalation to restraints.

3. Exactly what restraint position and equipment should be used, and the need for this use to be uniform throughout the system.[37]

4. When an outside limit is reached, and the specific further options available (e.g., hospitalization).

5. The nagging problem of the few inmates who continue to self-mutilate when released and whose lives are in jeopardy without extended restraint, constant surveillance, or successful treatment.[38]

6. Separate policies regarding the use of (1) clinical (or therapeutic) restraints and (2) use of force restraints. These issues may be addressed in separate sections of the policy, but separate policies are preferable.

To conclude, it is plain that mechanical restraints (and isolation) legally may be used with mentally ill prisoners. The prisoner has a liberty interest in the avoidance of such intrusive and frequently terrifying measures and resort to them should be available only when other measures have not or seemingly will not work.

The application cannot continue beyond the emergency. Training of staff in the application of restraints is vital and one of the benefits of clearly separating the clinical from the security use of restraints is the need for a special sensitivity to the mentally ill or suicidal inmate. Where the same special response team is used, it is likely that the approach used for the disruptive inmate will prevail. I have watched such procedures where the officer in charge repeated to a plainly hallucinating inmate, "I'm ordering you for the seventh time to turn around and cuff up!" The inmate continued to pray aloud to Jesus. Five men in battle gear then rushed in and easily subdued the nearly naked 150-pound inmate and took him to a nearby "safe cell." The inmate was completely subdued and passive by then; mumbling only fragments of religious babble.

The officers placed him on the bed and in four-point restraints—following policy and procedure. Need I say more?

---

and mechanical restraints are emergency, control measures and surely the same criteria, for example, should apply.

[37] In Coleman v. Wilson, 912 F. Supp. 1282, 1314 (E.D. Cal. 1995), the record showed that the use of restraint varied among prisons, but a state regulation on point and other measures defused any finding of unconstitutionality.

[38] Consider the inmate who cuts open his stomach and actually exposes his inner parts. He does this repeatedly, is stitched repeatedly, and further surgery becomes dubious. There should be a policy for this outlyer, but it must not drive basic policy. There should be a standardized solution (e.g., constant watch), but again the off-the-chart problem should not drive solutions to the more common problems associated with acute and temporary situations. This situation was one I actually encountered in which officials tried boxing gloves, partial restraints, everything they could think of. The inmate simply tore off the stitches and officials repeated the awful process of repair. The doctors said they could no longer stitch him. I have no further information.

Chapter 13

Disciplinary Proceedings and Mental Illness

¶ 13.1 REASONABLE ACCOMMODATION DIFFICULTIES

Prison disciplinary proceedings often are a lightning rod for exacerbating tensions between security and mental health staff. This seems particularly true when the inmate is housed in a residential treatment unit. Mental health staff may see an inmate's acting out as symptomatic of the illness; security may see a person harming another or destroying property, knowing right from wrong and requiring punishment.[1] Prosecution is an option in prison, of course. This chapter focuses on whether to initiate internal disciplinary proceedings or treat at least some behavior as "acting out."

Training and the involvement of security staff in the treatment team will go a long way toward reaching reasonable accommodation. In my experience, however, some of the problems are so deeply rooted that they are not likely ever to be fully resolved. For some inmates the issues go to the very heart of the prison experience. For example, repeated infractions and findings of guilt invariably lead to a gradual tightening of an inmate's security status. This in turn often leads to transfer to a state's highest security facilities. *Pelican Bay*[2] is simply an extreme example of this.

The toughest prisons and the most secure cell blocks within them are too often candidates for the toughest, and often sickest, inmates, and creation of this sort of psychiatric ghetto is in no one's best interests. Is this situation legally permissible? In all likelihood, yes. Does it deserve additional analysis and accommodation? Most certainly, yes.

In a 1989 study, Hans Toch and Douglas Grant point out that prison disciplinary systems too often contain an insufficient number of dispositional options—essential-

---

[1] In one of the few articles dealing with response options where psychiatric inpatients engage in acts of violence, author Stephen Rachlin reviews the conflicting perspectives that prosecution encourages responsibility but subverts therapeutic alliances. He concludes that prosecution must remain an option as a last resort. Stephen Rachlin, *The Prosecution of Violent Psychiatric Inpatients: One Respectable Intervention*, 22 BULL. AM. ACAD. PSYCHIATRY LAW 239 (1994).

[2] Madrid v. Gomez, 899 F. Supp. 1146 (N.D. Cal. 1995). Referred to as *Pelican Bay*, this case is discussed in Chapter 7, ¶ 7.3[2]–7.3[2][d]; Chapter 11, ¶ 11.2, and elsewhere in this book.

ly, discipline or mental health, with little flexibility on combining the two. In addition, they suggest that while hearing staff may resort to mental health referrals, they do so infrequently and miss priceless opportunities for obtaining needed help.[3]

Policy questions abound in this area, unaided by much in the way of empirical data.[4] For example, if a disciplinary process is designed to achieve punishment and deterrence, one must ask about the legitimacy of punishing someone who had no control over his conduct or perhaps no appreciation of its wrongfulness. One must also question the pursuit of individual deterrence when it is clear that a particular inmate is not deterrable.

One might argue that even when an individual acts out of a hallucinatory or delusional framework, general deterrence can still be achieved, and especially so in the closed world of prison where information travels with lightening speed.

Lawyers and nonlawyers alike appear to avoid the complexities of the responsibility dilemma. Where nonlawyers appear to focus on dispositional alternatives, lawyers likely debate procedural due process or competence (or triability), with perhaps a nod at the unavailability of a "disciplinary insanity defense."

Serious legal questions surfaced about 10 years ago in judicial proceedings challenging both the legality of conducting a disciplinary proceeding when an inmate may be unable to defend himself and the general unavailability of mental disability as a defense.[5] There were concessions, generally off the record, that an inmate's mental illness was taken into account either to diminish culpability or, more often, to determine the sanction. Much depends on the seriousness of the conduct and the identity of the victim. Assaults on staff universally are treated differently than inmate-inmate assaults.

The essence of the initial challenge is the argument that there is a federally grounded due process right to a fair hearing in at least some prison disciplinary proceedings.[6] At a minimum, the argument goes, the accused inmate has a right to participate physically and mentally in the hearing and offer defenses and matters in explanation or mitigation. Unless the inmate is able to understand the charges and to aid in the defense—unless he is competent—then it is fundamentally unfair to conduct a disciplinary proceeding.[7]

---

[3] Hans Toch & J. Douglas Grant, *Mental Illness in Prison: Disciplinary Responses to Eccentric Violations*, in THE AMERICAN PRISON (Goodstein & MacKenzie, eds. 1989), pp. 216–219.

[4] Toch and Grant review the few studies then available in this area.

[5] Anderson v. Coughlin, No. 86 Civ. 8879 (S.D.N.Y. Nov. 17, 1986) (references in the text are drawn from the pleadings in the case and not from any judicial decision). Prisoner Legal Services of New York raised both these issues in a lawsuit seeking declaratory and injunctive relief.

[6] *See* Wolff v. McDonnell, 418 U.S. 539 (1974); Sandin v. Conner, 115 S. Ct. 2293 (1995), shifts the analysis here somewhat. A *Wolff*-hearing is required when good time credits may be lost or where an "atypical, significant deprivation" is imposed. *See* discussion of this in Chapter 3, especially ¶ 3.7[1], 3.7[2]. Extended disciplinary segregation has been allowed without a *Wolff* hearing, courts deciding that this is not atypical or significant. Thus, if there is no hearing required, it is difficult to argue that the right to participate requires physical and mental presence.

[7] In a criminal trial, if a defendant is found incompetent to be tried the government can, and most often does, commit the accused for treatment. Thus in the prison setting, a decision to delay a hearing would effectively also be a decision to seek treatment. *See* Jackson v. Indiana, 406 U.S. 715 (1972).

¶ 13.2 COMPETENCE AND INSANITY

Competency is a synonym for "triability," whereas the proposed mental disability defense (actually a hybrid form of insanity defense) is a synonym for responsibility. If an inmate is sufficiently mentally ill at the time of the alleged infraction and also lacks the capacity to know or appreciate either the nature or consequences of his conduct or its wrongfulness, then, it is argued, the inmate cannot be punished. The inmate is not culpable and surely not deterrable. To punish such an inmate, it is claimed, constitutes cruel and unusual punishment.[8]

To summarize, these legal claims seek either to delay a disciplinary proceeding until the inmate is competent or to deny the right to "convict" and impose punishment on the inmate who is irresponsible as a result of mental disease. An important third point is the desirability of factoring into the disposition information pertaining to the inmate's mental health.

In a case challenging New York State's handling of these issues, the inmates' legal complaint raised several allegations. One inmate with a long history of suicidal behavior and with severe psychosis was disciplined for striking an officer who attempted to remove the inmate from his cell. Another inmate was disciplined for threatening suicide shortly after being returned to prison from a mental hospital. He continued to threaten suicide and eventually did mutilate himself several times. Disciplinary action continued between stays at a mental hospital. One of the more shocking allegations involved a 24-year-old transsexual who attempted suicide four times at the jail while awaiting transfer to a prison. While imprisoned, the inmate continued to attempt suicide and also attempted to remove his penis and testicles, finally succeeding in removing a testicle by making an incision with a part of a ballpoint pen. The inmate faced serious disciplinary charges as a result of this conduct.[9]

Concededly, the cases just mentioned are extreme. However, they are hardly isolated. Whether or not such inmate claims are fully substantiated, they do represent the type of case that calls for a decision on competency and responsibility. Although the law is unsettled in this area, most would likely agree in principle that it is fundamentally unfair to try someone incapable of either understanding the charge or presenting a defense, and it is unfair as well as cruel to punish someone for conduct that he cannot appreciate or control. Such punishment, it is argued, serves no valid purpose. And certainly the punishment by definition does not deter.

The consequences of recognizing competency and the more difficult problems of responsibility in a prison disciplinary proceeding are not as threatening as might first appear. That is, there is no loss or impairment of custody. Whether incompetent or irresponsible, the inmate may be placed in a secure treatment environment and sub-

---

[8] Similar issues abound in the juvenile justice system. There is no clear Supreme Court authority, nor any consensus among the states, on whether a juvenile may raise an insanity defense or even the right to assert trial incompetency. To the extent that the juvenile system is viewed as a punishment system, insanity and incompetence are recognized. Viewing juvenile justice in the older, rehabilitative mode discounts the need for incompetence, and certainly insanity, as hindering access to treatment. *See* Loren Warboys & Shannon Wilbur, *Mental Health Issues in Juvenile Justice*, in Law, Mental Health, and Mental Disorder (Bruce D. Sales & Daniel W. Shumar, eds. 1996), pp. 510–512.

[9] These accounts are taken from *Anderson v. Coughlin, supra* note 4.

jected to the control deemed necessary. There will be the marginal cases, and there will be those who "fake it." The answer to these problems may be that the possibility of abuse ought not to dominate the search for acceptable general principles and fair procedures.

Among prison officials with whom I talk, the major concern with excusing misconduct is that it offers others an invitation to engage in similar misconduct. This is an aspect of the ubiquitous concern for control and security, and I do not take it lightly. However, as the number of seriously ill inmates grows, this is not a problem that may be discussed only behind closed doors.

Every jurisdiction should formulate a policy on these questions and, in addition, create mechanisms whereby marginally competent inmates in disciplinary proceedings are afforded even more assistance at a hearing than would be afforded the normal inmate. For example, a lay advocate or even counsel could assist instead of a prison employee. Rules governing triability and responsibility can be kept simple and workable without requiring expert testimony. Cases like *Anderson* represent inmates with a record of hospitalizations and bizarre and destructive behavior, in which there is enough evidence available to reach an informed opinion. A jurisdiction having its own rules and policy need not simply await judicial intervention. Special attention should be given to the mentally retarded inmate whose disability will likely have more of an effect on competence to be tried than on responsibility for the alleged infraction.

William J. Rold, an attorney who is quite active in correctional health care, has formulated a list of 14 administrative procedures designed to be protective of the rights of mentally disordered prisoners.[10] The first 5 are general but the remainder, which are set out below, deal with discipline.

> Review by mental health professional of mental health status of inmates before placement in segregation and regularly while in segregation.
>
> Prohibit the placement or maintenance in solitary confinement of inmates with severe mental disorders or current psychotic disability.
>
> Provide opportunity for inmates to submit proof of mental health factors underlying misconduct.
>
> Make counsel available for inmates unable to assist themselves.
>
> Make it an affirmative duty of hearing officers to inquire into the mental health status of the inmate when the issue is presented fairly, even if the inmate fails to raise it.
>
> Inquire into the consequences of mental health treatment of proposed dispositions and use of clinically appropriate sanctions.
>
> Make available a variety of disciplinary dispositions that take into account the mental health cases for behavior, including dismissal of charges.
>
> Limit the maximum time spent in punitive segregation, as adopted by many states.
>
> Review the mental status of inmates discharged from psychiatric hospitalization who "owe" segregation time before returning them to solitary confinement.[11]

---

[10] William J. Rold, Consideration of Mental Health Factors in Inmate Discipline, Correct Care 4F (1992).

[11] Id.

It is curious that the author says nothing about competence (or triability) and recommends counsel, certainly not legally required and while perhaps an ideal, a mandate few systems will voluntarily undertake. However, the focus on disposition and attention to the disorder is commendable.

¶ 13.3 REASONABLE ACCOMMODATION AT WORK

[1] The Ohio Approach

In Ohio, a workable, and perhaps transitional, accommodation has been reached regarding disciplinary proceeding for incompetent inmates.[12] Where an inmate is on a mental health caseload or otherwise diagnosed as mentally ill, the prison disciplinary process must take into account the inmate's mental illness, medication, and treatment needs.

On occasion, a hearing officer, acting more like a committing magistrate than a judge, may simply refuse to process "a ticket." The charge remains of record but the offending inmate with mental illness is dealt with on a psychiatric basis. The most compelling reasons for this diversion are that (1) the inmate has not been compliant with his medication; (2) the offending behavior is consistent with the noncompliance and illness; and (3) the charge is not terribly serious.[13]

Where a hearing is held there may be personal input from a mental health worker, most often the person who works with the inmate. The worker will discuss the illness, medication and the behavior, and make recommendations to the disciplinary committee about a suitable disposition in the event of a finding of guilt.

Having observed dozens of these proceedings, I believe there is a reasonable accommodation at work. The training the staff receives regarding the symptoms of mental illness, side effects of medication, and consequences of noncompliance is a critical factor here. Security staff has softened its rigid views on the need to punish, while mental health staff are more alert to authentic security concerns.

Obviously, there is a certain lack of symmetry, or fairness if you will, in ever punishing a person for that which they cannot control. The case law, however, rather plainly would not require an administrative insanity defense, and prison systems would not now easily tolerate it. Thus, the world of reasonable accommodation takes over and produces an Ohio-like procedure.

Training of staff in Ohio includes distinguishing an insanity defense from a situation in which a person's behavior is involuntary. I have described Tourette's Disorder to staff and asked how they felt about charging an afflicted inmate with "verbal disrespect" or "disregarding a lawful order."

Where the afflicted inmate's verbal tic involves repeated obscenities, known as Coprolalia, the involuntary behavior takes on yet another dimension. The trainees invariably express the view that "it wouldn't be right to punish those guys." It takes only a little more effort, then, to distinguish involuntary and rightly unpunishable behavior from mental disorder-driven behavior and the availability of discipline.

---

[12] This account of the Ohio procedure is based on my experience there as a monitor for mental health services.

[13] Striking an officer invariably leads to a hearing, whereas "disrespect" may not. Pushing (versus-punching) an inmate is a borderline infraction.

This is not to suggest that such training solves the problem, but it does serve to highlight the distinction between involuntary behavior and voluntary behavior driven by mental illness. One hopes that this heightens sensitivity and creates some pockets of discretion in what is essentially an area of law dominated by strict liability.

[2] No Disciplinary Proceeding—Incompetency

Where an inmate is unable to comprehend the charges, offer a coherent defense, or offer a coherent explanation, then a disciplinary proceeding should not go forward. A few questions are all that it usually takes: Do you know where you are? What you are charged with? What might happen if you are found guilty? Inappropriate answers equate with incompetence.

Incompetency leads to delay, not dismissal. There should be a clearly expressed outside time limit to such delay, with treatment obligations imposed, and regular review of the matter.

I concede that this is a "cutting-edge" issue that rarely receives much discussion. This does not detract from its importance or the regularity with which this problem surfaces. There is a certain danger in "going public" with these issues, especially in more humane or sophisticated prison systems where informal, sensitive handling is the norm.

On the other hand, there should be some effort to establish consistency and to be openly fair in these difficult matters. In the same fashion that prison officials rightly worry about sending a message that some harmful conduct may be excused, officials should work to send a message that disciplinary proceedings are fair.

Chapter 14

Suicide

¶ 14.1 THE PROBLEM

Custodial suicides involve the most extreme manifestation of inmate despair; they cause the most hardened of staff untold grief and psychological trauma; and they are statistically significant, especially so in jails. Lindsay Hayes, perhaps the country's top expert in the field, reports that the rate of suicides in prison throughout the country during the past 10 years was 20.6 deaths per 100,000—a rate more than 50 percent greater than that of the general population, yet far below the rate of jail suicides.[1] Jail suicides run at least 400 percent above prison suicides.[2] Interestingly, states with

---

[1] LINDSAY M. HAYES, PRISON SUICIDE: AN OVERVIEW AND GUIDE TO PREVENTION (N.I.C. 1995), p. 31 [hereinafter PRISON SUICIDE].

[2] *See, e.g.,* SOURCE BOOK FOR CRIMINAL JUSTICE STATISTICS: 1994; and HENRY J. STEADMAN, et al.,

smaller prison populations have a much higher rate of suicide, often more than two and one-half times the national average.[3] Hayes has detected a steady decline in prison suicides since 1985, although 1993 was a high year and whether it signaled a reversal or was aberrational is uncertain.[4]

For our purposes, statistical purity is not important. What is important is the undoubted prominence of suicide in our custodial facilities, and that we attempt to understand the applicable law on point. As a keynote to what follows, I would argue that the law of custodial suicide places an unseemly premium on the ignorance of custodians, that is, an ignorance of the readily accepted factors that are predictive of suicide. This is one area in which I would argue that policy makers and custodians go their own way—that they not be content to adhere only to the lowest common denominator of the law.

Professor Hans Toch, perhaps our most prominent scholar of prison violence, describes the social-psychological dimension of inmate self-injury:

> Contrary to stereotypes, most inmate self-injuries reflect concrete and intense personal breakdowns. Most frequently, these are crises of self-doubt, hopelessness, fear, or abandonment. There are also psychotic crises—problems of self-management, tension, delusions, or panic. At best, self-directed violence mirrors helplessness, and involves coping problems with no perceived solution. Crises vary with type of population. They are more prevalent among youths than among older inmates, and among white and Latin inmates. Prisons feature different crises than jails; married inmates, for instance, feel more vulnerable in jail, while single inmates suffer more heavily in prison. Ethnic, sex, and age groups differ in their special vulnerabilities. Latin inmates, for example, are often acutely upset if they feel abandoned by relatives; women have problems with loneliness, or with the management of their feelings.
>
> Prisons as living environments cannot control the stresses they may tend to produce. Different inmates react to different aspects of their imprisonment as particularly stressful. While some men are susceptible to the press of isolation, others react to overcrowding, conflict, coldness, or the aggressive challenges of peers.
>
> Whatever the shape of a man's crisis, the institution has no truck with it when the inmate reacts with self-inflicted violence. The yard's measure of esteem is manliness. Self-injury means despair, and despair is unmanly. The inmate-in-crisis must deny his problems to survive. Others must deny them too. If problems are recognized, the inmate is stigmatized. If they are not recognized, he is abandoned.[5]

THE MENTALLY ILL IN JAIL: PLANNING FOR ESSENTIAL SERVICES (1989), p. 153, which reports that suicide is the leading cause of death in jails and lock-ups in New York state and the nation; the rate was 5 times higher than for state prison inmates.

[3] PRISON SUICIDE, *supra* note 1, p. 31.

[4] PRISON SUICIDE, *supra* note 1, pp. 31–32.

[5] *See* HANS TOCH, CORRECTIONS: A HUMANISTIC APPROACH (1997), Ch. 16. Some courts explicitly balance a type of least intrusive intervention approach against the acceptance of some risk of suicide.

[1] Need for Reasonable Objectives

With the adoption of certain jail and prison procedures and with changes in operations and structure, it is conceivable that custodial suicides can be eliminated.[6] This would entail such measures as regular strip and body cavity searches, unremitting visual and auditory surveillance (including cells that afford no privacy), extraordinary measures as to clothing and personal possessions, in-depth screening and counseling, and broadly shared risk information.[7]

A person who is constantly observed and deprived of any device that can be used to cause death is an unlikely candidate for suicide. However, the tariff for such an approach in terms of its over-inclusiveness should be viewed as prohibitive: it includes ending all individual privacy and most attributes of human dignity, as well as the dubious allocation of limited dollars. The elimination of custodial suicide is not a reasonable objective whether viewed from a cost-benefit analysis or as a matter of social policy. We must ask instead, what policy objectives are reasonable and attainable concerning custodial suicide? What roles do the courts have in fashioning and enforcing rules designed to *reduce*—not eliminate—custodial suicide and to provide just compensation where liability is established?

[2] Plaintiffs' Legal Claims

Without some actual knowledge of an individual's potential for committing suicide, custodians simply have no constitutionally based liability and any ensuing litigation may never reach the complex questions associated with a particular facility's preventive measures.

Custodial suicide litigation seeking damages may occur in the federal courts in the form of a civil rights action or in the state courts in the form of a wrongful death action.[8] Federal actions constitute the vast majority of the reported cases. In a federal action, the plaintiffs must show that the defendants acted under color of state law (usually not difficult to do), that the decedent or survivor was deprived of some federally protected right (usually quite difficult to do), and that the denial of such a right created liability (now almost impossible to do). The federal courts have made the liability requirements for custodial suicide so onerous that many plaintiffs' claims will not escape a motion for summary judgment.

That is, given some freedom from restraint and intensive surveillance, some tragedies will occur. *See* Estate of Max G. Cole v. Fromm, 97 F.3d 254, 261 (7th Cir. 1996).

[6] The latest data is for 1996 and it shows 297 suicides out of a total of 611 deaths. The southern jails were the clear leaders in suicides. SOURCE BOOK FOR CRIMINAL JUSTICE STATISTICS (1982), p. 528. The Source Book may be found on the World Wide Web at: http://www.albany.edu/sourcebook. The administrator of Menard Psychiatric Center, a part of the Illinois Department of Corrections, reports that 40 percent of their admissions involve suicidal behavior. Hardy, *Dealing with the Mentally and Emotionally Disturbed*, 44 CORRECTIONS TODAY 16, 18 (1984).

[7] Much of the material that follows is adapted from Fred Cohen, *Liability for Custodial Suicide: The Information Base Requirements*, 4 JAIL SUICIDE UPDATE 1–11 (1992). Reproduced with permission of the National Center on Institutions and Alternatives.

[8] *See* William D. O'Leary, *Custodial Suicide: Evolving Liability Considerations*, 60 PSYCHIATRIC QUARTERLY 31, 34–36 (1989), in which O'Leary clearly describes the differences between a civil rights action under 42 U.S.C. 1983 and a state court wrongful death action as a negligence action sounding in tort.

The custodian's legal duty will always be preventive. Even where a case employs the language of a duty to seek medical or psychiatric care, the claim ultimately will be failure to obtain adequate care or failure to obtain any care at all (i.e., a preventive obligation).

The plaintiff's claim invariably will charge the defendants with one or more of the following failures to act or omissions:

- Failure to properly screen

- Failure to convey information relevant to suicide potential

- Failure to recognize signs and symptoms of suicide

- Failure to provide a safe environment

- Failure to train

- Failure to act promptly or properly after the act of suicide

- Failure to search or remove implements or material suitable for suicide

- Design failure

- Failure to provide appropriate treatment (nearly always limited to prison versus jail cases)

¶ 14.2 LIABILITY: GENERAL STANDARDS AND RULES

The reported federal decisions are beginning to coalesce around the requisite standards of liability, and certain general legal rules are now regularly repeated. They are:

1. *Custodians.* Custodians—whether they be police at a lockup, sheriffs at a jail, or correctional officials at a prison—are not insurers of the life and safety of those in their charge. While there clearly are constitutional duties to preserve life and to provide medical or mental health care, these duties do not translate into some guarantee of safety, health, and the continuity of life.

2. *Deliberate indifference.* The standard for liability in the federal courts is the now familiar deliberate indifference requirement which, at a minimum, means culpability beyond mere negligence. The defendants must be shown to have had actual knowledge of a particular vulnerability to suicide; this knowledge must create a strong likelihood, as opposed to the possibility, of suicide; and this "strong likelihood" must be so obvious that a lay person would easily recognize the need for some preventive action.[9] Parenthetically, the courts seem to be unaware of the fact that they are borrowing the "obvious to a layman" phrase (or test) from prison and jail mental health cases, which state that a mental illness or medical need is serious if it would be obvious to a lay person that treatment was needed.[10]

---

[9] *See* Colburn v. Upper Darby Twp., 946 F.2d 1017, 1024–1025 (3d. Cir. 1991) [known as Colburn II, distinguishing it from an earlier decision to remand, 836 F.2d 663 (3d Cir. 1988), *cert. denied,* 489 U.S. 1065 (1989)].

[10] Ramos v. Lamm, 639 F.2d 559, 575 (10th Cir. 1980), is one of the earliest decisions to use this

A custodial suicide per se is not conclusive proof of deliberate indifference. If it were, then custodians would in fact be required to provide suicide-proof institutions.[11]

3. *Intake screening.* The general right of detainees to receive basic medical or mental health care does not place upon jail officials the responsibility to screen every detainee for suicidal tendencies.[12] A high percentage of detainees arrive at a lockup or jail under the influence of alcohol or some other drug, and judicial decisions questionably now hold that being "under the influence" alone does not enhance the custodian's duty to screen or to take extraordinary suicide preventive measures.[13]

By failing to mandate some screening, the federal courts, perhaps inadvertently, have placed a dubious premium on custodial ignorance. Custodians are now in the untenable position of being held to higher standards when they seek out and obtain suicide-relevant knowledge. This could actually retard efforts to obtain information or to use the increasingly popular, effective, and easy-to-use suicide screening instruments, and should be regarded both as wretched policy and as antitherapeutic.

Professor David Wexler has developed an approach to mental health law—of which custodial suicide clearly is a part—which he entitles *Therapeutic Jurisprudence.* Simply put, this jurisprudence looks at a legal decision as a social force that may produce therapeutic or antitherapeutic results. For us, the question is whether or not a premium on custodial ignorance is consistent with the need for early identification and a mental health/life preserving response. Clearly, a premium on ignorance is an antitherapeutic legal rule. The preservation of life as a goal is far better served by insisting at least on some gross screening followed by more intensive screening where a given number of "hits" occurs. Hits include being drunk, young, male, agitated, "hesitation marks," and the like.[14]

4. *No prior suicide attempt.* Absent a threat to commit suicide that is, or must be, taken seriously or knowledge that the individual has in fact attempted suicide in the recent past, the courts are extremely reluctant to impose liability.[15]

Indeed, the Eleventh Circuit Court of Appeals recently stated, "[I]n the absence of a previous threat or an earlier attempt at suicide, we know of no federal court in the

---

phrase, now regularly and uncritically repeated by the federal courts. For a full discussion, *see* FRED COHEN, LEGAL ISSUES AND THE MENTALLY DISORDERED PRISONER 58–63 (NIC, 1988). Only "serious" medical or psychological needs evoke a constitutional duty of appropriate care.

[11] *See* Rellegert v. Cape Girardeau County, Mo., 924 F.2d 794, 796 (8th Cir. 1991), on the issue of suicide as inconclusive proof of deliberate indifference.

[12] *See* Belcher v. Oliver, 898 F.2d 32, 34–35 (4th Cir. 1990), citing also to five other circuits as supportive of this view.

[13] *See, e.g.,* Belcher, 898 F.2d at 35.

[14] *See* DAVID B. WEXLER & BRUCE J. WINICK, ESSAYS IN THERAPEUTIC JURISPRUDENCE (1991), Ch.2. *See also* Freedman v. City of Allentown, Pa., 853 F.2d 1111, 1118–1119 (3d Cir. 1988) (Judge Brotman concurring and dissenting on duty of a trained officer who sees certain scars to recognize them as "hesitation marks.")

[15] *See* Bell v. Stigers, 937 F.2d 1340 (8th Cir. 1991), reversing the district court judge who listened to a tape of the detainee threatening to commit suicide and characterized it as a voice of despair. The Court of Appeals instead described it as a single, off-hand comment about shooting oneself where no weapon is available. 937 F.2d at 1344. This court also stressed that the brain-damaged, suicide attempt survivor had not threatened or attempted suicide before. 937 F.2d at 1343–1344.

nation that has concluded that official conduct in failing to prevent a suicide constitutes deliberate indifference."[16] As stringent as that standard is, some courts will not find liability even after a suicide threat that clearly should have been taken seriously. In *Zwalesky v. Manistee Co., Mich.*,[17] an intoxicated, violent, threatening detainee, who was hitting his head against the police car's protective screen, threatened suicide. He fulfilled the threat within one and one-half hours of detention, and the court granted immunity to the defendants. That is, it found that no special precautions seemed in order.

Zwalesky aside, the law seems clearly established that custodians must take some measures to prevent suicide once they know that a suicide is highly probable. There is, however, a continuing lack of clarity concerning what those measures must be.[18] The nature of the risk normally defines the legal duty. Thus, appropriate measures will range from removal of personal items, to close surveillance, use of double-celling, counseling, and so on.

[1] *Farmer v. Brennan* and Suicide

Farmer v. Brennan[19] once again rears its head and we are led to examine its impact on custodial suicide. Recall that in defining deliberate indifference, *Farmer* opted for a criminal recklessness-actual knowledge test.[20] But Professor James E. Robertson and others have concluded that "knowledge of a high risk of suicide no longer must be individually specific before deliberate indifference can be found."[21] Robertson states that after *Farmer*, inferences as to what jailers knew can be drawn from various sources, including circumstantial evidence regarding suicidality found in jail records, training manuals, and screening devices.[22]

Actually, I always believed that even pre-*Farmer* inferences of knowledge could be drawn from those sources if it could be shown they had been consulted. This is true even of a jail's own records showing that an individual had attempted suicide in that very jail. The problem seemed to center on defendants' denials of having consulted any information source and the courts' persistent failure to insist on a duty to consult even readily available, relevant information. My preference would be that an inference

---

[16] Edwards v. Gilbert, 867 F.2d 1271, 1275 (11th Cir. 1989). The opinion suggests that there was only one reported decision suggesting that deliberate indifference could exist where no prior suicide threat or attempt existed: Brewer v. Perrin, 132 Mich. App. 520, 349 N.W.2d 198 (1984). At least one subsequent decision, Simmons v. City of Philadelphia, 947 F.2d 1042 (3rd Cir. 1991), is somewhat contrary to the *Edwards* pronouncement in that the decedent did not appear to have attempted or threatened suicide prior to hanging himself in a police lockup. The verdict for the plaintiff-mother was upheld, however, despite her failure to establish deliberate indifference due to the city's failure to properly pursue an objection. 947 F.2d at 1088.

[17] 749 F. Supp. 815 (W.D. Mich. 1990).

[18] Rellegert v. Cape Girardeau County, Mo., *supra* note 11.

[19] 511 U.S. 825 (1994).

[20] *Farmer*, 511 U.S.at 838. *See* discussion of *Farmer,* and of recklessness and actual knowledge, in Chapter 4, ¶¶ 4.3[2] amd 4.3[4]. *See also* ¶ 14.6[2].

[21] James E. Robertson, *Jailers' Liability for Custodial Suicide After* Farmer v. Brennan, 6 Jail Suicide/Mental Health Update 1 (1996).

[22] Robertson, *supra* note 21, at 3.

of knowledge be allowed on a showing of ready availability but not actual consultation.

I am doubtful, but hopeful, that courts may treat readily available suicide-relevant information as subject to an inference of knowledge from circumstantial evidence. As we proceed to a review of the pre and post-*Farmer v. Brennan* case law, I cannot locate a decision post-*Farmer* in which a plaintiff prevails who might not also have prevailed before the *Farmer* decision.

Some readers may instinctively find it odd that a third person can be liable for the self-destructive acts of another. We may then ask: why should one party be held liable for another person's intentional act of self-destruction? This question is not answered by referring only to the human and environmental factors that may be important contributing factors in explaining or predicting suicide. Understanding the cause of an event need not create a basis for blame. But it is *blame* the federal courts insist on. Following the lead of the Supreme Court, the federal courts read the Eighth and Fourteenth Amendments as aimed strictly at official abuse of power, not at inaction or inadvertence that may infer abuse.[23]

[2] Custody Itself Creates Potential Responsibility

The legal foundation for governmental liability here is having an individual in actual physical custody. In *DeShaney v. Winnebago County Department of Social Services*,[24] the Supreme Court held that while government has no affirmative obligation to provide services, when government holds a person against his will there is a corresponding duty to assume some responsibility for his safety and general well-being. A special relationship marked by dependency thus arises, and the custodian and his inmate are no longer legal strangers.[25]

If a person in confinement manages to slit his wrists, the custodian is plainly under a duty to take reasonable steps to staunch the bleeding and rapidly obtain medical care. This post-injury duty stems from the fact of custody and obvious need; it does not turn on who created the medical urgency.[26]

Does the post-injury duty to ameliorate the harm or to have taken some measures to prevent the self-injury depend on the precise legal basis for custody? Jails and lock-ups, after all, house people awaiting booking, bail, trial, and transfers (to a prison as a probation or parole violator or to a mental institution), people in "protective custody," and people serving relatively short sentences.

The short answer to the question just posed is: The legal basis (or rationale) for custody is not determinative of the custodian's duty to prevent suicide or to take rea-

---

[23] *See, e.g.,* Wilson v. Seiter, 111 S. Ct. 2321 (1991).

[24] 489 U.S. 189 (1989).

[25] In City of Revere v. Massachusetts Gen. Hosp., 463 U.S. 239 (1983), the Court affirmed the duty of care owed to a fleeing felon who was shot and wounded by the police. Custody was created at the moment of disablement, and the duty was to obtain life-preserving and/or pain reducing medical care.

[26] In Guglielmoni v. Alexander, 583 F. Supp. 821, 826–827 (D. Conn. 1984), the defendants actually argued that a self-inflicted harm is not attributable to the state. The court rebuffed the argument. Of course, the responsibility question is relevant for a host of other legal issues, including criminal charges, if the cause was an assault by another.

sonable steps in the face of a suicide attempt. The constitutional source of the duty may vary, depending on the captive's legal status, but the duty itself is constant.

In *Buffington v. Baltimore Co., Md.*,[27] police held the decedent in what they termed protective custody and then claimed that this status released them from any custodial obligations to prevent harm. The Court of Appeals answered, "Nothing in the Court's rationale [citing to *DeShaney*] for finding that some affirmative duty arises once the state takes custody of an individual can be read to imply that the existence of the duty somehow turns on the reason for taking custody."[28]

In one recent case, a detainee was hospitalized, placed on suicide watch, and still managed to commit suicide by asphyxiation using a plastic hamper liner.[29] In holding for the defendants, the district court took no official notice of the status of the person as either detainee or patient, while also finding there was no high risk of suicide and no deliberate indifference in failing to perceive a risk of suicide with this instrumentality![30]

Suppose a detainee is being held illegally in that he was arrested without a warrant and not promptly brought before a magistrate for arraignment? The Eighth Circuit, correctly in my view, recently held that illegal incarceration for seven days cannot constitute proximate causation for custodial suicide without some evidence that the defendants knew or should have known that some preventive action was necessary.[31] The failure to promptly arraign, known as a *Gerstein*[32]-*Riverside*[33] violation, may have evidentiary consequences; there might be a recovery of nominal damages for the illegal detention; but without *more*, there is no liability for a suicide.

What might constitute the "more" necessary for liability? First, the entire package of liability issues that are determinative of any custodial suicide must be present. Second, I am convinced (1) that liability should attach where the decedent became increasingly agitated due to his illegal confinement, (2) that he might have been released on bail if promptly arraigned, and (3) that this agitation was proven to be the trigger of the suicide.[34]

One final point on the actual custody issue: There are a few state court decisions that establish a tort law basis for liability for suicide when there is no actual custody. For example, in *Eisel v. Board of Education*,[35] a Maryland court held that school counselors have a duty to use reasonable means to attempt to prevent a suicide when they

---

[27] 913 F.2d 113 (4th Cir. 1990).

[28] Buffington, 913 F.2d at 199; *see also* Simmons v. City of Phila., *supra* note 16 (decedent was said to be in protective custody).

[29] Estate of Max G. Cole v. Fromm, 941 F. Supp. 776 (S.D. Ind. 1995).

[30] Cole, 941 F. Supp. at 785.

[31] Wayland v. City of Springdale, Ark., 933 F.2d 668, 691 (8th Cir. 1991).

[32] Gerstein v. Pugh, 420 U.S. 103 (1975).

[33] County of Riverside v. McLaughlin, 500 U.S. 44 (1991).

[34] In one sense, it would not matter why a detainee became agitated if the agitation was of a sufficient nature and degree to trigger a suicide alarm. Why the decedent became agitated might well influence a jury in the direction of establishing liability.

[35] 597 A.2d 447 (1991). This is based exclusively on state law, and while it is unique and interesting, it is only of parenthetical interest to the thrust of this chapter.

are on notice of a child or adolescent student's suicidal intent. This, of course, is based on a state court's interpretation of state law as it relates to a wrongful death and survivor action. The court understood that this was a novel holding and that it is rare to find liability for noncustodial suicide in the analogous situation of therapists, church pastors who counsel, and lawyers who advise.[36]

The Supreme Court has clearly established that in our context the Cruel and Unusual Punishment Clause of the Eighth Amendment applies only to persons in actual physical confinement after conviction of a crime, while the Due Process Clause of the Fourteenth Amendment applies to the custody-related claims of detainees.[37] Conviction provides a lawful basis for punishment that may not be cruel or unusual, while a person who has not been convicted may not be punished at all.[38]

As a general proposition, the same criteria are applied under both the Fourteenth and the Eighth Amendments to resolve claims to medical and psychiatric care as well as claims involving custodial suicide. As one court recently put it in a custodial suicide case, "The Fourteenth Amendment right of pretrial detainees, like the Eighth Amendment right of convicted prisoners, requires that governmental officials not be deliberately indifferent to any serious medical needs of detainees."[39]

In *Hare v. City of Corinth*,[40] the Eleventh Circuit chose to resolve a dilemma of its own making in its resolution of suicide cases. Where a detainee sought recovery on a failure to protect theory, the court used a deliberate indifference test, but where the suicide was treated as a medical or mental health failure, the court applied a more lenient, reasonableness test.[41] The court issued a long, convoluted opinion, making frequent errors along the way, but ultimately settling on deliberate indifference as the mental requirement for both theories of recovery.[42]

[3] Prevention and Treatment Obligations—the Unconvicted

If there are to be any differences between the convicted and the unconvicted, one would think that the unconvicted have a stronger claim to legal protection. While that

---

[36] *See* Swenson, *Legal Liability for a Patient's Suicide*, 14 J. PSYCHIATRY & L. 409 (1986). The author points out that failure to care for obvious suicide risks is at the top of the list of reasons for malpractice suits against psychiatrists.

[37] *See* Bell v. Wolfish, 441 U.S. 520 (1979). What I mean by "in our context" is the rights of those in confinement. The Cruel and Unusual Punishment doctrine has been applied, e.g., to the discipline of school children, the death penalty, proportionality in sentencing, whether a person may be punished at all, and so on.

[38] Some courts will be explicit and state that denial of required medical or psychiatric care, or the failure to prevent suicide, may amount to punishment. *See* Kocienski v. City of Bayonne, 757 F. Supp. 457, 462 (D.N.J. 1991).

[39] Belcher v. Oliver, *supra* note 12, 898 F.2d at 34.

[40] 74 F.3d 633 (5th Cir. 1996) (en banc).

[41] Hare, 74 F.3d at 640.

[42] Hare, 74 F.3d at 646. At page 649, the sentence structure is so shattered it is difficult to know what is being communicated. The court suggests that *DeShaney* raises questions of mental element, which it does not; it deals only with the scope of the duty—actual custody—not how one assigns liability thereafter. In any event, when the verbal dust settles, the Eleventh Circuit is in line with other federal jurisdictions.

may occur at some unconscious level of decision-making, the reported decisions now consistently recognize that while jails and prisons are different places with different populations and missions, the constitutional criteria for resolving custodial suicide cases are the same.[43] As I will develop shortly, I believe the courts have ignored some major differences in the duty owed persons in jail versus the duty owed those in prison and have missed the opportunity to impose appropriately different obligations. In particular, I refer to prevention and treatment obligations.

Before turning to a further elaboration of constitutional criteria, one further point of foundational law deserves mention. Consistent with the great bulk of the literature and reported cases, I have been using the term pretrial detainee to refer to all persons in penal confinement before conviction. This approach is not entirely accurate and courts may recognize this in the near future. There is a point in the criminal justice process where a person is no longer an arrestee but where he also may not yet be a detainee. That point would follow a lawful arrest[44] and include confinement during the booking process and while awaiting arraignment. It may also include confinement where an arrest is illegal as not being based on probable cause.

If this interim pre-pre-trial detainee status is accorded a distinct status, then a custodial suicide claim might be brought under the Fourth Amendment and subject to search and seizure analysis. This, in turn, may make it somewhat easier to establish a claim, if it is judged by a reasonableness rather than a deliberate indifference standard. Put somewhat differently, an interim status suicide claim may go forward on proof that exceeds negligence but still falls short of the more onerous standard of deliberate indifference. At the least, this could allow a plaintiff's claim to escape summary judgment and reach a jury.[45]

¶ 14.3 THEORIES OF LIABILITY

There are three theories of liability presently used in custodial suicide cases, and all must eventually link themselves to the demanding test of deliberate indifference.[46] These theories are:

1. Failure to provide medical or mental health care for a serious medical (or more likely) psychological disorder;

2. Failure to provide a non-life-threatening (or safe) environment; and

3. Failure to train.

---

[43] A person who has been convicted and is in jail awaiting sentence is neither a pretrial detainee nor held under a criminal sentence. However, with Due Process and Eighth Amendment claims analyzed in the same fashion, it may not be vital to clarify this status. *See* Edwards v. Gilbert, 867 F.2d 1271, 1274 (11th Cir. 1989), on a convicted but unsentenced juvenile's suicide in an adult jail.

[44] Whether the existence of a warrant might be important is unclear.

[45] *See* Jones v. DuPage, 700 F. Supp. 965 (N.D. Ill. 1988); *see also* Graham v. Connor, 490 U.S. 386 (1989) for the Court's analysis of use of force issues and the Fourth Amendment. In Daniels v. Williams, 474 U.S. 327 (1986), and Davidson v. Canon, 474 U.S. 344 (1986), the Court rejected negligence as a basis for damages under a Section 1983 (civil rights action) claim.

[46] Where the Fourth Amendment is used as a basis for liability, a reasonableness test might apply (as discussed above).

The first two theories are far and away the most popular. With the Court's recent decisions in *Farmer v. Brennan*,[47] *Wilson v. Seiter*,[48] and its earlier decisions in *Estelle v. Gamble*[49] and *City of Canton v. Harris*,[50] deliberate indifference is the state of mind requirement for prison (and presumably jail) condition cases, failure to train claims, and also medical/psychiatric claims.[51]

[1] Failure to Provide Care and Failure to Protect

The reported decisions are confused on the precise boundaries of these competing theories and this is especially so for a "failure to protect" claim and a failure to provide medical/psychiatric care claim. When courts analyze a custodial suicide case along mental health care lines, they seem implicitly to accept suicide as caused by some mental aberration: "Sane persons do not ordinarily kill themselves," stated one early court.[52]

In civil commitment law, modern statutes require a finding of mental illness that also creates a substantial danger of the person causing serious harm to himself or others. Suicide ideation, and certainly a recent attempt to commit suicide, serve as adequate bases for a "dangerous to self" commitment in most jurisdictions.[53]

Professor David Wexler argues that persons who attempt suicide are by no means always mentally incompetent at the time of attempt. Should we save only those who appear to be incompetent and allow the competent the choice of dying at their own hand? Should we honor future valid consents from a rescued but ungrateful incompetent?[54]

The fact that custodial suicide cases present interesting questions concerning commitability, and the fact that viewing suicide exclusively as an act of madness or incompetence is dubious, does not affect the custodian's duty to preserve life. As noted earlier, that basic duty flows from custodial obligations and does not depend on the legal basis for custody, the cause or source of the harm or threatened harm, or the

---

[47] *Supra* note 19.

[48] 501 U.S. 294 (1991).

[49] 429 U.S. 97 (1976).

[50] 489 U.S. 378 (1989).

[51] There are cases dealing with a claim of inadequate aid after a suicide has been attempted. While such a claim may argue that life could have been saved, it is not focused on prevention of the suicidal act. *See, e.g.,* Estate of Cartwright v. City of Concord, Calif., 856 F.2d 1437 (9th Cir. 1988), also involving an unsuccessful claim of inadequate post-hanging investigation and preservation of evidence.

[52] Wychoff v. Mutual Life Ins. Co., 147 P.2d 227, 229 (1944). At common law, suicides were punishable by ignominious burial and forfeiture of chattels. A widely held belief that mental illness "caused" suicide probably accounts for its gradual legal destigmitization. *See* Kate Bloch, *The Role of Law in Suicide Prevention: Beyond Civil Commitment—Bystander's Duty to Report Suicide Threats,* 39 STANFORD L. REV., 929 (1989). *See also* Stephen Morse, *A Preference for Liberty: The Case Against Involuntary Commitment of the Mentally Disordered,* 70 CALIF. L. REV., 54, 59–65 (1982), arguing generally that the assertion that the crazy behavior of mentally disordered persons is compelled in contrast to the freely chosen behavior of normal persons is a belief based on common sense assumptions and not scientific evidence.

[53] *See* SAM BRAKEL, et al., THE MENTALLY DISABLED AND THE LAW, 3d. ed. (American Bar Foundation, 1985), Ch.2. This is the single best reference book available on the mentally ill and the law.

[54] DAVID WEXLER, MENTAL HEALTH LAW: MAJOR ISSUES (1981), pp. 45–47.

acceptance of any particular theory as explaining the harm or threat thereof. However, if one accepts suicide as invariably a sign of serious mental illness, the *nature* of the custodian's duty changes. This may have significant consequences for the particular duty owed the individual and its duration. The duty owed, in turn, may also be seen as varying with the nature of the facility.

[2] Treatment vs. Protection

As we have repeatedly seen, a serious mental illness calls for treatment. A suicide threat calls first for prevention and then, perhaps, treatment. However one ultimately defines treatment, it has longer term objectives and it is more involved than the protection of the individual from himself. The latter duty evokes an insulating function and carries with it no implications for "getting better." Treatment, on the other hand, clearly is an intervention based on a clinical diagnosis and designed to relieve needless pain or suffering and to ultimately ameliorate or cure a particular condition.[55]

Jails and lockups are inherently short-term holding facilities. Longer-term treatment based on a medical model of causation for suicide is far more appropriate for prison, yet it is regularly and uncritically incorporated into the reported decisions involving short-term facilities.

I am not arguing here that mental illness is more or less likely to explain suicides or suicide attempts in prison. I am arguing that longer-term confinement breeds longer term obligations along with the additional time to arrive at more discriminating causal assessments. Thus, with more time for more discriminating diagnosis and assessment and a longer-term relationship, I would expect mental illness as a cause and as dictating a response to be more at home in prison than jail.[56]

[3] Actual Knowledge

Viero v. Buffano[57] raises a number of interesting questions on the knowledge aspect of liability. A 14-year-old boy who had been in a psychiatric hospital for 33 days before being committed to a juvenile facility, who spoke of suicide at his intake screening, and who was prescribed but then not given Ritalin, committed suicide. The case is factually complicated but Judge Shadur did see at least one point clearly:

> Defendants miss the point that there are potentially two independent paths to recovery here . . .. For instance, [defendants] argue that because "Ritalin is not

---

[55] *See* FRED COHEN, THE LAW OF DEPRIVATION OF LIBERTY (1991), pp. 107–122, for various perspectives on treatment.

[56] Robert Rubenstein, et al., *On Attempted Suicide*, 79 A.M.A. ARCHIVES OF NEUROLOGY & PSYCHIATRY, 103, 111 (1958), conclude that attempted suicide is not an effort to die but rather an effort to improve one's life. Anecdotal evidence I have acquired suggests that some, perhaps many, threats or attempts at custodial suicide are either pleas for help or a manipulative effort to obtain a mental health placement that would not otherwise be available. When asked for legal advice on point I always urge that errors be made on the side of taking the threat or aborted effort seriously.

[57] 925 F. Supp. 1374 (N.D. Ill. 1996).

to be prescribed for an adolescent diagnosed as suffering from major depression," defendants' failure to ensure that Rosario received Ritalin could not have led to his suicide. That may perhaps be so (although defendants have offered no evidence to support their assertion), but such reasoning perpetuates a mistake made by defendants' throughout their filings. Two possible grounds for liability exist here: defendants' failure to ensure that Rosario's serious medical needs were met, and defendants' failure to protect Rosario from committing suicide. Defendants do not recognize that the former need not be related to the latter for Viero [the mother] to recover under Section 1983 (though the measures of damages would be very difficult). On the other hand Viero could argue that the reason Rosario committed suicide was that he was mentally unstable because he had not been given Ritalin, nor had he been given access to mental health professional since he arrived at St. Charles. But Viero could also independently argue that defendants' failure to ensure that Rosario received Ritalin and had mental health counseling caused harm to him independent of his suicide. Of course any recovery on the latter theory would be limited to the harm suffered by Rosario without regard to his suicide (e.g., pain and suffering), but she could recover on that theory nonetheless.[58]

While Judge Shadur did see the separate routes to recovery more clearly than most, his observation on recovery for the alleged medical or mental health failure may be misleading. That is, recovery for suicide based on either of the twin theories should be the same. There is, however, a third point lurking here: the plaintiff-mother might recover for the pain and suffering associated with the medical-mental health failure *independent* of the suicide. This might occur if a fact-finder did not find the risk of suicide serious or sufficiently obvious but did find deliberate indifference as to the medication, failure to counsel, and failure to utilize existing information.

[4] Limitations of Deliberate Indifference Standard

In *Zwalesky v. Manistee Co.*,[59] the decedent was arrested on a complaint of spousal abuse. He was drunk, swore and yelled in the police car, banged his head on the car's screen, and threatened to kill his relatives and himself. The decedent was placed in a so-called detoxification cell and about 90 minutes later was discovered to be dead, hanging by his shirt from a conduit pipe in the cell.

The trial judge granted summary judgment for all the jail-connected employees, finding they were immune from suit because there was no showing of any clearly established right possessed by the decedent that reasonable public officials should have known.[60] *Zwalesky* involves the two theories of liability discussed above: denial of medical care and denial of the right to be free from unsafe confinement. The court

---

[58] Viero, 925 F. Supp. at 1382 n.18.
[59] Zwaleski, *supra* note 17, 749 F. Supp. 815.
[60] Zwaleski, *supra* note 17, 749 F. Supp. at 818.

stated that the right actually asserted was a detainee's right to be screened for suicidal tendencies and then to have appropriate preventive measures taken. The court said that the general right to medical care was not sufficient to establish a clear constitutional right to be screened for psychological problems.[61]

Of course, the court ignored the fact that this individual, who may be in the interim status between arrestee and detainee, actually threatened to do violence to others and himself. Thus, this case did not raise the general issue of psychological/suicide screening and did not involve fine distinctions of underlying cause. Indeed, this was not a case in which the court discussed the authenticity of the suicide threat. The case fits so many of the standard factors on the jail suicide profile developed by the National Center on Institutions and Alternatives (NCIA), as well as the most demanding informational requirements for a suicide alert, that it dramatically illustrates the strictures of deliberate indifference and judicial confusion on liability theories.[62]

The court went on to hold that the exercise of professional judgment did not require prison (or jail) officials to make accommodations for potential suicide attempts and that the failure to include suicide prevention procedures for processing incoming detainees did not violate any clearly established constitutional rights.[63]

This is about as tough as it gets for plaintiffs and about as forgiving as it gets for custodians. *Zwalesky* should not have been analyzed as a general screening case and it need not have involved any immediate claims to remedial medical or psychiatric care. The most reasonable claim would have been to the standard and inexpensive measures associated with a suicide watch and removal of any implements of potential self-destruction.

Hypothetically, if this suicide victim had survived and then been convicted and sentenced to prison, I would then argue that at a minimum:

- The suicide-attempt information should accompany him to prison;

- Prison authorities have a heightened diagnostic-evaluative obligation at reception; and

- If suicide ideation continued, it would be reasonable to then diagnose a serious illness calling for appropriate mental health care and a protective process and environment.

In other words, the authorities would be put on clear notice of a high suicide risk. While general screening in jails may not be mandated, there would still exist an obligation here of "information transfer" and a consequent "suicide alert."

In *Belcher v. Oliver*,[64] the Fourth Circuit adopted the position that "The general right of pretrial detainees to receive basic medical care does not place upon jail offi-

---

[61] Zwalesky, *supra* note 17, 749 F. Supp. at 819.

[62] *See* Fred Cohen, *Custodial Suicides: Common Source of Litigation—But Cases Can Be Defended,* in I CORRECTIONAL L. REP. 50 (1989).

[63] Zwaleski, *supra* note 17, 749 F. Supp. at 820.

[64] Belcher, *supra* note 12, 898 F.2d 32.

cials the responsibility to screen every detainee for suicidal tendencies."[65] In so doing, the court aligned itself with earlier decisions by the Third, Fifth, Sixth, Ninth and Eleventh Circuits. At first blush, such a position may seem to be unduly harsh and not sufficiently protective of persons in confinement. However, millions of persons are processed annually through jails and lockups and many are held only for a brief time while awaiting arraignment, release on bond, sobering up, a relative, and so on. Courts are reluctant to allow highly intrusive searches of arrestees without reference to the reason for arrest, the special characteristics of the arrestee, and the projected duration of confinement.[66] A similar approach that apportions privacy protection based on such factors may also support an approach that effectively limits the custodian's obligations to develop certain information, including suicide-relevant information.

However, once again, the courts generally seem to misapprehend the issues. Even if we stipulate to the correctness of "no general duty to screen," that does not mean there is no duty to screen or assess persons presenting certain characteristics or who are members of a particular at-risk group more vulnerable to suicide.

Reasonable people may well disagree about what characteristics or signs in what combination should create the duty to develop further information, but it does not seem reasonable to adopt the *Belcher* "no duty at all" position and then shut down the debate. The *Zwalesky* hypothetical discussed above surely is an example of where a duty should exist.

In the context of a decision to deprive a person of his liberty, serious questions are—and should be—raised about the ability of experts to predict dangerousness to self or others.[67] In our context, liberty invariably has been taken and the question is the preservation of life and health.[68] With jail and lockup suicides tending to occur in isolation, early in the confinement, by relatively young, white, males who are "high," who have not been screened, and who then "hang up" in the early morning hours, how much effort and training would it take to use these factors as triggers for additional screening and/or special precautions?[69] Very little, it would seem.

Any errors in screening and short-term precautions would likely impose little cost on the facility and hardly any dignitarian costs on the person in custody. Yet, the courts are moving in a direction that positively discourages the development of either information or expertise. Plainly, *Farmer v. Brennan*[70] will not likely reverse that trend.

---

[65] Belcher, 898 F.2d at 34–35.

[66] *See* Wilkes v. Borough of Clayton, 696 F. Supp. 144 (D.N.J. 1988), discussed at 1 CORRECTIONAL L. REP. 14 (1989) (decisions on automatic strip searches are noted).

[67] *See* Fred Cohen, *supra* note 55, at 325–338, for a collection of material questioning the ability of "experts" to predict dangerousness. *See* Foucha v. Louisiana, 504 U.S. 71 (1992), on the issue of confining the non-mentally ill but dangerous offender.

[68] I mention "health" because there are cases in which a suicide attempt is foiled, but not before serious and permanent brain damage occurs. *See, e.g.,* Rich v. City of Mayfield Heights, 955 F.2d 1092 (6th Cir. 1992) (no right to be cut down immediately when discovered hanging, with delay resulting in physical and mental disabilities).

[69] One cost is related to the additional demand on security manpower if an officer is required to engage in a close watch—let us say every 15 minutes—and is then unavailable for other duties. If a constant watch is required, the demand is even more obvious.

[70] *Supra* note 19.

¶ 14.4 THE INFORMATION PROBLEM IN DELIBERATE INDIFFERENCE STANDARD

[1] Inference of Actual Knowledge

In *Freedman v. City of Allentown, Pennsylvania*,[71] we encounter a variation on the *Belcher* formula. *Belcher* (and the several cases in line with it) deals with the custodial duty to screen and develop information, whereas *Freedman* deals with the obligation to *interpret* certain signs as indicative of a suicide risk. In *Freedman*, an officer observed scars on the confined individual's wrists and inside his elbows and neck—signs generally indicative of prior suicide attempts—but failed to interpret them as indicia of suicidal tendencies. The scars were prominent. The court stated, "[W]e will assume that a reasonably competent prison official should have known and identified these marks as 'suicide hesitation cuts'. . .. Even if so, the failure to recognize them as such, without more, amounts only to negligence and therefore fails to support a claim."[72]

Judge Brotman, dissenting in part, pointed out that a detective questioned Freedman for over two and one-half hours and asked about scars that he then displayed. Characterizing the majority's position as an unilluminating conclusion, the dissent went on to state:

> I remain unconvinced that Detective Balliet's inability to recognize the telltale signs of a high risk individual can never amount to "recklessness." I fail to see how the majority can be so resolute in its position without knowing the extent of the police officer's background and training in detecting suicide risks and in suicide prevention, in addition to his prior experience with prisoners who have taken their own lives or attempted unsuccessfully to do so. None of the information concerning the officer's knowledge, experience and professional competence would likely be known even to the most diligent civil rights plaintiff at the pleadings stage, and, therefore, he should be entitled to adduce such pertinent facts through discovery.
>
> For example, discovery might reveal that Detective Balliet was a veteran police officer who had received extensive training in suicide prevention and had become well-versed in detecting the indicia of suicidal propensities. It is not unlikely that such a veteran officer would have seen bodily markings similar to the ones on the decedent's body in the course of his duties, nor is it improbable that he would have come into contact with a prisoner bearing such markings who had committed or attempted to commit suicide. Surely a reasonable jury could conclude that a police officer possessing such knowledge, training, and experience acted "in disregard of a known or obvious risk that was so great as to make it highly probable that harm would follow." See W. Page Keeton, *Prosser and Keeton on Torts* Sec. 34, at 3213 (5th ed. 1984).[73]

---

[71] 853 F.2d 1111 (3d Cir. 1988).

[72] Freedman, 853 F.2d at 1116.

[73] Id. Obviously, Judge Brotman succeeds quite well in expressing my own sentiments.

Nonetheless, the majority view prevailed and the plaintiff's case was dismissed. Here, then, we have obvious and objective signs that might easily have alerted the custodians to the need for effective preventive measures. The majority, however, refused to impose a constitutional duty of knowledge in the interpretive sense on police officers and, presumably, jailers. This, it seems, is the sort of permissible inference from circumstantial evidence that Justice Souter had in mind in *Farmer v. Brennan.*[74] That is, the officer's prior experience and training, once established, plus what he saw (the scars), could easily lead to an inference of actual knowledge of risk.

[2] Failure to Train or to Create Policy

Does the *Freedman* majority approach place a premium on ignorance or does it encourage possible life-saving information? Obviously, the majority opinion favors ignorance and, not so obviously, so does the dissent. Judge Brotman's speculation about discovery possibly producing information on training and expertise and thus creating the potential for deliberate indifference may also be taken to mean that if no such training or indicia of competence was forthcoming, then the officer's ignorance bars recovery. That is, sound legal policy here may be to insist on this type of training in the face of the regularity and seriousness of custodial suicide.

Have we reached a point in time when jail and lockup suicides are so prevalent, and the steps necessary to prevent or drastically reduce these tragedies so well known and affordable, that a constitutional obligation of at least minimal training is now in order? I believe so, but not only is support for this lacking in the leading decisions, the courts actually induce ignorance by rewarding it.

In *City of Canton v. Harris,*[75] the Supreme Court outlined the conditions under which a municipality might be liable for a custom or policy of failure to train. The municipality itself, not its agents, must be the direct cause of the violation, and the failure to train must amount to deliberate indifference to the rights of persons with whom the agency comes into contact. There must be a deliberate choice to follow a course of action from among various alternatives and there must be a direct link between a specific deficiency in training and the ultimate injury. Failure to train claims will not succeed simply by showing that harm might have been avoided with more or better training.

Putting a lethal weapon into the hands of a police officer with no training in its handling and no clear policy on deadly force is probably the clearest example of a potentially successful failure to train lawsuit. I would suggest that with so many custodial suicides, with so much predictive information readily available and usable by anyone sufficiently competent to work in corrections or law enforcement, and with prevention measures available at no significant cost, it is time for *Canton* to be applied to this area. At a minimum, where a facility has experienced a recent custodial suicide, this should be taken as prima facie evidence of a need for some training.[76]

---

[74] *Supra* note 19; *see also* Mullins v. Stratton, 878 F. Supp. 1016, 1021 (E.D. Ky. 1995) (failure to recognize a scar as evidence of a prior suicide attempt was not deliberate indifference).

[75] 489 U.S. 378 (1989).

[76] *See* Zinnerman v. Burch, 494 U.S. 113 (1990), for the proposition that forseeable risks (here, that "voluntary" patients may not be competent) call for protective processes.

Returning to the *Freedman* scenario, the issue there will be characterized as information interpretation. That is, the officer had relevant information—the multiple, severe scars—and the issue was his alleged failure to understand their significance. We might again note that even if this information had been properly translated into an awareness of a high probability of suicide, the plaintiffs would still have been required to prove that the response, or lack thereof, was constitutionally deficient—that is, deliberately indifferent.

The *Freedman* information-characterization problem has arisen in other recent cases. In *Bell v. Stigers*,[77] an 18-year-old DWI arrestee told the booking officer that he thought he would shoot himself. The booking officer apparently bantered with the youth and replied that it was too bad, but he did not have a gun handy. The officer did not check a suicide box on the booking form and he also failed to remove the young man's belt when placing him in a solitary cell. The decedent was found hanging about an hour later; he was cut down and survived with permanent brain damage and physical injuries.[78]

The trial judge had refused the defendant's request for summary judgment after listening to a tape of the exchange with the booking officer and finding a note of despondency in the youth's voice.[79] The Court of Appeals, however, with one dissent, held, "A single off-hand comment about shooting oneself when no gun is available cannot reasonably constitute a serious suicide threat."[80] The court held that the "off-hand" comment even as bolstered by the detainee's fitting a suicide profile cannot support the "strong likelihood of suicide" requirement for liability. At best, there is negligence here and summary judgment was ordered.[81]

In another decision,[82] a life-threatening, domestic violence scene ended with the arrest of the plaintiff's paramour who was drunk at the time. The plaintiff told the arresting officer that earlier she heard the decedent say, "If I only had the guts." She interpreted that to mean, "If I only had the guts I would shoot myself with this gun." The plaintiff had told the arresting office of her interpretation of the decedent's earlier words. The officer knew of the violence and intoxication, yet took no suicide precautions. Jail officials violated their own rules on cell monitoring and were disciplined for their dereliction in the wake of the decedent's suicide.[83]

The court, however, granted the defendants summary judgment, characterizing the earlier threat as a vague reference to suicide, analogous to the *Bell v. Stigers* "off-hand" comment about wanting a gun. The court seems to vacillate between treating the decedent's reference to 'having the guts' either as an ambiguous suicide threat or a suicide threat that was reasonably clear but not actionable without any clear history of suicide attempts or suicide ideation.[84]

---

[77] 937 F.2d 1340 (8th Cir. 1990).

[78] Id.

[79] Bell v. County of Washington, Iowa, 741 F. Supp. 1354, 1359 (S.D. Iowa, 1990).

[80] Bell, 937 F.2d at 1344.

[81] Id.

[82] Christian v. Stanczak, 769 F. Supp. 317, 319 (E.D. Mo. 1991). At the time of the threat, the decedent did have a weapon.

[83] Christian, 769 F. Supp. at 322.

[84] Id.

Kocienski v. City of Bayonne[85] is yet another variation on the Freedman information-interpretation problem. Here, the plaintiff's sister, one Garity, was arrested and jailed on theft charges. About 10 hours thereafter she committed suicide, hanging herself with her panty hose.

The decedent had a history of contact with the defendant police department, including earlier information that she was suicidal and may have overdosed on drugs. Two weeks previously, the plaintiff obtained a restraining order to protect her from possible violence at the hands of her sister. The order had the word "psychiatric" clearly written on it. The plaintiff left the order with the police department and called the next day to make certain her sister's last name was on the order. The suicide occurred soon thereafter.[86]

The court held that an officer's failure to discern suicidal tendencies from the face of the restraining order—i.e., the word "psychiatric"—is at most negligence. Referring to *Freedman,* the court stated, "The failure to recognize signs far more indicative of potential suicide than that which (the officer) 'failed' to recognize has constituted negligence only."[87]

Thus, in the context of the deliberate indifference standard, the federal courts place only a nominal burden of information interpretation on the police and other custodial officials. The information aspect of the deliberate indifference test has yet other dimensions to which we now turn.

[3] No Passing or Sharing of Information—The "Hand-Off" Issue

Freedman includes one additional dimension. *Freedman* held that there was no constitutional duty imposed on a trained police officer to recognize large and prominent scars as "hesitation marks" and it also held that no liability attached due to the failure of the decedent's probation officer, who knew of Freedman's prior suicide attempts, to inform the detective questioning the decedent.[88] Even if the officer was at the jail during the questioning and chose not to convey the information about suicidal tendencies, this did not amount to showing reckless indifference to Freedman's rights.[89]

This aspect of *Freedman* relates to a continuing problem that I will characterize as a "hand-off" problem. Hand-off problems occur, for example, where there is a shift change and the incoming staff are not given suicide-relevant information by the outgoing shift; where an arresting or transporting officer has such information and does not pass it along; or where a known suicide risk simply moves through the conveyor belt of the criminal justice system and there is no intra- or interagency sharing of such information. The hand-off problem speaks directly to the now discarded "should have known" aspect of the deliberate indifference test: defendants knew or *should have known* of a particular vulnerability to suicide.

---

[85] 757 F. Supp. 457 (D.N.J. 1991).

[86] Kocienski, 757 F. Supp. at 460.

[87] Kocienski, 757 F. Supp. at 464. This decision has other aspects as well, such as the violation of police rules in failing to remove panty hose.

[88] Freedman, 853 F.2d at 1117.

[89] Id.

In *Buffington v. Baltimore Co., Md.*[90] the record is clear that police officers had received repeated and unambiguous information that James Buffington was drunk, in possession of firearms, and dangerously suicidal. At booking, James was handcuffed to the rail near the booking desk in accordance with local practice. Officers Gaigalas and Tucker came on duty shortly thereafter and took James to an isolation cell without removing his clothing and with no monitoring. The young man hung himself in less than an hour. Officer Gaigalas admitted that he knew James was suicidal when he took him to the cell after previously giving a contrary deposition which he now admits was deliberately and knowingly false.[91]

This is one of the few cases in which the plaintiffs prevailed in a custodial suicide claim, and it is basically because the new shift officers were in fact informed of James' suicidal tendencies but then did everything wrong. As the plaintiff's expert Joseph Rowan testified, "I strongly feel that this is the worst case of handling of a suicide case that I have ever seen."[92]

In *Buffington*, the threat of suicide was clear, it was repeated to the authorities, but then ignored. Suppose that law enforcement officials, like the probation officer in *Freedman*, simply fail to convey information they have concerning suicide risks?

In the frequently cited *Partridge v. Two Unknown Police Officers of Houston*,[93] a young man was arrested on burglary-theft charges and became hysterical during on-scene questioning. The boy's father told a sergeant on the scene that his son previously had experienced a "nervous breakdown" and he pointed out two medical bracelets on the boy's wrists. In response, it was suggested that the father contact a psychiatrist or get a letter. The boy was agitated and violent while being transported in the patrol car. He banged his head on the partition but calmed down a bit at the station. The arresting officers communicated none of this to anyone at the jail. The young man was placed in a solitary cell and three hours later hanged himself with his socks. Booking officers were unaware of clinical records kept four doors away showing a suicide attempt during an earlier arrest.

The Fifth Circuit, in a revised opinion, viewed the above facts as stating grounds for a cause of action and overruled the lower court's dismissal of the complaint. The court's analysis turned almost exclusively on deliberate indifference to medical/psychiatric needs with virtually no discussion of the need to protect such an arrestee or detainee from himself.[94] Even under this analysis, the court assumed that police will and should communicate unambiguous suicide information about an arrestee to jail staff.

We should also note that in *Partridge* the amendment complaint claimed that suicide is a known risk in jails; the jail provided no special training about suicide, no written policy or procedural manual; police personnel had no protocol for access to jail clinical data; and there was inadequate staffing, no television monitoring, no reg-

---

[90] 913 F.2d 113 (4th Cir. 1990).

[91] Buffington, 913 F.2d at 117.

[92] Id.

[93] 791 F.2d 1182 (5th Cir. 1986).

[94] Whether *Partridge* survives *Farmer v. Brennan* is yet another matter. *See* Hare v. City of Corinth, 74 F.3d 633 (5th Cir. 1996) (en banc), suggesting that *Partridge* appeared to rely on a deliberate indifference standard while other Fifth Circuit decisions of that area were confused and inconsistent.

ular cell-checking and no sharing of relevant information. These details represent a basic checklist of what a plaintiff's attorney is going to pursue and, therefore, represent questions to which a custodial facility better have acceptable answers.

In *Partridge,* we focus on the arresting officers making the direct hand-off of the arrestee to booking officers. In *Freedman,* the probation officer appeared not to have any direct role in the interrogation and subsequent processing of the decedent. Information relevant to suicide prevention was possessed in both cases, but it is possible to distinguish the obligation to convey such information based on the direct versus indirect hand-off roles of the participants.

In *Lewis v. Parish of Terrebone,*[95] a most bizarre set of circumstances culminated in the suicide death of a man placed in isolation as punishment for striking a deputy who had driven him back to the jail after a mental examination at a hospital. Prior to the assault, the deputy placed an envelope containing the examining psychiatrist's advice on a desk near the defendant warden.[96] The envelope remained unopened until Lewis was found dead. It contained a diagnosis that he was suicidal and the specific suicide precautions that should be taken. The warden actually knew other facts that were also strongly suggestive of suicide. The failure to inform himself, however, of an available medical opinion seemed most persuasive in upholding a jury verdict for Lewis' survivors.[97]

McDuffie v. Hopper[98] is yet another example of the personal representative of a prisoner who committed suicide surviving a motion for summary judgment. The decedent, an Alabama prisoner for over 17 years, had a long, documented history of hallucinations and at least four prior suicide attempts. Shortly before his death by a hanging while in an isolation cell, the decedent's actions and requests were strongly indicative of suicidal thoughts, yet the prison mental health specialists abruptly terminated his massive doses of Thorazine and provided no substitute or monitoring.[99]

Plaintiffs charged Correctional Medical Services (CMS) with discontinuing medication to cut costs.[100] Relying on the plaintiff's expert, a tactic that surprised the judge as much as it probably does the reader,[101] the court had little trouble finding sufficient evidence of deliberate indifference to escape a motion for summary judgment.[102]

Thus, where there is clear and unequivocal information regarding a person's suicidal tendencies—and that information must relate to a clinical diagnosis, a fairly recent suicide attempt, or an unequivocal threat—and no special precautions are taken, plaintiffs have a fair chance to escape summary judgment and prevail before a

---

[95] 894 F.2d 142 (5th Cir. 1990).

[96] Lewis, 894 F.2d at 144.

[97] The jury awarded no compensatory damages and only $6,279.00 punitive damages, the cost of the funeral. The Court of Appeals remanded for further findings on damages. 894 F.2d at 150.

[98] 982 F. Supp. 817 (M.D. Ala. 1997).

[99] McDuffie, 982 F. Supp. at 820.

[100] CMS, perhaps the largest private mental health care provider to corrections, had the state-wide contract for prison mental health services.

[101] McDuffie, 982 F. Supp. at 827.

[102] There was also evidence of failure to contact doctors who previously treated the decedent, that the cell housing the inmate increased the severity of the mental illness, and that there simply was no rationale for reducing (or eliminating) the medication.

jury. Where the suicide-relevant information is even slightly ambiguous, the courts tend to treat a failure to alert or a misinterpretation as negligence, at best.

In a recent decision from the Sixth Circuit Court of Appeals,[103] a Michigan inmate committed suicide by overdosing on his prescribed, psychotropic medication. The treating mental health professionals had medical records indicating the decedent's clinical depression and suicidal thought; they knew he had attempted suicide on prior occasions (once by medication overdose); and they knew he had been placed on liquid medication and was severely depressed.[104]

The majority rebuffed the attempt by defendants to characterize this claim as a failure to screen. Obviously, the events had moved beyond screening and a knowledge base equating with a high degree of risk existed.

The most damaging aspect of defendant's position is the evidence that liquid medication (v. tablets) was not dispensed at pill call because "it would take a longer amount of time."[105] This surely sounds an alarm to all correctional mental health providers concerning the conduct of pill call. I often encounter hoarding by "checking" the pills because the nurse is rushed or harried; inmates may receive the wrong medication or wrong dosage; records are poorly maintained, and so on.

Convenience simply cannot be the deciding factor in dispensing potentially lethal drugs. *Williams* certainly testifies to that fact.

What I have termed the information "hand-off" problem certainly is not clearly resolved by the reported decisions. In *Elliott v. Cheshire County, N.H.,*[106] for example, a young man with a long history of mental health problems, and most recently diagnosed as schizophrenic, assaulted his mother. Trooper Ranhoff responded to the parents' call for police, and while he was told that the son had mental health problems and was schizophrenic, he was not told of the son's two prior threats to commit suicide.[107]

The trooper, however, did not inform the intake officer of what he knew of the arrestee's mental illness, and the intake officer asked no questions on point. A few days later, after some very strange and suicide-suggestive behavior, the boy committed suicide while in custody. The reviewing court found that the trooper did not know of the decedent's prior suicide threats and that the boy's demeanor did not suggest suicide. The court simply ignored the fact that Ranhoff was given the boy's mental health information and knew of the diagnosis of schizophrenia.[108]

Elliott seems to straddle the *Freedman* information-interpretation category and the "hand-off" category. Clearly, not every schizophrenic is a custodial suicide risk and not every narrative of mental health problems suggests a suicide alert. However, when an arresting officer has information of the sort possessed by Ranhoff and fails to hand it off to a booking officer, and where that officer asks no suicide screening questions, this surely is extremely poor practice. Whether it is deliberate indifference,

---

[103] Williams v. Mehra, 135 F.3d 1105 (6th Cir. 1998).

[104] Williams, 135 F.3d at 1107–1113.

[105] Williams, 135 F.3d at 1113 n.6.

[106] 940 F.2d 7 (1st Cir. 1991).

[107] Elliott, 940 F.2d at 9.

[108] Elliott, 940 F.2d at 12. The case was remanded on possible liability for jail officials based on post-confinement behavior of the decedent. *See also* Hare v. City of Corinth, *supra* note 94, in which there is a dispute concerning transmission of suicide-relevant information during a shift change at a Mississippi jail.

of course, is another matter. Courts are inclined to label it negligence and, in so doing, once again give support to ignorance and dissembling.

[4] Professional Evasion

With the courts tending to reward ignorance, a pernicious practice may be developing. A psychologist on contract to a jail informed me that when asked to do a work-up on an arrestee or a detainee, he will never use the word suicide in a report. He may order further tests, seek to obtain medication, or even prescribe a watch but it will not be called a suicide watch.

He has been led to believe that by using the word suicide he may be exposing himself and his colleagues to an easily avoided liability. Is he correct? In *Dobson v. Magnusson*,[109] an escapee was returned to prison and a sergeant placed the prisoner on a 15-minute suicide watch. A psychologist then examined Dobson and found no indication of an intent to die although "he might engage in injurious behavior."[110] He continued the 15-minute watch as a precaution.

The requisite check-ups were not made and in that interim a distraught Dobson committed suicide. The court stated, "We agree with the district court . . . that it [missing two checks] could not be thought so faulty as to indicate indifference, deliberate or otherwise. If this watch had been . . . a suicide watch, we might feel differently . . . ."[111]

[5] Risk and Causation Issues

Hardin v. Hayes[112] involved a decedent who (1) called police, (2) then kicked in the squad car door, and (3) was seen in jail the next day smearing vomit on herself, beating her head on the bars, and stabbing herself and an officer with a pen.[113] Following a mental health examination, as civil commitment papers were being drawn, she was observed putting her head under water in the sink, eating feces, falling down, and then collapsing and dying. She died from asphyxiation, having swallowed a small bar of soap and failing to dislodge it.

Hardin's estate sued the city and a number of city and county officials. The sheriff and the Chief of Police settled on the first day of trial, and the jury returned a verdict for the city finding neither deliberate indifference nor negligence. The trial judge ordered a new trial; the city appealed and the appellate court found that in ordering a new trial the trial judge abused his discretion.

We should note that the plaintiff abandoned the suicide claim during the trial, no longer asserting that the death was a suicide, and argued instead that the City was liable for Hardin's anguish during confinement. With all this in mind, *Hardin* still leaves open a very interesting risk question. Assuming that the one and one-half day

---

[109] 923 F.2d 229 (1st Cir. 1991).

[110] Dobson, 923 F.2d at 230.

[111] Dobson, 923 F.2d at 231. Judgment for all defendants was affirmed. The decision was not clear concerning whether there was a significant difference between a "watch" and a "suicide watch."

[112] 52 F.3d 934 (11th Cir. 1995).

[113] Hardin, 52 F.3d at 937.

delay in obtaining treatment was unreasonable, one must still ask whether that delay is causally related to the risk of death by asphyxiation from the ingestion of soap. Apparently, the plaintiff's medical expert uncovered only two self-inflicted jail deaths through ingestion of foreign objects in a sample of 400 deaths. The court of appeals found it reasonable for a jury to conclude that the delay in getting care was not unreasonable in light of the knowledge of harm.[114]

Hardin, then, may be seen as a good teaching case from the standpoint of risk and causation analysis. That is, even where it is crystal clear that a detainee is very ill and destructive, if no care is provided and self-inflicted death ensues, the manner or instrumentability of death needs to be placed within the scope of the risk. For example, if Hardin had tripped and fallen in her cell and died from head injuries, one would have the same analytical problem.

¶ 14.5 THE SALVI SUICIDE

Perhaps the most dramatic and poignant custodial suicide in recent years was that of John Salvi, who was confined in Massachusetts' Walpole Prison. Walpole is a maximum security facility where Salvi and the majority of the 820 inmates were in lockdown, which is cell confinement for 22-23 hours a day. Salvi caused his death by placing a plastic bag around his head and binding his head and hands with shoelaces tied in a series of slip-knots.[115]

Salvi will be remembered for entering the Planned Parenthood clinic in Brookline, Massachusetts on December 30, 1994, killing a receptionist and wounding others, then going to another Brookline clinic where he killed another person and wounded others, and finally appearing the next day at a clinic in Virginia where he sprayed a clinic's lobby with rifle bullets. He was apprehended driving away from that scene.

I still recall my initial impressions about Salvi, impressions generated basically by media accounts. Salvi reportedly ranted about a diabolical Masonic conspiracy aimed at Catholics; his writings are hopelessly erroneous and crazily illogical. His pre-homicide conduct showed a young man in psychological free-fall, and yet he was found competent and sane.[116]

Almost a dozen psychiatrists and psychologists examined Salvi and he still managed to pass through the few clumsy legal devices available to divert the seriously mentally ill from the full rigors of the criminal justice process.[117] When Salvi arrived at the prison gates one official reportedly stated, "He was a sane, healthy inmate."[118] He received virtually no mental health care despite his mother's entreaties and the

---

[114] Hardin, 52 F.3d at 940.

[115] Much of what follows is derived from a comprehensive report requested by the Massachusetts Department of Corrections and prepared by the University of Massachusetts Medical Center Department of Psychiatry. *See* Report on the Psychiatric Management of John Salvi In Massachusetts Department of Correctional Facilities, *1995-1996* (Jan. 31, 1997), pp.1–45 [hereinafter "Salvi Report].

[116] *See* Eileen McNamara, *Nobody Cares He Was Insane,* Boston Globe, Nov. 30, 1996, B1.

[117] Those devices are incompetency and insanity. *See* Steven Kurkjian & John Ellement, *No Mental Health Treatment Offered,* Boston Globe, Nov. 30, 1996, A1.

[118] Id. Perhaps a spontaneous cure occurred.

efforts of his counsel.[119] Salvi reportedly was seen only once by a psychiatrist from the time of his conviction until his death, and then only because a doctor was curious about the celebrity inmate. He received some nominal supportive counseling but was neither evaluated nor treated.

Since Salvi's survivors indicate they will not bring suit, and the Salvi Report indicates we will never know if the errors in management and treatment led to his death, we too are left to speculate. The Salvi Report offers the following as a basis for its expert opinions.

1. Mr. Salvi's "blunted" affect (i.e., a severely reduced intensity in emotional expressiveness).

2. Mr. Salvi's generally "guarded" demeanor, suggesting suspiciousness and distrust, if not frank paranoia.

3. Mr. Salvi's social isolation and withdrawal.

4. Mr. Salvi's apparently paranoid, delusional concerns about being poisoned as suggested by the following:

    a. Refusal of many meals and extensive purchasing of food in canteens at BHS and in prison;

    b. Informing his mother that people were trying to poison him, causing him to prefer only "sealed" food;

    c. Reported statements to Attorney Carney that the Norfolk County Correctional Center was trying to poison him, and Mr. Salvi's request that Attorney Carney get a chemical analysis on a piece of ham that Mr. Salvi had saved.

5. Mr. Salvi's evasive responses to clinicians, regarding any history of hearing voices, suggesting that he did experience auditory hallucinations.

6. Mr. Salvi's assaultive and bizarre behavior while incarcerated, including hanging a wet rag, plastic container and a chain of elastic bands from his penis.

3. Mr. Salvi's often perseverative, rambling, and disorganized thinking noted by some observers and present in his writings.

4. The above findings appear to represent a deterioration in functioning for Mr. Salvi. He had no reported history of psychiatric disturbance prior to the time leading up to and following his crime.[120]

Using Salvi, then, only as a stalking horse for analytical purposes, much as I did with *Hardin*, let me engage in some speculation. As indicated, the *Farmer* test for

---

[119] *See also* Fred Cohen, *Offenders with Mental Disorders in the Criminal Justice—Correctional Process*, in LAW, MENTAL HEALTH, AND MENTAL DISORDER (Bruce D. Sales & Daniel W. Shuman, eds. 1996), Ch. 19, for a discussion of legal mechanisms that may divert mentally ill offenders.
[120] Salvi Report, *supra* note 15, p.26.

deliberate indifference now requires that the responsible official "knows of and disregards an excessive risk to inmate health or safety; the official must both be aware of facts from which the inference could be drawn that a substantial risk of serious harm exists and that he must also draw the inference."[121]

As I previously noted, the *Farmer* Court indicated that actual knowledge may be inferred from an obvious risk, although officials may attempt to show lack of awareness of even obvious risks. In addition, a defendant may not escape liability for failure to verify underlying facts or for refusal to confirm inferences of risk he strongly believed were true.[122]

Subjective states of mind, like deliberate indifference, are not demonstrated by some sort of culpability x-ray. Without a "confession," inference remains the primary tool for reaching conclusions about any mental state. The Salvi records available to me do not reveal any suicide threats made to corrections officials, but they do reveal a pattern of behavior so clearly consistent with mental illness that the four experts who prepared the Salvi Report, although they presumably never met the decedent, confidently found him to have been psychotic.

Stipulating that psychosis is a correct diagnosis, does it follow (1) that Salvi should have been given treatment *and* (2) that the apparent failure to provide even minimal mental health care was the proximate cause of the suicide? The case is probably easily made that Massachusetts prison officials were deliberately indifferent to Salvi's psychosis. If that psychosis had manifested itself as driving Salvi to self-destruction, then a causal link would likely exist between what was known and what was at risk. Again, the record does not clearly support that inference.

This is analogous to a Louisiana case where a jail inmate, under care for depression and on psychotropic medication, was able to remove a gun from an officer's car and kill himself.[123] The inmate-trustee was allowed to wash these cars and he obtained the gun by popping open the glove compartment. The decedent had given no hint of suicidal thinking. The Louisiana Appellate Court held that if the weapon had been taken as part of an escape and used in that connection, the result might be different. The act of suicide was found to be neither foreseeable nor easily associated with any breach of duty owed the decedent.[124]

Not every diagnosis of mental illness and consequent failure to provide adequate mental health care is deliberate indifference as to the serious risk of suicide. Whether there may be liability for the anguish and disintegration associated with the untreated mental illness is, of course, another matter. How the matter is resolved, of course, has critical implications for the measure of damages available. As noted earlier, liability for custodial suicide will likely be based on a theory of failure to provide medical or mental health care or failure to protect the individual from committing suicide.[125] Deliberate indifference is required for liability under either theory but the duties imposed on correction officials are quite different.

---

[121] Farmer v. Brennan, *supra* note 19, 511 U.S. at 838.

[122] Farmer, *supra* note 19, 511 U.S. at 843 n.8.

[123] Misenheimer v. West Baton Rouge Parish Sheriff's Office, 677 So. 2d 159 (La. App. 1996).

[124] Id.

[125] *See* Viero v. Buffano, *supra* note 57, 925 F. Supp. at 1382 n.18.

Thus, where the theory of liability is a failure to provide appropriate and mandatory mental health care, it must be shown that the decedent had a serious and either untreated or inadequately treated mental illness which illness itself included the serious risk of suicide. From the preventative standpoint, that is a far more expensive option than the essentially insulating-from-harm requirement built into the duty to protect theory of liability. Once the suicide alarm goes off and there is an obvious and imminent risk thereof, protective measures focus on the design and furnishings of the crisis cell, observation, type of clothing and bedding available, possible use of restraints, availability of first aid material and a cutting tool, a procedure for ameliorative cell entry, and so on.

All of these measures are designed to be preventative or to reduce the risk of harm associated with a suicide attempt. There is no requirement of healing, or of altering the internal, psychological state of the person at risk. The threshold, of course, is the nature and quality of the information that generates the duty to protect an individual from himself.

¶ 14.6 RISKS AND DUTIES

[1] Seriousness of Threat

In *Heggs v. Grant*,[126] the decedent was brought to jail drunk. After communicating initial denials during intake screening, Ms. Heggs then threatened to kill herself on learning she would be detained. She then retracted the threat, stating that she was only joking. She also refused an offer of hospital care. The lieutenant directly involved with her had known the decedent for some 15 years and indicated that he had not otherwise known her to be suicidal. This lieutenant placed Ms. Heggs in a cell by herself without a blanket, sheet, or mattress but left her with her clothing. The other items were removed as a safeguard against fire or property destruction.[127] She was subject to 15-minute vision checks, which did occur, but she still managed to successfully hang herself with her socks.

The federal court of appeals held that the law did not and does not require that defendants do anything more or differently. The officers' evaluation of her risk potential and her overall situation required no further preventative action or training.[128]

If the plaintiffs in *Heggs* hoped to prevail they would have had to win the battle on the seriousness of the threat and somehow show that while the threat was serious, the recanting was not. Even with this showing, the plaintiff would also have to show that the regular observation and clothing left with the decedent in the cell amounted to deliberate indifference.[129] This they failed to do, and indeed it would be difficult to

---

[126] 73 F.3d 317 (11th Cir. 1996).

[127] A cynic might suggest that this is very convenient testimony, akin to a mental health professional requesting only a watch. Testimony that the cell was stripped because of a concern for suicide would have elicited: "And if you thought her to be at risk for suicide, why not a constant watch? Why leave her with clothes that could be used for hanging?"

[128] Heggs, 73 F.3d at 320.

[129] The plaintiff's best argument would have been that constant observation was required and would have been preventative. Removal of clothing, except for a belt and shoelaces, is not usually recommended. *See* PRISON SUICIDE, *supra* n.1.

do within the framework of the *Farmer* requirement of actual knowledge of an imminent threat to commit suicide.

[2] Actual Knowledge

Williams v. Lee Co. Alabama[130] involved an obviously mentally ill detainee and a somewhat ambiguous threat to commit suicide. Once again, the defendants prevailed. Williams had sought to be detoxified at a medical facility but then left without authority. He was taken into custody by order of a probate court and taken to jail on a temporary "mental hold" pending the probate court hearing.[131] Jail officials had a probate court form stating that Williams was believed to be mentally ill and a present danger of substantial harm to himself, and that he recently left a hospital without authorization.

Williams was under constant observation for two days and then moved to a single cell where he was checked every 15 or 20 minutes. An Officer Jones visited Williams in his cell and Williams said, " I'm not going to make it. If I don't do it myself, somebody else will." Jones left and reportedly reflected on this statement and then sagely concluded that it was a threat of self-harm. Whether Jones's supervisors were told of this remains disputed but it is clear that 15 or 20 minutes later Jones found Williams hanging by a sheet from a sprinkler in the ceiling.

The federal appeals court affirmed summary judgment here finding no possibility of showing deliberate indifference. "A reasonable official would have no reason to assume from routine booking information that a prisoner brought with him a strong, or any, likelihood of suicide."[132]

In this brief opinion there is no mention of the need for mental health care while the decedent was in jail and one may only presume that none was provided. The court did note that this was the first suicide at this jail and that William's cell had specially constructed non-moveable furniture with the sprinkler head some 10 feet from the floor.[133]

It remains a mystery to me how this court could first recite the facts known to jail officials—the clear statement of mental illness and "dangerousness"—and then conclude that there was no reason to assume any likelihood of suicide. If the reference is somehow to the more limited information obtained in the routine booking process it may make a bit more sense, but it obviously does not matter how one characterizes the information—it was available and presumably known. The only substantial question should have been: given a clear risk of imminent self-harm or suicide, were jail officials deliberately indifferent in light of that information? Should there have been an immediate mental health intervention? Should there have been constant observation?

---

[130] 78 F.3d 491 (11th Cir. 1996).

[131] This process is not unusual, since the local jail may be the only readily available custodial facility for persons who are homeless or dangerous and facing a commitment hearing. The reference to Williams as a "detainee" is a bit of a stretch but serves to distinguish him from a convicted inmate.

[132] Williams, 78 F.3d at 493.

[133] Of course, without knowing how easy it was to access the sprinkler head, presumably by standing on the furniture, these points are not very helpful. That this is the first suicide in this jail is relevant, but it is not determinative of liability on facts such as those in *Williams*. Id.

In *Olivas v. Denver*,[134] the decedent hung himself with leg irons that authorities had actually left on the bars of his cell. Officer Mitchell, with others, had responded to a domestic disturbance call in which the decedent's girlfriend told them that the decedent was drunk, threatening violence, and was in the bathroom ready to cut his wrists. Blood drops were observed. Concerning Officer Mitchell, the court found there was enough evidence of actual knowledge of suicide risk for the plaintiffs to escape summary judgment. The Chief of Police was found to have immunity without a showing that there had been a series of suicide attempts or knowledge of a serious risk of suicide in police substations.

This would seem to be a case where actual knowledge of the risk is plain and the means of suicide closely linked to deliberate indifference. And yet, even here the defendants argued that the case should not even go to trial; and the right to a trial, it should be clear, is all that was won here.

[3] Professional Judgment Issues

Estate of Max G. Cole v. Fromm,[135] discussed earlier in this chapter, raises some interesting issues. In this case, the detainee committed suicide while hospitalized by placing a plastic bag used as the liner for a clothes hamper over his head and suffocating to death. This detainee was reporting suicidal thoughts, but apparently they were not couched in terms of present intention. The decedent was on a suicide precaution watch, but not a close watch, based on medical judgment. This form of suicide—using a bag from a clothes hamper liner—had never before been encountered at this hospital, and there was evidence that it generally was very rare in custodial suicides.

Are we able to say that there was a risk of suicide, based on the decedent's words, and that the use of plastic bags in an area accessible by patients on suicide watch represented a suicide risk as to the means employed? The answer would appear to be yes.

However, the Seventh Circuit Court of Appeals was concerned with a "strong likelihood" versus a "mere possibility" and in the use of this measure of probability, the court joined the requirement of a high risk of the event with a high risk regarding the means employed. That there is "some risk" did not require the adoption of all preventive measures, according to the court.[136]

The court relied importantly on *Youngberg v. Romeo*[137] first to setup and then to resolve important policy disputes. The initial question here relates to the significance of the exercise of medical, or professional, judgment. A doctor concluded that the decedent was not a high risk of suicide, with the very restrictive precautions attendant to that decision.[138]

An expert for the plaintiffs was prepared to disagree both as to the risk of suicide and the risk attendant to access of the plastic bag actually employed. Relying on

---

[134] 929 F. Supp. 1329 (D. Colo. 1996).

[135] 941 F. Supp. 776 (S.D. Ind. 1995), *aff'd*, 94 F.3d 254 (7th Cir. 1996).

[136] Cole, 94 F.3d at 260.

[137] 457 U.S. 307 (1982). *See* Chapter 6, ¶ 6.2[4], and Chapter 7, ¶ 7.2[5][c], regarding *Romeo* and issues of professional judgment and staff training.

[138] Cole, 94 F.3d at 257.

Romeo, the court stated: "[D]eliberate indifference may be inferred based upon a medical professionals' erroneous treatment decision only when the medical professional's decision is such a substantial departure from accepted professional judgment, practice, or standards as to demonstrate that the person responsible did not base the decision on such a judgment."[139]

This effectively precludes reliance on another, basically opposed, medical opinion even if other experts would, in a sense, vote with the latter opinion. Courts view this is a mere disagreement of professional judgment, with correctional (or here, hospital) authorities able to rely on the sole, contrary view so long as professional judgment was exercised.

The second use of *Romeo* here relates to the policy issue of personal freedom versus bodily restraint to prevent death. Noting that detainees have a limited right to avoid personal restraint[140] and a right to avoid injury, the court stated:

> When faced with treatment of an individual in state custody, a medical professional must consider conflicting rights. Cole had a right to be free from restraint, but this right was not absolute; it ended at the point at which his freedom of restraint posed the substantial risk that he would seriously injure or kill himself. At that point, Cole had a right to appropriate treatment, including bodily restraint. Where these conflicting medical rights intersect is a matter of medical judgment. In making this judgment, the medical professional must balance the need for treatment against competing concerns—i.e., preventing unnecessary treatment, the need for freedom from unnecessary restraint, etc. Surely, if defendants bound, gagged, and immobilized like Hannibal Lecter every patient for the sole purpose of preventing the patients from injuring themselves, then Cole would not have been able to access the plastic bags. At the same time, however, defendants would have violated Cole's right to be free from bodily restraint because the doctor would have failed to exercise medical judgment. *Youngberg* and *Farmer* both require medical professionals to exercise medical judgment. The right to be free from bodily restraint is breached when an individual is restrained unless the decision was made pursuant to an appropriate exercise of judgment by a health professional. If the decision is made by a professional, it is presumptively valid. We find that the same standard applied to allegations of improper medical treatment as evidence of "deliberate indifference."[141]

In *Cole,* the issue of duty to provide a safe environment focused on the availability of the plastic bags. Some of the defendants conceded that they knew such bags could be used to commit suicide and all of the nursing defendants admitted they would have confiscated a plastic bag from Cole if they had seen him obtain it, which they did not.[142]

---

[139] Cole, 94 F.3d at 262.

[140] Id. The court failed to note that this aspect of *Romeo* requires an analysis as to whether or not a detainee is being punished.

[141] Id. (citations omitted).

[142] Cole, 94 F.3d at 258.

Regarding the possibility of deliberate indifference on the safety issue, the court stated:

> There is no evidence, however, that any defendant perceived the presence of the plastic bags in the BU2 unit to be a danger to Cole or other patients. In addition, no person who had worked in the BU2 unit, visited it, or inspected it had ever recognized that the bags posed a risk to the patients and no person had called such risk to the Hospital's attention. Finally, there was no evidence that any BU2 unit patient had ever tried to harm himself or herself with a plastic bag prior to Cole's suicide.[143]

Cole, then, is not a case about the failure to obtain relevant information, nor is it about having some information that actually indicates prior suicide attempts (e.g., scars on the wrists)[144] but that is not interpreted properly. This is a case where the decedent is believed to be a suicide risk *and* the accessible implement used to commit suicide is believed to be an object which is dangerous in the hands of a suicidal person. Why then is summary judgment for the defendants affirmed?

Expert opinion existed to the effect that the risk was not "serious"—meaning imminent, in my view—and that while the bags were dangerous, the danger factor relates to the imminence of the danger of suicide. If this sounds rather strained, it is a view shared with this author.

Indeed, I find the entire analysis by the *Cole* court flawed, and especially so in denying the plaintiffs an opportunity for a trial by a jury. If professional judgment, as here, is used to trump compelling evidence supportive of deliberate indifference, then the possibility of recovery in such cases becomes even more illusory.[145] The professional judgment standard as used in *Cole* becomes a proxy for the older "hands-off" doctrine and substitutes a concern with who decides for the more substantive basis of *how* the decision is made.[146]

To conclude this Chapter, I might end very much as I began: suicide is a statistically significant problem in custodial facilities; there is a body of accessible literature that provides suicide risk profiles and preventive measures; and there is a body of case law that places a premium on the ignorance of the custodian, which makes it very difficult for plaintiffs to prevail. Accepting as accurate that there is no constitutional obligation to screen for suicide potential all persons detained in jail, courts should impose an obligation to "screen" when information relevant to suicide (or with medical problems) comes to their attention.

---

[143] Id. The BU2 unit is, of course, the unit where the suicide occurred.

[144] *See* Mullins v. Stratton, *supra* note 74, 878 F. Supp. at 1020.

[145] Other decisions in suicide that utilize the professional judgment standard are Zwalesky v. Manistee Co., Mich., *supra* note 17, 749 F. Supp. at 819; Danese v. Asman, 875 F.2d 1239, 1243 (6th Cir. 1989) *cert. denied,* 494 U.S. 1027 (1990).

[146] "Hands-off" is simply a way to describe a judicial policy of deference to various decision-makers. It attaches an almost impenetrable presumption of correctness, for example, to the decisions of doctors, wardens, sheriffs, police officers, and the like. For an excellent analysis of these matters, *see* Susan Stefan, *Leaving Civil Rights to the "Experts"; From Defense to Abdication Under the Professional Judgment Standard,* 102 YALE L.J. 639 (1992).

¶ 14.7 KEY TO SUICIDE PREVENTION

The key to suicide prevention lies in staff training, intake screening in prison and the more limited screening discussed above in jails, having a suicide precaution plan in place, appropriate housing, access to appropriate emergency and other skilled care, and having a quality assurance program in place. Prisons appear to have made progress in the last decade and attention now should focus on jails and the significant bundle of problems noted here.

Chapter 15

Pretrial Detainees

¶ 15.1 CONSTITUTIONAL SOURCE OF RIGHTS

Many of the issues discussed in this chapter have been identified or discussed elsewhere in this book; this chapter provides sharper focus on these issues. To begin, virtually everything discussed thus far concerning legal issues and the mentally disordered offender applies to convicted prisoners as well as to pretrial detainees. *Bell v. Wolfish*[1] mortally wounded a judicial trend to recognize more rights in the detainee than in the convicted. Before *Bell,* some courts had determined that detainees retain the rights of unincarcerated individuals and can be deprived of their liberty only to the extent the deprivation inhered in confinement itself or was justified by compelling necessity.[2] *Bell's* full impact would not be felt immediately, but its portent was very clear.

[1] Due Process Right to No Punishment

Justice Rehnquist, writing for the court in *Bell,* found no constitutional basis for the compelling necessity standard, granting only that detainees may not be punished:

> Not every disability imposed during pretrial detention amounts to "punishment" in the constitutional sense, however. Once the Government has exercised its conceded authority to detain a person pending trial, it obviously is entitled to employ devices that are calculated to effectuate this detention. Traditionally, this has meant confinement in a facility which, no matter how modern or how antiquated, results in restricting the movement of a detainee in a manner in which he would not be restricted if he simply were free to walk

---

[1] 441 U.S. 520 (1979).
[2] *See, e.g.,* Brenneman v. Madigan, 343 F. Supp. 128, 142 (N.D. Cal. 1972).

the streets pending trial. Whether it be called a jail, a prison, or a custodial center, the purpose of the facility is to detain. Loss of freedom of choice and privacy are inherent incidents of confinement in such a facility. And the fact that such detention interferes with the detainee's understandable desire to live as comfortably as possible and with as little restraint as possible during confinement does not convert the conditions or restrictions of detention into "punishment."[3]

Pretrial detainees, then, have a due process right not to be punished, while convicted inmates have an Eighth Amendment right not to be punished in a cruel and unusual manner. As we have seen, a convicted inmate's claim to medical and psychological care is grounded in the Eighth Amendment, while a detainee's similar claim is grounded in the Due Process Clause. Although the constitutional source of the right clearly is different, is there a difference in the nature and level of care required?

A 1986 decision of the Fifth Circuit Court of Appeals deals directly with our problem, holding:

> *Estelle v. Gamble* applied its standard of medical care to prisoners who had actually been convicted. The holding was based on a convicted prisoner's Eighth Amendment right to be free from cruel and unusual punishment. A pretrial detainee, however, has a Fourteenth Amendment Due Process right to be free from punishment altogether. *Bell v. Wolfish* held that in determining whether a particular condition accompanying pretrial detention amounts to a denial of due process, the court must decide whether the condition is imposed for the purpose of punishment or whether it is but an incident of some other legitimate governmental purpose. If a particular condition of pretrial detention is reasonably related to a legitimate governmental objective, it does not, without more, amount to punishment. "[I]f a restriction or condition is not reasonably related to a legitimate goal—*if it is arbitrary or purposeless*—a court permissibly may infer that the purpose of the government action is punishment that may not constitutionally be inflicted upon detainees qua detainees."
>
> As we noted in our earlier opinion: Pretrial detainees are often entitled to greater protection than convicted persons. See *Bell v. Wolfish*; *Jones v. Diamond*, 5 Cir. 1981, 636 F.2d 1364, 1368 ('The due process clause accords pretrial detainees rights not enjoyed by convicted inmates.") Although "[t]he standard by which to measure the medical attention that must be afforded pretrial detainees has never been spelled out," *Jones v. Diamond*, 636 F.2d at 1378, both this Circuit and other circuits have held that pretrial detainees are entitled to at least the level of medical care set forth in *Estelle*. The Fourth Circuit has explicitly used an Eighth Amendment standard to assess a pretrial detainee's allegations of inadequate medical care.[4]

---

[3] Bell, 441 U.S. at 531–535.

[4] Partridge v. Two Unknown Police Officers of Houston, 791 F.2d 1182, 1186 (5th Cir. 1986) (emphasis in original).

Certainly one portion of the above quotation remains accurate: detainees are entitled to *at least* the same level of medical (also mental health) care as convicted inmates. On the other hand, over time the "at least" has come to mean "about the same." There are some judicial expressions of uncertainty,[5] but the weight of decisional authority equates the convicted and the detainee.[6]

In *Murphy v. Walker*,[7] the court held that detainees have greater protection with regard to punitive shackling and use of restraints. However that may be, on the question of medical or mental health care it is fair to say that due process and the cruel and unusual punishment standards use the same legal doctrine, including *Farmer v. Brennan's*[8] definition of deliberate indifference, and the outcomes are the same.

[2] Minimally Adequate Care and Protection

In *City of Revere v. Massachusetts General Hospital*,[9] the Supreme Court was confronted with the question of who should absorb the cost of medical care administered to a detainee who was shot and wounded by police during his arrest. In deciding that the allocation of costs is a matter of state law, the Court held:

> The Due Process Clause, however, does require the responsible government or governmental agency to provide medical care to persons, such as Kivlin, who have been injured while apprehended by the police. In fact, the due process rights of a person in Kivlin's situation are at least as great as the Eighth Amendment protections available to a convicted prisoner. See *Bell v. Wolfish*. We need not define, in this case, Revere's due process obligation to pretrial detainees or to other persons in its care who require medical attention. Whatever the standard may be, Revere fulfilled its constitutional obligation by seeing that Kivlin was taken promptly to a hospital that provided the treatment necessary for his injury. And as long as the governmental entity ensures that the medical care needed is in fact provided, the Constitution does not dictate how the cost of that care should be allocated as between the entity and the provider of the care.[10]

The nature of the facility, the duration of the stay, special problems of suicide and substance abuse, and similar matters strongly suggest that jails need different approaches and programs than prisons. The principle of minimally adequate care

---

[5] Carnell v. Grimm, 74 F.3d 977 (9th Cir. 1980).

[6] Hare v. City of Corinth, Miss., 74 F.3d 633, 643 (5th Cir. 1996) (en banc); Cottrell v. Caldwell, 85 F.3d 1480, 1490 (11th Cir. 1996); Swan by Carello v. Daniels, 923 F. Supp. 626 (D. Del. 1995), holding also that failure to follow contractual standards of care, NCCHC criteria, was not also deliberate indifference.

[7] 51 F.3d 714, 717 (7th Cir. 1995).

[8] 511 U.S. 825 (1994).

[9] 463 U.S. 239 (1983).

[10] City of Revere, 463 U.S. at 244–245 (citations omitted). Plainly, the Court's statement places the detainee's right to medical care in the Due Process Clause and indicates, in agreement with the text, that a detainee's rights are at least as great as the rights of the convicted.

clearly applies, including the debated question of classification, records, careful and restricted use of isolation, suicide prevention, and emergency care.[11]

In *Dawson v. Kendrick*,[12] the district court used the *Bell* standard to uphold detainee restrictions where they helped ensure the inmates' presence at trial or aided in the effective management of the facility. The Mercer County Jail did not have routine psychological testing. Prisoners with mental or emotional problems were sent into the general population; there was no detoxification program; and there were no arrangements for psychiatric or psychological assistance.[13] This litany of "not available," along with generally poor conditions, was found to be inadequate.[14]

In a number of somewhat earlier detainee cases, courts recognized the due process source of the claimed right and then explicitly tested the constitutional adequacy of conditions according to the *Estelle* "deliberate indifference" standard. For example, on remand a district court found "as a matter of fact that the care of the mentally ill in the Allegheny County Jail is woefully inadequate . . . to the extent of 'deliberate indifference.'"[15] The jail had no mechanism for screening new admittees, no observation or diagnostic area for new inmates, no segregation of seriously disturbed inmates, and no monitoring of medication. The court also found that one-quarter to one-third of the 450 to 500 detainees were seriously mentally ill and that there was no staff psychiatrist, psychologist, or psychiatric social worker to deal with them.[16] In its decree, the court ordered the jail to establish procedures to care for these inmates, to transfer them to other institutions when necessary, and to adopt a means of monitoring the dispensing and handling of medication.[17]

Decisions rendered before 1979, when *Bell v. Wolfish* was decided, must, of course, be read closely to determine whether the court was applying a type of strict necessity test on behalf of detainees. This is especially so on such questions as double-bunking, reading material, strip searches, and the like. There is less of a problem with medical and psychological needs. No one seriously speaks of the need to closely examine inmate claims to be free of infectious diseases, to be free of inmate violence, to have care for their mental illness, or to be protected from one's own self-destructive violence.

Decisions rendered after *Bell* and before 1994, when *Farmer v. Brennan* was decided, also must be read closely to determine which version of deliberate indiffer-

---

[11] *See* Jones v. Diamond, 636 F.2d 1364 (5th Cir. 1981), *overruled*; International Woodworkers v. Champion Int'l Corp., 790 F.2d 1174 (5th Cir. 1986). For a valuable study on current practices in jail mental health law, *see* Henry Steadman, et al., Developing Jail Mental Health Services: Practice and Principles (U.S. Dept. Health & Human Servs., 1986). *See also* Karen M. Abram & Linda A. Teplin, *Co-Occurring Disorders Among Mentally Ill Jail Detainees: Implications for Public Policy*, 46 Am. Psychologist 1036 (1991), arguing that mentally ill persons with co-occuring substance abuse problem or antisocial personalities (e.g., schizophrenics who are also alcoholics) are particularly vulnerable to arrest, primarily due to a lack of other alternatives. Part of this call for reform is to enhance the jail's role in identifying and then diverting or referring the detainee to a treatment site.

[12] 527 F. Supp. 1252 (S.D. W.Va. 1981).

[13] Dawson, 527 F. Supp. at 1273.

[14] *See* Lareau v. Manson, 651 F.2d 96 (2d. Cir. 1981), for a discussion of due process and Eighth Amendment standards.

[15] Inmates of Allegheny County Jail v. Pierce, 487 F. Supp. 638, 642–643 (W.D. Pa. 1980).

[16] Inmates of Allegheny, 487 F. Supp. at 641.

[17] Inmates of Allegheny, 487 F. Supp. at 644.

ence was being applied. As a general proposition, where a constitutional violation of medical or mental health care was found, the general conditions have been so egregious, so life-threatening, that pre- or post-*Farmer* deliberate indifference would have been found.

¶ 15.2 SCREENING AND RECEPTION

[1] No Screening

The case law of the 1970s and 80s is replete with decisions concerned with initial screening and reception. For example, in *Campbell v. McGruder*[18] the court found there was no staff psychiatrist at the jail and that the jail was not equipped to house, care for, or treat psychiatric patients. The Court of Appeals substantially upheld the lower court's order and spoke to the jail's reception (not intake screening) process:

> In the event an inmate displays unusual behavior suggestive of possible mental illness, such behavior shall be immediately reported to the medical staff. The inmate will be seen by a psychiatrist within twenty-four (24) hours. If the inmate is found to be mentally ill, he will be transferred within forty-eight (48) hours of such finding to a hospital having appropriate facilities for the care and treatment of the mentally ill.[19]

In *Jones v. Wittenburg*,[20] the inmate challenged the conditions of the Lucas County Jail. Mental health care was among the challenged conditions and was found lacking by the court because the jail had no psychiatrist. The court said that although various needs of inmates with special needs were being met, "psychiatrist services are needed in order to meet the special needs of inmates suffering from psychological and psychiatric maladies."[21]

Alberti v. Sheriff of Harris County, Texas[22] involved a successful challenge to jail conditions. The court ordered an immediate screening program to detect psychological and psychiatric problems.[23] In addition, the jail officials were ordered to find a new location to house mentally ill and mentally disturbed inmates.[24]

[2] No Passing of Information

The situation in Houston apparently had not materially improved 11 years later. As discussed in Chapter 14, the parents of a detainee who committed suicide in the

---

[18] 580 F.2d 521, 549 (D.C. Cir. 1978).

[19] Campbell, 580 F.2d at 548–549. The order was amended for additional flexibility on the 48-hour time limit.

[20] 509 F. Supp. 653 (N.D. Ohio 1980).

[21] Jones, 509 F. Supp. at 687.

[22] 406 F. Supp. 649 (S.D. Tex. 1975).

[23] Alberti, 406 F. Supp. at 677.

[24] Id.

municipal jail successfully brought a suit for damages.[25] The gist of the claim was that the defendants deliberately adopted a policy of indifference to the medical needs of detained persons, and that they consequently failed to render aid to the plaintiffs' son, who clearly displayed suicidal tendencies.[26]

Recall that while the boy was being arrested, his father told the police that the boy had previously suffered a nervous breakdown, and when the father directed their attention to the medical bracelets the boy wore, the police suggested that a letter from the boy's psychiatrist would likely result in his release.[27]

The boy became very agitated on the trip to the jail. He banged his head on the police car divider. On arriving at the station the officers told no one of the aberrant behavior. The young man was placed in solitary confinement and three hours later he hanged himself with a pair of socks tied around the upper bars of his cell.[28]

In reviewing the adequacy of the complaint, the Fifth Circuit found that the claim rested squarely on the jail's systematic lack of adequate care for detainees, including: failure to alert to the risk of suicide, absence of a written policy or procedure manual, no sharing of the jail clinic's personnel records, inadequate staffing, no regular cell-checking procedures, failure of personnel to alert to the decedent's behavior, and failure to adequately train staff.[29]

[3] Overcrowding

Yet another dramatic case involving a detainee's suicide exposes further dimensions of the jailor's duties.[30] The decedent was a passenger in a car involved in an accident. Highly intoxicated at the time, the young man was arrested at the scene on a disorderly conduct charge.[31] The decedent's parents offered proof that a deputy hit their son and dragged him to the booking area. He was dragged and repeatedly struck on the way to a cell where he was stripped naked. This cell was without a mattress, pillow or blanket. The decedent began to yell and, in reaction, officers dragged him to an isolation cell where he continued to scream and beat his head on the bars. He cried for a doctor. Several hours after the arrest, the young man was found dead as a result of hanging himself with bedsheets.[32]

The defense argued that the plaintiff's assertion of overcrowded and under manned conditions at the jail was not relevant. This the court easily dismissed, find-

---

[25] Partridge v. Two Unknown Police Officers of Houston, *supra* note 4. *See* Chapter 14, ¶ 14.4[3] for a fuller discussion of this case.

[26] Partridge, *supra* note 4, 791 F.2d at 1183.

[27] Partridge, *supra* note 4, 791 F.2d at 1184.

[28] Id. Police also were unaware that the boy had attempted suicide during an earlier confinement; these records were four doors away from the booking desk.

[29] Partridge, *supra* note 4, 791 F.2d at 1184–1185. The matter was remanded, one of the crucial issues being whether the alleged indifference was a custom or a policy of the municipality. *See* Monell v. Department of Soc. Servs., 436 U.S. 658 (1978).

[30] Strandell v. Jackson County, 634 F. Supp. 824 (S.D. Ill. 1986).

[31] Id.

[32] Strandell, 634 F. Supp. at 827. It must be emphasized that the government moved to dismiss the complaint and the facts noted in the text are merely the bare allegations of the plaintiff parents.

ing that the conditions complained of might easily contribute to an utter disregard of the detainee's right to care and to freedom from harm.[33] Again, this is a clear warning to local government that when overcrowding contributes to conditions which effectively deny care and safety to those in their charge, the consequences in terms of liability may be compelling.

Strandell is interesting also because the court found that:

> The Illinois County Jail Standards provide that detainees shall be assigned to suitable quarters, that emotionally disturbed detainees shall be kept under constant supervision, and that "suspected disturbed" detainees shall be immediately examined by a physician. Ill. Admin., Reg. ch. IV and VII (7/11/80). The Court concludes that the mandatory language of these regulations creates a protected liberty interest in an expectation of certain minimal standards and treatment. The Court further finds that plaintiffs' complaint sufficiently alleges a deprivation of that liberty interest in violation of the fourteenth amendment.[34]

[4] Duty to Screen

One significant area of conflict between jails and prisons, however, relates to intake screening and evaluation. Henry Steadman and his colleagues write:

> All of the standards rank intake screening as one of the most significant mental health services that a jail can offer (it is ranked as "important" by the AMA and "essential" by the other two organizations). This assessment is usually described as a three-part process. First, the booking officer should review any papers or records that accompany the prisoner. The second step involves asking the inmate a series of questions about his or her mental health history. The questions should determine whether the individual has ever attempted suicide, been admitted to a psychiatric hospital, or committed acts of sexual deviancy. The officer should also try to ascertain whether there is a pattern of violence or of substance abuse and whether the inmate is currently taking any medication. Finally, the officer should record any visual observation of the inmate's behavior. Of particular interest are signs of delusions, hallucinations, peculiar speech and posturing, disorganization, depression, memory deficits, and evidence of self-mutilation. In addition to developing standards for the intake process, the AMA has prepared a model form for the specific purpose of screening incoming prisoners.

Although the implementation of a screening procedure is widely encour-

---

[33] Strandell, 634 F. Supp. at 828. *See* Matzker v. Herr, 748 F.2d 1142 (7th Cir. 1984); Madden v. City of Meriden, 602 F. Supp. 1160 (D. Conn. 1985); Soto v. City of Sacramento, 567 F. Supp. 662 (E.D. Cal. 1983).

[34] 634 F. Supp. at 829. After Sandin v. Conner, 515 U.S. 472 (1995), the liberty interest analysis in the text is essentially invalid. Local rules would be admissible but not determinative of the duty. The decision, however, would likely stand merely on a "deliberate indifference" basis without the need to rely on Illinois law.

aged, it is designed only to identify disturbed inmates who respond to mental health questions accurately or who manifest overt signs of mental illness while being booked. It is thus possible that inmates with serious psychiatric problems will still go undetected. It is also possible that the stress of the jail environment or uncertainty about an upcoming trial will cause some prisoners to break down after they have been admitted. One strategy to identify all inmates in need of services is the training of correction officers to recognize the symptoms of mental illness. Another, which the standards unanimously recommended, is that inmates be granted unhindered access to medical and mental health personnel. Inmates should receive written notice at the time of admission of the procedures to be followed for requesting psychological services. The AMA and ACA also recommended that thorough health assessment be completed for each inmate within 14 days after arrival at the facility. The exam should be primarily medical in orientation, although the opportunity should be used to collect additional information for completing the psychiatric history.

Formal evaluation can be of an emergency or nonemergency nature. The AMA and AACP recommend that an assessment of an inmate referred for comprehensive psychological evaluations on a nonemergency basis be completed within 14 days. In an emergency, there is a consensus that the inmate should be held in a special area with constant supervision by trained personnel while waiting to receive professional attention. According to the AMA and ACA, no more than 12 hours should elapse before emergency care is rendered. The AACP sets a deadline of 24 hours.[35]

What the experts urge and what various standards recommend is relevant but not determinative of constitutional rights. *Belcher v. Oliver*,[36] discussed in Chapter 14, is very certain that there is no constitutional obligation to screen every detainee for suicidal tendencies. On the other hand, I have argued that there does appear to be such a duty imposed on prison authorities.[37]

If the law is more demanding of prisons than jails, more protective of inmates than detainees, then we have the uncomfortable irony of being the least protective where it is needed most. Of course, there are daunting dimensions to the problem in mandating intake screening in jails, or even lock ups, with the millions of annual intakes.

Stipulating to the accuracy of the law as summarized in *Belcher*, as noted above, there remains some wiggle-room for plaintiffs. That is, where detainees present themselves in obvious crisis, perhaps with medication that almost uniformly is seized and not returned, and where nothing preventive or ameliorative is done, a case of deliberate indifference may be made.

---

[35] HENRY J. STEADMAN, et al., THE MENTALLY ILL IN JAIL: PLANNING FOR ESSENTIAL SERVICES (1989), pp. 34–35. (AACP is the American Association of Correctional Psychologists.) *See also* LINDSAY M. HAYES, PRISON SUICIDE: AN OVERVIEW AND GUIDE TO PREVENTION (N.I.C. 1995), p.19, finding that intake screening and assessment is the key to prevention. It is doubtful whether this type of liberty analysis would prevail today.

[36] 898 F.2d 32 (4th Cir. 1990). *See* discussion in Chapter 14, ¶ 14.3[4].

[37] *See* Chapter 5 generally on the problems of deficient or nonexistent screening programs.

The literature is rich with examples of jails that have screening and evaluation components to identify the mentally ill and the suicidal. Larger jails can develop screening and in-house care. Smaller and more rural facilities need to enter into working agreements with local or state mental health boards and community mental health facilities. A regional mental health approach may be possible, perhaps even with mobile response units.[38]

I am acutely aware of having moved from legal standards to suggestions on how to operate jails in a more humane and effective fashion. Those who wish to operate at the law's least common denominator obviously are free to do so. Those who wish to take a step beyond in this complex area of detainee rights have some guidance.

¶ 15.3 THE L.A. COUNTY JAIL FINDINGS

A September 1997 U.S. Department of Justice investigation of the Los Angeles jail system, with its eight facilities and 18,500 inmates, tells its own screening and education story:

> We believe that the Jail's provision of mental heath care is constitutionally inadequate in numerous aspects. The Jail fails to identify adequately inmates with serious mental illnesses and does not adequately treat those inmates it has identified as mentally ill. Some inmates with mental illnesses enter the Jail without their illnesses being discovered, others report their mental illnesses, but are then "lost" in the Jail system, misclassified and placed in unsafe housing, or transferred repeatedly between facilities. For many mentally ill inmates who are properly identified, the treatment they receive is below constitutional minimum standards. They too often wait dangerously long periods before being evaluated or prescribed medication, have their illnesses misdiagnosed and their medications improperly administered. Mentally ill inmates are housed in conditions that often exacerbate their condition and they are not permitted to participate in the same programs as other inmates, even where their mental illness would allow such participation. They are the victims of predatory behavior at the hands of other inmates and have been abused by correctional staff. Clinical response to suicidal inmates is delayed, on occasion with tragic results, and suicidal inmates are placed in housing that permits them to act on their suicidal ideation.
>
> The reason for the poor state of mental health care in the Jail is manifold. The number of inmates in need of mental health care overwhelms available staff resources. The Jail's systems of medical record keeping and inmate tracking and classification are deficient to the point that custody and mental health staff cannot adequately access information necessary to provide appropriate care. The Jail does not adequately prevent abuse of mentally ill inmates and does not adequately investigate allegations of such abuse when it occurs. Many current custody policies are obstacles to the provision of adequate mental health care. A lack of adequate training of custody staff in dealing with

---

[38] *See* STEADMAN, et al., *supra* n. 11, Ch. 7.

inmates with mental illnesses negatively impacts the provision of mental health care. The chronic overpopulation in the Jail results in insufficient housing and treatment space, further exacerbating the Jail's inadequate system of mental health care.[39]

This is about as pervasive as legal criticism may be about a jail's mental health program. While the Report does argue that there must be intake screening and evaluation, it does point out a wholesale failure to identify, and thus treat, those with serious mental illness. After that, treatment is nominal, misdiagnosis rampant, housing improper, programs limited, victimization rampant, records poor, and training inadequate. This most certainly is a wake-up call to all large jails and a caution for smaller facilities.

In conclusion, then, an analysis of numerous decisions fails to disclose any sharp distinction between pretrial detainees and convicts on the factors considered relevant where medical or psychological services are challenged. More often than not, the courts use the standards developed under the Eighth Amendment as the standards by which to decide the due process right.[40]

For all practical purposes, and subject to the special problems noted earlier, the rights of detainees and sentenced inmates in the area of psychiatric care appear to be the same.

¶ 15.4 SEPARATION OF DETAINEES FROM CONVICTS

While detainees perhaps should be separated from convicted prisoners,[41] today jail inmates are likely to be housed according to standard classification, or risk, factors. Their illnesses must be identified in a reasonable fashion, and the mentally ill must be provided with access to mental health professionals. Some cases also make it clear that "It would be an unfortunate precedent that would allow prison officials to examine a detainee or prisoner once and to rely henceforth on the results of that examination."[42] Thus, post-examination or post-classification behavior or an opinion from an outside doctor may well call for a different custodial or treatment response. The risk of suicide and the problems of detoxification are inherently greater in jails than in prisons. Thus, while the legal principle of the right to care remains constant, the required response naturally will vary with the facility and the nature of the problem.

---

[39] Letter from Isabella Katz Pinzler, Acting Assistant Attorney General, Civil Rights Division, to Joanne Sturges, L.A. County Executive, dated Sept. 5, 1997 regarding CRIPA Investigation of Mental Health Services in the Los Angeles Jail. (CRIPA is the Civil Rights of Institutionalized Persons Act.)

[40] Some cases distinguish to some extent housing minima for detainees from that of convicts. In Lareau v. Manson, 651 F.2d 96, 108–109 (2d Cir. 1981), the court argued that sentenced inmates could be subjected to marginally passable living conditions for a longer period of time than pretrial detainees. Steinke v. Washington Co., 903 F. Supp. 1403 (D. Or. 1995), dealt with private space for attorney-client conferences; Mitchell v. Dupnick, 75 F. 3d 517 (9th Cir. 1995), found detainees entitled to a due process hearing before being disciplined; Antonelli v. Sheehan, 81 F.3d 1422 (7th Cir. 1996), discusses 17 items claimed by detainees and contains an interesting comparative analysis; Nerren v. Livingston Police Dept., 86 F.3d 469 (5th Cir. 1996), contains a use of force analysis.

[41] Palmigiano v. Garrahy, 443 F. Supp. 956, 971 (D.R.I. 1977), remanded on the issue of deadlines, 599 F.2d 17 (1st Cir. 1979).

[42] Consent Decree, Downs v. Martin, slip op. (S.D. Ga. 1986).

Chapter 16

Mentally Retarded Offenders

¶ 16.1 NATURE OF THE PROBLEM

No one seems to deny the sorry plight of the mentally retarded inmate. Numerous mental health professionals, when interviewed, agreed that as bad as it is in most prisons for the mentally ill, it is always worse for the retarded inmate. Questions about programs prompt an empty smile—there usually are none. My own more recent experiences with prisons confirm the truth of these interviews.

In a 1979 study, Miles Santamour and Bernadette West offered a description of the problems of the mentally retarded inmate that remains accurate:

1. In prison, the retarded offender is slower to adjust to routine, has more difficulty in learning regulations, and accumulates more rule infractions, which, in turn, affect housing, parole, and other related matters.
2. Retarded inmates rarely take part in rehabilitation programs because of their desire to mask their deficiencies.
3. They often are the brunt of practical jokes and sexual harassment.
4. Such inmates are more often denied parole, serving on the average two to three years longer than other prisoners for the same offense.[1]

In addition to being manipulated and victimized by the general population, a more

---

[1] MILES B. SANTAMOUR & BERNADETTE WEST, RETARDATION AND CRIMINAL JUSTICE: A TRAINING MANUAL FOR CRIMINAL JUSTICE PERSONNEL (President's Committee on Mental Retardation, 1979), p.14.

recent study suggests that mentally retarded inmates are disproportionately placed into menial jobs and are more likely to be the recipient of more disciplinary action than the general population.[2]

[1] Retardation Defined

There does seem to be more agreement about the definition of mental retardation than that of mental illness. The American Association on Mental Deficiency (AAMD) promulgates the following definition: "Mental retardation refers to significantly sub-average general intellectual functioning existing concurrently with deficits in adaptive behavior and manifested during the developmental period."[3]

As is well known, intellectual functioning is quantified and the upper boundary of mental retardation is set, perhaps arbitrarily, at an IQ level of 70. However, to be classified as mentally retarded, the intellectual deficit must be accompanied by

significant limitations in an individual's effectiveness in meeting the standards of maturation, learning, personal independence, and/or social responsibility that are expected for his or her age level and cultural group, as determined by clinical assessment and, usually, standardized scales.[4]

There is general agreement that mental retardation manifests itself at an early age. Indeed, an arbitrary cutoff age of 18 has been established.[5] Mentally retarded people are classified as mild, moderate, severe, and profound. Mildly retarded people make up perhaps 89 percent of all those classified, having IQ scores in the 50 to 55 range.[6]

It is very difficult to know just how many mentally retarded persons there are in our prisons. One study estimates that about 2 percent of our prison population is retarded. At the time of the Denkowski study there were 7,600 inmates regarded as mentally retarded out of a national prison population of 378,400.[7] A more recent study concluded that somewhere between 1 to 3 percent of the New York State prison population met the federal statutory definition for having developmental disabilities.[8]

---

[2] George Denkowski & Kathryn Denkowski, *The Mentally Retarded Offender in the State Prison System: Identification, Prevalence, Adjustment and Rehabilitation*, 12 CRIM. JUST. & BEHAV. 55, 62–63 (1985).

[3] CLASSIFICATION IN MENTAL RETARDATION (American Association on Mental Deficiency, H. Grossman, ed. 1983), p.1.

[4] AAMD, *supra* note 3, p.11. Most prison systems use a 69 or 70 IQ level as their cut-off point for classification of an inmate as retarded.

[5] James Ellis & Ruth Luckasson, *Mentally Retarded Criminal Defendants*, 53 GEO. WASH. L. REV. 414, 422 (1985). This is an excellent article to consult for an analysis of the impact of the *ABA Criminal Justice Mental Health Standards* (1984), on the retarded offender.

[6] Ellis & Luckasson, *supra* note 5, at 423.

[7] Denkowski & Denkowski, *supra* note 2, at 66. Today, the number would likely be over 10,000; the 2 percent estimate actually is three percentage points below the estimate for mentally retarded persons in the general population.

[8] *Inmates with Developmental Disabilities in New York State Correctional Facilities* (New York State Commission on Quality of Care for the Mentally Disabled, 1991) [hereinafter New York State Study]. The federal criteria require a significant limitation in at least three of seven life skill areas: self-care, receptive and expressive language, learning, mobility, independent living, and self-sufficiency.

[2] Learning Disabled Inmates

If we shift definitionally and conceptually to inmates with learning disabilities, then a three-state study completed in 1983 showed that the average inmate left school after tenth grade but performed more than three years below grade level; 42 percent had some form of learning deficiency, and of this group 82 percent (420 inmates) had specific learning disabilities.[9] The average IQ of learning deficient inmates was dramatically lower than that of non-learning deficient inmates.[10]

[3] Conviction—Competency Issues

There are many good policy and operational reasons for wanting to know about the extent of mental retardation, developmental disabilities, and learning disabilities found in a captive population. One might wish to institute remedial education and habilitation programs, or, more broadly, devise better techniques of diversion. Our concern, however, is the more limited one of looking at the legal claims to some form of care—whether denominated treatment, habilitation, rehabilitation, or training—available to this "at risk" population.

Initially, there is a problem simply understanding why so many mentally retarded inmates avoid the various "kick-outs" and avenues of diversion that exist in the criminal justice system.[11] It is understandable that the marginally retarded, comprising the mild to moderate categories previously noted, simply may escape detection.[12] However, it is difficult to imagine how persons in the low moderate range, and certainly in the severe and profound range, are found competent to stand trial or to enter a guilty plea.

In 1984, I did an evaluation of the mental health and mental retardation services in the South Carolina prison system. One of the most impressive features of this system was the Developmentally Disabled Unit (known as the Stephens Unit). The unit contained 32 residential beds and could serve an additional 15 inmates on a nonresidential basis.

While precise figures were not available, some of the inmates tested in the IQ range of 40, and virtually every inmate had previously been through the state's Department of Mental Retardation. A fair number had been convicted of assault committed while institutionalized and the conviction served, in effect, as a way to transfer these residents from a school to a prison.

I observed one inmate wearing a leather cap to cover his open skull; he had no hands and was severely facially disfigured. He was obviously well below mild retardation. How might such a person receive a fair trial or competently enter a guilty plea?

---

[9] Raymond Bell, et al., *The Findings of and Recommendations of The National Study on Learning Deficiencies in Adult Inmates*, 35 J. CORRECTIONAL EDUC. 35, 129–137 (1984).

[10] Id.

[11] By "kick-outs" I refer to such mechanisms as grand jury refusal to indict, discretionary nonenforcement or refusal to prosecute, and determinations of incompetence to stand trial. By diversion I simply mean placement in programs in lieu of prosecution, conviction, or confinement.

[12] *See* Richard Allen, *The Retarded Offender: Unrecognized in Court and Untreated in Prison*, 32 FED. PROBATION 22 (Sept. 1968).

How could the mandated defense attorney fail to raise competence and how could a judge impose a criminal sentence under these circumstances?[13]

I detected no venality in all of this. My impression is that it was understood that programs available in the prison were better than those available elsewhere. Lawyers, judges, and expert witnesses understood that and used the criminal conviction as a device by which to help, not hurt. The great majority of these inmates had never worked. In prison they were taught to wash cars and to perform janitorial duties and farm labor. In addition, inmates learned basic life skills such as cooking, using the telephone, dressing, and so on.

The terrible irony is that with very limited bed space and staff, only the most severely retarded inmates receive services. The humane but dubious use of the prison as a "community resource" effectively prevents other retarded inmates—the most educable—from receiving services.[14]

Penal administrators indicate that their most common management problem with the retarded inmate is that they require almost constant and individualized staff attention, which badly strains already thin resources.[15]

¶ 16.2 LEGAL RIGHT TO CARE OR PROTECTION

We turn now to the mentally retarded person as an inmate and begin the legal inquiry. As indicated, people do not suddenly become retarded in prison (although it is generally agreed that a person may indeed become mentally ill in prison). Thus, at the outset we encounter a group of prospective inmates who are prime candidates for diversion—that is, for placement in appropriate settings with the requisite level of security and adequate programming. Until such placement efforts are made, we must confront the reality of perhaps 2 percent of the prison population being classified as mentally retarded.[16] Does the mentally retarded inmate have a constitutional right to treatment and, if so, what is the source of such a right?

The question is an interesting one and the answer is not entirely clear. *Estelle v. Gamble*[17] most certainly is the constitutional basis of an inmate's minimal claims to treatment for a serious mental disorder. The *Estelle* analysis, and subsequent judicial extension from physical to mental disorders, does not clearly include or exclude those

---

[13] The *ABA Mental Health Standards*, § 7-4.1(b) (1984), sets out the test for competence to stand trial and recognizes retardation as an appropriate basis for such a finding. Among the major problems here is whether a retarded person ever will gain sufficient competence to be tried.

[14] The South Carolina Program is treated as a model program in PROGRAMMING FOR MENTALLY RETARDED AND LEARNING DISABLED INMATES: A GUIDE FOR CORRECTIONAL ADMINISTRATORS (National Institute of Corrections, 1989) [hereinafter PROGRAM FOR THE MENTALLY RETARDED], 74–81.

[15] Barbara Rowan, *Corrections*, in THE MENTALLY RETARDED CITIZEN AND THE LAW 650, 661 (President's Committee on Mental Retardation, M. Kindred, ed. 1976).

[16] I.Q. scores of 69 or below on a standardized test is the generally acceptable measure for identifying the mentally retarded. *See* Barbara Rowan & Thomas Courtless, THE MENTALLY RETARDED OFFENDER (N.I.M.H. 1967).

[17] 429 U.S. 97 (1976). *See* Chapter 4, ¶¶ 4.1[1], 4.1[2]. *See also* Stephen Morse, *A Preference for Liberty: The Case Against Involuntary Commitment of the Mentally Disordered*, 70 CAL. L. REV. 54 (1982), for an insightful discussion of the assumptions and consequences of viewing "craziness" as indicating incompetence, lack of control, or treatability.

who are only mentally retarded. The American Psychiatric Association recently argued that:

> [T]he word "habilitation" . . . is commonly used to refer to programs for the mentally retarded because mental retardation is . . . a learning disability and training impairment rather than an illness . . . .. [T]he principal focus of habilitation is upon training and development of needed skills.[18]

With mental retardation excluded from the sickness (or disease) model, the retarded inmate's claims to help, whatever such help is called, seems also outside the scope of the *Estelle* rule. That, however, is not the end of the matter.

[1] The Involuntarily Committed

In *Youngberg v. Romeo,*[19] the Supreme Court for the first time considered the substantive, constitutional rights of involuntarily committed mentally retarded persons. Romeo, a profoundly retarded adult, did not challenge the legitimacy of his initial commitment or seek release. He claimed that the defendants unduly restrained him for prolonged periods of time and that he was entitled to damages for their failure to provide him with appropriate treatment or programs for his mental retardation.[20]

In analyzing Romeo's claims and then fashioning an extraordinarily narrow ground for relief, Justice Powell, for the Court, looked at the rights of prison inmates as the handiest analogue from which to establish Romeo's rights. That is, persons convicted of crimes and sentenced to prison have the weakest claims to any substantive rights, but if a prisoner should possess a legal right then, the argument goes, surely those who are unconvicted, yet confined, possess at least the same right.

The Court recognized that the right to personal security is an historic liberty interest, protected by due process, and not extinguished even by penal confinement.[21] The Court also recognized freedom from undue bodily restraint as a fundamental liberty interest which also survives criminal conviction and incarceration.[22] Justice Powell wrote

> that Romeo is entitled to such minimally adequate care, or training, as may be needed to protect his liberty interests in safety and freedom from unreasonable restraint. What is reasonable is determined by the judgment exercised by qualified professionals. Indeed, so long as such judgment is exercised, constitutional minima have been met.[23]

The Court expanded on the definition of professional decision-maker as follows:

---

[18] Brief of the American Psychiatric Association as *Amicus Curiae*, at 4, n.1, quoted in Youngberg v. Romeo, 457 U.S. 307, 309 n.1 (1982).

[19] Romeo, 457 U.S. at 309.

[20] Romeo, 457 U.S. at 311. Treatment was used synonymously with habilitation.

[21] Romeo, 457 U.S. at 315.

[22] Id.

[23] Romeo, 457 U.S. at 322.

By professional decision-maker, we mean a person competent, whether by education, training or experience, to make the particular decision at issue. Long term treatment decisions normally should be made by persons with degrees in medicine or nursing, or with appropriate training in areas such as psychology, physical therapy, or the care and training of the retarded. Of course, day-to-day decisions regarding care—including decisions that must be made without delay—necessarily will be made in many instances by employees without formal training but who are subject to the supervision of qualified persons.[24]

Exactly what all this means for the mentally retarded citizen in civil confinement is hardly clear.[25] To the extent that this narrow right to training equates with treatment/habilitation, the training need not aim at achieving the resident's ultimate freedom or even maximizing whatever life skills potential the individual has. The training is required only to minimize the use of physical restraints and to maximize freedom from needless physical jeopardy. And those who prescribe the training are protected as long as they exercise judgment—not necessarily good judgment, simply judgment.

Justice Powell also stated, "Persons who have been involuntarily committed are entitled to more considerate treatment and conditions of confinement than criminals whose conditions of confinement are designed to punish."[26] Thus the question arises whether *Romeo* indirectly creates any rights for mentally retarded prisoners? The answer, it seems, is yes. The practical consequence, it seems, is very little.

[2] Basis of Claim to Help

[a] Due Process

The mentally retarded inmate's claim to "help" cannot easily be derived from a disease model, nor may it comfortably rest on a preparation for release-type argument. The latter argument was not dealt with in *Romeo*, and it has a sufficient ring of rehabilitation to face speedy rejection unless encompassed by other glaringly deficient conditions in a given penal system.

Although there are a large number of retarded offenders in prison—perhaps three times the ratio to the population at large—the vast majority of such inmates, as noted, seem to be only mildly retarded.[27] Should a person as profoundly retarded as Romeo appear at the prison gates (an I.Q. of between 8 and 10, who cannot talk or exercise

---

[24] Romeo, 457 U.S. at 322 n.30.

[25] *See, e.g.,* the several interpretations discussed in Rennie v. Klein, 720 F.2d 266 (3d Cir. 1983). *See also* David Wexler, *Seclusion and Restraint: Lessons from Law, Psychiatry and Psychology*, 5 INT'L J. L. & PSYCHIATRY 285 (1982), which emphasizes the vast discretion ceded professionals in the use of restraints.

[26] Romeo, 457 U.S. at 321–322; the Justice cites Estelle v. Gamble, *supra* note 17, to support this proposition.

[27] Santamour & West, *supra* note 1. Indeed, the point seems to be that the vast majority clearly are educable.

basic self-care skills), then there must have been an earlier profound miscarriage of justice. The most elemental concepts of criminal responsibility, and certainly of competence to be tried, would seem to have been violated.

It should again be noted that, unlike mental illness, no one suggests that imprisonment may cause retardation. Clearly, already minimal skills may deteriorate and vulnerability may increase, but prison does not *cause* retardation.

Mentally retarded inmates' special claim to help is derived from their due process rights to physical safety and freedom from undue restraint. This, of course, is far from an obligation to assist the inmate in the mastery of basic social and cognitive skills as part of a systematic, individualized plan.[28] It is, indeed, a right to a non-life threatening environment and membership in a class of particularly vulnerable inmates.

Farmer v. Brennan[29] once again must make an appearance in this work. I hasten to add that *Farmer* did not invent a prisoner's right to a non-life threatening environment; it brought a modern imprimatur to an existing right. Clearly, detainees and prisoners who are retarded—and the more profound and obvious, the more clear the duty—are entitled to personal safety.

Farmer, of course, reaffirmed the requirement of deliberate indifference for liability while defining that mental state as actual knowledge of a high degree of risk. Prison officials may be found deliberately indifferent if they fail to isolate, or otherwise protect, prisoners who are obvious victims. *Farmer* itself involved a feminine-appearing transsexual who was raped.

Other cases claiming personal safety have involved a sex offender placed in an unsupervised holding cell,[30] the transfer of a mentally ill inmate to an overcrowded general population with no mental health care,[31] a failure to safeguard a known informant,[32] and a legally blind inmate placed in the general population.[33]

[b] Eighth Amendment Habilitation Right

The *Ruiz v. Estelle*[34] decision from Texas early on set the tone for judicial consideration of the mentally retarded inmate. Judge Justice found that between 10 and 15 percent of TDC inmates were retarded and that they were distributed throughout the TDC system. The Judge echoed Santamour and West concerning the retarded inmates' special problems and added that:

---

[28] Appendix A, containing the survey of various standards in this area, reveals that the mentally ill and the retarded offender are, more often than not, joined for purposes of establishing a right to appropriate care. *See* Clark v. California, 123 F. 3d 1267 (7th Cir. 1997), allowing a suit brought under the Americans With Disabilities Act on behalf of the inmates suffering from developmental disabilities to go forward in face of the state's claims of immunity.

[29] 511 U.S. 825 (1994). One may still argue that detainees are entitled to greater safety than convicted prisoners.

[30] Swoffard v. Mandrell, 969 F.2d 547, 549 (7th Cir. 1992).

[31] Cortes-Quinones v. Jiminez-Nettleship, 842 F.2d 556, 559–560 (1st Cir. 1988).

[32] Gullatte v. Potts, 654 F.2d 1007, 1013 (5th Cir. 1981).

[33] Harris v. O'Grady, 803 F. Supp. 1361, 1366 (N.D. Ill. 1992). There are a host of decisions involving the failure to separate known aggressive inmates from potential victims.

[34] 503 F. Supp. 1265 (S.D. Tex. 1980), *aff'd in part*, 679 F.2d 1115 (5th Cir. 1982), *cert. denied*, 460 U.S. 1042 (1983).

1. They are abnormally prone to injury, [sic] many of which are job-related.
2. They are decidedly disadvantaged when appearing before a Disciplinary Committee and this raises basic problems of fairness and the special need for assistance.[35]

Judge Justice did not hesitate to find a constitutional basis for the lack of special care afforded mentally retarded inmates. He stated:

The evidence shows that TDC has failed to meet its constitutional obligation to provide minimally adequate conditions of incarceration for mentally retarded inmates. Their special habilitation needs are practically unrecognized by TDC officials, and they are subjected to a living environment which they cannot understand and in which they cannot succeed. Moreover, prison officials have done little to protect these mentally handicapped inmates from the type of abuse and physical harm which they suffer at the hands of other prisoners. Their conduct is judged by the same standards applicable to prisoners with average mental ability, and they are frequently punished for actions, the import of which they do not comprehend.[36]

The Judge's constitutional rationale is located in the Eighth Amendment and his view that:

Those whose needs are more specialized or complex than the average inmate's may not be denied their eighth amendment rights to adequate living conditions, protections from physical harm, and medical treatment by being forced to fit into a mold constructed for persons of average intelligence and physical mobility.[37]

Obviously, there is some confusion and inconsistency here. It is one thing to find living conditions constituting cruel and unusual punishment based, in part, on the special characteristics of the confined individuals. Indeed, that conclusion was important earlier in this work in analyzing the use of isolation cells for the mentally disordered inmate.[38] It is another thing, however, to find that an absence of habilitation efforts is a constitutional deficiency and then order programs that are designed to do more than safeguard personal security.

The *desirability* of habilitation is not the issue here. The issue is whether *Ruiz* requires habilitation as a primary constitutional right—and thus exceeds the *Romeo* mandate for the civilly confined—or whether a lack of habilitation efforts and programs, along with other conditions contributing to endangerment, culminates in an Eighth Amendment violation.

In fashioning relief, the objective of ameliorating dangerous conditions inherent-

---

[35] Ruiz, 503 F. Supp. at 1344.
[36] Ruiz, 503 F. Supp. at 1346.
[37] Ruiz, 503 F. Supp. at 1345.
[38] *See* Chapter 11 on the effects of isolation on certain suicide risks.

ly requires fewer resources and less effort than the objective of affirmative advancement for the impaired inmate. Implementation of *Ruiz* by the TDC now includes special education programs, occupational therapy, and coping skills development. Inmates are now uniformly tested and screened, and if found retarded are placed in an Intellectually Impaired Offender Program and housed in special units.[39] Thus, while Judge Justice's constitutional analysis may be less than clear, perhaps flawed, the implementation phase in Texas appears to encompass elements of both habilitation and personal security.

[c] Classifying and Recordkeeping Obligations

In *Kendrick v. Bland,*[40] another federal district court ordered the creation of a basic training course for correctional officers designed to develop skills in identifying and reacting to mentally ill and mentally retarded inmates. That type of an order, whether designed to prevent harm or identify habilitation needs, has much to commend it. Indeed, it may profitably be viewed as an aspect of the more encompassing task of classification. The need for a regular and adequate system of classification is not limited to possible mental or physical illnesses.

A retarded inmate who may be particularly vulnerable, or violent, should be identified and dealt with. This may be limited to protective measures or, if legally mandated, may include habilitation efforts. In either case there is a legal duty at least to use standard testing procedures.

The creation and maintenance of adequate records is also a vital component of the basic right to treatment.[41] Records are necessary to preserve test data, diagnosis, treatment and rehabilitation plans and activities, and to preserve the continuity of such efforts. Adequate records for the retarded inmate, whether to ensure habilitation or safety, would seem to be as legally and professionally desirable as for the mentally ill inmate.

The mentally retarded inmate is more than occasionally recognized by courts as having special needs and requiring special attention.[42] Judicial concerns have centered on classification systems—on adequate testing—to identify these vulnerable inmates.[43] Programs or habilitation activities are more likely to be mandated as part of an overall order to improve prison conditions in general, and medical care in particular.

---

[39] Interview with James Shaddock, former Chief Psychologist, Texas Dept. of Corrections, Jan. 9, 1984. The Texas program, driven by *Ruiz,* is now listed as a model in Programming for the Mentally Retarded and Learning Disabled Inmates: A Guide for Correctional Administrators (National Institute of Corrections, 1989).

[40] 541 F. Supp. 21, 48 (W.D. Ken. 1981).

[41] *See* Chapter 10.

[42] Newman v. Alabama, 349 F. Supp. 278, 284 (M.D. Ala. 1972), *aff'd in part,* 503 F.2d 1320 (5th Cir. 1974), *cert. denied,* 421 U.S. 948 (1975), is one of the earliest decisions to order the identification of mentally retarded inmates and require transfer from prison when necessary. *Accord,* Laaman v. Helgemoe, 437 F. Supp. 269, 328 (D.N.H. 1977).

[43] The National Commission on Correctional Health Care (NCCHC) at § 25 (1988) recommends the Weschler Adult Intelligence Scale test, or something similar, as part of the intake and screening admission process.

¶ 16.3 POLICY ALTERNATIVES

There is virtually no dissent from the proposition that many mentally retarded inmates are part of a highly vulnerable population. Their vulnerability ranges from sexual and economic exploitation to being co-opted as drug runners. The major debate today is whether to mainstream such inmates or place them in Special Needs Units, at least for housing, with programming available off the living unit.

A New York State study notes two special units in the New York penal system that offer a measure of protection but do not provide habilitation or rehabilitation programs. A concern for minimal programs, stigma, and impairment of parole opportunities led the Commission to state:

> These factors lead the Commission to be wary of recommending more aggressive efforts to identify inmates who may be developmentally disabled and to develop programs for separate treatment of these inmates. We believe that the professional staffing and resources of the existing special units need to be augmented to enable them to provide adequate habilitative and rehabilitative programs to meet the needs of developmentally disabled inmates. We also support plans for modest expansion of this program of special units to meet the needs of additional developmentally disabled inmates who may be particularly vulnerable in the general prison population. In that connection, we support the plan of the Department of Correctional Services to open a new special unit to prepare inmates with special needs for parole.[44]

¶ 16.4 CRIMINAL RESPONSIBILITY ISSUES

In concluding this topic, it seems appropriate to again shift the focus from the mentally retarded inmate to the mentally retarded accused. One must be concerned about the relatively large number of inmates believed to be mentally retarded and wonder how they came to be in prison. Are mentally retarded offenders entitled to special exemption or at least special consideration on the threshold issue of criminal responsibility? Professor Richard C. Allen points out:

> Historically, society has pursued three alternative courses with the mentally retarded offender: we have ignored his limitations and special needs; or we have sought to tailor traditional criminal law processes to fit them; we have grouped him with psychopaths, sociopaths, and sex deviates in a kind of conventicle of the outcast and hopeless.[45]

Allen's proposal suggests the creation of an Exceptional Offenders' Court, modeled on the Juvenile Court, and he appears to have proposed it without the caution dic-

---

[44] New York State Study, *supra* note 8.

[45] Richard Allen, *Reaction Comment to S. Fox, The Criminal Reform Movement*, in THE MENTALLY RETARDED CITIZEN AND THE LAW, *supra* note 15, pp. 627, 645.

tated by the contemporary state of juvenile justice or defective delinquency-type laws. The point, however, is that now the mentally retarded are not given special doctrinal attention in the criminal law.[46] And it is not clear that the retarded, especially the marginally retarded, would profit from such doctrinal attention. The risk, of course, is to further stereotype, discriminate, and remove incentives for the exercise of individual responsibility.

Persons who are severely retarded are not proper subjects for prosecution or imprisonment, nor are they found in great numbers in prison.[47] Our concern is with the disproportionately high percentage of moderately retarded inmates who are processed through the criminal justice system and find themselves in prison and in need of protection. Systems that go further (e.g., South Carolina's) do so without the whip of judicial mandates and obviously there is nothing wrong with that.

As a matter of law, sensible practice, and common decency, mentally retarded inmates are people who require special care and attention.

---

[46] Jackson v. Indiana, 406 U.S. 715 (1972), deals with important questions of competency to be tried and concerns itself with the plight of a severely disabled accused. Competence—the ability to aid counsel and grasp the essence of the charges—is not limited in focus to mental retardation.

[47] Interviews and informal discussion with numerous clinicians affiliated with dozens of prison systems confirms this view. Inmates with I.Q.s ranging from the 50s on up represent the great majority of the retarded or learning disabled persons found in prisons.

Chapter 17

Transfer of Inmates for Treatment

¶ 17.1 PROCEDURAL CLAIMS—EARLIER CASES

The choice of where to provide an inmate with needed treatment, like the selection of a preferred treatment provider or modality, raises few if any legal issues. Policy questions, yes! Robert Levinson once described the prison system as the system that cannot say no[1] and the individual with a "mixed" diagnosis as the persona non grata in all settings. Prisoner A, he writes, may be "crazy" in prison and "sane" in the state hospital. A mental health facility in the Department of Mental Hygiene may have regulations or priorities that make it nearly impossible to accept an inmate for treatment.[2] To this we might add that studies disclose that civil hospitalization staff are under immediate and persistent pressure to discharge civilly committed patients.[3] Prison officials are not so fortunate with regard to discharge.

The procedure for moving an inmate from place to place for needed treatment

---

[1] Robert Levinson, *The System That Cannot Say No*, AM. PSYCHOLOGIST 811 (July 1984).

[2] Id.

[3] T. Howard Stone, *Therapeutic Implications of Incarceration for Persons with Severe Mental Disorders: Searching for Rational Health Policy*, 24 AM. J. CRIM. L. 283, 294 (1997), citing to studies on point.

may create some significant legal issues. In 1980 the Supreme Court decided *Vitek v. Jones*,[4] which now governs the procedural requirements that apply to transfers from prisons to mental treatment facilities. Not surprisingly, *Vitek* left open a good many questions while answering others. In order to grasp the significance and the ambiguity of *Vitek,* it will be useful to briefly discuss earlier decisions on transfer and related issues and then return to *Vitek* itself.

[1] Right to Equal Protection

The 1966 case of *Baxstrom v. Herold*[5] is the earliest Supreme Court decision most related to *Vitek,* yet it is easily distinguishable. Baxstrom was convicted of assault and sentenced to a New York prison. When he was nearing the end of his relatively short sentence, a petition was filed in the local Surrogate's Court stating that Baxstrom's prison term was about to expire but that he remained mentally ill, and requesting civil commitment to Dannemora State Hospital.

Baxstrom appeared alone in the judge's chambers and was allowed to ask a few questions before his commitment. The Supreme Court determined that Baxstrom was denied equal protection under the law (1) in not having the opportunity for jury review that is available to all other civil committees in New York, and (2) as a separate violation, in being confined in a facility housing the "dangerously mentally ill" without the judicial determination of dangerousness required for all others so confined.[6]

It should be emphasized that since this decision was based on equal protection grounds, its analytical basis is strictly comparative and, thus, the case does not create independent rights. That is, *Baxstrom* did *not* decide there is a constitutional right to a determination of dangerousness. It did hold that where a jurisdiction elects to provide the right to a jury in a civil commitment proceeding, and designates a facility for housing those found to be dangerous, then whether a person is nearing the end of a prison term is not relevant to the availability of a jury trial or a finding of dangerousness. The state cannot base post-sentence confinement on a person's criminal sentence. Chief Justice Warren wrote:

> Where the State has provided for a judicial proceeding to determine the dangerous propensities of all others civilly committed to an institution of the Department of Correction, it may not deny this right to a person . . . solely on the ground that he was nearing the expiration of a prison term. . . . A person with a past criminal record is presently entitled to a hearing on the question whether he is dangerously mentally ill so long as he is not in prison at the time civil commitment proceedings are instituted. Given this distinction, all semblance of rationality of the classification, purportedly based upon criminal propensities, disappears.[7]

---

[4] 445 U.S. 480 (1980).

[5] 383 U.S. 107 (1966).

[6] Baxstrom, 383 U.S. at 110.

[7] Baxstrom, 383 U.S. at 114–115. For interesting follow-up data on this decision, *see* Hunt & Wiley, *Operation Baxstrom After One Year*, 129 AM. J. PSYCHIATRY 974 (1968); and Steadman & Keveles, *The*

In a somewhat generous reading of *Baxstrom,* the Second Circuit Court of Appeals extended the decision to cover those New York prison inmates being transferred to a mental hospital during the term of their criminal sentence.[8] A distinguishing feature of *Baxstrom* is that it turned on the state acquiring a basis other than the criminal sentence for the post-sentence confinement of the person.

Schuster, shortly after charging prison officials with corruption, was transferred to a mental hospital where he remained for many years. Consistent with the de facto policy in many jurisdictions, he was never seriously reviewed for parole during his confinement in a corrections-administered mental health facility.[9]

The Second Circuit concluded that prison inmates had an equal protection right to be committed by substantially the same procedures as those available to free persons subjected to an involuntary commitment proceeding. Judge Kaufman's analysis tracked *Baxstrom* in determining that the procedures used for commitment are not dependent on the place where the alleged mentally ill persons happen to be. According to Judge Kaufman, being on the street or in prison is not determinative of procedural fairness in civil commitment. That is *not* the approach, however, taken more recently, and more authoritatively, by the Court in *Vitek.*

[2] Prison-to-Prison Transfers: No Right to Due Process

Baxstrom involved a prison-to-mental hospital transfer, whereas *Meachum v. Fano,*[10] a 1976 decision, involved an inter-prison transfer. *Meachum,* however, provides an important part of the overall procedural framework needed to fully grasp *Vitek,* especially some of its open questions. In *Meachum,* the question before the Court was straightforward: does the Due Process Clause of the Fourteenth Amendment entitle a state prisoner to a hearing when transferred to a prison with less favorable conditions, without a state law conditioning such a transfer on proof of misconduct or the occurrence of other events?[11]

The Court found that a prisoner had no right to any form of due process, and in so finding surprised a number of lawyers. Why? Just two years earlier, the Supreme Court determined that where a state prisoner was faced with disciplinary charges that might result in a loss of good-time credits or in a form of solitary confinement, the prisoner was entitled to (1) advance, written notice prior to a hearing before an impartial tribunal, and (2) a written statement of reasons for any adverse decision.[12]

Community Adjustment and Criminal Activity of the Baxstrom Patients: 1966–970, 129 AM. J. PSYCHIATRY 304 (1972).

[8] United States *ex rel.* Schuster v. Herold, 410 F.2d 1071 (2d Cir. 1969), *cert. denied,* 396 U.S. 847 (1969).

[9] United States *ex rel.* Schuster v. Herold, 410 F.2d at 1081.

[10] 427 U.S. 215 (1976).

[11] Meachum, 427 U.S. at 216. *Meachum* would be decided the same way today, although the liberty interest implications of part of the analysis are no longer viable in light of Sandin v. Conner, 515 U.S. 472 (1995).

[12] Wolff v. McDonnell, 418 U.S. 539 (1974). The reach of *Wolff* has now been seriously limited by Sandin v. Connor, *supra* note 11. *See* discussion in Chapter 3, ¶ 3.7[1]–3.7[3], making it clear that loss of good time credits still requires a *Wolff* hearing.

The pre-*Meachum* thinking was that a prison-to-prison transfer, and especially a punitive transfer, which rather clearly was the situation in *Meachum,* was not functionally distinct from a general population-to-isolation, intra-prison transfer. Indeed, if anything, moving from a minimum or medium security prison and being some distance from family and friends, losing a job, and facing strange, new and possibly threatening fellow inmates often is a more grievous loss than certain forms of disciplinary confinement.[13]

No matter. The Court found no constitutionally protected interest residing either in state law or the Constitution itself. We learned that not even grievous losses will invariably invoke the safeguards of procedural due process.

¶ 17.2 CREATION OF LIBERTY INTEREST—*VITEK*

Returning to *Vitek,* the question asked at the outset was: does the Nebraska statute create a liberty interest that the state might later withdraw or is the Constitution itself the source of any such liberty interests? The statute at issue in *Vitek* reads as follows:

> When a physician designated by the Director of Correctional Services finds that a person committed to the department suffers from a physical disease or defect, or when a physician or psychologist designated by the director finds that a person committed to the department suffers from a mental disease or defect, the chief executive officer may order such person to be segregated from other persons in the facility. If the physician or psychologist is of the opinion that the person cannot be given proper treatment in that facility, the director may arrange for his transfer or examination, study, and treatment at any medical-correctional facility, or to another institution in the Department of Public Institutions where proper treatment is available. A person who is so transferred shall remain subject to the jurisdiction and custody of the Department of Correctional Services and shall be returned to the department when, prior to the expiration of his sentence, treatment in such facility is no longer necessary.[14]

Justice White agreed with the lower courts that this statute created a liberty interest.

> Section 83-180(1) provides that if a designated physician finds that a prisoner "suffers from a mental disease or defect" in prison, the Director of Correctional Services may transfer a prisoner to a mental hospital. The District Court also found that in practice prisoners are transferred to a mental hospital only if it is determined that they suffer from a mental disease or defect that cannot adequately be treated within the penal complex. This

---

[13] In New York State, *Wolff* procedures have applied to "keep-lock," which is simply being confined in your own cell and temporarily taken out of the normal prison routine. *See* Powell v. Ward, 487 F. Supp. 917 (S.D.N.Y. 1980), *cert. denied*, 454 U.S. 832 (1981).

[14] Neb. Rev. Stat. § 83-180(1).

"objective expectation, firmly fixed in state law and official Penal Complex practice," that a prisoner would not be transferred unless he suffered from a mental disease or defect that would not be adequately treated in the prison, gave Jones a liberty interest that entitled him to the benefits of appropriate procedures in connection with determining the conditions that warranted his transfer to a mental hospital. Under our cases, this conclusion of the District Court is unexceptional.[15]

[1] Liberty Interest Rationale

This dated analysis would not be encountered in the new due process world of *Sandin v. Connor*.[16] Objective expectations are not within the new due process calculus, only "atypical and significant hardships." *Vitek* itself, however, survives because the Court found essentially that it also addressed a qualitative change in confinement ruling:

> None of our decisions holds that conviction for a crime entitles a State not only to confine the convicted person but also to determine that he has a mental illness and to subject him involuntarily to institutional care in a mental hospital. Such consequences visited on the prisoner are qualitatively different from the punishment characteristically suffered by a person convicted of crime. Our cases recognize as much and reflect an understanding that involuntary commitment to a mental hospital is not within the range of conditions of confinement to which a prison sentence subjects an individual . . ..
>
> A criminal conviction and sentence of imprisonment extinguish an individual's right to freedom from confinement for the term of his sentence, but they do not authorize the State to classify him as mentally ill and to subject him to involuntary psychiatric treatment without affording him additional due process protections.
>
> In light of the findings made by the District Court, Jones' involuntary transfer to the Lincoln Regional Center pursuant to Sec. 83-180, for the purpose of psychiatric treatment, implicated a liberty interest protected by the Due Process Clause. Many of the restrictions on the prisoner's freedom of action at the Lincoln Regional Center by themselves might not constitute the deprivation of a liberty interest retained by a prisoner. . . . But here, the stigmatizing consequence of a transfer to a mental hospital for involuntary psychiatric treatment, coupled with the subjection of the prisoner to mandatory behavior modification as a treatment for mental illness, constitute the kind of deprivation of liberty that requires procedural protections.[17]

Thus, the combination of stigma (obviously not welcomed by mental health advocates), a qualitative alteration in the conditions of confinement, and being subjected

---

[15] Vitek, *supra* note 4, 445 U.S. at 489–490.

[16] *Supra* note 11.

[17] Vitek, *supra* note 4, 445 U.S. at 493–494.

to mandatory behavior modification programs[18] combined to create a liberty interest traceable to the Fourteenth Amendment Due Process Clause. There was no need to rely on the now discarded state-created liberty interest analysis because the interest at stake was deemed so vital as to have an independent source in the Constitution itself. This, of course, is not to say that a prison-to-mental hospital transfer cannot be done, only that certain minimal procedural safeguards apply.

[2] Mandated Procedural Safeguards

Vitek requires the following minimal procedural safeguards where there is a contested prison-to-mental hospital transfer:

1. Written notice to the prisoner that a transfer to a mental hospital is being considered.

2. A hearing, sufficiently after the notice to permit the prisoner to prepare, at which disclosure to the prisoner is made of the evidence being relied on for the transfer and where the prisoner receives an opportunity to be heard in person and to present documentary evidence.

3. An opportunity at the hearing for the defense to present testimony of witnesses and to confront and cross-examine witnesses called by the state, except upon a finding, not arbitrarily made, of good cause for not permitting such presentation, confrontation, or cross-examination.

4. An independent decision-maker ("This person need not come from outside the prison or hospital administration.").

5. A written statement by the decision-maker as to the evidence relied on and the reasons for transferring the inmate.

6. Availability of "qualified and independent assistance" furnished by the State, if the inmate is financially unable to furnish his own. (No right to legal counsel, however).

7. Effective and timely notice of all the foregoing rights.[19]

Unlike the Second Circuit's analysis in *Schuster*, the Supreme Court did not rely on equal protection and it did not procedurally equate prisoner transfers with free person commitments. Professor Michael Churgin correctly points out that the Court opted for a parole-revocation model, requiring far less than a "full blown" trial but considerably more than the *Wolff* disciplinary hearing model.[20]

---

[18] The behavior modification referred to in *Vitek* apparently was Thorazine; *see Vitek v. Jones*, Transcript of Oral Argument at 29 (April 24, 1978).

[19] For elaboration, *see* Michael Churgin, *The Transfer of Inmates to Mental Health Facilities*, in MENTALLY DISORDERED OFFENDERS (J. Monahan & H. Steadman, eds. 1983), pp. 218–219. *See* James Ellis & Ruth Luckasson, *Mentally Retarded Defendants*, 53 GEO. WASH. L. REV. 414, 483–484 (1985), for a discussion of the law and policy of transferring the mentally retarded inmate.

[20] Churgin, *supra* note 19, at 221.

Churgin correctly considers an administrative hearing procedure constitutionally permissible, but he believes it may be wiser to rely on the regular civil commitment processes because often there is no decision-making body resembling a parole board available to prisoners. This approach clearly makes available the entire range of statutory commitments, from emergency to voluntary, from shorter to longer terms.[21] On the other hand, *Vitek* does not preclude emergency or voluntary admissions and the duration of commitment is discretionary within the maximum term of the sentence.

The American Bar Association Standards create yet another option entitled "court ordered transfer." If an inmate seeks admission but the mental health or retardation facility rejects the application, then a petition for a court-ordered transfer may be filed, with the adverse parties being the inmate and institution of choice.[22]

Vitek proves interesting in its unwillingness to place a societal interest on the balancing scales and also in its unwillingness to abjectly defer to professional judgment. Since the issue is not liberty *vel non* but the choice of a place of confinement, the Court properly did not address community safety or fear issues.

[3] The Problem of Emergency Transfers

It would have been very easy in *Vitek* for the Court to succumb to claims of professional judgment. The argument would be that mental health care in prisons is a very scarce and expensive commodity. This strongly suggests that a self-regulating mechanism is in place. Further, inmates rarely resist such transfers; indeed, the contrary is true. Many inmates, it can be argued, prefer the relative comfort, security, at times higher pay, and frequently better treatment available in a mental hospital. Thus, *Vitek* is simply an arm-chair libertarian's decision solving presently nonexistent problems. It is a decision, it is argued, in which we may easily trust a doctor's judgment.

In point of fact, much of the above argument actually rings true. As I also state about forced medication,[23] while the Court's protective decision ought not to be denegrated, it simply does not strike at a presently significant problem. In my experience, there are far more problems involved (1) in gaining timely admission to a hospital-type facility than in protecting resisting inmates; (2) in retaining the inmate-patient for a sufficient time for treatment to take hold; and (3) in identifying the manipulators who pursue the secondary gains available in being hospitalized. It is fair rebuttal to argue that the existence and acceptance of *Vitek*—and it is widely known and observed in the corrections community—is the reason there are few, if any, issues about inappropriate or punitive hospitalizations. That, indeed, also may be accurate.

In many jurisdictions, an emergency commitment (or more accurately admission) procedure is consistently used to admit inmates to a psychiatric hospital. This sidesteps any *Vitek* procedure and, in states like New York, any pre-admission, judicial hearing. When a hearing is subsequently held it is consistently in front of the same

---

[21] In New York State, the most seriously ill inmates are transferred to Central New York State Psychiatric Center at Marcy. Many of those transfers are done on an emergency basis, thus obviating any pretransfer court procedures. The average stay for this population of 180 inmate-patients is about 70 days.

[22] Criminal Justice Mental Health Standards 7-10.4 (A.B.A., 1984).

[23] *See* Chapter 9 on forced medication.

local court and it is a court likely to have grown, shall we say, increasingly friendly to the state's position.

. *Vitek* plainly does not apply in an emergency situation or, as we shall see, where the transfer is for a clinical evaluation.[24] What is an emergency, and what is its duration, are important but also separable questions. While it may be relatively easy to define a clinical evaluation, there surely is a point in time at which a diagnostic procedure shades into a treatment intervention, thereby raising *Vitek* issues.

Hafemeister and Petrila point out that *Vitek's* allowance of "the use of an independent decision maker without legal training has only been sporadically utilized, with the review of a transfer recommendation generally provided by the judiciary."[25] They also suggest that state courts do look closely, when they look at all.[26]

¶ 17.3 ISSUES NOT RESOLVED BY *VITEK*

Important questions concerning prison to mental hospital transfer were not answered by *Vitek*. These are:

1. Does *Vitek* apply to mental health facilities administered by corrections or is it limited to outside mental health facilities? In a multi-prison state, would *Vitek* apply to a transfer from a prison without mental health facilities to one with such facilities? Would it apply to an intra-prison transfer to a treatment unit?[27]

2. What criteria and what evidentiary standards must (or should) apply?

3. Does *Vitek* impose any durational limits short of the criminal sentence? If *Vitek* procedures equate with civil commitment procedures (and standards), then may the inmate be confined beyond the prison term?

4. May the transferred inmate be denied good time credits or consideration, if eligible, for parole?

5. What is the legal status of the transferred inmate while in the treatment facility? Is he or she a prisoner in a hospital or a patient in a hospital?

---

[24] Thomas L. Hafemeister & John Petrila, in *Treating the Mentally Disordered Offender; Society's Uncertain, Conflicted, and Changing Views*, 21 FLA. ST. U.L. REV. 731, 829 (1994), worry that emergency procedures relying on a showing of imminent danger accommodate needless deterioration. They argue for more timely and appropriate interventions. With a sympathetic judge, many things are possible, including a flexible opinion as to "imminent danger" and the comfort of knowing a challenge to admission will be rare, indeed.

[25] Hafemeister, *supra* note 24, at 826.

[26] The authors cite appropriately In re Foster, 426 N.W. 2d 374 (Iowa 1988) (initial review of transfer decision under Iowa state law provided by a "judicial hospitalization referee"—which is a licensed attorney appointed by the courts—a judge, or a magistrate). This review is the same as that used for reviewing applications for involuntary hospitalization in general; *see* Iowa Code Ann. § 229.21 (West 1985). They also cite the tough criteria in In re Moll, 347 N.W.2d 67, 70 (Minn. Ct. App. 1984) ("Under the commitment statute, it is the trial court, not a medical expert, that must determine whether a person is mentally ill."); and Harmon v. McNutt, 587 P.2d 537 (Wash. 1978) (judicial hearing mandated prior to transfer in nonemergency).

[27] *See* Okumoto v. Lattin, 649 F. Supp. 55 (D. Nev. 1986), for a discussion but no clear resolution on this matter. The court did not evaluate the characteristics of a prison mental health unit.

These issues are discussed in the paragraphs that follow.

[1] Facilities Encompassed

The Court in *Vitek* provided no clear answer on precisely what types of facilities are covered, although the opinion makes numerous references to a *mental hospital.* However, reading *Vitek* as limited to mental-health hospitals seems inconsistent with the Court's rationale and would have little actual impact.[28] The Court's concern in *Vitek* was with involuntary psychiatric care and the compounding effect of adding the label "mental illness" to that of "convict." Where such treatment is attempted and which agency is responsible for the facility or service seem irrelevant.

The results of a major research project led the authors to conclude "that if *Vitek* is not applied to prison-operated mental health facilities, its impact will be severely limited."[29] Conducting a study of psychiatric transfers in six states, the authors discovered that five of the six states transferred nearly all (86 percent) of their mentally disordered inmates to mental health facilities within corrections, that three of these states had changed to this pattern since 1978, and that the mental health facilities in corrections were not drastically different from their mental-health-operated counterparts.[30] Thus, *Vitek* should be read as applicable to prison-to-mental hospital transfers as well as prison-to-prison hospital transfers.

A very interesting decision involving the North Carolina prison system dealt with this and other related questions. In *Baugh v. Woodard,*[31] the court began its analysis of the problem, stating: "[W]e do not distinguish, for the purpose of compliance with *Vitek,* inpatient mental treatment hospital facilities whether operated by the prison system, as in the case here, or by another state agency as in *Vitek.*"[32]

The basic issue for decision in *Baugh* involved the timing and the place of the hearing required by *Vitek.* Putting to one side emergency transfers, the reviewing court disagreed with the district court and held that due process does not require a hearing on the propriety of an inmate's involuntary mental health transfer *prior* to the inmate's physical transfer from the unit where he is currently housed. As long as the requisite hearing is held promptly after the physical transfer and before admission and start of treatment, then due process is satisfied.[33]

Very plainly, the court's purpose in this decision was not to impede either emergency transfer for short-term care of the acutely ill or transfer for diagnostic or observational purposes. *Baugh* seems to be a workable solution to these problems and fits comfortably within the letter and spirit of *Vitek.*

Suppose that an inmate is serving time in a prison that has what in New York is called a satellite unit, or in Ohio is called a residential treatment unit: a mental health unit used for inpatient type services, diagnostic procedures, and short-term, acute

---

[28] *See* Churgin, *supra* note 16, at 226.

[29] Eliot Hartstone, et al., Vitek *and Beyond: The Empirical Context of Prison-to-Hospital Transfers,* 45 LAW & CONTEMP. PROBS. 125, 130 (1982).

[30] Hartstone, et al., *supra* note 29, at 130–131.

[31] 808 F.2d 333 (4th Cir. 1987).

[32] Baugh, 808 F.2d at 335 n.2.

[33] Baugh, 808 F.2d at 336–337.

care. Does transfer to such a unit trigger a *Vitek* problem? Is this more like an administrative transfer, which may be virtually free of procedural demands?[34] The answer is not very clear.

The critical factors appear to be the probability of stigma, a drastic change in confinement,[35] and enforced treatment. On balance, *Vitek* seems applicable where the admission is not diagnostic and treatment of the acute case exceeds a brief (e.g., 10-day) stay. While it is difficult to read *Vitek* any other way, actual practice, and perhaps optional policy, points in another direction. Movement into and out of this nonhospital setting, albeit with residential treatment beds, tends to follow the example of gaining access to the prison's infirmary: that is, it is based strictly on clinical judgment.

To be more specific, the units referred to are not primarily for diagnosis; they are for treatment. A diagnosis of mental illness likely will precede, indeed be prerequisite to admission; the treatment of choice likely will be psychotropic medication; and the admission may be from any institution in the system, including the facility.[36] Inmates confined there likely will move through a levels system with entry and intermediate levels highly restrictive. Depending on the system, involuntary medication may or may not take place on the unit.[37]

In *Okumoto v. Latlin*,[38] a Nevada prisoner was transferred from one prison to another prison's psychiatric unit. The complaining inmate relied on *Vitek* in his legal action concerning lack of due process. While denying the plaintiff's motion for summary judgment, the court stated that at the time he had not shown enough to render *Vitek* applicable.[39] The judge also stated: "The plaintiff has not shown that the move to unit four rendered his treatment outside the range of conditions of confinement to which a prison sentence subjects an individual."[40] This obviously was not a *Vitek* issue; the questions were whether the inmate had been labeled mentally ill and was subject to the possibility of "behavior modification."[41]

The point ultimately is that *Vitek's* rationale plainly applies in these intermediate-type care facilities. Is it applied? Not in my experience. Is the practice under legal siege? Not in my experience. Should it be? I will leave that for others, indicating only that I would not be the lawyer bringing such a challenge.

[2] Criteria for Transfer

What criteria for transfer and evidentiary standards apply to a *Vitek* transfer? This is another question not resolved by *Vitek*. Where an equal protection analogue is

---

[34] *See* Meachum v. Fano, *supra* note 10.

[35] Satellite units in New York often have very secure cells, and inmates have been confined in such isolation and security for over three months. Ohio inmates may actually serve their entire prison term in a residential treatment unit, although shorter terms are the norm.

[36] *See* Appendix D for Ohio's procedure on point, along with a description of the level system used in the residential treatment unit.

[37] Ohio now permits an involuntary order obtained at the hospital to follow the inmate to such a unit, and it is beginning to experiment with obtaining original orders for use on the unit.

[38] Okumoto, *supra* note 27.

[39] Okumoto, *supra* note 27, 649 F. Supp. at 58.

[40] Id.

[41] In Witzke v. Johnson, 656 F. Supp. 294 (W.D. Mich. 987), the court held *Vitek* applicable where a prisoner was transferred to a mental hospital despite his not yet having been subjected to unwanted treatment.

employed and inmates are dealt with like any one else during confinement, the answer is clear—the criteria and procedures are the same. This is true, for example, as a result of legislation in New York State.[42]

In light of *Vitek's* silence on criteria, analysis should begin with the already impaired legal status of the inmate. The choice here is not liberty versus confinement. Since liberty already has been taken, the fundamental questions are the nature and objectives of confinement. Arguments in support of a rigorous dangerousness standard for civil commitment lack the same force when applied in the prison context. Some courts find that the traditional "need of care and treatment" standard is unconstitutionally overbroad and vague in light of *O'Connor v. Donaldson*.[43] On the other hand, Professor Churgin argues:

> Once a proper procedure is utilized and the individual inmate is found to be both mentally ill and in need of some treatment, any other requirement might be superfluous. The Supreme Court hinted as much in *Vitek* by repeated references to the determination required by the Nebraska statute, a finding of mental illness and a benefit in being transferred to the mental health facility.[44]

The Court also did not address the burden of proof required in a *Vitek*-mandated hearing. In this situation the primary concern is the risk-of-error problem. *Addington v. Texas*[45] determined that civil commitment proceedings required the state to prove commitability by proof that is at least clear and convincing. On the other hand, the Court deferred to medical judgment and a presumed identity of interest when parents sought to commit their children.[46]

The handiest analogue here appears to be the *Addington* standard of "clear and convincing." The Court's basic premise in *Addington* is the individual interest in avoiding arbitrary classifications as mentally ill. The risk of error in an authentic *Vitek* situation appears sufficiently substantial to warrant *Addington's* evidentiary safeguards against error.[47]

[3] Durational Limits

Vitek rather clearly imposes no durational limits on confinement of the transferred inmate. Statutes also are of little assistance here. Thus, how long an inmate remains in

---

[42] *See* N.Y. Correct. Law § 402 (1) (McKinney Supp. 1983–1984).

[43] 422 U.S. 563 (1975). *See, e.g.,* Commonwealth ex rel. Finken v. Roop, 339 A.2d 764 (1975), *cert. denied*, 424 U.S. 960 (9176). In Kolender v. Lawson, 461 U.S. 352, 357 (1983), Justice O'Conner indicated that the vagueness doctrine focuses on arbitrary enforcement rather than on notice to the persons arguably affected. This approach, of course, strengthens vagueness claims in this area.

[44] Churgin, *supra* note 19, at 228. This clearly seems correct. Another author argues that the state *should* show dangerousness. Gottlieb, Vitek v. Jones: *Transfer of Prisoners to Mental Institutions*, 8 AM. J. L. & MED. 175, 206 (1982).

[45] 441 U.S. 418 (1979).

[46] Parham v. J.R., 442 U.S. 584 (1979). The Court also found that social welfare agencies may be presumed to act in the best interests of their wards when they move for admission to a psychiatric hospital.

[47] Addington, *supra* note 45. In Jones v. United States, 463 U.S. 354 (1983), the court refused to apply *Addington* standards to commitment following a not guilty by reason of insanity verdict. For a

a mental health facility is a question of policy or clinical judgment *as long as the confinement does not exceed the maximum term of the criminal sentence.*

If civil commitment procedures are used and the state gains authority to hold indefinitely, then in the absence of any countervailing state law, the transferee could be held beyond the term of the sentence. In New York, for example, the director of a hospital to which an inmate may be committed may apply for a new commitment at the expiration of the prison sentence.[48] The general rule, however, seems to be that the maximum duration of an inmate's hospitalization is linked to the length of the prison term.

Another durational issue that seems not to have been litigated but that arises with some regularity in practice relates to the expiration of time between the transfer/commitment hearing and the actual transfer. If the mental health facility has no bed space or simply engages in delaying tactics, then one should ask, when does the determination of mental illness and commitability become stale? Three weeks? Two months? Six months? There is no clear answer, but the principles that apply seem clear:

1. The determination of a present condition and treatment need that is not inherently stable—such as mental illness—does have inherent limits.

2. The longer the delay between the determination and the requisite action—transfer and care—the more dubious the continued validity of the earlier determination.

[4] Transfers for Evaluation

The reported decisions consistently hold that a prison-to-mental hospital transfer for psychiatric evaluation is not within the compass of *Vitek. Trapnell v. Ralston*[49] is one of the clearest cases to support the proposition. In *Trapnell,* the federal prisoner was transferred from Leavenworth to the Medical Center in Springfield. The inmate refused to allow any examination or any proferred treatment. Indeed, he was returned to prison within two days.[50]

Reiterating a position taken in another case, but rendered by a different panel, the court stated: "*Vitek* addresses indefinite commitment and not a transfer for medical or psychological evaluation."[51] Such a temporary transfer places no more of an imposition on a prisoner than does a transfer for administrative reasons.[52]

---

critical review of *Addington, see* DAVID WEXLER, MENTAL HEALTH LAW: MAJOR ISSUES (1981), pp. 59–68. In State v. Harris, 463 N.W. 2d 829 (Neb. 1990), the court dealt with a post-conviction, mentally disordered sex offender proceeding on the question of the requisite procedure, including burden of proof, and found *Vitek* an apt analogy. Recognizing *Vitek's* silence on the burden of proof, the court did accept "clear and convincing" as recommended here in the text.

[48] N.Y. Correct. Law § 404 (1) (McKinney Supp. 1983–1984).

[49] 819 F.2d 182 (8th Cir. 1987).

[50] Id.

[51] United States v. Jones, 811 F.2d 444 (9th Cir. 1987), involving statutory interpretation as well as *Vitek; see also* United States v. Horne, 955 F. Supp. 1141 (D. Minn. 1997), for a full discussion of a transfer for treatment under 18 U.S.C. § 4245, especially the evidentiary support therefore.

[52] Trapnell, *supra* note 49, 819 F.2d at 184.

[5] Good Time Credits and Parole Eligibility

With regard to good time credits and parole eligibility, the ABA Standards resolve the problems with commendable clarity:

(a) A prisoner in a mental health or mental retardation facility is entitled to earn good time credits on the same terms as offenders in adult correctional facilities.

(b) A prisoner in a mental health or mental retardation facility should be eligible for parole release consideration on the same terms as offenders in adult correctional facilities.

(c) If otherwise qualified for parole, a prisoner should not be denied parole solely because the prisoner had or is receiving treatment or habilitation in a mental health or retardation facility.

(d) If otherwise qualified for parole, a prisoner who would benefit from outpatient treatment or habilitation should not be denied parole for that reason.[53]

With few exceptions, the courts that have dealt with the good time credit issue have determined that prisoners may and do lose the opportunity to earn good time credits after a determination of mental illness ("insanity" in the older cases) and some form of hospitalization. In *Bush v. Ciccone*,[54] for example, the court dealt with federal law and determined that good time credits are suspended for prisoners found "insane" by a Board of Examiners. The federal statute reads as follows:

A board of examiners for each Federal penal and correctional institution shall examine any inmate of the institution alleged to be insane or of unsound mind or otherwise defective and report their findings and the facts on which they are based to the Attorney General.

The Attorney General, upon receiving such report, may direct the warden or superintendent or other official having custody of the prisoner to cause such prisoner to be removed to the United States hospital for defective delinquents or to any other institution authorized by law to receive insane persons charged with or convicted of offenses against the United States, to be kept until in the judgment of the superintendent of said hospital, the prisoner shall be restored to sanity or health or until the maximum sentence without reduction for good time or commutation of sentence, shall have been served.[55]

Bush relied on *Urban v. Settle*,[56] which found that a prisoner:

who has been removed to a hospital for defective delinquents under 18 U.S.C.A. Sec. 4241 is not entitled to have further good conduct accruals made

---

[53] Criminal Justice Mental Health Standards, 7-10.10 (A.B.A., 1984); *see also* 2 MENTAL DISABILITY L. REP. 669–670 (1978).

[54] 325 F. Supp. 699 (W.D. Mo. 1971).

[55] 18 U.S.C. § 4241.

[56] 298 F.2d 592 (8th Cir. 1962).

or become operative for conditional release purposes until, in the judgment of the superintendent of the hospital, he has become restored to sanity or health. If, in the judgment of the superintendent, he does not become so restored, he is entitled to be kept in the hospital, under Sec. 4241, until his maximum sentence is served. He cannot, in this situation, ordinarily seek his release from the hospital until one or the other of these two contingencies has occurred.

Within the power of Congress to control the care and treatment of all federal prisoners, it necessarily may set up such appropriate administrative machinery for dealing with this problem as it sees fit, without leaving the way open to a prisoner to have the judgment of the officials to whom that responsibility has been entrusted subjected to judicial examination, except as some right otherwise of a prisoner may be violated.[57]

Sawyer v. Sigler[58] is an important case that runs contrary to most other decisions. Nebraska apparently denied statutory good time credits to prisoners found to be *physically unable* to work. This was viewed as forcing prisoners to choose between constitutionally required medical care and statutory good time. The judge concluded:

I am compelled to declare that the policy of denying statutory good time to persons physically unable to perform work, when that physical inability does not result from misconduct on the part of the prisoner, is contrary to the equal protection clause of the Fourteenth Amendment of the Constitution of the United States and to enjoin the enforcement of the policy to that extent.

Meritorious good time, as opposed to "statutory good time" stands on a different footing. The granting of meritorious good time is permissive under the statute, rather than mandatory. There is nothing in the evidence to indicate a deliberate or purposeful discrimination against the petitioners with respect to meritorious good time. Indeed, there is no evidence as to what the practice is in awarding meritorious good time to persons who are not physically infirm. The mandatory nature of the statute with respect to meritorious good time sets no standard, so evidence of actual practice must provide guidelines and no such evidence was here presented. The burden in that respect being upon the petitioners, I hold that they have not carried their burden of showing impermissible discrimination in the granting of meritorious good time.[59]

If we may interpolate this approach to mental disability—and it is difficult to imagine why not—then in a system where good time accrues either for good behavior or employment, an inmate undergoing mental health treatment should not be

---

[57] Urban, 298 F.2d at 593.

[58] 320 F. Supp. 690 (D. Neb. 1970), *aff'd,* 445 F.2d 818 (8th Cir. 1971).

[59] Sawyer, 320 F. Supp. at 699. *See* Moss v. Clark, 886 F.2d 686 (4th Cir. 1989), holding that a District of Columbia prisoner transferred to a federal prison due to overcrowding was entitled to earn the more favorable good time credits available under the D.C. Code. That is, the less favorable federal good time law applied, costing Moss some three years of additional confinement. This differential treatment is found to be rationally related to the legitimate governmental purpose of relieving overcrowding.

deprived of the opportunity to earn such credits.[60] However, where a state denied good time credits to defendants who first were hospitalized, found untreatable, then sentenced to prison, the Washington Supreme Court upheld the deprivation.[61] This was based on the Washington statute and a finding that equal protection was not violated despite the fact that the defendants were actually confined for a longer period of time, counting the hospital evaluation time, than others who were sent immediately to prison.

There is, of course, no right to good time credits in the sense that a state must adopt such a system of rewards and sentence reduction. However, where good time laws exist, inmates ought not to be prevented from earning credits on irrational or discriminatory grounds. That is the essence of the reasoning in *Sawyer,* which seems eminently sound in general and also as applied to mentally disordered inmates undergoing treatment.

As we know, *Bowring v. Godwin*[62] is one of the earliest decisions to clearly apply the *Estelle v. Gamble*[63] right to medical care to psychiatric and psychological treatment. In *Bowring,* a parole board denied release on parole, at least partially because of the inmate's mental condition, which was judged sufficiently impaired to make success on parole problematic. The reason for the denial then became the basis for a limited right to treatment.[64]

This encounter between mental disorder and parole resembles, but is distinguishable from, the issue of denial of parole during the course of treatment. The overt denial of parole, or a mandated hearing, is distinguishable as well from the common practice of simply denying parole to inmates in treatment.[65] In *Sites v. McKenzie,*[66] the

---

[60] It should be clear that this discussion centers on the opportunity to earn such credits and not on the problem of forfeiting credits already accrued. *See* Wolff v. McDonald, *supra* note 12; Preiser v. Rodriguez, 411 U.S. 475 (1973) (a prisoner's challenge to the loss of good time is within the core of a habeas corpus challenge); King v. Edgar, 1996 WL 705256 (N.D. Ill. 1996) (an inmate allegedly suffering with schizophrenia not improperly denied good time credits attached to participation in a prison educational program he was not eligible for). Sandin v. Conner, *supra* note 12, does not, of course, affect the right to earn or continue to earn good time credits. It does reaffirm the need for *Wolff* due process on the revocation thereof.

[61] In re Bordens, 786 P.2d 789 (Wash. 1990). *See* Murray v. Lopez, 529 A.2d 1302 (Conn. 1987), holding that where a sex offender was ordered to serve a criminal sentence in prison, Connecticut law required credit for presentence jail good time as well as prison good time credits. The time spent in the hospital was viewed as imprisonment for statutory construction purposes. California courts took yet another view, in People v. Sage, 611 P.2d 874 (Cal. 1980), finding there was no entitlement to good conduct credit for the term a sex offender was hospitalized, but there was a right to presentence credits as a detainee-felon.

[62] 551 F.2d 44 (4th Cir. 1977).

[63] 429 U.S. 97 (1976).

[64] Bowring, 551 F.2d at 46. By implication, the treatment was to be aimed at "parole readiness."

[65] Inmates undergoing mental health treatment consistently serve longer terms than their counterparts who are not so labeled or treated. *See* Frank J. Porporino & Laurence Motiuk, *The Prison Careers of Mentally Disordered Offenders,* 18 INT'L J.L. & PSYCHIATRY 29, 42 (1995); Robert Miller & Jeffrey Metzner, *Psychiatric Stigma in Correctional Facilities,* 22 BULL AM. ACAD. PSYCHIATRY L. 621, 626 (1994). Parole officials are entitled to quasi-judicial immunity from liability for actions taken in granting, denying, or revoking parole; *see* Fendler v. United States Parole Comm'n, 714 F.2d 975, 980 (9th Cir. 1985).

[66] 423 F. Supp. 1190 (N.D. W.Va. 1976).

only decision found directly on point, the court dealt with a 76-year-old inmate who had been incarcerated for 45 years either in the West Virginia Penitentiary or Weston State Hospital. Although the inmate was first eligible for parole in 1941, his first parole interview was "slightly" delayed and not granted until 1970.[67] The judge cited a West Virginia regulation, which states: "Prisoners confined in mental institutions for observation and psychiatric treatment will not be interviewed by the Parole Board until it has received a complete report from the institution showing that there has been a recovery from the mental illness or disturbance."[68]

The judge reasoned that this regulation had the effect of creating an irrebuttable presumption of dangerousness, or at least unfitness, for release into society. From there the decision confounded the problem of release from an order of civil commitment with the problem of consideration for release on parole. The ruling itself, however, was mercifully clear:

> Accordingly, to grant parole hearings to prisoners not confined in mental institutions and to deny parole consideration to the Plaintiff because he was in Weston State Hospital was unequal and unfair.
>
> Thus, it is clear that this regulation is unconstitutional because it denies prisoners in mental institutions the equal protection of the law.[69]

Presumably what the court meant was that whether this inmate was properly or improperly in a mental hospital, that alone should not be an absolute bar to parole consideration. No case law was cited for this unique holding, and no effort was made to articulate the equal protection analysis being employed. However, since there was no right to parole,[70] we may infer that the court used a form of the rational basis test[71] and compared one group of prisoners (in prison) with another group of prisoners (in a mental treatment facility).

The question that should have been articulated is whether there is a reasonable relationship between confinement in a mental hospital and parole eligibility. In effect, *Sites* found that there is not. There seems to be no barrier to a parole board taking into account an inmate's mental condition whether the inmate remains in prison or is in a treatment facility. However, an explicit bar to release based on hospitalization per se is indeed suspect in light of equal protection analysis and the result in *Sites*.[72]

[6] Rights Subsequent to Transfer

We turn now to an infrequently litigated but potentially serious question: after a prisoner has been transferred to a mental health facility, does he acquire any substan-

---

[67] Sites, 423 F. Supp. at 1992.

[68] Sites, 423 F. Supp. at 1194.

[69] Sites, 423 F. Supp. at 1194–1195.

[70] Greenholtz v. Inmates of the Neb. Penal & Correct. Complex, 442 U.S. 1 (1979).

[71] *See, e.g.,* Dandridge v. Williams, 397 U.S. 471 (1970).

[72] *See* Vance v. Holland, 355 S.E 2d 396 (W.Va. 1987), holding that the parole board abused its discretion in denying parole interviews mandated by statute because of the inmate's extensive prison disciplinary history. This, of course, is all too common with seriously mentally ill prisoners.

tive or procedural rights to resist return to prison? The great weight of the case law is that the inmate-patient acquires neither substantive nor procedural rights. It should be clear that his Eighth Amendment claims to adequate care—the deliberate indifference test—remain intact, along with a challenge to the adequacy of care available at the receiving prison. These issues are independent of transfer claims. *Burchett v. Bower*[73] appears to be the only case to the contrary.

In *Burchett*, the district court finessed the question of a federally based right to treatment by determining that Arizona state law invested this inmate-patient with a right to treatment.[74] Once the right to treatment was resolved, the court determined that as a "right" or "benefit," termination could not occur without some type of hearing before the retransfer. The court did not decide whether an administrative hearing with judicial review or only judicial review would meet constitutional standards.[75]

In *Jackson v. Fair*,[76] a state prisoner serving three consecutive life sentences for murder was in custody of the Massachusetts Department of Correction. After some time he was committed to the high security Bridgewater State Hospital, where he resisted returning to prison. Under local law all civil commitments were valid only for a year, so in a sense the issue here was a demand for retention or recommitment. The challenged transfer was purely administrative, without even notice.

Jackson raised a couple of points of interest, although a reverse-*Vitek* argument seems not to have been pushed. First, the plaintiff argued that the transfer violated a fundamental liberty interest akin to the interest created in the retention of parole status.[77] The court rejected the analogy and noted that not a single case was cited upholding a challenge to release from a psychiatric facility, and that there was no alternative source for recognizing this supposed liberty interest.[78] As suggested above, the court stated: "[T]here is no recognized right to treatment for prisoners that differs from the Eighth Amendment . . . ."[79] In effect, the claim of a right to remain in a treatment facility is treated here, and generally elsewhere, as a claim of right to the location of care, which is a consistently losing argument.

In Re Hurt[80] occupies a sort of middle ground on retransfer. A prisoner challenged his transfer from St. Elizabeth's Hospital to Lorton Correctional Complex. Although this prisoner had had a judicial hearing on retransfer, he claimed that it did not meet due process standards. Hurt's claim was that the interest at stake in such a hearing was the right to treatment, a right long recognized in the District of Columbia. The court agreed that Hurt had the right to treatment but did not agree that was the issue:

---

[73] 355 F. Supp. 1278 (D. Ariz. 1973). In Angell v. Henneberry, 607 A.2d 590 (Md. App. 1992), the court found that under the peculiarity of Maryland's Defective Delinquency Law, a prisoner had a liberty interest in remaining at Patuxent. This is a hybrid decision.

[74] Burchett, 355 F. Supp. at 1281.

[75] Burchett, 355 F. Supp. at 1282.

[76] 846 F.2d 811 (1st Cir. 1988).

[77] *See* Greenholtz v. Inmates of the Neb. Penal & Correct. Complex, *supra* note 70, holding that due process is required to revoke parole.

[78] Jackson, 846 F.2d at 816.

[79] Id.

[80] 437 A.2d 590 (D.C. Cir. 1981).

The record makes plain the fact that appellant would continue to receive treatment in the form of daily dosages of Thorazine while at the Lorton Correctional Complex, and that he would be under the care of mental health professionals at that facility. What is therefore actually at stake is only the locus of treatment.

With the question before us thus presented, we cannot accept appellant's contention that the opportunity for a hearing which he was afforded was any less than he is entitled to under the Constitution or the pertinent statute.[81]

The statutory provision relevant to returning a prisoner to the custody of the Department of Corrections reads as follows:

> When any person confined in a hospital for the mentally ill while serving sentence shall be restored to mental health within the opinion of the superintendent of the hospital, the superintendent shall certify such fact to the Director of the Department of Corrections of the District of Columbia and such certification shall be sufficient to deliver such person to such Director according to his request.[82]

Because Hurt already had been transferred and retransferred twice, the appellate court viewed the court-ordered hearing actually held as appropriate to these special circumstances and actually more than required by the Constitution or by statute. A *Vitek* hearing was deemed unnecessary in these circumstances. Specifically reserved was the question presented where a prisoner who is transferred to a mental hospital for treatment is then returned to the prison population but without further care or treatment.[83]

More typical of judicial handling of this matter is the pre-*Vitek* decision in *Cruz v. Ward*.[84] Here, New York prisoners challenged their administrative transfers from Matteawan State Hospital to prison as violative of their due process rights. Although New York provided elaborate procedures for the prison-to-hospital transfer, the court required or provided no hearing procedures on retransfer.[85]

Over the strong dissent of Judge Kaufman, the court decided that there was no indication that these were punitive transfers.[86] In rejecting the claim to due process procedures, the court suggested that for these uniquely medical judgments, to have hearings, a statement of reasons, and legal counsel might do more harm than good. It also rejected a request that guidelines be adopted and observed.[87]

---

[81] Hurt, 437 A.2d at 593.

[82] D.C. Code Ann. § 24-303(b) (1973).

[83] Hurt, *supra* note 80. *See* Bailey v. Noot, 324 N.W. 2d 164 (Minn. 1982), for a discussion of statutory authority to transfer a patient committed to a security hospital to a prison; authority was denied. *See also* State v. Fotakos, 599 A.2d 753 (Del. Super. 1991), in which a defendant was transferred from the state hospital to prison for the remainder of his prison term; the court discussed substantive propriety and simply accepted the lawfulness of the statutorily authorized administrative transfer.

[84] 558 F. 2d 658 (2d Cir. 1977), *cert. denied*, 434 U.S. 1018 (1978).

[85] Cruz, 558 F.2d at 662.

[86] Id.

[87] Id.

The dissent found that the challenged transfers often were punitive, and that the record disclosed an almost sadistic propensity to shuttle unruly inmates from Matteawan to stripped cells in the prison system.[88]

Ultimately, the substantive problem in this area is whether an inmate is receiving at least the minimal right to treatment afforded by the Constitution or, perhaps, more expansive rights provided by state law. As stated earlier, there is no cognizable right in the inmate as to the place of care, only a right to minimal care. Indeed, even where state law expresses a policy of care in the least restrictive environment, this may not be viewed as a constitutionally protected right to remain in a mental health care facility and to resist return to jail.[89]

The conservative approach here is to argue that a hearing is required prior to transfer to a mental hospital because of the additional stigma and possibility of enforced treatment. On return from the hospital, the inmate is not further disadvantaged or additionally stigmatized.[90] Whatever right to treatment he or she had remains intact.

A less conservative view would stress the possibility for abuse, as did Judge Kaufman in *Cruz*. The argument for a hearing would be to provide some opportunity to challenge clinical or medical judgment and to determine whether statutory criteria were met. However that may be, as a matter of policy some opportunity for retransfer challenges may be the better part of wisdom and actually may be more meaningful than a pretransfer hearing.

[7] Beyond Mental Hospitals

The Ninth Circuit recently expanded *Vitek* to an area well beyond the confines of the original decision. In *Neal v. Shimoda*,[91] Hawaii state prisoners challenged the application to them of that state's newly enacted (1993) Sex Offender Treatment Program (SOTP).

The inmates claimed that the SOTP violated their due process in that their administrative classification as sex offenders, and consequent assignment to the program which must be completed as a precondition to parole eligibility, implicates a liberty interest subject to due process protection. Once unilaterally labeled a sex offender, the inmate loses eligibility for furlough or favorable housing and must complete the SOTP as a pre-condition to parole eligibility.

In this aspect of the case the inmates insisted that a hearing is required before such negative consequences may be imposed. The Ninth Circuit, relying on a *Vitek* analogy, agreed with the inmate claim in the case of the plaintiff who was charged with, but not convicted of, a sex offense.[92] Where an inmate has been convicted of a sex offense,

---

[88] Cruz, 558 F.2d at 663, 665.

[89] Santori v. Fong, 484 F. Supp. 1029 (E.D. Pa. 1980), holding no right to a hearing for a pretrial detainee on the retransfer decision.

[90] In Price v. State, 716 P.2d 324 (Wyo. 1986), the Supreme Court of Wyoming held that an order transferring a defendant from the state hospital to the state prison to serve the remainder of his sentence was not appealable. There is no liberty interest in the reverse-*Vitek* situation. 716 P.2d at 329.

[91] 131 F.3d 818 (9th Cir. 1997). The plaintiffs raised interesting questions concerning the Ex Post Facto clause which were resolved, incorrectly in my view, against them.

[92] Neal, 131 F.3d at 830.

and nowhere is that defined, then the conviction is said to provide all the post-conviction process that was due. The case of the reasoning employed is as follows:

> The liberty interest implicated by the establishment of the SOTP is not merely the requirement that sex offenders complete the specified treatment program. If that were all that was at stake, we could probably not say that a liberty interest had been created, given the fact that prisons frequently maintain treatment and behavioral modification programs (such as anger management or alcohol abuse classes) that have long withstood legal challenge. The liberty interest at stake in this case is similar in form and scope to the interest at stake in *Vitek*: the stigmatizing consequences of the attachment of the "sex offender" label coupled with the subjection of the targeted inmate to a mandatory treatment program whose successful completion is a precondition for parole eligibility creates the kind of deprivations of liberty that require procedural protections. Inmates like Neal and Martinez are entitled to the benefits of these procedures before being labeled as sex offenders and subjected to the requirements of SOTP.[93]

After this rather strained approach to liberty interest analysis, the court incomprehensibly relied on *Sandin v. Conner*[94] as a basis for imposing the procedural requirements of a disciplinary hearing[95] instead of the more demanding requirements set out in *Vitek* itself.

The court found that being labeled mentally ill and a sex offender are stigmatic equals for the purpose of due process analysis. In addition, the mandated treatment as a precondition to parole eligibility is the functional equivalent of the enforced treatment alluded to in *Vitek*. The result here may have some lurking fairness to it but the Ninth Circuit's reasoning and use of authority is so flawed that this decision will not likely attract other courts.

For example, how could the court so easily dismiss mandated substance abuse or anger management programs? Surely, it is not status elevating to be labeled an addict or a violent inmate. In any event, *Vitek* lives and it has a somewhat new home in *Neal v. Shimoda*.

---

[93] Id.

[94] *Supra* note 11.

[95] Wolff v. McDonnell, *supra* note 12, requires little more than written, advance notice, an impartial tribunal, and a written statement of reasons for the finding. *Sandin* clearly was concerned with restraints imposed on prisoners which may be an atypical and significant hardship. *Vitek* was concerned with a qualitative alternation in the prisoner's regimen.

Appendix A

Standards: Legal Issues and the Mentally Disordered Inmate

The chart on the following pages compares the standards applicable to mentally disordered inmates promulgated by six major organizations. (A blank column indicates that the organization has not issued a standard on that topic.)

Key to Column Heads

ABA—American Bar Association
ACA—American Correctional Association
Am. Psychiatric—American Psychiatric Association
Am. Psychological—American Psychological Association
APHA—American Public Health Association
NCCHC—National Commission on Correctional Health Care

Access to Treatment and Habilitation

ABA	ACA	Am. Psychiatric	Am. Psychological	APHA	NCCHC
Mental health and mental retardation services need to be available within the adult correctional facility for offenders whose mental illness or retardation is not severe enough to necessitate commitment to a mental health or retardation facility (Standard 7-9.7(a), p. 479).

Correctional facilities should provide a range of mental health and mental retardation services for prisoners and should have adequately trained personnel readily available to provide such services (Std. 7-10.2(a), p. 510). | Written policy, procedure, and practice provide for unimpeded access to health care and for a system of processing complaints regarding health care. These policies are communicated orally and in writing to inmates on arrival and are put in language clearly understood by each inmate (3-4331M, p. 110).

Written policy, procedure and practice specify the provision of mental health services for inmates. These services include, but are not limited to, those provided by qualified mental health professionals who meet the educational and license/ certification criteria specified by their respective professional discipline (3-4336, p. 112). | The fundamental policy goal should be to provide the same level of mental health services to patients in the criminal justice process as are available in the community. This principle should be regarded as a general goal of the provision of services as would be expected to be available in the average community (B.1.a, p. 5), along with timely and effective access to mental health care. These principles and guidelines for psychiatric services in jails and prisons seek to assure access by setting out the parameters of access in the form of appropriate screening, referral, and mental health evaluation and treatment (F.4, p. 11). | Each psychological service unit is guided by a set of procedural guidelines for the delivery of psychological services. Depending on the nature of the setting, and whenever feasible, providers are expected to provide a statement of procedural guidelines in oral and/or written form that can be understood by users as well as the sanctioners. This statement may describe the current methods, forms, procedures, and techniques being used to achieve the objectives and goals for psychological services. | Mental health services, both diagnostic and therapeutic, must be made available to all incarcerated persons (p. 35). | Access to health care services is essential. Written policy and defined procedures require, and actual practice evidences, that information about access to health care services be communicated orally and in writing to inmates, in a form and language they understand, upon their arrival in the prison (P-32, p. 41). |

Treatment Refusal

ABA	ACA	Am. Psychiatric	Am. Psychological	APHA	NCCHC
A prisoner, unless involuntarily transferred to a mental health or mental retardation facility, should be permitted to decline habilitation or mental health treatment except: when required by order of the court, or when reasonably believed to be necessary in an emergency to save the life of the person or to prevent permanent and serious damage to the person's health. An involuntarily transferred prisoner has the same right to refuse treatment or habilitation as a civilly committed person in that jurisdiction (Std. 7-10.9(a)(b), p. 526).	Inmates shall have the option of refusing to participate in any rehabilitation or treatment program except basic adult education and programs ordered by the sentencing court, the paroling authority, or the required statute (3-4395, p.55).	Policies concerning the right to refuse treatment should conform with the rules and procedures of the jurisdiction in which the facility is located (D.2, p. 8).		The state (jurisdiction) may not mandate treatment for any inmate, unless an inmate, by reason of mental disability as determined by a licensed health professional, poses a clear and present danger of grave injury to himself, or to others, including exacerbation of symptoms by pathological-ly-based refusal of treatment. The precise language must be determined by references to each state's standard for civil commitment. Then, and only then, may intervention be mandated, but only with the least dramatic measures: (a) in response to an immediate emergency; or (b) on a continuing basis, only after civil judi-cial direction by the appropri-ate court, in which proceeding the individual is accorded an independent psychiatric evalu-ation and the protections of due process safeguards (p. 42).	*Right to refuse treatment* (important). Written policies and defined procedures allow, and actual practice evidences, that an inmate can refuse, in writing, health treatment and care (P-65, p. 77).

Emergency

ABA	ACA	Am. Psychiatric	Am. Psychological	APHA	NCCHC
	Written policy, procedure, and practice provide for 24-hour emergency medical, dental, and mental health care availability as outlined in a written plan. (List of criteria available if needed) (3-4350M, p. 118).	Mental health evaluation or an appropriate alternative response shall be provided no more than 24 hours from the time of referral. In case of urgency, provision shall be made for immediate evaluation upon referral (D.1.b.3.a, p. 28). Emergency treatment includes transfer to special medical/psychiatric housing units, transfer to inpatient psychiatric units, use of psychotropic medications, and special observation. In certain cases, verbal counseling or verbal therapy may be the treatment of choice. The duration of emergency treatment services will generally not exceed 72 hours, after which time these interventions would become included under treatment services (D.2.a.2, p. 29). Essential mental health services include: (1) training of correctional staff by a psychiatrist and other mental health professionals to recognize an inmate in a state of crisis; (2) availability of a psychiatrist to consult with on a 24-hour basis with reference to inmate management; (3) 24-hour availability of a qualified physician to prescribe emergency medications when indicated (D.2.b, p. 30).		It shall be the responsibility of the Mental Health Unit to insure that a program is developed that will be capable of responding 24 hours a day, 7 days a week, to inmates in acute emotional or mental distress. This program shall include the screening of all inmates for mental health problems on admission to the facility; the capability for immediate hospitalization of severely psychotic individuals or suicide risks; the availability of appropriate housing areas in the institution for mental health observation and suicide watch and alcohol and drug withdrawal; and the training of medical and correctional staff in the recognition of the signs and symptoms of mental and emotional disorders as well as the signs of alcohol and drug intoxication and withdrawal (p. 36).	*Hospital and specialized ambulatory care* (important). The prison has written arrangements for providing hospital and specialized ambulatory care for medical and mental illnesses in facilities that meet state licensure requirements for hospital care (P-29, p. 33). *Emergency services* (essential). Written policy and defined procedures require, and actual practices evidence, that the prison provide 24-hour emergency health care, outlined in a written plan that includes arrangements for the following: emergency evaluation of the inmate from within the facility when required; use of an emergency medical vehicle; use of one or more designated hospital emergency departments or other appropriate facilities; emergency on-call physician and dentist services when the emergency health care facility is not located nearby; and security procedures for the immediate transfer of inmates when necessary (P-42, p. 50).

Diagnosis

ABA	ACA	Am. Psychiatric	Am. Psychological	APHA	NCCHC
	Written policy, procedure, and practice require medical, dental, and mental health screening to be performed by health trained or qualified health care personnel on all inmates, excluding intrasystem transfers, on the inmate's arrival at the facility. This screening includes inquiry into mental health problems, and past and present treatment or hospitalization for mental disturbance or suicide (3-4343M, p. 114).	Receiving mental health screening will be carried out immediately upon arrival to the prison and will include a review of pertinent records accompanying the inmate. It will also include inquiry into past mental health treatment and screening questions designed to identify the signs of severe emotional, intellectual, and/or behavioral problems such as hallucinations, suicidal and/or homicidal thinking, severe thought disorganization, or bizarre behavior. Receiving mental health screening should be performed by a qualified mental health professional or trained correctional officer at the time of admission (D.1.b.1.a & c, p. 27).		Every individual upon entering custody in a correctional institution must be given an initial medical assessment by trained medical personnel. Specific determination must be made that the inmate can be safely kept at the facility and does not need further health evaluation or immediate treatment beyond the scope of the facility. [T]he unpredictable nature of the early custody situation and the institutional responsibility for the welfare of all inmates dictate that all be evaluated immediately upon entry and more completely after seven days in custody (p. 1). Each inmate admitted to the facility must be screened for withdrawal from alcohol and drugs as part of the intake medical screening (p. 37).	*Receiving screening* (essential). Written policy and defined procedures require screening to be performed by qualified health care personnel on all inmates (including transfers) immediately on their arrival at the prison. Persons who are mentally unstable or who are otherwise urgently in need of medical attention are referred immediately for emergency care. If they are referred to a community hospital, their admission or return to the prison is predicated on written medical clearance. The receiving screening findings are recorded on a printed form approved by the health authority. At a minimum, the screening process includes the following:
	Written policy, procedure, and practice require that all intrasystem transfers receive a health screening by health-trained qualified health care personnel immediately on arrival at the institution. This screening includes inquiry into whether the inmate is being treated for a mental health problem or has a current mental health complaint (3-4344, p. 115).	Intake mental health screening should take place within 7 days of admission to a prison or reception center. The intake mental health screening should be performed by a member of the health care staff (D.1.b.2.a &c, p. 28).			(1) Inquiry into current and past illnesses, health problems, and conditions, including mental health; (2) observation of the following: behavior (which includes state of consciousness), mental status (including suicide ideation), appearance, conduct, tremors, [other indicators of medical problems], and needle marks or other indications of drug abuse; (3) notation of the disposition of the patient, such as immediate referral to an appropriate health care ser-
	Written policy, procedure, and practice require that each inmate, excluding intrasystem transfers, is completed within 14 days after arrival at the facility. If there is documented evidence of a health appraisal within the previous 90 days, a new health appraisal is not required except as determined by the designated health authority (3-4345, p. 116).				

(cont'd)

Diagnosis (cont'd)

ABA	ACA	Am. Psychiatric	Am. Psychological	APHA	NCCHC
					vice, placement in the general inmate population, and the later referral to an appropriate health care service, or placement in the inmate population; (4) documentation of the date and time when referral/placement actually takes place (P-31, p. 39). *Health assessment* (essential). Written policy and defined procedures require, and actual practice evidences, the following: (1) A full health assessment is completed for each inmate as soon as possible after arrival in consideration of results from the receiving screening process, but not later than 7 calendar days after the inmate arrives at the prison, and includes: a review of the receiving screening results; the collection of additional data to complete the medical, dental, and mental health histories; a physical examination, including comments about mental status (P-34, p. 42). *Mental health evaluation* (essential). Written policies and defined procedures require, and actual practice evidences, post-admission evaluation of all inmates by qualified mental health personnel (physicians, psychiatrists, dentists, psychologists, nurses, physician assistants, psychiatric social workers, and others who by virtue of their education, credentials,

Diagnosis (cont'd)

ABA	ACA	Am. Psychiatric	Am. Psychological	APHA	NCCHC
					and experience are permitted by law to evaluate and care for the mental health needs of patients) within 14 calendar days of admission. Results of the evaluation become part of the inmate's health record. Inmates found to be suffering from serious mental illness or developmental disability are referred for care. Those who require acute mental health services beyond that available at the prison or whose adaptation to the correctional environment is significantly impaired are transferred to an appropriate facility as soon as the need for such treatment is determined by qualified mental health personnel. A written list of referral services exists (P-35, p.44).

Modalities/Treatment Plan

ABA	ACA	Am. Psychiatric	Am. Psychological	APHA	NCCHC
Committed severely mentally ill or seriously mentally retarded prisoners should be entitled to the same kind of periodic review by the institution providing treatment or habilitation and by the court as provided for involuntary civil committees. The purpose of this review is solely to determine if treatment or habilitation in a mental health or mental retardation facility is still necessary (Std. 7-10.6, p. 521).	Written policy, procedure, and practice provide for a special health program for inmates requiring close medical supervision. A written, individual treatment plan, which includes direction to health care and other personnel regarding their roles in the care and supervision of the patient, is developed for each such inmate by the appropriate physician, dentist, or qualified mental health practitioner (3-4355, p. 120). Written policy, procedure, and practice provide for a written inmate classification plan. The plan specifies the objectives of the classification system and methods for achieving them, and it provides a monitoring and evaluation mechanism to determine whether the objectives are being met. The plan is reviewed at least annually and updated as needed (3-4282, p. 95).	Mental health treatment is a multidisciplinary approach to mental illness which includes, but is not limited to, the following: (a) an acute care program, (b) a chronic care program, (c) a transitional care program, and (d) and outpatient treatment program. Treatment modalities shall be provided consistent with generally accepted psychiatric practices and with institutional requirements (F.5, p. 11-12). Given the relatively long-term nature of prison confinement, a wider range of mental health treatment modalities will be called for. These include preparation of a written, individualized treatment plan for all inmates receiving mental health services (D.3.a.5, p. 30) [and] 7-day-a-week mental health coverage, which includes 24-hour availability of consultation with a psychiatrist. Unless otherwise demonstrated as unnecessary, the presence of a psychiatrist on site should be at least once a week. Larger facilities with in-patient care will require considerably more on-site psychiatric coverage (D3.a.4, p. 30).	Psychologists develop plans for psychological services appropriate to the problems presented to the users. Ideally, a plan for intervention or consultation is in written form and serves a basis for accountability. Regardless of the type of setting or users involved, a plan that describes the psychological services indicated and the manner in which they will be provided is developed and agreed to by the providers and users (2.3.2, p. 6).	Direct treatment services must be provided in a context of varied modalities, with the availability of all treatment forms commonly used in the national setting (p.36).	*Special needs treatment plans* (essential). Written policy and defined procedures guide the care of inmates with special needs requiring close medical supervision and/or multi-disciplinary care. Included among special needs patients are the following: inmates with special mental health needs (including self-mutilators, sex offenders, the aggressive mentally ill, and substance abusers) and the developmentally disabled. For each of these special needs patients, there is a written treatment plan, developed by a physician or other qualified health practitioner. The plan includes (as applicable) instructions about diet, exercise, adaptation to the correctional environment, mediation, the type and frequency of diagnostic testing, and the frequency of follow-up for medical evaluation and adjustment of treatment modality (P-50, p. 61).

Medication

ABA	ACA	Am. Psychiatric	Am. Psychological	APHA	NCCHC
	Written policy, procedure, and practice provide for the proper management of pharmaceuticals and address the following subjects: prescription practices, including the following requirements: (1) psychotropic medications are prescribed only when clinically indicated as one face of a program of therapy; (2) "stop order" time periods are required for all medications; and (3) the prescribing provider reevaluates a prescription before its renewal (3-434, p.113). Written policy, procedure, and practice govern the administration of involuntary psychotropic drugs in compliance with the applicable laws of the jurisdiction (2-4322-1, p. 54 of 1994 Supplement). Psychotropic drugs such as antidepressants, and drugs requiring parental administration, are prescribed only by a physician or authorized health provider by agreement with the physician and then only following a physical examination of an inmate by the health provider. Such drugs are administered by the responsible physician, qualified health personnel, or health-trained personnel under the direction of the health authority (3-4342, p. 114).	The full range of psychopharmaceutical agents should be available to the practitioner in the correctional setting. The use of particular medications and any limitations on such use will depend on the particular facility and the types of patients served. The use of anti-psychotics, antidepressants, lithium, and other generally used medications are to be administered as necessary. Investigational new drugs must be used only as part of an externally monitored protocol approved by the Food and Drug Administration (F.5.c., p. 13). Given the relatively long-term nature of prison confinement, a wider range of mental health treatment modalities will be called for. These include the availability of a full range of psychotropic medications. Prescribing and monitoring of psychotropic medications is carried out by a qualified psychiatrist except in emergency situations, when a non-psychiatrist physician may prescribe these medications. Psychiatrists, along with the facility's pharmacy, should develop and monitor procedures to assure that psychotropic medications are appropriately distributed (D.3.a.6, p. 30).		In all instances, psychotropic medication must be prescribed only by a psychiatrist in accordance with generally accepted pharmacological principals and contemporary national standards. Any patient placed on psychotropic medication must have biochemical monitoring where indicated and evaluation of efficacy in all cases. Psychotropic medication shall be dispensed only when clinically indicated. Every inmate receiving psychotropic medication shall be seen and evaluated by a psychiatrist at least once a week until stabilized, and thereafter at least every two weeks. Female inmates shall be informed of the potential risks of taking psychotropic medication while pregnant (p.40).	Pharmaceuticals (essential). 5,(e) Automatic drug stop orders or required review of all orders for DEA-controlled substances, psychotropic drugs, or any other drug that should be restricted because it lends itself to abuse or for any other reason dictating that patient compliance be monitored. (h) The prescribing of psychotropic or behavior-modifying medications shall apply only when clinically indicated (as one facet of a program of therapy) and not for disciplinary reasons (P-30, p.34). Forced psychotropic medication (essential). Written policy and defined procedures guide the use of forced psychotropic medication. This policy and these procedures, while governed by the laws applicable in the jurisdiction, include requirements for authorization by a physician and specification of the duration of the regimen; for the when, where, and how the procedures may be used; and for the treatment plan goals for less restrictive treatment alternatives as soon as possible. Actual practice is consistent with the policy and procedures. *(cont'd)*

Medication (*cont'd*)

ABA	ACA	Am. Psychiatric	Am. Psychological	APHA	NCCHC
					Discussion: Though the right to refuse treatment is inherent in the notion of informed consent, exceptions may arise in psychiatric emergencies. State laws vary on this matter, but as a rule, forced psychotropic medication should be employed only under the following conditions: (1) the inmate poses an imminent or immediate threat of danger to himself or others; (2) all less restrictive or intrusive measures have been employed or have been judged by the treating physician or psychiatrist to be inadequate; (3) the physician or psychiatrist clearly documents in the medical records the inmate's condition, the treatment proposed, and the reason for the proposed forcing of medication, including other treatments attempted; (4) in all cases except emergencies, a documented consultation with another psychiatrist or physician, obtained before the forcing of medication, and with the treatment plan addressing the withdrawal of medication as soon as possible; (5) where possible, a review of orders for forced medication through independent psychiatric evaluation and a safeguarding of the inmate's right to due process (P-67, p.79).

Situs

ABA	ACA	Am. Psychiatric	Am. Psychological	APHA	NCCHC
Severely mentally ill or seriously mentally retarded sentenced offenders should be treated in a mental health or mental retardation facility, preferably under the supervision of the jurisdiction's department of mental health or mental retardation, in accordance with standards 7-9.8 and 7-9.9 (7-9.7 (b), p. 479).					*Mental health evaluation* (discussion). Acutely suicidal and psychotic inmates are emergencies and should be placed immediately in a treatment setting within the prison if one is available, or transferred to an appropriate facility if not. Less seriously disturbed inmates should be housed in a specially designated area with frequent observation by qualified health professionals when available, or by health-trained correctional personnel (P-35, p. 44).

Staff (Training & Ratio)

ABA	ACA	Am. Psychiatric	Am. Psychological	APHA	NCCHC
	The staffing requirements for all categories of personnel are determined on an ongoing basis to ensure that inmates have access to staff, programs and services (3-4050, p.14). Written policy, procedure, and practice provide that all professional specialist employees who have inmate contact receive 40 hours of training in addition to orientation training during their first year of employment and 40 hours of training each year thereafter (3-4082, p.24). Written policy, procedure, and practice provide for a minimum of one social service staff person for each 100 inmates (3-4385, p. 130).	[S]taffing levels are virtually impossible to set with any objective formula and standard that has general applicability. Rather, staffing levels may be assessed for a particular facility based on a clinical determination that adequate mental health services may be, or are, provided by a particular number of various types of professional staff providing the services (B.2.b, p. 6). Ideally, the practitioner should receive specialty education and training at various levels before undertaking employment in a correctional setting. Education and training in correctional psychiatry should be available in medical schools and psychiatric residencies. The correctional psychiatrist should seek out relevant courses as continuing medical education, or, at a minimum, the literature that is to be found in textbooks and journals (C.2. p. 7). Given the relatively long-term nature of prison confinement, a wider range of mental health treatment modalities will be called for.	Each psychological service unit offering psychological services has available at least one professional psychologist and as many more professional psychologists as are necessary to assure the quality of services offered (1.1, p.3). A psychological service unit strives to include sufficient numbers of professional psychologists and support personnel to achieve its goals, objectives, and purposes (2.1.2, p. 4).	Because medical and correctional personnel are in frequent and close contact with the inmate population, they shall receive special training from the mental health staff in the identification of individuals with possible emotional and mental disorders (a list of criteria is available if needed) (p.38).	*Staffing levels* (important). There is a written staffing plan that assures that a sufficient number of qualified health personnel of varying types are available to provide adequate evaluation and treatment consistent with contemporary standards of care. *Discussion:* The number and types of health care professionals required at a facility depend on the size of the facility, the types (medical, nursing, dental, mental health) and scope (outpatient, specialty care, inpatient) of services delivered, the needs of the inmate population, and the organizational structure (e.g., hours of service, use of assistants, scheduling). Also, special consideration should be given to the number of inmates in segregated housing, since the more restricted inmates' movement is, the more demands there are on staff time. These factors should be addressed in the facility's health service staffing plan. It is important to ensure that there is sufficient physician time. It is recommended that there be at least one full-time-equivalent physician in prison with an average daily population of 750 or greater (P-20, p. 23).

Staff (Training & Ratio) (cont'd)

ABA	ACA	Am. Psychiatric	Am. Psychological	APHA	NCCHC
					Orientation training for health services staff (important). Written policy and defined procedures require, and actual practice evidences, that all health services staff, within 90 days of their employment, complete a formal orientation program that has been designed in consultation with, and annually approved by, the health authority. Completion of the orientation is documented and kept on file (P-21, p. 24).
					Continuing education for qualified health services personnel (essential). Written policy and defined procedures, approved by the health authority, provide that all qualified health services personnel annually receive at least 12 hours of continuing education or staff development that is appropriate to their positions. In addition, all health services personnel must have current training in cardiopulmonary resuscitation (CPR). Completion of the annual training and current CPR training is documented for each health services employee and retained on file (P-22, p. 25).
					Training for correctional officers (essential). Written policy and a training program established or approved by the

(cont'd)

Staff (Training & Ratio) (cont'd)

ABA	ACA	Am. Psychiatric	Am. Psychological	APHA	NCCHC
					responsible health authority in cooperation with the prison administrator guide the health related training of all correctional officers who work with inmates. Training is continuous (i.e., each officer is trained at least every two years), documented, and includes at least the following areas: recognizing chronic medical or disabling conditions (such as mental illness) (P-23, p. 25). *Medication administration training* (essential). Written policy and defined procedures guide the training of personnel who administer medication, and require training from or approval by the responsible physician and the prison administrator, or their designees, regarding matters of security, accountability for administering medications in a timely manner according to physicians' orders, and recording the administration of medications in a manner and on a form approved by the health authority (P-24, p. 26).

Transfer Criteria

ABA	ACA	Am. Psychiatric	Am. Psychological	APHA	NCCHC
Prisoners who require mental health treatment or mental retardation habilitation not available in the correctional facility should be transferred to a mental health or mental retardation facility, preferably under the appropriate security provisions to a facility where such care is available (3-4360, p. 121). Inmates who are severely disturbed and/or mentally retarded are referred for placement in appropriate noncorrectional facilities or in units specially designated for handling this type individual (3-4367, p. 124).	Patients who need health care beyond the resources available in the facility, as determined by the responsible physician, are transferred to a mental health or mental retardation facility, preferably under the supervision of the jurisdiction's department of mental health or mental retardation, pursuant to the procedures set forth in the applicable standards (7-10.2(b), p. 510).	Discharge and/or transfer planning are those mental health services by which inmates in need of further mental health services at a time of transfer to another institution or discharge to the community are assured of continuity of care. The following elements should be met before a patient is discharged or transferred: (a) criteria are contained in a written policy approved by both the mental health authority and the correctional facility administration; (b) medications or other special treatments required en route and specific written instructions for administration are furnished to transportation staff; (c) appropriate mental health records accompany the patient with precautions to protect confidentiality (D.4.a. & b, p. 31).			*Patient transport discussion* (important). When transferring an inmate to another prison, his/her medical and mental health needs should be reviewed before the transfer. Aspects to consider in transferring these patients include suitability for travel based on medical evaluation, preparation of a summary copy of pertinent health information, medication or other therapy required en route, and instructions to transporting personnel regarding medication or other special treatment (P-33, pp. 41-42). *Mental health evaluation* (essential). Inmates found to be suffering from serious mental illness or developmental disability are immediately referred for care. Those who require acute mental health services beyond those available at the prison or whose adaptation to the correctional environment is significantly impaired are transferred to an appropriate facility as soon as the need for such treatment is determined by qualified mental health personnel. Qualified mental health personnel include physicians, psychiatrists, dentists, psychologists, nurses, physician *(cont'd)*

Transfer Criteria (cont'd)

ABA	ACA	Am. Psychiatric	Am. Psychological	APHA	NCCHC
					assistants, psychiatric social workers, and others who, by virtue of their education, credentials, and experience, are permitted by law to evaluate and care for the mental health needs of patients.

Involuntary Transfer: Procedures Due

ABA	ACA	Am. Psychiatric	Am. Psychological	APHA	NCCHC
If correction officials believe a prisoner is severely mentally ill or seriously mentally retarded and requires treatment in a mental health or mental retardation facility and the prisoner objects to such placement, involuntary transfer proceedings should be instituted. At a minimum, involuntary transfer hearings for prisoners should provide the following procedural protections: (1) the right to legal counsel, furnished by the state if the prisoner is financially unable to secure counsel; (2) the right to be present, to be heard in person, and to produce documented evidence; (3) the right to call and cross-examine witnesses; (4) the right to review mental evaluation reports; and (5) the right to be notified of the foregoing rights. In order to commit the prisoner, the judge must find by clear and convincing evidence that the prisoner meets the criteria for involuntary commitment and cannot be given proper treatment or habilitation in prison. Expert testimony as to whether a prisoner is severely mentally ill or seriously mentally retarded and requires treatment or habilitation in a mental facility should be admissible (7-10.5, pp. 517-518).	Transfers that result in an inmate's placement in a non-correctional institution or in a special unit within the institution specifically designated for the care and treatment of the severely mentally ill or mentally retarded follow due process procedures as specified in law prior to the move being effected (3-4368, p. 124).		There is a mutually acceptable understanding between a provider and a user or that user's responsible agent regarding the delivery of services. A psychologist discusses the plan for the provision of psychological services with the user, noting the procedures that will be used and respective responsibilities of provider and user. This interaction is repeated whenever major changes occur in the plan for service. This understanding may be oral or written, but in any event, the psychologist documents the nature of the understanding (2.3.3, p. 6).		

Emergency Transfer

ABA	ACA	Am. Psychiatric
If in respect to any prisoner a need for emergency intervention exists, the chief executive officer of the prison or that officer's designee may authorize immediate transfer to a mental health or mental retardation facility provided that an involuntary transfer hearing is initiated not later than 48 hours after the transfer is effected. An emergency exists when the chief executive officer of the correctional facility, or that officer's designee, reasonably believes that an immediate transfer is necessary to prevent serious injury to the prisoner or to protect the safety of other persons (7-10.7(a)(b): p. 523).	In emergency situations, a hearing is held as soon as possible after transfer (3-4368, p. 124).	Discharge planning and transfer planning operations are carried out in a timely fashion by regularly assigned, qualified mental health personnel (D.4.b.1, p. 31).

Custodial Discipline

ABA	ACA	Am. Psychiatric	Am. Psychological	APHA	NCCHC
	Written policy and practice require that except in emergencies, there shall be joint consultation between the warden/superintendent (or designee) and the responsible physician (or designee) before taking action regarding identified mentally ill or retarded patients in the following areas: housing assignments, program assignments, and disciplinary measures. When an emergency action is required, joint consultation to review the appropriateness of the action must occur as soon as possible, but no later than the next working day (3-4369, p. 124).	Particular attention must be devoted to distinctions between the use of modalities for custodial-administrative purposes and for mental health/therapeutic purposes (F5.d.1, p. 14). The effective delivery of mental health services in correction settings requires that there be a balance between security and treatment needs. It must be emphasized that there is no inherent conflict between security and treatment. It is universally recognized that good treatment is good security and vice versa (H.1, p. 15).		Restraints may not be ordered for punitive purposes (p. 41). No reward, privilege or punishment should be contingent on mental health treatment (p.43).	
	Written policy, procedure, and practice provide that single occupancy cells/rooms shall be available when indicated for the following: inmates with severe mental disabilities and inmates suffering from serious mental illness (2-4129-1, 1994 Supplement, p. 34).				
	A classification system is used to divide the occupants into groups that reduce the probability of assault and disruptive behavior. The classification system, at a minimum, evaluates the following: mental and emotional stability, escape history, and medical status (2-4129, 1994 Supplement, p. 34).				

Assignments—Housing and Program Due

ABA	ACA	Am. Psychiatric	Am. Psychological	APHA	NCCHC
	Written policy and practice require that except in emergencies, there shall be joint consultation between the warden/superintendent (or designee) and the responsible physician (or designee) before taking action regarding identified mentally ill or retarded patients in the following areas: housing assignments, program assignments, disciplinary measures. When an emergency action has been required, joint consultation to review the appropriateness of the action occurs as soon as possible, but no later than the next working day (3-4369, p. 124).	Severely mentally ill inmates should not be housed in correctional facilities unless the following conditions are met: (a) sanitary and humane environment; (b) written procedures for adequate observation; (c) adequate allocation of resources for the prevention of suicide and assault; (d) medical and mental health staff available to provide adequate treatment and supervision. When these conditions cannot be met, patients are transferred to an appropriate mental health facility according to written policy approved by the appropriate mental health authority and the correctional facility administration (F.5, p. 12).			
	Written policy, procedure and practice provide that single occupancy cells/rooms shall be available when indicated for the following: inmates with severe mental disabilities and inmates suffering from serious mental illness (2-4129-1, 1994 Supplement, p. 34).	Given the relatively long-term nature of prison confinement, a wider range of mental health modalities will be called for. These include available beds, either in the prison or in an outside hospital, for inmates in need of psychiatric hospitalization (D.3.a.3, p. 30).			
	A classification system is used to divide the occupants into groups that reduce the probability of assault and disruptive behavior. The classification system, at a minimum, evaluates the following: mental and emotional stability, escape history, and medical status (2-4129, 1994 Supplement, p. 34).				

Isolation/Restraint

ABA	ACA	Am. Psychiatric	Am. Psychological	APHA	NCCHC
	Written policy, procedure and practice provide that when an offender is placed in a four-point restraint ... advance approval must be obtained from the warden/superintendent or designee. Approval must also be obtained from the designated health authority or designee (2-4185-1, 1994 Supplement, p. 43). Instruments of restraint such as handcuffs, irons, and straight jackets are never applied as punishment (3-4183, p. 60). Four-point restraints should be used only in extreme instances and only when other types of restraints have proven to be ineffective (2-4185-1, 1994 Supplement, p. 43). Written policy, procedure, and practice govern the use of restraints for medical and psychiatric purposes. At a minimum, the policy will address the following: conditions under which restraints may be used, types of restraints to be applied for specific conditions, identification of person or persons who may authorize the use of restraints, and monitoring procedures for inmates in restraints. When restraints are *(cont'd)*	Some of the special issues to be considered in using seclusion and restraints as adjuncts to mental health treatment services in jails and prisons are: (1) The necessity of having written guidelines for the use of seclusion and restraints. Guidelines include criteria and indications for use, as well as staff responsibilities, limitations on time, periodic evaluations, etc. as they apply to that specific facility. Particular attention must be devoted to distinctions between the use of these modalities for custodial-administrative purposes and for mental health therapeutic purposes. (2) Orientation of patients should include a careful delineation of the policies on seclusion and restraints. (3) Custodial staff as well as mental health staff should receive special and continuing education in regard to these policies and procedures (F.5.d, pp. 13-14).		The use of restraints shall be instituted only when all attempts to calm the inmate have failed and when, in the judgment of a psychiatrist or physician, the threat of serious injury to self and others is so severe as to warrant such a response. Restraints shall be used only on the order of a psychiatrist, physician, or licensed health care professional (a list of criteria is available if needed) (p. 41).	*Health evaluation of inmate in disciplinary segregation* (essential). Written policy and defined procedures require, and actual practice evidences, that all inmates who are segregated from the general population for disciplinary reasons are evaluated by qualified health care personnel before their placement in segregation, and daily while in segregation, to determine their health status. The preplacement health evaluations and the daily encounter are document in the inmate's health record. *Discussion:* The intent of this standard is to ensure that the inmate's health status does not decline while in segregation. For these reasons, the responsible physician should be involved in the development of segregation policies and procedures. Owing to the possibility of injury and depression during segregation, the daily evaluations should include notation of bruises or other trauma markings, comments regarding the inmate's attitude and outlook (particularly as they might relate to suicide intention) and any health complaints. Inmates placed in segregation who have been *(cont'd)*

Isolation/Restraint (cont'd)

ABA	ACA	Am. Psychiatric	Am. Psychological	APHA	NCCHC
	part of a health care treatment regimen, the restraints should be those that would be appropriate for the general public within the jurisdiction. Written policy should identify the authorization needed and when, where, and how restraints may be used and for how long (2-4312, 1994 Supplement, p. 53). Written policy, procedure, and practice provide that a qualified mental health professional personally interviews and prepares a written report on any inmate remaining in segregation for more than 30 days. If confinement continues beyond 30 days, a mental health assessment by a qualified mental health professional is made at least every 3 months —more frequently if prescribed by the chief medical authority (3-4244, 1994 Supplement, p. 71).				receiving mental health treatment should be evaluated by mental health personnel within 24 hours after being placed in segregation. The evaluation should be documented and placed in the health record (P-43, p. 51). *Medical restraints and therapeutic seclusion* (essential). Written policy and defined procedures guide, and actual practice evidences, the appropriate use of medical restraints and therapeutic seclusion for patients under treatment for a mental illness. They specify the type(s) of restraint that may be used and when, where, how, and for how long restraints or seclusion may be used. Use is authorized in each case by a physician, on reaching the conclusion that no other less restrictive treatment is appropriate. For restrained or secluded patients, the treatment plan addresses the goal of removing the inmate from restraint or seclusion as soon as possible. The health care staff does not participate in the nonmedical restraint of inmates except for monitoring their health status.

Isolation/Restraint (cont'd)

ABA	ACA	Am. Psychiatric	Am. Psychological	APHA	NCCHC
					Discussion: The standard applies to those situations where restraints are a part of health care treatment. Generally, an order for therapeutic restraint should not exceed 12 hours. There should be 15 minute checks by trained personnel or qualified health professionals. The same kind of restraints that would be appropriate for individuals treated in the community (e.g., fleece-lined leather, rubber, or canvas hand and leg restraints and straightjacket) may likewise be used for medically restraining incarcerated individuals. Metal or hard plastic devices should not be used for therapeutic restraint. Persons should not be restrained in an unnatural position (e.g., hog-tied, facedown, spread-eagled) (P-66, p. 78).

Consent: Applicability and Components

ABA	ACA	Am. Psychiatric	Am. Psychological	APHA	NCCHC
	Written policy, procedure, and practice provide that all informed consent standards in the jurisdiction are observed and documented for inmate care. When health care is rendered against the patient's will, it is in accord with state and federal laws and regulations (3-4372, p. 125).	The principles of informed consent as embodied in the ethical guidelines of the American Psychiatric Association (i.e., the APA's Annotations Especially Applicable to Psychiatry to the AMA's Principles of Medical Ethics) remain applicable to patients in lock-ups, jails, and prisons. The patient should participate, to the extent possible, in decisions about evaluations and treatment. Psychiatrists should offer to discuss with their patients the nature, purposes, risks, and benefits of the potential types of treatment (D.2, p. 8).	Written policy and practices prohibit the use of inmates for medical, pharmaceutical, or cosmetic experiments. This policy does not preclude individual treatment of an inmate based on his or her need for a specific medical procedure that is not generally available. An individual's treatment with a new medical procedure by his or her physician should be undertaken only after the inmate has received full explanation of the positive and negative features of the treatment (3-4373, p. 126).		Informed consent (important). Written policy and defined procedure require, and actual practice evidences, that all examinations, treatments, and procedures are governed by informed consent practice applicable in the state. The informed consent of next of kin, guardian, or legal custodian applies when required by law (P-64, p. 77).

Confidentiality: Applicability

ABA	ACA	Am. Psychiatric	Am. Psychological	APHA	NCCHC
		A distinction must be drawn between information obtained by a mental health professional in the course of treatment and information obtained from the inmate in the course of forensic or other evaluation for non-treatment purposes. In the latter case, the usual rules in regard to confidentiality may not apply. It is the responsibility of the evaluating mental health professional to clearly set forth any such limitations to the evaluee as part of the informed consent process. Similarly, in treatment situations, the mental health professional must clearly specify any limits on the usual precepts of confidentiality before initiating treatment, except in emergencies. This notice may be presented in general terms, as applying to situations where the patient or the institution may be at risk. In the following situations, the usual rules of confidentiality may not be applicable: (a) where the patient is suicidal; (b) where the patient is homicidal or assaultive; or (c) where the patient presents risk of escape or the creation of internal disorder or riot.

This list is not meant to be all inclusive and can be supple- | Psychologists establish and maintain the confidentiality of information about the user of services, whether obtained by themselves or by those they supervise. If directed otherwise by statute, by regulations with the force of law, or by court order, psychologists seek a resolution that is both ethically and legally feasible and appropriate. Users are informed in advance of any limits in the setting for maintaining the confidentiality of psychological information. When the user's intention to waive confidentiality is judged by a professional psychologist to be contrary to the user's best interest or to be in conflict with that person's legal or civil rights, it is the responsibility of the psychologist to discuss the implications of releasing the psychological information and to assist the user in limiting disclosure by specifying the nature of the information, the recipients, and the time period during which the release is in effect, recognizing however, that the ultimate decision concerning the release of the information is that of the user (2.3.7, p. 6). | Full confidentiality of all information obtained in the course of treatment should be maintained at all times, with the only exceptions being normal legal and moral obligations to respond to a clear and present danger of grave injury to the inmate or others, or the single issue of escape. In all therapeutic relationships, the mental health professional shall explain the guarantee of confidentiality, including the precise delineation of the limits and periodically review the guarantee and its limits, to insure continued awareness. The inmate who reveals information that falls outside the guarantee of confidentiality shall be told, before the disclosure, that such information will be disclosed. If informing the inmate of the therapist's intent to disclose information will increase the likelihood of grave injury to self or others, the therapist may delay informing the treated inmate of that disclosure (p. 45). | Confidentiality of health information (essential). Written policy provides that the physician or his or her designee has access to information contained in the inmate's confinement record when the physician believes such information may be relevant to the inmate's health and course of treatment. This same policy also specifies the circumstances when correctional staff should be advised of an inmate's health status in order to preserve the health and safety of the inmate, other inmates, or the correctional staff. Actual practice is consistent with this policy (P-61, p. 72). |

(cont'd)

Confidentiality: Applicability (cont'd)

ABA	ACA	Am. Psychiatric	Am. Psychological	APHA	NCCHC
		mented in accordance with the special needs of the patients of the institution. Additionally, certain situations that are part of the mental health treatment process may require changes from the usual rules of confidentiality (e.g., a patient receiving psychotropic medication or a patient requiring transfer to a treatment facility outside the prison). Whatever the limitations being placed on the usual rules of confidentiality, as expressed in the various codes of ethics that apply, those rules generally should prevail. The exceptions relate to the legal, ethical, and moral obligations to respond to clear and present dangers of physical injury and the single issue of escape (E.2, pp. 8-9).			

Confidentiality: Records

ABA	ACA	Am. Psychiatric	Am. Psychological	APHA	NCCHC
	Written policy and procedure uphold the principle of confidentiality of the health record and support of the following requirements: (1) the active health record is maintained separately from the confinement case record; (2) access to the health record is controlled by the health authority; and (3) the health authority shares with the superintendent/warden information regarding an inmate's medical management, security, and ability to participate in programs (3-4377, p. 127).	Written policies and procedures, approved by the medical authority of the facility, govern the transfer of medical records and medical information (D.4.b.4, p. 31).	Psychologists establish and maintain a system that protects the confidentiality of their user's records. All people who are supervised by psychologists (including nonprofessional personnel and students) and who have access to records of psychological services are also expected to maintain this confidentiality of information. Users have the right to information in their agency records and to be informed as to any regulations that govern the release of such information. However, the records are the property of the psychologist at the facility in which the psychologist works and are, therefore, under the control of the psychologist or of the facility. Users have the right to examine such psychological records. Preferably, the examination should be in the presence of a psychologist who judges how best to explain the material in a meaningful and useful manner (2.3.7, p. 6).	Mental health data shall be entered into the unit health records to be handled in accordance with the provisions of the Health Records section of these standards. The mental health data shall be restricted to the facts of treatment, diagnosis, prognosis, treatment plan, and medication. Sensitive or highly personal data shall not be included in the medical record (pp. 45-46).	*Confidentiality of health records* (essential). Written policy and defined procedures establish, and actual practice evidences, the principle of confidentiality of health records. Health records stored in the prison are maintained under security conditions, separate from custody records, and access to health records is controlled by the health authority consistent with applicable local, state, and federal law (P-60, p. 72).

Confidentiality: Third Party

ABA	ACA	Am. Psychiatric	Am. Psychological	APHA	NCCHC
	The institution uses a "release of information consent form" that complies with applicable federal and state regulations. Unless the release of information is required by statute, the inmate signs the consent form before the release of information and a copy of the form is maintained in the inmate's case record (3-4096, p. 30). Health record information is transmitted to specific and designated physicians or medical facilities in the community, on written authorization of the inmate (3-4378, p. 128).	It is suitable for the mental health professional to share confidential information with facility administrators when the information relates to the medical management of the patient, to security issues, or to the patient's ability to participate in programs (E.2, p. 9).	Psychologists do not release confidential information except with the written consent of the user involved, or of his or her legal representative, guardian, or other holder of the privilege on behalf of the user, and only after being assured by whatever means that may be required that the user has been assisted in understanding the implications of the release. Even after the consent has been obtained for the release, psychologists clearly identify such information as confidential for the recipient of the information (2.3.7, p. 6).		*Transfer of health records* (important). Written policy and defined procedure require, and actual practice evidences, that when an inmate is transferred to another correctional facility within the same correctional system, the inmate's health record is sent to the facility to which the inmate is transferred either before or at the same time as the inmate. Written authorization by the inmate is required for the transfer outside the correctional system of medical records and information, unless otherwise provided by law or administrative regulation. Summaries or copies of the inmate's health record are sent with the inmate on referral to an off-site health care provider (P-62, p. 73). *Continuity of care* (important). Written policy and defined procedure require, and actual practice evidences, continuity of care from admission to the prison through discharge from it, including referral to the community resource when indicated. Medical, mental health, and dental providers within the correctional setting also should regularly share information about the care and treatment of patients. A single health record that documents medical, mental health, and dental care is preferable (P-41, p. 49).

Suicide Prevention

ABA	ACA	Am. Psychiatric	Am. Psychological	APHA	NCCHC
	There is a written suicide prevention and intervention program that is reviewed and approved by qualified medical or mental health professionals. All staff with responsibility for inmate supervision are trained in the implementation of the program (3-4364, p. 123).			Suicide is a major cause of death among detainees and prisoners. Health providers must be trained to recognize warning signs and must devise appropriate plans to safeguard life. Inmates are especially at risk for suicide when first admitted to jail. Whereas correctional authorities have responsibility for safe custody, health staff possess the training and expertise to recognize signs of depression and aberrant behavior, which may include suicidal intent (a list of criteria is available if needed)(p. 39).	Suicide prevention (essential). The prison has a written policy, defined procedures, and a program for identifying and responding to suicidal individuals. The program components include: identification, training, assessment, monitoring, housing referral, communication intervention, notification reporting, and review. Discussion: Key components of a suicide prevention program include the following: (1) Identification. The receiving screening form should contain observations and interview items related to the inmate's potential suicide risk. (2) Training. All staff members who work with inmates should be trained to recognize verbal and behavioral cues that indicate potential suicide. (3) Assessment. Assessment should be conducted by a qualified mental health professional, who designates the inmate's level of suicide risk. (4) Monitoring. The plan should specify the facility's procedure for monitoring an inmate who has been identified as potentially suicidal. Regular, documented supervision should be maintained.

(cont'd)

Suicide Prevention (cont'd)				
ABA	ACA	Am. Psychiatric	Am. Psychological	NCCHC
				(5) *Housing.* A suicidal inmate should not be housed or left alone unless constant supervision can be maintained. If a sufficiently large staff is not available so that constant supervision can be provided when needed, the inmate should not be isolated. Rather, he or she should be housed with another resident or in a dormitory and checked every 10 to 15 minutes by correctional staff. The room should be as nearly suicide proof as possible (that is, without protrusions of any kind that would enable the inmate to hang himself or herself).
				(6) *Referral.* The plan should specify the procedures for referring potentially suicidal inmates and attempted suicides to mental health care provides or facilities.
				(7) *Communication.* Procedures for communication between health care and correctional personnel regarding the status of the inmate should be in place to provide clear and current information.
				(8) *Intervention.* The plan should address how to handle a suicide in progress, including appropriate first-aid measures.

Suicide Prevention (cont'd)

ABA	ACA	Am. Psychiatric	Am. Psychological	APHA	NCCHC
					(9) *Notification.* Procedures should be in place for notifying prison administrators, outside authorities, and family members of potential, attempted, or completed suicides. (10) *Reporting.* Procedure for documenting the identification and monitoring of potential suicides should be detailed, as should procedures for reporting a completed suicide. (11) *Review.* The plan should specify procedures for medical and administrative review if a suicide does occur (P-54, p. 65).

Miscellaneous

ABA	ACA	Am. Psychiatric	Am. Psychological	APHA	NCCHC
			Providers of psychological services avoid any action that will violate or diminish the legal and civil rights of users or of others who may be affected by their actions (2.2.2, p. 5).		

Appendix B

Landmark Cases on Inmate Mental Health Care

[Editor's Note: This appendix provides extensive excerpts from three landmark cases concerning inmates' rights and recourses in the area of mental health care: Casey v. Lewis *(beginning on page App. B-2),* Madrid v. Gomez *(beginning on page App. B-40), and* Coleman v. Wilson *(beginning on page App. B-104). Excised material (discussion not relevant to our purpose in this book) is indicated by the use of three asterixes (***). Footnote numbers in these excerpts are not consecutive because we have abridged the cases; the note numbers shown match the note numbers in the full text of each case. Official page numbers for the quoted material are indicated in bold and are preceded by an asterisk (*1479), should you need to cite to the case.]*

CASEY V. LEWIS
834 F. Supp. 1477 (1993)
U.S. District Court
D. Arizona
March 19, 1993

***

*1479

FINDINGS OF FACT AND
CONCLUSIONS OF LAW *** MENTAL
HEALTH CARE

MUECKE, District Judge.

Having considered the evidence presented by the parties relevant to the *** mental health care issues in this case, the Court concludes as follows:

Background

This action was filed on January 12, 1990. The plaintiff class alleges that the defendants are deliberately indifferent to their serious health care needs including *** mental health care needs. The plaintiff class further alleges that the defendants discriminate against female prisoners in the delivery of mental health services. Defendants respond that their health care system complies with constitutional standards.

Findings of Fact

I. DEPARTMENT OF CORRECTIONS

At the time of trial in this action, January of 1992, the Arizona Department of Corrections (ADOC) consisted of nine prison facilities within the state of Arizona. On January 22, 1992, the total male population was 14,424 and the total female population was 922 inmates.[1] The nine facilities had the following populations on January 22, 1992:[2]

Douglas	1,957	[Florence *cont'd*]	
Gila Unit		CB6	
Mohave Unit		SMU	
Maricopa Unit		Rynning Unit	
Cochise Unit		Fort Grant	632
Papago DWI Unit		Globe 120	
Florence	4,727	Perryville	2,210
Women's Division		Santa Cruz Unit	
Central Unit		San Juan Unit	
North Unit		San Pedro Unit	
South Unit		Santa Maria Unit	
East Unit		Phoenix	962
SPU		Alhambra	

---

[1] Keeney testimony, 1/27/1992, p. 11-12.
[2] Keeney testimony, 1/27/1992, p. 11-12; Defendants' Exhibit 950.

[Phoenix *cont'd*]		[Tuscon *cont'd*]	
Flamenco		Santa Maria Unit	
Aspen DWI		Winslow	1,308
Picacho[3]	203	Kaibab Unit	
Stafford	476	North Unit	
Tucson	2,398	South Unit	
Cimmaron Unit		Coronado Unit	
Echo Unit		Yuma	243

*1480 The facilities are classified for security purposes as level one (minimum security) through five (maximum security).

***

*1483

3. *Mental*

In 1990, there were 18,356 psychiatrist/patient encounters and 111,624 mental health encounters by psychologists or other mental health staff; 621,393 prescriptions dispensed and 231,035 psychotropic medications dispensed.[34] In 1991, there were 19,071 psychiatrist/patient encounters; 109,689 mental health encounters;[35] 678,673 prescriptions dispensed;[36] and 70,332 psychotropic medications dispensed.[37] Psychotropic medication usage went down in 1991 when Benadryl and Vistaril were eliminated from the definition of a psychotropic medication because they are used for nonpsychotropic purposes.[38]

C. Experts

Both plaintiffs and defendants presented expert testimony regarding whether the medical care system met the serious medical needs of the inmates. Plaintiffs presented the testimony of two experts. One of plaintiffs' experts was Dr. Kim Thorburn. Dr. Thorburn reviewed the medical facilities at SMU in Florence, Douglas and Tucson.[39] Dr. Thorburn was guided in her testimony principally by the community standard for the delivery of health services. Additionally, she was guided by the National Commission on Correctional Health Care standards and the American Public Health Association standards.[40] The National Commission on Correctional Health Care Standards consist of 71 goal standards for correctional health care that are "quite high."[41] There are no correctional health standards that are more stringent or more difficult to fulfill than the National Commission on Correctional Health Care Standards.[42] The National Commission on Correctional Health Care has a certification program for institutions that meet the standards.[43] According to Dr. Thorburn, the prison system that meets the National Commission standards has a fairly decent system of health care delivery.[44]

Plaintiffs' other expert, Charles Braslow, evaluated the health services at Phoenix, Perryville and

---

[3] Picacho is a separate facility near the Florence complex. Because the Picacho facility inmates obtain medical care from the Florence Complex, it will be considered part of the Florence facility for purposes of the medical/dental/mental health care issues.

[34] Defendants' Exhibit 927, p. 1.

[35] Defendants' Exhibit 927, p. 1.

[36] Defendants' Exhibit 927, p. 1.

[37] Defendants' Exhibit 927, p. 1.

[38] Lutz testimony, 1/6/1992, p. 55, line 15-p. 56, line 9.

[39] Thorburn testimony, 11/20/1991, p. 40, lines 12-13.

[40] Thorburn testimony, 11/20/1991, p. 43, lines 13-23.

[41] Warren testimony, 1/28/1992, p. 147, lines 10-11.

[42] Warren testimony, 1/28/1992, p. 145, lines 19-25.

[43] Warren testimony, 1/28/1992, p. 144, line 14-p. 145, line 25.

[44] Thorburn testimony, 11/20/1991, p. 176, lines 5-8.

Florence, with the exception of SMU.[45] Dr. Braslow evaluated the health care within ADOC based on the general community standard for acceptable medical practice. This standard is a nationwide standard.[46] Dr. Braslow selected records by going through sick call lists, medication lists and pulling files with color coded markers indicating a particular disease.[47] Dr. Braslow did not do a physical examination on any of the inmates.[48]

Defendants' medical expert was Dr. Michael Warren. Dr. Warren is a physician *1484 who is a faculty member at the University of Texas. The University provides consultation and treatment care for inmates in the Texas Department of Corrections and supplies the top personnel to the Texas DOC for medical purposes. Dr. Warren was also the acting deputy director for health services for the Texas Department of Corrections for two years beginning in 1986.[49] To form his opinions, Dr. Warren reviewed policies and procedures and the map to determine the facilities and their locations. Over a period of six days, Dr. Warren visited Alhambra, ACW, Douglas, Tucson, Florence and Perryville. Dr. Warren also met with staff that he considered to be "key staff," including Dr. Lutz. To measure the system, he relied on the standards of the National Commission on Correctional Health Care.[50]

***

*1484

There are approximately 196 nurses within the Arizona Department of Corrections. Each institution has its own nursing supervisor.[59] Thirty-two of the nurses are specifically psychiatric (psych) nurses. Although the state qualification for a psych nurse II is that they have at least one year of psych nurse experience, psych nurses are not hired unless they have at least three to five years of psych experience or exposure.[60]

***

*1494

3. *Use of Sick Call System*

a. Sick Call System

Defendants provide *** mental health care through a sick call system. An inmate can go to sick call and see a nurse at a pre-established day and time. In the event inmates have an illness or problem and it is not on a day with the established sick call, they can notify the correctional service officer that they need to be seen by a provider. The correctional service officer relays the request to nursing. Therefore, based upon the seriousness of the problem, an inmate can be seen seven days a week.[188]

---

[45] Braslow testimony, 11/25/1991, p. 13, lines 8-14.

[46] Braslow testimony, 11/25/1991, p. 14, lines 20-25; 11/26/1991 p. 76, lines 3-13.

[47] Braslow testimony, 11/26/1991, p. 169, lines 7-24.

[48] Braslow testimony, 11/26/1991, p. 176, lines 19-21. A physician who examines a patient is in a better position to diagnose and treat an illness than a physician who simply reads a record or report. *Id.* p. 34, lines 6-9.

[49] Warren testimony, 1/28/1992, p. 133, line 15—p. 139, line 25.

[50] Warren testimony, 1/28/1992, p. 141, line 13—p. 150, line 18.

[59] Turner testimony, 1/9/1992, p. 39, lines 4-10.

[60] Turner testimony, 1/9/1992, p. 48, lines 18-25.

[188] Lutz testimony, 1/6/1992, p. 70, lines 1-7.

b. Problems with Sick Call System

Numerous problems exist with the sick call system. The system discourages use because inmates may stand in line two to three hours.[189] If inmates leave the line, they may not see the provider. In Douglas, once an inmate checks in he cannot leave the area.[190] In the Perryville Santa Maria Unit, after they sign up for sick call, the inmates must wait outside the units until seen.[191] Once an inmate signs up for sick call, she must stay in the area or she will be considered a refusal.[192]

***

*1502

8. *Problems with Security Involvement in Health Care*

The most serious problems with health care occur because of security involvement in health care. In some cases, lack of security staff causes delays in treatment of *** mental health care.[297] Lack of security staff and transportation also delay care provided outside of the prison.[298] Defendants are aware of the insufficient security staff and transportation problems.[299]

***

Finally, security staff are allowed to overrule medical judgments of health staff. For example, a psychiatrist can recommend that a prisoner be released from lockdown for mental health reasons, but security may overrule that medical order.[307]

***

*1511

IV. MENTAL HEALTH CARE SYSTEM

A. Generally

1. *General Administration*

The Department of Corrections formerly divided the psychologist and psychology associates between Health Services and Adult Services. There were psychologists in both Health Services and Adult

---

[189] Lutz testimony, 1/6/1992, p. 71, lines 4-8.

[190] Plaintiffs' Exhibit 248dd.

[191] Plaintiffs' Exhibit 248dd 8/3, 8/1989.

[192] Plaintiffs' Exhibit 248dd 8/3, 8/1989.

[297] Plaintiffs' Exhibit 33e, note 3/7/1990; Plaintiffs Exhibit 249ppp; Plaintiffs' Exhibit 250xx; Plaintiffs' Exhibit 31k, notes 10/23/1990, 11/8/1990, 11/9/1990, 11/28/1990, 11/30/1990, 12/5/1990; Plaintiffs' Exhibit 24k, note 9/14/1990; Plaintiffs' Exhibit 30h, note 10/1/1990; Plaintiffs Exhibit 19hh, Plaintiffs' Exhibit 574, p. 52, note 7/2/1990; Plaintiffs' Exhibit 247de; Plaintiffs' Exhibit 28n, note, 10/11/1989; Hanson deposition, 10/24/1990, p. 62, line 17—p. 63, line 10; Hanson testimony, 1/9/1992, p. 127, lines 6-17.

[298] Plaintiffs' Exhibits 150; 142; 146; 159; 160; 163; and 164.

[299] Plaintiffs Exhibit 117, Plaintiffs' Exhibit 50; Lewis deposition, 2/28/1991, p. 56, lines 13-22; Scalzo deposition, 11/13/1990, p. 38, lines 7-23; Guy testimony 1/8/1992, p.165, lines 11-17; Norrish deposition, 10/24/1990, p. 75, lines 10-19; Jolley testimony 1/15/1992, p. 45, line 22—p. 46, line 3.

[307] Plaintiffs' Exhibit 309, p. 118, lines 17-25; *See also*, Findings of Fact in *Arnold v. Lewis*, 91-1809 (consolidated into this case).

Services.[430] As of January 1, 1992, all psychologists in the Department of Corrections report to Health Services.[431]

*1512

2. *Experts*

Plaintiffs' mental health expert, Cassandra Newkirk, toured the facilities at Phoenix, Tucson, Perryville, Douglas and Florence.[432] Dr. Newkirk formulated her opinion in part by reviewing the medical records of certain inmates. Some of the records were chosen at random and others were reviewed after she had obtained signed releases from inmates. Dr. Newkirk reviewed a total of 95 inmate records.[433] Dr. Newkirk interviewed some inmates but did not review their medical records. She interviewed other inmates along with their medical records.[434]

Defendants' expert, Dr. Roberta Stellman, is a board certified psychiatrist and an expert in the mental health delivery system in a correctional setting.[435] Dr. Stellman provided psychiatric services for the New Mexico Department of Corrections for eight years ending September 1991.[436] While working for the New Mexico Department of Corrections, Dr. Stellman provided clinical services to inmates who were classified as maximum security prisoners.[437]

3. *Intake Procedure*

a. Male Inmates

The Department of Corrections has a routine procedure for intake of new male inmates. A portion of that procedure focuses on identifying mental health problems. The nursing staff screens the new inmates by asking specific questions about history of mental illness, self injury, substance abuse, and hospitalizations. The inmates receive psychological testing that may pick up either major deficits in intel-

---

[430] Newkirk testimony, 11/21/1991, p. 175, lines 10-19.

[431] Garabedian testimony, 1/7/1992, p. 219, lines 14-22. Dr. Stellman found that this fragmentation of the mental health staff was cumbersome and impaired communication. Dr. Newkirk found a lack of communication between the two groups of mental health professionals, as well as some duplication. Dr. Warren similarly perceived this division to be a problem, and recommended that all psychologists be in the Health Services Division. Warren testimony, 11/29/1992, p. 92, line 25—p. 93, line 7. The separation of mental health professionals into two different divisions of the Department also caused significant problems with record-keeping. Lang deposition, 10/25/1990, p. 31, line 25—p. 32, line 23; Hanson testimony, 1/9/1992, p. 128, line 24—p. 129, lines 1-8; Sloboda deposition, 10/29/1990, p. 32, lines 3-17; Cassady deposition, p. 60, line 21—p. 61, line 24; Stellman testimony, 1/28/1992, p. 42, lines 3-7. Thus, Dr. Stellman found that the division of mental health staff made it difficult to get a complete picture of mental health services. Dr. Stellman believes that the consolidation of mental health staff under Health Services will improve continuity of documentation and increase accountability.

[432] Newkirk testimony, 1/21/1992, p. 83, line 19—p. 84, line 1.

[433] Newkirk testimony, 11/22/1991, p. 44, lines 5-7.

[434] Newkirk testimony 11/22/1991, p. 45, line 25—p. 46, line 8.

[435] Stellman testimony, 1/27/1992, p. 93, lines 4-12, p. 102, lines 11-15.

[436] Stellman testimony, 1/27/1992, p. 95, line 10, p. 96, line 3. The American Correctional Association has accredited the delivery of health care, including mental health care, at the New Mexico Department of Corrections. Stellman testimony, 1/27/1992, p. 99, lines 9-19. The New Mexico Department of Corrections has been under a Federal Consent Decree for approximately ten years. The mental health monitor for the special master in the case has recommended that mental health services and medical services be moved up to a lower level of monitoring because of the improvements in those areas. Dr. Stellman is familiar with how the federal court has proceeded with the case and with how the monitors have surveyed and critiqued the New Mexico Department of Corrections. Stellman testimony, 1/28/92, p. 1, line 16—p. 2, line 15. Dr. Stellman was retained as an expert by a special master appointed by the District Court in Jacksonville, Florida for a class action lawsuit against the Florida Department of Corrections. Dr. Stellman served as a team leader for several multi-disciplinary survey teams that reviewed specific prisons in Florida to see if they had come into compliance with guidelines set down by the District Court. Stellman testimony, 1/27/1992, p. 103, line 6, p. 104, line 22.

[437] Stellman testimony, 1/28/1992, p. 114, line 22, p. 115, line 9.

lectual functioning or psychological distress. The inmates have ready access to the psychiatrist and the psychologist at the intake facility [Alhambra].[438]

b. Female Inmates

The Santa Maria Unit lacks a system to identify and evaluate female inmates with mental illness upon intake. In addition, ADOC does not obtain past psychiatric records *1513 of inmates.[439] Because the Perryville facility does not have a full-time psychiatrist, it is left to staff to identify an inmate who is seriously mentally ill. Staff then initiate transfer or treatment based on a verbal order.[440] At Perryville, Dr. Lang found a tendency by security staff to bring inappropriate referrals to mental health. These were prisoners security did not want to handle, so they would "dump them on the mental health person," thus taking time away from those prisoners who genuinely needed services.[441]

c. Identification and Treatment of Inmates with Serious Mental Health Problems

Defendants fail to identify seriously mentally ill prisoners in their custody, so that those prisoners might receive treatment. According to the ADOC Mental Health Services Manual, review of a prisoner's medical record upon arrival at an institution is a main source of mental health referrals.[442] Dr. Busfield believes that evaluating persons who have a recent history of mental illness, even if they are not on medication, is "professionally responsible" and "only prudent."[443] However, such reviews are not routinely performed. At SMU, not all arriving prisoners are assessed to determine whether they have mental problems.[444] Mr. Hanson, the psychiatric nurse, does not see every prisoner who comes to SMU who is on psychotropic medication or has a history of mental illness.[445] Similarly, at Douglas, Dr. Centric does not know if he routinely sees all prisoners who come to the facility with a history of mental illness or on psychotropic medication, because when he sees a prisoner, he does not know the reason for the appointment, unless he asks the prisoner.[446]

As a result of the lack of systems to identify them, seriously mentally ill prisoners go undetected in the prisons, and do not receive treatment. Plaintiffs presented evidence of the following inmates who did not receive treatment:

Henry Simms, a prisoner at Douglas, was quite psychotic when Dr. Newkirk saw him, and was out of touch with reality during the entire interview.[447] Although he had a history of hospitalization at Baker Ward, the ADOC psychiatric hospital, he had been transferred to Douglas and not followed by mental health staff at that facility.[448] His record contained two notes from psychological associates, in 1987 and 1988, noting his unusual or psychotic behavior and stating that he needed treatment. However, there was no evidence that he had received treatment by the time Dr. Newkirk saw him in August of 1990.[449]

Defendants' expert, Dr. Stellman, testified that at the time she reviewed Mr. Simms' chart, there was no evidence that he was having any acute problems.[450] Dr. Stellman was "uncomfortable" with Mr. Simms' record. According to Dr. Stellman, Mr. Simms had been at Douglas many years; was a chronic paranoid schizophrenic; and by the nature of his disease, he had refused treatment. He would periodi-

---

[438] Stellman testimony, 1/27/1992, p. 141, line 9, p. 143, line 3.

[439] See, Arnold v. Lewis, CIV 91-1808 [Consolidated into this case] Findings of Fact and Conclusions of Law, p. 15.

[440] Stellman testimony, 1/27/1992, p. 143, lines 4-21.

[441] Lang deposition, 10/25/1990, p. 44, lines 12-21.

[442] Plaintiffs' Exhibit 1(2), pp. 23-24.

[443] Busfield deposition, 10/26/1990, p. 22, lines 3-16.

[444] Hanson testimony, 1/9/1992, p. 121, line 25, p. 122, lines 1-3.

[445] Hanson deposition, 10/24/1990, p. 15, line 11—p. 18, line 20.

[446] Centric deposition, p. 27, lines 9-23.

[447] Newkirk testimony, 11/21/1991, p. 100, line 25—p. 101, line 7.

[448] Newkirk testimony, 11/21/1991, p. 101, lines 8-13.

[449] Newkirk testimony, 11/21/1991, p. 101, lines 13-20.

[450] Stellman testimony, 1/28/1992, p. 24, lines 1-2.

cally decompensate, or his mental condition would worsen, and be called to the attention of staff.[451] Dr. Stellman *1514 was disturbed by the fact that the most recent note in the chart was several years old.[452] There was no indication in the record that anyone had responded to this note, which was a referral to mental health.[453] Dr. Stellman requested that the nursing director have Mr. Simms seen by the physician the following day.[454]

Another such inmate was Mr. Bryce, a prisoner who was on psychotropic medications when he was transferred from SMU to Douglas.[455] He had a history of prior suicidal gestures.[456] According to his medical record, Mr. Bryce was not seen by a psychiatrist at Douglas between June 1989 and April 1990. His record from Adult Services was not available.[457] In Dr. Stellman's opinion, it would be desirable for a prisoner who is on psychotropic medication and is transferred to be evaluated at the receiving facility regarding his or her need or desire to continue the medication; this should be noted in the record.[458] Dr. Stellman testified that in her opinion Mr. Bryce suffered an adjustment reaction to the facility, rather than a mental illness.[459]

When she visited Perryville, Dr. Newkirk found inmate Michael Tyler in a lockdown unit/isolation cell. He was psychotic at the time, and was hearing voices.[460] A review of his record showed that he had a history of psychiatric illness, and had previously been on psychotropic medication while in ADOC, but his medication had been discontinued.[461] Although he was psychotic when Dr. Newkirk saw him, his record revealed that he had only been seen by psych associates when he was in lockdown.[462] He had not been seen by a psychiatrist in several months.[463]

Dr. Newkirk also testified about Ms. Velah, a woman with a 22-year history of depression and other psychiatric problems. Inmate Velah was in lockup at the Perryville Santa Maria Unit.[464] Although a psychological report done shortly prior to her incarceration showed a history of psychiatric problems and treatment, there was no indication in her record that she had had psychiatric evaluation upon her entry into the prison system.[465]

Another prisoner, Tommy Wilson, was acutely ill and psychotic when he entered the system, and was evaluated at Alhambra and sent to the Perryville facility.[466] While at Perryville, he was not seen by any mental health staff; nor was he given psychotropic medication. After he decompensated, he was transferred to SPU.[467]

Inmate Alex Heil's October 26, 1989 assessment report states that the Perryville prisoner suffers from substantial depression, dysthymic disorder or neurotic depression, and needs to see a competent provider. *1515 However, he was not seen by psychiatrist until July 5, 1990.[468]

Inmate Hayes entered the ADOC in 1986. A psychological assessment in August of 1986 diagnosed him as having serious mental illnesses, including schizophrenia, paranoid type, schizoaffective disorder, and schizophrenia, undifferentiated type.[469] The 1986 assessment report indicated that Mr. Hayes "shows severe depression and extreme anxiety."[470] On November 25, 1987, a mental health team review indicat-

[451] Stellman testimony, 1/28/1992, p. 22, line 25, p. 23, lines 1-8.
[452] Stellman testimony, 1/28/1992, p. 23, lines 12-14.
[453] Stellman testimony, 1/28/1992, p. 71, lines 3-14.
[454] Stellman testimony, 1/28/1992, p. 23, lines 15-18.
[455] Stellman testimony, 1/28/1992, p. 72, lines 5-12.
[456] Stellman testimony, 1/28/1992, p. 74, lines 16-17.
[457] Stellman testimony, 1/28/1992, p. 72, lines 18-19, p. 73, lines 10-16.
[458] Stellman testimony, 1/28/1992, p. 74, lines 8-24.
[459] Stellman testimony, 1/28/1992, p. 119, lines 1-25.
[460] Newkirk testimony, 11/21/1991, p. 98, lines 15-19.
[461] Newkirk testimony, 11/21/1991, p. 98, line 20—p. 99, lines 1-4.
[462] Newkirk testimony, 11/22/1991, p. 54, lines 1-7.
[463] Newkirk testimony, 11/21/1991, p. 98, line 20—p. 99, line 4.
[464] Newkirk testimony, 11/21/1991, p. 101, line 25—p. 102, line 1.
[465] Newkirk testimony, 11/21/1991, p. 102, lines 7-22.
[466] Newkirk testimony, 11/21/1991, p. 153, lines 16-24.
[467] Newkirk testimony, 11/21/1991, p. 53, lines 23-25.
[468] Plaintiffs' Exhibit 35b.
[469] Plaintiffs' Exhibit 264qq, pp. 94-100.
[470] Plaintiffs' Exhibit 264qq, p. 95.

ed that he had a history of mental illness, especially depression and possible schizophrenia, with three suicide attempts. On December 28, 1987, he was evaluated and the medical records note a direction to "r/o [rule out] atypical depression."[471] The March 5, 1988 note states "r/o major depression, r/o atypical depression."[472] On March 22, 1989, Dr. Gopolan evaluated the prisoner after Mr. Hayes' complaint of depression but again found no mental illness.[473] Mr. Hayes began receiving treatment from mental health on April 28, 1989 when he complained of feeling depressed.[474] He also signed a no intent to harm document, indicating that he was not suicidal.[475] He was given medication for depression.[476] On August 7, 1989, he was put on suicide watch because he was hoarding his medication.[477] On August 9, 1989, his medication was discontinued by Dr. Pera based on the report of hoarding, but without a face-to-face evaluation.[478]

At the time Dr. Newkirk saw Mr. Hayes in CB6, he had not been seen by mental health in approximately one year.[479] He was psychotic. On questioning, he said he was hearing voices. He was anxious and tense, exhibiting the type of tension often seen in paranoid prisoners.[480] He had a past history of violence against women and was in CB6 at that time for allegedly assaulting a female staff member.[481]

Inmate Cordray was an inmate at the Perryville Santa Maria Unit when Dr. Newkirk interviewed her. The inmate said she was depressed and had been unable to see a psychiatrist.[482] Her medical record revealed a history of untreated depression. On December 26, 1989, she cut her wrists and was referred to mental health by officers to Dr. Lang and the CPOII.[483] She was seen by a nurse on December 27, 1989 who obtained telephone orders for medication from Dr. Palmer and referred her to psychology but not mental health (psychiatry).[484] There was no follow-up of this incident noted in the medical record.[485] On May 7, 1990, she was seen by a nurse who quoted her as saying she "was about to go off."[486] She was not seen by a psychiatrist until August 11, 1990.[487]

*1516 Inmate Lewis was treated for depression while in jail, prior to her incarceration at ADOC, between April 16, 1990 and July 3, 1990. She requested mental health services at Perryville, Santa Maria Unit and was evaluated by Dr. Pera on August 14, 1990. Dr. Pera gave her a prescription and diagnosed her as having an adjustment reaction. On August 21, 1991, without seeing the prisoner, Dr. Pera indicated there was no need for renewal of the prescription. She was subsequently transferred to ASPC-Florence, Women's Division and on November 1, 1990 referred herself to mental health. She was hearing voices, "very paranoid," and "very nervous." She was seen regularly after that by Dr. Busfield for depression.[488]

4. *System for Providing Care to Mentally Ill Inmates Who Decompensate*

The mental health staff learns about an inmate who decompensates in his housing area through a number of ways. First, the inmate may initiate a request to the medical department requesting to see the

---

[471] Plaintiffs' Exhibit 264qq, pp. 81, 88.

[472] Plaintiffs' Exhibit 264qq, p. 79.

[473] Plaintiffs' Exhibit 264qq, p. 74; Stellman testimony, 2/7/1992, p. 124, lines 8-17.

[474] Plaintiffs' Exhibit 264qq, p. 72.

[475] Plaintiffs' Exhibit 264qq, p. 73.

[476] Plaintiffs' Exhibit 264qq, pp. 70, 71.

[477] Plaintiffs' Exhibit 264qq, p. 67.

[478] Plaintiffs' Exhibit 264qq, p. 69.

[479] Newkirk testimony, 11/21/1991, p. 95, line 22—p. 96, line 5.

[480] Newkirk testimony, 11/21/1991, p. 95, lines 1-16.

[481] Newkirk testimony, 11/21/1991, p. 96, lines 12-16, p. 97, lines 6- 10.

[482] Newkirk testimony, 11/21/1991, p. 99, lines 9-13.

[483] Plaintiffs' Exhibit 264vv, pp. 63, 64.

[484] Newkirk testimony, 11/21/1991, p. 99, lines 14-20; Stellman testimony, 2/7/1992, p. 140, lines 14-25; Plaintiffs' Exhibit 264vv, p. 21.

[485] Newkirk testimony, 11/21/1991, p. 99, lines 20-22.

[486] Plaintiffs' Exhibit 264vv, p. 18.

[487] Plaintiffs' Exhibit 264vv, p. 62.

[488] Plaintiffs' Exhibit 24e.

psychiatrist or be put on the psych line. Second, an inmate may make the same request to the CPO or the psych associate assigned to his unit. Third, requests for treatment are initiated by security officers or the warden at the facility. Finally, other inmates bring problems to the attention of the staff.[489]

If an inmate begins to decompensate within a facility in the Arizona Department of Corrections, a correctional service officer or nurse will make an assessment and could make a referral to the on-site psychiatrist or psychologist. If there is no on-site psychiatrist or psychologist, the officer or nurse may call the licensed correctional mental health facility in Phoenix.[490] At that point, an individual male may be referred to the Baker Ward for seventy-two hour mental health evaluation.[491]

Pursuant to policy, if a patient fails to pick up a psychotropic medication, the nurse or psychiatric nurse should determine why the individual did not pick up their medication. The nurse will either have the inmate brought to them or go to their cell to find out why the medication was not picked up by the inmate. If the inmate continues to refuse to take the medication and has not decompensated, a right of refusal form is witnessed and signed either by the inmate or by two witnesses.[492]

B. Mental Health Facilities

1. *Phoenix*

a. Alhambra, Flamenco, and ACW facilities

The mental health component of the Alhambra facility is the maximum security special psychiatric hospital for male inmates known as Baker or B Ward. B Ward is licensed by the Arizona Health Services Division of Licensing as a special psychiatric hospital. Annually, B Ward must meet the same criteria as any other psychiatric hospital to retain its license. The hospital is licensed for forty beds and has a useful capacity of thirty-six beds.[493] Male inmates may be involuntarily committed to B Ward pursuant to state law procedures.[494]

Also at the Alhambra facility is the Flamenco Mental Health Center. Flamenco Mental Health Center is licensed by the State of Arizona as a mental health residential facility. A mental health residential facility has lesser requirements than a special psychiatric hospital and is intended for patients who are more stable.[495] Flamenco is a medium custody facility with three male wards and ***1517** one female ward.[496] G Ward, one of the four wards in Flamenco, is used to house mentally ill female inmates. G Ward was activated in 1990 and has a bed capacity of twenty inmates.[497] Psychiatrists and psychologists provide treatment to inmates incarcerated at Baker Ward, Flamenco, and G Ward.[498]

Plaintiffs admit that the mental health treatment provided at Alhambra and the Arizona Center for Women (ACW) meet the serious mental health needs of inmates.[499]

b. Aspen

Although Dr. Garabedian supervises mental health services at Aspen, neither he nor the psychological associates under his supervision provide mental health services to the Aspen DWI Unit.[500]

---

[489] Stellman testimony, p. 33, line 7, p. 35, line 5.

[490] Lutz testimony, 1/6/1992, p. 61, lines 4-18.

[491] Lutz testimony, 1/6/1992, p. 61, line 21—p. 62, line 3.

[492] Lutz testimony, 1/6/1992, p. 59, line 15—p. 60, line 15.

[493] Garabedian testimony, 1/7/1992, p. 212, line 16—p. 213, line 14.

[494] Garabedian testimony, 1/7/1992, p. 213, lines 17-25.

[495] Garabedian testimony, 1/7/1992, p. 213, lines 4-14; p. 215, lines 20-15.

[496] Garabedian testimony, 1/7/1992, p. 216, line 1.

[497] Garabedian testimony, 1/7/1992, p. 214, line 21—p. 215, line 3.

[498] Garabedian testimony, 1/7/1992, p. 217, lines 8-17.

[499] PTS, uncontested Facts 12-13; R.T. of 11/21/1991, p. 93, lines 17- 21; Plaintiffs' Response to Request for Admissions.

[500] Garabedian testimony, 1/7/1992, p. 231, lines 8-16.

Rather, inmates requiring mental health treatment are transported about 300 feet from Aspen to Alhambra.[501]

In addition, Aspen provides its own programs through outside providers.[502] Those programs include everything from 12-step programs to life skills and to how to make it on the streets.[503]

2. Florence (excluding SMU)

Mr. Veloz is the mental health coordinator who is responsible for mental health services throughout the Florence complex, with the exception of SMU.[504]

a. SPU in Florence

The Special Programs Unit (SPU) in Florence is a halfway house for mentally ill and retarded male inmates who, under Arizona law, cannot be admitted to any of the mental health treatment facilities. SPU provides services to male inmates who are seriously mentally ill, severely mentally retarded, or who suffer from organic illness.[505] Inmates housed at SPU may receive mental health treatment and programming.[506]

The SPU has a capacity of 139 beds. The SPU facility is a dormitory style facility with an open yard where the inmates can be out most of the time.[507] The SPU is not classified in terms of a level of custody, but rather accepts inmates based on their mental health needs.[508]

The SPU takes a team approach to the delivery of mental health care. Master level therapists, CPOs, and registered nurses[509] offer group therapies in anger management, communication skills, current events, and sexual dysfunction. The groups consist of five to ten patients, and the facility offers six groups per week. The facility also has groups on self-awareness, self-esteem, current events, substance abuse education, choices and changes, coping with frustration, beyond depression, rational emotive therapy, and Alcohol and Narcotics Anonymous.[510]

The psychologist conducts group therapy and psychological evaluations for the parole board and for developing treatment plans. The psychologist also holds individual therapy or assessments with inmates. The SPU offers individual counseling and appointments *1518 with the psychologist virtually every day.[511] In addition, the psychiatrist, psych associates, and at times registered nurses at SPU provide individual therapy to the inmates at SPU. About 90% of the inmates requiring treatment are seen by psychiatrists or masters level care providers weekly.[512]

The SPU has a recreation therapy room where the inmates can watch television or videotapes, participate in arts and crafts, play games, or read.[513] Recreational therapy is offered two hours a day.[514] The facility also offers educational support, and 24-hour crisis intervention.[515]

The Department has a policy for assigning inmates to the SPU once they are referred for placement to the facility. When the mental health staff receives a referral, they discuss the referral. The staff then composes a Mental Health Admissions Board made up of two mental health professionals and one cor-

---

[501] Garabedian testimony, 1/7/1992, p. 241, lines 1-6.
[502] Garabedian testimony, 1/7/1992, p. 231, line 20—p. 232, line 2.
[503] Garabedian testimony, 1/7/1992, p. 231, lines 16-26.
[504] Veloz testimony, 1/9/1992, p. 139, lines 18-24.
[505] Busfield testimony, 1/9/1992, p. 24, lines 8-20.
[506] Garabedian testimony, 1/7/1992, p. 216, line 17—p. 217, line 2.
[507] Veloz testimony, 1/9/1992, p. 142, lines 4-11.
[508] Veloz testimony, 1/9/1992, p. 141, line 23—p. 142, line 3.
[509] Veloz testimony, 1/9/1992, p. 162, lines 1-15.
[510] Veloz testimony, 1/9/1992, p. 154, line 20—p. 156, line 22.
[511] Veloz testimony, 1/9/1992, p. 151, line 22—p. 152, line 8.
[512] Veloz testimony, 1/9/1992, p. 162, line 18—p. 163, line 17.
[513] Veloz testimony, 1/9/1992, p. 154, line 20—p. 156, line 22.
[514] Veloz testimony, 1/9/1992, p. 159, line 9—p. 160, line 5.
[515] Veloz testimony, 1/9/1992, p. 159, line 9—p. 160, line 5.

rections officer that goes to the facility where the inmate is assigned and performs a cursory mental status exam. The Admissions Board also reviews the medical and institutional file to determine whether the inmate's behavior is a management problem.[516]

The medical records of all patients coming to the SPU are reviewed by a psychiatrist when the medical records show that the inmate either has or has had emotional difficulties.[517] As part of the mental status exam, the mental health team determines whether the inmate has experienced auditory problems or visual hallucinations. Staff look at the inmate's gait and perform other exams necessary to assess whether the inmate is seriously impaired and belongs in a chronic unit like the SPU or if he is acute enough to be considered for admission to the psychiatric hospital B ward. The mental health team also determines whether the inmate can function in an open yard dormitory setting and whether the inmate has a history of repeated aggressive behavior against either other inmates or corrections employees.[518] If an inmate requires institutional care but is not a candidate for the SPU because of a history of assaultive behavior, the inmate is referred to B Ward at Alhambra.[519]

The majority of the inmates at SPU that receive medications are receiving psychotropic medications. The psychiatric nurse gives out those medications dose by dose.[520]

The Department of Corrections has no SPU for women. Women who require the intermediate mental health care offered to the men at the SPU can be treated at G Ward.[521]

Some of the inmates decompensate at SPU.[522] For example, Dr. Stellman observed Phillip Gonzales in CB6 and noted that he had had frequent moves between **1519** SPU and Baker Ward for decompensation.[523] Plaintiffs allege that this decompensation is caused by lack of programming or staff. However, the nature of mental illness, which follows a cyclical pattern, may be the cause of such decompensation.[524]

b. Women's Division in Florence

Inmates at the Women's Division obtain care through sick call which is conducted twice a week and a provider line which is conducted three days a week.[525] Inmates at the Women's Division are referred to a psychiatrist through the psychiatric nurse. Counselors and security staff members advise the nurse about women who need assistance. The nurse also has open office hours where female inmates come to speak with her, and she determines whether the inmate requires a psychiatric evaluation.[526]

3. *SMU in Florence*

a. Referral System

SMU conducts a psych line once a week.[527] Inmates at SMU are scheduled for appointments with the psychiatrist through various ways. First, the psychologist or the psychotherapist can refer the inmate

---

[516] Veloz testimony, 1/9/1992, p. 145, lines 1-24.

[517] Busfield testimony, 1/9/1992, p. 25, line 18—p. 28, line 9.

[518] Veloz testimony, 1/9/1992, p. 146, line 21—p. 147, line 21.

[519] Veloz testimony, 1/9/1992, p. 148, lines 14-25.

[520] Cory testimony, 1/14/1992, p. 12, lines 1-19.

[521] Garabedian testimony, 1/7/1992, p. 218, line 24—p. 219, line 13.

[522] Plaintiffs' Exhibit 199, SPU treatment team briefing, 1/15/90 (prisoner Phelan decompensating, has become more agitated; broke out counselor's office window; placed in Central Unit isolation on 15-minute precaution), 2/7/90 (inmate Boykin decompensating and paranoid), 2/22/90 (inmate Green decompensating; Dr. Pera increased medications), 3/2/90 (inmate Cooksey decompensating badly), 3/30/90 (inmate Mokake decompensating, voicing suicidal ideas), 5/15/90 (Inmate Gholson has decompensated badly; "totally out of it;" sent to B-ward yesterday), 5/16/90 (inmate Tucker "decompensating badly; rambling speech, disoriented," "wandering around lost").

[523] Stellman testimony, 1/28/1992, p. 107, lines 7-20.

[524] Stellman testimony, 1/27/1992, p. 163, line 1—p. 164, line 9.

[525] Cory testimony, 1/14/92, p. 12, lines 1-19.

[526] Busfield testimony, 1/9/1992, p. 14, lines 14-24.

[527] Hanson testimony, 1/9/1992, p. 93, lines 2-7.

for psychiatric care. A new inmate may be referred for psychiatric care if one of the nurses reviews his chart and finds a significant history of mental health care or determines that the inmate is on medications. The inmates can pick up self-referral forms from the nurse. The inmate also may be referred by a CPO or by other nurses.[528]

When a referral comes in, the psychiatric nurse goes to the inmate's cell and talks with him face-to-face to determine how quickly the inmate needs to be scheduled for an appointment.[529] If the patient is referred because of medications, the psych nurse contacts the pharmacy and ensures that the inmate receives his medications promptly. He or she then advises the inmate when his medications will be arriving and when he will be seeing the psychiatrist. When an inmate is referred because of a significant history of mental illness, the psych nurse visits with the inmate and makes a clinical judgment of the inmate's condition.[530]

b. Medications

The psychiatric patients at the SMU receive their psychiatric medications by unit dosage. Each day the medications are put in individual envelopes and delivered to the inmate at his cell.[531] If an inmate refuses to take his prescribed medication, the person dispensing the medication will work with the inmate, remind him why the medication was ordered, and explain the consequences of his refusing to take the medication. If the inmate continues to refuse to take his medication, the refusal generally is noted on the med sheet. After a period of time, at the next appointment, the med sheets are looked at and sometimes the nurse again tries to negotiate with the patient.[532]

c. Mental Health Programming

SMU has very little programming for seriously mentally ill inmates. At the time of his deposition on January 31, 1991, Dr. Pushkash indicated the mental health programming in the SMU consisted of one therapy group involving four prisoners, a levels system for prisoners with behavioral problems, and individual therapy.[533] At the time of trial, SMU *1520 provided a group therapy program, the levels system, the pod for self-abusive inmates, and a bibliotherapy program.[534]

The levels system program is a behavioral modification/levels system program in which sixteen inmates are eligible to participate at any given time. The inmates proceed through a four phase system based on their behavior. As the inmates proceed through the phases, they accumulate points and privileges, such as being able to "buy" extra time out of their cells.[535] The levels system was actually implemented by security officers. Some of the officers had received forty hours of training. However, due to turnover, other officers had been assigned to the levels system unit but received no training. In addition, in 1991, defendants were not developing a training program for officers.[536] Dr. Newkirk testified that such training is very important because the levels system deals with behaviors in a treatment modality.[537] Further, Dr. Stellman testified that officers should have some mental health training from a mental health professional, especially in suicide prevention, how to deal with assaultive patients, side effects of psychiatric medications and general training regarding the program being implemented.[538]

At the time of his deposition on January 31, 1991, Dr. Pushkash also indicated that SMU had a prob-

---

[528] Hanson testimony, 1/9/1992, p. 91, line 17—p. 92, line 4.

[529] Hanson testimony, 1/9/1992, p. 92, line 8—p. 93, line 7.

[530] Hanson testimony, 1/9/1992, p. 93, line 17—p. 94, line 25.

[531] Hanson testimony, 1/9/1992, p. 96, line 25—p. 97, line 7.

[532] Hanson testimony, 1/9/1992, p. 98, line 22—p. 99, line 23.

[533] Pushkash deposition, 1/31/1991, p. 25, lines 14-22, p. 17, lines 14-25, p. 18, line 1.

[534] Hanson testimony, 1/9/1992, p. 105, line 25—p. 106, line 23.

[535] Hanson testimony, 1/9/1992, p. 104, line 23—p. 105, line 17.

[536] Newkirk testimony, 1/21/1991, p. 11, lines 12-22, p. 116, lines 1- 5; Pushkash deposition, 1/31/1991, p. 48, line 12—p. 49, line 4.

[537] Newkirk testimony, 11/22/1991, p. 116, lines 6-8.

[538] Stellman testimony, 1/28/1992, p. 28, line 18—p. 29, line 7.

lem with suicidal and self-abusing prisoners. He had developed an outline for a housing pod for these prisoners that had been submitted to Warden Crist, but he had not heard whether it had been approved at the time of his deposition.[539] This self-abuser pod was established in 1991 or early 1992 at SMU to set aside those people who had some kind of emotional disorder, not necessarily a mental illness, while they were at SMU.[540]

4. *Tucson*

Inmates in the Tucson facility may obtain referrals for psychiatric treatment through a number of ways. First, an inmate can write a kite or an inmate letter if he feels the need for psychiatric care. Second, the nurses or general medical providers can refer an inmate after the inmate expresses a need for care or the medical providers observe a need for care. Third, the psychologist interviewing inmates for other reasons may observe that the inmate is having an emotional problem. Fourth, when inmates are transferred from other prisons, they are evaluated on arrival or shortly thereafter if they have either a current or past history of mental illness.[541]

Inmates with histories of psychiatric illness are seen by a psychiatrist within ten days. If an inmate in the Tucson complex requests early in the week, on Monday or Tuesday, to be seen by a psychiatrist, he will be seen that week.[542] Otherwise, he will be seen the next week.[543] Priority is given to scheduling appointments with inmates who are displaying psychiatric difficulties. At the appointment, the psychiatrist determines whether the inmate has stabilized and whether he needs medical care. If the inmate needs a more comprehensive diagnostic evaluation than the psychiatrist can perform, the psychiatrist at B Ward is contacted. After *1521 consultation, the inmate most likely will be transferred to Alhambra.[544]

5. *Yuma*

The Yuma facility has no psychiatric services.[545] It also has no psychologists.[546] This facility is a full duty work camp with a capacity of 250 inmates.[547] Thus, inmates who need mental health services are not assigned to Yuma. If inmates with mental health problems are assigned to Yuma, they are transferred within forty-eight to seventy-two hours.[548]

C. Staffing Problems

1. *Numbers and Vacancies of Staff*

Plaintiffs expert, Dr. Newkirk, testified that defendants fail to provide sufficient staff to diagnose and treat the serious mental health needs of the prisoners in their custody.[549] With the exception of Alhambra, none of defendants' facilities has a full-time psychiatrist.[550]

Defendants clearly have a shortage of mental health staff. In recent years, the prisoner population

---

[539] Pushkash deposition, 1/31/1991, p. 28, line 1—p. 29, line 15.

[540] Stellman testimony, 1/28/1992, p. 35, line 17—p. 36, line 7. The self-abuser pod was established about a year or a year and one-half prior to Mr. Hanson's testimony in January 9, 1992 and had no mental health staff assigned to it at the time of trial. Hanson testimony, 1/9/1992, p. 115, lines 17-24.

[541] Busfield testimony, 1/9/1992, p. 10, line 18—p. 11, line 15.

[542] Jolley testimony, 1/15/1992, p. 32, line 25—p. 33, line 6.

[543] Jolley testimony, 1/15/1992, p. 33, line 6.

[544] Busfield testimony, 1/9/1992, p. 28, line 12, p. 29, line 4.

[545] Charles deposition, 10/23/1990, p. 9, lines 13-14.

[546] Keeney deposition, 11/14/1990, p. 60, lines 2-12.

[547] Keeney testimony, 1/27/1992, p. 22, lines 16-19.

[548] Charles deposition, 10/23/1990, p. 9, lines 15-20.

[549] Newkirk testimony, 11/21/1991, p. 160, line 24—p. 161, line 1.

[550] PTS, uncontested Fact A9.

has grown, and this has increased the need for psychological services.[551] In January of 1988, ADOC's prisoner population was 10,877. Four years later, in January of 1992, it had grown to 15,346.[552] As a result, the prisoner-to-staff ratio is too high to allow the mental health staff to do thorough work.[553] Caseloads are too heavy, and there is a tendency for mental health staff to "burn out."[554]

Shortages of mental health staff are found throughout the system. At the time of trial [November 1991-February 1992], the position of the mental health program manager, the person responsible for mental health services throughout the Department, had been vacant since July of 1990.[555] Defendants' expert, Dr. Stellman, noted staffing shortages at some of the facilities.[556] She believes that the vacant mental health positions in the SMU, Perryville and Tucson facilities should be filled;[557] that the number of psychological associates in outlying areas should be increased; and that each major prison should have one or two more psychological associates.[558]

a. Florence

As of October, 1990, the Florence complex, excluding SMU, had no psychologists.[559] Mr. Veloz has repeatedly requested additional mental health positions for the Florence complex, including psychiatrists, psychologists, and psychological associates. However, at the time of trial, he had not received any of these positions.[560] In fact, since 1986, there have been no new mental health positions at **1522** Florence, except SMU.[561] Because in recent years the legislature has allocated money only for new prisons, Dr. Veloz has found himself "borrowing and stealing" staff from the budgets for new prisons.[562] During Dr. Stellman's tour of Florence, Mr. Veloz told her that the mental health staffing of the facility is "sub-average."[563] Dr. Stellman believes that Florence should have two full-time psychiatrists.[564] However, in October of 1990, the facility had one and one-sixth full time equivalent psychiatrists.[565]

As of October of 1990, there were either two or three psychologist positions vacant, and they had been vacant for over a year.[566] When Dr. Warren visited Florence, all three psychologist positions were vacant.[567] Similarly, at the time of trial, there were two psychologist positions vacant at Florence.[568]

(1) Florence—SPU

SPU has a psychiatrist, psychiatric nurses, counselors, and security officers.[569] As of October 1990, there was no psychologist at SPU.[570] The psychological associates at the SPU are supervised by the doctor level psychologist. The psych associates provide orientation to new inmates about the services pro-

---

[551] Veloz testimony, 1/9/1992, p. 181, lines 15-21, p. 182, lines 5-14 ("we find it very difficult to keep up with the population growth"); Keeney, deposition, 11/14/1990, p. 59, lines 1-7.

[552] Plaintiffs' Exhibit 191; Keeney testimony, 1/27/1992, p. 12, lines 20-22.

[553] Lang deposition, 10/25/1990, p. 26, line 6—p. 27, line 13.

[554] Lang deposition, 10/25/1990, p. 45, line 5, p. 46, lines 1-3.

[555] Lutz testimony, 1/6/1992, p. 36, lines 5-11, 25, p. 37, lines 1-10.

[556] Stellman testimony, 1/28/1992, p. 61, lines 9-12.

[557] Stellman testimony, 1/27/1992, p. 187, lines 14-18, p. 196, lines 1-5.

[558] Stellman testimony, 1/27/1992, p. 196, lines 5-11; 1/28/92, p. 66, lines 17-21.

[559] Veloz testimony, 1/9/1992, p. 179, line 6.

[560] Veloz testimony, 1/9/1992, p. 180, lines 2-14.

[561] Veloz deposition, 10/25/1990, p. 5, lines 3-4; p. 21, lines 3-7.

[562] Veloz testimony, 1/9/1992, p. 166, line 18—p. 167, line 15.

[563] Stellman testimony, 1/28/1992, p. 66, lines 1-4.

[564] Stellman testimony, 1/28/1992, p. 67, lines 2-5.

[565] Norrish deposition, 10/24/1990, p. 17, lines 13-22.

[566] Veloz deposition, 10/25/1990, p. 14, line 10—p. 16, line 24.

[567] Warren testimony, 1/29/1992, p. 93, lines 8-11.

[568] Veloz testimony, 1/9/1992, p. 165, lines 15-21.

[569] Garabedian testimony, 1/7/1992, p. 217, lines 37.

[570] Veloz deposition, 10/25/1990, p. 68, line 25—p. 69, line 4.

vided by the Mental Health Department. The psych associates run groups, do individual therapy, and ensure that inmates are not decompensating in the dorm. The psych associates also introduce the inmates to the psychiatric nurse, who does a nursing evaluation, schedules appointments for the psychiatrist, and ensures that the necessary paperwork is done so that the inmate can attend the appointment.[571] SPU also utilizes a recreational therapist at SPU, who is a certified recreation professional, to work with the lowest functioning inmates in the yard.[572]

(2) Florence—SMU

Although SMU has the capacity to house 895 male inmates,[573] at the time of trial, a psychiatric social worker and a psychiatric nurse were the only mental health staff at SMU.[574] There were no psychologists.[575] A psychiatrist [Dr. Gopalan] visits SMU for three days every two weeks. This schedule is such that there are nine consecutive days when he is not at the facility.[576]

Mr. Hanson, the psychiatric nurse, believes SMU needs two psychologists.[577] Turnover is "pretty high" among mental health staff at SMU.[578] Mr. Hanson is sometimes unable to do formal rounds because of *1523 the demands on his time.[579] Shortly before trial, the psychiatrist line at SMU was decreased from one and a half days a week to one day a week, as the Rynning unit was demanding more staff time.[580] When Dr. Stellman visited SMU, Dr. Pushkash, a psychologist, told her that the psychiatric coverage at the facility needs to be increased to three days per week.[581] Dr. Gopalan and Dr. Menendez, both psychiatrists, agree that sixteen to twenty hours per week would be a minimum for conscientious coverage.[582]

(3) Women's Unit

The Florence women's facility has one half day a week of psychiatrist time.[583] It is not clear whether the women have access to a psychologist.[584]

b. Tucson

The Tucson facility has four or five institutional psychologists as part of its mental health staff.[585] Tucson also has one half-time psychiatrist, Dr. Busfield.[586] Dr. Busfield visits the Tucson prison Tuesday, Wednesday and Friday of one week and then Tuesday and Friday of the next week.[587] By contrast to the Tucson facility, Dr. Stellman testified that the Penitentiary of New Mexico, with only about 1,000 prisoners, has two half-time psychiatrists.[588] Dr. Stellman believes that a facility the size of Tucson should have a full-time psychiatrist.[589]

---

[571] Veloz testimony, 1/9/1992, p. 152, line 9—p. 154, line 19. In maximum security prisons, the psych nurses also do out-patient. The recreational therapist at SPU is a certified recreation-professional who also works with the lowest functioning inmates in the yard. Id.

[572] Veloz testimony, 1/9/1992, p. 152, line 9—p. 154, line 19.

[573] Keeney testimony, 1/27/1992, p. 18, lines 20-23.

[574] Hanson testimony, 1/9/1992, p. 117, lines 10-25.

[575] Hanson testimony, 1/9/1992, p. 116, lines 17-21.

[576] Hanson deposition, 10/24/1990, p. 7, lines 4-14.

[577] Hanson testimony, 1/9/1992, p. 118, lines 8-18.

[578] Hanson testimony, 1/9/1992, p. 118, line 19—p. 119, line 1.

[579] Plaintiffs' Exhibit 193, September 1989.

[580] Hanson testimony, 1/9/1992, p. 113, line 21—p. 114, line 9.

[581] Stellman testimony, 1/28/92, p. 66, line 22—p. 67, line 1.

[582] Plaintiffs' Exhibit 193, October 1989.

[583] Busfield testimony, 1/9/1992, p. 15, lines 1-17.

[584] Busfield testimony, 1/9/1992, p. 35, lines 6-8.

[585] Busfield testimony, 1/9/1992, p. 22, line 17—p. 23, line 10.

[586] Jolley testimony, 1/15/1992, p. 32, lines 14-18.

[587] Jolley testimony, 1/15/1992, p. 32, lines 14-24.

[588] Stellman testimony, 1/28/1992, p. 48, line 15—p. 49, line 4.

[589] Stellman testimony, 1/28/1992, p. 69, lines 5-12.

Numerous vacancies exist in Tucson. Except for an eight-month period, the Tucson facility has not had a psychiatric nurse since at least October of 1990.[590] There is a Ph.D. psychologist position that has been vacant for over a year.[591] Another psychologist position had been vacant for a year and a half, but was filled in approximately November of 1991.[592]

Dr. Stellman also noted that there were some mental health positions that were frozen; she believes these positions should be unfrozen and filled.[593]

c. Douglas

The Douglas facility, which houses 1,957 inmates,[594] is visited by a psychiatrist, Dr. Centric, approximately one day a month, although sometimes more than a month elapses between his visits.[595] Dr. Centric gives orders for prescriptions over the telephone.[596] He does no therapy at Douglas, except in the sense of psychopharmacologic management.[597] This arrangement was characterized by the Douglas Facility Health Administrator as a "band-aid."[598] Prior to *1524 1990, there was no psychiatrist at Douglas at all.[599]

Douglas has no Ph.D. psychologist. There is such a position, but it has never been filled.[600] Psychological associates should not treat patients without the supervision of a Ph.D. psychologist.[601] ADOC policy also requires that psychological associates be supervised by a Ph.D.-level psychologist.[602] Although the psych associates are now supervised by a Ph.D. psychologist,[603] until recently the psychological associates were supervised by Steven Sloboda, who does not have Ph.D. in psychology.[604]

d. Perryville

As of October 23, 1990, Perryville had three psychologists and one psychologist vacancy.[605] At that time, the San Pedro Unit had no psychologist, only a psych associate.[606] Dr. Cassady, a psychologist at Perryville, believes a psychologist should be available to the San Pedro Unit.[607]

In October of 1990, the psychiatrist position at the Perryville facility had been vacant for approximately eighteen months.[608] The position was finally filled effective December 31, 1991, after being vacant for two and a half years.[609] Because Perryville did not have a full-time psychiatrist at the time of her evaluation, Dr. Stellman expressed concern that, if a prisoner were acutely mentally ill, it might be necessary to initiate treatment or a transfer based on a verbal order, or based on the judgment of the general medical physician.[610] Dr. Stellman believes that the Perryville facility needs a psychiatric nurse and

---

[590] Busfield testimony, 1/9/1992, p. 15, line 24—p. 17, line 16.
[591] Jolley testimony, 1/15/1992, p. 31, lines 7-25.
[592] Jolley testimony, 1/15/1992, p. 39, lines 6-9.
[593] Stellman testimony, 1/28/1992, p. 69, lines 13-23.
[594] Keeney testimony, 1/27/1992, p. 11, line 22—p. 12, line 15.
[595] Centric deposition, p. 9, lines 3-13, p. 46, lines 2-18.
[596] Schwegler testimony, 1/13/1992, p. 43, lines 1-8.
[597] Centric deposition, p. 10, lines 19-25, p. 11, lines 1-3.
[598] Schwegler testimony, 1/13/1992, p. 25, line 14-25, p. 26, lines 14-19.
[599] Schwegler testimony, 1/13/1992, p. 25, lines 14-24.
[600] Schwegler testimony, 1/13/1992, p. 42, lines 8-17.
[601] Newkirk testimony, 11/21/91, p. 132, lines 12-22.
[602] Newkirk testimony, 11/22/91, p. 79, lines 24-25, p. 80, lines 1-12. *See also* Garabedian testimony, 1/7/1992, p. 209, lines 6-8 (the law requires that a psychological associate be supervised by a Ph.D. psychologist).
[603] Schwegler testimony, 1/13/1992, p. 41, lines 16-17.
[604] Schwegler testimony, 1/13/1992, p. 42, lines 2-7.
[605] Cassady deposition, 10/23/1990, p. 13, lines 173; p. 21, lines 2-18.
[606] Cassady deposition, 10/23/1990, p. 55, lines 18-24.
[607] Cassady deposition, 10/23/1990, p. 55, line 18—p. 57, line 1.
[608] Charles deposition, 10/23/1990, p. 27, line 25, p. 28, lines 1-4.
[609] Charles testimony, 1/7/1992, p. 136, line 20—p. 137, line 24.
[610] Stellman testimony, 1/27/1992, p. 143, lines 8-15.

a full-time psychiatrist and that a psychiatrist working only two days a week is not adequate.[611] Perryville gained a psychiatric nurse position in the summer of 1991.[612]

When Dr. Lang was a psychologist at Perryville, he was not able to see all the prisoners who asked to see him.[613] It was also difficult to have prisoners evaluated for the mental health ward at Alhambra because of the lack of psychiatric staff.[614]

e. Winslow

The Winslow facility, with a capacity of 1,321 inmates,[615] has no psychiatrist.[616] Rather, a psychiatrist [Dr. Busfield] visits the facility once a quarter. In the interim, prescriptions for psychotropic medications are written by a nurse practitioner.[617] On **1525** his visit to the facility in January 1991, Dr. Busfield saw 60 prisoners in two days.[618] Before January of 1991, Winslow had no access to a psychiatrist at all. Rather, patients were seen by a nurse practitioner.[619] According to Dr. Newkirk, a psychiatrist should visit on at least a monthly basis, in order to prescribe and monitor psychotropic medications.[620]

Inmates with serious mental illness should not be classified to the Winslow facility.[621] At the time Dr. Stellman toured, Dr. Busfield was touring the state and pulling mentally ill prisoners to the four main prisons of Tucson, Florence, Perryville and Phoenix.[622]

2. Impact of Inadequate Staffing

Defendants admit that they have requested further staff and could function better with those staff.[623]

As a result of inadequate staffing, defendants fail to meet the serious mental health needs of prisoners. For example, a prisoner at Tucson had his treatment discontinued after seeing a psychologist weekly for two months. The record indicated that the psychologist had to stop seeing him because of a

---

[611] Stellman testimony, 1/28/1992, p. 61, lines 13-16, 19-23.

[612] Charles testimony, 1/7/1992, p. 136, lines 15-19.

[613] Lang deposition, 10/25/1990, p. 56, lines 16-25.

[614] Lang deposition, 10/25/1990, p. 45, lines 1-6.

[615] Keeney testimony, 1/27/1992, p. 14.

[616] Lutz testimony, 1/6/1992, p. 61, lines 4-10.

[617] Sanders deposition, 4/8/1991, p. 41, lines 5-16.

[618] Sanders deposition, 4/8/1992, p. 47, lines 4-8.

[619] Sanders deposition, 4/8/1991, p. 53, lines 13-23.

[620] Newkirk testimony, 1/22/1991, p. 8, lines 2-23.

[621] Stellman testimony, 1/27/1992, p. 190, lines 1-8.

[622] Stellman testimony, 1/27/1992, p. 190, lines 8-11.

[623] Plaintiffs' Exhibit 49, SPU treatment team meeting, 8/7/89 (discussion of lifting hiring freeze on psychologist II positions); 8/10/89; 8/24/89; and 9/7/89 (clinical practicum canceled due to lack of staff); 10/11/89 (in two weeks, SPU will have no psychiatrist unless one as been provided by then); Plaintiffs; Exhibit 50, Executive Staff Meeting Minutes, ASPC-Florence, 1/18/89, p. 3 (problems with mental health staffing—"we are struggling with staffing the Psych area. There are no psychologists in the state that can work with the Department and we can't get a cert. list. If we advertise nationwide, it'll take months before we can get someone hired."); ASPC-Winslow, 8/1/89, p. 5 (Alhambra psychiatrist does not want to authorize medications for Winslow prisoners; unclear what psychological associates are to do about prescribing medications. Warden states "it looks like the psychiatrist position will be frozen, so problems like this will continue to occur"); Plaintiffs' Exhibit 196 (memo from SMU deputy warden Upchurch acknowledging severe shortage of mental health staff); Keeney deposition, 11/14/1990, p. 58, lines 19-25 (Associate Director Keeney has expressed the view that more psychologists and psychological associates are needed); Plaintiffs' Exhibit 232, 11/6/89 letter from Director Lewis (psychiatric services at Perryville and Florence are performed by three staff psychiatrists who are unable to meet the demand for their services. These institutions have two frozen psychiatrist positions); Plaintiffs' Exhibit 243bcl (as of 3/29/89, no psychiatrist assigned to Perryville); Plaintiffs' Exhibit 255bq (as of 11/90, Winslow is trying to recruit a psychiatrist); Plaintiffs' Exhibit 279, ASPC-Florence, 4/4/90, p. 5 (lack of trained mental health staff); Plaintiffs' Exhibit 84E, ASPC-Winslow Quality Assurance Audit Summary, 4/17/91, p. 1 (no psychiatrist at this facility; prisoners must be referred to Alhambra. This is not appropriate for those with only behavioral problems); p. 2 (lack of mental health staff, although Winslow has prisoners with serious men-

drastic increase in the psychologist's caseload.[624] Another prisoner, who had a long history of mental health problems and treatment, was unable to be followed monthly by a psychologist while he was at the Winslow facility.[625] An inmate at Santa Maria in Perryville *1526 was unable to see the psychiatrist for some time due to the psychiatrist's caseload.[626]

Dr. Newkirk found inadequate programming at the Special Program Unit because of a lack of staff.[627] Dr. Newkirk believes that SPU needs more staff in order to provide more intensive programming such as one-on-one counseling and group therapy.[628] The mental health staff of the SPU are not separate from that of the rest of the Florence complex. Staff at SPU are responsible for delivering mental health services throughout Florence, with the exception of the SMU.[629] SPU has been short-staffed, in part because SPU staff were diverted to other units in the Florence complex.[630] The treatment team briefings log indicated that staff were performing duties in other units, for example, doing psych (psychiatrist) line in CB6.[631] This limits the ability to have groups and intensive one-on-one therapy.[632] Further, prisoners are excluded from groups because they are full.[633]

Because of high prisoner-to-staff ratios, SPU mental health staff have had to develop a triage (priority) system.[634] Except for a crisis intervention program, there is no 24-hour mental health coverage at SPU.[635] SPU always has a waiting list for admission.[636]

Due to staff shortages at Baker and Flamenco, the ADOC is sometimes unable to have the maximum number of prisoners assigned to those facilities.[637]

The lack of mental health staff at Douglas results in delays in treating prisoners and a lack of follow-up services.[638] Mr. Sloboda has repeatedly requested additional mental health staff.[639] Dr. Stellman believes that the staffing at Douglas is not adequate to deal with the serious needs of mentally ill prisoners.[640] In April of 1991, Dr. Busfield identified five prisoners at Douglas who were seriously mentally ill and should not be housed at that facility.[641]

---

tal health problems, on psychotropic medication); Plaintiffs' Exhibit 309, p. 127, line 24 (Dr. Pera sees 100 patients a week, a situation he characterizes as "ludicrous"); Stewart testimony, 1/16/92, p. 62, lines 19-25 (DOC has tried but has not been able to hire administrative staff so that medical health professionals are freed up to provide direct care because the Legislature will not appropriate money). Plaintiffs' Exhibit 116, 3/8/89 memo from Veloz to Facility Health Administrator Norrish (not enough staff for Women's Division, Central, and SPU. Only two psychiatric nurses to cover Women's, South, East, and North Units; no psychologist, psychological associate, or psychotherapist. Central and Women's continue to impose a strain on limited staff resources with increasing requests for services and crisis intervention).

[624] Newkirk testimony, 11/21/1991, p. 161, lines 6, 13-24.

[625] Newkirk testimony, 11/22/91, p. 8, line 24—p. 9, line 13; Plaintiffs' Exhibit 28n, notes 3/9/89, 4/20/89 [inmate Banich] (Florence–North prisoner not seen by psychiatrist due to lack of time, but psychiatrist renewed medication).

[626] Plaintiffs' Exhibit 249ew (Perryville–Santa Maria prisoner [Michelle McNeil] complains of stress and depression; staff responds that there are too many prisoners on psychiatrist's caseload, and prisoner will not be seen for "some time").

[627] Newkirk testimony, 11/21/1991, p. 116, lines 9-24.

[628] Newkirk testimony, 11/21/1991, p. 166, line 25—p. 167, line 2.

[629] Newkirk testimony, 11/21/1991, p. 116, line 25, p. 117, lines 1-5.

[630] Newkirk testimony, 11/21/1991, p. 166, lines 3-13.

[631] Newkirk testimony, 11/21/1991, p. 117, lines 10-12, 16-20; Plaintiffs' Exhibit 199; Stellman testimony, 1/27/1992, p. 160, lines 13- 25, p. 161, line 1 (description of psych nurses indicated they had other duties in Florence).

[632] Newkirk testimony, 11/21/1991, p. 117, lines 5-9.

[633] Veloz testimony, 1/9/1992, p. 161, lines 9-20; Veloz deposition, 10/25/1990, p. 44, lines 24-25, p. 45, lines 1-5 (there are lists of prisoners waiting to get into groups that are full).

[634] Veloz testimony, 1/9/1992, p. 162, line 25—p. 163, line 2.

[635] Veloz deposition, 10/25/1990, p. 31, lines 15-18.

[636] Veloz testimony, 1/9/1992, p. 149, lines 18-23.

[637] Plaintiffs' Exhibit 232 (more staff would allow the department to increase Baker's census from 21 to approximately thirty-eight and Flamenco from its level of 46 to its maximum of 125).

[638] Sloboda deposition, 10/29/1990, p. 31, lines 7-25, p. 32, lines 1- 7.

[639] Sloboda deposition, 10/29/1990, p. 39, lines 12-24.

[640] Stellman testimony, 1/28/1992, p. 69, line 24—p. 70, line 2.

[641] Stellman testimony, 1/28/1992, p. 70, lines 3-7.

D. Delays in Assessment and Treatment

Prisoners with serious mental health problems experience delays in receiving treatment that are potentially dangerous and cause the prisoners to endure unnecessary psychological pain. Dr. Stellman testified that, optimally, assessments by mental health professionals should be done by the next day ***1527** when a prisoner complains of hearing voices or complains of feeling anxious, tense, or about to explode.[642] A person with serious mental health complaints should be seen within a few days of making complaints.[643]

1. *Delays in Commitment to a Mental Hospital*

Prisoners in need of commitment to a mental hospital have experienced prolonged delays in being transferred to a state hospital. Plaintiffs presented the following examples of delays in commitment to a mental hospital:[644] In 1991, a prisoner at Perryville was in lockdown for two months in a four feet by four feet cell. The prisoner was only allowed out of the cell one hour per day in cuffs and chains. However, the prisoner was not transferred to the state hospital for two months until April of 1991.[645]

In another instance, Dr. Fernandez indicated that a female inmate at Perryville-Santa Maria needed a transfer to a mental hospital on March 1, 1988, but the patient did not receive a transfer until April 12, 1988.[646] Part of the time prior to transfer, the patient was kept in lockdown.[647] At the time the patient was finally admitted to the state hospital, she was reporting paranoia and had active hallucinations and delusions.[648]

In another instance with the same inmate on March 8, 1989, the staff indicated that there was a plan to transfer the patient as an involuntary admission to the Arizona State Hospital.[649] The patient was paranoid, with grandiose illusions and had severely impaired insight into her illness.[650] The patient was not transferred but two months later placed in lockdown for eleven and one-half months.[651] She was not admitted to the hospital until April 27, 1990.[652]

In a third instance with the same inmate, Dr. Pera noted plans on May 28, June 4 and June 11 to commit this patient to the state hospital. On June 5, Dr. Pera signed an affidavit that she was a danger to herself and others, but she was not committed until August 1, 1991.[653] It took up to a week or two for this patient to be seen by a psychiatrist while she was in lockdown.[654]

On July 11, 1990, a male inmate in Central Unit was found to be delusional and staff were attempting to get him to Baker Ward for treatment.[655] On July 27, 1990, he was still in the Central Unit on watch swallow and waiting to be seen by Dr. Busfield on August 9, 1990.[656]

2. *Delays in Evaluation and Treatment by a Psychiatrist*

At Tucson, it may take several days to a week for a prisoner to be seen by a psychiatrist.[657] This delay does not appear to be unusual. Plaintiffs presented numerous examples of inmates who requested mental health care, but provision of that care was delayed:

---

[642] Stellman testimony, 1/28/1992, p. 89, lines 1-8.

[643] Stellman testimony, 1/28/1992, p. 89, line 1—p. 90, line 22.

[644] *See also*, Finding of Fact and Conclusions of Law, *Arnold v. Lewis*, 91-1808.

[645] Plaintiffs' Exhibit 309, p. 112, lines 7-25.

[646] Plaintiffs' Exhibit 311, p. 267, lines 11-17.

[647] Plaintiffs' Exhibit 311, p. 268, lines 14-17.

[648] Plaintiffs' Exhibit 311, p. 269, lines 6-13.

[649] Plaintiffs' Exhibit 311, p. 269, line 18—p. 270, line 4.

[650] Plaintiffs' Exhibit 311, p. 270, lines 10-17.

[651] Plaintiffs' Exhibit 311, p. 270, lines 22-25.

[652] Plaintiffs' Exhibit 311, p. 270, lines 5-9; *See also Arnold v. Lewis*, 91-1808, Findings of Fact and Conclusions of Law.

[653] Plaintiffs' Exhibit 311, p. 271, lines 1-8; p. 272, lines 2-8.

[654] Plaintiffs' Exhibit 312, p. 42, lines 9-12.

[655] "Staff is continuing trying to get inmate to B-Ward for treatment." Plaintiffs' Exhibit 199, 7/11/1990.

[656] Plaintiffs' Exhibit 199, 7/11/90 and 7/27/90.

[657] Jolley testimony, 1/15/1992, p. 33, lines 1-6.

In October and November of 1990, an inmate in SMU filed a series of grievances asking to see a doctor. In one grievance, he indicated that he was hearing voices and that **1528** they were giving him headaches. In three other grievances, he indicated that he had an immediate need to see staff. Staff responded to all four grievances by telling him to see the nurse at sick call.[658]

In another instance, the records of a prisoner at Winslow show an intake examination noting a history of mood instability.[659] On February 20, 1991, he asked to see a psychiatrist.[660] On March 20, 1991, his records note that a consult from Dr. Springer, a psychologist, was reviewed, and that he was scheduled for Dr. Busfield's next visit.[661] On April 14, 1991, medical staff received a call from security staff that the prisoner was acting strangely; he said there was something in his room, and he was hiding in the corner. The LPN referred the inmate to a provider for a consultation for his paranoid ideation. On the same date, eighty-nine pills were confiscated from the prisoner.[662] On April 15, 1991, the medical unit received a call from a psychological associate, who said Dr. Springer felt that the patient was going to "go off." The staff on the same day received another call from security staff indicating that the prisoner was complaining of anxiety and "going crazy," and was asking to see the psychiatrist. Security staff was advised to contact psychology; it was noted that the prisoner would be seen by a psychologist that day.[663] A note on April 17, 1991 stated that the prisoner was being followed by Dr. Springer. Later the same day, security called to say that the prisoner had threatened to hurt himself. The medical unit advised security staff to monitor the prisoner's behavior and advise the medical staff if there was any change in behavior.[664]

Another inmate at SPU was seen by a psychological associate on approximately July 17, 1990, who indicated that the prisoner wanted to see a psychiatrist. The prisoner denied suicidal intent or ideation. The prisoner had a history of treatment for depression. The prisoner was subsequently transferred to the Central Unit at Florence, where he again requested to see the psychiatrist for depression. He had great difficulty receiving treatment until Dr. Lutz intervened.[665]

In addition, plaintiffs presented the following examples through the inmate grievances:[666]

On January 30, 1991 a female inmate at Perryville Santa Maria Unit was told that too many patients were in the psychiatrist's caseload and the psychiatrist could not see the prisoner for "some time."[667]

In another instance, on September 12, 1990, a prisoner at the Perryville Santa Maria Unit reported that she was experiencing a family crisis and was falling apart, and that she wanted to see someone before the scheduled appointment in three weeks. The staff responded that the patient would remain on Dr. Pera's list. The appointment that had been made was for the "soonest time available."[668]

On March 20, 1991, another prisoner at Perryville, Santa Maria indicated that she wanted to be seen as soon as possible because her medications were not helping her depression and she was in a destructive state of mind. In response, a staff member indicated that Dr. Pera had not been at the facility and he was behind in his caseload, with "many, many" patients who needed to be seen before the prisoner who filed the grievance. The grievance response further **1529** indicated that Dr. Pera would try to get to the prisoner in two weeks if possible.[669]

On March 31, 1990, another Santa Maria inmate complained of problems sleeping and feeling really stressed and like she was "going off" after her prescription was discontinued. On April 27, 1990, the grievance response directed the prisoner to see the nurse at sick call to be referred to the unit psychologist or psychiatrist.[670]

---

[658] Plaintiffs' Exhibit 19cc, 11/18/90; 11/21/90, 11/24/90, 10/7/90, 10/12/90.

[659] Plaintiffs' Exhibit 287c, note 4/12/90.

[660] Plaintiffs' Exhibit 287c note 2/20/91.

[661] Plaintiffs' Exhibit 287c, note 3/20/91.

[662] Plaintiffs' Exhibit 287c, notes 4/14/91.

[663] Plaintiffs' Exhibit 287c, notes 4/15/91.

[664] Plaintiffs' Exhibit 287c, note 4/17/91.

[665] Newkirk testimony, 11/21/1991, p. 110, lines 6-24; Plaintiffs' Exhibit 199, 7/17/90, p. 3.

[666] These are admissible for the defendants' responses to the grievances but not for the truth of the inmates' complaints.

[667] Plaintiffs' Exhibit 249ew, 1/30/91.

[668] Plaintiffs' Exhibit 249fg, 9/12/90 (kite); 9/20/90 (response).

[669] Plaintiffs' Exhibit 249ga, 3/20/91 (kite); 3/22/91 (response).

[670] Plaintiffs' Exhibit 249gz, 3/31/90 (kite); 4/27/90 (response).

On July 19, 1990 a prisoner at Perryville-Santa Maria filed a grievance asking for an appointment with a psychiatrist. She filed a second kite on August 6, 1990. On August 8, 1990, she was told she was on Dr. Pera's psych line for an appointment. On August 20, 1990, she was scheduled for an appointment with Dr. Pera.[671]

In another case, on April 9, 1990, a prisoner at Santa Maria requested to see Dr. Fernandez, stating that she was depressed and wanted her prescription renewed. On April 27, 1990, the grievance response indicated that she was scheduled to be re-evaluated in the "near future."[672]

E. Inappropriate Use of Lockdown Facilities

1. *Use of Lockdown as an Alternative to Mental Health Care*

The SMU and CB6 in Florence are not mental health facilities, but rather are maximum security lockup units.[673] Neither SMU nor CB6 are appropriate for the seriously mentally ill because they have insufficient programming for psychotics or those with major depressions.[674] According to Dr. Stellman, it is inappropriate to house an acutely psychotic prisoner in segregation facilities such as CB6, SMU and the women's detention unit at Perryville for more than three days.[675] The only time it is appropriate to put a suicidal or self-abusive prisoner in isolation cells in a non-treatment facility is if it is an emergency, there is absolutely no other place to put them, and they are there for only a short time with a maximum of twenty-four to forty-eight hours.[676] Dr. Pera recognizes that people have objected to the use of lockdown for mental health patients, but states that "economic conditions are such we cannot seem to change the system."[677] Dr. Fernandez, the clinical director for the ADOC Psychiatric Hospital for men (Baker Ward), indicated that lockdown damages people rather than helping them.[678]

Seriously mentally ill prisoners are routinely assigned to SMU and CB6 and placed in detention or isolation cells in non-mental health facilities throughout the ADOC for longer than three days. Isolation is used throughout the ADOC for prisoners with acute mental health problems. Dr. Schwegler, the Facility Health Administrator at Douglas, indicated that prisoners have been put in lockdown and retained there for five to seven days, awaiting transfer to the mental health facility in Phoenix.[679]

a. Female Inmates

Female prisoners exhibiting mental health problems necessitating psychiatric intervention are assigned to lockdown at the Santa Maria Unit in Perryville and retained for more than three days. Examples of such ***1530** lockdown include inmate Legg,[680] Brown,[681] Caltevedt,[682] Bloomfield,[683] and Martinez.[684] *See also Arnold v. Lewis*, 91-1808. Dr. Pera, the psychiatrist responsible for providing psy-

---

[671] Plaintiffs' Exhibits 249ho and 249hp.

[672] Plaintiffs' Exhibit 249fn, 4/9/90 (kite); 4/27/90 (grievance).

[673] Newkirk testimony, 11/21/1991, p. 111, lines 5, 17-18.

[674] Newkirk testimony, 11/21/1991, p. 111, lines 20-21.

[675] Stellman testimony, 1/28/1992, p. 80, line 9—p. 81, line 1.

[676] Newkirk testimony, 11/21/1991, p. 168, lines 1-22.

[677] Plaintiffs' Exhibit 309, p. 127, lines 8-22.

[678] Plaintiffs' Exhibit 309, p. 129, lines 5-13, p. 153, lines 1-3.

[679] Schwegler deposition, 10/29/1990, p. 56, lines 24-25, p. 57, lines 1-21.

[680] Plaintiffs' Exhibit 281(7), 9/12/90 (Legg placed on special watch in lockdown by Dr. Pera on 9/12/90 and retained through 9/22/90).

[681] Plaintiffs' Exhibit 281(7), 12/31/90 (Brown in lockdown per Sergeant from 12/31/90 at least through 1/11/91 until seen by Dr. Pera).

[682] Plaintiffs' Exhibit 281(7), 3/2/91 (Caltevedt put in lockdown on special 30 minute watch (changed to fifteen minute watch on 3/5/91) until seen by Dr. Pera; on watch until 3/13/91).

[683] Plaintiffs' Exhibit 281(7), 3/8/90 (Bloomfield on watch until seen by "psych;" maintained to 3/13/91).

[684] Plaintiffs' Exhibit 281(7), 3/16/91 (Martel Martinez in lockdown on 3/16/1991 until seen by Dr. Pera; still in lockdown as of 3/26/91).

chiatric services at Perryville testified that he sees approximately seven to eight women in lockdown per week.[685] He only sees people in lockdown who are put there because of mental health problems.[686] Some of these are women with significant mental illnesses who are in need of hospitalization.[687]

b. Male Inmates

(1) CB6

CB6 is frequently used to house acutely mentally ill prisoners for longer than three days. Plaintiffs presented numerous examples of seriously mentally ill inmates housed in CB6 including inmates Munk, Mitchell, Brown, Honeycutt, Johnson, Tucker and Autrey:

On April 11, 1989, in Central Unit, Inmate Munk was placed on ten-minute watch in a holding cell and stripped after threatening to eat light bulbs.[688] On April 12, 1989, Inmate Munk was placed in isolation and stripped. He was "still hostile; smearing feces; and jumped on an officer." He was then sent to CB6.[689] On April 14, 1989, Munk was seen by Dr. Pera in CB6. Dr. Pera determined that he was still a behavior problem and should be seen again.[690] On April 17, 1989, Munk was still in CB6, "in observation" with "no change."[691] On April 18, 1989, Munk was still in CB6 and Dr. Pera placed him in four points and released him when he took his medication.[692] On May 10, 1989, Munk was still in CB6.[693]

On September 21, 1989, Inmate Mitchell was on seclusion watch in an observation cell in CB6. He "denied hallucinations or suicide ideations but [was] still very hyper." The notes indicated that the inmate would remain in CB6 until he calmed down.[694]

In another instance, records for October 10, 1989 indicate that Inmate Brown was in CB6, was given a shot of Prolixin by Dr. Pera, would remain at CB6 until "more stable" and then the Admission Team would reevaluate.[695] On October 13, 1989, Inmate Brown was in CB6 where he remained delusional ["Brown remains delusional; appears the same and a little less mellow; Dr. Pera *1531 will see today, needs to be seen daily."].[696] On October 17, 1989, Brown was brought back to SPU from CB6.[697]

On November 22, 1989, Inmate Honeycutt, while in Central Unit, cut himself seriously and was hospitalized at Maricopa Medical Center. However, he was refused admission to Baker Ward (Alhambra) for psychiatric evaluation and returned to Central Unit where he was placed on isolation and transferred to CB6. Inmate Honeycutt remained in CB6 until December 2, 1989 when he was sent to Flamenco for 72 hour evaluation.[698]

In CB6, on March 21, 1990, inmate Johnson was "delusional, out of contact with reality," and was being monitored by mental health staff.[699]

---

[685] Plaintiffs' Exhibit 309, p. 5, lines 8-10, p. 67, lines 22-25.

[686] Plaintiffs' Exhibit 309, p. 68, lines 8-10.

[687] Plaintiffs' Exhibit 309, lines 20-23, p. 6, lines 18 5, p. 7, lines 23-25, p. 8, lines 2, 14-25, p. 9, lines 1-6 (Daisy Brown is a schizophrenic prisoner who was assigned to Santa Maria Unit; placed in lockdown in July 1991 when displaying inappropriate and dangerous behavior such as smearing feces, refusing to talk, refusing to eat); p. 139, lines 22-23, p. 151, lines 16-25, p. 152, lines 1-12 (Guittiere, a woman Dr. Fernandez diagnosed with schizophrenia, paranoid type, was in lockdown in Perryville for more than a month before she was transferred to Flamenco); p. 112, lines 19 (Helen Brown stayed in lockdown two months after Dr. Pera requested she be transferred to the hospital); Garabedian testimony, 1/15/1992, p. 234, lines 10-13 (Helen Brown spent long periods of time in lockup because she would become psychotic).

[688] Plaintiffs' Exhibit 49, 4/11/89.

[689] Plaintiffs' Exhibit 49, 4/12/89.

[690] Plaintiffs' Exhibit 49, 4/14/89.

[691] Plaintiffs' Exhibit 49, 4/17/89.

[692] Plaintiffs' Exhibit 49, 4/18/89.

[693] Plaintiffs' Exhibit 49, 4/19-21/89, 4/25/89, 5/10/89.

[694] Plaintiffs' Exhibit 49, 9/21/89.

[695] Plaintiffs' Exhibit 49, 10/10/89.

[696] Plaintiffs' Exhibit 49, 10/13/89.

[697] Plaintiffs' Exhibit 49, 10/18/89.

[698] Plaintiffs' Exhibit 49, 11/22/89, 11/27/89, 2/12/89.

[699] Plaintiffs' Exhibit 199, 3/21/90, 3/23/90, 3/26/90.

In May of 1990, inmate Tucker was decompensating in SPU. He had rambling speech, was disoriented and was wandering around lost. Tucker was sent to CB6, where he remained for five days.[700]

Inmate Mike Autrey was found dead from hanging in a cell in CB6 on December 27, 1989. He had made several suicide attempts in the past while in the custody of the ADOC, but was never admitted to Baker or SPU for more intensive evaluation or treatment.[701] He was placed in CB6 or SMU when he made these suicide attempts rather than receiving more intensive treatment.[702] There were times when he refused treatment; however, no psychiatrist ever recommended he go to any treatment facility.[703] He was followed by mental health and a psychiatric nurse had seen him and requested he be placed on the psychiatrist's line, but he had "adamantly" refused.[704] Although the psychiatric nurse had identified a need for him to see a psychiatrist, this was not forced on him. Perhaps if that had been done, he would not have committed suicide.[705] The general standard in recommending involuntary hospitalization is whether a person is a danger to self or others.[706] The department, under its own policies, could have involuntarily hospitalized him.[707]

(2) SMU

Seriously mentally ill prisoners are also housed in the Special Management Unit (SMU). Examples of such inmates include inmates Barge;[708] Gooden;[709] Arvizu;[710] *1532 Verheim;[711] Jones[712] and Trotter.[713] Mr. Veloz indicates that there are people who are not appropriate for Baker and Flamenco and cannot function in SPU because they are too assaultive and present management problems. These inmates probably would be assigned to SMU.[714]

Defendants also house self-abusive prisoners in SMU. From her review of records, Dr. Newkirk identified the following self-abusive prisoners who were inappropriately housed at SMU:[715]

---

[700] Plaintiffs' Exhibit 199, 5/16/90, 5/17/90, 5/18/90, 5/21/90.

[701] Newkirk testimony, 11/21/1991, p. 109, lines 10-20.

[702] Newkirk testimony, 11/21/1991, p. 109, line 21—p. 110, line 3.

[703] Newkirk testimony, 11/22/1991, p. 68, lines 2-9, p. 84, lines 3-11.

[704] Stellman testimony, 1/27/1992, p. 144, lines 17-22.

[705] Stellman testimony, 1/27/1992, p. 145, lines 7-10.

[706] Newkirk testimony, 11/22/1991, p. 84, line 21—p. 85, line 6.

[707] Plaintiffs' Exhibit 120.

[708] Plaintiffs' Exhibit 49, 2/10/89 (Barge in holding cell for six days, "acting crazy at Alhambra, still erratic"), Plaintiffs' Exhibit 49, 2/27/89 (Barge in holding cell; standing orders that if he refuses medication three times in a row he be placed automatically in the holding cell), Plaintiffs' Exhibit 49, 2/28/89 (Barge in holding cell, taking medication intermittently, doing better but degenerates; will keep in holding cell until stable), Plaintiffs' Exhibit 49, 3/21/89 (Barge had been sent to Alhambra but refused to talk to anyone there so being returned to SMU for documentation and possible involuntary hospitalization).

[709] Plaintiffs' Exhibit 49, 2/23/89 (Gooden's eyes were bright; totally unresponsive; talking gibberish; left on ten-minute close watch), 2/28/89 (Gooden is doing well but not well enough to put back in cell; medications will be doubled today; remains in restraints).

[710] Plaintiffs' Exhibit 49, 2/27/89 (Arvizu is "totally out of it;" given shot of Benadryl and four-pointed), 2/28/89 (Arvizu still four-pointed; tried to take a shower but security had to forcibly remove from shower; will try to get him back to Alhambra), 3/2/89 (Arvizu is still in holding cell on close watch; Dr. Menendez started him on medication; in full restraints, arms and ankles are swollen badly), 3/7/89 (Arvizu still in bad shape), 3/31/89 (Arvizu going to Alhambra today).

[711] Plaintiffs' Exhibit 49, 3/15/89 (Verheim is hallucinating; wants to come to SPU; file shows assaultive).

[712] Plaintiff's Exhibit 49, 10/10/89 (Jones placed in observation cell [holding cell] threatening self-abuse), 10/11/89 (Jones appears to be suffering from paranoia), 10/12/89 (Jones still in holding cell; still refusing to sign "no self harm" contract), 10/13/89 (Jones hung himself with sheet; banged head), 10/16/89 (Jones escalated to stage of being terrified, sent to Maricopa Medical Center), 10/17/89 (Jones sent to Baker from Maricopa Medical Center).

[713] Roy Trotter would sometimes become extremely explosive. Because of his psychotic behavior, he was being seen by mental health. But he was constantly in and out of lockup facilities and was housed at SMU. Newkirk testimony, 11/21/1991, p. 169, lines 10-15.

[714] Veloz deposition, 10/25/1990, p. 72, line 10—p. 73, line 12; Plaintiffs' Exhibit 49, 2/17/1989, p. 2.

[715] Newkirk testimony, 11/21/1991, p. 167, line 16—p. 169, line 4, p. 170, line 1.

Ralph Lara had a history of swallowing razor blades. He had been in and out of isolation cells and lockup cells because of his self-abusive behavior.[716]

William Morrows had been at SPU and CB6, and had to be isolated on several occasions because of his self-destructive behavior, which staff believed to be secondary to his psychiatric history.[717]

Frank Bartholic was a self-abusive prisoner housed at SMU.[718] He was placed in a holding cell and shackled because he threatened to harm himself.[719] Mr. Bartholic was put in lockdown on at least four occasions in 1989.[720] On one occasion, he was kept in lockdown for three and a half days.[721]

On December 7, 1989, Mr. Sanchez swallowed a piece of a razor blade. Medical staff refused to have him brought to the health unit; instead, they told the officer to check for blood.[722] Two weeks later, Mr. Sanchez cut himself on the chest.[723] The following month he tried to cut himself and was moved to the holding cell; he was heard saying that the Devil was talking to him.[724] On July 29, 1990, he cut his neck with a razor.[725]

Another inmate, Mr. Estrada, cut himself four times within a three-month period.[726] He also set fires in his cell.[727] He was seen by mental health after some, but not all, of these incidents.[728]

Other such self-abusive inmates include inmate Hinds, Barge, Villareal, Mendez, *1533 Deutsch, and Jones.[729]

When a prisoner circulates in and out of the holding cell, it indicates that the prisoner has a psychiatric problem that is not being adequately addressed.[730] It is also disruptive to the functioning of the unit, because prisoners in holding cells are often placed on a 10 or 15 minute watch, and the programming of the prisoner is disrupted.[731] Mr. Bartholic is an example of a prisoner who circulates in and out of the holding cell[732] because his behavioral problem is not being addressed. His record shows that a decision was made that he only needed to be seen by mental health when in a crisis, so the psychiatrist stopped seeing him on a regular basis. Nothing has been done in a treatment modality to decrease the self-destructive behavior.[733] Thus, Mr. Bartholic has attempted suicide four times while in ADOC custody; the last three of these attempts took place while he was housed at SMU.[734]

---

[716] Newkirk testimony, 11/21/1991, p. 169, lines 7-10.

[717] Newkirk testimony, 11/21/1991, p. 169, lines 16-19.

[718] Newkirk testimony, 11/21/1991, p. 170, lines 9-14.

[719] Newkirk testimony, 11/21/1991, p. 170, line 22—p. 171, line 1.

[720] Stellman testimony, 1/27/1992, p. 199, lines 11-14.

[721] Newkirk testimony, 11/22/1991, p. 6, lines 17-19, p. 7, lines 3-8.

[722] Plaintiffs' Exhibit 19ooo, incident report 12/7/89.

[723] Plaintiffs' Exhibit 19ooo, incident report 12/20/89.

[724] Plaintiffs' Exhibit 19ooo, incident report 1/27/90.

[725] Plaintiffs' Exhibit 19ooo, use of force report 7/29/90. Exh. 19uuu, incident report 12/14/90.

[726] Plaintiffs' Exhibit 19uu, incident reports 10/29/90, 12/14/90, 12/28/90, 1/2/91.

[727] Plaintiffs Exhibit 19uu, incident reports 5/25/90, 9/18/90.

[728] Plaintiffs Exhibit 19uu, incident reports 5/25/90, 9/18/90.

[729] Plaintiffs' Exhibit 49, SPU staff briefing, 2/10/89 (Hinds attempted to strangle self, is "real threat to self;" transferred from Perryville to SMU and put in holding cell in restraints); 2/21/89 (Barge throwing self against wall and banging head; refused medication; stripped and four-pointed); 2/23/89 (Villareal pulled out all sutures; treated and put back in holding cell in restraints); 2/23/89 (Mendez taken off close watch last night, then made six-inch slash on his arm); 8/22/89 (Deutsch hit head so hard he opened deep gash and was taken to Maricopa Medical Center for treatment); 10/13/89 (Jones tried to hang himself with a sheet; upon return from hospital, ripped helmet off and rammed head into wall, causing bleeding); 10/16/89 (Jones had huge hematoma on head from ramming into cell wall; sent to Maricopa Medical Center); 10/17/89 (Jones transferred to B-ward from Maricopa Medical Center).

[730] Newkirk testimony, 11/21/1991, p. 173, lines 9-13.

[731] Newkirk testimony, 11/21/1991, p. 173, lines 3-8.

[732] In this section, the terms "holding cell," "lockup," and "lockdown" are used interchangeably. The SMU holding cell is smaller than a regular cell, and is triangular in shape. A bench that serves as a bed is bolted to the wall, and there is a toilet. Newkirk testimony, 11/21/1991, p. 171, lines 17-23. Dr. Newkirk described it as a "very small, cramped space." Newkirk testimony, 11/21/1991, p. 171, line 3. A prisoner is usually placed in the cell wearing only his undershorts. He may be given a blanket, but nothing else. Newkirk testimony, 11/21/1991, p. 72, lines 20- 24.

[733] Newkirk testimony, 11/21/1991, p. 173, line 18—p. 174, line 4.

[734] Bartholic testimony, 12/17/1991, p. 176, lines 4-16.

Defendants know that SMU is not suitable for self-abusive prisoners.[735] In late 1990 or early 1991, a pod for self-abusive prisoners was established at SMU. However, that pod has no mental health staff assigned to it.[736] Moreover, Mr. Hanson, the SMU psychiatric nurse, does not know "whether there is any real specific programming provided for it, other than the fact that it gets more individual attention."[737]

Prisoners who continue to have serious mental health problems are discharged from Baker Ward and sent to SMU. Johnny Johnson, a prisoner who swallowed razor blades, lacerating his esophagus, was returned to SMU with a discharge summary of "very, high risk of suicide."[738] Another prisoner, Hanlon, jumped off a rail on the second floor with a rope around his neck. The suicide attempt was unsuccessful because the rope broke. Dr. Gopalan indicated the inmate had a history of serious suicide attempts, a volatile bipolar disorder, was a chronic suicide risk, and needed placement in licensed mental health facility such as B Ward or Flamenco.[739]

The mental health staff at SMU refer prisoners to Baker, when they "decompensate and become quite disturbed," and to SPU. However, pursuant to Director Lewis' policy, prisoners living in urine and feces for two or *1534 three days are no longer allowed to go to Baker Ward.[740] Moreover, not all prisoners referred to SPU and Baker are accepted.[741] When accepted, inmates still may have to wait in SMU for more than three days before transfer.[742] Inmate Simpson is an example of a prisoner who had to wait for his transfer. He was referred for admission to SPU on May 4, 1990. On May 9, 1990, Mr. Hanson called SPU and indicated the prisoner was acting "very strange." On May 17, 1990, Mr. Simpson was still in SMU, with a plan that he be moved to SPU that day.

(3) *Other Facilities*

There are other facilities that improperly house seriously mentally ill prisoners in lock-down. In North Unit, in September of 1989, Inmate Oliveras was "acutely psychotic; responding to auditory and hallucinatory ideations." Dr. Pera decreased medication and sent the inmate to Central Unit isolation on a ten-minute watch.[743] On March 2, 1991, Inmate Weathersby was in Winslow lockdown unit and exhibiting bizarre and self-destructive behavior including urinating on cell floor, flooding the cell and cutting his wrists. He was not transferred to Alhambra until March 6, 1991.[744]

There are also self-abusive prisoners inappropriately housed at other facilities including inmate Thomas who was housed at Douglas, inmate Honeycutt who was housed at Central Unit and CB6, inmate Smith who was housed at Winslow, inmate Maxwell who was housed at CB6, and inmate Bronkinson who was housed in Tucson detention.[745]

---

[735] Plaintiffs' Exhibit 176, SMU mental health team minutes, 7/19/90, (remarks of Dr. Gopalan); Plaintiffs' Exhibit 177, SMU mental health team minutes, 8/15/90.

[736] Hanson testimony, 1/9/1992, p. 115, lines 7-24.

[737] Hanson testimony, 1/9/1992, p. 106, lines 8-19.

[738] Plaintiffs' Exhibit 176, p. 2.

[739] Plaintiffs' Exhibit 199, 7/12/90 (Hanlon referred to SPU by Tim Hanson on recommendation from Dr. Gopalan).

[740] Plaintiffs' Exhibit 176, p. 3.

[741] Stellman testimony, 1/28/1992, p. 86, lines 21-25 (Dr. Pushkash has asked for acutely mentally ill prisoners to be transferred to Baker who have not been accepted); Pushkash deposition, p. 27, lines 10-19, p. 28, lines 8-20.

[742] Pushkash deposition, p. 27, lines 10-19, p. 28, lines 8-20.

[743] Plaintiffs' Exhibit 49, Cochise Detention Unit Log, 9/13/89; Exh. 281(10) (prisoners on suicide watch: 3/2/90 3/5/90 [Olivas]; 3/7/90 to 3/12/90 [Smart].

[744] Plaintiffs' Exhibit 95, 3/2/91-3/6/91.

[745] Plaintiffs' Exhibit 49, SPU staff briefing, 8/22/89 (Thomas at Douglas ordered back to SPU by Dr. Scalzo; Mr. Veloz noted that prisoner had made a serious suicide attempt, and should be sent to Alhambra psychiatric hospital; Dr. Menendez agrees); 11/22/89 (Honeycutt in Central Unit cut himself seriously and sent to hospital); 11/27/89 (Dr. Menendez refuses to accept Honeycutt at Baker; he is returned to Central Unit with a recommendation he go to CB6); 12/11/89 (Honeycutt in CB6 cut himself and sent to hospital); Plaintiffs' Exhibit 52, Winslow weekly summary of outside referrals, 3/25/91-3/31/91 (Smith attempted suicide; sent to hospital to have neck sutured); Plaintiffs' Exhibit 199, SPU treatment team briefings, 3/19/90 (Maxwell in CB6 attempted overdose; air evacuated to hospital); Plaintiffs' Exhibit 281(9), Tucson Complex Detention Unit Log, 1/20/91, 2033-2130 (medical staff in unit for Bronkinson, who injured himself; he was later sent to Rincon, D-wing).

F. Problems Prescribing Medication

1. *Monitoring of Medication*

Plaintiffs allege that ADOC fails to appropriately monitor the prescription of psychotropic medication. A patient on psychotropic medication should be seen by a psychiatrist on a monthly basis to review the prescription.[746] Dr. Stellman does not know of an ADOC policy that requires patients on psychotropic medications to be monitored.[747] Pursuant to ADOC Policy 704.1, a psychotropic prescription is valid for only sixty days.[748] The HSB Monthly Activity Reports for Safford for 1989 and 1990 indicate that patients are prescribed or continued on psychotropic medications without a face-to-face evaluation by a psychiatrist, because the reports show a larger number of prisoners on psychotropic medication than the number of prisoners seen by a psychiatrist.[749] Similarly, the HBS Monthly Activity Reports for Ft. Grant for 1989 and 1990 indicate that patients at that institution are also prescribed or continued on psychotropic medications ***1535** without a face-to-face evaluation by a psychiatrist.[750]

The same practice exists at Winslow[751] and Douglas.[752] At Winslow, psychological associates, who are master's level mental health providers, call Dr. Menendez to prescribe Thorazine. Dr. Menendez prescribes Thorazine based on these conversations without evaluating the patient in person. Plaintiffs presented the following example: On November 29, 1990, staff responded to a prisoner grievance at Winslow regarding the failure to monitor patients on psychotropics by indicating that "[b]oth ASPC-W Health Services and HSB are aware of this problem. We are both trying to recruit a psychiatrist for ASPC-W and are in touch with a psychiatrist in the Phoenix area institutions for consultation. DOC psychiatrists are presently developing guidelines concerning the prescribing of psychotropic drugs and for evaluating non-drug needs of inmates in the mental health area."[753]

2. *Delays in Receipt of Medications*

Inmates experience delays in the receipt of prescribed psychotropic medication. The following are examples of such delays:

In February of 1990, a patient at the Central Unit had psychotropic medications ordered but did not receive them for a month.[754] On March 27, 1989, prescriptions at SPU for several medications expired but no physician could be located to renew the prescriptions.[755]

A prisoner saw Dr. Fernandez at Perryville-Santa Maria on December 27, 1989. As of January 31, 1990, she had not received a prescription. She was told she would be rescheduled for Dr. Fernandez' next visit to Santa Maria on February 19, 1990.[756]

A patient transferred to Perryville-Santa Maria indicated in a grievance that she had not received her prescription from ACW. In response to the patient's grievance, she was told on November 9 that the medication had been ordered and she was placed on a psych line for an appointment with Dr. Pera.[757]

On August 8, 1990, a prisoner filed a grievance indicating that the medication had been received, but in the wrong dosage. The staff subsequently responded that he was now receiving the correct dosage prescribed by Dr. Pera.[758]

---

[746] Newkirk testimony, 11/22/1991, p. 7, line 25, p. 8, lines 1- 23.

[747] Stellman testimony, 1/28/1992, p. 77, line 21—p. 78, line 2.

[748] Stellman testimony, 1/28/1992, p. 60, lines 29-14.

[749] Plaintiffs' Exhibit 147, 1/89-12/89, 1/90-12/90.

[750] Plaintiffs' Exhibit 148, 7/89-12/89, 1/90-3/90.

[751] Plaintiffs' Exhibit 151, 1/89-12/89; 1/90-8/90, 10/90-12/90.

[752] Plaintiffs' Exhibit 169, 2/89-11/89, 1/90/90, 4/90-6/90, 12/90.

[753] Plaintiffs' Exhibit 255bq, 11/5/90.

[754] Plaintiffs' Exhibit 199, 2/1/90.

[755] Plaintiffs' Exhibit 49, 3/22/89.

[756] Plaintiffs' Exhibit 244ppp, 1/17/90 (grievance); 1/31/90 (response).

[757] Plaintiffs' Exhibit 249fc, 11/6/90.

[758] Plaintiffs' Exhibit 249bk, 8/8/90.

On April 4, 1989, a prisoner at Perryville-Santa Cruz was told, in response to a grievance, that "there is no guarantee that the prescription will be delivered at the time due to varied circumstances in our environment."[759]

Prisoners who were transferred may be without their medications for a period of time. If an inmate is transferred from one facility to another, such as from Alhambra to SMU, and the inmate is on medications, in order to maintain the continuity of care, a psychiatric nurse sees the patient then makes an assessment.[760] For example, if someone comes into SMU on a Friday afternoon, he probably will not receive his medication until Monday.[761]

3. *Discontinuing Medications Without Face-to-Face Interviews*

Defendants sometimes discontinue a prisoner's psychotropic medications based on a laboratory report that the level of medication in the prisoner's blood is low, without conducting a face-to-face interview with the prisoner. ***1536**[762] It is important to monitor blood levels for inmates taking psychotropic medications to ascertain whether the dosage is in the therapeutic range or is toxic.[763] The other use of blood level monitoring is to check on compliance with the medication to see if someone is really taking the doses that are prescribed.[764] It is important for the mental health professional to know whether an inmate is really taking his psychotropic medication because it affects the safety of all the people in the population.[765] Blood level monitoring is an acceptable practice both in and out of a correctional setting in the areas of psychiatry.[766] In some situations, it is appropriate to discontinue psychotropic medications based on low blood levels.[767]

Discontinuing medication based solely on blood levels is not appropriate because a number of factors can cause blood levels to vary.[768] For example, other medications the prisoner is taking can distort the blood levels, as can the functioning of the patient's liver.[769] In particular, blood levels for antipsychotic drugs are not reliable.[770]

Before taking a prisoner off psychotropic medication, the mental health staff should look at the prisoner's clinical functioning.[771] If a prisoner's blood level is low, and the practitioner suspects the prisoner may not be taking the medication, there are alternatives to stopping the medication. For example, the prisoner can be watched while taking the medicine, or it can be given in liquid or injection form.[772] In any event, psychotropic medication should not be stopped for noncompliance unless the noncompliance is documented in the chart, the prisoner's behavior is under control, and the practitioner has had a face-to-face interview with the prisoner.[773] Dr. Stellman agreed that in her own general practice she would not discontinue medication without seeing the prisoner.[774]

The practice of discontinuing psychotropic medications based on blood levels, without a face-to-face interview, has caused mentally ill prisoners to decompensate. Plaintiffs presented the following examples of inmates who decompensated after their medications were discontinued based only on blood levels.

---

[759] Plaintiffs' Exhibit 250ao, 4/4/89.

[760] Hanson testimony, 1/9/1992, p. 25, lines 6-16.

[761] Hanson testimony, 1/9/1992, p. 96, lines 1-9.

[762] Newkirk testimony, 11/21/1991, p. 124, lines 10-17.

[763] Stellman testimony, 1/27/1992, p. 112, lines 19-25.

[764] Stellman testimony, 1/27/1992, p. 113, lines 1-4.

[765] Stellman testimony, 1/27/1992, p. 113, lines 5-7.

[766] Stellman testimony, 1/27/1992, p. 113, lines 18-21.

[767] Stellman testimony, 1/27/1992, p. 145, line 23—p. 146, line 4.

[768] Newkirk testimony, 11/21/91, p. 131, lines 10-14.

[769] Newkirk testimony, 11/21/91, p. 131, lines 15-18.

[770] Newkirk testimony, 11/21/1991, p. 132, lines 4-6.

[771] Newkirk testimony, 11/21/1991, p. 131, lines 18-20.

[772] Newkirk testimony, 11/21/1991, p. 131, lines 21-24; 11/22/91, p. 59, lines 20-25, p. 60, lines 1-11; Stellman testimony, 1/27/92, p. 114, line 15—p. 115, line 3.

[773] Newkirk testimony, 11/21/1991, p. 59, lines 9-16, p. 63, lines 16- 22, p. 79, lines 12-16.

[774] Stellman testimony, 1/28/92, p. 51, line 23—p. 52, line 9.

Mr. Ezell was a prisoner at Douglas with a history of swallowing razor blades.[775] He was taking Thorazine, but based on his blood levels, the psychiatrist suspected he was not taking the medication, so it was stopped, without having Mr. Ezell actually seen by a psychiatrist.[776] He was placed on a suicide watch, and was eventually transferred to Douglas.[777] There is no indication that the psychiatrist offered to give Mr. Ezell his medication in injection form, to alleviate any **1537** concerns about possible hoarding.[778] Mr. Ezell's medication was later reinstated.[779] Dr. Stellman testified that the doctor's actions in this case were warranted based on the fact that Mr. Ezell had a history of swallowing razor blades and on one occasion he overdosed on a psychotropic medication while at Flamenco.[780] In addition, Mr. Ezell was placed in an observation cell so he could be watched closely by mental health.[781]

Mr. Rossi, a prisoner in CB6, had been seen by mental health for some time, and was taking medication for tension and irritability.[782] He had previously been diagnosed as a paranoid schizophrenic.[783] His prescription was discontinued based on low blood levels. By the time Dr. Newkirk saw him, he was complaining of being quite tense and irritable.[784] After the prescription was discontinued, mental health staff did not evaluate Mr. Rossi to determine if he was able to function without the medication.[785] Ten days after the medication was stopped, a physician noted Mr. Rossi's agitation, and prescribed Benadryl.[786]

Dr. Stellman testified that Mr. Rossi's medical chart indicated that he appeared to be a management problem rather than a mental health illness.[787] According to Dr. Stellman, the treatment plan was to begin to decrease the medication and reevaluate the inmates.[788] Despite full levels of antipsychotic medication, blood levels repeatedly returned as below therapeutic, indicating that Mr. Rossi was not taking his medication.[789] Despite the low blood levels, Mr. Rossi was not evidencing acute mental illness or decompensation. Thus, Dr. Stellman believed that he did not need the drugs.[790] Further, after discontinuation of his medication, Mr. Rossi was seen by a psychiatrist on September 13, 1990.[791] There was no indication in the medical chart to indicate that Mr. Rossi was suffering from a psychotic illness upon discontinuation of his medication.[792]

Dr. Newkirk also reviewed the record of Mr. Villario in CB6. According to his record, he had had psychotic episodes and been out of touch with reality, sometimes to the point of smearing feces on the wall.[793] On one occasion, the physician suspected that he was not taking his medication; a blood level was ordered, and when the result was low, Mr. Villario's prescription for Navane was discontinued.[794] Approximately two weeks later, he began to complain of hearing voices, and appeared to be psychotic. He was then placed on Thorazine.[795]

---

[775] Newkirk testimony, 11/21/1991, p. 125, lines 6-10.
[776] Newkirk testimony, 11/21/1991, p. 125, lines 10-15; Stellman testimony, 1/27/1992, p. 146, line 16—p. 147, line 1.
[777] Newkirk testimony, 11/21/1991, p. 129, lines 14-16.
[778] Stellman testimony, 1/28/1992, p. 128, lines 9-19.
[779] Stellman testimony, 1/27/1992, p. 147, lines 9-10.
[780] Stellman testimony, 1/27/1992, p. 147, lines 9-15.
[781] Stellman testimony, 1/27/1992, p. 147, lines 15-25.
[782] Newkirk testimony, 11/21/1991, p. 129, lines 17-24.
[783] Stellman testimony, 1/28/1992, p. 131, lines 10-16.
[784] Newkirk testimony, 11/21/1991, p. 129, line 24—p. 130, line 1.
[785] Newkirk testimony, 11/21/1991, p. 130, lines 2-8.
[786] Newkirk testimony, 11/22/1991, p. 63, line 22—p. 64, line 8.
[787] Stellman testimony, 1/27/1992, p. 150, lines 14-15.
[788] Stellman testimony, 1/27/1992, p. 150, lines 16-17.
[789] Stellman testimony, 1/27/1992, p. 151, lines 1-25.
[790] Stellman testimony, 1/27/1992, p. 152, lines 7-25.
[791] Stellman testimony, 1/27/1992, p. 153, line 23—p. 154, line 2.
[792] Stellman testimony, 1/27/1992, p. 154, lines 2-15.
[793] Newkirk testimony, 11/21/1991, p. 130, lines 12-21.
[794] Newkirk testimony, 11/21/1991, p. 130, lines 22-25.
[795] Newkirk testimony, 11/21/1991, p. 130, line 25, p. 131, line 2.

G. Equal Protection

Defendants do not provide female prisoners with mental health facilities and programming *1538 comparable to those offered to male prisoners.

1. *B Ward*

There are no facilities for the involuntary commitment of women in ADOC such as the Baker Ward for men.[796] While male prisoners can be committed involuntarily to Baker Ward, an ADOC psychiatric hospital, until recently ADOC had no facility to which females could be committed involuntarily.[797] Thus, women would be committed to the Arizona State Hospital (ASH), where they would remain for a very short period before being returned to prison, where they would often be placed in lockup. Dr. Garabedian characterized this as a "vicious cycle." Due to a recent statutory change, female prisoners can now be committed either to ASH or to G-ward.[798] This statutory change took effect in September 1991; both Dr. Garabedian and Executive Assistant Director Stewart lobbied for its passage.[799] Although the female inmates can now be involuntarily committed to Flamenco, it does not provide the higher level of care provided in Baker Ward, which is a licensed psychiatric hospital.

2. *Flamenco*

Flamenco is designed to provide psychiatric treatment and custody to prisoners who are acutely disturbed and/or psychotic and require voluntary placement in a correctional psychiatric setting.[800] Flamenco has three wards for male prisoners. Each of these wards serves a different purpose; K is the acute unit, J is sub-acute, and I is the "functional" unit.[801] At Flamenco, male prisoners can progress from the J to I ward and then into SPU or general population. The purpose of this phase program is to provide each prisoner the care appropriate to his needs, and to encourage improvement in the prisoner.[802]

There is only a single ward at Flamenco for female prisoners. G-ward was opened in May or June of 1990.[803] Before that time, there was no facility at Alhambra for women with serious mental illness. Rather, ADOC staff would petition to have such persons committed to the Arizona State Hospital (ASH).[804] G-ward "gets uncomfortable" when its population reaches sixteen or seventeen; its average census is fifteen or sixteen, although it has gone as high as eighteen.[805]

The programming available to women in G-ward is markedly inferior to that available in the male wards at Flamenco. For example, the men have a large occupational therapy area with various kinds of equipment; the women receive occupational therapy in the unit, and a limited amount of supplies can be brought to the unit.[806] Men have many more opportunities for occupational therapy than women.[807] Occupational therapy is important for the mentally ill, as it helps improve socialization with peers.[808] There are other inequalities in the programming offered to men and women at Flamenco. These inequities are clear from the mental health activity reports. For example in April of 1990, men were offered basketball, volleyball, computer training, communication training, stress management, *1539 anger control, work crew, and current events. Women were offered aerobics.[809] In June of 1990, men were offered com-

[796] Newkirk testimony, 11/21/1991, p. 103, line 6—p. 104, line 23.
[797] Newkirk testimony, 11/21/1991, p. 103, lines 19-2; Plaintiffs' Exhibit 1(2), pp. 37-38, 42.
[798] Garabedian testimony, 1/7/1992, p. 214, lines 9-20.
[799] Garabedian testimony, 1/7/1992, p. 224, line 4—p. 225, line 11.
[800] Plaintiffs' Exhibit 1(3), p. 17.
[801] Plaintiffs' Exhibit 1(3), p. 20.
[802] Plaintiffs' Exhibit 1(3), p. 21.
[803] Guy deposition, 10/22/1990, p. 13, lines 8-25, p. 14, lines 1-7.
[804] Charles deposition, 10/23/1990, p. 43, line 19—p. 44, line 2.
[805] Garabedian testimony, p. 215, 1/7/1992, lines 1-7, p. 225, lines 13-19.
[806] Newkirk testimony, 11/21/1991, p. 103, line 24—p. 104, line 15; Garabedian testimony, 1/7/1992, p. 219, lines 23-25, p. 220, lines 1- 3, p. 229, lines 4-10.
[807] Garabedian testimony, 1/7/1992, p. 229, lines 8-10.
[808] Newkirk testimony, 11/21/1991, p. 104, line 16—p. 105, line 3.
[809] Plaintiffs' Exhibit 239, Mental Health Activity Report, Baker/Flamenco, 4/90.

puter training, basketball, walking, volleyball, work crew, values training, and basic hygiene. Women were offered board games, movies, and "Women Who Love Too Much."[810]

3. *SPU*

There is no progressive unit or level system for women as there is for men at Florence SPU.[811] The principle of the level system for men is to house prisoners with similar levels of functioning in the same unit; by contrast, G-ward may house a mixture of levels, ranging from those who are actively psychotic to those who are ready to enter general population.[812]

The Special Program Unit (SPU) is a special living unit where mentally ill prisoners are housed, and specially trained staff provide mental health programming. Some prisoners, who would have difficulty living in general population, are placed in SPU long-term; for others, it is an acute, transitional unit.[813] However, SPU is a male unit; there is no similar facility for female prisoners.[814] Women who need SPU-type care may be treated in G-ward.[815] Thus, for example, if a male prisoner at Florence had some kind of breakdown, he would be sent to SPU. However, if a female prisoner were in the same situation, there would really be no place to house her pending an evaluation; she would probably be placed in isolation.[816]

Conversely, chronically mentally ill women who are stabilized while on G-ward go back to general population; similarly situated men may go either to population or to SPU. Mr. Garabedian testified that "we have one more option with the men."[817] According to Dr. Newkirk, after being stabilized in a Baker-type unit, it would be important for a prisoner like H.B. to be placed in an SPU-type unit.[818] Dr. Newkirk opined that she needs long-term chronic care, but such care is not available for women in ADOC.[819] There are other examples of female prisoners, including Ms. Cordra and Ms. Velah, who would be appropriate candidates for an intermediate care facility, if one were available.[820]

4. *Impact*

The consequences of the lack of equivalent mental health facilities for women are illustrated by the case of H.B. See Findings of Fact and Conclusions of Law in *Arnold v. Lewis*, 91-1808. Rather than receiving treatment for their mental illness, female inmates are locked down in the Santa Maria Unit in Perryville. *Id.* For ten years, the defendants have neglected to treat H.B.'s severe mental illness [schizophrenia, chronic, paranoid type]. Rather, her treatment has followed a pattern of lock-down for prolonged periods of time with denial of mental health treatment during lock-down. As a result, her mental condition deteriorates and she is eventually transferred to Flamenco or ASH. When her condition is under control, she is released to general population and again locked down, sometimes within 24 to 72 hours.[821] Defendants have placed her in *1540 lock-down to punish her for behavior that was a result of her mental illness; failed to monitor her medications; and failed to transfer her to ASH when mental health staff recommended transfers.[822] The mental health care system at Santa Maria is inadequate to meet her needs because it lacks staff so that she can be seen by a psychiatrist or psychologist, especially in lock-down.[823]

---

[810] Plaintiffs' Exhibit 239, Mental Health Activity Report, Baker/Flamenco, 6/90.
[811] Garabedian testimony, 1/7/1992, p. 225, lines 20-25, p. 226, lines 1-9.
[812] Garabedian testimony, 1/7/1992, p. 226, lines 10-20.
[813] Newkirk testimony, 11/21/1991, p. 105, line 17—p. 106, line 11.
[814] Newkirk testimony, 11/21/1991, p. 105, lines 12-16.
[815] Garabedian testimony, 1/7/1992, p. 218, line 21—p. 219, lines 6.
[816] Norrish deposition, 10/24/1990, p. 63, lines 11-21; p. 64, lines 7-24.
[817] Garabedian testimony, 1/7/1992, p. 229, line 11—p. 230, line 13.
[818] Newkirk testimony, 11/21/1991, p. 107, lines 4-25.
[819] Newkirk testimony, 11/21/1991, p. 98, lines 8-14.
[820] Newkirk testimony, 11/21/1991, p. 106, line 22—p. 107, line 1.
[821] *See Arnold v. Lewis*, 91-1808, Findings of Fact and Conclusions of Law, pp. 4-9.
[822] *See Arnold v. Lewis*, 91-1808, Findings of Fact and Conclusions of Law, pp. 5-14.
[823] *See Arnold v. Lewis*, 91-1808, Findings of Fact and Conclusions of Law, pp. 15-19, 25.

V. POST-FILING CHANGES

This lawsuit was filed on January 12, 1990. Since that time, the defendants have taken numerous steps in an attempt to remedy the following specific problems identified by plaintiffs:

***

*1542

   B. Mental Health Care

In September and October 1990, defendants promulgated four major documents governing mental health care, including the Alhambra/Flamenco Treatment Program (9/1990), the Mental Health Services Manual (9/1990), the Staff Training Manual (10/1990) and the Training and Development Manual (19/1990).[856]

In late 1990, defendants established the policy requiring mental health staff to follow up when a prisoner fails to pick up his or her unit dose of psychotropic medication.[857]

In approximately April of 1991, Dr. Busfield was identifying mentally ill prisoners throughout the system and having them reclassified and transferred to Florence, Tucson, or Perryville. He found five seriously mentally ill prisoners in Douglas who should not have been at that facility.[858] The purpose of this process was to move mentally ill prisoners to facilities where they would have greater access to trained staff, including psychologists, psychiatrists and psychiatric nurses.[859]

Effective January 1, 1992, all ADOC psychologists have been consolidated under the Health Services Bureau.[860] Previously, psychologists had been assigned to two different divisions in ADOC.[861]

In 1990, SMU implemented the residential program for emotionally disturbed prisoners with a levels system.[862]

Defendants have removed the "socialization chair" from the Special Program Unit (SPU), and discontinued its use.[863] Formerly, prisoners were placed in this chair and sometimes restrained.[864]

Defendants have discontinued use of the behavioral control area or "pens" at SPU. These were outdoor fenced areas adjacent to one of the dormitories, and contained no toilet facilities or equipment of any kind.[865] Prisoners were placed in this area for various reasons.[866] Dr. Newkirk was critical of the pens. She was especially concerned about prisoners being placed there in mid-day because the pens afforded no shelter from the sun and most psychotropic medications increase sensitivity to sunlight.[867] She also stated that prisoners in the pens should have *1543 access to water and toilet facilities.[868] Indeed, at least one prisoner appeared to suffer adverse health consequences while in the pen.[869] The behavioral control area was eliminated shortly after the deposition of Esteban v. Veloz, Mental Health Coordinator at Florence.[870]

---

[856] Plaintiffs' Exhibit 1.

[857] Lutz testimony, p. 59, line 15—p. 60, line 1, p. 150, line 9—p. 151, line 6.

[858] Stellman testimony, 1/28/1992, p. 70, lines 3-13.

[859] Stellman testimony, 1/27/1992, p. 190, lines 13-16.

[860] Stewart testimony, 1/16/1992, p. 68, lines 6-14.

[861] Stewart testimony, 1/16/1992, p. 67, lines 5-12.

[862] Defendants Exhibit 184.

[863] Stipulation, p. 35, § IV.

[864] See, e.g., Plaintiffs' Exhibit 49, SPU briefing, 3/3/89 (Gonzalez placed in chair and restrained), 9/12/1989 (Barber put in chair).

[865] Newkirk testimony, 11/22/1991, p. 10, line 21—p. 11, line 5.

[866] See, e.g., Plaintiffs' Exhibit 49, Florence-SPU treatment team briefing, 2/24/1989 (Davenport put in pen due to "abnoxious [sic] behavior"); Plaintiffs' Exhibit 199, 8/22/1990 (Duniphin placed in pen because he was "extremely paranoid"), 9/11/1990 (Gurr placed in pen after shoving officer), 9/18/90 (Martin in pen after fighting).

[867] Newkirk testimony, 11/22/1991, p. 13, lines 13-22.

[868] Newkirk testimony, 11/22/1991, p. 13, line 23—p. 14, line 1.

[869] Plaintiffs' Exhibit 49, SPU treatment team briefing, 2/16/1989 (prisoner Lopez found to be non-responsive with a heart rate of 46 while in the pen, and taken to health unit; diagnosis unknown).

[870] Veloz testimony, 1/9/1992, p. 173, line 20—p. 174, line 7.

Conclusions of Law

I. 8TH AMENDMENT CRUEL AND UNUSUAL PUNISHMENT CLAIMS

Plaintiffs allege that the medical, dental and mental health care systems violate the inmates' eighth amendment rights to be free from cruel and unusual punishment.

In order to prevail on a civil rights claim under 42 U.S.C. § 1983 because of inadequate medical care in violation of the eighth amendment right to be free from cruel and unusual punishment, a prisoner must establish "acts or omissions sufficiently harmful to evidence deliberate indifference to serious medical needs.'" *Estelle v. Gamble*, 429 U.S. 97, 106, 97 S.Ct. 285, 291-92, 50 L.Ed.2d 251 (1976); *Toussaint v. McCarthy*, 801 F.2d 1080, 1111 (9th Cir.1986), *cert. denied*, 481 U.S. 1069, 107 S.Ct. 2462, 95 L.Ed.2d 871 (1987). The indifference must be substantial to violate the constitution. *Jones v. Johnson*, 781 F.2d 769, 771 (9th Cir.1986). Generally, mere claims of "indifference," "negligence," or "medical malpractice" do not support a claim under 42 U.S.C. § 1983. *Estelle*, 429 U.S. at 106, 97 S.Ct. at 292; *Broughton v. Cutter Laboratories*, 622 F.2d 458, 460 (9th Cir.1980). Nor does a difference in medical opinion amount to deliberate indifference. *Sanchez v. Vild*, 891 F.2d 240, 242 (9th Cir.1989); *Franklin v. State of Oregon*, 662 F.2d 1337, 1344 (9th Cir.1981) (difference of opinion between patient and medical authorities).

Prison officials are deliberately indifferent to a prisoner's serious medical needs when they deny, delay or intentionally interfere with medical treatment. *Wood v. Housewright*, 900 F.2d 1332, 1334 (9th Cir.1990). However, a mere delay in medical care, without more, is insufficient to state a claim against prison officials for deliberate indifference. *See May v. Enomoto*, 633 F.2d 164, 167 (9th Cir.1980); *Shapley v. Nevada Bd. of State Prison Comm'rs*, 766 F.2d 404, 407 (9th Cir.1985). A delay in treatment does not constitute a violation of the eighth amendment unless the delay caused substantial harm. *Wood v. Housewright*, 900 F.2d at 1335. In cases in which the system's constitutionality is at issue, deliberate indifference to the serious medical needs of prisoners may also be "evidenced by repeated examples of negligent acts which disclose a pattern of conduct by the prison medical staff" or by "proving there are such systemic and gross deficiencies in staffing, facilities, equipment or procedures that the inmate population is effectively denied access to adequate medical care." *Wellman v. Faulkner*, 715 F.2d 269, 272 (7th Cir.1983), *cert. denied*, 468 U.S. 1217, 104 S.Ct. 3587, 82 L.Ed.2d 885.

The Ninth Circuit set forth the eighth amendment standards for physical, dental and medical care systems in *Hoptowit v. Ray*, 682 F.2d 1237, 1253 (9th Cir.1982) as follows:

> The Eighth Amendment requires that prison officials provide a system of ready access to adequate medical care. Prison officials show deliberate indifference to serious medical needs if prisoners are unable to make their medical problems known to medical staff. [Citation omitted] Access to the medical staff has no meaning if the medical staff is not competent to deal with ***1544** the prisoners' problems. The medical staff must be competent to examine prisoners and diagnose illnesses. It must be able to treat medical problems or refer prisoners to others who can. Such referrals may be to other physicians within the prison, or to physicians or facilities outside the prison if there is reasonably speedy access to those other physicians or facilities. In keeping with these requirements, the prison must provide an adequate system for responding to emergencies. If outside facilities are too remote or too inaccessible to handle emergencies promptly and adequately, then the prison must provide adequate facilities and staff to handle emergencies within the prison. These requirements apply to physical, dental and mental health. *Hoptowit*, 682 F.2d at 1253.

Courts may consider expert opinions to determine the constitutional requirements. However, such opinions do not ordinarily establish constitutional minimums. *See, Bell v. Wolfish*, 441 U.S. 520, 543-44,

---

[1] A serious medical need is "one that has been diagnosed by a physician as requiring treatment or one that is so obvious that a lay person would easily recognize the necessity for a doctor's attention." *Monmouth County Corr. Inst. Inmates v. Lanzaro*, 834 F.2d 326, 347 (3rd Cir.1987). Similarly, a serious dental need is one that causes "pain, discomfort or threat to good health." *Dean v. Coughlin* 623 F.Supp. 392, 404 (S.D.N.Y.1985).

n. 27, 99 S.Ct. 1861, 1876, n. 27, 60 L.Ed.2d 447 (1979); *Rhodes v. Chapman*, 452 U.S. 337, 348, 101 S.Ct. 2392, 2400, n. 13, 69 L.Ed.2d 59 (1981).

Officials can be held liable for their failure to implement a proper mental health care program or failure to adequately train or supervise subordinates. *Greason v. Kemp*, 891 F.2d 829, 836-37 (11th Cir.1990).[2]

***

*1545

Relevant to mental health care, Director Lewis stated:

> Currently the limitation in staff at Flamenco and the Psychiatric Hospital limits the number of inmates that can be effectively treated. Authorizing funding for three CPO positions at the Psychiatric Hospital, will allow us to increase the census from the current level of 21 to approximately 38. In addition, authorizing funds to fill positions assigned to Flamenco will allow us to increase the census from the current level of 46 to its maximum of 125. Plaintiffs' Exhibit 232.

This lack of staff results in delays in the assessment and treatment of inmates' medical and dental needs. Generally, such delays must result in substantial harm to rise to the level of an individual constitutional violation. *Wood v. Housewright*, 900 F.2d at 1335. Plaintiffs did not establish injury to all of the inmates as a result of those delays. Yet, defendants should be aware that each instance of delay in care due to lack of staffing could rise to the level of a constitutional violation if the inmate suffers serious harm. *Wood v. Housewright*, 900 F.2d at 1335. Further, such repeated examples of delays or negligence may result in constitutional violations. *Wellman*, 715 F.2d at 272.

Since the filing of this action, defendants have acquired additional staff and filled some of the vacant positions. However, the problem of inadequate numbers of staff still exists. Both plaintiffs' and defendants' experts testified at trial that the defendants still needed more medical staff. Defendants admit that they could provide better care with additional medical staff. Further, although they have increased the numbers of staff since the filing of this action, there is no guarantee that those positions will remain funded.

***

*1547

B. Mental Health Care System

1. Problems with the Mental Care System

Plaintiffs have established numerous problems with the mental health care system provided to inmates by the ADOC. Plaintiffs allege that as a result of these problems, the mental health care system is inadequate to treat the serious mental health care needs of inmates.

---

[2] Generally, supervisory officials cannot be held liable under the theory of respondeat superior. *Monell v. Dept. of Social Services*, 436 U.S. 658, 691, 98 S.Ct. 2018, 2036, 56 L.Ed.2d 611 (1978). Rather, plaintiff must establish that the official personally participated in the constitutional deprivation or that a state supervisory official was aware of the widespread abuses and with deliberate indifference to the inmate's constitutional rights failed to take action to prevent further misconduct. *King v. Atiyeh*, 814 F.2d 565, 568 (9th Cir.1987); *Monell*, 436 U.S. at 691, 98 S.Ct. at 2036; *Williams v. Cash*, 836 F.2d 1318, 1320 (11th Cir.1988); *Fundiller v. City of Cooper City*, 777 F.2d 1436, 1443 (11th Cir.1985). However, officials may be independently liable under § 1983. *Id.*

a. Intake Procedure

ADOC lacks a system and the psychiatric staff to identify and evaluate female inmates with serious mental illnesses when those inmates come into the system. Thus, at the Perryville Santa Maria Unit, unqualified security staff must identify seriously ill inmates so that they may receive treatment.[4]

Defendants have also implemented a policy that provides for reviews of inmates' medical records upon transfer to other facilities. However, such reviews are not routinely performed due to shortages of staff. Therefore, seriously mentally ill male and female inmates do not receive treatment until they request treatment or regress to the point that security staff recognize the illness or lock them down for the behavior caused by the mental illness. Thus, mentally ill inmates are unable to make their problems known to staff and their constitutional rights are violated. *Hoptowit*, 682 F.2d at 1253.

b. Staffing Problems

Defendants fail to provide sufficient mental health staff to diagnose and treat the serious mental health needs of inmates. The experts agreed that shortages of mental health staff existed within the facilities. Alhambra is the only facility that has a full-time psychiatrist. The facilities also lack an adequate number of psychologists. SPU lacks sufficient staff to consistently provide all of the programs to the inmates that need such programs. The staff shortage has also resulted in no 24-hour mental health coverage at SPU. Further, there is always a waiting list of inmates for admission to SPU. ***1548** Because of inadequate numbers of staff, the existing staff cannot adequately treat inmates and their constitutional rights are violated. *Hoptowit*, 682 F.2d at 1253.

The staffing problem exists partly because the Legislature will not fund positions and partly because ADOC has vacancies in positions that have been funded. Defendants admit that they have requested further staff and could function better with those staff. However, lack of funding is not a defense to eighth amendment violations. *Jones v. Johnson*, 781 F.2d 769, 771 (9th Cir.1986); *Harris v. Thigpen*, 941 F.2d 1495, 1509 (11th Cir.1991).

c. Programming for Mentally Ill Inmates

ADOC provides insufficient mental health programming at SMU. At the time of filing of this action, little or no programming existed at SMU. At the time of trial, more programming existed. However, programming for mentally ill inmates at SMU is still insufficient. The levels system behavioral modification program is implemented by security officers who are untrained both in mental health care and in the program they are implementing.

d. Delays in Assessment and Treatment

Inmates with serious mental health needs experience unacceptable delays in assessment and treatment. Assessments by mental health professionals should be made within a few days of an inmate's complaint of hearing voices or feeling anxious, tense or "about to explode." Because of staffing shortages and inadequate policies, such assessments are rarely made by mental health personnel. Rather, inmates' mental health care is consistently delayed. Inmates experience delays [in] assessment, treatment and in commitment to mental hospitals (Baker Ward for men or ASH for women). When inmates act out because of their mental illness, they are locked down. While in lockdown, inmates generally wait months for transfer to the mental hospital. In addition, it may take several days to a week for inmates to see a psychiatrist.

e. Inappropriate Use of Lockdown

Rather than providing timely mental health care to inmates with serious mental illnesses, defendants lock down those inmates in the higher security facilities such as SMU and CB6 for men and Santa Maria

---

[4] Defendants have established a routine intake procedure for males at Alhambra. In addition, Alhambra has the mental health staff available for the system.

detention for women. Yet, both the plaintiffs' and defendants' experts agreed that it is inappropriate to house acutely psychotic inmates in segregation facilities for more than three days. Further, psychiatrists employed by the ADOC, Drs. Pera and Fernandez,[5] admit that lockdown damages, rather than helps, mentally ill inmates. Despite their knowledge of the harm to seriously mentally ill inmates, ADOC routinely assigns or transfers seriously mentally ill inmates to SMU, CB6 and Santa Maria lockdown. The inmates remain in lockdown for more than three days. In most cases, the inmates are locked down because of the behavior resulting from their mental illness. In addition, the inmates are locked down on orders of security rather than medical personnel. According to Dr. Pera, economic conditions prevent this system from being changed.[6] Even when inmates are referred for transfer to mental health facilities, they remain in lockdown for more than three days waiting a transfer. Defendants also discharge inmates with serious mental illnesses from Baker ward and send them to SMU. Because they are assaultive or a behavior problem, they are not eligible for treatment at SPU.

During lockdown, inmates are provided improper mental health care or no mental health care. Inmates with serious mental illnesses who have been locked down should receive almost immediate psychiatric follow-up.[7] Further, inmates that are locked down should be seen daily by a psychiatrist.[8] Daily checks by nurses are insufficient care and according to Dr. Garcia are "not treatment at *1549 all."[9] Yet, inmates in lock-down for their mental illnesses are not seen by a psychiatrist either immediately for an evaluation or daily. Rather, security staff, or possibly the nurses, perform health and welfare checks. Most of the logs from the facilities indicate that security staff performs the welfare checks on these inmates.

The most egregious example of the inappropriate use of lockdown is H.B., who was locked down for approximately 11 and 1/2 months in the Perryville Santa Maria Unit.[10] During that time, she was seen only nine times by the psychiatrist. During her ten years of custody, she has been locked down numerous times for her mental health condition. Yet, she has never received immediate psychiatric evaluation. During these times, she was actively psychotic and hallucinating. H.B. is not the only inmate in this condition in Santa Maria. Dr. Pera testified that at any one time there were several seriously mentally ill inmates locked down in Santa Maria.

Defendants also inappropriately house self-abusive inmates in SMU, despite their knowledge that SMU is not suitable for self-abusive inmates. Since the filing of this action, defendants have established the self-abuser pod. However, they have not established that the pod is appropriately staffed or fully operational. At the time of trial, the psychiatric nurse at SMU did not know if there was any specific programming for the unit, other than the fact that the individuals received more attention.

This use of lockdown as an alternative to mental health care for inmates with serious mental illnesses clearly rises to the level of deliberate indifference to the serious mental health needs of the inmates and violates their constitutional rights to be free from cruel and unusual punishment.

f. Medication

Defendants do not properly monitor the prescription of psychotropic medication. Despite the expert testimony that inmates on psychotropic medication should be seen on a monthly basis, ADOC prescribes, continues and discontinues psychotropic medication without face to face evaluations by the psychiatrists.

Defendants also have no system or method to insure that inmates take medications. The only policy presented at trial requires the nurse to talk to the inmate to convince him or her to take the medications and then note the refusal on the chart. The policy does not require that the inmate be seen by a psychiatrist.

---

[5] *See, Arnold v. Lewis*, 91-1808, p. 3. (consolidated into this action).

[6] Budgetary constraints are not a defense to liability for deliberate indifference to inmates' serious medical care needs. *Jones v. Johnson,* 781 F.2d 769, 771 (9th Cir.1986); *Harris v. Thigpen*, 941 F.2d 1495, 1509 (11th Cir.1991).

[7] *See Arnold v. Lewis*, p. 8.

[8] *See Arnold v. Lewis*, p. 9.

[9] *See Arnold v. Lewis*, p. 9.

[10] *See, Arnold v. Lewis*, CIV 91-1808, Findings of Fact and Conclusions of Law. The *Arnold* case, including the Findings of Fact and Conclusions of Law, has been consolidated into this case.

2. *Constitutionality of the Mental Care System*

The mental health care provided at B Ward, Flamenco and Alhambra meets the serious mental health needs of inmates. If defendants had adequate staff to provide all of the programs at SPU,[11] the mental health care would meet the serious mental health needs of the male inmates incarcerated in that facility. Unfortunately, SPU also lacks staff and the capacity to house all of the inmates that qualify for such care.

However, the overwhelming evidence establishes that the defendants are deliberately indifferent to the serious mental health care needs of the inmates in other institutions throughout the state. Seriously mentally ill inmates are housed in most[12] of the other facilities. Such inmates tend to be concentrated in the lockdown facilities of SMU, CB6 and Santa Maria in Perryville. Those facilities have inadequate mental health staff and programming for inmates. Rather than providing mental health care for these inmates, *1550 security staff lock inmates down for prolonged periods of time because of the behavior that is the result of their mental illnesses. During lockdown the inmates are provided little or no mental health care by psychiatrists or psychologists.

Because of the lack of staff and programming, inmates do not have "ready access" to mental health care. Severely mentally ill inmates cannot make their needs known to mental health staff. Untrained security staff assess inmates' mental health. Further, referrals to B Ward, Flamenco, and ASH are not "reasonably speedy." Inmates remain in lockdown for days to months waiting for transfer to these facilities. Although psychological staff request transfers, they are not consistently carried out by security staff. All of these problems result in deliberate indifference to inmates serious mental health needs such that the inmates' constitutional rights to be free from cruel and unusual punishment are violated by the defendants.

The fact that the lack of staff and programming is partially a result of lack of funding from the Legislature is not a defense to these constitutional violations. *Jones*, 781 F.2d at 771; *Harris*, 941 F.2d at 1509.

The system for female inmates is even worse than for male inmates because female inmates have no SPU or transitional facility. Rather, female inmates are returned to general population and are generally locked down for behavior caused by their mental illness. Sometimes, the lockdown reoccurs within 24 to 72 hours of return to general population. Seriously ill female inmates are limited to the G Ward with its 15 to 17 beds or transferred outside ADOC to ASH. Even at G Ward, female inmates receive less programming than that provided to males.

The Court finds the treatment of seriously mentally ill inmates to be appalling. Rather than providing treatment for serious mental illnesses, ADOC punishes these inmates by locking them down in small, bare segregation cells for their actions that are the result of their mental illnesses. These inmates are left in segregation without mental health care. Many times the inmates, such as H.B. are in a highly psychotic state, terrified because of hallucinations, such as monsters, gorillas or the devil in her cell.[13] Nor does it appear that H.B. is the exceptional case as seven to eight mentally ill women may be locked down at the Santa Maria Unit in Perryville at any one time and may remain there for months without care. In addition, such treatment is common for male inmates in other lockdown facilities or units in the state including SMU and CB6. The Court considers this treatment of any human being to be inexcusable and cruel and unusual punishment in violation of the eighth amendment of the Constitution.

II. EQUAL PROTECTION CLAIM

Plaintiffs also allege that defendants discriminate against female inmates in the delivery of mental health care in violation of the equal protection clause.

---

[11] After the filing of this action and Dr. Newkirk's (plaintiffs' expert) review of SPU, that facility eliminated the socialization chair and pens. Use of these treatments rises to the level of deliberate indifference to the serious medical/mental health care needs of inmates. Placing inmates into unshaded pens outside in the Arizona heat without bathroom facilities and water is clearly cruel and unusual punishment in violation of the eighth amendment.

[12] Defendants presented evidence that seriously mentally ill inmates are not housed in the work camp type of facilities such as Yuma.

[13] In fact, one psychiatric expert stated he wouldn't treat his dog the way the defendants treated H.B. *Arnold v. Lewis*, Exhibit A at 125.

The equal protection clause states that no State shall "deny to any person within its jurisdiction the equal protection of the laws." Thus, all similarly situated persons should be treated alike. *City of Cleburne, Tex. v. Cleburne Living Center*, 473 U.S. 432, 439, 105 S.Ct. 3249, 3253, 87 L.Ed.2d 313 (1985). Gender based differences require a heightened standard of review. A party seeking to uphold dissimilar treatment based on gender must show an "exceedingly persuasive justification." *Kirchberg v. Feenstra*, 450 U.S. 455, 461, 101 S.Ct. 1195, 1199, 67 L.Ed.2d 428 (1981). To withstand constitutional challenges, classifications based on gender must serve as important governmental objectives and must be substantially related to achievement of those objectives. *Craig v. Boren*, 429 U.S. 190, 198, 97 S.Ct. 451, 457, 50 L.Ed.2d 397; *McCoy v. Nevada Dept. of Prisons*, 776 F.Supp. 521, 523 (D.Nev.1991). Under this standard of review, female inmates must be treated "in parity" with male inmates. *McCoy*, 776 F.Supp. at 523.

*1551 Defendants clearly provide, because there are fewer women in the system, fewer mental health services for women than they provide for men within the prison system. In addition, the lack of these mental health services for women result in more egregious cases of deliberate indifference to the women's mental health needs.

For men, defendants provide a psychiatric hospital within the ADOC. Women are given access to the ASH, which is not within ADOC. Inmates cannot remain in ASH during the period of incarceration unless they were found innocent by reason of insanity. Thus, women inmates are discharged after a short period of time, returned to general population and often again locked down. After September of 1991, women inmates can be involuntarily committed to G Ward. However, it is not a psychiatric hospital.

At Flamenco, men are provided more advanced programming and facilities than women. Men can progress in a phase program from the acute unit to the sub-acute unit and then into SPU or general population. Women of all levels are treated in G ward. Men have better access to occupational therapy with more equipment and supplies. In addition, mental health activities logs indicate that men are offered more substantive programs such as computer training, communication training, stress management and anger control. However, at the same time, women are offered aerobics, board games, movies and "Women Who Love Too Much."

ADOC also has the SPU progressive unit for men, but no comparable unit for women. Thus, ADOC houses men with other men of similar levels of functioning. However, women of all levels of functioning are housed together at G Ward. As a result, chronically ill women who are stabilized are returned to general population; act out when then are provided little or no mental health care; are locked down [sometimes within 24 to 72 hours]; remain in lockdown where they decompensate and eventually, after a serious delay, return to Flamenco or ASH. Yet, chronically ill men who are not assaultive are allowed to progress back to general population, through the SPU facility. Dr. Newkirk identified female inmates that needed long-term chronic care that could benefit from an SPU-type of unit for women.

Defendants argue that the additional units, like SPU, are necessary for men because they are more predatory, and more likely to pick on weaker male inmates. However, such considerations do not justify the unequal treatment in the provision of mental health care. The Court does not consider that the different care serves any "important governmental objectives" so that the disparity could be constitutional. Clearly, the unequal treatment results in even more egregious denials of mental health care for seriously ill female inmates violating those inmates' equal protection rights under the constitution in addition to their rights under the eighth amendment.

Defendants also argue that female inmates receive the same number of beds in mental health facilities in proportion to the number of inmates within the system. However, this argument ignores the very clear differences in care and the impact of that unequal treatment.

III. INJUNCTIVE RELIEF

"The basis for injunctive relief in the federal courts has always been irreparable injury and the inadequacy of legal remedies." *Weinberger v. Romero-Barcelo*, 456 U.S. 305, 312, 102 S.Ct. 1798, 1803, 72 L.Ed.2d 91 (1982). Such determination requires a balancing between the conveniences of the parties and possible injuries to them as they may be affected by the granting or withholding of the injunction. *Yakus v. United States*, 321 U.S. 414, 410, 64 S.Ct. 660, 675, 88 L.Ed. 834 (1944).

Because of the lack of a constitutional mental health care system, inmates have suffered harm in the past and such harm is likely to reoccur absent injunctive relief. Because of economic conditions, ADOC will continue to lockdown inmates as an alternative to mental health care. As a result inmates' mental conditions will consistently deteriorate and they will suffer from hallucinations that seem very real and terrifying or they will harm themselves or others. Based on the continuing cycle of lack of treatment, the *1552 harm is likely to reoccur. On the other hand, the only harm to defendants is additional costs to hire staff and implement programs. However, if these inmates are provided proper mental health care, security staff should be relieved of the time consuming problems caused when inmates become violent or assaultive due to mental illness. In addition, security staff should be relieved of the duty of performing health and welfare checks, which disrupt security duties and require that security personnel perform medical duties which they are not qualified to perform.

Because the harm and potential harm to the inmates for this lack of care clearly outweighs the harm to defendants, the Court has determined that injunctive relief is appropriate.[14]

ORDER

***

II. MENTAL HEALTH CARE SYSTEM

The court could work out a plan to remedy the deficiencies in the mental health system. However, it would be more appropriate and the Court would prefer that the parties, along with their various experts, work out the procedures and remedies to remedy those deficiencies. The parties, along with their experts and the staff and administration of ADOC know better than the Court what policies and changes will be effective solutions in the particular prisons. The court further notes that defendants cannot make such changes without cooperation from the Legislature and that attempts to provide an adequate system have been thwarted by inadequate appropriations.

The other alternative to this procedure would be for the Court to appoint a special master and/or expert. However, appointment of a special master and/or expert could *1553 result in delays and additional expenses. Therefore, it is preferable that the parties work out the remedies.

IT IS THEREFORE ORDERED THAT:

(1) No later than *May 31, 1993*, counsel shall meet and discuss possible proposals to remedy the deficiencies in the mental health care system.

(2) No later than *September 30, 1993*, the parties shall jointly file a proposed plan to remedy the deficiencies in the mental health care system. The plan shall address the following issues:

A. STAFF: The plan shall provide for sufficient numbers of qualified staff to provide evaluation, diagnosis and treatment of mental health problems of inmates. The plan shall also provide for recruitment and incentives for such staff to assure that defendants are able to fill staff positions with qualified persons.

B. FACILITIES: The plan shall provide for the development of sufficient and adequate mental health housing facilities for male and female inmates who are unable to function in general population facilities to prevent their retention in segregated facilities for medically inappropriate periods of time. The plan should provide for appropriate facilities for those mentally ill inmates that are too assaultive or are behavior problems such that they are not placed in SPU. The plan should also provide for the development of appropriate seclusion rooms for special housing units, such as SPU, to assure that defendants do not revert to utilization of the socialization chair or behavior pens or transfer inmates to isolation cells in nonmental health units such as CB6, SMU or other lockdown or detention units.

C. MEDICATIONS: The plan shall include written policies for the administration and monitoring of psychotropic medications by qualified mental health professionals.

D. EQUAL PROTECTION: The plan shall provide for the development of mental health programming for women, comparable to that provided for men.

---

[14] Injunctions and other court orders are not so inflexible that they can never be changed without time consuming court proceedings. If changes in circumstances justify changes in the injunctions or orders, this Court is agreeable to necessary changes that defendants have discussed with plaintiffs. In fact, should counsel agree by stipulation to changes in the injunction or orders, the Court is willing to amend the injunction or orders without conducting court hearings. The parties are reminded that the appropriate way to seek changes is the method applied by the Ninth Circuit recently in *Hook v. State of Arizona*, 972 F.2d 1012 (9th Cir.1992).

MADRID v. GOMEZ
889 F. Supp. 1146 (1995)
U.S. District Court
N.D. California
Jan. 10, 1995

*1154 FINDINGS OF FACT, CONCLUSIONS OF LAW, AND ORDER

THELTON E. HENDERSON, Chief Judge.

*1155

I.

INTRODUCTION

Plaintiffs represent a class of all prisoners who are, or will be, incarcerated by the State of California Department of Corrections at Pelican Bay State Prison, which is located in the remote northwest corner of California, seven miles northeast of Crescent City and 363 miles north of San Francisco. Pursuant to the civil rights statute 42 U.S.C. § 1983,[1] plaintiffs challenge the constitutionality of a broad range of conditions and practices that intimately affect almost every facet of their prison life. They seek redress from the Court in the form of injunctive and declaratory relief.

Although referred to in the singular, Pelican Bay State Prison ("Pelican Bay") actually consists of three completely separate facilities. The first is a maximum security prison which houses approximately 2,000 "general population" maximum security inmates. The daily routine for these inmates is comparable to that in other maximum security prisons in California. The second is the Security Housing Unit, commonly referred to as the "SHU." Located in a completely separate complex inside the security perimeter, the SHU has gained a well-deserved reputation as a place which, by design, imposes conditions far harsher than those anywhere else in the California prison system. The roughly 1,000-1,500 inmates confined in the SHU remain isolated in windowless cells for 22 and 1/2 hours each day, and are denied access to prison work programs and group exercise yards.

Assignment to the SHU is not based on the inmate's underlying offense; rather, SHU cells are reserved for those inmates in the California prison system who become affiliated with a prison gang or commit serious disciplinary infractions once in prison. They represent, according to a phrase coined by defendants, "the worst of the worst." Finally, there is a small minimum security facility that houses approximately 200 prisoners. All in all, there are between 3,500 and 3,900 prisoners confined at Pelican Bay on any given day.

Just over five years old, Pelican Bay was activated on December 1, 1989. Considered a "prison of the future," the buildings are modern in design, and employ cutting-edge technology and security devices. This, then, is not a case about inadequate or deteriorating physical conditions. There are no rat-infested cells, antiquated buildings, or unsanitary supplies. Rather, plaintiffs contend that behind the newly-minted walls and shiny equipment lies a prison that is coldly indifferent to the limited, but basic and elemental, rights that incarcerated persons—including "the worst of the worst"—retain under the *1156 First, Eighth, and Fourteenth amendments of our United States Constitution. In particular, plaintiffs allege that defendants (1) condone a pattern and practice of using excessive force against inmates, (2) fail to provide inmates with adequate medical care, (3) fail to provide inmates with adequate mental health care, (4) impose inhumane conditions in the Security Housing Unit, (5) utilize cell-assignment procedures that expose inmates to an unreasonable risk of assault from other inmates, (6) fail to provide adequate procedural safeguards when segregating prison gang affiliates in the Security Housing Unit, and (7) fail to provide inmates with adequate access to the courts.

---

[1] 42 U.S.C. § 1983 provides that "Every person who, under color of any statute, ordinance, regulation, custom, or usage, of any State . . . subjects or causes to be subjected, any citizen of the United States or other person within the jurisdiction thereof to the deprivation of any rights, privileges, or immunities secured by the Constitution and laws, shall be liable to the party injured in an action at law, suit in equity, or other proper proceeding for redress."

Named in their official capacity as defendants are Pelican Bay Warden Charles Marshall, Chief Deputy Warden Terry Peetz, Chief Medical Officer A.M. Astorga, and James Gomez, Director of the California Department of Corrections ("CDC").[2] They deny that any of plaintiffs' allegations have merit, and assert that Pelican Bay operates well within constitutional limits in each of the areas outlined above. Moreover, they argue, Pelican Bay, and the SHU in particular, does exactly what it was designed to do: it isolates the most brutal and disruptive elements of the inmate population while reducing violence in California state prisons overall.

The case was tried before the Court between September 14 and December 1, 1993. Immediately prior to the trial, the Court spent two days touring Pelican Bay, accompanied by counsel for both parties and prison officials. During the course of the trial, the Court heard testimony from 57 lay witnesses, including class members, defendants, and correctional employees at all levels. It also received into evidence over 6,000 exhibits, including documents, tape recordings, and photographs, as well as thousands of pages of deposition excerpts.[3]

The Court recognizes that neither the inmates at Pelican Bay nor the Department of Corrections personnel can be considered neutral witnesses. For reasons that are self-evident, class members, as well as defendants and other prison staff, are interested in the outcome of the case. We also take into account the undeniable presence of a "code of silence" at Pelican Bay. As the evidence clearly shows, this unwritten but widely understood code is designed to encourage prison employees to remain silent regarding the improper behavior of their fellow employees, particularly where excessive force has been alleged. Those who defy the code risk retaliation and harassment.[4] We have considered *1157 all of the above, as well as the manner and demeanor of the witnesses, in assessing witness credibility and making our factual findings.

The Court was also aided by the testimony of ten experts in the areas of medicine, psychiatry, psychology, and prison management and operation.[5] With respect to the claims regarding excessive force

---

[2] On January 5, 1995, the Court was notified by defendants' counsel that three of the defendants have retired or resigned from their positions, and that new officials have been named in their place: Warden Marshall has been succeeded by interim Warden J.S. Stainer; Chief Deputy Warden Peetz has been succeeded by Chief Deputy Warden Robert L. Ayers, and Chief Medical Officer Astorga has been succeeded by interim Chief Medical Officer Dr. David Cooper.

[3] Aside from a limited group of documents, discovery in this action closed on February 26, 1993. *See* April 21, 1993 Order at 2-4. Accordingly, the evidence presented in this case primarily concerns incidents and events that occurred between December 1989 and February 1993.

[4] Several prison staff admitted to a code of silence problem. For example, one Program Administrator agreed, in his deposition, that a code of silence "frequently" operates among officers of Pelican Bay, and that this fact can make it difficult, as a supervisor, to determine what really happened during an incident. Helsel Tr. 21-3577 (quoting deposition). Notably, in open court this same administrator was reluctant to testify about the code of silence; after agreeing that he knew "what the code of silence is at Pelican Bay," he was asked if it operates frequently, to which he would respond only that "I don't know how to answer that." Helsel Tr. 21-3576. The Chief Deputy Warden also acknowledged the code of silence, *see* Peetz Tr. 19-3243 (Q: "Do you have concerns that there is a code of silence among staff at Pelican Bay?" A: "Yes. I have at times, yes"), as did former Program Administrator Rippetoe. *See* Rippetoe Depo. at 197-98 ("I believe that there's always been a code amongst peers to protect each other, okay, whether it be law enforcement official [sic], whether it be, you know—it's no greater in the prison setting. Yes, I think that there is that."). Captain Jenkins also acknowledged that the code of silence has hampered his investigations of excessive force at Pelican Bay. Tr. 2-288. Defendant Gomez similarly agreed that lack of candor can impede some investigations at Pelican Bay: "There are people that . . . are not forthcoming . . . that are not as honest as they should be, and that makes an investigation more difficult to prove." Tr. 28-4653.

We also observed at trial that prison staff frequently could not recall the identity of other staff whom they testified did or said certain things, although other details were easily recalled. Prison staff also report to internal investigators, with notable frequency, that they had just looked the other way, been distracted by something else, or had their visibility impaired at the moment the alleged misuse of force was said to have occurred. *See, e.g.*, Trial Exh. P-3083 at 79046 ("Officer Bare claimed that he was unable to observe what was happening . . . because the helmet he was wearing . . . blocked his view.").

Those who violate the code of silence risk hostility from other prison staff. After Sergeant Cox testified that he witnessed an inmate being hit on the head with the butt of a 38 millimeter gas gun, he was recalled as a witness. He testified that, after his appearance at trial, he had been told by various senior staff (whom he would not name unless ordered by the Court) that he had been a snitch and that he should "watch his back" and that "the administration wasn't very happy with me." Cox Tr. 18-17. Similarly, Officer Powers made the following comments to an internal inves-

and cell assignment practices, plaintiffs presented three experts: Charles Fenton, a former warden of two maximum security prisons,[6] Steve Martin, who spent more than 20 years working in varying capacities for the Texas Department of Corrections,[7] and Vince Nathan, who has worked for nearly 20 years as a court-appointed monitor and expert in prison cases.[8] *1158 Defendants presented two experts: Daniel McCarthy, who worked for almost 40 years in varying capacities for the California Department of Corrections, most recently as its Director,[9] and Larry DuBois, the Commissioner of the Massachusetts Department of Corrections.[10]

---

tigator: "what do I say; you know the position I'm in . . . about ratting off that, how am I going to work here any more. . . . [I]f an officer 'rats' on a fellow officer, that officer becomes an outcast." Trial Exh. P-3084 at 79860. Captain Jenkins also agreed that he has "seen evidence of the situation where an officer reports another officer and is not too long thereafter reported upon himself," and that this "has been an issue" at Pelican Bay. Tr. 2-290.

[5] The direct testimony of all experts was submitted by way of declaration, supplemented by two hours of live testimony. The parties were also permitted unlimited live cross examination and redirect examination.

Defendants filed a motion to strike portions of the declaration submitted by one of plaintiffs' experts, Dr. Craig Haney, asserting that (1) ¶¶s 56-61 should be stricken as inadmissible legal opinion outside Haney's area of expertise, and (2) that all inmate statements contained in the declaration should be stricken as inadmissible hearsay. With respect to the latter, defendants stipulate that the statements may be admitted to show the basis of Dr. Haney's opinions, but not for the truth of the matters asserted.

We conclude that this motion should be denied. With respect to the inmate statements specified as numbers 1-32 in plaintiffs' supplemental opposition, such statements are admissible under Fed. R. Evid. 803(3) to show the declarant's then existing mental, emotional or physical condition. With respect to the inmate statements specified as numbers 32-49, plaintiffs have clarified that they are not offering such statements to show the truth of the matter asserted therein, and thus they do not constitute hearsay. Finally, the objection to ¶¶ 56-61 appears moot given that plaintiffs do not rely on the opinions set forth in these paragraphs in their proposed findings of fact and conclusions of law; nor has the Court otherwise considered them in making its findings of fact or conclusions of law.

[6] Charles Fenton worked for the Federal Bureau of Prisons for 27 years prior to his retirement in 1980, and served as Warden of the federal prison at Marion, Illinois (which during Fenton's tenure housed those inmates posing the greatest security risk in the federal prison system, although ethnic prison gangs had not yet emerged as a significant presence). Fenton also served as warden at the federal maximum security prison at Lewisburg, Pennsylvania, and as the first warden at a new federal prison in Wisconsin. Since 1980, Fenton has served as a consultant for the Massachusetts Department of Corrections. He has also testified as an expert for the defense in prison lawsuits filed in several states. Notably, this is the first time that Fenton has ever testified on behalf of an inmate class.

[7] Steve Martin has more than 20 years experience in prison management and policy and holds two degrees in correctional science. He has worked as a correctional officer at a maximum security prison, as chief legal representative for the Texas Department of Corrections, and as Chief of Staff to the Director of the Texas Department of Corrections (the third ranking operational officer in the department). Since leaving the Texas department in 1985, Martin has served as a consultant for prison systems in California, Texas, Nebraska, and Ohio; he currently serves on the Texas Punishment Standards Commission.

[8] Vince Nathan, a lawyer by training and former law professor, has served as a court-appointed expert and monitor in a number of cases challenging prison conditions. He served as a court monitor in the seminal *Ruiz v. Estelle* litigation, 503 F.Supp. 1265 (S.D.Tex.1980), *aff'd in part and rev'd in part*, 679 F.2d 1115 (5th Cir.1982) (involving, *inter alia*, staff misuse of force in the Texas correctional system), and *Guthrie v. Evans*, 93 F.R.D. 390 (S.D.Ga.1981) (involving Georgia State Prison). Nathan has also worked as a court-appointed monitor in the Puerto Rico and Michigan prison systems, and as a court-designated expert consultant in litigation involving Rhode Island prisons. He has also done consulting work for the National Institute of Corrections and the New Mexico and Arkansas Departments of Corrections. In *Fisher v. Koehler*, 692 F.Supp. 1519, 1522 n. 6 (S.D.N.Y.1988), *aff'd*, 902 F.2d 2 (2d Cir.1990), Judge Lasker observed that Nathan "has the reputation as one of the most knowledgeable experts in his field."

[9] Daniel McCarthy was employed for almost forty years by the California Department of Corrections before his retirement in 1987. During that time, he worked as the Director of the California Department of Corrections for four years, and as the Warden of California Men's Colony for 12 years. His earlier positions included Deputy Superintendent at the California Men's Colony, Correctional Administrator at the California Correctional Institution in Tehachapi, California, Program Administrator at the California Medical Facility in Vacaville, California, Assistant Departmental Training Officer at Departmental Headquarters, Assistant Departmental Transportation Officer at Departmental Headquarters, In-Service Training Officer and Correctional Sergeant at California Medical Facility, and Correctional Officer at San Quentin.

[10] Larry DuBois has been in the field of corrections for over 20 years. He has previously served as the Warden at the Federal Correctional Institution in Englewood, Colorado, and at a facility in Lexington, Kentucky. Other prior posi-

With respect to the claims concerning medical care, mental health care, and conditions in the SHU, plaintiffs presented Dr. Armond Start, an associate professor at the University of Wisconsin Medical School and former director of health care services for the Oklahoma and Texas prison systems,[11] Dr. Stuart Grassian, a psychiatrist and faculty member at Harvard Medical School and expert on the effects of solitary confinement,[12] and Dr. Craig Haney, a professor of psychology at the University of California at Santa Cruz, who has specialized in the psychological effects of incarceration.[13] Defendants **1159** presented Dr. Jay Harness, a professor of surgery at the University of California at Davis and former director of health care services for the Michigan prison system,[14] and Dr. Joel Dvoskin, a clinical psychologist and director of the Bureau of Forensic Services for the New York State Office of Mental Health.[15]

---

tions include Associate Warden at federal correctional facilities in Talladega, Alabama and Marion, Illinois, and Regional Director for the Federal Bureau of Prisons. After his retirement, and before accepting his present position, he worked for three months assisting a Fulton County, Georgia facility on issues pertaining to overcrowding and staffing.

[11] Dr. Armond Start is an Associate Professor at the University of Wisconsin Medical School, where, in 1991, he founded the National Center for Correctional Health Care Studies. He obtained his M.D. in 1957 from the University of Michigan, and has been "Board Certified" as a pediatrician since 1964. Dr. Start also received an M.P.H. from the University of Oklahoma College of Health in 1977. After twelve years in private practice, Dr. Start served as the Director of the Division of Communicable Disease Control for the Oklahoma State Department of Health from 1975 to 1977. From 1977 to 1983 he served as the Medical Director of the Oklahoma Department of Corrections. At that time, he became the Director of Health Care for the Texas Department of Corrections, then the largest correctional system in the United States.

Dr. Start has reviewed over one hundred jails and prisons over the course of his career. He has acted as a correctional medical consultant or expert witness on numerous occasions. Notably, he was retained by the California Department of Corrections in *Gates v. Deukmejian*, a case concerning medical care at the California Medical Facility in Vacaville.

[12] Dr. Stuart Grassian has been a faculty member at Harvard Medical School since 1974 and a "Board Certified" psychiatrist since 1979. He obtained his M.D. in 1973 from New York University Medical School. In addition to his teaching, Dr. Grassian maintains a private practice, is the Psychiatric Director at the Melrose Wakefield Hospital Day Treatment Program for Addictions, and serves as a supervising psychiatrist in the Outpatient Department at the New England Memorial Hospital in Stoneham, Massachusetts. From 1977 to 1980 he was also Director of Inpatient Services at a community mental health center, where he was responsible for implementing policies regarding staffing, quality assurance, and supervision of psychiatric residents and other mental health professionals. He had similar responsibilities when he served as Chief of Staff (1991-92) and Director of Adult Inpatient Services (1980-84) at the New England Memorial Hospital. He has also testified as an expert witness in other prison litigation. Dr. Grassian has published two articles on the psychological effects of solitary confinement. Grassian & Friedman, *Effects of Sensory Deprivation in Psychiatric Seclusion and Solitary Confinement*, 8 Int'l J. of Law & Psychiatry 49 (1986); Grassian, *Psychopathological Effects of Solitary Confinement*, 140 Amer.J. of Psychiatry 1450 (1983).

[13] Dr. Craig William Haney is a Professor of Psychology and Director of the Program in Legal Studies at the University of Santa Cruz, where he has been teaching for the past 16 years. Dr. Haney earned both his Ph.D. in Social Psychology and his J.D. from Stanford University in 1978. He has published over 40 articles and book chapters on topics in law and psychology, including works on the conditions of confinement and the psychological effects of incarceration. Dr. Haney has testified as an expert witness in prison litigation in state and federal courts in California, Washington, and Illinois.

[14] Dr. Jay Harness received his medical degree in 1969 from the University of Michigan Medical School, and has been a "Board Certified" surgeon since 1970. Since 1992, Dr. Harness has been a Professor of Surgery at the University of California, Davis Medical School, and is also Chief of Surgical Oncology at Highland General Hospital in Oakland, California. From 1975 to 1985 Dr. Harness was the Director of the Office of Health Care for the Michigan Department of Corrections. He has served, *inter alia*, as a member of the American Medical Association's ("AMA's") Advisory Committee to improve medical care at correctional institutions, as the chairman of the AMA's National Consultant Advisory Group on accreditation of jails, and AS Chairman of the Board of Directors for the National Commission on Correctional Health Care. Dr. Harness has also served as a consultant on correctional health care for both the United States Department of Justice and for attorney generals in several states.

[15] Dr. Joel Dvoskin, a clinical psychologist, obtained his Ph.D. from the University of Arizona in 1981. Since 1984, he has directed the Bureau of Forensic Services for the New York State Office of Mental Health. In that position, he has line authority for, among other things, inpatient services at three large forensic hospitals and two regional forensic units, and all mental health services in New York state prisons. Since 1988, he has held the title of Associate Commissioner for Forensic Services in the New York State Office of Mental Health.

Dr. Dvoskin was previously employed, *inter alia*, as the Acting Executive Director of the Kirby Forensic

We are mindful that the opinions of experts are entitled to little weight in determining whether a condition is "cruel and unusual punishment" under the Eighth Amendment. *Toussaint v. McCarthy (Toussaint IV)*, 801 F.2d 1080, 1107 n. 28 (9th Cir.1986). As such, we have not relied upon expert opinion to make this ultimate legal determination. It is appropriate, however, for this Court to consider expert opinion in assessing subsidiary issues which inform the court's final determination. For example, expert opinion may be properly considered in assessing the effects of challenged conditions or practices. *See Helling v. McKinney*, 509 U.S. 25, —, 113 S.Ct. 2475, 2482, 125 L.Ed.2d 22 (1993) (making reference to the "scientific and statistical inquir[ies]" that will be used to determine the seriousness of the harm caused by challenged conditions); *Jordan v. Gardner*, 986 F.2d 1521, 1526 (9th Cir.1993) (en banc) (relying on expert testimony to establish psychological impact of challenged measure on inmates). *See also Slakan v. Porter*, 737 F.2d 368, 378 (4th Cir.1984) (correctional expert's opinions concerning punitive nature of prison's water hosing practices properly admitted).

After the trial was completed, in December 1993, the parties filed proposed findings of fact and conclusions of law on January 28 and February 1, 1994. The case was taken under submission at that time.

II.

FINDINGS OF FACT

A. *EXCESSIVE FORCE*

***

*1166

Inmate Dortch

Vaughn Dortch, a mentally ill inmate, suffered second-and third-degree burns over one-third of his body when he was given a bath in scalding water in the prison infirmary. The week before the incident Dortch bit an officer. Dortch had also created a nuisance by smearing himself and his cell with his own fecal matter. Although there was a shower near Dortch's cell, which would have provided a more efficient method of cleaning Dortch than a bath (even assuming Dortch was uncooperative), the officers instead forcibly escorted Dortch to a bathtub in the SHU infirmary, located some distance away in another ***1167** complex.[26]

According to Barbara Kuroda, the nurse on duty at the infirmary, a Medical Technical Assistant arrived shortly before Dortch, and was asked if he "want [ed] part of this bath," to which he responded, yes, he would take some of the "brush end," referring to a hard bristle brush which is wrapped in a towel and used to clean an inmate. Tr. 1-144. Five or six correctional officers then arrived with Dortch. Although a nurse would normally run the water for a therapeutic bath, Dortch's bath was managed solely by correctional staff.

Kuroda later observed, from her nurse's station, that Dortch was in the bathtub with his hands cuffed behind his back, with an officer pushing down on his shoulder and holding his arms in place. Subsequently, another officer came into the nurse's station and made a call. Kuroda's unrebutted testimony is that she overheard the officer say about Dortch, who is African-American, that it "looks like we're going to have a white boy before this is through, that his skin is so dirty and so rotten, it's all fallen off." Tr. 1-154. Concerned by this remark, Kuroda walked over toward the tub, and saw Dortch stand-

---

Psychiatric Center, a new maximum security forensic psychiatric hospital in New York, and by the Arizona State Prison system, where he served as a psychologist, supervising psychologist, and Inmate Management Administrator. He has acted as a consultant to approximately 18 jurisdictions regarding the provision of mental health care to incarcerated persons. He has also worked in prisons and prison hospitals in Massachusetts.

[26] Indeed, there is no indication that Dortch requested a bath over a shower. Rather, because of Dortch's uncooperativeness, custody staff was unable to successfully dress him, and he arrived at the SHU infirmary essentially nude, except for his restraints and part of a blue isolation gown that was wrapped around his upper torso.

ing with his back to her. She testified that, from just below the buttocks down, his skin had peeled off and was hanging in large clumps around his legs, which had turned white with some redness. Even then, in a shocking show of indifference, the officers made no effort to seek any medical assistance or advice. Instead, it appeared to Kuroda that the officers were simply dressing Dortch to return him to his cell. When Kuroda told them they could not return him in that condition, Officer Williams responded, in a manner described by Kuroda as disparaging and challenging, that Dortch had been living in his own feces and urine for three months, and if he was going to get infected, he would have been already. Williams added, however, that if Kuroda wanted to admit him, she could do the paperwork. Dortch then either fell, or began falling, to the floor from weakness, at which point Kuroda had Dortch taken to the emergency room. Although Dortch was not evidencing any pain at this point, Kuroda testified that this did not surprise her. Because severe burns destroy the surrounding nerve endings, the victim does not experience any pain until the nerves began to mend. Dortch was ultimately transported to a hospital burn center for treatment.

Based on the record before us, we can not say that any of the staff involved in the incident specifically intended the severity of the burns inflicted upon Dortch. It is unclear whether the officers knew the actual temperature of the water or the full extent of the burns that were being inflicted.[27] Nor did Dortch yell out in pain to alert the officers.[28] On the other hand, officers were observed holding Dortch down in the tub, and the burns he was experiencing must have been visible.

Although we assume, for purposes of this case, that those involved did not intend to inflict third-degree burns, it is nonetheless clear, from all of the surrounding circumstances, that Dortch was given the bath primarily as a punitive measure and for the purpose of inflicting some degree of pain, in retaliation for, and perhaps out of frustration with, his prior offensive conduct.

***

*1168

(2) Use of Fetal Restraints

The fetal restraint, also known as "restraint control status" or "hog-tying," is a particular type of in-cell restraint. Utilized numerous times until late 1991 or mid 1992, the fetal restraint procedure involves handcuffing an inmate's hands at the front of his body, placing him in leg irons, and then drawing a chain between the handcuffs and legs until only a few inches separate the bound wrists and ankles. At least one officer, however, handcuffed inmates in the back, so that the inmate's arms were behind his back and his ankles were up around his handcuffs. The fetal restraint was applied most commonly in response to an inmate kicking his cell door, although it was utilized on other occasions as well.

Plaintiffs' medical expert confirmed inmate testimony that being in this position without the ability to stretch one's legs or arms would, over time, likely cause considerable pain,[30] and could pose a serious health risk to inmates with respiratory ailments. Thus, unlike four- or five-point restraints, which completely prevent any disruptive movement without imposing pain or health risks, fetal restraints can inflict significant pain and yet not fully secure the inmate.

Notably, no expert at trial defended the use of fetal restraints. Plaintiffs' expert described such restraints as a painful, repugnant, humiliating punishment, and termed their level of use at Pelican Bay

---

[27] Shortly after the incident, a nurse returned to the tub. The water had been drained but she turned it on to test the temperature at the hottest setting, which was 140 degrees. A device has since been installed that prevents the water from reaching such a high temperature.

[28] According to the evidence in the record, Dortch maintained his silence because he knew that some retaliation would be coming for his having bitten an officer the week before, and he was determined to "take it like a man" and not let them enjoy it. However, there is also some evidence that Dortch passed out in the tub at some point, which would have alerted the officers.

[30] One inmate testified that "each time [in fetal restraints], it's very painful, because you in a cramped-up position and you unable to . . . relax one way or another because you cramped up, because you—you pulling on your . . . arms, your legs. You know, you pulling one way or another, you pulling." Jones Tr. 3-521-22.

"unprecedented" in modern corrections.[31] Martin Tr. 18-1351 Defendants' expert Daniel McCarthy testified that he had never previously used or seen anyone use a fetal restraint in his forty years in the California Department of Corrections, and did not believe that it would be an acceptable technique. Defendants' other expert, Larry DuBois, also stated that he had never used a fetal restraint and that he had not been asked to express an opinion regarding its use.

***

*1169

Inmates restrained in fetal restraints were at times also chained to toilets or other fixed objects, particularly during program administrator Rippetoe's tenure in the SHU. Although there is directly conflicting testimony regarding the extent of this practice, the Court finds that it was more than merely an occasional occurrence. Sergeant Cox testified credibly that during the limited period that he was working overtime in the SHU, he personally observed, over the course of different shifts, ten to twelve inmates who were in fetal restraints and chained to stationary objects. Some staff, including Sergeant Cox, objected to this practice, and one SHU program administrator testified that he "never ha[s] and never would" authorize such a practice. Lopez Tr. 14-2196. Sergeant Cox testified, however, that his objections were dismissed out of hand. When he asked Rippetoe why they were engaging in this practice, he responded "because we can do it." Tr. 15-2345. When he raised the issue with Associate Warden Garcia, he was told "this is Pelican Bay State Prison, and if you don't like it, get out . . . [W]e're going to do it our way." Tr. 15-2347.

Prison records indicate that fetal restraints were used in dozens of instances between January 1990 and August 1992.[33] Such restraints were imposed from anywhere between a few minutes to 24 hours, with most instances falling in the three to six hour range. Current written SHU policies permit use of fetal restraints for up to 12 hours without obtaining consent of the Warden. Whether an inmate would be freed from the restraints in order to eat or use the toilet was left to the discretion of individual staff.

At trial, defendants did not attempt to justify the fetal restraint as an appropriate response to the kicking of cell doors *per se*, although current SHU policy permits the use of fetal restraints for cell door kicking. Trial Exh. D-49 at 18307.[34] Indeed, although cell door kicking is a common occurrence, no lay or expert witness was able to identify any other prison that resorted to fetal restraints in response.

Rather, defendants testified that the use of fetal restraints for kicking doors was necessary because a weakness in the metal in the ***1170** door retainer at the bottom of each cell made cell doors vulnerable to metal fatigue in the event of continued kicking. Various prison officials testified that they became aware of this problem when the prison opened (in December 1989), and that the practice of using fetal restraints stopped once the doors were fixed in December 1991.

Integrity of cell doors is, of course, a critical security concern. However, we are not persuaded by the record that repairs to address the metal fatigue problem were not undertaken until late 1991. Although defendant Peetz testified that repair work on the cell doors occurred between approximately June and December 1991, it appears that these repairs primarily concerned another door problem involving the pneumatic locking mechanism, which was not discovered until sometime in 1991.

---

[31] Plaintiffs' expert Vince Nathan similarly described the use of these forms of restraint as "unnecessary, ineffective, excessive, and altogether lacking in any legitimate penological value." Nathan Decl. at 91.

[33] Under governing SHU policy, staff were directed to fill out a form in all cases where they used a restraint in a manner that matches the description of the fetal restraint described above. Trial Exh. D-49 at 18182, subsection (K). The record shows that between January 1990 and August 1992, over 170 "Attachment A" forms were filled out. In many of these forms, the staff did not specifically use the phrase "fetal restraints." However, this does not mean that fetal restraints were not in fact used. First, it does not appear that the policy required staff to fill out "Attachment A" unless they were using a restraint that was equivalent to a fetal restraint. Second, neither the policy nor Attachment A ever refer specifically to the term "fetal restraint" or require that such term be used. Even assuming, however, that some of the Attachment A forms did not involve use of fetal restraints, the Court finds that usage of the restraint was substantial between January 1990 and August 1992.

[34] It also permits use of fetal restraints for destruction of property or any conduct that "may incite other inmates." Trial Exh. D-49 at 18307.

***

More fundamentally, however, we are not persuaded that the use of fetal restraints was necessary or primarily prompted by legitimate penological purposes. The "D" wing of the SHU and the "C" wing of the SHU suffered from the same metal defect, and housed roughly the same number of inmates (physically the two wings are mirror images of each other). Yet, during the period that inmates in C-SHU were fetally restrained on dozens of occasions, fetal restraints were used in D-SHU less than 5 times. Given that defendants offered no basis for concluding that the inmates in D-SHU would be less likely to kick their cell doors than in C-SHU, this discrepancy in numbers is a compelling indication that the utilization of fetal restraints was not necessary to maintain security.

Moreover, fetal restraints did not even effectively prevent continued kicking of cell doors. As Captain Scribner agreed, it was "clear that if an inmate wanted to kick the door while he had his [fetal restraint] chains on . . . he could do so," and in fact it appeared to him that an inmate might end up kicking the door even harder after he was restrained. Scribner also testified that such an inmate could still get "enough of a kick" that he could compromise the integrity of the door. Scribner Tr. 7-1241, 6-1120. Indeed, it is clear that the continued ability to kick only escalated the need for more restraints, such that there was a practice, albeit relatively short-lived, of locking an already fetally-restrained inmate to his toilet—a practice which Lieutenant Carl agreed was in violation of governing California regulations. Carl Depo. at 291-92.

The use of fetal restraints in response to the kicking of doors becomes particularly suspect when it is considered that a far more effective, yet less painful, alternative was available. As plaintiffs' expert Steve Martin emphasized without contradiction, from a custody standpoint, the most effective means of preventing an inmate from kicking a cell door is to place him in full restraints: "you put a man in a four-point, five-point restraint, he's not going to kick a door." Tr. 8-1350. And, as noted above, full restraints accomplish this result without inflicting discomfort and pain. Nonetheless, there is no indication in the record that defendants ever considered full restraints as an alternative at any point between December 1989 and December 1991.

In short, it is undisputed that the fetal restraint, which requires an obvious contortion *1171 of normal body position, can cause considerable pain over time. It is also undisputed that this restraint failed to effectively prevent the kicking of doors, and that other more effective and less painful alternatives were available and known to defendants. Nonetheless, in one section of the SHU, fetal restraints were often the response of first resort to cell door kicking for a period of at least two years.

We do not, and need not, find that every application of the fetal restraint at Pelican Bay was punitive in nature. Nor do we address the facial validity of the prison's fetal restraint rule. However, the record and particular circumstances presented here convince us that there was a practice of using fetal restraints at Pelican Bay for solely punitive rather than good faith security purposes.

(3) Cagings

Another use of force at Pelican Bay that is punitive in character is the confinement of naked or partially dressed inmates in outdoor holding cages during inclement weather. These cages, approximately the size of a telephone booth, and constructed of weave mesh metal, are designed to provide a temporary holding place for an inmate, and are positioned at various locations around the prison. Inmates confined in the cages are exposed to the elements as well as public view.

Violet Baker, a former educational program supervisor at Pelican Bay, gave a frank and credible account of one such incident. She testified that one day in late January or early February, she was walking from her office toward another facility. It was very cold (she was wearing gloves and a heavy jacket), and it was pouring rain. She observed two African-American inmates being held naked in two cages. When she passed by again one hour later, one inmate was still there, and she observed that he was covered with goose bumps. He said he was freezing, and asked her to request a pair of shorts and a T-shirt. She then saw an officer coming in her direction. When she looked at him, he looked back and just shrugged his shoulders, saying it was "Lieutenant's order." When she determined that it was Lieutenant Slayton on duty, she let the matter drop. Although the incident upset her, Slayton had a reputation for causing problems if crossed, and she did not want her educational program or teachers to suffer by her interference in this matter.

In another such incident, inmate Johnny Barnes testified credibly that he was caged naked in one of the outdoor holding cages on a "misty" day. Although he was bleeding from his nose and mouth after a physical altercation with several correctional officers, Barnes was held in the outdoor cage for an hour and a half without receiving medical attention. In public view of whoever passed by, Barnes recalled that he felt like he was "just a[n] animal or something." Tr. 10-1529.

Lieutenant Slayton at first denied that there was "ever any occasion" when an inmate was held in a holding cell completely nude. Tr. 20-3363. However, he later testified that there were instances where inmates were briefly held naked in cages, but insisted that they were dressed as soon as possible. Providing inmates with clothes was a priority, he testified, because of the inclement weather, and because "it's just a common dignity." Tr. 20-3364.

Clearly, there are times when prison officials will need to take an inmate's clothes, as potential evidence after an incident, or for other justifiable purposes. And we agree with Lieutenant Slayton that providing substitute clothes is not only a matter of health and safety in inclement weather, but a matter of common dignity, given the public placement of the cages and the routine presence of female staff. However, his testimony that the inmates were never caged naked for more than brief periods lacks credibility in light of his inconsistent testimony on this point, as well as the credible testimony of Violet Baker and Johnny Barnes.

Moreover, some of these cages are visible from the main administrative offices for the yard (including the Lieutenant's office), and are in full view of anyone who crosses the yard. Thus, it is apparent that such naked cagings would be known to, and thus implicitly, if not explicitly, condoned by supervisory *1172 staff. Indeed, the incident to which Violet Baker testified was clearly ordered by mid-level supervisory staff, as opposed to a renegade officer.

Such incidents may be relatively infrequent. Baker testified that she had never seen anyone naked in the cages except for that one day.[36] However, as Martin observed, this is the type of incident that is not typically memorialized in reports, making it difficult to determine how often it occurs. Notably, neither of the above incidents were documented, which leads the Court to conclude that there likely have been other undocumented instances as well. The reaction of the correctional officer to Baker's inquiry suggests that this was not considered an extraordinary or unique event.

Leaving inmates in outdoor cages for any significant period—as if animals in a zoo—offends even the most elementary notions of common decency and dignity. It also fails to serve any legitimate penological purpose in any kind of weather, much less cold and rainy weather. The fact that it occurred at all exhibits a callous and malicious intent to inflict gratuitous humiliation and punishment.

(4) Cell Extractions

(i) *Overview*

The forcible removal of an inmate from his cell—also known as a "cell extraction"—is indisputably an essential tool in maintaining security in any prison. There will clearly be occasions when security concerns mandate that an inmate be removed from his cell against his will, such as where the inmate is suspected of harboring contraband, or has had an altercation with a cellmate. Such a forcible removal can be accomplished by various means. Staff who are completely unarmed, or armed only with a mattress or shield, can use sheer weight and numbers to overwhelm the inmate.[37] At the other extreme, staff can be highly armed, even during routine extractions, as is the case at Pelican Bay.

Indeed, the cell extraction process at Pelican Bay is an undeniably violent maneuver which can involve several weapons, including 38 millimeter gas guns, tasers, short metal batons, and mace. It also results in frequent injuries and infliction of pain. As Chief Deputy Warden Peetz summed it up, "cell extractions are a very, very violent maneuver . . .. Inmates get hurt and staff get hurt, and it's just the nature of the thing." Tr. 20-3316. As such, witnesses for both sides agree that cell extractions should be

---

[36] At the time of trial, Baker had been on medical leave as of March of 1993; it is unclear how long she had been employed at Pelican Bay prior to that time.

[37] For example, in Georgia State Prison, only hands-on force and restraints are used in cell extractions; in Texas, staff are limited to handcuffs, belly chains, leg irons and straight jackets, unless the inmate is armed, in which case the baton, shield and/or mace may also be used. Texas staff may only use tasers if separate requirements for use of lethal force are also met.

performed only when necessary. Indeed, under normal circumstances, an inmate should not be extracted absent an imminent risk to the safety and security of the institution. Scribner Tr. 7-1211.

***

*1178.

Viewed separately, the high level of force deployed as a routine practice, the string of significant injuries, and the unnecessarily high number of cell extractions, could each raise a legitimate concern. Combined, however, they are potent evidence that cell extractions at Pelican Bay have too often been considered, not as tools to be used sparingly in response to threats to prison security, but as opportunities to punish, and inflict pain upon, the inmate population for what were often minor rules violations. The evasive and cursory nature of incident reports, discussed *supra*, further reinforces this conclusion.

(5) Lethal Force

The California Department of Corrections has for many years integrated firearms into its system of maintaining security, both inside and outside of housing units.[51] Pelican Bay is no exception. It employs a variety of firearms to maintain control inside the general population maximum security housing units and exercise yards and inside the SHU.[52] The general population yards are ***1179** observed by an armed officer in a central tower overlooking the entire yard, as well as by armed officers in control booths in each housing unit, who oversee daily activities through windows that look onto the yard.[53] The housing units in both the maximum security general population units and the SHU are monitored by armed officers in the control booths. In the former, the armed officers have a direct line of sight into the cells, while in the SHU, armed control booth officers have a direct line of sight into the common pod area outside of the cells but not into the cells themselves.

Notably, other large prison systems, such as New York, Texas, Ohio, and the Federal Bureau of Prisons, manage their prisons (except for the perimeters) without the use of any firearms. Indeed, reliance on firearms in housing units (either general population or security housing units) and exercise yards to maintain control and break up incidents is unusual. Defendant Gomez was aware of only one other state, Nevada, which employs firearms inside housing units.

The record does not, however, support a finding that the decision to deploy firearms at Pelican Bay in and of itself constitutes a policy or practice of excessive force. Whether firearms should be integrated into a prison's security system is a matter best left to the sound discretion of prison administrators. However, given that every use of a firearm creates the potential for death or serious bodily injury—not only for the intended victim but for others nearby as well—a policy of arming prison staff can easily lead to the application of excessive force.

Recognizing this, governing regulations prohibit the use of firearms except when "absolutely necessary," i.e., "only as a last resort after other reasonable and available resources have been considered and exhausted or are determined to be clearly inappropriate in view of the immediate need to use armed force." Cal.Code Regs. § 3276(b); *see also* Trial Exh. D-37, California Department of Corrections Operations Manual (referred to as "DOM") at 55050.8 ("Employees shall not discharge a firearm . . . except under [certain specified] circumstances and only after all other reasonable means fail"). The evi-

---

[51] This practice appears at least in part designed to compensate for the fact that California is ranked 47th in the nation in the number of correctional officers per inmate. Gomez. Tr. 28-4612-13. Defendant's expert McCarthy also hypothesized that "I guess we [in California] were [in] the wild west days there and never got out." Tr. 15-2539-40.

[52] The firearms used at Pelican Bay are: (1) the Ruger Mini-14 .223 caliber rifle, (2) the Heckler & Koch Model 94 ("H & K 94") 9 millimeter carbine, using the Glaser Safety Slug, (3) the Smith & Wesson .38 caliber revolver, and (4) the Remington 12-gauge pump shotgun. Firearms were discharged 177 times in 129 incidents between the time the prison opened and September 9, 1993. Of the 177 shots fired, 23 were intended to be for effect (i.e. were fired with the intent to hit a person), 152 were intended to be warning shots, and 2 were accidental. 109 shots were fired outdoors and 68 indoors. Of the 152 warning shots, 13 caused or were alleged to have caused inmate injuries from ricochets or bullet fragments.

[53] The general population yards are also supervised by unarmed staff who patrol the yard on the ground.

dence showed, however, that staff have resorted to firearms too quickly—before any life threatening situation has developed—rather than reserving such lethal force as "the force of last resort."[54]

Based on the evidence presented, we conclude that firearms at Pelican Bay have been used unnecessarily, and in some cases, recklessly.[55] *1180 However, in contrast to the instances of excessive force discussed in the sections above, the record before us does not demonstrate that lethal force has been applied maliciously for the purpose of causing harm, rather than in a good faith effort to restore order, on more than the isolated occasion. Rather, it appears that, in many instances, officers resorted first to lethal force because prison administrators failed to supply them with alternative weapons or because prison policies promoted the use of lethal force. See, e.g., notes 67, 64 and accompanying text, infra. These facts, however, explain more than just the actions of staff. They also reveal that defendants are strikingly unconcerned that lethal force may be applied even when a lesser degree of force would be sufficient.

***

*1181 Based on the evidence regarding specific incidents and practices, and the opinions of prison experts, the Court is convinced that the instances of force being used excessively and for the purpose of causing harm are of sufficient scope, variety, and number to constitute a pattern. Plaintiffs have convincingly documented a staggering number of instances in which prison personnel applied unjustifiably high levels of force, both pursuant to, and in contravention of, official prison policies. Simply put, the evidence before the Court is proof of the most powerful, unambiguous kind that a pattern of excessive force has become an undeniable reality at Pelican Bay.[57]

2. *Inadequacies in the Systems for Regulating the Use of Force*

There is no dispute among the parties that the use of force must be carefully regulated and controlled

---

[54] For example, control booth officers in the SHU have resorted to semi automatic rifles to break up an unarmed fight between inmates on the pod because no gas gun or taser or mace is kept in the control booth. Instead, at least through June of 1992, the gas gun was stored in the corridor control, notwithstanding the fact that the SHU operating procedure contemplates that the control booth officer would have access to a gas gun. Similarly, at least as of June of 1992, it was not expected that staff would attempt to break up unarmed inmate fights in SHU pods through use of cell extraction teams before resorting to lethal force.

In one instance, two inmates were fighting in the SHU pod while approximately ten officers, some with batons, stood on the other side of the pod door. However, they were not allowed to intervene absent specific orders from a lieutenant or sergeant, neither of whom had arrived by the time the control booth officer felt action was necessary to stop the fight. Given this, and the absence of a gas gun, the control booth officer testified that his only alternatives for breaking up the unarmed fistfight were to shout warnings or use his firearm. Brodeur Tr. 24-4014-15. As a result, inmate Ashker was shot in the arm. He later developed an aneurysm in the arm, which, because of lack of treatment, ultimately necessitated an airlift for emergency surgery. Start Decl. at 174-175.

Another inmate fistfight a month before trial resulted in an inmate named Jose Padilla being shot and wounded. On this occasion, as previously, the inmates were unarmed and were fighting in the pod, in clear view of the control booth officer. As before, backup officers were waiting at the pod door for the supervisor with a gas gun to arrive. In this instance, there were three backup officers at the time of the shot and there were three inmates involved in the fight. Once again, the control booth officer did not believe that she could allow the fight to continue, and had no alternative available other than to use her firearm. She therefore shot Mr. Padilla in the hip, causing him to sustain extensive trauma to his hip and necessitating an air evacuation.

[55] The records produced in this action show that three prisoners have been killed, two of whom were not the person at whom the shooting officer was aiming. Another 20 inmates have been hit by bullets or bullet fragments; six of these inmates appear from the prison records to have been uninvolved bystanders, and another three appear not to have been the aggressor. When defendants' expert reviewed reports from three separate shooting incidents between March and August 1993 (involving six inmates and 10 separate shots), he concluded that none of the reports set forth sufficient facts to justify any of the shots and that, upon receipt, he would have referred the reports to an investigative unit. Trial Ex. P-1267, P-4900, and P-5599; DuBois Tr. 29-4770-71, 74, 75, 79-80.

[57] If anything, that pattern is, in reality, stronger than reflected in the findings here, given the operative code of silence and the fact that the testimony by prison staff often seemed calculated to reveal no more than necessary. Inadequacies in the supervision of the use of force and the investigatory process also obscure the full parameters of the pattern. Certainly, much has transpired at Pelican Bay of which the Court will never know.

in order to prevent abuses against inmates, as well as to ensure the overall safety and security of the prison. As Fenton explained:

> In running a penitentiary, a high security prison, force is a necessary element. It must be used when it's appropriate and when it's required. But it is the most dangerous and potentially destructive function that takes place in a prison. Not only can it destroy or seriously injure the people it's directed against, but it can do enormous damage to . . . the spirit and morale of the inmate body [and] to the staff. . ... The use of force can be enormously dangerous. For that reason, it ought to be absolutely seriously monitored.

Tr. 5-766. Indeed, there was no evidence suggesting that the failure to adequately monitor or regulate the use of force would serve any legitimate penological purpose or otherwise advance the security of a prison.

A system that adequately monitors and regulates the use of force consists of five components: (a) written policies that clearly identify for line staff when and how much force is appropriate under different circumstances; (b) training of correctional officers regarding the proper use of force; (c) supervision of the use of force to ensure that it is consonant with departmental and institutional policies and procedures; (d) investigation of possible misuses of force; and (e) officer discipline for the misuse of force. Nathan Tr. 13-1999-2000; Nathan Decl. at 15; *see also Fisher v. Koehler*, 692 F.Supp. 1519, 1551 (S.D.N.Y.1988), *aff'd*, 902 F.2d 2 (2nd Cir.1990).

Each of these interrelated components builds upon and reinforces the others. Thus, adequate written policies provide the necessary framework for properly training staff and evaluating subsequent conduct. Yet, written policies alone serve little purpose unless staff are trained as to their content. Adequate supervision and investigation are necessary to ensure that, in practice, staff are properly implementing written policies and principles learned through training. Finally, a meaningful disciplinary system is essential, for if there are no sanctions imposed for misconduct, the prison's "policies and procedures . . . become a dead letter." Nathan Tr. 13-2003.

The evidence shows that the system for controlling use of force at Pelican Bay suffers from serious deficiencies, particularly with respect to the supervisory and investigatory components described above. The Court also finds that these deficiencies, known and tolerated by defendants, are a significant cause of the misuse of force at Pelican Bay.

***

*1184

. . . As a result, staff resorted to lethal force in the general population units before exhausting lesser alternatives. For example, if an assault continued after the control booth officer opened the cell door to allow one inmate a chance to exit, the control booth officer would immediately attempt to control the assault with a firearm, by firing either a warning shot or a shot for effect.[64]

***

*1185 Perhaps of most concern, the Court finds the deficiencies in certain written policies, described above, symptomatic of a more general disregard for the importance of written policies. The

---

[64] As a result of the CDC task force study, Pelican Bay adopted a post order that provides for the following alternative before resort to lethal force: "A cell extraction team shall be utilized for those inmates continuing to fight after being ordered to stop. The cell extraction team shall be deployed in accordance with established procedures. In an extreme emergency, in order to prevent the death or great bodily injury of an innocent cell partner, floor staff will vacate the affected section. Floor staff will notify the Control Officer of the immediate need for armed force. The Control Officer will then attempt to control the assault with the use of armed force in compliance with DOM 55050." Trial Exh. D-58 at 52886. Warden Marshall also testified that the current practice is that, in the event of a cell fight, the control booth officer waits until staff arrives, and then when the door is opened, staff goes in and breaks up the fight. Marshall Tr. at 22-3808. Marshall also testified that in the event lethal force is used, the control booth officer may fire a warning shot or a shot for effect. We note, however, that the post order does not give any specific guidance as to where such warning shots should be fired.

Court notes that, as of the date of trial, a number of officially sanctioned policy changes still had not been memorialized in written form, thus creating a schism between the prison's written policies and its actual operating procedure.[65] Notably, the current written operation policy for the SHU has remained "under revision" since 1990. Scribner Tr. 7-1214-15. Although this means that senior staff sometimes find themselves directing line officers to rely on "unapproved" revised policy, *see, e.g.,* Helsel Tr. at 21-3565-66, no prison staff at trial evinced any concern over the fact that the SHU was operating under an outdated written policy with no apparent date set for the issuance of a current version.

As might be expected, the lack of completeness and consistency in written policies relating to the use of force, and the lack of importance ascribed to written policies in general, have also served to undermine the legitimacy of those written policies that are in effect. It was not uncommon for staff to testify that they were unaware of written policies,[66] or for the evidence to show that a written policy was simply not followed, whether by design or because of a simple lack of familiarity.[67]

***

*1186

c. *Supervision of the Use of Force*

Adequate supervision is probably the most critical component of any system that regulates the use of force: not only does it serve as an immediate check on any abuses, but it also creates an atmosphere that encourages responsible conduct. At the same time, adequate supervision ensures that sufficient force is used to maintain security for staff and inmates.

At trial, defendants' witnesses readily acknowledged the importance of providing effective supervision over the use of force. The evidence, however, shows that senior prison administrators have, for the most part, abdicated their responsibility in this crucial area. Indeed, Pelican Bay's approach to the use of force is often so passive that plaintiffs' expert concluded that there is a "near total absence of meaningful supervision" of the application of force at Pelican Bay. Nathan Tr. 13-2039.

***

*1187

---

[65] For example, policy changes regarding fetal restraints, staff response to meal tray retentions, and use of tasers have never been memorialized in writing. Of course, practices that are not formalized in written policies are also more susceptible to change. For example, although Chief Deputy Warden Peetz testified that the rule was now that fetal restraints were "completely discontinued," Tr. 20-57, Program Administrator Helsel testified that he was led to believe that he still had "some latitude" or "discretion" in this area. Tr. 21-67.

[66] For example, Program Administrator Lopez was unaware at the time of his deposition in 1993 whether Pelican Bay even had written policies describing when cell extractions are appropriate. Tr. 14-2186. Similarly, Officer Brodeur did not recall seeing the written operational policy for the SHU until the time of his deposition. Tr. 24-4017. Captain Scribner provided another example, stating that when he was assigned as a full-time lieutenant in the SHU, he was not required to read the post orders for his subordinate staff, and could not recall what they said about warning shots. Scribner Depo. at 107-08. He also testified that extractions generally were appropriate only if there was an imminent threat to safety or security, but was unsure what written policy, if any, set forth that standard. Tr. 7-14. Nor could he recall whether there were any written procedures governing the use of fetal restraints. Tr. 7-38.

[67] For example, although the SHU operating procedure contemplates that the control booth officer will have access to a gas gun, control booths do not contain such guns. Specifically, the SHU operating procedure provides that in the event of a violent cell fight in the SHU, the control booth officer is to open the cell door in order to allow the victim to exit the cell into the pod, which the procedure notes, will also "give the gun officer a clear field of fire, if required." If the fight continues into the pod, and assuming no weapon is observed, "the first weapon of choice should be the 37-mm gun utilizing the single rubber baton round 264-R. Obviously, the firing of this round *will be from the control booth*, not from the floor. In directing this shot, staff are advised to avoid any direct hits, but rather should ricochet it around." Trial Ex. D-49 at 18289 (emphasis added). Notwithstanding the above, the only weapon available to officers in the SHU control booths is the H & K 9-millimeter rifle. As a consequence, significant injuries have been inflicted when control booth officers have resorted to using rifles. *See* note 54, *supra*. No explanation was offered at trial as to why gas guns have not been stationed in the control booths. Other examples of staff actions which contravened written policy include leaving an inmate in fetal restraints on the bunk instead of on the floor, and using fetal restraints with the hands and ankles tied behind the back instead of in the front.

The Court finds that supervision of the use of non-lethal force at Pelican Bay is strikingly deficient. The breakdown in supervision reveals itself in a number of ways. First, senior administrators permit, or even encourage, officers to submit overly general incident reports, a practice which both parties' experts criticized as making it impossible to evaluate the propriety of staff conduct. As defendants' expert stated, "[the incident reports] appear to be generic in nature. They're—they're not reports that I, as a Commissioner in Massachusetts . . . looked at as . . . covering the whole event but more in terms of describing what happened very generically." DuBois Tr. 29-4713. It is not unusual for a report to gloss over events and inmate injuries by reporting little more than the team "gained control" and "applied mechanical restraints." See, e.g., Trial Exh. P-4925 at 3208. Other reports provide more detail but still lack sufficient information to enable a supervisor to determine what occurred. See Martin Decl. at 64-65, 158 (pattern of sanitized reports is "simply undeniable."). In still other cases, the reports of different officers are suspiciously identical.[73]

The fact that such reports are routinely accepted leaves the clear inference that senior prison administrators not only have little concern as to what actually occurred, but that they affirmatively approve of such reports. Notably, one sergeant testified that his supervisor wanted reports to be "vague and non-specific," because otherwise those higher up the chain of command would not accept them. Cox Tr. 15-49.

Second, it is not unusual for prison administrators to turn a blind eye when an incident report clearly calls for further inmate sustained serious injuries that are either unexplained or suspiciously explained.

***

* 1190

(2) Supervision of the Use of Lethal Force

Given Pelican Bay's substantial reliance on firearms, and the fact that every firing of these weapons potentially inflicts serious injury or death, effective supervision over the use of firearms is particularly critical. The evidence shows, however, that despite a facially complex system for reviewing the use of firearms, the lax attitude toward the use of non-lethal force, described above, is equally evident in the area of lethal force. Indeed, meaningful firearm supervision of the kind that actually protects human beings is almost non-existent.

***

*1198 The Court does not intend to suggest that special circumstances may not warrant leniency in a particular case or that a Warden should not be permitted to exercise his or her discretion in this regard. What the record reflects at Pelican Bay, however, is an institution that lacks serious commitment to disciplining or controlling the behavior of staff who misuse force against inmates.

***

[5] However the fact that a prison may be new does not excuse defendants' obligation to operate it in a constitutionally acceptable manner, an obligation which defendant Gomez testified he understood. Tr. 28-4629. Thus, we have attempted to discern to what extent the pattern of excessive force and breakdown in the systems for controlling use of force can be attributed to the "growing pains" of a new facility (that is, good faith errors or mistakes), and to what extent defendants were not only aware of the problems and the consequences, but deliberately chose to ignore them. We conclude that while the newness of the facility may explain some of the problems identified in the findings above, defendants are largely culpable for the pattern of excessive force at Pelican Bay.

***

---

[73] For example, the reports of two baton men assigned to the cell extractions of two cellmates (inmates Molano and Moreno) utilize identical language except for changing the name of the inmate. When questioned about this at trial, one of the baton men admitted that he had "no explanation" of how that occurred. Owens Tr. 28-4581.

The record also demonstrates that this risk was consciously disregarded, evincing, at the very least, an attitude of deliberate indifference. Although defendants have ceased some of the practices complained of by plaintiffs,[99] such changes, which post-date the filing ***1199** of this class action, were likely motivated by this litigation, and at least as of the time of trial, had not been cemented in any formal written policy. As such, they may well be transitory in nature, and the Court is not persuaded that such changes would not be undone in the absence of court intervention. Nor has any prison official ever suggested that such changes were made to address problems concerning the use of excessive force. On the contrary, defendants never acknowledged that there was a genuine problem to be addressed and always offered other reasons to explain these changes in practice. Moreover, defendants never offered the Court any firm or clear assurances that such changes would be permanent. Accordingly, the Court is not convinced that these recent changes represent a serious commitment by defendants to end the pattern of excessive force.

Rather, the great weight of the evidence indicates that the misuse of force against inmates was something that prison administrators preferred to disregard or ignore. Although defendants acknowledged that regulation of the use of force is important if abuses are to be minimized or avoided, they made no serious effort to operate the prison in a manner that would effectively regulate and control the use of force. As detailed in section II(A)(2) above, defendants failed to provide (1) clear and authoritative use of force policies, (2) any meaningful supervision of the use of force, (3) a bona fide investigatory process into allegations of misuse of force, or (4) consistent imposition of discipline in those cases in which misuse of force was found. While a failure in one area might not raise any particular inference, the glaring deficiencies in all of the above areas convinces us that such deficiencies are not accidental but the result of deliberate indifference.[100]

This indifference was underscored when senior administrators were questioned about particular incidents. For example, when the Warden was questioned about the circumstances surrounding an inmate who suffered a broken jaw, he evinced no concern that neither he nor the investigative report could satisfactorily explain why there had been "blood on the floor." *See* note 94, *supra*. Similarly, when the Chief Deputy Warden was questioned about an incident report that all experts agreed should be investigated, he saw nothing of concern. *See* section II(A)(2)(c)(1), *supra* [omitted here]. Given all of the above, we readily find that defendants were deliberately indifferent to the risk of serious injury to inmates.

Plaintiffs' experts also convincingly testified that the degree of excessive force found at Pelican Bay and the deficient systems to control the use of force reflect a management practice that is designed to inflict unnecessary pain and suffering. Fenton, for example, stated that "this is the first I had ever heard of an administrative organization where prisoners were, on a fairly systematic basis, cruelly treated as an administrative device. I've never seen . . . that before." Tr. 5-734. Similarly, Nathan described Pelican Bay as "a lawless, violent place" where "defendants have knowingly allowed grossly inappropriate use of force to occur as a deliberate management policy." Nathan Tr. at 13-2051; Decl. at 13. *See also* Martin Tr. 8-1377 ("they've got some folks out there obsessed . . . with pain and with sending this . . . message to the rest of the system: that you will hurt and you will experience sheer pain if you come to Pelican Bay").[101]

We agree that the extent to which force is misused at Pelican Bay, combined with the flagrant and pervasive failures in defendants' systems for controlling the use of force reveal more than just deliberate indifference: they reveal an affirmative management strategy to permit the use of excessive force for the purposes of punishment and deterrence. For example, when defendants manifest no concern that the SHU has no current official operating policy, when they fail to explain ***1200** why SHU control booth officers are not provided with gas guns as a non-lethal alternative to rifles, when they let highly suspicious incident and investigative reports go unchallenged, and when they promote the code of silence by failing to support those who come forward, they lead us to conclude that they have implicitly sanctioned the misuse of force and acted with a knowing willingness that harm occur. Of course, these points only touch on some of the evidence discussed in the Court's findings that bears on this point. All together, it paints a picture of a prison that all too often uses force, not only in good faith efforts to restore and maintain order, but also for the very purpose of inflicting punishment and pain.

---

[99] For example, inmates are no longer routinely subjected to full-scale cell extractions in the event a meal tray is withheld, tasers are no longer routinely used, and fetal restraints are no longer utilized with any frequency, if at all.

[100] While another inference would be simple incompetence, there is no evidence in the record to support the conclusion that defendants, with lengthy careers in corrections, could not perform their responsibilities in a competent manner.

[101] From the context of his testimony, it is clear that Martin's colloquial reference to "some folks" was not a reference to a few renegade officers but to the management level officials at the prison.

B. *MEDICAL HEALTH CARE*

Plaintiffs contend that Pelican Bay has a constitutionally inadequate system for delivering medical care. At trial, the Court heard testimony from two expert witnesses. Dr. Armond Start, testifying for the plaintiffs, based his opinion on an extensive examination of Pelican Bay's medical care system. In addition to touring the prison and interviewing both inmates and prison personnel, he has reviewed over 130 prisoner medical records[102] and a random sample of 3000 sick call slips. He also examined the depositions of Department of Corrections staff and read numerous other documents such as grievance forms and records from hospitals and other third party health care providers. In all, Dr. Start spent more than 300 hours evaluating the health care system at Pelican Bay. Start Tr. 11-1703.

Dr. Jay Harness, the defendants' expert, evaluated Pelican Bay's delivery of medical care by touring the facility, reviewing documents and depositions, including that of Dr. Start, and reviewing eight prisoner medical records. Dr. Harness testified that his entire evaluation took around thirty or thirty-one hours. Harness Tr. 19-3089-90.[103]

The Court also heard testimony from Nadim Khoury, the Assistant Deputy Director for Health Care Services for the California Department of Corrections, Kyle McKinsey, Deputy Director for Health Care Services with the Department of Corrections, and Pelican Bay physician Dr. David Cooper. Nurses, the head Medical Technical Assistant, and several inmates also presented testimony, and the Court received deposition testimony from other health care providers at Pelican Bay. The Court also carefully reviewed well over a thousand pages of documentary evidence submitted by both parties.

The evidence before the Court compels us to find that the medical care system at Pelican Bay does not meet minimum constitutional standards. We agree with plaintiffs' expert, Dr. Start, who concluded that "the entire system is grossly inadequate and unsatisfactory in meeting the health care needs of the inmate population. Indeed, . . . [it is] deplorably inadequate." Start Decl. at 4.[104] As described below, the record reveals systemic, unremedied deficiencies in the system for delivering health care at Pelican Bay which render that system incapable of meeting inmates' serious medical needs. Moreover, we find that the evidence reflects defendants' deliberate indifference to those needs.

1. *Serious Need for Medical Services*

There is no doubt that inmates at Pelican Bay have serious medical needs. Like the population at large, prisoners entering the facility suffer from diseases such as asthma, hypertension, epilepsy, diabetes, tuberculosis and lupus. Once at Pelican Bay, inmates experience the full spectrum of medical problems, ranging from the routine to the life-threatening, including loss of hearing, abdominal pains, fractures, kidney stones, lacerations and gunshot wounds. Dr. Cooper, a physician and surgeon at Pelican Bay, stated ***1201** that inmates experience more serious levels of illness than patients he sees in private practice. Cooper Tr. 14-2259. In addition, many serious health disorders are overrepresented in the prison population. Start Decl. at 11 (seizure disorders, diabetes, asthma, chronic obstructive pulmonary disease, trauma, hypertension and cardiac problems are disproportionally present, as are risk factors for communicable diseases). In addition, inmates in the SHU generally need more medical care than those in the general prison population. Khoury Tr. 10-1588. Inmates clearly have medical needs that are genuine, frequent, and serious.

2. *Systemic Deficiencies in the Delivery of Health Care*

a. *Staffing Levels*

Both sides agree that the presence of sufficient, qualified medical staff is indispensable to the provision of adequate medical care. However, Pelican Bay has from its opening operated without enough doctors and properly trained and supervised medical personnel to meet the needs of the inmate population. This numerical inadequacy contributes significantly to the failure of the medical system as a whole.

Dr. Nadim Khoury, the former Chief of Medical Services for the CDC, was called as an adverse wit-

---

[102] Defendants have argued that Dr. Start's sample was "biased" because he examined records that plaintiffs felt reflected deficiencies in the medical care system. However, plaintiffs assert not that Dr. Start's sample was random, but that it was a focused study which highlighted systemic problems at Pelican Bay.

[103] The qualifications of both Dr. Armond Start and Dr. Jay Harness are set out in section I, supra.

[104] References herein are to Dr. Start's declaration filed on January 14, 1994.

ness by the plaintiffs. He confirmed that CDC policy is to require a ratio of 1 physician for every 550 inmates. Khoury Tr. 10- 1587. Notwithstanding this established policy, of which the Warden was well aware,[105] defendants elected to open the prison in December of 1989 without a single physician on staff. Instead, when Pelican Bay opened, the only physician available to inmates was a Crescent City emergency room physician who worked at the facility one day per week. Astorga Depo. at 28. Since then, the number of physicians and other medical personnel on staff has grown, but has not kept pace with the needs of the inmates. For example, by the end of January 1990, one M.D., five registered nurses, and sixteen Medical Technical Assistants ("MTAs")[106] had been hired for a prison population of approximately 1,300, a physician/inmate ratio of 1:1,300. By January of 1991, the staff had increased moderately to include three physicians, six nurses, and 24 MTAs, but the inmate population had grown to over 3,500 inmates. Thus the grossly inadequate physician/inmate ratio remained almost constant at approximately 1:1,166. These conditions amounted to an "extreme shortage of staff," such that medical personnel were "spread too thin to really be able to give very much individual attention to inmates." Lara Depo. at 35, 73. Even the defendants' medical expert, Dr. Harness, admitted in exquisite understatement that the initial staffing levels were "incomplete." Harness Decl. at 11.

Support staff repeatedly voiced to supervisors their concerns about insufficient staffing; one MTA testified that she remembers asking "[e]verybody [—] [s]enior MTAs, doctors []" for more MTAs to be hired. Gollihar Depo. at 63. A supervising nurse testified that in 1992 she needed and requested more nurses "to deal with the increased acuity of the inmates," but her request was denied because of a hiring freeze. S. Bliesner Tr. 26-4262-63. In fact, physicians openly referred to staffing shortages to justify inadequate care. For instance, after one inmate complained after a seven month delay in removing his cysts, Dr. Astorga answered that the facility was "125% short of doctors." Start Decl., Exh. E at 7091. The lack of staff has had predictable effects, from delays in medical treatment, discussed below, to tragic oversights, as when the medical staff "missed" a inmate's ruptured appendix. Ruble Depo. at 63.

By January 1, 1993, over three years after the prison opened, there were five doctors, seven nurses (and one open position), and 26 *1202 MTAs providing medical care for 3898 prisoners, a doctor/inmate ratio of approximately 1:780. By the time of trial another doctor had been added, yet the medical staff is still unable to serve the sheer number of inmates who need medical attention. As one MTA notes, it is "almost impossible to keep up with the demand of patient care services." Simmons Depo. at 49. MTAs and doctors, including Dr. Astorga, agree that Pelican Bay is still "short of physicians," Astorga Depo. at 100, and some doctors have expressed a wish for more doctors, more nurses, and more MTAs. As Dr. Start concluded, Pelican Bay "continues to have . . . an inadequate number of health care staff to provide necessary services to the inmate population there." Start Decl. at 5. In combination with Pelican Bay's other medical shortcomings, understaffing clearly contributes to the systemic failure of medical services.

b. Inadequate Training and Supervision

What medical staff does exist must be properly supervised and trained in order to be effective, but "medical training at Pelican Bay is virtually non-existent and supervision is woefully deficient." Start Decl. at 92. Dr. Start testified to the importance of prison staff staying updated on changes in health care management. Although facilities can offer in-house ("in-service") programs on topics such as management of emergencies or tuberculosis, "[t]here is none of that in existence at Pelican Bay." Start Tr. 11-1742. Pelican Bay medical personnel at all levels have identified this lack of training as a problem. MTAs have repeatedly requested additional training, one even going so far as to file a grievance protesting the lack of continuing medical education. Carter Depo. at 182-83. Dr. Gard, a physician at Pelican Bay, recognized a ongoing need to train MTAs to handle emergency situations. Gard Depo. at 71.

Particularly noteworthy is an absence of "drills to practice emergency care and [a lack of] instruction given for basic emergency procedures which is particularly disturbing because of the frequency of trauma." Start Decl. at 96. The need for training in emergency procedures is especially clear in light of instances in which MTAs have mishandled emergency situations. Dr. Start highlighted several such

---

[105] See Marshall Tr. 22-3826.

[106] MTAs are licensed vocational nurses. They are qualified, when directed and supervised by a physician, to administer medications by hypodermic injection, withdraw blood, start and superimpose intravenous fluids, administer tuberculin and other skin tests and various immunizations. Cal.Bus. & Prof.Code §§ 2860.5-2860.7. They are not specifically licensed to perform a triage function, although some MTAs may have triage training. Many MTAs at Pelican Bay have worked as corpsmen in the military.

examples; in one instance, an MTA waited until inmate Roger Hernandez was carried to a clinic on a gurney before CPR was initiated. Carter Depo. at 95-96; Trial Exh. P-3053 at 32679. In several other cases, MTAs improperly treated inmates who were in shock. *See* Start Decl. at 98-102.

Even more troubling than the absence of training programs is the basic lack of physician supervision of MTAs. MTAs play a critical role in inmates' medical treatment by performing initial triage.[107] When inmates need medical assistance, they fill out a sick call slip which is collected from a central location once a day by an MTA.[108] The MTA then reviews the slips to determine whether the illness requires emergency treatment or can be treated at a later time. Unbelievably, MTAs perform this vital triage function without an organized form of supervision.[109] Dr. Cooper, a physician and surgeon at Pelican Bay, testified that he was unaware of any protocol that "specifies any way to review or supervise the performance of an MTA in triaging medical slips." Cooper Tr. 14-2308. In fact, there is very little supervision in general: Dr. Start concluded that there is "no evidence that the physicians who are ultimately responsible for what kind of care is delivered . . . are supervising the nurses and, more importantly, the correctional medical technicians, the MTAs." Start Tr. 11-1742-43.

Clearly, there is a need to supervise medical staff; even defendant's expert Dr. Harness agreed that "physicians need to be monitoring what MTAs are doing." Harness Tr. 19-3102-03. The record is replete with instances in which MTAs inappropriately refused ***1203** to refer inmates to doctors or exceeded the scope of their competence.[110] For instance, one inmate complained to an MTA of ear pain and hearing loss. Despite being unqualified to do so, the MTA nevertheless examined the inmate's ears, Start Decl. at 373, and noted that one ear canal was completely occluded with wax. However, she did not refer the inmate to a physician or for treatment. When the inmate finally saw a physician more than a week later, the physician was unable to examine the eardrum because the ear canal was still occluded with wax. Trial Exh. P-637 at 27624. Another inmate was told by two MTAs that he needed no further treatment for a facial fracture when, in fact, the fracture actually required surgery. Trial Exh. P-430 at 2968-69, 2947. In another case, when an inmate exhausted his asthma inhaler before his prescription ran out (usually a sign that asthma is worsening and an indication that the patient should be seen by a physician), an MTA chose to "counsel" the inmate simply not to use the inhaler so frequently. Start Decl. at 200; Trial Exh. P-535 at 16118, 16124. There is no supervisory process in place to correct these errors or prevent them in the future.

c. *Medical Records*

The medical records system at Pelican Bay is nothing short of disastrous. Accurate and complete medical records are essential to adequate medical care. Providers must know the patient's medical history, allergies, medications, and past courses of therapy in order to properly diagnose and treat current problems. Without accurate and thorough records, providers continually run the risk of prescribing contraindicated medications, failing to notice ongoing illnesses, or ordering inappropriate or even dangerous courses of treatment. Despite these dangers, and defendants' knowledge of them, the Pelican Bay medical records system "is outrageously disorganized, making it almost impossible to understand what is happening to the patient, which in turn prevents the inmate from obtaining health care."[111] Start Decl. at 89.

Several problems contribute to the utter failure of the medical records system. First, recordkeeping personnel at Pelican Bay are both too few and insufficiently trained. Even though the task of maintaining medical records is onerous and complex, records staff receive no specialized instruction beyond on-

---

[107] Triage is a sorting system which is used to assign priorities to medical complaints based on urgency and seriousness.

[108] As Dr. Cooper noted, inmates can also call out to custodial staff—properly characterized as "scream[ing] for help." Cooper Tr. 14-2305.

[109] Head MTAs do lead "debriefing" after some emergencies; however, isolated debriefing cannot take the place of regular, structured evaluation of MTA performance.

[110] A 1991 audit of Pelican Bay commented that a written policy "appeared" to sanction MTA-written orders, and that it "appeared" that medications were routinely being renewed by MTAs. Trial Exh. P-3334 at 32538-39. Both of these activities exceed the scope of MTA and LVN *licensure* as well as competence.

[111] The Court finds Dr. Start's opinion on the adequacy of medical records much more credible than that of Dr. Harness. Dr. Harness reviewed only eight files and stated that the records were sufficient, but conceded on the stand that one of the eight records was incomplete. Dr. Start, on the other hand, examined well over 100 patient files.

the-job training. In addition, there are simply too few people on staff to oversee the records of over 3,500 inmates.[112] Even Dr. Astorga stated that he was unsatisfied with recordkeeping personnel levels. Astorga Depo. at 135.

Second, patient records are stored in a central recordkeeping area separate from where inmates are examined in satellite clinics. As a result, records are often delayed.[113] Providers are often forced to risk treating patients without consulting their medical records at all—a practice, in the words of one MTA, tantamount to "flying by the seat of *1204 your pants." Carter Depo. at 182.[114]

Third, and most important, the notes that *have* been made in patient records by physicians and medical support staff are disorganized, incomplete, sometimes contradictory, and inadequate. As Dr. Khoury acknowledged, it is a basic, fundamental principle of medical practice to document everything the provider does. Khoury Tr. 10-1636. Nevertheless, the record is replete with examples of charts without medical histories, with no record of examinations, no management plan, orders for tests with no record of results, test results with no record of why, when, or by whom the test was ordered, and so forth.[115] Even aside from the shortcomings of each individual entry, the entire system "ought to be better organized," as defendants' expert admitted. Harness Tr. 19-3110. There is no uniform note-taking format, no system for correlating physicians' orders and progress notes, and no auditing of medical records, despite a warning in a 1991 audit that recordkeeping audits and better record managing were needed. Trial Exh. P-3334 at 32533. These ongoing problems led Dr. Start to declare that he was "impressed over and over again with the gross deficiency of the records system." Start Decl. at 89.

d. *Screening*

By examining inmates as they enter the facility, providers can identify those patients who need uninterrupted medication, catch prisoners' previously unnoticed medical problems early on, and discover potential medical emergencies among newly-arrived inmates. Providers can also prevent from being admitted to the prison's general population those who pose a threat to the health and safety of others (such as inmates with communicable diseases).

---

[112] Dr. Harness, the defendants' medical expert, agreed with the following statement in a budget request prepared in 1992:

> [A]dditional clerical staff is essential. The current staffing level is inadequate to provide even the normal daily coordination of medical and psychiatric appointments, purging of medical records, reviewing of intake records for compliance including appropriate follow up, and auditing of records for completeness prior to transferring. It is imperative that all of these tasks be done timely to maintain the continuity of medical care being delivered.

Trial Exh. D-148 at 49178; Harness Tr. 19-3127.

[113] Defendants were formally warned that this practice has "a negative impact upon the care provided to inmate patients" in a 1991 audit by the Department of Corrections. Trial Exh. P-3334 at 32551.

[114] In addition to delays within the institution, up to one quarter of new inmates arrive at Pelican Bay without their medical records. In 1992 Dr. Astorga sent a memo to Dr. Khoury, describing how records often arrive a week late and how "[t]he results of the lack of this vital information can be disastrous, creating litigation, as well as medical, problems." Trial Exh. P-4225 at 51647.

[115] For instance, Dr. Start described the medical records of inmate Harold Van Horn in his declaration. The chart shows several bouts of starting and discontinuing pharmaceutical treatment of the patient's seizure disorder, and then shows:

> [O]n 11/14/91 Dr. Johns signs order to discontinue Dilantin and lower bunk precautions (looks like Gordon, MTA, wrote it). On 11/15/91 there is a typed note from Dr. Johns giving inmate lower bunk because 'medical condition.' Which is the correct order? On 11/22/91 the patient complains of seizure, requests medicine (Med. Order Sheet shows he's been getting it 11/4-11/30!) On 12/9/91 and 12/18/91 there are similar requests but no evidence that he did see an M.D.

Start Decl. at 312 (references to Trial Ex. P-625 omitted). Dr. Start describes the records of another inmate, Glenn Turner, as follows:

Despite the importance of initial health screenings, Pelican Bay has failed to provide consistent or meaningful screening of incoming prisoners. First, physicians are not involved at all in initial screenings; nurses examine the medical records of arriving inmates if the records are available, and only MTAs screen inmates in person. Astorga Depo. at 99-100. Usually inmates simply answer questions without being actually examined. Dr. Astorga admitted that there is no practice of conducting routine physical examinations at the prison. Astorga Depo. at 99-100. Dr. Start found telling evidence *1205 of inadequate screening when he surveyed 130 patient files:[116] only 10 percent of inmates transferring into Pelican Bay had an adequate medical history taken,[117] 34 percent had no intake history performed at all, and a mere 4 percent had any kind of physical examination or assessment. Start Decl. at 20-21. Such superficial intake screenings plainly cannot elicit accurate or complete medical profiles of incoming inmates.

***

e. *Access to Medical Care*

Inmates must be afforded access in a timely fashion to medical providers who are qualified to treat their illnesses. However, prisoners at Pelican Bay often experience significant and unnecessary delays in obtaining access to physicians. In many instances, they are denied access altogether. For inmates *1206 with serious or painful symptoms, delays lasting days or even weeks can cause unnecessary suffering, exacerbate illness, and have life-threatening medical consequences.

As discussed above, inmates who want medical care submit sick call slips, which are then read and analyzed by MTAs. MTAs determine whether and when the inmate will be allowed to see a physician— often solely on the basis of what is written on the sick call slip. *See* E. Thayer Tr. 25-4204. If the MTA feels that the inmate should see a physician, the inmate is placed on a "doctor's line," the rough equivalent of having an appointment. Thus, MTAs function as a "gatekeeper" through which inmates must pass before they can have access to a doctor. Yet, as discussed above in section II(B)(2)(b), *supra*, MTAs have insufficient training and supervision to perform this vital function. Moreover, Pelican Bay has no written protocol or triage training to help MTAs determine who needs to be evaluated by a nurse or physician or how urgently care is needed. As one MTA put it, the decision whether to send an inmate to a clinic is "pretty much . . . left to our judgment." Griffin Depo. at 16.

The record shows that, over and over, MTAs have inappropriately used that judgment to deny pris-

---

Low white blood cell count noted in M.D. notes. The progress note of 8/27/90 indicates that the physician was concerned about the possibility of diabetes—a chem panel was ordered. Subsequent visits to the physician on 10/1/91 and 10/24/91 [—] no mention is made of the chem panel which was ordered to rule out diabetes. On the 10/1/91 visit to the physician the 'patient concerned about chronic low white blood count—desires complete blood count (CBC)[;] also wants to get weighed.' On 10/5/91 the inmate was weighed. On 10/24/91 the patient was seen by the physician, 'Inmate concerned for low white blood count (WBC)-3.3. WBC discussed with patient and he is apparently reassured.'

In my opinion, the three physician notes are in violation of the California Medical Malpractice Act because they do not contain the basic elements expected of a physician encounter. There is no progress note follow up on the chem panel to rule out diabetes. There is no history regarding the reason why the patient was concerned about his WBC. Was the patient worried about HIV infection? The medical record indicates a history of drug abuse. [. . .]

Start Decl. at 309-10 (references to Trial Exh. P-623 omitted). These instances are typical of the many analyses of medical charts in the record.

[116] Dr. Start examined 130 charts which were selected because the patient had experienced some health care problem. The sample of these files was blind with respect to screenings; those selected were, if anything, more likely than a completely random sample to have been screened, since those patients had reason to come in contact with the Pelican Bay medical staff. Dr. Start collected data both on the proportion of inmate transfers to the prison in which an intake screening was performed, and on screening of inmates for contagious diseases.

[117] Dr. Start testified that two "fairly typical" examples of incomplete intake histories included "one inmate whose history had no mention of his hypertension, intravenous drug use, ulcers or the presence of a bullet lodged in his spine with nerve injury, and another who had no mention of his being HIV positive or having had extensive neck surgery." Start Decl. at 19-20.

oners access to medical care. Prisoners complaining of symptoms as serious as chest pain, severe abdominal pain, coughing up blood, and seizures are often made to wait for regular appointments or denied access to a physician altogether. For instance, MTA Griffin, who described her own position at Pelican Bay as "sort of a glorified delivery person," Griffin Depo. at 17, recounted what MTAs do when prisoners have seizures: "We monitor them and if we feel that they need to be sent, then they're sent. Otherwise, if they're alert, oriented and their vital signs are stable and they haven't voided on themselves, then we just let them be and tell them to get in touch with us if they have any problems." *Id.* at 41.[122]

***

Sergeant Cox testified about another disturbing instance in which an MTA effectively denied an inmate timely access to appropriate medical care. Cox responded to an alarm for an inmate fight and arrived to see an inmate bleeding profusely with bruises on his neck. It took an MTA 18 minutes to arrive on the scene after being called on the radio. Cox suspected that one of the inmates had been raped; he testified that he told the MTA it was "obvious" that "the guy's probably been raped." Cox Tr. 18-3004. Despite Cox's protestations, the MTA refused to examine the inmate or refer him to a doctor and merely wiped up the inmate's blood. Sergeant Cox testified that he went to the watch commander: "I explained to the watch commander, hey I even did a—performed an unclothed body search on this man. There was fluids coming out of his rectum that wasn't supposed to be. And all she did was put the inmates in ad seg [administrative segregation]." Cox Tr. 18-3005.

Even when inmates presenting serious medical problems are put on the doctor's line *1207 by MTAs, prisoners experience delays ranging from significant to appalling before they actually see a physician. Understaffing has created a constant backlog of inmates vying for appointments. For instance, in 1991, when Pelican Bay was particularly short of doctors, inmates waited to see a doctor for as long as four to six weeks. Inmate Arturo Castillo's experience exemplifies the outrageous delays typical of Pelican Bay's early years. After suffering a serious scalp laceration, Castillo was treated with surgical staples at Sutter Coast Hospital and then returned to his cell after a week's recuperation in the prison infirmary. Castillo subsequently told an MTA that his wound had become painful, dirty, and itchy, and even filed a grievance, but the MTA merely told him he could see a doctor in two weeks. Castillo received no medical attention at all until weeks after he complained, when a piece of his scalp finally became so severely infected that it fell off. Castillo Tr. 1-102-04; Trial Exh. P-667 at 4407-08, 4415.

Although improved staffing levels have reduced delays in access to physicians, such delays still pose a significant problem. MTA Ruble testified that by 1992 medical staff had "got it down to the point where we were running two weeks and sometimes one week" for an appointment. Ruble Depo. at 59; *see also* Elliott Depo. at 57 (one to two week wait in December 1992). As late as July 26, 1992, there were 242 prisoners on the waiting list to see a doctor. Start Decl., Exh. U at 8905. While it is impossible to discern from the record how long the *average* delay in treatment was at the time of trial,[123] the record is still filled with examples of unacceptable delays in access to physicians and treatment.[124]

***

---

[122] For a description of the effects of seizures, see Dr. Start's description of the treatment of Tyler Henderson, section II(B)(2)(f) at p. 1209-1210, *infra.*

[123] Dr. Start conducted a survey of over 3000 sick call slips to determine the average number of days inmates waited for an appointment. He examined all of the sick call slips submitted in June and July of 1992 for Facility A (590 slips), May 1991 for Facility C (1053 slips), and May through August of 1990 for Facility D (1300 slips). The time period for each facility was chosen randomly.

Each sick call slip was examined for symptoms that Pelican Bay doctors identified as requiring immediate or same-day referral to a physician: cardiac symptoms, significant abdominal pain, and unresolved bleeding. Start Decl. at 31. Dr. Start found that the average delay before a physician appointment for cardiac symptoms was 11.27 days; for unresolved bleeding, 12.75 days; for abdominal pain, 16.8 days. *Id.*

While these figures show abysmal delays in patient treatment, they may not reflect the current state of medical care at Pelican Bay. Access to medical care has improved since 1990, and since nearly half of the slips examined are from that year, the data generated by Dr. Start does not represent or indicate current periods of delay.

[124] In addition, access to specialists is limited. Most of the specialists to whom inmates are referred are located up to 90 miles away, and several types of specialists are simply not available in the community surrounding Pelican Bay. Cooper Tr. 14-2261-62.

Inmate access to appropriate treatment is even further impeded by delays in lab testing. The record is rife with examples of lab tests that are ordered but never performed, performed only after unexplained and lengthy delays, or performed and never reported. A particularly notable example of delayed lab testing was observed by Dr. Start. Of the eight inmates who had positive tuberculosis tests in the sample of records he examined,[125] the average amount of time before performance of a chest X-ray (which would indicate whether inmates had active TB and were contagious) was 47 days. Start Tr. 11-1710. This was so even though Pelican Bay had an X-ray machine on site. *Id.* *1208 Diagnosis and treatment of inmates' conditions is pointlessly deferred because of the prison's inadequate system for ordering, performing, and reporting lab tests.

Finally, prisoners' access to emergency treatment is impeded by both lack of expertise on the part of medical staff and custody concerns. As Dr. Start observed, "[o]ne principle of basic emergency medicine is that the difference between whether one saves or loses the patient depends on what treatment is given quickly at the scene of the accident." Start Decl. at 98. However, as discussed above, there are no protocols for handling emergencies at Pelican Bay, and MTAs receive virtually no training in emergency techniques or handling trauma.[126] In addition, access to emergency treatment is often delayed for significant periods because a transportation team or chase car is unavailable to follow ambulances leaving Pelican Bay.[127] Thus the ambulance transporting inmate Ricky Hurtado, who had been stabbed in the neck and shoulder, was delayed for twenty minutes before it could leave Pelican Bay. Start Decl., Exh. G at 1158; Ray Norris, having sustained a severe head injury, endured a twenty-eight minute delay; *id.* at 57; Roman Davis, experiencing respiratory difficulties, suffered a forty minute delay while waiting for a transportation team and paperwork; *id.* at 969, 971; and so forth. These life-threatening delays in delivering emergency services because custody staff is disorganized or understaffed are constitutionally unacceptable.

f. *Lack of Quality Control Procedures*

Although the quality of medical care provided to inmates at Pelican Bay often falls dramatically below community standards, medical staff and administrators have taken no effective steps to systematically review the care provided or to supervise the physicians providing it.

As Dr. Khoury noted, peer review[128] is a "very important" way for practitioners to "review and upgrade care they provide." Khoury Tr. 10-1625-26. However, at the time of trial Pelican Bay had no formal peer review process through which physicians could review and discuss each others' work. Although defendants insist that they have a "peer review committee," this committee merely performs a function known as "utilization review"—a process of approving or denying requests for particular medical procedures, such as consultation or surgery.[129] *See* Cooper Tr. 14-2279-2282; McKinsey Tr. 26-4291-92. This review, in essence a cost/benefit analysis, is a far cry from the mutual evaluation and learning process ordinarily called peer review. It is no wonder, then, that defendants' own expert, Dr. Harness, could not "recall" a peer review process at Pelican Bay. Harness Tr. 19-3117.

Another basic procedure that helps medical staff learn from experience and avoid fatal mistakes is

---

[125] *See* section II(B)(2)(d), *supra.*

[126] *See* section II(B)(2)(b), *supra.*

[127] When a medical emergency arises, the medical staff informs the watch commander. The watch commander in turn calls an ambulance and assembles a transportation team, which follows the ambulance in order to prevent escape attempts.

[128] Peer review is a process through which physicians confidentially review each others' work by evaluating individual cases and discussing the medical care provided.

[129] The minutes of the committee's meetings provide unambiguous evidence of the nature of the "review" conducted. For example, the "Orthopedics" section of the minutes entitled "Medical Peer Review Meeting, July 22, 1993" reads in part as follows:

HART C49090 Mr. Hart is referred for evaluation of a symptomatic ganglion cyst, right foot. Repeated aspiration has been performed. Patient of Dr. Winslow. This has been DEFERRED.
CRAPO H17375 Mr. Crapo is referred for evaluation of proven intraarticular chondromalacia, symptomatic, with locking and chronic recurring pain. Patient of Dr. Cooper. This has been GRANTED.

Trial Exh. D 286 at 42637.

the performance of a "death review," an investigation and report on each death that occurs in custody. However, the medical staff at Pelican Bay does not conduct death reviews. This is the case even though Dr. Astorga, the Chief Medical Officer, thinks death reviews would be a "good idea," and testified that he saw no reason, administrative or budgetary, why they could not be performed. Astorga Depo. at 721.

*1209 Of most concern is the fact that Pelican Bay has no formal quality assurance program.[130] Dr. Harness agreed that quality assurance is "standard practice in virtually any health care facility in the country" and a "fundamental part" of the provision of health care. Harness Tr. 19-3117. Although the Pelican Bay medical staff has organized a Quality Control committee, Dr. Cooper admitted that at the time of trial it had not yet met. Cooper Tr. 14-2282. Defendants argue that quality control measures are planned for the future, and offered the testimony of Kyle McKinsey[131] to that effect. McKinsey testified that a Quality Program Unit will be charged with three tasks, one of which is "to insure that in the field over time we have quality assurance programs in place in all of our institutions."[132] McKinsey Tr. 26-4291. McKinsey projected that it would take until 1995 for the Quality Program Unit merely to develop formal standards against which medical care can be evaluated, and even longer to actually implement the program. *Id.* at 4317-18. In addition, McKinsey stated that he hoped to have formal peer review instituted as part of quality assurance "eventually, resources being available." *Id.* at 4292. Thus, Pelican Bay has yet to implement quality assurance within the facility itself, and the Department of Corrections has barely set in motion the machinery that may or may not someday yield effective quality assurance programs.

Failure to institute quality control procedures has had predictable consequences: grossly inadequate care is neither disciplined nor redressed. For instance, one physician was reprimanded by the Medical Board of California, which stated in a 1992 letter that the history and physical examination he performed on one inmate "were of such brevity as to not demonstrate a level of care that is considered within the community standard in the State of California." Trial Exh. P-553 at 6890. Although Dr. Astorga testified he did not recall receiving a copy of the letter, he did remember one of several complaints by Pelican Bay staff that the doctor appeared to be intoxicated on the job. Astorga Depo. at 597-98. Dr. Astorga took no disciplinary action other than talking to the physician.

Similarly, a system for review of the numerous avoidable inmate illnesses, as well as inmate deaths, would have underscored the systemic deficiencies in the Pelican Bay health care system. For example, the care received by Tyler Henderson displayed, in Dr. Start's words, "a long and well-documented history of neglect, inappropriate evaluations, and sub-standard care" that led to his death at age 24. Start Decl. at 53. When he arrived at Pelican Bay in August of 1990, Henderson did not receive his seizure medication for several days, even though he had a cyst on his brain and a significant seizure disorder. Dr. Start characterized Henderson's treatment as reflected in his chart:

> Seizures are destructive to the brain, and, except for very rare circumstances, preventable and controllable. If a treatable spell of seizures continues uncontrolled, the patient dies. Even very frequent, but self-limited, seizures have serious repercussions—black-outs, trauma to the patient, the risk of aspiration pneumonia, and short and long-term memory loss. No one knows exactly how many seizures is too many . . ..
>
> In the case of Tyler Henderson, this patient was having prolonged periods of as many documented seizures as two a day, or three or four a week . . . [h]e was having frequent, recognized seizures that were not being treated. He was often just ***1210** left in his cell after a seizure, or taken to the infirmary just until he woke up, then returned to his cell. In multiple instances, he was only evaluated by an MTA, and no drug levels were drawn. [The] dosing of his medications and checking of blood level was haphazard, at best . . . Poignantly, he had appealed for transfer on the basis of inadequate medical care July 29, 1991—citing "occasional blackouts." His appeal was denied . . ..

---

[130] Quality assurance is a review by someone in a supervisory capacity of care delivered in the past to determine whether it meets desired standards. For example, quality assurance may be conducted by reviewing a sample of records to evaluate the outcome of medical care provided. In fact, Dr. Harness stated that the evaluation of records performed by plaintiffs' expert, Dr. Start, was an "excellent" quality assurance analysis. Harness Tr. 19-3119.

[131] McKinsey is the Deputy Director of the Department of Corrections' new Division of Health Care Services. Health care administration has been reorganized and a new Program and Systems Development department will oversee mental health, physical medicine, public health, planning, and quality program units. McKinsey Tr. 26-4287-92.

[132] The unit will also oversee utilization review and examine litigation issues.

Patients who have difficult-to-control seizures may need more than one medicine, higher levels of a specific medicine, or may be resistant to one class of medicine. Tyler's medication dosing when he came to PBSP suggested that he could have difficult-to-control seizures because he was on two types of medicines, and one of the two was a less-commonly-used type of seizure medication. If a doctor knows that a patient has difficult to control seizures, this information prompts aggressive therapy and evaluation when a seizure occurs, close monitoring of blood levels and care in changing a proven regimen. None of these basic elements of care are present in the "care" this inmate received at Pelican Bay. In addition, had the physicians obtained his old medical records (and there is no evidence of any attempt to do so), they may have found that he was resistant to one of the other types of medications. Furthermore, negligence in follow-up and monitoring of his drug levels resulted in Tyler receiving toxic doses of seizure medicine (Trial Ex. P-488 at 17052). Physician notes referred to "probable malingering" (Trial Ex. P-488 at 17036) in spite of overwhelming evidence to the contrary.

Start Decl. at 54-56. Tyler Henderson died in his cell on March 15, 1992 of probable cerebral anoxia due to epileptic seizures. As defendants' expert conceded, Mr. Henderson's case raises serious concerns about "physician involvement in the care" of the patient. Harness Tr. 19-3102. Again, review of this file would have accentuated the urgent need for organized files, adequate staffing, competent medication management, and closer supervision of MTAs, and thus helped to avoid similar problems in the future.

***

g. *Treatment Provided*

*1212

Perhaps the most graphic example of inadequate medical care is that received by inmate Vaughn Dortch. The scalding of Dortch in the infirmary tub is discussed in section II(A)(1)(a)(1), *supra*. Dortch had received second- and third-degree burns that eventually required skin grafts on his legs and buttocks, surgical excision of part of his scrotum, and extensive physical therapy. Start Decl. at 42. However, despite patently obvious indications that Dortch was burned, Dr. Astorga and Dr. Gard attempted to minimize or deny the full extent of his injuries, saying that Dortch merely had "dead skin," Trial Exh. P-1219 at 29848, or "exfoliation." Trial Exh. P-444 at 258. His transfer to the hospital was delayed over an hour, until he went into shock and his blood pressure became dangerously low because medical staff had not started fluid resuscitation. Kuroda Depo. at 69-73, Start Decl. at 47. However, in a memorandum written the day after the scalding, Dr. Gard states that medical staff immediately recognized Dortch's burns and sent him to the hospital.[136] Trial Exh. P-444 at 352.

The Court agrees with Dr. Start's report that "there is a rampant pattern of improper or inadequate care that nearly defies belief." Start Decl. at 5. Not only has each discrete deficiency discussed above (inadequate recordkeeping, lack of supervision, and so forth) created unnecessary pain and suffering, but the deficiencies compound each other to render the provision of adequate care nearly impossible.[137] The many instances of grossly inadequate care are the utterly predictable result of systemic failures in Pelican Bay's medical services.

3. *Defendants' State of Mind*

The record amply demonstrates defendants' unresponsiveness to the health needs of inmates at Pelican Bay. Some of defendants' comments, actions, and policies show such disregard for inmates' pain

---

[136] Dr. Start described in detail the grossly inadequate medical care Dortch received while medical staff busied themselves attempting to minimize the ramifications of the incident. Start Decl. at 37-48.

[137] In a system that is already understaffed, for example, having to decipher disorganized records reduces the amount of time physicians can spend with each patient; if no quality control is in place, no one will stop MTAs from inappropriately "diagnosing" sick inmates as malingerers.

and suffering that they shock the conscience. For instance, Pelican Bay has an informal policy of treating inmates engaging in hunger strikes simply by weighing them once a week until they lose 20 percent of their body weight. *See* Griffin Depo. at 74-75. MTA logs contain ***1213** unabashed notations such as "[c]omplains of chest pain. Hah!" Start Decl., Exh. U at 8498, revealing medical staff's often flippant attitudes toward inmates' pain and suffering. Occurrences like these led Dr. Start to state that "[b]ased on my experience in eighteen years of correctional health care, I cannot think of a prison that more completely embodies a callous indifference toward inmate health needs." Start Decl. at 117.

Sheer callousness aside, defendants' behavior unambiguously evinces a conscious disregard for inmates' serious medical needs. Defendants knew that the plaintiffs had serious medical needs, knew that the medical system at Pelican Bay was inadequate to serve those needs, and nevertheless failed to remedy the gross and obvious deficiencies of the system.

Defendants' attitude toward staffing typifies their deliberate indifference to the clear dangers created by Pelican Bay's medical system. Even though Chief Deputy Warden Peetz was authorized to hire 3.5 physicians when the facility opened, the prison began operation without a physician on staff. Incredibly, Warden Marshall stated that he believed Pelican Bay could provide adequate medical care to the inmates without a doctor on site, despite the fact that he had never worked in a prison without a full time physician. Marshall Tr. 22-26.

The defendants have instituted some changes, but they have often been cosmetic at best. For instance, medical staff knew full well that because of the disorganization of the medication distribution system, inmates often did not receive prescribed medications. Minutes of the prison's Pharmaceutical Committee record Dr. Cooper's comments that "too many mistakes were being made, too many medications were not being taken care of routinely, [there were] too many delays, and too many 602's [inmate grievances] [were] coming through because of inmates not getting medications." Trial Exh. D-283 at 61283 (meeting minutes for April 1992). The Committee grappled with the problem and "solved" it by abdicating responsibility for medication renewal: Dr. Cooper testified that "[w]e've resolved the method of . . . the patient achieving his refills. We've taken the responsibility from a memory of the medical technician and placed it on the . . . individual patient to recognize that they're running low on their medicines and they have to ask for a refill." Cooper Tr. 14-2273-74. Even defendants' expert, Dr. Harness, could not bring himself to say that this "solution" was acceptable.[138]

Other systemic deficiencies of the health care system have remained virtually untouched. For example, the 1991 Department of Corrections audit warned medical staff that the record-keeping system posed a danger to patients. Trial Exh. P-3334 at 32551-52. Doctors were constantly reminded of the problem. *See, e.g.,* Trial Exh. P-404 at 3339 (medical record reading "I have no old chart on this patient to document his problems"). However, there have been no efforts to reform the system.

Pelican Bay doctors also continue to endanger inmates by testing them for tuberculosis without consulting medical records.[139] Before the 1992 tuberculosis screening, Dr. Johns suggested to medical staff that they consult records before applying tuberculosis skin tests. Dr. Cooper knew it was "improper" to retest inmates who had previously tested positive. Cooper Tr. 14-2302. This danger notwithstanding, inmates were tested without medical records that might reveal previous positive test results.

The absence of quality assurance programs and peer review and the lack of supervision of doctors and support staff bespeaks a striking indifference to the quality of care provided. This indifference is illustrated by Pelican Bay's reaction when one of its doctors was reprimanded by the state Medical Examination Board: As Dr. Start noted, "a letter from the licensing board identifying a deficiency should create an explosion of corrective action. It appears from the record that ***1214** no one paid any attention to this letter."[140] Start Decl. at 77.

We find that defendants had abundant knowledge of the inadequacies of medical care at Pelican Bay.

---

[138] *See* Harness Tr. 19-3116. Dr. Harness gave protracted and evasive answers to plaintiffs' requests for his professional opinion of the policy. He did, however, conclude that "[i]t's an area that clearly needs improvement. There's no question about that." *Id.* at 3115.

[139] *See* discussion section II(B)(2)(d), *supra*.

[140] Dr. Astorga testified that he did not recall reading or receiving a copy of the letter (even though it bears a stamp indicating it was received by his office). Astorga Depo. 868. Even if this were the case, that such an important matter could go unnoticed by the Chief Medical Officer is itself a scathing indictment of the administration and supervision of the medical staff.

That knowledge is reflected in records of complaints by prisoners and staff, audit reports, and budget requests that allude to the risk of harm (and of litigation) if conditions are not ameliorated. We find that by failing to remedy deficiencies in health care, Pelican Bay medical staff did not merely create a risk of harm to inmates but practically insured that inmates would endure unnecessary pain, suffering, debilitating disease, and even death. We agree with Dr. Start's opinion that "[t]he fact that a new prison with contemporary medical facilities nevertheless could be so shockingly deficient in its provision of health care is . . . a terrible indictment of the defendants, and compellingly illustrates what . . . is their stunning indifference to the health care needs of the prisoners at Pelican Bay." Start Decl. at 4.

C. *MENTAL HEALTH CARE*

Plaintiffs contend that when Pelican Bay opened—with no psychiatrist on staff—the system for delivering mental health care was grossly inadequate. Although staffing has since improved, plaintiffs argue that continued understaffing, along with other chronic problems, continues to render the delivery of mental health care constitutionally inadequate. They also argue that defendants have been deliberately indifferent to the mental health needs of the Pelican Bay prison population.

At trial, plaintiffs relied upon two expert witnesses who gave testimony relating to mental health care, as well as conditions in the SHU. The first, Dr. Stuart Grassian, spent two weeks at Pelican Bay, one in September 1991 and one in May 1993. During this time, he toured the prison, spoke informally with prison personnel, and conducted 69 interviews with 55 inmates (14 were interviewed twice). He also reviewed the medical files of most of these inmates, depositions of Pelican Bay health professionals, and other documents. At trial, Dr. Grassian estimated that he had reviewed "18 U- Haul boxes [of documents] at last count." Tr. 12-1862. The second expert, Dr. Craig Haney, visited Pelican Bay on September 16, 1992 and January 6, 1993, at which time he toured the prison and spoke informally with prison personnel. He also separately conducted formal interviews with 65 inmates, reviewed depositions of Pelican Bay mental health professionals, and examined an extensive number of documents and files.

Defendants' expert, Dr. Joel Dvoskin, visited Pelican Bay for one day in April 1992, and then again for one day in January 1993. On both occasions he toured the facilities and spoke informally with inmates and staff. He also comprehensively reviewed approximately eleven inmate medical files, along with selected parts of other medical files. He also reviewed selected CDC training materials.[141]

In addition to the expert witnesses, the Court heard from various mental health professionals presently or formerly employed at Pelican Bay or by the CDC. The parties also submitted into evidence deposition excerpts and extensive documentary evidence. Taken together, this testimonial and documentary evidence amply demonstrates that the mental health care system at Pelican Bay falls dramatically short of minimum constitutional standards.

Plaintiffs' expert, Dr. Grassian, described the mental health services at Pelican Bay as "grossly inadequate." Decl. at 5; *id.* at 158, 166-67 (system of psychiatric care is "manifestly deficient" and fails to meet "the most minimal standards for adequate psychiatric care").[142] Even defendants' expert, Dr. Dvoskin, could find no cause to endorse the *1215 mental health system at Pelican Bay. He testified that, as of the time he visited Pelican Bay, he could not represent to the Court that the mental health care delivery system was "adequate" or met constitutional standards. Tr. at 27-4431-32. Indeed, as detailed below, the evidence plainly shows that there have been, and continue to be, chronic and pervasive problems with the delivery of mental health care at Pelican Bay. It also reveals defendants' deliberate indifference to the serious mental health needs of inmates.

1. *The Need for Mental Health Services at Pelican Bay*

A significant number of inmates at Pelican Bay, in both the SHU and the general population section of the prison, suffer from serious mental health problems. A survey done by Dr. Nadim Khoury's[143] office

---

[141] The expert qualifications of Doctors Grassian, Haney, and Dvoskin are set out in section I, *supra.*

[142] Page references for Dr. Grassian's declaration refer to the copy of his declaration filed January 4, 1994.

[143] At the time of this survey, Dr. Khoury held the position of Chief of Medical Services with responsibility for overseeing health care operations for the California Department of Corrections.

in August 1990 estimated that there were at least 208 inmates at Pelican Bay who were either psychotic or psychotic in partial remission.[144] Trial Exh. P-3820.[145] Dr. Sheff estimated that during his tenure at Pelican Bay from April 1992 to February 1993, there were between 200 and 300 mentally ill inmates requiring psychiatric intervention at any given time, and that between 5 and 10 percent of incoming inmates were mentally ill or had some need to continue medication. Tr. 25-4103-04. *See also* Grassian Decl. at 4-5 (expressing his opinion that he had met numerous acutely psychotic inmates during his interviews in the Pelican Bay SHU); Haney Decl. at 55 n. 20 (finding that out of 40 random interviews in the SHU, close to one-third suffered from what appeared to be psychotic symptoms or had been placed on anti-psychotic medication)[146]; Ruggles Tr. 17-2905 (senior staff psychologist stating that there are a "considerable" number of inmates at Pelican Bay with organic brain damage).

As Warden Marshall described in an August 1991 budget request, the high incidence of mentally ill inmates at Pelican Bay is predictable because mentally ill inmates frequently exhibit behavioral problems, and inmates with a history of misconduct are often transferred to Pelican Bay:

> [A] large number of psychiatrically disabled inmates exhibit violent and problematic behavior as part of their symptomatology. Consequently, these inmates present a history of severe disciplinary and assaultive behavior that is considered an endangerment to themselves, other inmates, staff, and prison security . . .. Pelican Bay was constructed to house those inmates considered to be the most violent and problematic . . .. By virtue of its mission, Pelican Bay now houses most of the psychiatrically disabled inmates who have a history of violent and assaultive behavior.

Trial Exh. P-4602 at 49197-98; *id.* at 49198 ("Current departmental security needs dictate that institutions transfer problematic psychiatrically-disabled inmates to Pelican Bay as soon as medically possible, since they cannot be accommodated anywhere else"). *See also* Dvoskin Tr. at 27-4443-44 (observing that there seemed to be more inmates with mental illness in higher security prisons because of classification, disciplinary, and service delivery practices); Haney Decl. at 68 (inmates unable to manage their psychiatric disorders often incur rules violations).

*1216 This same budget request also noted that "[b]ecause of inadequate outpatient services at Pelican Bay, these inmates usually decompensate quickly and require intensive psychiatric care and/or readmission to inpatient care." Trial Exh. P-4602 at 49198. Warden Marshall further observed that a "cursory review" showed that there were 214 inmates on psychotropic medication alone, and that "according to referrals by medical doctors and other staff, there are more than 100 other inmates in immediate need who should be seen and receive ongoing psychiatric treatment." *Id.*[147]

The need for substantial mental health services at Pelican Bay is heightened by the presence of the SHU, which houses approximately 1,500 persons. As detailed more fully in section II(D)(2), *infra*, the conditions in the SHU are sufficiently severe that they lead to serious psychiatric consequences for some

---

[144] A patient who is "psychotic" has a major mental disorder with current symptoms. The diagnosis also includes inmates who are acutely suicidal. A patient who is "psychotic in partial remission" is still psychotic but shows some improvement. Trial Exh. P-3820.

[145] This figure probably substantially underestimated the number of psychotic inmates at Pelican Bay. *See* Trial Exh. P-4602 at 49198 (memorandum from Warden Marshall to Dr. Khoury noting that estimate of at least 200 active psychotic inmates "does not include those inmates who are otherwise severely or moderately disabled, and those who have, thus far, remained undiagnosed"); Rose Depo. at 28 (figure was an underestimate based on his experience as staff psychologist at Pelican Bay).

[146] Page references for Dr. Haney's declaration refer to the copy of his declaration filed September 14, 1993.

[147] Dr. Khoury suggested that budget requests, known as "Budget Change Proposals," simply represent hyperbolic attempts to secure additional funds and should be given little weight. Even assuming, however, that a budget request is written to highlight, rather than minimize, problems, we decline to assume that Warden Marshall submitted a request that was false in any serious respect. Rather, considering all of the evidence in this case, it is clear that the request was essentially accurate.

Dr. Khoury also testified that he does not believe that there have ever been any inmates in the SHU who suffer from a serious mental disorder. Khoury Tr. 10-1579. This testimony is not credible in light of the overwhelming evidence in the record to the contrary. More generally, the Court found Dr. Khoury's attempts to minimize the mental health needs of inmates at Pelican Bay unconvincing in light of his defensive demeanor and evasive responses to many questions.

inmates. As Dr. Grassian concluded, "[f]or some, SHU confinement has severely exacerbated a previously existing mental condition," while other inmates developed mental illness symptoms not apparent before confinement in the SHU. Grassian Decl. at 4. Defendants' expert also acknowledged that there are some people who "can't handle" segregation in the SHU. "Typically, those are people who have a pre-existing disorder that is called borderline personality disorder, and there—there's a fair amount of consistent observation that those folks, when they're locked up [in segregation] may have a tendency to experience some transient psychoses, which means just a brief psychosis that quickly resolves itself *when they're removed from the lockdown [segregation] situation.*" Dvoskin Tr. 27-4374-75 (emphasis added). Inmates with chronic longstanding depression, chronic schizophrenia, or any other longstanding, severe mental illness are also at a higher risk of deteriorating in the SHU. Dvoskin Tr. 27-4473-74. Pelican Bay senior staff psychologist Ted Ruggles also observed a connection between placement in the SHU and the mental health of certain inmates: "There was a psychiatric deterioration that occurred in correlation with placement on SHU [with some inmates], and I'm not altogether certain what caused it." Ruggles Tr. 17-2914. A memorandum prepared in September 1989 by the Institutions Division of the CDC also underscored the substantial need for psychiatric services in the SHU, particularly where the prison fails to screen out inmates who may be vulnerable to developing serious mental disorders. Trial Exh. P-3390.

Given the above, it was manifest that operation of the SHU would require close psychiatric monitoring and substantial psychiatric services. Haney Decl. at 67 (the need for psychiatric screening and monitoring in the SHU can not be overemphasized); *see also* Dvoskin Decl. at 11 (while "*some* inmates with mental illness can be adequately treated in the [SHU], *if the necessary services are available . . . [, t]he most basic need is for observation* [by a mental health practitioner] to insure that their mental illness is not being exacerbated by the tighter confinement and more restrictive socialization") (emphasis added). Significantly, Dr. Grassian found numerous acutely psychotic inmates in the SHU in need of immediate, hospital-level, inpatient treatment. Grassian Decl. at 45-104.

2. *Systemic Deficiencies in the Delivery of Mental Health Care*

a. *Staffing Levels*

When Pelican Bay began operations in December 1989, it was severely understaffed and ill-equipped to respond to the mental *1217 health needs of the inmate population, which quickly grew from 1,287 inmates on January 1, 1990 to over 3,500 inmates by January 1, 1991. From December 1989 until April 1992, the total mental health staff employed at Pelican Bay consisted of either one or two psychologists. The result was nothing short of a mental health care crisis. One of the initial staff psychologists described his day as "running as fast as I can putting out as many fires as I could." Rose *Coleman* Depo. at 31.[148] When asked "what was a fire," Rose responded as follows: "Well, I mean, these were very serious cases that demanded attention and my time was taken up taking care of crisis intervention . . . [which involved] acutely psychotic, acting-out inmates." *Id.* at 32. Even with these frantic efforts by Rose, acutely psychotic inmates failed to receive treatment for an "unacceptable period of time" on "a regular basis." *Id.* at 34. "[I]f a patient did not [engage in] very flagrant behavior, aggressive violent behavior or suicidal behavior, they could stay in that cell for a long period of time, just nobody pays that much attention to them . . .. [M]onths maybe." *Id.* at 35.

Until April 1992—almost 2 and 1/2 years after the prison opened—there was *no* resident psychiatrist at Pelican Bay with the exception of a psychiatrist who submitted his resignation after working for one month. Trial Exh. P-3121.[149] Instead, defendants attempted to obtain visiting psychiatrists from other

---

[148] *Coleman* refers to the related case, *Coleman v. Wilson*, Civ-0520 LKK (E.D.Cal.), a class action challenging the constitutional adequacy of mental health services at all California prisons, including Pelican Bay, but excluding San Quentin and the California Medical Facility at Vacaville.

[149] In his letter of resignation, Dr. Simonds stated that "I am leaving because in this new position I will not be able to provide safe and adequate services, given the limited resources, and where there exist too many situations in which my license could be place [sic] in jeopardy." Trial Exh. P-3816. Dr. Simonds expressed particular frustration over the fact that inmates often refused to cooperate in physical examinations or other examinations, thus making it difficult for him to practice psychiatry in the manner he had envisioned. Trial Exh. P-4092. At that time, as well as now, Pelican Bay had no procedures for providing involuntary medication to inmates. *See* section II(C)(2)(e), *infra*.

institutions for two to five days each month. *Id.* However, even this sparse coverage was not always obtained. When Dr. Baker, one of the visiting psychiatrists, was asked whether he came to Pelican Bay one week a month he responded: "It was very irregular based upon the need and my ability to extricate myself from [California Medical Facility]." Baker *Coleman* Depo. at 20. He believes that for at least a year, he was the only visiting psychiatrist. *Id.* at 21. As senior staff psychologist Ted Ruggles recalled, psychiatrists from other institutions visited only "periodically." Tr. 17-2904. In November 1990, Warden Marshall sent the Deputy Director of Institutions a memorandum stating that there were currently five federal court cases regarding the lack of psychiatric care at Pelican Bay, and that the system of "bor-row[ing], on occasion, psychiatrists from existing institutions" was "generally a hit and miss method." Trial Exh. P-4737. Finally, in January 1992, psychiatrists from different institutions were assigned to Pelican Bay each week; however, this was still a wholly inadequate, stop-gap measure. Even in July of 1992, with two full-time psychiatrists at Pelican Bay, many mentally ill inmates went without adequate psychiatric treatment.

By the time of trial, and under the pressure of litigation in different courts, the mental health staff at Pelican Bay had slowly climbed to nine clinicians: a chief psychiatrist and two staff psychiatrists, a senior psychologist and three staff psychologists, and two licensed social workers. There are also two MTAs, one office technician, and a medical transcriber.

As experts for both sides agree, however, this level of staffing remains insufficient to provide adequate mental health services for the population at Pelican Bay. Grassian Decl. at 166; Dvoskin Tr. 27-4411 (current staffing "probably not" adequate). At his deposition in January 1993, staff psychologist Dr. Ruggles testified that the provision of services is still primarily crisis-oriented, with emphasis on crisis intervention stabilization in cases where inmates are exhibiting disruptive, ***1218** bizarre or aberrant behavior, making suicidal statements or gestures, or experiencing a personal family crisis. Ruggles *Coleman* Depo. at 36-38.[150] Treatment for seriously ill inmates is primarily limited to medication management through use of antipsychotic or psychotropic drugs,[151] and intensive outpatient treatment is not available. The lack of staffing is particularly problematic in the SHU. As Dr. Dvoskin testified, current staffing levels are not sufficient to enable the mental health staff to quickly and effectively respond when inmates exhibit serious mental health problems in the SHU. Tr. 27-4475-76.

Defendants recently approved an additional 6.9 mental health positions for Pelican Bay, which would include a psychiatrist, a psychologist, a registered nurse, a senior MTA, and an additional health records technician. However, at the time of trial, none of these positions had been filled. Moreover, even defendants' expert would not confirm that this additional staffing, which would increase the mental health staff to 16, would provide an adequate level of care, stating that "I can't give [a] definitive answer without actually seeing [the staff] in place. . . . [It] might well be enough or it might not." Dvoskin Tr. 27-4411-4412; *id.* at 27-4476 (noting that if the 6.9 additional positions are filled, "they're getting clos-er, but I would still have questions about it").[152]

Needless to say, the lack of adequate staffing severely impacts the level of care received by inmates. As Dr. Grassian testified, "staffing shortages [at Pelican Bay] have led inexorably to inadequate access to care, inappropriate and shoddy medication management and monitoring, and chaotic record-keeping." Grassian Decl. at 166. Dr. Grassian further concluded that "[t]hese failures, taken together, violate even the most minimal standards for adequate psychiatric care." *Id.* at 167.

---

[150] At trial, Dr. Ruggles stated that they are "beginning" to see people in non crisis contexts as well and that, as of late, he is able to see people "as often as I need to." Tr. 17-2906-08. While the level of care may have improved since Dr. Ruggles's deposition, the Court is not convinced that the description he gave at that time does not remain largely accurate.

[151] The therapeutic benefits of psychotropic or anti-psychotic drugs is "well documented." *Washington v. Harper*, 494 U.S. 210, 226 n. 9, 229-30, 110 S.Ct. 1028, 1039 n. 9, 1041, 108 L.Ed.2d 178 (1990). There are, however, poten-tially serious or dangerous side effects including acute dystonia, a severe involuntary spasm of the upper body, tongue, throat or eyes (which is reversible); akathesia, which is characterized by restlessness and inability to sit still; neu-roleptic malignant syndrome, a relatively rare condition which causes cardiac dysfunction and possibly death; and tar-dive dyskinesia, a potentially irreversible neurological disorder which results in involuntary, uncontrollable move-ments of various muscles, especially around the face. *Id.*

[152] Notably, a study prepared by Scarlett Karp and Associates for the California Department of Corrections, to which Dvoskin contributed as a consultant for Scarlett Karp, recommended that the mental health staff at Pelican Bay be increased to 38, a figure which he suggested at his deposition was roughly 10 percent over the amount that would be required to provide minimally adequate mental health care. Dvoskin Depo. at 423; Tr. 27-4414.

b. *Screening and Referrals*

It is important that a mental health care system effectively identify those inmates in need of mental health services, both upon their arrival at the prison and during their incarceration. While mentally competent inmates can be relied upon to self-report most medical ailments, mentally ill prisoners may not seek out help where the nature of their mental illness makes them unable to recognize their illness or ask for assistance. Nor are family or friends usually around to notice developing mental problems or help inmates seek treatment.

For almost three years, Pelican Bay did not have an organized screening system at all. As Dr. Baker described, "[u]ntil the advent of our own MTA system, which we have instituted within the last three months [as of January 1993], there really was not an organized way of picking up on problems and feeding them to us. It happened. We had no control over it. It was a passive rather dependent situation which we really didn't have anyone out there who was a member of our staff to pick up on problems and follow them through." Baker *Coleman* Depo. at 26. Thus, many mentally ill inmates did not receive any mental health care until they were grossly psychotic and/or exhibited flagrant or *1219 suicidal behavior. Those who had serious mental illnesses but exhibited less unusual outward behavior might suffer in their cells for weeks or months without detection. *See also* Trial Exh. P-3161 at 83788 (1991 CDC audit finding that Pelican Bay was "seriously lacking" in the "timely identification" of inmates with psychiatric concerns).

The current system, while a significant improvement, still does not provide for "adequate[ ]" early intervention. Dvoskin Tr. 27-4456. The MTAs who briefly screen incoming inmates typically do not have the necessary training and background to recognize psychiatric illnesses. Staffing shortages also create gaps in the screening process, which are further exacerbated when staff are absent because of illness or vacation. As Dr. Dvoskin observed, "it would . . . certainly not be unlikely that [mentally ill] people would be missed upon transfer [from one prison to another]." Tr. 27-4458.

For those inmates already confined at Pelican Bay, the prison relies on referrals from custody staff or the inmate. Mental health staff who participate in classification committee reviews can also initiate referrals, and MTAs have contact with inmates taking psychotropic medication. Staff psychiatrists and psychologists, however, rarely visit the cellblocks in the SHU.

While custody staff can often provide useful information regarding an inmate's conduct and are instructed to report unusual behavior,[153] they are not adequately trained to identify mental illness. Nor do all custody staff consistently refer abnormal behavior. Defendants' expert also observed that the lack of mental health staff leads custody staff to impose a higher referral threshold than appropriate. Dvoskin Tr. 27-4462. As a consequence, custody staff essentially make medical judgments that should be reserved for clinicians, and some inmates are not given appropriate early treatment that could prevent or alleviate a severe psychiatric disorder.

As defendants' expert noted, the need for effective screening and monitoring in the SHU is particularly critical in order to ensure that inmates suffering from mental illness are not experiencing a deterioration in their condition. Dvoskin Decl. at 11; Tr. at 27-4475 (emphasizing the importance of responding quickly if symptoms begin to emerge). The same holds true with respect to inmates who do not have a demonstrated history of psychiatric illness.

In the New York system administered by Dr. Dvoskin, mental health staff make regular rounds (10 hours per week) in each segregation unit (with between 30-110 inmates) "to identify problems before they become anything remotely like mental illness" and to reduce stress among inmates and staff. Dvoskin Tr. 27-4421; 4466-4468. When Dr. Dvoskin recommended such rounds to the Warden or the Chief Deputy Warden at Pelican Bay, he was told that lack of staff precluded such a program in the SHU. Tr. 27-4468; Dvoskin Decl. at 11. In addition, there is no policy requiring *any* periodic psychological evaluations of SHU inmates. Peetz. Tr. 20-3330-31.

c. *Psychiatric Records*

The ability to provide appropriate psychiatric treatment at Pelican Bay is also impeded by the poor condition of inmate psychiatric records. First, the psychiatric records that are forwarded from other insti-

---

[153] One of the courses taught at the R.A. McGee Correctional Training Center for new correctional officers is a three hour class entitled "Unusual Inmate Behavior." Trial Exh. D-327.

tutions are often sketchy, and important information, including prior psychiatric hospitalizations, is sometimes missing. Second, once the records arrive at Pelican Bay, they are poorly maintained. Notes of mental health examinations are often cursory, and documentation of monitoring is "very chaotic and haphazard in many of the cases" reviewed by Dr. Grassian. Grassian Tr. 12-1903. Entries sometimes fail to account for prior diagnoses; mental health staff "just put[ ] in another diagnosis with no comment on the fact that there's a discrepancy here so that, you know, you see a person five times, he's got five diagnoses." *Id.* at 1904. Also, suicide watch records are made in the infirmary record rather than in the medical record, and psychiatric services staff do not receive these records from the infirmary.

*1220 d. *Delays in Transfers for Inpatient and Outpatient Care*

Pelican Bay does not offer psychiatric inpatient or intensive psychiatric outpatient treatment for mentally disturbed inmates. Inmates ill enough to require inpatient care[154] must be transferred to another institution such as the California Medical Facility ("CMF") in Vacaville or Atascadero State Hospital. Inmates needing intensive outpatient care must be transferred to CMF or the California Men's Colony ("CMC"). At Pelican Bay, several inmates each month may be referred out for either inpatient or intensive outpatient evaluation and treatment.

Traditionally, there have been exceedingly long delays in the transfer of inmates needing inpatient treatment. In June 1991, defendants' audit found that "[m]ajor problems exist in the transfer of medical and psychiatric patients from the Pelican Bay State Prison to the California Medical Facility–Vacaville." Trial Exh. P-3161 at 83807. Inmates needing either inpatient or outpatient care could wait up to three months before they were transferred from Pelican Bay, during which time they failed to receive appropriate psychiatric care. According to former staff psychologist Rollin Rose, at one point, the mental health staff was so seldom successful in getting inmates into CMF that they just "gave up [trying] after a while" except in "very extreme" cases. Rose *Coleman* Depo. at 57-58.

The transfer process has considerably improved for inmates needing inpatient care, a fact that former staff psychiatrist Bruce Baker attributed to the initiation of "these legal actions" and the arrival of Chief Psychiatrist Albert Sheff. Baker *Coleman* Depo. at 41-42. Inmates needing "immediate" inpatient care are now generally transferred to CMF in three days, although this is sometimes stretched to five or six days. Referrals to CMF for intensive outpatient treatment still take at least a month and sometimes two or three months. While inmates awaiting transfer may continue to be seen periodically by clinicians at Pelican Bay, in most cases they are not receiving the services necessary to provide them with appropriate treatment.

It is not uncommon for inmates transferred to another site for inpatient or intensive outpatient treatment to later be returned to Pelican Bay in essentially the same condition. As staff psychologist Rose described, "[w]ell, of course, they were sent to, referred to CMF in the first place because it was felt that they had serious psychiatric problems that we could not treat at Pelican Bay. And then several months later, we would get them back more or less in the same condition." Rose *Coleman* Depo. at 54. Other inmates return from CMF or CMC in an improved condition but then regress. According to Dr. Sheff, about half of the inmates transferred back to Pelican Bay from CMF "[do] not do well." Tr. 25-4177.

---

[154] Inmates needing inpatient care are generally categorized as either Category I, J, or K inmates. Category I inmates are inmates who, because of serious mental illness, are unable to function within a particular prison setting and require psychiatric inpatient treatment. A determination that an inmate needs to be treated on an inpatient basis might be made "only after crisis intervention steps to try to control the symptomatology with medication and/or brief psychotherapy." Sheff Tr. 25-4106.

Category J inmates are those who have a residual or chronic mental illness and may have problems functioning in a particular prison setting; they require a supportive rather than acute inpatient treatment. Category K prisoners are those who have similar sorts of problems as Category J prisoners, but whose problems are due to mental retardation.

Clinicians at Pelican Bay can not formally designate an inmate as falling within either Category I, J, or K; that designation can only be made by California Department of Mental Health practitioners at CMF or Atascadero State Hospital. The mental health staff at Pelican Bay can only refer an inmate who they believe should be categorized as Category I, J, or K to CMF or Atascadero State Hospital for evaluation and treatment.

e. *Lack of Procedures for Necessary Involuntary Psychiatric Treatment*

There are occasions where, in the medical judgment of a psychiatrist, a seriously ill patient is clearly in need of anti-psychotic medication, but is too paranoid and frightened to cooperate in his or her own treatment and thus refuses medication. The Supreme Court recently ruled that a state may, ***1221** consistent with constitutional guarantees, involuntarily treat an inmate with antipsychotic drugs if the inmate is dangerous to himself or others and the treatment is in the inmate's medical interest as determined by medical professionals. *Washington v. Harper*, 494 U.S. 210, 223-29, 110 S.Ct. 1028, 1038-40, 108 L.Ed.2d 178 (1990). The inmate, however, is entitled to a hearing before medical professionals to ensure that the decision to medicate the inmate against his will is neither arbitrary nor erroneous. *Id.* at 227-29, 110 S.Ct. at 1040; *cf. Keyhea v. Rushen*, 178 Cal.App.3d 526, 223 Cal.Rptr. 746, 755-56 & n. 3 (1986) (prisoners are entitled to judicial determination of their competency to refuse treatment before they can be subjected to long-term [over 10 days] involuntary psychotropic medication).

At Pelican Bay, there are no protocols or procedures in place for administering involuntary psychiatric medication. Instead, inmates needing involuntary medication must be transferred to CMF for inpatient treatment. However, as noted, this process usually takes three days, and sometimes longer, during which time the inmate is not involuntarily medicated. Thus, inmates in acute distress often suffer for an extended period of time before they receive treatment that should be provided immediately.

There are also inmates who need and would benefit from involuntary medication, but who are not transferred to a facility offering such treatment on account of security concerns. For example, Inmate A[155] is an inmate who was suffering from delusional beliefs and auditory command hallucinations telling him to commit violent acts. When Dr. Grassian interviewed the inmate in September 1992, he found him to be "severely mentally ill, incompetent to appreciate his need for treatment, and a danger to himself and others." Grassian Decl. at 51; Tr. 12-1900-02. Dr. Grassian was informed, however, that the inmate's security needs required him to remain at Pelican Bay. Inmates like Inmate A are essentially trapped in a Catch-22: they are too psychotic to consent to treatment, yet their psychosis makes them too "dangerous" for a transfer to a facility where they could receive treatment that would potentially reduce their security risk. *See also* Astorga Depo. at 753-54 (acknowledging "Catch-22" situation of inmates whose custodial needs preclude transfer).

f. *Failure to Involve Mental Health Staff in Housing Decisions*

There are instances where it may be critical, from a medical standpoint, to alter an inmate's housing assignment (e.g., from the SHU to another environment or from double to single cell housing), in order to effectively address an inmate's serious mental health problems. With respect to the SHU, Dr. Grassian concluded that some inmates in the SHU have experienced a severe exacerbation of existing mental conditions or the onset of mental illness, and that "many of the acute symptoms suffered by these inmates are likely to subside upon termination of SHU confinement." Grassian Decl. at 4. Dr. Dvoskin also testified that, except for "very, very rare exceptions," inmates who are in acute psychiatric distress or suicidal depressions should not be housed in the SHU. Tr. 27-4473.

Nonetheless, Pelican Bay psychiatrists and psychologists are not, as a practical matter, allowed input into cell housing decisions, even when the inmate is suffering acute symptoms and the mental health staff believe that a change in housing conditions is potentially necessary to the effective treatment of the inmate's disorder. Defendants' complete failure to consider the mental health needs of inmates in making housing decisions seriously compromises the ability of the mental health clinicians to effectively and adequately treat their patients.[156]

---

[155] For privacy purposes, specific inmates will be referred to by letter rather than by name in this section.

[156] As noted earlier, *see* note 151, *supra*, certain psychotropic drugs are extremely potent and may have serious adverse side effects. Thus, while the use of such drugs may reduce symptoms of mental illness, this is not an adequate treatment or long term solution if the mental health staff are of the opinion that the underlying source of the illness is continued exposure to conditions in the SHU.

*1222 g. *Suicide Prevention*

While prison staff receive a modicum of suicide prevention training, there is no comprehensive suicide prevention program in place. As part of their basic training, new correctional officers take a three-hour course entitled "Unusual Inmate Behavior," which includes a short section on how to identify inmates susceptible to suicide and what to do after identifying such an inmate or discovering an attempted suicide. Trial Exh. D-327. In June 1992, a "Suicide Prevention Handbook" was distributed to all Pelican Bay staff, and they were required to read the handbook and complete an accompanying quiz. Trial Exh. D- 297. There has also been some additional in-service training; however, it appears to have taken place on a sporadic basis.

h. *Quality Assurance*

As described in section II(B)(2)(f), *supra*, a Quality Assurance program is designed to enable a medical institution or department to review, on an ongoing basis, staff medical decisions and practices in order to assess whether corrective measures are necessary or appropriate. Such a program is considered "standard practice" in virtually every health care facility in the country and is considered a "fundamental part" of a health care operation. Harness Tr. 19-3117.

At least as of trial, however, Pelican Bay, after almost four years of operation, still had not implemented a Quality Assurance program for its mental health staff. Former staff psychologist Rollin Rose explained that he never tried to discuss this particular point with Dr. Astorga, Pelican Bay's Chief Medical Officer, because "there are certain issues that just wouldn't be very fruitful to discuss with Dr. Astorga and that was probably one of them." Rose *Coleman* Depo. at 78-79.

i. *Treatment Provided*

For those inmates that are seen by the mental health staff,[157] the combined effect of staffing shortages and other problems discussed above has inevitably led to numerous instances of grossly deficient treatment. As Warden Marshall stated in a 1991 budget request, "Pelican Bay's design staffing is not adequate to even identify all of the psychiatrically disabled inmates, much less provide the mandated mental health treatment." Trial Exh. P-4602 at 49198. A 1991 CDC audit also concluded that Pelican Bay was "seriously lacking in the . . . treatment and tracking of inmates diagnosed as having psychiatric concerns. . . . The deficiencies exist[ ] particularly in the areas of appropriate follow-up treatment and/or transfer to more suitable housing." Moreover, serious problems continue to persist, notwithstanding the modest staffing increases. *See* Dvoskin Tr. at 27-4456 (current system does not provide adequate stabilization and symptom management); Grassian Tr. at 12-1904 ("the follow-up of psychiatric staff is . . . often extremely chaotic [and] sporadic").

The pain, suffering, and deterioration experienced by inmates who fail to receive appropriate treatment for their mental disorders is substantial. In the case of an inmate suffering a serious psychotic break, the impact can be enormous. As Dr. Grassian described, "I've had patients who've lived through psychotic breaks of that magnitude [observed at Pelican Bay]. And it is a scarring experience for years, probably for the rest of their lives, to feel that out of control and that agitated and that terrified, to know how absolutely terrified you can be, to know how absolutely out of control you can be. It is a very scarring, frightening experience that people live with, and there are prisoners suffering . . . it day after day." Tr. 12-1973-74.

*1223 While the deficiencies in defendants' system of mental health care are felt prison-wide, the

---

[157] The nine clinicians currently employed at Pelican Bay see inmates for evaluation after referral in a "psychiatric line," "psychology line" or "clinical social worker line" on certain days of the week in each different section of the prison. The lines operate like a clinic, with the MTA arranging for a set number of inmates to be seen on each line. A clinician sees about eight to twelve inmates on each line, with the psychiatry lines being somewhat longer. Follow-up review and treatment is handled by the "treatment team" for either the SHU or the General Population section of the prison. The treatment team includes the Chief Psychiatrist, any clinicians assigned to a particular housing unit, the MTA assigned to the housing unit, and custody staff including correctional counselors and program administrators, who are the senior managers of the prison housing facilities.

problems are especially severe in the SHU. At least three factors have contributed to this result. The first stems from the very mission of the SHU, which is to house the most dangerous and disruptive inmates. Since, as discussed above, inmates suffering from mental illness are more likely to engage in disruptive conduct, significant numbers of mentally ill inmates within the California prison system are ultimately transferred to the Pelican Bay SHU. Second, the severity of the environment and restrictions in the SHU often cause mentally ill inmates to seriously deteriorate; other inmates who are otherwise able to psychologically cope with normal prison routines may also begin decompensating in the SHU. Third, defendants chose to provide only limited psychiatric services to inmates in the SHU. Aside from the obvious limitations which ensue from lack of staffing, discussed above, defendants have made no effort to provide appropriate treatment for inmates suffering from major mental disorders. The prison is not equipped to provide *any* inpatient or intensive outpatient treatment or involuntary medication. At the same time, delays prevent urgently needed care from being provided off-site as well. While inpatient care can be provided elsewhere in 3 to 5 days, this does not help the inmate who needs immediate hospitalization or involuntary medication. Similarly, a one- to three-month delay effectively denies adequate treatment for the seriously ill inmate needing immediate intensive outpatient treatment. And in some cases, security concerns preclude any transfer at all.

In short, defendants created a prison which, given its mission, size, and nature, would necessarily and inevitably result in an extensive demand for mental health services—perhaps more so than any other California facility; yet, at the same time, they scarcely bothered to furnish mental health services at all, and then only at a level more appropriate to a facility much smaller in size and modest in mission.

It is not surprising, then, that during his 69 interviews with 50 SHU inmates in September of 1992 and May of 1993, Dr. Grassian found that 17 of those inmates were acutely psychotic and not receiving appropriate treatment for their condition. As detailed at length in Dr. Grassian's declaration at pages 25 and 45 through 104, medical staff often failed to conduct adequate mental examinations, ignored past medical history or failed to obtain a proper history, made contradictory or inconsistent diagnoses, and engaged in only a superficial review and diagnosis. A number of inmates were in need of immediate involuntary medication and/or hospital-level inpatient treatment; some were the most severely ill people Dr. Grassian has encountered in his research and observations.

The following examples are illustrative of some of the glaring problems found in the delivery of mental health care at Pelican Bay:

Inmate B

Inmate B is a 38 year-old white male with a history of childhood sexual abuse, intermittent paranoia, periods of depression, and prior psychiatric hospitalization. Grassian Decl. at 66. When Dr. Grassian interviewed him in May 1993, he was "quite obviously paranoid and psychotic." *Id.* Among other things, he was suffering from auditory and visual hallucinations and delusional ideas. Inmate B reported to Dr. Grassian that:

> [T]he [custody staff] are growing marijuana. They killed someone. They cut each other off in conversation day by day. . . . I'm on Stelazine (an antipsychotic) because of audio and visual hallucinations. I hear radio transmissions, background hiss. If I have difficulty sleeping it gets worse. I see patterns on the wall, shadows get brighter. The hallucinations get more intense with less sleep.

Id. at 66-67. Inmate B also believed that his body had been transported by "astral projection" to a place where it was invaded and mutilated. *Id.* at 67. Although the severity of his illness warranted transfer to a psychiatric hospital, he was simply receiving medication adjustments on "roughly a monthly basis." *Id.* at 66-67.

*1224 *Inmate C*

In September 1992, Dr. Grassian found Inmate C to be in an acute catatonic state requiring immediate hospitalization and antipsychotic medication. He was in a fixed, immobile posture, staring "bug-eyed" at the walls and ceiling, with his posture punctuated by "sudden jerking movements of his eyes and body, giving the clear impression that he was responding defensively to frightening internal (hallu-cinatory) stimuli." Grassian Decl. at 46. This type of catatonic posturing is "usually associated with an inner state of absolute abject terror." Grassian Tr. 12-1908. Over the years, Dr. Grassian has seen many patients in a similar state, especially in his experience with psychiatric inpatients, and has learned to "regard it as a psychiatric emergency of the first magnitude, a living nightmare which even after the acute episode is successfully treated, produces deep lasting emotional scars." Grassian Decl. at 46-47. Such a patient should be immediately hospitalized and treated with antipsychotic medication under very close supervision.

Inmate C had been on antipsychotic medications continuously since 1991, and had previously been diagnosed as suffering from various mental disorders by several mental health professionals. Dr. Grassian also noted that accurately feigning a state of acute catatonia is something that few, if any, can achieve. Grassian Decl. at 49. Nonetheless, Pelican Bay staff suspected Inmate C of malingering. Grassian Decl. at 47-49. When Dr. Grassian returned to Pelican Bay in May 1993, Inmate C was still psychotic and hal-lucinatory.

Dr. Grassian found that Inmate C's situation is one that particularly shocks the conscience. "[T]here has been no consistency regarding the clinicians who saw him, nor was there adequate supportive psy-chotherapeutic contact: he appears to have been seen only a handful of times during the entire period. Finally, there was no consistency from visit to visit as to diagnosis. He was at various times diagnosed as suffering from schizophrenia . . ., organic hallucinosis, a personality disorder, an organic mental disor-der, or to be malingering. There is no continuity in these assessments; it is as though each interview was a unique event unrelated to prior contacts." Grassian Decl. at 49-50.

Inmate D

Inmate D was housed at Corcoran State Prison prior to his transfer to the Pelican Bay SHU in April 1990. While at Corcoran, he was treated with the antipsychotic medication Mellaril and the mood-stabi-lizing medication Lithium. In a psychiatric summary dated March 28, 1990, just three weeks prior to Inmate D's transfer to Pelican Bay, it was specifically noted that Mellaril helped stop the prisoner's audi-tory hallucinations and his inability to concentrate, and that Lithium helped him control his temper. Trial Exh. P-643 at 69169.

Once at Pelican Bay, however, Inmate D was not provided any psychiatric treatment until September 1990, five months after his transfer. When the inmate complained that he had trouble controlling his anger and aggressive behavior, the staff psychologist noted that the inmate's file was unavailable for review to check his psychiatric history and psychotropic medications. As a result of the inmate's com-plaint, a psychiatrist who apparently never saw Inmate D nor reviewed his records prescribed Lithium and an antidepressant, Elavil. He was not prescribed Mellaril, the other major medication he had received at Corcoran. Five months later, in January 1991, he simply stopped receiving medication, for no reason apparent in the record. Inmate D was not seen again until March 1993, over two years later. At that time, a social worker interviewed him briefly and referred him to a psychiatrist, who wrote in his record: "[unintelligible] and wants legal relief from all the harassment from inmates. No mental disorder. Not asking for treatment. Plan—no treatment—no follow-up." Trial Exh. P-643 at 69167. There is no indica-tion that the psychiatrist ever considered Inmate D's psychiatric history. By May of 1993, Inmate D was in a grossly deteriorated mental state. Just days before he was interviewed by Dr. Grassian, he was placed on Lithium, but not Mellaril or any other antipsychotic medication. Based on his May 1993 interview, Dr. Grassian concluded that Inmate D was seriously ill and suffering from obsessional thoughts of vio-lence, impulsive *1225 violence, paranoia, severe anxiety, massive difficulty with concentration, recur-rent dissociative confusional episodes, and perceptual distortions. Grassian Decl. at 43, 128- 32.

Inmate E

Inmate E was previously incarcerated by the California Youth Authority ("CYA") beginning in 1987. There he underwent extensive psychiatric evaluation and testing for his pedophilia. Although he was described by CYA psychiatrists as "moody, depressed, narcissistic, and very immature," Trial Exh. P-173 at 24680, and diagnosed as having pedophilic impulses that were out of control, *id.* at 24681, clinicians found no evidence that he had a psychotic disorder.

However, Inmate E became overtly psychotic and suicidal after being placed in the Pelican Bay SHU in 1991. He was evaluated in April 1992 after he wrote a suicide note in his own blood. Inmate E report-ed that he was "hearing voices" and the examining doctor described him as "obviously very psychotic." Trial Exh. P-694 at 3675. Although Inmate E claimed the next day that some of his behavior was "a fake," he almost immediately thereafter reported "hearing voices," then "flipped out," according to an MTA. *Id.* The inmate was prescribed Mellaril and remained in the infirmary for two weeks. However, he was discharged to custody by Dr. Sheff in early May with the notation, "no meds, no psych problems noted." *Id.* at 3676.

Inmate E continued to have psychotic or suicidal episodes; Pelican Bay staff seemingly vacillated between treating his psychotic episodes as such and dismissing them as manipulation. In late May the inmate again stated that he wanted to kill himself, and then later retracted; Dr. Mandel felt he had no psychiatric disorders and recommended that the inmate be disciplined for manipulation of the system. Trial Exh. P-694 at 3662. In July of 1992, Inmate E was found to have multiple superficial lacerations on his forearm and was "talking nonsensically." *Id.* at 3648-49. Dr. Baker noted that the inmate was having panic attacks and that voices were telling him to hurt himself. By August he had deteriorated further, and Dr. Baker characterized him as having a "schizophrenic" episode with "disjointed" thinking after he described hearing voices and receiving messages from a computer at the base of his neck. Trial Exh. P-497 at 993. Nevertheless, only five days after Dr. Baker's evaluation, another staff psychologist diagnosed Inmate E as having no significant mental disorder. *Id.* at 990.

When Dr. Grassian subsequently interviewed Inmate E, the inmate was still grossly psychotic and incoherent. He told Dr. Grassian,

> "I see or hear things. I have been hypnotized since April 13th by Cybernetics. I can't even explain it without being hooked up with polygraph tests. It's like frequency tests. A bunch of people come up to me and talk about why I have to kill myself. Things I've thought of, things I've seen, animals and stuff like that. It's frightening. They tried to kill me. They used sounds, send emotions through my body and my body shakes . . . I'm tired of people talking in my head. I was mentally clear before . . . sometimes I get so confused, I don't even know what's going on."

Grassian Decl. 54. The lack of coherent approach to this clearly psychotic inmate is not atypical.

Undoubtedly, there are some inmates who attempt to feign mental illness, and who are justifiably considered "malingerers." The Court also acknowledges that the identification of simulated symptoms may sometimes involve difficult judgment calls. It is clear, however, that an overburdened, and sometimes indifferent, mental health staff is far too quick to dismiss an inmate as a "malingerer" and thus deny him needed treatment, a fact that is illustrated by some of the above examples. Indeed, Dr. Grassian found "an almost obsessive preoccupation by staff members with the possibility that an inmate might be manipulating, which significantly impairs their capacity to recognize severe mental illness." Grassian Decl. at 56; Tr. 12-1979-80. There is also evidence that inmates are labeled malingerers even though the inmate has been prescribed strong antipsychotic medications, which should not be ***1226** taken unless medically necessary, given the potentially dangerous side effects.[158]

3. *Defendants' State of Mind*

The record in this case reveals a deliberate, and often shocking, disregard for the serious mental health needs of inmates at Pelican Bay.

It is certainly "known" that there are inmates with serious mental disorders "throughout" the California prison population. McKinsey Tr. 26-4326. Indeed, the evidence before the Court demonstrates that it would be patently obvious to any experienced prison administrator that operating a maximum security facility with a population of 3,500 inmates, which includes, as everyone concedes, the "worst of the worst," would create a need for substantial mental health services. Defendants also knew, given Dr.

---

[158] *See* note 151, *supra.* As Dr. Grassian also notes, the act of "malingering" may itself be a symptom of mental illness. An inmate "faking" a symptom complained of may well be so ill in another sense that he is desperately seeking help in any way possible. Also, a patient may both be manipulating and at the same time very ill. "Both things can go on in the same individual. . . . [A] person can be very ill and that could be why they're manipulating." Grassian Tr. 12-1979. The medical records, however, do not indicate that these possibilities have been considered when an inmate is characterized as a "malingerer."

Khoury's September 1989 memorandum, that the need for substantial mental health services would be particularly acute given the presence of the SHU, which soon housed approximately 1,500 inmates. It would also be equally obvious that the failure to provide such services would cause considerable pain and suffering. Indeed, these facts are so obvious that we find that defendants clearly knew of them.

At the same time, defendants were made aware that there would be "minimal psychiatric services available to . . . SHU inmates unless they . . . [became] actively psychotic and thus . . . [were] eligible for transfer to another prison." See Trial Exh. P-4220 at 5; Park Tr. 11-1681.[159] They were also aware that when Pelican Bay opened in December 1989, with no psychiatrist on staff, the prison was operating without sufficient mental health care services, see, e.g., Peetz Tr. at 20-3250, and that serious mental health needs were continuing to go unmet in the months and years thereafter.

Associate Warden Peetz, for example, acknowledged that he "was aware that we had inadequate resources to deal with people that were having mental problems." Tr. 20-3332. This knowledge is also reflected by internal audits and budget requests for additional staff submitted by Warden Marshall, which plainly highlighted a number of serious deficiencies in the delivery of mental health care.

Defendants' response to the lack of adequate mental health care—and particularly the response of defendant Gomez, who has overall responsibility for the California Department of Corrections—reflects a deplorable, and clearly conscious, disregard for the serious mental health needs of inmates. For example, defendants suggest that, despite lacking a staff psychiatrist—or any semblance of a mental health care program—they were nonetheless justified in opening Pelican Bay, given their "contingency plan" of providing mental health services through periodic visits from psychiatrists at other institutions. However, this plan was so clearly and grossly deficient that it only highlights defendants' striking indifference to the mental health of thousands of persons in their custody.[160]

Prodded by this litigation, as well as litigation in the Coleman case, supra, defendants slowly improved staffing levels over the last two years. However, even this response has *1227 been tepid. As discussed above, staffing levels, as of the time of trial, still remained seriously deficient. Nor is it a sufficient response to simply plead that recruitment of doctors is difficult. Defendants certainly knew before Pelican Bay opened that its remote location would present obstacles to attracting professional mental health staff. Moreover, recruitment difficulties do not excuse compliance with constitutional mandates. See Wellman v. Faulkner, 715 F.2d 269, 273 (7th Cir.1983) (failure of prison to fill authorized position for two years weighs "more heavily against the state than for it"). Rather, they simply require that defendants make additional efforts to compensate for their choice of location for the prison—yet those efforts to date can only be described as half-hearted and weak in substance.

In addition to defendants' slack response to the lack of staffing, defendants have shown little interest in addressing other systemic problems in the delivery of mental health care at Pelican Bay discussed above. For example, defendants have failed to implement a quality assurance program or make serious efforts to provide needed treatment for inmates who, for security reasons, can not be transferred to another institution for inpatient or intensive outpatient treatment.

Defendants emphasize that they have begun plans for initiating a new Health Care Services Division within the Department of Corrections, and that the purpose of this reform is to improve the quality of medical and mental health care and ensure consistent, cost-effective care. While such reform is a step in the right direction, it does not excuse defendants' deliberate indifference to the mental health needs of inmates at Pelican Bay over the last five years.[161]

D. CONDITIONS IN THE SECURITY HOUSING UNIT

The SHU at Pelican Bay is a separate, self-contained complex that operates as the "maxi SHU" for all of California's state prisons. Located within the prison's security perimeter, it is designed to house

---

[159] Trial Exhibit P-4220, which contains a report on Pelican Bay prepared by a Special Consultant for the California Legislature Joint Committee on Prison Construction and Operations, was circulated to the CDC and discussed at a hearing attended by high-ranking CDC officials.

[160] Dr. Khoury maintained that psychiatric staffing at Pelican Bay was not necessary during the initial phase of its operation because the Department of Corrections did not send more than a handful of mentally ill prisoners to Pelican Bay. However, the overwhelming evidence demonstrates that there was no policy, and certainly no enforced policy, of excluding mentally ill inmates from Pelican Bay. Furthermore, Dr. Khoury's contention completely fails to address the needs of those inmates who may develop mental illness after their transfer to Pelican Bay.

[161] Notably, the Legislative Analyst's Office made the following observations in its analysis of the 1992/93 Budget:

1,052 inmates, but has sufficient beds to hold double that number, or 2,104. At the time of trial, the SHU was authorized by the CDC to operate at 150 percent of capacity, bringing the total number of inmates confined in the SHU to approximately 1,500. Roughly two-thirds (or 1,000) of those inmates are double celled, and the remaining 500 inmates are single celled.[162]

For the most part, these 1,500 inmates are considered by the CDC to be the most disruptive or potentially dangerous inmates in the California prison system. *See* Trial Exh. D-130 (designating SHU as housing "of choice" for inmates "who are the greatest threat to prison security and safety"). Roughly half of the 1,500 are inmates who have violated prison rules, usually by possessing a weapon, attempting an escape, or assaulting or participating in an assault on other inmates or staff. They are transferred temporarily to the SHU to serve a set term as punishment for their rule violation(s). The next largest group (numbering around 600) consists of inmates whom the CDC has determined are affiliated with a prison gang. They are assigned to the SHU for indeterminate terms—that is, they will remain in the SHU indefinitely up to the maximum length of their sentence (which, for some prisoners, may mean 10 or 15 years, or the duration of *1228 their life).[163] Another sizeable group consists of inmates who are neither gang affiliated nor serving a term for violation of a disciplinary rule; rather they are persons whom prison administrators believe should nonetheless be segregated because of general concerns regarding assaultive or disruptive behavior. These inmates may also remain in the SHU indefinitely. Finally, there are some inmates who are at risk of assault from other inmates and so are housed in the SHU for their own safety. Again, these inmates may remain in the SHU for an indefinite time.[164]

Security Housing Units (sometimes referred to as Disciplinary Control Units, Special Management Units, or other similar names) are a common feature in American prisons; their unifying characteristic is that they segregate inmates from other "general population" prisoners and subject them to greater restrictions and fewer privileges. The degree of segregation and restrictions may vary, however, depending on a variety of factors, including penal philosophy and the underlying reason for the inmate's segregation.

Plaintiffs claim that at Pelican Bay, the degree of segregation is so extreme, and the restrictions so severe, that the conditions in the SHU inflict psychological trauma on inmates confined there, and in some cases, deprive inmates of sanity itself. They further contend that defendants have been deliberately indifferent to the mental health risks posed by the conditions in the SHU. In the remainder of this section, we address: (1) the conditions in the SHU, (2) the impact of SHU conditions on mental health, and (3) defendants' state of mind.

1. *Conditions in the SHU*

a. *Physical Description*

The SHU is a low-level grey structure that roughly resembles a large "X" in shape. There are two separate but physically connected wings which are referred to as the "C" SHU and the "D" SHU. Both

---

Too Little Planning, Too Much Litigation. Our review indicates that, although the CDC has made some improvements in administration of its medical programs, the programs are too often characterized by a lack of adequate long-term planning, and 'crisis management,' often brought about by litigation. For example, the CDC's justification for two significant budget proposals—restructuring of the existing psychiatric outpatient program and authorization to build a new health care facility at CIW—are based on consent decrees and court orders.

The lack of long-term planning has been apparent over the years . . . .. Trial Exh. P-3958 at 32.

[162] Statewide, there are approximately 2,300 inmates who are held in security housing units, a figure which represents roughly two percent of the California prison population (which totalled 119,000 as of November 1993). Besides the Pelican Bay SHU, defendants also operate smaller SHUs at the New Folsom and Corcoran state prisons.

[163] Earlier release from the SHU may be secured only if the inmate successfully completes what is referred to as a "debriefing process." This process requires the inmate to furnish detailed information regarding other prison gang members or gang activity. *See* section II(F), *infra* [omitted here].

[164] As of November 1992, there were 675 prisoners serving determinate terms for disciplinary rule violations, 485 prisoners serving indeterminate terms for prison gang membership or association, 200 prisoners serving indeterminate terms due to concerns regarding their assaultive or disruptive behavior, and 62 prisoners serving indeterminate terms to avoid risks to their own safety. In October 1993, the number of inmates serving indeterminate terms for prison gang affiliation was 625.

wings, which are virtually identical, are divided into "cell blocks", each of which consists of eight "pods" containing eight cells each. Each pod is divided into two short tiers, with four cells opening onto an upper tier and four cells opening onto a lower tier.

Each cell is 80 square feet and comes equipped with two built-in bunks and a toilet-sink unit. Cell doors are made of heavy gauge perforated metal; this design prevents objects from being thrown through the door but also significantly blocks vision and light. A skylight in each pod does allow some natural light to enter the tier area adjacent to the cells; however, cells are primarily lit with a fluorescent light that can be operated by the inmate. Each cell block is supervised and guarded by a separate control station which is staffed by armed correctional officers and separated from the pods by an electronically controlled metal gate. The officers also electronically control the opening and closing of the cell doors.

Patterned after a "Special Management Unit" in Florence, Arizona (albeit with some modifications), the SHU interior is designed to reduce visual stimulation. *See* Trial Exh P-3814 at 3955. The cellblocks are marked throughout by a dull sameness in design and color. The cells are windowless; the walls are white concrete. When inside the cell, all one can see through the perforated metal door is another white wall.

A small exercise pen with cement floors and walls is attached to the end of each pod. Because the walls are 20 feet high, they preclude any view of the outside world. The top of the pen is covered partly by a screen and partly by a plastic rain cover, thus providing ***1229** access to some fresh air. However, given their cell-like design and physical attachment to the pod itself, the pens are more suggestive of satellite cells than areas for exercise or recreation.

The overall effect of the SHU is one of stark sterility and unremitting monotony. Inmates can spend years without ever seeing any aspect of the outside world except for a small patch of sky. One inmate fairly described the SHU as being "like a space capsule where one is shot into space and left in isolation." Lopez Tr. 1-49.

b. *Social Isolation*

Inmates in the SHU can go weeks, months or potentially years with little or no opportunity for normal social contact with other people. Regardless of the reason for their assignment to the SHU, all SHU inmates remain confined to their cells for 22 and 1/2 hours of each day. Food trays are passed through a narrow food port in the cell door. Inmates eat all meals in their cells. Opportunities for social interaction with other prisoners or vocational staff are essentially precluded. Inmates are not allowed to participate in prison job opportunities or any other prison recreational or educational programs. Nor is group exercise allowed. Inmates who are single celled exercise alone. Inmates who are double celled exercise with their cellmate or alone if the cellmate chooses not to exercise. No recreational equipment is provided. As the Court observed during its tour of the SHU, some inmates spend the time simply pacing around the edges of the pen; the image created is hauntingly similar to that of caged felines pacing in a zoo. Inmates in adjoining cells can hear but not see each other.

Interaction with correctional staff is kept to an absolute minimum. According to defendants' expert, the SHU has "attempted to reduce physical contact between inmates and staff to the extent possible, as much probably [as] anyplace I've seen in a segregation environment." Dvoskin Tr. 27-4391. For example, when an inmate leaves his cell to go to the exercise pen, the door is opened automatically by the control booth officer. Once in the tier area, the inmate must strip naked in front of the control booth; the door to the exercise pen is also controlled electronically. In addition, the contact that correctional staff do have with inmates often occurs in a routinized setting while inmates are in handcuffs and waist and ankle chains, such as during an escort from the cell to another point in the prison. As previously found, there is also a pattern of correctional officers using excessive force against inmates. *See* section II(A)(1), *supra*. The resulting tension in the SHU has further limited the ability of inmates and staff to engage in normal and constructive interactions.

The social isolation, however, is not complete. Inmates may leave their pod area on certain specified occasions; however, such opportunities may be infrequent and generally provide only a limited type of interaction.[165] For example, inmates may leave their pod periodically to go to the law library; however, they are assigned to an individual library cell and have little interaction with other inmates or library staff. Inmates may also leave their pod to receive visitors or their attorney; however, all visits are con-

---

[165] For security reasons, inmates are always restrained in handcuffs and/or waist and ankle chains any time they leave the pod area.

ducted by telephone through a thick glass window, precluding opportunity for human touch. Moreover, because of Pelican Bay's distance from metropolitan areas, many inmates get either few visitors or none at all. Inmates also attend periodic on-site classification committee meetings, and those who become ill may leave their pod for diagnosis or treatment by the medical or mental health staff. Inmates may also request a counseling, prayer or Bible study visit from a religious volunteer under a program operated by the Pelican Bay chaplain.[166]

Roughly two-thirds of the inmates are double celled; however, this does not compensate for the otherwise severe level of social *1230 isolation in the SHU. The combination of being in extremely close proximity with one other person, while other avenues for normal social interaction are virtually precluded, often makes any long-term, normal relationship with the cellmate impossible. Instead, two persons housed together in this type of forced, constant intimacy have an "enormously high risk of becoming paranoid, hostile, and potentially violent towards each other." Grassian Tr. 12-1857; Haney Tr. 6-89. The existence of a cellmate is thus unlikely to provide an opportunity for sustained positive or normal social contact.

In sum, those incarcerated in the SHU for any length of time are severely deprived of normal human contact regardless of whether they are single or double celled. As former Warden Fenton testified, conditions in the SHU amount to a "virtual total deprivation, including, insofar as possible, deprivation of human contact." Tr. 5-808.

c. *Privileges*

SHU inmates are allowed certain limited privileges which provide a source of environmental stimulation. For the most part, however, they do not involve direct human interaction. Inmates with funds may purchase radios and televisions, and an Arts Film Program is shown on a closed circuit television channel. These televisions and/or radios provide one of the few sources of stimulation or link with the outside world. However, not all inmates possess a television or radio. Inmates may send and receive mail (no phone calls are permitted), read books, and participate in a Bible correspondence class. In recent months, prison administrators have also allowed the mental health staff to provide inmates with reading materials on relaxation techniques. Not all inmates, however, are literate. Inmates may also keep certain personal property in their cells and make purchases through the prison canteen. They are also permitted three showers per week. Other privileges previously mentioned are non-contact visits, participation in the chaplain's religious visitor program, and an exercise period five times each week.

d. *Comparison to Other SHUs*

While it is difficult to assess exactly how conditions in the Pelican Bay SHU compare to other security housing units, there is little doubt that, by any measuring stick, the Pelican Bay SHU by design lies on the harsh end of the SHU spectrum. Plaintiffs' expert Craig Haney, who has toured 20 to 25 segregation units, concluded that inmates at Pelican Bay are more isolated than inmates in any other segregation unit he has experienced. He noted that "[t]he only place that comes close is the federal penitentiary at Marion. But even Marion in some ways is a different and a less-isolated environment than this one." Tr. 6-988. Defendants' expert Dvoskin testified that SHU conditions at Pelican Bay are the conditions "of segregation as they exist in American prisons." However, he acknowledged that some SHUs provide more "privileges and freedom" than others, and that "Pelican Bay has clearly, on that continuum, decided to err on the side of physical safety rather than . . . increased privileges and freedom and increased staff to inmate contact." Tr. 27-4389-90.

2. *Impact of SHU Conditions on Mental Health*

Social science and clinical literature have consistently reported that when human beings are subjected to social isolation and reduced environmental stimulation, they may deteriorate mentally and in

---

[166] Although the record is somewhat unclear, it appears that the religious volunteers conduct their visits while standing outside the cell door. On some occasions, the inmate may be taken to a holding cell in another area which affords greater privacy.

some cases develop psychiatric disturbances. These include perceptual distortions, hallucinations, hyper-responsivity to external stimuli, aggressive fantasies, overt paranoia, inability to concentrate, and problems with impulse control. This response has been observed not only in the extreme case where a subject in a clinical setting is completely isolated in a dark soundproofed room or immersed in water, but in a variety of other contexts. For example, similar effects have been observed in hostages, prisoners of war, patients undergoing long-term immobilization in a hospital, and pilots flying long solo flights. While acute symptoms tend to subside after normal stimulation or conditions are returned, some people may sustain long-term effects. This series of symptoms has been discussed using varying terminology; however, one common label is "Reduced Environmental Stimulation," or "RES." According to Dr. Grassian, **1231** the complex of symptoms associated with RES is rarely, if ever, observed in other psychotic syndromes or in humans not subject to RES, a point which defendants did not refute with any specificity.

There is also an ample and growing body of evidence that this phenomenon may occur among persons in solitary or segregated confinement—persons who are, by definition, subject to a significant degree of social isolation and reduced environmental stimulation. Early experiments with complete solitary confinement in American and European penitentiaries in the late 1700's and 1800's led to numerous reports of psychiatric disturbances. *See* Grassian Decl. at 11-16. In 1890, the Supreme Court described the experience with one such facility, the Walnut Street Penitentiary in Philadelphia, in *In re Medley*, 134 U.S. 160, 10 S.Ct. 384, 33 L.Ed. 835 (1890):

> The peculiarities of this system were the complete isolation of the prisoner from all human society, and his confinement in a cell of considerable size, so arranged that he had no direct intercourse with or sight of any human being, and no employment or instruction. Other prisons on the same plan, which were less liberal in the size of their cells and the perfection of their appliances, were erected in Massachusetts, New Jersey, Maryland and some of the other States. But experience demonstrated that there were serious objections to it. A considerable number of the prisoners fell, after even a short confinement, into a semi-fatuous condition, from which it was next to impossible to arouse them, and others became violently insane; others, still, committed suicide; while those who stood the ordeal better were not generally reformed, and in most cases did not recover sufficient mental activity to be of any subsequent service to the community. It became evident that some changes must be made in the system, and the separate system was originated by the Philadelphia Society for Ameliorating the Miseries of Public Prisons, founded in 1787.

Id. at 168, 10 S.Ct. at 386 (emphasis deleted). More recent studies have also documented the potential adverse mental health effects of solitary or segregated confinement. As the Seventh Circuit noted in *Davenport v. DeRobertis*, 844 F.2d 1310, 1316 (7th Cir.1988), "there is plenty of medical and psychological literature concerning the ill effects of solitary confinement (of which segregation is a variant)" (citing Grassian, *Psychopathological Effects of Solitary Confinement*, 140 American Journal of Psychiatry 1450 (1983)).[167]

Defendants' expert Dr. Dvoskin acknowledged that it is "possible" that a "syndrome" could be associated with segregated conditions in confinement, although he does not believe there is sufficient data to support "an exact syndrome." Tr. 27-4373-74. Dr. Dvoskin has, however, used the term "AD SEG [Administrative Segregation] Syndrome" or other terms in his work to describe those people who "can't handle" segregation or find "segregation intolerable." Tr. 27-4374. Dr. Sheff, the former chief psychiatrist at Pelican Bay, also testified that he observed prisoners at Pelican Bay demonstrating the RES "symptom complex," although he did not observe it in a "large number" of the patients with whom he interacted.[168]

---

[167] *See also* Grassian & Friedman, *Effects of Sensory Deprivation in Psychiatric Seclusion and Solitary Confinement*, 8 Int'l Journal of Law & Psychiatry 49 (1986); Brodsky and Scoggin, *Inmates in Protective Custody: First Data on Emotional Effects*, 1 Forensic Reports 267 (1988); Toch, *Mosaic of Despair: Human Breakdowns in Prison*, Washington, D.C.: American Psychological Association, 1992; Benjamin & Lux, *Solitary Confinement as Psychological Punishment*, 13 Cal.W.L.Rev. 265, 268-277 and citations therein (1977); Grassian Decl. at 15-18, and bibliography attached thereto; Haney Decl., Appendix D.

[168] Dr. Sheff also testified that he did not attribute the complex he observed to conditions in the SHU; however,

Regardless of whether there is an "exact syndrome" associated with incarceration in solitary confinement or security housing units, the Court is well satisfied that a severe *1232 reduction in environmental stimulation and social isolation can have serious psychiatric consequences for some people, and that these consequences are typically manifested in the symptoms identified above.

Turning to the case at bar, it is clear that confinement in the Pelican Bay SHU severely deprives inmates of normal human contact and substantially reduces their level of environmental stimulation, as detailed above. It is also clear that there are a significant number of inmates in the Pelican Bay SHU that are suffering from serious mental illness. *See* section II(C)(1), *supra*. At least one Pelican Bay psychologist, Dr. Ruggles, also observed that there was a "psychiatric deterioration that occurred in correlation with placement . . . [in the] SHU." Tr. 17-2914. He did not, however, explain the nature of the deterioration or know the cause. *Id.* Indeed, the critical question is whether any of the psychiatric problems being experienced by SHU inmates are attributable to conditions in the SHU as opposed to other factors, and if so, the extent and degree of such problems.

To address these issues, Dr. Grassian conducted in-depth interviews with 50 inmates in the SHU over the course of two weeks (in September 1992 and May 1993), and reviewed their medical records. Fourteen inmates were interviewed twice. The inmates were not chosen randomly but were selected because there was some basis to believe that they might be experiencing psychiatric problems.[169]

Dr. Grassian concluded that in forty of the fifty inmates, SHU conditions had either massively exacerbated a previous psychiatric illness or precipitated psychiatric symptoms associated with RES conditions. Grassian Tr. 12-1862-63, 1891-92. Of these 40 inmates, 17 were actively psychotic and/or acutely suicidal and in urgent need of inpatient hospital treatment. The other 23 suffered serious psychopathological reactions to the SHU. Grassian Decl. at 25. Of the 40 seriously ill inmates, 28 suffered from perceptual disturbances, 35 had problems with concentration, 22 experienced intrusive obsessional thoughts, 29 suffered from paranoia, 28 had impulse dyscontrol, 25 had anxiety/panic disorder, and 24 suffered from overt psychotic disorganization. Ten of the 50 inmates did not appear to be experiencing any significant psychiatric deterioration attributable to the SHU. Grassian Tr. 12-1862-3.

Dr. Grassian concluded that an inmate's symptoms were attributable to the SHU only where the inmate's records indicated that the symptoms, or the exacerbation of mental illness, surfaced after confinement in the SHU, and where the inmate was experiencing a constellation of symptoms that is rarely found outside conditions of social isolation and restricted environmental stimulation.

A few examples of Dr. Grassian's findings are summarized as follows:

Inmate 1[170]

Inmate 1, whose records indicate a history of psychiatric illness as an adolescent, was placed in the SHU in November 1990. By April 1992, he was suffering from a paranoid hallucinatory psychosis. He was convinced his food was being poisoned, and was drinking from his toilet and refusing to eat. He reported having auditory and visual hallucinations, claimed that a microphone had been placed in his cell, and was experiencing extreme anxiety. Pelican Bay staff initially asserted that he was malingering, but then also prescribed powerful antipsychotic medicine. A visiting psychiatrist concluded that he had classical symptoms of paranoid schizophrenia and was not being manipulative. On August 28, 1992, he was admitted to the infirmary on suicide watch. At that time, a staff psychiatrist diagnosed him as suffering from chronic undifferentiated schizophrenia and recommended that he be *1233 transferred to CMF-Vacaville for evaluation and treatment. When Dr. Grassian interviewed him on September 17, 1992, Inmate 1 was still in the SHU, actively psychotic and delusionally fearful of being killed. He was eventually transferred to CMF-Vacaville in November, where his clinical state dramatically improved and his psychotic symptoms remitted. The evaluation there indicated that he was: "an immature, needy emotionally underdeveloped young man who simply cannot cope psychologically with the situation that

---

he explains that he "did not take a scientific research attitude towards the symptom complex but treated the symptoms as they appeared and treated inmates as individuals, not guiding myself according to whether there was a need to remove the person from a noxious stimulus or not." Tr. 25-4115-16.

[169] When asked to focus on the psychological aspects of the environment, defendants' expert undertook a similar approach. While touring the prison, he specifically tried to find the people who were most in need. It "was not meant to be a random selection survey." Dvoskin Tr. 27-4369.

[170] For privacy purposes, specific inmates will be referred to by number rather than by name in this section.

he has made for himself and which he probably never anticipated. . . . He is genuinely afraid, even panicked, by the Pelican Bay SHU, which seems to have crushed him." Because his mental state improved at CMF-Vacaville, he was transferred back to the SHU in March of 1993. When Dr. Grassian interviewed him a second time in May of 1993, Inmate 1 had again degenerated into a psychotic state; he was agitated, terrified, and hallucinatory. Grassian Decl. at 38-39, 61-64.

Inmate 2

In December 1986, while at the SHU in Folsom Prison, Inmate 2 developed a brief confusional psychosis and saw "little black fuzzy things." Other than this, his records do not indicate any psychiatric history prior to his incarceration. Prior to his transfer to Pelican Bay, he asked for psychiatric help for his quick and uncontrollable temper and because he had attempted suicide in the past. The examining doctor concluded he did not have a psychiatric problem and recommended no treatment.

Within several weeks of his transfer to the SHU, he had difficulty with insomnia, suicidal and homicidal thoughts, and claustrophobic fears. He was given a low dose of an antidepressant medication. Inmate 2 subsequently developed an overt confusional, paranoid psychosis. At one point he had a severe psychotic episode, during which he became severely confused and hallucinatory; he was eventually cell extracted when he began kicking his cell door in a highly agitated state.[171] He continued to experience a fear and preoccupation with "entities" and "demons." In July and August of 1992, a staff psychologist assessed him as being in no apparent distress with normal behavior. However, when Dr. Grassian interviewed him in September, he found that Inmate 2 was continuing to suffer from a preoccupation with "entities" and intense fear. In a second interview the following May, Dr. Grassian found that Inmate 2's thinking was more disorganized than it had been the previous September. He reported "I still have trouble with entities and demons—evil spirits—comic books I read are about the antichrist. I can see them through the walls, black evil. Used to be real heavy. If you pay attention to them, you give in. Mostly it is the devil—no doubt about it. . . . Got to fight back. . . ." He also described increasing obsessive fears and anxiety about his health: "I fear I'm going to die. I trip on it. I can't sleep O.K., I can't relax. My back hurts, my neck hurts. . . ." Grassian Decl. at 56-61.

Inmate 3

Inmate 3 has been housed almost continually in the SHU since October 1991. He is unable to read or write and has a history of cognitive difficulties, severe emotional volatility and impulsivity, and wrist cutting. He was psychiatrically hospitalized in 1987. He is "precisely the type of individual most vulnerable to becoming psychotically disorganized in [the] SHU." Grassian Decl. at 110. Once in the SHU his mental state deteriorated. Dr. Grassian found that he was suffering, among other things, from acute psychotic disorganization, perceptual distortions ("like on Television, if things get closer to you, it makes me think I'm going crazy"), and obsessional ruminations. Grassian Decl. at 41, 108-110. He was eventually prescribed a mood stabilizing medication in August of 1992. *Id.* at 109-10.

Inmate 4

Inmate 4 arrived at the Pelican Bay SHU already vulnerable to decompensation. He was institutionalized for much of his childhood and adolescence in state psychiatric hospitals, suffering from developmental disability, a seizure disorder, and behavioral problems, but until his transfer to the SHU in May of 1992, he seemed to have had few **1234** behavioral disturbances since 1988. Given his psychiatric history, however, Dr. Grassian noted that "it is not at all surprising that within just a few weeks of his incarceration at Pelican Bay [SHU], he became increasingly psychotic, increasingly agitated, and increasingly out of control." Decl. at 145.

On June 8, 1992, an MTA was called to Inmate 4's cell after he had ripped the sprinkler head off of the ceiling of his cell and tried to swallow it. He had also attempted to gouge his wrists with a broken plastic spoon. He was, according to Dr. Fulton, "in severe distress, suffering from auditory and visual hal-

---

[171] *See* section II(A)(1)(4), *supra*, for a description of a cell extraction.

lucinations." Trial Exh. P-480 at 3532. Although the inmate was put on suicide watch in the infirmary, he was later released to the SHU. By the end of July the inmate again felt as if he was "tripping out . . . losing it," and told an MTA that he planned to hurt himself. *Id.* at 3419. On August 1, 1992, custody officers noticed that he was extremely agitated and tearing up his mattress; on August 13, he was found kicking his cell door in an attempt to escape from "demons"; on August 25, the inmate injured himself by banging his handcuffed hands against the cell wall while trying to hit the "demons."

The inmate's psychotic behavior escalated over the next few days. MTAs and correctional officers reported that at times they found him "out of control," screaming, or incoherent. Trial Exh. P-480 at 3414, P-158 at 19344. The inmate repeatedly said that he was being attacked by demons and that he would try to kill himself to get away from them. He was observed crying in the corner of his cell on August 29, and an MTA noted that "[the] inmate appears sincere in his suicidal ideation." Trial Exh. P-158 at 19517. On September 9, he again tried to kill himself by swallowing a piece of the fire sprinkler.

When Dr. Grassian interviewed Inmate 4 less than a week after his last suicide attempt, the inmate was disheveled, despondent, and desperate. He explained that "my heart starts racing, I get dizzy spells, scared, nervous, shaking, crying. I hear voices telling me to tear up my mattress. Demons come out. I see them. . . . I never saw them before SHU." Grassian Decl. at 148. Inmate 4 was eventually recommended for transfer to the California Medical Facility at Vacaville by the Pelican Bay staff.

In a separate study undertaken by Dr. Haney, 100 randomly chosen SHU inmates were interviewed using a highly structured questionnaire format.[172] Inmates were asked a series of 27 questions, mostly drawn from existing literature relating to RES, which focused on symptoms of psychological distress and the negative effects of prolonged social isolation, including confused thought process, hallucinations, irrational anger, emotional flatness, violent fantasies, social withdrawal, oversensitivity to stimuli, and chronic depression. The study included a control question—whether the inmate had experienced a tingling sensation in the ends of fingers or toes, which is not a symptom of psychological trauma or a psychopathological effect of social isolation. The results showed that a majority of SHU inmates reported a number of the above symptoms, and that many reported "a constellation of symptoms that appears to be related to developing mood or emotional disorders—concerns over emotional flatness or losing ability to feel, swings in emotional responding, and feelings of depressions or sadness that did not easily go away." Dr. Haney also found that "sizeable minorities" reported symptoms that are typically only associated with more extreme forms of psychopathology—hallucinations, perceptual distortions, and thoughts of suicide. Haney Decl. at 42.[173]

*1235 On its face, the study does not indicate that a majority of SHU inmates are experiencing the "more extreme" types of symptoms associated with severe isolation and reduced environmental stimulation. The study also does not specify either the frequency or the degree to which the reported symptoms were experienced; thus, it is difficult to exactly assess the extent of the mental trauma being reported by most inmates. The study also did not review inmate records to compare symptoms reported outside the SHU or otherwise include a control study of non-SHU inmates. The relatively high response to the control question (19 percent) also suggests that the response level may include some exaggeration.[174]

Notwithstanding the above, the study is not without some probative value. First, it strongly suggests that many of the symptoms observed by Dr. Grassian are not isolated to the inmates he interviewed but are also likely experienced to some degree by other inmates in the SHU. The study also suggests that the more severe symptoms are only experienced by a minority of the SHU population.

---

[172] Dr. Haney originally interviewed 65 inmates for approximately one hour each; 40 of the 65 inmates were randomly selected while 25 were preselected. Because a high number of prisoners spontaneously complained about various negative psychological and psychiatric symptoms in the SHU, which correlated with published literature discussing extreme forms of social deprivation and psychological trauma, Dr. Haney independently decided to conduct the more systematic random study described above.

[173] The 100 SHU inmates exhibited the following symptoms: talking to self (63%), hallucinations (41%), ruminations (88%), violent fantasies (61%), oversensitivity to stimuli (86%), perceptual distortions (44%), irrational anger (88%), confused thought process (84%), emotional flatness (73%), mood/emotional swings (71%), chronic depression (77%), suicidal thoughts (27%), overall deterioration (67%), and social withdrawal (83%). Haney Decl. at 37, 41.

[174] Dr. Haney hypothesized that the relatively high response to the control question could have been caused by the fact that the lack of activity in the SHU may have led some inmates to experience circulatory problems, one symptom of which is a tingling sensation in fingers or toes.

Based on studies undertaken in this case, and the entirety of the record bearing on this claim, the Court finds that many, if not most, inmates in the SHU experience some degree of psychological trauma in reaction to their extreme social isolation and the severely restricted environmental stimulation in the SHU. As one court recently observed in connection with an Illinois state prison, "the record shows, what anyway seems pretty obvious, that isolating a human being from other human beings year after year or even month after month can cause substantial psychological damage, even if the isolation is not total." *Davenport v. DeRobertis*, 844 F.2d 1310, 1313 (7th Cir.), *cert. denied*, 488 U.S. 908, 109 S.Ct. 260, 102 L.Ed.2d 248 (1988).

It is also equally clear that although the SHU conditions are relatively extreme, they do not have a uniform effect on all inmates. For an occasional inmate, the SHU environment may actually prove beneficial. For others, the adverse psychological impact of the SHU will be relatively moderate. They may experience some symptoms but not others, and/or experience those symptoms to a minor or moderate degree. As Dr. Grassian testified, "[t]here clearly are people who are able to tolerate solitary confinement [or] small-group confinement and manifest only some of the symptoms. They don't reach the point of psychotic disorganization that we see in some of the other prisoners." Tr. 12-1869. For some, however, the conditions in the Pelican Bay SHU will likely lead to serious mental illness[175] or a massive exacerbation of existing mental illness.[176]

The experts are essentially in agreement with respect to the types of persons that are most likely to suffer a serious mental injury from continued exposure to the conditions in the Pelican Bay SHU. Probably most vulnerable are inmates already suffering from mental illness. Dr. Haney testified that prisoners suffering from severe mental disorders should never be subjected to conditions that are as harsh as those imposed in the Pelican Bay SHU. Haney Decl. at 67. Defendants' expert Dr. Dvoskin agreed that segregation may exacerbate pre-existing mental illness and that inmates who are in acute psychiatric distress or suicidal depressions should not be placed in the SHU, absent a few "very, very rare exceptions." Tr. 27-4466, 4473-74.

*1236 Certain inmates who are not already mentally ill are also at high risk for incurring serious psychiatric problems, including becoming psychotic, if exposed to the SHU for any significant duration. As defendants' expert conceded, there are certain people who simply "can [no]t handle" a place like the Pelican Bay SHU. Persons at a higher risk of mentally deteriorating in the SHU are those who suffer from prior psychiatric problems, borderline personality disorder, chronic depression, chronic schizophrenia, brain damage or mental retardation, or an impulse-ridden personality. Dvoskin Tr. 27-4374-75, 4473-74; Grassian Tr. 12-1869-71, 1882. Consistent with the above, most of the inmates identified by Dr. Grassian as experiencing serious adverse consequences from the SHU were either already suffering from mental illness or fall within one of the above categories. In contrast, persons with "mature, healthy personality functioning and of at least average intelligence" are best able to tolerate SHU-like conditions. Grassian Decl. at 21; *see also* Tr. 12-1870. Significantly, the CDC's own Mental Health Services Branch recommended excluding from the Pelican Bay SHU "all inmates who have demonstrated evidence of serious mental illness or inmates who are assessed by mental health staff as likely to suffer a serious mental health problem if subjected to RES conditions." Trial Exh. P-4495 at 3951.

3. *Defendants' State of Mind*

Defendants were aware that the SHU had, "by design, [been] constructed so that the inmates' environmental stimulation would be minimized," Trial Exh. P-4495 at 3948, and that inmates would be subjected to virtually total social isolation. For example, defendants knew, among other things, that inmates in the SHU would have very little direct human contact with staff or inmates, other than possibly a cellmate, for potentially years on end, that visitors would be infrequent, and that there would be no window or view of the outside world from either the exercise pen or the cell.

---

[175] Serious forms of mental illness are "frequently characterized by breaks with reality or perceptions of reality that lead the individual to serious disruption of normal functioning if not treated." Sheff Tr. 24-4117.

[176] Undoubtedly, the lack of adequate mental health care has aggravated the psychiatric problems of many inmates; we are not persuaded, however, that this fully explains the serious psychiatric distress being suffered by certain inmates in the SHU. Rather, in many of the cases addressed by Dr. Grassian, the suffering is attributable, in substantial or significant part, to conditions in the SHU.

Defendants were also aware that such conditions could pose a significant risk to the mental health of inmates, particularly for those who are mentally ill or otherwise at a high risk for suffering substantial mental deterioration in the SHU. Defendant Marshall, for example, knew before the SHU opened that RES was a potential risk for inmates, and had "some concerns that [mental decompensation in the SHU] was always a possibility." Tr. 22-3821; *see also* Trial Exh. P-4596 at 81280. The CDC's Mental Health Services Branch ("MHSB") addressed the potential effects of RES on inmates confined in the Pelican Bay SHU in a September 1989 memorandum entitled "Possible Effects of Reduced Environmental Stimulation on Inmates Confined to the Pelican Bay State Prison." Trial. Exh. P-4495. That memorandum recommended excluding from the SHU all inmates who were either seriously mentally ill or assessed as likely to suffer a serious mental health problem if subject to RES conditions. Trial Exh. P-4495 at 3951.

The recommendation was largely based on a "dramatic contrast" between two other SHUs which also impose substantial restrictions on human contact and environmental stimulation—one in Marion, Illinois and the other in Florence, Arizona (which served as the model for Pelican Bay). *Id.* at 3950; Trial Exh. P-3814 at 3954-55. The MHSB report found that the Marion SHU, which excludes mentally ill inmates and those whom the mental health staff feel are at risk for developing a serious psychiatric condition, does not experience a "significant level of psychological decompensation as a result of RES." *Id.* However, the Florence SHU, which does not exclude such persons, has experienced "a significantly greater level of adverse behavioral and psychiatric consequences than the Marion facility. In particular, [Florence] cites experiencing problems with their Borderline Personality Disorder inmates who had an increased frequency of suicidal behavior." *Id.*

As the record shows, however, the MHSB recommendation was essentially disregarded. As time progressed, defendants were aware that some inmates were developing serious psychiatric problems or suffering a serious exacerbation of an existing mental illness after transfer to the SHU. Notwithstanding *1237 this experience, and defendants' knowledge that RES conditions have the potential for adversely affecting inmate mental health, defendants made no effort to investigate or address whether SHU conditions were adversely affecting inmates suffering from serious psychiatric problems. Nor is there any indication that the MHSB recommendation was given any serious consideration. Rather, inmates who were suffering severe effects from conditions in the SHU were, for the most part, simply medicated with psychotropic drugs or ignored.

***

*1244

III.

CONCLUSIONS OF LAW

A. *EIGHTH AMENDMENT OVERVIEW*

By virtue of their conviction, inmates forfeit many of their constitutional liberties and rights: they are isolated in prisons, and subject to stringent restrictions that govern every aspect of their daily lives. Nonetheless, those who have transgressed the law are still fellow human beings—most of whom will one day return to society.[195] Even those prisoners at the "bottom of the social heap . . . have, nonetheless, a human dignity." *Toussaint v. McCarthy (Toussaint VI)*, 926 F.2d 800, 801 (9th Cir.1990), *cert. denied*, 502 U.S. 874, 112 S.Ct. 213, 116 L.Ed.2d 171 (1991). In recognition of this fundamental principle, our jurisprudence is clear: while incarceration may extinguish or curtail many rights, the Eighth Amendment's protection *1245 against cruel and unusual punishment still retains its "full force" behind prison doors. *Michenfelder v. Sumner*, 860 F.2d 328, 335 (9th Cir.1988).

It is a right animated by "broad and idealistic concepts of dignity, civilized standards, humanity, and decency." *Estelle v. Gamble*, 429 U.S. 97, 102, 97 S.Ct. 285, 290, 50 L.Ed.2d 251 (1976); *see also*

---

[195] The Director of the CDC estimates that there are 80,000 prisoners entering the California prison system each year and approximately 70,000 who are released.

Hudson v. McMillian, 503 U.S. 1, 11, 112 S.Ct. 995, 1001, 117 L.Ed.2d 156 (1992); *Patchette v. Nix*, 952 F.2d 158, 163 (8th Cir.1991) (Eighth Amendment " 'draw[s] its meaning from the evolving standards of decency that mark the process of a maturing society' "); *Michenfelder*, 860 F.2d at 335; *Spain v. Procunier*, 600 F.2d 189, 200 (9th Cir.1979) (Eighth Amendment is based on the "fundamental premise that prisoners are not to be treated as less than human beings"). It is a right that recognizes that in a country such as ours, which aspires to the highest standards of civilization, there is simply no place for abuse and mistreatment, even in the darkest of jailhouse cells.

Consistent with these humanitarian concepts, our courts have long acknowledged that when the State, by imprisonment, prevents a person from caring for himself, the Constitution imposes " 'a corresponding duty to assume some responsibility for his safety and general well being.' " *Helling v. McKinney*, 509 U.S. 25, 113 S.Ct. 2475, 2480, 125 L.Ed.2d 22 (1993). "[H]aving stripped [prisoners] of virtually every means of self-protection and foreclosed their access to outside aid," society may not simply lock away offenders and let "the state of nature take its course." *Farmer v. Brennan*, 511 U.S. 825, 114 S.Ct. 1970, 1977, 128 L.Ed.2d 811 (1994). Rather, government officials must ensure that prisons, while perhaps "restrictive and even harsh," *Rhodes v. Chapman*, 452 U.S. 337, 347, 101 S.Ct. 2392, 2399, 69 L.Ed.2d 59 (1981), do not degenerate into places that violate basic standards of decency and humanity. In short, while the Eighth Amendment " 'does not mandate comfortable prisons' . . . neither does it permit inhumane ones." *Farmer*, 511 U.S. at —, 114 S.Ct. at 1976 (citation omitted).

Thus, it is well past dispute that the Eighth Amendment requires that prison officials provide inmates with such minimum essentials as adequate food, shelter, clothing, medical care, and safety.

> When the State by the affirmative exercise of its power so restrains an individual's liberty that it renders him unable to care for himself, and at the same time fails to provide for his basic human needs—e.g. food, clothing, shelter, medical care, and reasonable safety—it transgresses the substantive limits on state action set by the Eighth Amendment.

Helling, 509 U.S. at —, 113 S.Ct. at 2475 (quoting *DeShaney v. Winnebago County Dep't. of Social Services*, 489 U.S. 189, 199-200, 109 S.Ct. 998, 1005-06, 103 L.Ed.2d 249 (1989)); *see also Farmer*, 511 U.S. at —, 114 S.Ct. at 1976; *Toussaint v. McCarthy (Toussaint IV)*, 801 F.2d 1080, 1107 (9th Cir.1986) ("human needs that prison officials must satisfy include food, clothing, sanitation, medical care, and personal safety"), *cert. denied*, 481 U.S. 1069, 107 S.Ct. 2462, 95 L.Ed.2d 871 (1987).

The Eighth Amendment also prohibits those who operate our prisons from using "excessive physical force against inmates." *Farmer*, 511 U.S. at —, 114 S.Ct. at 1976; *Hoptowit v. Ray*, 682 F.2d 1237, 1246, 1250 (9th Cir.1982) (prison officials have "a duty to take reasonable steps to protect inmates from physical abuse"); *see also Vaughan v. Ricketts*, 859 F.2d 736, 741 (9th Cir.1988), *cert. denied*, 490 U.S. 1012, 109 S.Ct. 1655, 104 L.Ed.2d 169 (1989) ("prison administrators' indifference to brutal behavior by guards toward inmates [is] sufficient to state an Eighth Amendment claim"). As courts have succinctly observed, "[p]ersons are sent to prison as punishment, not *for* punishment." *Gordon v. Faber*, 800 F.Supp. 797, 800 (N.D.Iowa 1992) (citation omitted), *aff'd*, 973 F.2d 686 (8th Cir.1992). "Being violently assaulted in prison is simply not 'part of the penalty that criminal offenders pay for their offenses against society.' " *Farmer*, 511 U.S. at —, 114 S.Ct. at 1977 (quoting *Rhodes*, 452 U.S. at 347, 101 S.Ct. at 2399).

In order to prevail on any Eighth Amendment claim alleging cruel and unusual ***1246** punishment, a plaintiff must satisfy two requirements:

> First, the deprivation alleged must be, objectively, sufficiently serious; a prison official's act or omission must result in the denial of the minimal civilized measure of life's necessities. For a claim . . . based on a failure to prevent harm, the inmate must show that he is incarcerated under conditions posing a substantial risk of serious harm . . ..
>
> The second requirement follows from the principle that only the unnecessary and wanton infliction of pain implicates the Eighth Amendment. To violate the Cruel and Unusual Punishments Clause, a prison official must have a sufficiently culpable state of mind.

Farmer, 511 U.S. at —, 114 S.Ct. at 1977 (internal quotations and citations omitted); *see also Wilson v. Seiter*, 501 U.S. 294, 297, 111 S.Ct. 2321, 2323, 115 L.Ed.2d 271 (1991). Thus, every Eighth Amendment claim embodies an objective and subjective component. *Wilson*, 501 U.S. at 297-98, 111 S.Ct. at 2323-2326. The former focuses on whether there has been a deprivation or infliction of pain serious enough to implicate constitutional concerns, while the latter requires inquiry into the defendant's state of mind to determine whether the infliction of pain was "unnecessary and wanton." *Jordan v. Gardner*, 986 F.2d 1521, 1525-28 (9th Cir.1993) (en banc).

In considering whether the objective component has been met, the Court must focus on discrete and essential human needs such as health, safety, food, warmth or exercise. *Wilson*, 501 U.S. at 304, 111 S.Ct. at 2327. "Courts may not find Eighth Amendment violations based on the 'totality of conditions' at a prison." *Hoptowit*, 682 F.2d at 1246 (quoting *Wright v. Rushen*, 642 F.2d 1129, 1132 (9th Cir.1981)). Thus, while courts may consider conditions in combination "when they have a mutually enforcing effect that produces the deprivation of a single, identifiable human need . . .[,] [n]othing so amorphous as 'overall conditions' can rise to the level of cruel and unusual punishment when no specific deprivation of a single human need exists." *Wilson*, 501 U.S. at 304-05, 111 S.Ct. at 2327. The question whether the objective component of an Eighth Amendment claim has been met presents an issue of law for the court to decide. *Hickey v. Reeder*, 12 F.3d 754, 756 (8th Cir.1993).

In contrast, the state of mind inquiry presents a question of fact, and is "subject to demonstration in the usual ways, including inference from circumstantial evidence." *Farmer*, 511 U.S. at —, 114 S.Ct. at 1981. For most Eighth Amendment claims, the plaintiff satisfies the culpability requirement by proving that the defendants' actions (or omissions) constitute "deliberate indifference." This "baseline" standard, *Jordan*, 986 F.2d at 1527, applies in cases alleging inadequate protection from injury from other inmates or inhumane conditions of confinement that deprive an inmate of a basic necessity of life, such as shelter, food, health or exercise. *See Farmer*, 511 U.S. at —, 114 S.Ct. at 1977; *Jordan*, 986 F.2d at 1528.

As the Supreme Court recently clarified, the test for determining "deliberate indifference" is essentially equivalent to the standard for establishing subjective recklessness in criminal cases. *Farmer*, 511 U.S. at —, 114 S.Ct. at 1980. Thus, the plaintiff must show that:

the [prison] official knows of and disregards an excessive risk to inmate health or safety; the official must both be aware of facts from which the inference could be drawn that a substantial risk of serious harm exists, and he must also draw the inference.

Id. at —, 114 S.Ct. at 1979. In other words, the defendant must "consciously disregard a substantial risk of serious harm." *Id.* at —, 114 S.Ct. at 1980 (internal quotation omitted). Such a standard presupposes that the defendant has not acted reasonably in the face of a known risk. Thus, a prison official can avoid liability if he "responded reasonably to the risk, even if the harm ultimately was not averted." *Id.* at —, 114 S.Ct. at 1982-83. "Whether one puts it in terms of duty or deliberate indifference, prison officials who act reasonably cannot be found liable under the Cruel and *1247 Unusual Punishments Clause." *Id.* at —, 114 S.Ct. at 1983.

In sum, deliberate indifference occurs where the prison official "knows that inmates face a substantial risk of serious harm and disregards that risk by failing to take reasonable measures to abate it." *Id.* at —, 114 S.Ct. at 1984. This standard does not require plaintiffs to "show that a prison official acted or failed to act believing that harm actually would befall an inmate; it is enough that the official acted or failed to act despite his knowledge of a substantial risk of serious harm." *Farmer*, 511 U.S. at —, 114 S.Ct. at 1981. Nor does this standard mean that "prison officials will be free to ignore obvious dangers." *Id.* While the obviousness of a risk is not conclusive, a factfinder may "conclude that a prison official knew of a substantial risk from the very fact that the risk was obvious." *Id.* at — and n. 8, 114 S.Ct. at 1981-82 and n. 8. Similarly, a defendant would "not escape liability if the evidence showed that he merely refused to verify underlying facts that he strongly suspected to be true, or declined to confirm inferences of risk that he strongly suspected to exist." *Id.* at — n. 8, 114 S.Ct. at 1982 n. 8; *see also McGill v. Duckworth*, 944 F.2d 344, 351 (7th Cir.1991) ("Going out of your way to avoid acquiring unwelcome knowledge is a species of intent"), *cert. denied*, 503 U.S. 907, 112 S.Ct. 1265, 117 L.Ed.2d 493 (1992).

Although the deliberate indifference standard governs most claims, an even higher degree of culpability must be shown in one type of claim: when an inmate seeks to hold an individual prison officer liable for using excessive physical force against the inmate during a particular incident. *Hudson*, 503 U.S. at 1, 112 S.Ct. at 995; *Whitley v. Albers*, 475 U.S. 312, 320, 106 S.Ct. 1078, 1084, 89 L.Ed.2d 251 (1986).

In *Whitley*, an inmate was shot and seriously wounded during the course of a prison riot. The inmate sought damages under 42 U.S.C. § 1983 against the individual prison guards and officials directly involved in the incident, alleging use of excessive force. 475 U.S. at 316-317, 106 S.Ct. at 1083. The Supreme Court held that in order to prevail, the plaintiff must show more than deliberate indifference;

he must show that the force used against him was applied, not in a "good faith effort to maintain or restore order, [but] maliciously and sadistically for the very purpose of causing harm." *Id.* at 320-21, 106 S.Ct. at 1085 (internal quotations omitted).

In 1992, the Supreme Court revisited the state of mind issue in *Hudson*, in which an inmate alleged that prison guards had beaten him for no reason during an escort. Extending *Whitley* beyond the context of a riot, the Supreme Court concluded that the "maliciousness" standard controlled, not just in major prison disturbances, but in smaller incidents as well. The Court held that "whenever prison officials stand accused of using excessive physical force . . . the core judicial inquiry is . . . whether force was applied in a good-faith effort to maintain or restore discipline, or maliciously and sadistically to cause harm." *Hudson*, 503 U.S. at 7, 112 S.Ct. at 999. Put another way, plaintiffs must show that "officials used force with 'a knowing willingness that [harm] occur.' " *Farmer*, 511 U.S. at —, 114 S.Ct. at 1978.

In determining whether the maliciousness standard has been met in any given case, the factfinder may draw inferences from circumstances surrounding the challenged conduct. To assist this process, the Supreme Court identified five factors that should be taken into consideration: (1) the extent of the injury suffered, (2) the need for the application of force, (3) the relationship between that need and the amount of force used, (4) the threat reasonably perceived by the responsible officials, and (5) any efforts made to temper the severity of a forceful response. *Hudson*, 503 U.S. at 7, 112 S.Ct. at 999; *Romano v. Howarth*, 998 F.2d 101, 105 (2nd Cir.1993).

B. *EXCESSIVE FORCE*

Plaintiffs advance two related but distinct theories of Eighth Amendment liability with respect to their excessive force claim. The first is that there is a pattern of prison staff using excessive force against inmates, and that defendants, in permitting this pattern to develop and persist, have acted not only with deliberate indifference, ***1248** but also with the malicious purpose of causing harm. The second is that defendants have failed to establish adequate systems for controlling use of force by prison staff against inmates—despite knowing the grave risks to inmate safety that this failure creates—and that inmates have suffered serious injuries as a result. Because we find that liability is established under the first theory, we do not address the second.[196]

---

[196] Unlike the first theory, plaintiffs' second theory does not depend on proof of a pattern of excessive force; rather, plaintiffs need only show that defendants' failure to adequately control the use of force, and their deliberate indifference to the risk to inmate safety that such failure poses, resulted in some serious inmate injuries. Plaintiffs have not identified any class-action excessive force case that has premised Eighth Amendment liability on this theory. Rather, evidence that prison administrators have failed to implement adequate use-of-force controls has been used, not to establish an independent basis for liability to the class, but to explain the underlying causes of a pattern of excessive force and to assess the defendants' state of mind. *See, e.g., Fisher v. Koehler*, 692 F.Supp. 1519, 1551 (S.D.N.Y.1988), *aff'd*, 902 F.2d 2 (2nd Cir.1990).

We note, however, that case precedent provides general support for such a theory. First, as the Ninth Circuit has ruled, "[p]rison officials have a duty to take reasonable steps to protect inmates from physical abuse" from prison guards. *Hoptowit*, 682 F.2d at 1250; *see also Slakan v. Porter*, 737 F. 2d 368, 377 (4th Cir. 1984), *cert. denied*, 470 U.S. 1035, 105 S.Ct. 1413, 84 L.Ed.2d 796 (1985) (prison administrators had firmly established duty to ensure that weapons were not misused against inmates).

Second, under 42 U.S.C. § 1983, municipalities can be found liable where the failure to train or supervise subordinates evinces deliberate indifference that leads to constitutional deprivations. *Canton v. Harris*, 489 U.S. 378, 390, 109 S.Ct. 1197, 1205, 103 L.Ed.2d 412 (1989) ("[I]t may happen that . . . the need for more or different training is so obvious, and the inadequacy so likely to result in the violation of constitutional rights, that the policy makers of the city can reasonably [be] said to have been deliberately indifferent to the need"); *Yharra v. Reno Thunderbird Mobile Home Village*, 723 F.2d 675, 680 (9th Cir. 1984). This doctrine of supervisory liability has also been applied in actions against state prison officials. *See, e.g., Walker v. Norris*, 917 F.2d 1449, 1455-56 (6th Cir. 1990) (applying supervisory liability theory in case against Tennessee state prison officials accused of allowing one inmate to kill another, but finding that evidence did not justify overturning directed verdict in their favor); *Slakan*, 737 F.2d at 370, 372-376 (affirming judgment against prison supervisory officials on ground that they were deliberately indifferent to a known risk of harm, as evidenced by their failure to provide prison guards with adequate training and guidance; *LaMarca v. Turner*, 995 F.2d 1526 (11th Cir. 1993), *cert. denied*, __ U.S. __, 114 S.Ct. 1189, 127 L.Ed.2d 539 (1994) (failure to supervise guards led to impermissible levels of violence between inmates, creating supervisory liability under Eighth Amendment). Of course, in the prison context, a showing of deliberate indifference must satisfy the subjective test enunciated in *Farmer*, rather than the objective standard contained in Canton. *Farmer*, __ U.S. at __, __-__, 114 S.Ct. at 1979, 1981-82.

***

*1252

a. *Pattern of Excessive Force*

The Court concludes that prisoners at Pelican Bay have been subjected to excessive force including assaults, beatings, and naked cagings in inclement weather—on a scale of sufficient proportions to demonstrate a pattern rather than a collection of isolated incidents. In reaching this conclusion, we note that plaintiffs need not show that the prison is a place "where sadistic guards regularly torture inmates without cause" or a "dark and evil world completely alien to the free world." *Fisher*, 692 F.Supp. at 1532, 1563 (internal quotations omitted); *Withers v. Levine*, 615 F.2d 158, 161 (4th Cir.), *cert. denied*, 449 U.S. 849, 101 S.Ct. 136, 66 L.Ed.2d 59 (1980) (plaintiff need not demonstrate a reign of violence and terror). On the other hand, plaintiffs must show more than a "mere collection of isolated and aberrant acts which are not characteristic of the institution[ ]." *Ruiz*, 503 F.Supp. at 1302.

As discussed in our findings, plaintiffs have amply shown that the misuse of force at *1253 Pelican Bay is not merely aberrational, but an inevitable and all too common consequence of defendants' actions and omissions which tolerate and encourage the use of grossly excessive and unnecessary force. *Fisher*, 692 F.Supp. at 1532. *See also Hoptowit*, 682 F.2d at 1249-50; *Ruiz*, 503 F.Supp. at 1302 (finding that violence by prison officers was routine and not restricted to dangerous situations).

***

*1254

The Court recognizes that correctional officers must react, sometimes quite forcefully, to subdue an uncooperative or combative inmate. Nothing herein is intended to detract from this basic proposition. However, it is not a license for correctional staff to immediately resort to the maximum, rather than the minimum, amount of force needed to restore order, and to do so with a knowing willingness that harm occur. *See Slakan*, 737 F.2d at 372 ("Even when a prisoner's conduct warrants some form of response, evolving norms of decency require prison officials to use techniques and procedures that are both humane and restrained."). At Pelican Bay, officers immediately resorted—with alarming regularity—to unnecessary and excessive force with the purpose of causing harm. Indeed, the degree of force used by correctional staff was often so far beyond any penological justification that it was clearly a pretext for inflicting punishment and pain.

***

*1255

3. *Conclusion*

While the Eighth Amendment will countenance prisons that are restrictive, and even harsh, it does not permit the pattern of needless and officially sanctioned brutality that has invaded operations at Pelican Bay. Not only have plaintiffs established a pattern of excessive force at Pelican Bay that has caused sufficient harm to demonstrate the "infliction of pain" on a classwide basis, but they have also shown that this pattern is attributable, not to inadvertence or mistake, but to defendants' deliberate indif-

---

Such supervisory liability is premised, not on a theory of *respondeat superior*, but rather on "a recognition that supervisory indifference or tacit authorization of subordinates' misconduct may be a causative factor in the constitutional injuries they inflict on those committed to their care." *Slakan*, 737 F.2d at 372. Indeed, just as a lack of training and supervision of municipal police officers can lead directly to unjustified and unnecessary injuries, the same is true for guards in state prisons. *See, e.g., LaMarca*, 995 F.2d at 1533 (failure to enforce procedures for investigating prison rapes "created an atmosphere of tolerance of rape which enhanced the risk that [such] incidents would occur"); *Slakan*, 737 F.2d at 376 (prison officials' failure to provide clear policies regarding use of water hoses left matter to guards' unbridled discretion, thus inviting abuses against inmates).

ference and knowing willingness that harm occur. It is a conclusion we do not reach lightly. On the contrary, it is with considerable reluctance and regret that we find violations of this nature within an institution of our state. We are persuaded, however, that the testimonial and documentary evidence permit no other result.

C. *MEDICAL AND MENTAL HEALTH CARE*

Like other conditions of confinement, medical care provided to inmates is subject to scrutiny under the Eighth Amendment's prohibition against cruel and unusual punishment. *Helling*, 509 U.S. at —, 113 S.Ct. at 2480; *Wilson*, 501 U.S. at 297, 111 S.Ct. at 2323. This does not mean, however, that every inattention to every medical need implicates the Constitution. Nor does the Eighth Amendment guarantee inmates the best medical care available. Rather, to establish Eighth Amendment liability, plaintiffs must demonstrate that prison officials are "deliberately indifferent" to "serious" medical needs of inmates. *Estelle*, 429 U.S. at 106, 97 S.Ct. at 292; *Toussaint IV*, 801 F.2d at 1111.

It is firmly established that "medical needs" include not only physical health needs, but mental health needs as well. *Hoptowit*, 682 F.2d at 1253; *Balla v. Idaho State Board of Corrections*, 595 F.Supp. 1558, 1576-77 (D.Idaho 1984). As far back as 1977, the Fourth Circuit observed that there is "no underlying distinction between the right to medical care for physical ills and its psychological or psychiatric counterpart. Modern science has rejected the notion that mental or emotional disturbances are the products of afflicted souls, hence beyond the purview of counseling, medication and therapy." *Bowring v. Godwin*, 551 F.2d 44, 47 (4th Cir.1977). Nor can it be questioned that deliberate indifference to a serious mental illness can precipitate as much, if not sometimes more, suffering and distress than indifference to a serious complaint of a solely physical nature. Thus the Ninth Circuit has held that "requirements for mental health care are the same as those for physical health care needs." *Doty v. County of Lassen* 37 F.3d 540, 546 (9th Cir.1994); *Cody v. Hillard*, 599 F.Supp. 1025, 1058 (D.S.D.1984) (adequacy of mental health care system "is governed by the same constitutional standard which applies when determining the adequacy of a prison's medical . . . system"), *aff'd in part and rev'd in part en banc*, 830 F.2d 912 (8th Cir.1987), *cert. denied*, 485 U.S. 906, 108 S.Ct. 1078, 99 L.Ed.2d 237 (1988).

It is clear, and defendants do not dispute, that members of the plaintiff class have "serious" medical and mental health needs.[201] *1256 Rather, the central issue is whether defendants have been deliberately indifferent to those needs. In class actions challenging the entire system of mental or medical health care, courts have traditionally held that deliberate indifference can be shown by proving either a pattern of negligent acts or serious systemic deficiencies in the prison's health care program:

> "[D]eliberate indifference" can be evidenced by 'repeated examples of negligent acts which disclose a pattern of conduct by the prison medical staff' *or* it can be demonstrated by "proving there are such systemic and gross deficiencies in staffing, facilities, equipment, or procedures that the inmate population is effectively denied access to adequate medical care."

Wellman, 715 F.2d at 272 (emphasis added) (citing *Ramos*, 639 F.2d at 575); *Casey v. Lewis*, 834 F.Supp. 1477, 1543 (D.Ariz.1993); *see also Hoptowit v. Ray*, 682 F.2d 1237, 1253 (9th Cir.1982) ("[M]edical services provided at the penitentiary are so deficient that they reflect a deliberate indifference to the serious medical needs of the prisoners"); *Todaro*, 565 F.2d at 52 ("systemic deficiencies in staffing, facilities or procedures [that] make unnecessary suffering inevitable" are evidence of "deliberate indifference").

As discussed above, however, the Supreme Court recently made it clear that the "deliberate indif-

---

[201] Indicia of "serious" medical need include "[t]he existence of an injury that a reasonable doctor or patient would find important and worthy of comment or treatment; the presence of a medical condition that significantly affects an individual's daily activities; or the existence of chronic and substantial pain." *McGuckin v. Smith* 974 F.2d 1050, 1059 1060 (9th Cir.1992). As the evidence shows, plaintiffs, as a class, clearly have serious medical needs. They also have serious mental health needs, in that members of the class suffer from mental disorders and illnesses that go beyond the mere stress or anxiety that is part of the "routine discomfort" of incarceration. *See Doty*, 37 F.3d at 546 (ailments such as nausea and depressed appetite caused by unresolved family situational stress not serious medical need); *Wellman v. Faulkner*, 715 F.2d 269, 272 (7th Cir.1983), *cert. denied*, 468 U.S. 1217, 104 S.Ct. 3587, 82 L.Ed.2d 885 (1984) ("Treatment of the mental disorders of mentally disturbed inmates is a 'serious medical need.' ")

ference" standard requires a showing of culpability that can not be inferred solely from objective conditions. *Farmer*, 511 U.S. at —, 114 S.Ct. at 1979-80. Rather, it can only be found where the defendant actually knows of, and yet disregards, an excessive risk to inmate health or safety. *Id.* at —, 114 S.Ct. at 1979. Accordingly, to prove deliberate indifference, plaintiffs must demonstrate not only that the levels of medical and mental health care are constitutionally inadequate from an objective standpoint—based on either a "pattern of negligent conduct" or "systemic deficiencies"—but also that defendants (1) knew the risk to inmate health that this inadequacy posed, and (2) acted with disregard for this risk. In short, plaintiffs must show that defendants " 'consciously disregard[ed]' a substantial risk of serious harm" to plaintiffs' health or safety. *Id.* at —, 114 S.Ct. at 1980. Accidental or inadvertent failure to provide adequate care will not suffice. *Ramos*, 639 F.2d at 575.

Plaintiffs have met this burden here, with respect to both the treatment of physical health needs and of mental health needs. As discussed below, they have shown that appalling systemic deficiencies render the mental health care system and the medical care system incapable of satisfying minimum constitutional standards. They have also shown that defendants have consciously disregarded the substantial risk of harm posed by these deficiencies. We therefore conclude that defendants have been deliberately indifferent to the serious mental and medical health needs of the population at Pelican Bay.

1. *Systemic Deficiencies in Medical and Mental Health Care Systems*

The Eighth Amendment does not require that prison officials provide the most desirable medical and mental health care; nor should judges simply "constitutionalize" the standards set forth by professional associations such as the American Medical Association or the American Public Health Association. *Hoptowit*, 682 F.2d at 1253; *see also Bell v. Wolfish*, 441 U.S. 520, 543-544 n. 27, 99 S.Ct. 1861, 1876 n. 27, 60 L.Ed.2d 447 (1979) (draft recommendations of the Department of Justice are not determinative of constitutional requirements). However, the Eighth Amendment does require that defendants "provide a system of ready access to adequate medical care." *Hoptowit*, 682 F.2d at 1253; *Casey*, 834 F.Supp. at 1545.

Courts have considered a number of factors which bear upon whether or not a system meets constitutional minima. First, prisoners must be able "to make their medical problems known to the medical staff." *Hoptowit*, 682 F.2d at 1253; *Casey* 834 F.Supp. at 1545. While a functioning sick call system can be effective for physical illnesses, there must be a "systematic program *1257 for screening and evaluating inmates in order to identify those who require mental health treatment." *Balla*, 595 F.Supp. at 1577 (quoting *Ruiz*, 503 F.Supp. at 1339). This is particularly so since "[s]everely mentally ill inmates cannot make their needs known to mental health staff" on their own. *Casey*, 834 F.Supp. at 1550.

Next, the facility must be sufficiently staffed. *Ramos*, 639 F.2d at 578 (staffing shortfalls effectively deny inmates access to diagnosis and treatment); *Lightfoot v. Walker*, 486 F.Supp. 504, 524-25 (S.D.Ill.1980) (finding that staff shortages render medical services below constitutional level); *French v. Owens*, 777 F.2d 1250, 1254 (7th Cir.1985), *cert. denied*, 479 U.S. 817, 107 S.Ct. 77, 93 L.Ed.2d 32 (1986) (gross deficiencies in staffing may constitute deliberate indifference). Mental health professionals must be employed in "sufficient numbers to identify and treat in an individualized manner those treatable inmates suffering from serious mental disorders." *Balla*, 595 F.Supp. at 1577 (quoting *Ruiz*, 503 F.Supp. at 1339); *see also Cabrales v. County of Los Angeles*, 864 F.2d 1454, 1461 (9th Cir.1988) (understaffing contributed to inmate's suicide because of a lack of diagnosis and treatment).

The prison may refer inmates to outside facilities for treatment; however, if defendants choose to refer inmates outside the prison, they must provide "reasonably speedy access" to these other facilities. *Hoptowit*, 682 F.2d at 1253. *See also Lightfoot*, 486 F.Supp. at 522 (finding unacceptable delays in transfer of residents in need of psychiatric care). For those inmates who are treated within the prison, access to medical treatment cannot be substantially delayed in a systematic manner. Although isolated instances of delay do not give rise to liability unless they have caused substantial harm to the inmate, *Wood v. Housewright*, 900 F.2d 1332, 1335 (9th Cir.1990), regular and significant delays in the delivery of medical care may be constitutionally unacceptable. *Casey*, 834 F.Supp. at 1545; *see also Hoptowit*, 682 F.2d at 1253 (must provide "ready" access); *Todaro v. Ward*, 431 F.Supp. 1129, 1146 (S.D.N.Y.1977) (substantially delayed access to treatment violates the constitution); *Balla*, 595 F.Supp. at 1567 (finding significant delays before seeing a doctor are part of violation).

Moreover, "the prison must provide an adequate system for responding to emergencies." *Hoptowit* 682 F.2d at 1253. Security staff (or lack thereof) should not dangerously delay access to emergency treatment. *See Casey*, 834 F.Supp. at 1502, 1545 (delay in access to treatment outside prison caused by lack of security and transportation staff is part of violation); *Ramos*, 639 F.2d at 577. If outside facilities are too distant to handle emergencies promptly, then the prison must provide "adequate facilities and staff to handle emergencies within the prison." *Hoptowit*, 682 F.2d at 1253. Staff must be adequately trained to cope with emergencies. *Palmigiano v. Garrahy*, 443 F.Supp. 956, 974 (D.R.I.1977) (nursing staff "not provided with guidance for use in commonly occurring emergencies" found inadequate); *Balla*, 595 F.Supp. at 1567 (lack of written procedures for emergencies an element of violation).

Health screenings are a necessary supplement to ordinary avenues of access to medical care. The facility should screen newly arrived inmates to identify potential medical problems and communicable diseases. *Lightfoot*, 486 F.Supp. at 524 ("Health care admission screening procedures, including a physical examination performed by a physician, are an essential element of a constitutionally adequate system"); *Tillery v. Owens*, 719 F.Supp. 1256, 1306 (W.D.Pa.1989), *aff'd*, 907 F.2d 418 (3rd Cir.1990) (three-minute intake physical performed by physician who does not touch inmates inadequate); *Hoptowit*, 682 F.2d at 1253 (failure to provide preventative health care or routine physical examinations part of violation). Screenings for communicable diseases should be sufficient to protect other inmates from infectious diseases. *See Lareau v. Manson*, 651 F.2d 96, 109 (2d Cir.1981) (failure to screen for communicable diseases poses a serious threat to well-being of other inmates and is sufficient to give rise to Eighth Amendment violation).

The requirement of ready access to adequate care precludes prison officials from preventing treatment which is medically necessary ***1258** in the judgment of the treating doctor. *Estelle*, 429 U.S. at 104-105, 97 S.Ct. at 291 (intentional interference with prescribed treatment manifests deliberate indifference); *Casey*, 834 F.Supp. at 1545.

Of course, "[a]ccess to the medical staff has no meaning if the medical staff is not competent to deal with the prisoners' problems." *Hoptowit*, 682 F.2d at 1253; *Cabrales*, 864 F.2d at 1461. While medical technical assistants or their equivalent may permissibly be the first to examine inmates with physical ailments, they must be properly trained to perform this function and adequately supervised. *Capps v. Atiyeh*, 559 F.Supp. 894, 912 (D.Or.1982); *see also Toussaint IV*, 801 F.2d at 1112 (unqualified personnel may not regularly engage in medical practice). Medical technicians cannot be "left to operate in a vacuum" without physician supervision or guidance from written protocols. *Capps*, 559 F.Supp. at 912; *Ramos*, 639 F.2d at 576 (constitutional violation where inadequately supervised medical providers misdiagnose or mistreat inmates, causing life-threatening situations and needless pain and suffering); *Palmigiano*, 443 F.Supp. at 974; *Newman v. Alabama*, 349 F.Supp. 278, 284 (M.D.Ala.1972); *Lightfoot*, 486 F.Supp. at 517. Moreover, staff should receive "in-service" training or continuing education to ensure that they are adequately trained. *See Capps*, 559 F.Supp. at 912 (lack of continuing education for staff part of violation); *Palmigiano*, 443 F.Supp. at 974 (lack of in-service training programs part of violation).

Certain procedures are also all but indispensable to providing adequate care. First, "[a] primary component of a minimally acceptable correctional health care system is the implementation of procedures to review the quality of medical care being provided." *Lightfoot*, 486 F.Supp. at 517-18. Reviews of records to evaluate the delivery of care are essential. *Capps*, 559 F.Supp. at 912 (lack of chart review is part of violation); *Lightfoot*, 486 F.Supp. at 517 (lack of chart review is element of violation); *Todaro*, 431 F.Supp. at 1160 (failure to audit system part of violation); *see also Palmigiano*, 443 F.Supp. at 975. In addition, peer review and death reviews should be instituted to improve the quality of care. *Capps*, 559 F.Supp. at 912 (lack of peer review part of violation); *Lightfoot* 486 F.Supp. at 517-18 (noting lack of peer review and expressing court's "alarm[ ]" at the "lack of regular system of review of deaths").

Medical records must be sufficiently organized and thorough to allow the provision of adequate care to inmates. *Hoptowit*, 682 F.2d at 1252-53 (deficient medical records part of violation); *Capps*, 559 F.Supp. at 912; *Casey*, 834 F.Supp. at 1503 (medical recordkeeping system deficient where "medical records are not always available at sick call treatment . . . [and] do not always have the appropriate or required documentation of treatment or assessment of medical problems"). Medical records that are "'inadequate, inaccurate and unprofessionally maintained'" constitute a " 'grave risk of unnecessary pain and suffering' in violation of the eighth amendment." *Cody*, 599 F.Supp. at 1057 (quoting *Burks v. Teasdale*, 492 F.Supp. 650, 676, 678 (W.D.Mo.1980)).

Finally, some constitutional minima are specific to mental health care. Psychotropic or behavior-altering medication should only be administered with appropriate supervision and periodic evaluation. *Ruiz*, 503 F.Supp. at 1339. In addition, there should be a basic program to identify, treat, and supervise inmates with suicidal tendencies, and mental health records should be adequately maintained. *Id.*; *see also Balla*, 595 F.Supp. at 1577.

The Court finds the delivery of both physical and mental health care at Pelican Bay to be constitutionally inadequate. The system of physical health care at Pelican Bay fails to provide "ready access to adequate medical care." *Hoptowit*, 682 F.2d at 1253. As discussed at length in the findings of fact, staffing levels, although improved after an abysmal start, are still insufficient. Training and supervision of medical staff, particularly during the critical triage process when MTAs decide if inmates may see a physician, is almost nonexistent. Intake health screening is woefully inadequate and screening for communicable diseases has been poorly implemented. *1259 Inmates often experience significant delays in receiving treatment. There are no protocols or training programs for dealing with emergencies or trauma, and the facility has no effective procedures for managing inmates' chronic illnesses. The medical record-keeping system is utterly deficient. Finally, there are no programs of substance in place to ensure that quality care is provided: Pelican Bay has no working quality control program, no genuine peer review, no death reviews. In combination, these systemic deficiencies in the provision of medical services make ready access to adequate medical care impossible at Pelican Bay.

Similarly, the mental health care system at Pelican Bay fails to provide "ready access to adequate [mental health] care." *Hoptowit*, 682 F.2d at 1253. As detailed in the findings of fact, staffing levels, once outrageously low, are still seriously deficient. Screening and referral mechanisms are inadequate. Inmates with serious mental health needs are not receiving adequate monitoring and treatment on far more than just isolated occasions, particularly in the SHU. Some acutely psychotic inmates are left to suffer, in a hallucinatory and distraught state, without being referred to needed inpatient or intensive outpatient treatment. Inmates that are referred to other institutions for inpatient or intensive outpatient care often experience significant delays—delays that become particularly troublesome given Pelican Bay's lack of procedures for involuntary administration of antipsychotic drugs. Certain mentally ill inmates may require temporary or permanent exclusion from the SHU in order to attain *and sustain* a psychiatric recovery; others may require temporary or permanent exclusion from the SHU to prevent a mental deterioration from progressing into a serious mental disorder. The professional mental health staff, however, is precluded from addressing such needs.

Defendants suggest that the mental health care provided at Pelican Bay should pass constitutional muster because it is not completely "systemless." Defendants also argue that they have a "system in place" to provide medical care. Clearly, a prison with "systemless" health care would not withstand Eighth Amendment scrutiny; this is not, however, the dispositive inquiry. Indeed, whether or not a prison has some medical or mental health care "system," unless it actually delivers ready access to adequate care it can not survive constitutional scrutiny.

In this case, the deficiencies discussed above and in the findings of fact show that the delivery of medical and mental health care at Pelican Bay is riddled with systemic and gross deficiencies—deficiencies which preclude ready access to adequate care. We therefore conclude, as we must, that defendants' system for providing mental health care and medical care fails to comport with minimum constitutional standards.

2. Defendants' State of Mind

Determination of the defendants' state of mind presents a question of fact. *Farmer*, 511 U.S. at —, 114 S.Ct. at 1981. As set forth in the findings of fact above, we conclude that defendants knew they were subjecting the inmate population to a substantial risk of serious harm by virtue of their utter failure to provide for adequate medical and mental health care. This finding is based on information of which defendants were aware, coupled with the fact that the need for medical and substantial psychiatric services at Pelican Bay, and the risks of failing to address this need, were patently obvious to defendants. *Id.* at —, 114 S.Ct. at 1981; *Hoptowit*, 682 F.2d at 1253 ("medical services provided at the penitentiary are so deficient that they reflect a deliberate indifference to the serious medical needs of the prisoners"); *Ramos*, 639 F.2d at 578 (staff shortages make "unnecessary suffering inevitable" and evince deliberate indifference).

Defendants' callous and deliberate indifference to inmates' needs is particularly evinced by their failure to institute any substantive quality control. Quality control procedures represent the first critical steps of self-evaluation that could help defendants remedy widespread deficiencies; yet, at the time of trial, there were still no such procedures in operation.

*1260 Defendant Gomez' actions, or lack thereof, after Pelican Bay became operational reveal a continuing, conscious disregard for the ongoing risk of harm to the mental health of inmates at Pelican Bay. Although some improvements have been made in recent years, they have not satisfactorily addressed the glaring deficiencies; further, we conclude that some of those improvements were prompted primarily by litigation. We find that the remaining deficiencies will not be cured absent some supervision by this Court.

3. *Conclusion*

In sum, plaintiffs have amply proven that the prison population at Pelican Bay has serious medical and mental health needs to which defendants have been deliberately indifferent. As was long ago established in *Estelle*, this unnecessary and wanton infliction of pain is inconsistent with contemporary standards of decency and violates the Eighth Amendment of the Constitution. *Estelle*, 429 U.S. at 103-104, 97 S.Ct. at 290-91.

D. *CONDITIONS IN THE SECURITY HOUSING UNIT*

There is no static test that determines whether conditions of confinement constitute cruel and unusual punishment. *Davenport v. DeRobertis*, 844 F.2d 1310, 1314-15 (7th Cir.), *cert. denied*, 488 U.S. 908, 109 S.Ct. 260, 102 L.Ed.2d 248 (1988). Rather, courts must assess whether the conditions are such that they are compatible with "civilized standards, humanity and decency." *Estelle*, 429 U.S. at 102, 97 S.Ct. at 290 (internal quotation omitted); *Young v. Quinlan*, 960 F.2d 351, 359 (3rd Cir.1992). These civilized standards are measured, not by reference to any fixed historical point, but by "the evolving standards of decency that mark the progress of a maturing society." *Rhodes*, 452 U.S. at 346, 101 S.Ct. at 2399. Of course, not every deficiency or inadequacy rises to the level of an Eighth Amendment violation. *Young*, 960 F.2d at 359. However, conditions that are "inhumane," *Farmer*, 511 U.S. at —, 114 S.Ct. at 1976, deprive inmates of "basic human needs," *Helling*, 509 U.S. at —, 113 S.Ct. at 2480-81, or fail to furnish a "minimal civilized measure of life's necessities," *Wilson*, 501 U.S. at 298, 111 S.Ct. at 2324; *Chandler v. Baird*, 926 F.2d 1057, 1064 (11th Cir.1991), are constitutionally wanting under contemporary Eighth Amendment standards. *Young*, 960 F.2d at 363-64.

At a minimum, these life necessities include adequate food, clothing, shelter, medical care and personal safety. *Farmer*, 511 U.S. at —, 114 S.Ct. at 1976; *Young*, 960 F.2d at 364 (including sanitation). However, no simplistic litany of conditions should preclude the "fact-intensive inquiry" required by Eighth Amendment standards. *Chandler*, 926 F.2d at 1064; *Toussaint v. McCarthy* (*Toussaint III*), 597 F.Supp. 1388, 1393 (N.D.Cal.1984), *aff'd in part and rev'd in part*, 801 F.2d 1080 (9th Cir.1986), *cert. denied*, 481 U.S. 1069, 107 S.Ct. 2462, 95 L.Ed.2d 871 (1981). Thus, although courts have often focused on the minimum needed to physically sustain life, such as shelter, food, and medical care, courts have also recognized that conditions that inflict serious mental pain or injury also implicate the Eighth Amendment. As the Third Circuit recently observed, "[t]he touchstone is the health of the inmate. While the prison administration may punish, it may not do so in a manner that threatens the physical *and mental health* of prisoners." *Young*, 960 F.2d at 364 (emphasis added).[202]

*1261 We thus cannot ignore, in judging challenged conditions of confinement, that all humans are composed of more than flesh and bone—even those who, because of unlawful and deviant behavior, must be locked away not only from their fellow citizens, but from other inmates as well. Mental health, just as much as physical health, is a mainstay of life. Indeed, it is beyond any serious dispute that mental health is a need as essential to a meaningful human existence as other basic physical demands our bodies may make for shelter, warmth or sanitation. As the Supreme Court has made quite clear, we can not, consistent with contemporary notions of humanity and decency, forcibly incarcerate prisoners under conditions that will, or very likely will, make them seriously physically ill. *Helling*, 509 U.S. 25, 113 S.Ct. 2475. Surely, these same standards will not tolerate conditions that are likely to make inmates seriously mentally ill.

In this case, plaintiffs do not claim that SHU conditions deprive inmates of adequate food, heat,

---

[202] *See also Hudson*, 503 U.S. at 16, 112 S.Ct. at 1004 (Blackmun, J., concurring) (observing that Supreme Court has not limited injury cognizable under the Eighth Amendment to physical injury and noting that "it is not hard to imagine inflictions of psychological harm—without corresponding physical harm—that might prove to be cruel and unusual punishment"); *Jordan*, 986 F.2d at 1531 (cross-gender body searches, which caused psychological suffering and were unnecessary and wanton, violated the Eighth Amendment); *Hoptowit*, 682 F.2d at 1253 (prison must provide adequate physical *and mental* health care); Id. at 1257-58 (finding that certain conditions "create[d] an extreme hazard to the physical and mental well-being of the prisoner") (emphases added); *Spain*, 600 F.2d at 199) (finding that prisons cannot deprive inmates of regular physical exercise because it is important not only to physical, but mental health as well); *id.* at 200 (observing that the "court's judgment must be informed by current and enlightened scientific opinion as to the conditions necessary to insure good physical *and mental* health for prisoners") (emphasis added). *But see Newman v. Alabama*, 559 F.2d 283, 291 (5th Cir.1977), *cert. denied*, 438 U.S. 915, 98 S.Ct. 3144, 57 L.Ed.2d 1160 (1978).

clothing, or sanitary conditions. Rather, plaintiffs allege that the conditions in the SHU, while sufficient to satisfy basic physical needs, pose a grave threat to the mental health of inmates. Specifically, plaintiffs contend that the conditions of extreme social isolation and reduced environmental stimulation in the SHU inflict psychological trauma, and in some cases deprive inmates of sanity itself. As such, they urge the Court to find that the SHU, as currently operated, deprives inmates of one of the "basic necessities of human existence." *Young*, 960 F.2d at 364. They further contend that defendants have been deliberately indifferent to the mental health risks posed by conditions in the SHU.[203] Defendants, on the other hand, contend that plaintiffs have failed to establish any link between the conditions in the SHU and mental illness and that, in any event, the conditions in the SHU comport with contemporary Eighth Amendment standards. This claim has generated considerable attention, not only because it raises issues of a very serious dimension but because the Pelican Bay SHU is considered a state-of-the-art, "modern day" SHU, and thus a potential forerunner for other similar units around the country.

Having given the matter careful deliberation, we conclude that the record and the law do not fully sustain the position advocated by either plaintiffs or defendants. As explained below, we are not persuaded that the SHU, as currently operated, violates Eighth Amendment standards vis-vis all inmates. We do find, however, that conditions in the SHU violate such standards when imposed on certain subgroups of the inmate population, and that defendants have been deliberately indifferent to the serious risks posed by subjecting such inmates to the SHU over extended periods of time.

1. *Whether Conditions in the SHU Are Sufficiently Injurious to Mental Health so as to Deprive Inmates of a Basic Necessity of Life*

We begin our analysis by underscoring that the general concept of segregating inmates for disciplinary or security reasons is a well-established and penologically justified practice. Indeed, segregation "may be a necessary tool of prison discipline, both to punish infractions and to control and perhaps protect inmates whose presence within the general population would create unmanageable risks." *Young*, 960 F.2d at 364. Thus, there is nothing *per se* improper about segregating inmates, even for lengthy or indefinite terms. *Toussaint v. Yockey*, 722 F.2d 1490, 1494 n. 6 (9th Cir.1984). There is also little question that prison gang activity and violence within California prisons are serious problems that require strong measures from prison administrators. The decision to segregate inmates who threaten the security of the general population falls well within defendants' far ranging discretion to manage California's prison population.

*1262 Defendants' discretion to determine the specific conditions of segregation is similarly broad. Given the "limitations of federalism and the narrowness of the Eighth Amendment" it is not the Court's function to pass judgment on the policy choices of prison officials. *Hoptowit*, 682 F.2d at 1246. Rather, prison administration is a matter "peculiarly within the province of the legislative and executive branches of government." *Turner v. Safley*, 482 U.S. 78, 84-85, 107 S.Ct. 2254, 2259, 96 L.Ed.2d 64 (1987). Defendants are thus entitled to design and operate the SHU consistent with the penal philosophy of their choosing, absent constitutional violations. *Peterkin v. Jeffes*, 855 F.2d 1021, 1033 (3rd Cir.1988). They may impose conditions that are " 'restrictive and even harsh' " *Farmer*, 511 U.S. at —, 114 S.Ct. at 1977 (quoting *Rhodes*, 452 U.S. at 347, 101 S.Ct. at 2399); they may emphasize idleness, deterrence, and deprivation over rehabilitation. This is not a matter for judicial review or concern unless the evidence demonstrates that conditions are so extreme as to violate basic concepts of humanity and deprive inmates of a minimal level of life's basic necessities. *Young*, 960 F.2d at 364 ("Segregated detention is not cruel and unusual punishment *per se*, as long as the conditions of confinement are not foul, inhuman or totally without penological justification"); *Toussaint III*, 597 F.Supp. at 1413-14 (although doubting wisdom of certain policies, the court observed that its function is "not to sit in judgment of the policy choices of state officials"). In short, absent a showing of constitutional infringement, courts may not substitute their judgment or otherwise interfere with decisions made by prison officials. *Peterkin*, 855 F.2d at 1033; *Hoptowit*, 682 F.2d at 1246.

It is equally clear that the very nature of prison confinement may have a deleterious impact on the mental state of prisoners, for reasons that are self-evident. Especially for those facing long sentences, "depression, hopelessness, frustration, and other such psychological states may well prove to be

---

[203] This claim is distinct from plaintiffs' claim that the prison has failed to provide adequate mental health care to inmates once they are in need of mental health treatment.

inevitable byproducts." *Jackson v. Meachum*, 699 F.2d 578, 584 (1st Cir.1983); *Davenport*, 844 F.2d at 1313 (it is "highly probable that the experience of being imprisoned inflicts psychological damage"). This is particularly true for inmates placed in segregation, given that they are, by definition, subjected to additional isolation beyond that experienced by other general population inmates. Such inmates, for example, are often excluded from participating in prison work and vocational programs, leaving them to endure a regimen of prolonged and forced idleness. The resulting extreme boredom may cause prisoners to suffer loneliness and "psychological pain." *Toussaint III*, 597 F.Supp. at 1414. Nonetheless, there is no right to recreational, vocational or rehabilitative programs. "The lack of these programs simply does not amount to the infliction of pain." *Toussaint IV*, 801 F.2d at 1106 (internal quotation omitted).

Thus, as the *Toussaint* case highlights, the "psychological pain" that results from idleness in segregation is not sufficient to implicate the Eighth Amendment, particularly where the exclusion from prison programs is not without some penological justification. *Toussaint IV*, 801 F.2d at 1108. As the district court observed in *Toussaint III*, "[a]t least in theory, each [inmate in segregated housing] has been selected for segregation on the basis of criteria indicating that he is in some way unfit or unsuited for intermingling with other inmates, whether because he has misbehaved, because he presents a threat to the safety of other inmates, or because he has requested isolation from other inmates for his own protection." *Toussaint III*, 597 F.Supp. at 1414.

Indeed, the import of *Toussaint* is that the mental impact of a challenged condition should be considered in conjunction with penological considerations. *Toussaint IV*, 801 F.2d at 1108. On the one hand, a condition that is sufficiently harmful to inmates or otherwise reprehensible to civilized society will at some point yield to constitutional constraints, even if the condition has some penological justification. Thus, defendants' insistence that the SHU is "working" as a secure environment for disruptive prisoners[204] ***1263** does not and cannot determine whether the SHU passes constitutional muster. No prison, for example, can deprive inmates of a basic human need, even though the underlying conditions might otherwise arguably promote some penological objective. "A punishment may be so below civilized norms as to be cruel and unusual no matter what its provocation." *O'Brien v. Moriarty*, 489 F.2d 941, 944 (1st Cir.1974). Sedating all inmates with a powerful medication that leaves them in a continual stupor would arguably reduce security risks; however, such a condition of confinement would clearly fail constitutional muster.

On the other hand, a condition or other prison measure that has little or no penological value may offend constitutional values upon a lower showing of injury or harm. *See Gordon*, 800 F.Supp. at 800 ("The lack of legitimate penological interest is relevant to the determination of whether the objective [Eighth Amendment] standard has been violated");[205] *see also Sheley v. Dugger*, 833 F.2d 1420, 1428 (11th Cir.1987) (Eighth Amendment "forbids inflictions of pain which are totally without penological justification") (internal quotation omitted).

In this case, the conditions at issue primarily affect three inmate populations: (1) those who are being disciplined for committing serious rules violations, (2) those who the CDC has determined are affiliated with a prison gang, and (3) those who are otherwise considered security risks because of disruptive or assaultive behavior. The severe restrictions on social interaction further defendants' legitimate interest in precluding opportunities for disruptive or gang related activity and assaults on other inmates or staff.[206] For those serving short-term disciplinary terms, they also serve a punitive function. Other aspects of the conditions in the SHU, however, appear tenuously related to legitimate penological inter-

---

[204] Defendants have presented the Pelican Bay SHU as a centerpiece of their program to decrease violence in the California prison system. However, evidence regarding the SHU's significance is inconclusive. Statistics submitted by the defendants show a consistent rate of decline in violence *since 1984*, five years before Pelican Bay opened its doors in December of 1989. See Trial Exh. D-80 at C003912 (1992 is "seventh year in a row that the rate of [violent] incidents has decreased"); *id.* at C003914 (downward trend in assaults on staff since 1984); *id.* at C003926-7 (the only recent significant drop in deaths per year occurred between 1987 and 1988).

[205] In *Gordon*, the inmate was exposed to sub-freezing weather without hat or gloves for over one hour. The court noted that the conduct at issue was not as harmful as a whipping or electrical shock; nonetheless, the pain inflicted was sufficient to violate the Eighth Amendment given, *inter alia*, the absence of any legitimate penological interest, and defendant's callous refusal to provide the hats and gloves although they were readily available. 800 F.Supp. at 800.

[206] Such measures may also have negative effects on security as well. For example, training materials for the CDC Correctional Training Center observe that "isolation of semi-sensory deprivation [sic]" and "dehumanizing incarceration" are two factors, among others, that increase violence by inmates. Trial Exh. P-3021. However, absent constitutional violations, it is for prison officials to determine what measures provide the best overall security for the prison.

ests, at least with respect to those inmates that are segregated in the SHU not as a disciplinary measure, but for other reasons. For example, it is not clear how the lack of an outside view, the extreme sterility of the environment, and the refusal to provide any recreational equipment in the exercise pen (even a handball) furthers any interest other than punishment, and defendants have not advanced one. Thus, in the Court's view, the totality of the SHU conditions may be harsher than necessary to accommodate the needs of the institution with respect to these populations. However, giving defendants the wide-ranging deference they are owed in these matters, we cannot say that the conditions overall lack any penological justification.

Accordingly, as was the case in *Toussaint*, plaintiffs cannot prevail on the instant claim simply by pointing to the generalized "psychological pain"—i.e. the loneliness, frustration, depression or extreme boredom—that inmates may experience by virtue of their confinement in the SHU. *Toussaint IV*, 801 F.2d at 1107-08; *see also Jackson*, 699 F.2d at 581 (where social isolation of segregated inmate "caused him to become depressed," district court could not order that daily interaction ***1264** with other inmates be provided). *Cf. Doty*, 37 F.3d at 546 ("mild stress-related ailments are the type of 'routine discomfort' that may result merely from incarceration" and do not constitute serious mental health need). The Eighth Amendment simply does not guarantee that inmates will not suffer some psychological effects from incarceration or segregation. *Jackson*, 699 F.2d at 583. However, if the particular conditions of segregation being challenged are such that they inflict a serious mental illness, greatly exacerbate mental illness, or deprive inmates of their sanity, then defendants have deprived inmates of a basic necessity of human existence—indeed, they have crossed into the realm of psychological torture.

Courts have recognized that conditions in segregation could cross this line, particularly, where the length of segregation is indefinite or long term. For example, in *Jackson*, the Court observed that "although depression, hopelessness, frustration, and other psychological states may well prove to be inevitable byproducts of lifelong incarceration, the threat of substantial, serious and possibly irreversible if not critical psychological illness together with prolonged or indefinite segregated confinement would increase the burden on prison authorities to explore feasible alternative custodial arrangements." 699 F.2d at 584-5; *see also O'Brien*, 489 F.2d at 944 (segregated confinement involving "neither *intolerable* isolation nor inadequate food, heat, sanitation, lighting or bedding" is not cruel and unusual) (emphasis added); *Grubbs v. Bradley*, 552 F.Supp. 1052, 1124 (M.D.Tenn.1982) ("[T]he mere fact that inmates may tend to degenerate as a result of incarceration is not actionable. On the other hand, if conditions are so bad that *serious* physical or psychological deterioration is inevitable, then the result is cruel and unusual punishment") (emphasis added).[207]

In short, while courts will reject Eighth Amendment claims where there is no persuasive evidence that the challenged conditions lead to serious mental injury,[208] where such injury can in fact be shown, Eighth Amendment protections clearly come into play. Thus, we must ask the following question: does the evidence before the Court demonstrate that the conditions in the Pelican Bay SHU inflict mental harm so serious or severe that they cross the constitutional line?

Clearly, the constellation of conditions at issue here go well beyond the simple absence of prison programs which formed the basis of the challenge in *Toussaint*. What plaintiffs object to is not merely an absence of programs, but a more universal deprivation of human contact and stimulation. As described more fully in the factual findings, this deprivation is achieved through various factors, including the stark physical environment, the lack of any window to the outside world, the geographically remote location of Pelican Bay, and the extreme degree of social isolation stemming from the tightly

---

[207] *See also Hutto v. Finney*, 437 U.S. 678, 686, 98 S.Ct. 2565, 2571, 57 L.Ed.2d 522 (1978) (length of confinement relevant to deciding whether confinement meets constitutional standards); *Young*, 960 F.2d at 364 ("The duration and conditions of segregated confinement cannot be ignored in deciding whether such confinement meets constitutional standards."); *Sheley*, 833 F.2d at 1429 (although the court has "been hesitant in the past to apply the Eighth Amendment to claims of physical and mental deterioration by prisoners in the general prison population . . . [the plaintiff's] twelve-year confinement in [solitary confinement] raises serious constitutional questions"); *Pepperling v. Crist*, 678 F.2d 787, 789 (9th Cir.1982) ("The deprivations associated with an institutional lock-up, including twenty-four hour confinement, and curtailment of all association, exercise and normal vocational and educational activity, may constitute a . . . violation of the Eighth Amendment, if they persist too long.").

[208] *See, e.g., Smith v. Coughlin*, 748 F.2d 783, 787 (2nd Cir.1984) (district court found that plaintiff was not suffering from any psychological damage as a result of conditions of confinement); *Sostre v. McGinnis*, 442 F.2d 178, 193 n. 24 (2nd Cir.1971) (no evidence of psychological injury to the health of the prisoner), *cert. denied*, 404, 405 U.S. 1049, 978, 92 S.Ct. 719, 1190, 30, 31 L.Ed.2d 740, 254 (1972); *Bruscino v. Carlson*, 654 F.Supp. 609, 621 (S.D.Ill.1987) (evidence presented did not support plaintiffs' claims regarding the mental effects of challenged conditions), *aff'd*, 854 F.2d 162 (7th Cir.1988), *cert. denied*, 491 U.S. 907, 109 S.Ct. 3193, 105 L.Ed.2d 701 (1989).

restricted contact with prison staff, inmates and others. As we have already noted, some of these conditions appear, at best, tenuously related to legitimate concerns. We must also ***1265** consider that many in the SHU face indefinite and potentially lengthy terms.[209]

As plaintiffs also point out, they need not show that *every* inmate will suffer a serious mental illness or injury that is attributable to conditions in the SHU. In *Helling*, 509 U.S. 25, 113 S.Ct. 2475, the plaintiff challenged a condition of confinement—his compelled exposure to second hand smoke—on the ground that it posed an unreasonable risk to his health. As the Supreme Court made plain, the plaintiff need not prove that every inmate would become ill from the second hand smoke. Rather, it indicated that the critical inquiry was whether (1) the risk involved was "unreasonable" in that the challenged conditions were "sure," "very likely" or "imminent[ly]" likely to cause "serious" damage to the inmate's future health, and (2) whether society considers the risk to be "so grave that it violates contemporary standards of decency to expose *anyone* unwillingly to such a risk." *Id.* at —, 113 S.Ct. at 2482. "In other words," the Court continued, "the prisoner must show that the risk of which he complains is not one that today's society chooses to tolerate." *Id.*[210]

Here, the record demonstrates that the conditions of extreme social isolation and reduced environmental stimulation found in the Pelican Bay SHU will likely inflict some degree of psychological trauma upon most inmates confined there for more than brief periods. Clearly, this impact is not to be trivialized; however, for many inmates, it does not appear that the degree of mental injury suffered significantly exceeds the kind of generalized psychological pain that courts have found compatible with Eighth Amendment standards. While a risk of a more serious injury is not non-existent, we are not persuaded, on the present record and given all the circumstances, that the risk of developing an injury to mental health of *sufficiently serious magnitude* due to current conditions in the SHU is high enough for the SHU population as a whole, to find that current conditions in the SHU are *per se* violative of the Eighth Amendment with respect to all potential inmates.

We cannot, however, say the same for certain categories of inmates: those who the record demonstrates are at a particularly high risk for suffering very serious or severe injury to their mental health, including overt paranoia, psychotic breaks with reality, or massive exacerbations of existing mental illness as a result of the conditions in the SHU. Such inmates consist of the already mentally ill, as well as persons with borderline personality disorders, brain damage or mental retardation, impulse-ridden personalities, or a history of prior psychiatric problems or chronic depression. For these inmates, placing them in the SHU is the mental equivalent of putting an asthmatic in a place with little air to breathe. The risk is high enough, and the consequences serious enough, that we have no hesitancy in finding that the risk is plainly "unreasonable." *Helling*, 509 U.S. at —, 113 S.Ct. at 2481. Such inmates are not required to endure the horrific suffering of a serious mental illness or major exacerbation of an existing mental illness before ***1266** obtaining relief. *Id.* at —, 113 S.Ct. at 2480-81.[211]

We are acutely aware that defendants are entitled to substantial deference with respect to their management of the SHU. However, subjecting individuals to conditions that are "very likely" to render them psychotic or otherwise inflict a serious mental illness or seriously exacerbate an existing mental ill-

---

[209] As the Supreme Court has made clear, conditions of confinement may establish an Eighth Amendment violation "in combination," even when each would not do so alone, "when they have a mutually enforcing effect that produces the deprivation of a single, identifiable human need." *Wilson*, 501 U.S. at 304, 111 S.Ct. at 2327. Thus, even though the challenged conditions in this case may not individually deprive an inmate of any basic human need or violate the Constitution, plaintiffs may attempt to show that, in combination, they deprive plaintiffs of an identifiable human need, which in this case is the inmate's sanity or mental health.

We also note that defendants have not disputed that the conditions at issue here are more restrictive than those that were in effect at San Quentin prison during the *Toussaint* litigation. For example, inmates there were permitted the opportunity for group exercise in a larger yard with equipment. Also, "movement throughout the institution was nowhere near as significantly controlled and surveilled as it is in Pelican Bay." Haney Tr. 6-1053; *see also* Haney Decl. at 59.

[210] Although *Helling* involved a risk to an inmate's physical health, it appears that the principles enunciated would apply in the context of mental health as well. This is consistent with the fact that courts have borrowed standards utilized in analyzing physical health care when evaluating the adequacy of mental health care. *See, e.g., Doty*, 37 F.3d at 546; *Cody*, 599 F.Supp. at 1058 (adequacy of mental health care system "is governed by the same constitutional standard which applies when determining the adequacy of a prison's medical . . . system").

[211] To the extent that other inmates not falling within these categories may develop a serious mental illness in response to conditions in the SHU, an adequate mental health care system should provide sufficient monitoring to be alert to such occurrences and have the ability to address them. *See* section II(C)(2)(a), *supra*.

ness can not be squared with evolving standards of humanity or decency, especially when certain aspects of those conditions appear to bear little relation to security concerns. A risk this grave—this shocking and indecent—simply has no place in civilized society. It is surely not one "today's society [would] choose[ ] to tolerate." *Id.* at —, 113 S.Ct. at 2482. Indeed, it is inconceivable that any representative portion of our society would put its imprimatur on a plan to subject the mentally ill and other inmates described above to the SHU, knowing that severe psychological consequences will most probably befall those inmates. Thus, with respect to this limited population of the inmate class, plaintiffs have established that continued confinement in the SHU, as it is currently constituted, deprives inmates of a minimal civilized level of one of life's necessities.

2. *Defendants' State of Mind*

The above conclusions do not end our inquiry. In addition to demonstrating an injury that is "sufficiently serious" to violate objective Eighth Amendment standards, plaintiffs must also satisfy the subjective component of the Eighth Amendment. Specifically, they must show that the alleged injury is attributable to defendants' "wanton" state of mind, and can therefore be fairly characterized as a form of cruel and unusual punishment. *Wilson*, 501 U.S. at 299, 111 S.Ct. at 2324.

Where, as here, the plaintiff contends that inhumane conditions are depriving inmates of their mental health, wantonness is established by proving that defendants have been deliberately indifferent to the risk of harm. *Farmer*, 511 U.S. at —, 114 S.Ct. at 1977 ("In prison-conditions cases [the relevant] state of mind is one of 'deliberate indifference' to inmate health or safety. . . ."); *Helling*, 509 U.S. at —, 113 S.Ct. at 2480 ("Whether one characterizes the treatment received by [the prisoner] as inhuman conditions of confinement, failure to attend to his medical needs, or a combination of both, it is appropriate to apply the deliberate indifference standard articulated in *Estelle*") (internal quotations omitted).[212]

Based on the Court's findings of fact, and the evidence presented, we conclude that defendants had actual subjective knowledge that the conditions in the SHU presented *1267 a substantial or excessive risk of harm with respect to inmates who were mentally ill or otherwise particularly vulnerable to conditions of extreme isolation and reduced environmental stimulation.[213] Yet defendants, in continued disregard for this risk, took no action to either exclude such inmates from the SHU, ameliorate the offending conditions with respect to these inmates, or otherwise seriously address the issue. This constitutes deliberate indifference. *Farmer*, 511 U.S. at —, 114 S.Ct. at 1979. As found above, defendants have also been deliberately indifferent to the lack of adequate mental health care provided to inmates at Pelican Bay, particularly in the SHU. *See* section II(C)(3), *supra*. This merely underscores defendants' callous lack of concern for the mental health of those inmates that are particularly at risk in the SHU.

---

[212] Notwithstanding the above authority, defendants make the novel argument that because the overall purpose of the SHU is related to the security of the prison system, the standard set forth in *Whitley*, 475 U.S. 312, 106 S.Ct. 1078, for evaluating the state of mind in claims of excessive force is applicable here. Thus, although this is a claim challenging the conditions of confinement rather than the use of excessive force, defendants argue, citing *LeMaire v. Maass*, 12 F.3d 1444 (9th Cir.1993), that no Eighth Amendment violation may be found unless plaintiffs show that defendants acted maliciously and sadistically for the very purpose of causing harm.

In *LeMaire*, the court stated that it would apply the "maliciousness" standard in evaluating specific measures undertaken to control a particular inmate confined in a "Disciplinary Segregation Unit" similar in purpose to the SHU. *Id.* The *LeMaire* court, however, distinguished that case from "prison condition cases": "What LeMaire complains of are not so much *conditions of confinement* or indifference to his medical needs which do not clash with important governmental responsibilities; instead his complaint is leveled at measured practices and sanctions either used in exigent circumstances or imposed with considerable due process, and *designed to alter LeMaire's manifestly murderous, dangerous* [conduct]." *Id.* at 1452-53 (emphasis added).

Here, plaintiffs are not challenging measures designed to respond to the particular behavior problems posed by a particular inmate. Rather, they are challenging routinized, basic conditions on the ground that they adversely affect serious mental health needs. We are not persuaded that *Whitley* was intended to stretch so far beyond its borders so as to govern the challenge to conditions presented here.

[213] Once defendants were aware of the risk, they were obligated to consider the risk seriously, and to conduct adequate inquiries. *See Farmer*, 511 U.S. at — n. 8, 114 S.Ct. at 1982 n. 8 (defendant may "not escape liability if the evidence showed that he merely refused to verify underlying facts that he strongly suspected to be true, or declined to confirm inference of risk that he strongly suspected to exist"). *Cf. Jordan*, 986 F.2d at 1529 (prison officials have duty to consider issue carefully and to "afford sufficient weight to the constitutional rights of individuals").

3. *Conclusion*

In sum, while the conditions in the SHU may press the outer bounds of what most humans can psychologically tolerate, the record does not satisfactorily demonstrate that there is a sufficiently high risk to all inmates of incurring a serious mental illness from exposure to conditions in the SHU to find that the conditions constitute a *per se* deprivation of a basic necessity of life. We emphasize, of course, that this determination is based on the current record and data before us. We cannot begin to speculate on the impact that Pelican Bay SHU conditions may have on inmates confined in the SHU for periods of 10 or 20 years or more; the inmates studied in connection with this action had generally been confined to the SHU for three years or less. We do, however, find, for the reasons stated above, that continued confinement in the SHU, under present conditions, constitutes cruel and unusual punishment in violation of the Eighth Amendment for two categories of inmates: those who are already mentally ill and those who, as identified above, are at an unreasonably high risk of suffering serious mental illness as a result of present conditions in the SHU. Defendants, of course, are not precluded from segregating either category of inmates from the remainder of the prison population where such segregation is otherwise justified; they simply can not segregate them under conditions as they currently exist in the Pelican Bay SHU.

***

*1279 IV.

SUMMARY

Throughout these proceedings, we have been acutely sensitive to the fact that our role in Eighth Amendment litigation is a limited one. Federal courts are not instruments for prison reform, and federal judges are not prison administrators. We must be careful not to stray into matters that our system of federalism reserves for the discretion of state officials. At the same time, we have no duty more important than that of enforcing constitutional rights, no matter how unpopular the cause or powerless the plaintiff. The challenge, then, in prison condition cases, is to uphold the Constitution in such a manner that respects the state's unique interest in managing its prison population. It is a challenge that requires us to draw constitutional lines when necessary, yet minimize any intrusion into state affairs.

It was with these principles in mind that we studied the voluminous record in this case and rendered our findings of fact and conclusions of law set forth above. And it is these principles that have compelled us to conclude that defendants have unmistakably crossed the constitutional line with respect to some of the claims raised by this action. In particular, defendants have failed to provide inmates at Pelican Bay with constitutionally adequate medical and mental health care, and have permitted and condoned a pattern of using excessive force, all in conscious disregard of the serious harm that these practices inflict. With respect to the SHU, defendants cross the constitutional line when they force certain subgroups of the prison population, including the mentally ill, to endure the conditions in the SHU, despite knowing that the *1280 likely consequence for such inmates is serious injury to their mental health, and despite the fact that certain conditions in the SHU have a relationship to legitimate security interests that is tangential at best.

As to the above matters, defendants have subjected plaintiffs to "unnecessary and wanton infliction of pain" in violation of the Eighth Amendment of the United States Constitution. We observe that while this simple phrase articulates the legal standard, dry words on paper can not adequately capture the senseless suffering and sometimes wretched misery that defendants' unconstitutional practices leave in their wake. The anguish of descending into serious mental illness, the pain of physical abuse, or the torment of having serious medical needs that simply go unmet is profoundly difficult, if not impossible, to fully fathom, no matter how long or detailed the trial record may be.

The record does not, however, sustain other allegations advanced by plaintiffs. Conditions in the SHU may well hover on the edge of what is humanly tolerable for those with normal resilience, particularly when endured for extended periods of time. They do not, however, violate exacting Eighth Amendment standards, except for the specific population subgroups identified in this opinion. We have also found for defendants with respect to plaintiffs' allegations regarding the use of force between inmates. Finally, with the exception of one issue, we have rejected plaintiffs' challenges to the procedures governing the assignment of prison gang members to the SHU for indeterminate terms.[229]

V.

APPROPRIATE RELIEF AND FURTHER PROCEEDINGS

Once constitutional violations have been found, federal courts have broad equitable powers to formulate appropriate relief. *Stone v. City and County of San Francisco*, 968 F.2d 850, 861 (9th Cir.1992), *cert. denied*, 506 U.S. 1081, 113 S.Ct. 1050, 122 L.Ed.2d 358 (1993); *Hoptowit*, 682 F.2d at 1245. We should only exercise, however, the least power necessary to accomplish this goal. Courts must " 'fashion a remedy that does no more and no less than correct [the] particular constitutional violation.' " *Doty*, 37 F.3d at 543; *Toussaint IV*, 801 F.2d at 1086 ("Injunctive relief against a state agency or official must be no broader than necessary to remedy the constitutional violation"). Such a remedy may include relief that the Constitution would not of its own force initially require, but only "if such relief is necessary to remedy a constitutional violation." *Toussaint IV*, 801 F.2d at 1087; *Gluth v. Kangas*, 951 F.2d 1504, 1510 n. 4 (9th Cir.1991).

To facilitate a remedy that both cures the constitutional deficiencies and minimizes intrusion into prison management, most district courts require the development and implementation of a remedial plan that is narrowly tailored to correct the specific constitutional violations at issue. *See, e.g., Casey*, 834 F.Supp. at 1552-53; *Lightfoot*, 486 F.Supp. at 527-528. We see no reason to deviate from this approach in the case at bar. Injunctive or equitable relief is appropriate, and indeed necessary, where there is a "contemporary violation of a nature likely to continue." *See Farmer*, 511 U.S. at —, 114 S.Ct. at 1983 (internal quotation omitted); *Williams v. Lane*, 851 F.2d 867, 885 (7th Cir.1988), *cert. denied*, 488 U.S. 1047, 109 S.Ct. 879, 102 L.Ed.2d 1001 (1989) ("District courts may . . . order appropriate injunctive relief to prevent any continuing deprivation of an inmate's constitutional rights"). We are firmly convinced that the constitutional violations identified above will not be fully redressed absent intervention by this Court.

In reaching this conclusion we have heeded the United States Supreme Court's recent admonition that, where injunctive relief is sought, the plaintiff must show not only that defendants possess the subjective state of mind necessary to establish Eighth Amendment ***1281** liability, but that this state of mind will persist beyond the instant litigation. *Farmer*, 511 U.S. at —, 114 S.Ct. at 1983. We must thus evaluate defendants "attitudes and conduct" not only as of the time the suit was filed, but also during the litigation and "into the future." *Farmer*, 511 U.S. at —, 114 S.Ct. at 1983.

Our assessment of defendants' current attitudes and conduct only reinforces our view that injunctive relief is not only appropriate in this case, but perhaps "indispensable, if constitutional dictates—not to mention considerations of basic humanity—are to be observed in the prison [ ]." *Stone*, 968 F.2d at 861. Throughout this litigation, defendants have shown no indication that they are committed to finding permanent solutions to problems of serious constitutional dimension. On the contrary, defendants have expended most of their energies attempting to deny or explain away the evidence of such problems. Even when defendants modify certain policies (as they have done in the use-of-force area), they do not argue that such changes evidence an intent to address the problems raised by this complaint; rather, defendants typically assert that they were precipitated by unrelated matters.[230]

---

[229] Plaintiffs have also alleged that defendants have denied inmates the constitutional right of meaningful access to the courts set out in *Bounds v. Smith*, 430 U.S. 817, 821, 97 S.Ct. 1491, 1494, 52 L.Ed.2d 72 (1977). We defer issuing a decision on this claim so that we can better consider recent Ninth Circuit case law on the subject, including *Vandelft v. Moses*, 31 F.3d 794 (9th Cir.1994), and *Casey v. Lewis*, 43 F.3d 1261 (9th Cir.1994).

[230] We also note that defendants' recent policy changes relating to the use of force do not moot plaintiffs' request for injunctive relief. In cases involving constitutional violations in prisons, courts have held that "[c]hanges made by defendants after a suit is filed do not remove the necessity for injunctive relief, for practices may be reinstated as swiftly as they were suspended." *Jones v. Diamond*, 636 F.2d 1364, 1375 (5th Cir.1981), *cert. dismissed*, 453 U.S. 950, 102 S.Ct. 27, 69 L.Ed.2d 1033 (1981), *and overruled on other grounds by Int'l Woodworkers of America v. Champion Int'l Corp.*, 790 F.2d 1174 (5th Cir.1986); *see also Gluth*, 951 F.2d at 1507; Gates v. Collier, 501 F.2d 1291, 1321 (5th Cir.1974); *Santiago v. Miles*, 774 F.Supp. 775, 793-95 (W.D.N.Y.1991) ("In cases involving challenges to prison practices, federal courts in this circuit have not been reluctant to issue injunctive relief in spite of substantial voluntary improvements by prison officials"); *Fisher*, 692 F.Supp. at 1565-66. Thus, the burden is on the defendants to prove "that the wrongs of the past could not reasonably be expected to recur." *Jones*, 636 F.2d at 1375; *LaMarca*,

In short, we glean no serious or genuine commitment to significantly improving the delivery of health care services, correcting the pattern of excessive force, or otherwise remedying the constitutional violations found herein which have caused, and continue to cause, significant harm to the plaintiffs. Indeed, the Court is left with the opinion that, even given the evidence presented at trial, defendants would still deny that any condition or practice at Pelican Bay raises any cause for concern, much less concern of a constitutional dimension.

Nor are we confident, given the history of other prison litigation, that defendants will promptly rectify constitutional deficiencies absent intervention by this Court. *See, e.g., Thompson v. Enomoto,* 915 F.2d 1383, 1387 (9th Cir.1990), *cert. denied,* 502 U.S. 1071, 112 S.Ct. 965, 117 L.Ed.2d 131 (1992) (Court Monitor reports showed that state prison officials had not complied with decree governing conditions for death row inmates in 1988 and 1989); *Gates v. Deukmejian,* No. Civ. S-1636 LKK (October 27, 1994 Order at 8) (finding state prison officials in contempt of decree after "four-year pattern of delay and obstruction regarding the planning and implementation of a satisfactory OPP [Outpatient Psychiatric Program]"). The Office of Legislative Analyst has also observed that defendants have failed over the years to undertake adequate planning to address the medical needs of inmates in California prisons. See Trial Exh. P-3958 at 32 ("Our review indicates that, although the CDC has made some improvements in administration of its medical programs, the programs are too often characterized by a lack of adequate long-term planning, and 'crisis management,' *1282 often brought about by litigation. . . . The lack of long-term planning has been apparent over the years.").

Considering all of the above, we conclude that injunctive relief is both necessary and appropriate to ensure an effective remedy of the constitutional violations at issue here. We also believe, given the above, that the participation of counsel for both parties, as well as a Special Master experienced in prison administration, will be essential to the formulation of a remedy that is both effective and narrowly tailored.

The appointment of a Special Master, with appropriately defined powers, is within both the inherent equitable powers of the court and the provisions of Rule 53 of the Federal Rules of Civil Procedure. *Ruiz,* 679 F.2d at 1159-62.

In this case, the assistance of a Special Master is clearly appropriate. Developing a comprehensive remedy in this case will be a complex undertaking involving issues of a technical and highly charged nature. The Court strongly believes that the participation of a well-qualified and impartial Special Master will greatly assist the Court in developing an appropriate remedy. The assistance of a Special Master will also be necessary to properly monitor the implementation of any remedy that this Court may order. Such a task will require a substantial expenditure of time and the expertise of someone experienced in prison administration. *See Stone,* 968 F.2d at 859 n. 18 (noting that federal courts "repeatedly have approved the use of Special Masters to monitor compliance with court orders and consent decrees") (citations omitted); Williams, 851 F.2d at 885 (appointment of a "knowledgeable and impartial special master to implement a just remedy consistent with the needs of prison security and legitimate penological goals should assure compliance with the court's ultimate decision"); *Ruiz,* 679 F.2d at 1159-62, 1165; *Mercer v. Mitchell,* 908 F.2d 763, 785 (11th Cir.1990) (district court appointed temporary Special Master to recommend remedial measures); *Armstrong v. O'Connell,* 416 F.Supp. 1325, 1340 (E.D.Wis.1976) (Special Master to assist in developing remedy in school desegregation case). We note that the court is "not required to await the failure or refusal of [prison officials] to comply with [a] decree before appointing an agent [under Rule 53] to implement it." *Ruiz,* 679 F.2d at 1161.

In addressing the scope and substance of the remedial plan, the parties and Special Master are reminded that "federal courts do not sit to supervise state prisons, the administration of which is of acute interest to the states." *Toussaint IV,* 801 F.2d. at 1087. However, it is also the duty and responsibility of this Court to ensure that constitutional rights are fully vindicated. Thus, the parties and Special Master should keep in mind that any equitable remedy must "strike a balance . . . that will both redress the constitutional violations found and yet accord appropriate deference to the defendants' interests in running their own institution." *Fisher,* 692 F.Supp. at 1567. This requires that any remedial plan be minimally intrusive and accord substantial deference to defendants' legitimate interest in managing a correctional

---

995 F.2d at 154142 (reforms enacted after filing of action challenging prison conditions do not preclude injunctive relief unless defendants show that the institution "would not return to its former, unconstitutionally deficient state"); *Santiago,* 774 F.Supp. at 794. For the reasons discussed in this Court's factual findings, the policy changes that have occurred in the use-of-force area appear not only litigation inspired but also transitory rather than permanent. We certainly are not persuaded that, absent injunctive relief, the prison would "not return to its former, unconstitutionally deficient state." *LaMarca,* 995 F.2d at 1541. Further, the policy changes at issue do not fully remedy the constitutional violations found herein.

facility. *Toussaint IV*, 801 F.2d at 1087 (court has duty to fashion least intrusive remedy that is still effective). Accordingly, defendants' policy preferences *must* be given deference unless doing so would preclude an effective remedy. *See Hoptowit*, 682 F.2d at 1254 (remedy "should permit, if possible within constitutional restraints, the prison officials to use the general approach that they find most effective and efficient").

Accordingly, and good cause appearing, it is HEREBY ORDERED that:

1. Defendants' February 11, 1994 Renewed Motion for Partial Judgment under Fed.R.Civ.P. 52(c), and to Strike Declarations of Grassian and Start, is denied.

2. The Court appoints Mr. Thomas F. Lonergan[231] to serve as a neutral Special *1283 Master, pursuant to Fed.R.Civ.P. 53 and the inherent powers of the Court, for the purpose of assisting the Court to fulfill its obligation to fashion an appropriate remedy and to monitor the implementation of that remedy. The specific duties and powers of the Monitor, along with other terms of his appointment, shall be governed by a separate order of reference to be issued forthwith.

3. As soon as practicable, counsel for plaintiffs and defendants shall begin working together jointly and in good faith, with the Special Master, to develop a satisfactory remedial plan that addresses the constitutional violations set forth in the accompanying conclusions of law.[232] The parties shall submit their proposed remedial plan to the Court within 120 days from the date of this order. The Special Master shall provide a progress report to the Court every 30 days and may recommend, for good cause, an extension of time beyond the 120 day deadline.

4. The Court fully anticipates that an appropriate remedial plan can be fashioned through the above process. In the event, however, that the parties are unable to develop a mutually acceptable remedial plan within the 120 day deadline (or such later deadline as the Court may allow by way of extension), the parties shall, no later than 7 days after such deadline, jointly submit to the Court any part(s) of such a plan that have been agreed to, or a statement that the parties were unable to agree on any aspect of a remedial plan. The Special Master shall then make recommendations to the Court with respect to any remaining areas of disagreement, after giving consideration to the input and concerns of both parties. Any such recommendations shall be consistent with the principles set forth above, and shall be filed and served no later than 30 days after the parties have jointly submitted any part(s) of the plan that have been agreed to (or a statement that no such agreement was possible). The parties shall have an opportunity to file any objections to the Special Master's recommendations within 10 days after such recommendations have been served and filed with the Court.

5. This Court shall retain jurisdiction over this action until such time as the Court is satisfied that all constitutional violations found herein have been fully and effectively remedied.

IT IS SO ORDERED.

---

[231] Thomas Lonergan previously served as a court-appointed Monitor for this Court, from December 1982 through June 1994, in *Cherco v. County of Sonoma*, which involved conditions at the Sonoma County Jail in Santa Rosa, California. He discharged his responsibilities as court Monitor in that case with utmost professionalism, integrity, diligence, and sensitivity to the concerns of all participants, and the Court has complete confidence in his ability to serve effectively as a Special Master in this case. He has also served as a court-appointed Special Master, Monitor or expert in 8 other cases including *Jordan v. Multnomah County* (United States District Court, Oregon), and *Fischer v. Winter* (United States District Court, N.D. California). He was employed by the Los Angeles County Sheriff's Department from 1963 until his retirement in 1980. He has a B.A. and M.A. in Political Science from California State University at Long Beach, and a Masters in Public Administration from Pepperdine University. He is a member of the American Correctional Association and served on its Legal Committee for four years.

[232] With respect to the provision of mental health care, the parties and Special Master should consider whether any remedy should be stayed pending further proceedings in *Coleman v. Wilson*, Civ S-0520 LKK (E.D.Cal). If not, any remedial plan should be carefully tailored to coordinate with proceedings in that action.

COLEMAN v. WILSON
912 F. Supp. 1282 (1995)
U.S. District Court
E.D. California
Sept. 13, 1995

***

*1293 *ORDER*

KARLTON, Chief Judge Emeritus.

Plaintiffs, state prisoners who suffer from serious mental disorders, brought suit under 42 U.S.C. § 1983 alleging that the mental health care provided at most institutions within the California Department of Corrections is so inadequate that their rights under the Eighth and Fourteenth Amendments to the United States Constitution are violated. Plaintiffs also raised a claim under the Rehabilitation Act, 29 U.S.C. § 794. Plaintiffs seek declaratory and prospective injunctive relief.

The named defendants are Pete Wilson, Governor of the State of California, Joseph Sandoval, Secretary of the Youth and Corrections Agency of the State of California, James Gomez, Director of the California Department of Corrections, Nadim Khoury, M.D., Assistant Deputy Director for Health Care Services for the California Department of Corrections, and John S. Zil, M.D., Chief of Psychiatric Services for the California Department of Corrections. All named defendants are sued in their official capacity.

The matter was referred to Chief Magistrate Judge John F. Moulds pursuant to 28 U.S.C. § 636(b)(1)(B) and Local Rule 302(c)(17). On October 22, 1991, Judge Moulds recommended certification as a class action pursuant to Rules 23(b)(1)(A), 23(b)(1)(B), and 23(b)(2) of the Federal Rules of Civil Procedure. On November 14, 1991, those findings and recommendations were adopted by this court, and a class was certified consisting of "all inmates with serious mental disorders who are now or who will in the future be confined within the California Department of Corrections (except the San Quentin State Prison, the Northern Reception Center at Vacaville and the California Medical Facility-Main at Vacaville)." (Order filed November 14, 1991, at 4-5.)

On June 6, 1994, the magistrate judge issued findings and recommendations on plaintiffs' § 1983 claims.[1] On July 25, 1994, defendants filed objections to the findings and recommendations ("Objections").[2] On September 13, 1994, plaintiffs filed a response to defendants' objections ("Plaintiffs' Response"). Plaintiffs' response was accompanied by declarations of Michael Bien (Bien Declaration) and Donald Specter (Specter Declaration) with appended exhibits. On November 7, 1994, defendants filed a closing brief ("Defendants' Closing Brief"), raising various evidentiary issues.

On March 25, 1995, this court remanded the matter to the magistrate judge because he had resolved the matter on constitutional grounds without first addressing the statutory claim. *See Lyng v. Northwest Indian Cemetery Protective Association, et al.*, 485 U.S. 439, 445, 108 S.Ct. 1319, 1323, 99 L.Ed.2d 534 (1988). Plaintiffs then moved to dismiss the Rehabilitation Act claim and the matter was returned to this court. Defendants were given an opportunity to comment on the terms and conditions of dismissal and plaintiffs were granted an opportunity to respond. Thereafter the Rehabilitation Act claim was dismissed and this court again turned to consideration of the merits.

Having concluded that the briefing on this matter exhausts the issues and thus resolution without oral argument is appropriate, *see* L.R. 230(h), the court now disposes of the matter.***

---

[1] Plaintiffs' claims regarding treatment of mentally retarded inmates have been dismissed by separate order.

[2] A corrected text of the objections was filed on August 2, 1994. Reference to defendants' objections throughout this opinion is a reference to the corrected text filed August 2, 1994.

***

*1296 II.

Summary of Findings and Recommendations

Undergirding the magistrate judge's recommendations were a series of legal conclusions. First he concluded that the Eighth Amendment requires the state to provide inmates with access to adequate mental health care. (Findings and Recommendations at 14.) Second, he concluded that there are six components required for a mental health care system to meet minimum constitutional requirements. (*Id.*).[8] Third, he determined that an Eighth Amendment claim based on inadequate medical care in prison is comprised of both an objective and a subjective component. (*Id.* at 15.) The objective component focuses on the degree of seriousness of the deprivation of medical care, while the subjective component focuses on whether defendants acted with "deliberate indifference" to serious medical needs. (*Id.*)

The magistrate judge was also required to propose factual findings. Although there are a great many specific findings, there are eight essential ones.

First, Judge Moulds found that defendants do not have an adequate mechanism for screening inmates for mental illness, either at the time of reception or during incarceration. He further found that the CDC has lacked adequate screening since at least 1987. (*Id.* at 31.)

Second, he found that the CDC is seriously and chronically understaffed in the area of mental health care. Indeed he found that there was no dispute in this regard. (*Id.* at 36.)

Third, he found that defendants have no effective method for insuring the competence of their mental health staff and, therefore, *1297 for insuring that inmates have access to competent care. (*Id.* at 42.)

Fourth, he found that "[t]here are significant delays in, and sometimes complete denial of, access to necessary medical attention, multiple problems with use and management of medication, and inappropriate use of involuntary medications." (*Id.*)

Fifth, he found that "the mental health status of class members is adversely impacted by inappropriate use of punitive measures without regard to the impact of such measures on their medical condition." (*Id.*)

Sixth, the magistrate judge found that the medical records system maintained by defendants is "extremely deficient." (*Id.* at 61.)

Seventh, the magistrate judge found that defendants have designed an adequate suicide prevention program and have taken many of the steps necessary to implement that program. (*Id.* at 75.) He also found, however, that the program has not yet been fully implemented at least in part because of the severe understaffing in mental health care. (*Id.*)

Finally, the magistrate judge found substantial evidence of defendants' deliberate indifference to the deficiencies in their system. (*Id.* at 75–76.)

Having concluded that the system for delivery of mental health care to members of the class maintained by the defendants violates the Eighth Amendment, the magistrate judge recommended a series of steps designed to redress the perceived constitutional violations. The majority of these recommendations would require defendants to develop and implement a series of forms, protocols, and plans in consultation with court-appointed experts. (*Id.* at 78–82.) Judge Moulds also recommended appointment of a special master for a period of three years to (1) consult with the court concerning the appointment of experts; (2) monitor compliance with court-ordered injunctive relief; (3) report to the court in twelve months on the adequacy of suicide prevention; and (4) perform such additional tasks as the court may deem necessary. (*Id.* at 78.)

---

[8] Those criteria are set out in n. 10, *infra*.

III.

Standard of Review of the Findings and Recommendations

The district court reviews *de novo* those portions of the proposed findings of fact to which objections have been made. 28 U.S.C. § 636(b)(1)(C); *McDonnell Douglas Corp. v. Commodore Business Machines*, 656 F.2d 1309, 1313 (9th 1981), *cert. denied*, 455 U.S. 920, 102 S.Ct. 1277, 71 L.Ed.2d 461 (1982). The court may, however, assume the correctness of that portion of the proposed findings of fact to which no objection has been made, and decide the matter on the applicable law. *See United States v. Remsing*, 874 F.2d 614, 617 (9th Cir.1989) (citing *Orand v. United States*, 602 F.2d 207, 208 (9th Cir.1979)). The magistrate judge's conclusions of law are reviewed *de novo*. *Barilla v. Ervin*, 886 F.2d 1514, 1518 (9th Cir.1989) (*citing Britt v. Simi Valley Unified Sch. Dist.*, 708 F.2d 452, 454 (9th Cir.1983)).

The court is not bound to adopt the magistrate judge's findings and recommendations; on the contrary, the court must exercise "sound judicial discretion" in making its own determination on the record. *United States v. Raddatz*, 447 U.S. 667, 675–76, 100 S.Ct. 2406, 2412–13, 65 L.Ed.2d 424 (1980). The court may accept, reject, or modify, in whole or in part, the magistrate judge's findings and recommendations. 28 U.S.C. § 636(b)(1)(C); *Remsing*, 874 F.2d at 617.

IV.

Substantive Standards

The Eighth Amendment to the United States Constitution imposes on the states an obligation to provide for the basic human needs of prison inmates. *Farmer v. Brennan*, 511 U.S. 825, —, 114 S.Ct. 1970, 1976, 128 L.Ed.2d 811 (1994).[9] While "[t]he Constitution 'does not mandate comfortable prisons,' . . . neither does it permit inhumane ones." *Id.* (citation omitted); *see also Helling v. McKinney*, 509 U.S. 25, —, ***1298** 113 S.Ct. 2475, 2480, 125 L.Ed.2d 22 (1993). The obligation to provide for the basic human needs of prisoners includes a requirement to provide access to adequate mental health care. *Doty v. County of Lassen*, 37 F.3d 540, 546 (9th Cir.1994); *Hoptowit*, 682 F.2d at 1253. If the state fails to meet this obligation, "it transgresses the substantive limits on state action set by the Eighth Amendment." *Helling*, 509 U.S. at —, 113 S.Ct. at 2480.

Where the allegations are that there has been a failure to provide adequate medical care, plaintiffs, to prove a violation of the Eighth Amendment, must demonstrate that defendants acted with "deliberate indifference" to their "serious medical needs." *Wilson v. Seiter*, 501 U.S. 294, 297, 111 S.Ct. 2321, 2323, 115 L.Ed.2d 271 (1991) (quoting *Estelle v. Gamble*, 429 U.S. 97, 106, 97 S.Ct. 285, 292, 50 L.Ed.2d 251 (1976)); *Doty*, 37 F.3d at 546. An Eighth Amendment violation is comprised of both an objective component and a subjective component. *See Wilson*, 501 U.S. at 298, 111 S.Ct. at 2324. The objective component turns on whether the deprivation of a particular medical need is "sufficiently serious." *Id.*; *see also McGuckin v. Smith*, 974 F.2d 1050, 1059 (9th Cir.1992). "The 'routine discomfort' that results from incarceration and which is 'part of the penalty that criminal offenders pay for their offenses against society' does not constitute a 'serious medical need.' " *Doty*, 37 F.3d at 546 (quoting *McGuckin*, 974 F.2d at 1059). Rather, a medical need is said to be "serious" for Eighth Amendment purposes, "if the failure to treat a prisoner's condition could result in further significant injury or the 'unnecessary and wanton infliction of pain.'" *McGuckin*, 974 F.2d at 1059 (citation omitted).

> The existence of an injury that a reasonable doctor or patient would find important and worthy of comment or treatment; the presence of a medical condition that significantly affects an individual's daily activities; or the existence of chronic and substantial pain are examples of indications that a prisoner has a 'serious' need for medical treatment.

Id. at 1059–60 (citations omitted).

---

[9] The Eighth Amendment provides: "Excessive bail shall not be required, nor excessive fines imposed, nor cruel and unusual punishments inflicted." U.S. Const. Amend. VIII.

The objective component of deliberate indifference is treated as a mixed question of law and fact in this circuit. *Doty*, 37 F.3d at 546. The etiology, symptoms, and diagnosis of medical conditions present questions of fact; whether a medical condition is a "serious medical need" for purposes of the Eighth Amendment is a legal conclusion to be drawn from established facts. *Id.*

In the context of this lawsuit, the objective component turns on whether the mental health care delivery system operated by defendants is so deficient that it deprives seriously mentally ill inmates of access to adequate mental health care. To analyze that question, the courts have focused on the presence or absence of six basic, essentially common sense, components of a minimally adequate prison mental health care delivery system. *Balla v. Idaho State Board of Corrections,* 595 F.Supp. 1558, 1577 (D.Idaho 1984) (citing *Ruiz v. Estelle*, 503 F.Supp. 1265, 1339 (S.D.Tex.1980)). As explained in detail below, the magistrate judge correctly identified those components and made appropriate findings concerning them.[10] (Findings and Recommendations at 14.)

Under present doctrine, even when inmates with serious mental illnesses are deprived of access to adequate mental health care, an Eighth Amendment violation is not shown unless defendants have acted with "deliberate indifference" to their need for such care. *See Wilson*, 501 U.S. at 303, 111 S.Ct. at 2327. "[A] prison official cannot be found liable under the Eighth Amendment for denying an inmate humane conditions of ***1299** confinement unless the official knows of and disregards an excessive risk to inmate health or safety; the official must both be aware of facts from which the inference could be drawn that a substantial risk of serious harm exists, and he must also draw the inference." *Farmer*, 511 U.S. at —, 114 S.Ct. at 1979.[11] As the Supreme Court recently explained, however, where the evidence before the district court proves the objective component of an Eighth Amendment violation, "the defendants could not plausibly persist in claiming lack of awareness, any more than prison officials who state during litigation that they will not take reasonable measures to abate an intolerable risk of which they are aware could claim to be subjectively blameless for purposes of the Eight Amendment . . . ." *Id.* at — n. 9, 114 S.Ct. at 1984 n. 9.

V.

Defendants' Objections

A. *Preliminary Observations*

The law provides for commitment to prison as punishment for the commission of serious crimes. Hence prisons are "places of involuntary confinement of persons who have demonstrated a proclivity for antisocial criminal, and often violent, behavior." *Hudson v. Palmer*, 468 U.S. 517, 526, 104 S.Ct. 3194, 3200, 82 L.Ed.2d 393 (1984). Administration of such institutions is no easy task. Moreover, in California that task has been complicated by the fact that prisons have also become the repository of an enormous number of the state's mentally ill. Thus in the matter at bar one of defendants' experts estimated that on

---

[10] The six components are: (1) a systematic program for screening and evaluating inmates to identify those in need of mental health care; (2) a treatment program that involves more than segregation and close supervision of mentally ill inmates; (3) employment of a sufficient number of trained mental health professionals; (4) maintenance of accurate, complete and confidential mental health treatment records; (5) administration of psychotropic medication only with appropriate supervision and periodic evaluation; and (6) a basic program to identify, treat, and supervise inmates at risk for suicide. *Balla v. Idaho State Board of Corrections*, 595 F.Supp. 1558, 1577 (D.Idaho 1984).

[11] The requirement of a subjective component is said to derive from the inherent meaning of the word "punishment," as connoting intentional conduct. *See Wilson v. Seiter*, 501 U.S. 294, 300, 111 S.Ct. 2321, 2325, 115 L.Ed.2d 271 (1991) (quoting *Duckworth v. Franzen*, 780 F.2d 645, 652 (7th Cir.1985) *cert. denied*, 479 U.S. 816, 107 S.Ct. 71, 93 L.Ed.2d 28 (1986)). The assertion, while expressed by Judge Posner with great firmness, is, at best, dubious. *See* Webster's Third New International Dictionary, at 1843 ("punishment . . . 3. severe, rough or disastrous treatment"). Moreover, even if the assertion had better linguistic support, it would not mandate the reductive examination of each occurrence for proof of the perpetrator's mental state required under the cases. The precondition for an Eighth Amendment claim is a formal judgment that imprisonment is an appropriate punishment. Thus everything that happens to a post-conviction prisoner is the result of an intentional effort to punish, and the only question which remains is whether the punishment actually experienced is cruel and unusual within the meaning the Eighth Amendment. Having noted my disagreement with both the principle and its rationale, it goes without saying that this court is bound by those cases and thus must apply those determinations, however much I think them in error.

any given day there are probably between 13,000 and 18,000 inmates in California's prisons in need of treatment because they suffer from serious mental disorders. (*See* Declaration of Joel A. Dvoskin (Dvoskin Declaration) at 6; Attachment to Letter from Karl S. Mayer, filed May 25, 1994.) As I noted above, under the Eighth Amendment such prisoners are entitled to adequate medical care. It is of course fundamental that neither the dimension of the task, nor its difficulty, excuses compliance with a constitutional mandate.

After a trial the magistrate judge found that the delivery of necessary care to the mentally ill inmates who comprise the plaintiff class was so deficient that it constituted a substantial violation of the federal Constitution. Defendants have interposed numerous objections to the magistrate judge's findings and recommendations. Their objections to Judge Moulds' findings and recommendations can be grouped into two categories. First, defendants contend that there are five "fundamental deficiencies" which pervade the findings and recommendations, herein characterized as "fundamental" objections. Second, defendants raise specific objections to the legal standard used by the magistrate judge to analyze defendants' state of mind and to several factual determinations that he made in the Findings and Recommendations. These are referred to as "specific" objections.[12]

*1300 B. *Fundamental Objections*

1. *Definition of Serious Mental Disorder*

Defendants object that the magistrate judge did not include a definition of "serious mental disorder" in the findings and recommendations. They suggest the absence of such a definition has two results, one evidentiary, the other substantive. As to the evidentiary issue they argue that without a more specific definition of "serious mental disorder," the connection between what a defendant knew and the defendant's response to that knowledge is "clouded." Defendants also contend that the absence of a specific definition of "serious mental disorder" precludes this court or anyone charged with implementing relief from determining who is a member of the class, and thus its extent or the requisites for relief. (Objections at 76.)[13]

The record in this action demonstrates that this objection is simply disingenuous. The class certified in this case, far from representing some amorphous enigma to defendants, describes a group of inmates who have been studied by the CDC for over eight years. Two of the major studies offered as evidence in this action, the Stirling Report and the Scarlett Carp Report, were based on data concerning the prevalence of inmates suffering from "serious mental disorders." (*See e.g.,* Plaintiffs' Exhibit 1 at ii-3, ii-7;

---

[12] In their objections, defendants raise for the first time a contention that class members confined at California Men's Colony (CMC) are bound by *Dohner v. McCarthy*, 635 F.Supp. 408 (C.D.Cal.1985), and the findings therein. Dohner was tried in 1985 and challenged various conditions of confinement; the class certified was "comprised of all inmates confined at CMC-East." *Id.* at 411. Individuals who are not members of a class are not bound by the judgment in a class action. 18 Wright, Miller & Cooper, Federal Practice and Procedure: Jurisdiction § 4455, at 473 (1981). The Dohner class did not include by its terms inmates who would in the future be housed at CMC-East, and there is no evidence that any inmates in the plaintiff class in this action were housed at CMC-East in 1985. Accordingly, there is no basis for concluding that members of the instant class are bound by the judgment in Dohner.

[13] The defendants raised the same objection in connection with class certification. *See* Defendants' Opposition to Plaintiffs' Motion for Class Certification, filed August 15, 1991 (Opposition), at 15-17; *see also* (Transcript of Proceedings on Plaintiffs' Motion for Class Certification, August 29, 1991, at, e.g., 2-4.). Defendants did not re-raise those arguments in their objections to the magistrate judge's findings and recommendations on class certification filed with this court. (*See* Objection to Magistrate Judge's Findings and Recommendations for Class Certification, and Request for Reconsideration by the Magistrate Judge or the Court, filed October 31, 1991.) Since that time defendants have not seriously pressed the issue, tendering only one sentence in their trial brief regarding the absence of an elaborate definition of serious mental disorder. (*See* Defendants' Trial Brief filed February 22, 1993, at 2.) Defendants' failure to object to the proposed class definition at the time of class certification arguably would, standing alone, suffice to support this court's conclusion that the objection is without merit. See *Gluth v. Kangas*, 951 F.2d 1504, 1509 (9th Cir.1991) (failure to object to class certification order and failure to provide trial court with amended or alternative findings sufficient to support denial of appeal from class certification order).

Defendants' Exhibit D1338 at i.)[14] These reports both concern themselves with the prevalence of, and the provision of mental health care services to, inmates who suffer from such disorders.[15]

Moreover, witnesses at trial had no trouble addressing the term. Thus, John O'Shaughnessy, Chief of Mental Health for the California Department of Corrections, testified that there is a clinical definition for the "seriously mentally disordered." (RT at 19:21.) In addition, one of defendants' experts, Dr. Koson, offered an opinion concerning the definition of serious mental disorder. (Declaration of Dennis F. Koson, M.D. (Koson Declaration) *1301 at 3.)[16] Defendants' other expert, Dr. Joel Dvoskin, discussed treatment for inmates suffering from "serious mental disorders" without any apparent need for further definition (Dvoskin Declaration, *passim*), and testified that "the level of need in the California Department of Corrections for treatment of serious mental disorder on any given day would be approximately 11 to 15 percent of the population." (Dvoskin Declaration at 6.)

Defendants' contention also fails because it ignores the relevant law. As noted above, Eighth Amendment jurisprudence addresses medical needs in both the physical and mental contexts, *see McGuckin*, 974 F.2d at 1059 and *Doty*, 37 F.3d at 546, and thus provides a legal gloss to the term. It is, of course, true that the legal conclusion that a medical condition constitutes a serious medical need is intertwined with a factual determination inherently dependent on clinical findings. That hardly renders the concept uncertain, although it does suggest the means of resolution of questions in a specific context.

The court concludes that the phrase "serious mental disorder" has a readily available definition in a medical context, in a legal context, and, as a result of at least two major studies conducted by or for the CDC, in a penological context. Accordingly, the court finds that defendants' objection that the term "serious mental disorder" lacks sufficient meaning to enable them to ascertain what the problem is, or to do what the Constitution requires of them, is without merit.

2. *Specification of Applicable Constitutional Minima*

Defendants' second "fundamental" objection is that the magistrate judge failed to specify the minimum for each, or any, of the elements of a constitutionally adequate mental health care delivery system. Defendants do not object to the elements of a constitutionally adequate delivery system as described by the magistrate judge, see n. 10 *supra*. Instead, defendants object to the magistrate judge's failure to quantify the specific level of services that the CDC must provide in order to satisfy the requirements of the federal Constitution. Defendants' argument, to the extent it reflects a serious legal position, as contrasted with mere obstructionism, does not convince.

The Constitution requires defendants to provide inmates in their custody with access to adequate mental health care. *Doty*, 37 F.3d at 546; *Hoptowit*, 682 F.2d at 1253. The basic components of a constitutionally adequate system have been described by the courts. See e.g., *Balla*, 595 F.Supp. at 1577 (quoting *Ruiz*, 503 F.Supp. at 1339). The Constitution does not, however, prescribe the precise mechanisms for satisfying its mandate to provide access to adequate mental health care. Moreover, in cases challenging conditions of prison confinement, courts must strike a careful balance between identification of

---

[14] These studies also used the term "severe" mental disorder. (*See, e.g.,* Plaintiff's Exhibit 1 at ii-7; Defendants' Exhibit D1338 at i.) The Stirling Report arose out of legislation which included a definition of "severe mental disorder." (Plaintiff's Exhibit 1 at ii-7.) It appears that the words "severe" and "serious" were used interchangeably. In any event, it is apparent that the phrase "serious mental disorder" is sufficiently specific to have concrete meaning in the contexts of both of these studies as well as among clinicians and officials in the CDC.

[15] The Stirling Report notes that "[t]he disorders providing the clearest operational indication of SMD according to the definition [in Penal Code § 2960] were taken to be Organic Brain Syndrome—Severe, Schizophrenia, Major Depression and the Bipolar Disorders. It is recognized that some offenders with nonpsychotic disorders may well be sufficiently impaired to meet the [relevant] criteria. The SMD operationalization is, therefore, a conservative criterion . . . ." (Plaintiffs' Exhibit 1 at ii-7.)

[16] Dr. Koson opined that "a person in state prison would have a serious mental disorder such as to require that he be given access to the continuum of mental health care services if currently or within the last three years, he or she has had a significant disorder of thought or mood which substantially impairs or substantially impaired reality testing, judgment, or behavior. A person would also suffer from a serious mental disorder if she or he currently does not have the ability to meet the functional requirements of prison life without psychiatric intervention, including psychotropic medication." (*Id.* at 3-4.)

constitutional deficiencies and deference to the exercise of the wide discretion enjoyed by prison administrators in the discharge of their duties. *See Toussaint v. McCarthy*, 801 F.2d 1080, 1086-87 (9th Cir.1986) *cert. denied*, 481 U.S. 1069, 107 S.Ct. 2462, 95 L.Ed.2d 871 (1987).[17] The need to strike that balance, common sense, and the clinical nature of the problem, all suggest that standards to insure compliance with the Eighth Amendment can only be developed contextually.

*1302 The magistrate judge relied on the six elements described in *Balla*, 595 F.Supp. at 1577, as the basic framework for a constitutionally adequate mental health care system. (Findings and Recommendations at 14, 29.) He found deficiencies of a constitutional magnitude in most of the necessary areas.[18] He did not, however, specify the exact mechanisms for screening inmates, or the number of staff that must be hired, or the specific level of competence that must be possessed by staff, or the precise methods of medication management to be used, or the manner of maintaining medical records. Indeed, it would have been error to do so. *See Hoptowit*, 682 F.2d at 1253-54. Rather, properly allowing for deference to the penological expertise of defendants, while recognizing the essentially medical nature of the problem, the magistrate judge essentially proposed leaving the matter to the creation of protocols, standards, procedures and forms to be developed by defendants in consultation with court appointed medical experts. For the reasons explained above that resolution appears wholly appropriate. Defendants' second objection is without merit.

3. *Individual Consideration of Deliberate Indifference*

Defendants contend that the magistrate judge failed to consider whether there was evidence that each defendant had acted with deliberate indifference to the serious medical needs of class members. The contention that the magistrate judge failed to consider the liability of each defendant individually is not supported by the record. While Judge Moulds did not make individual findings as to each defendant, he found that the defendants have acted with deliberate indifference. Defendants' contentions that the record does not support a finding of deliberate indifference as to each, or any defendant, is discussed *infra*.

4. *Reliance on Expert Opinion* [19]

Defendants' fourth "fundamental" objection pertains to expert testimony.[20] It takes essentially two forms. One addresses the weight accorded the evidence, and the other focuses on the legal use made by the magistrate judge of that evidence.[21]

---

[17] As Chief Judge Henderson recently observed, federal judges are not prison administrators nor does the Eighth Amendment provide a general power to reform state prisons. On the other hand the protection of the rights guaranteed by the federal constitution is the special responsibility of the federal judiciary. *See Madrid v. Gomez*, 889 F.Supp. 1146, 1279 (N.D.Cal.1995). It is within the parameters of both those truths that this, or any court resolving an Eighth Amendment case, must act.

[18] Judge Moulds did not specifically find a deficiency in the second area, i.e., the requirement of a treatment program involving more than segregation and close supervision.

[19] As used in this opinion, "expert testimony" refers to the testimony of those individuals identified as expert witnesses in the Findings and Recommendations at pages 5-12 and the appendix thereto.

[20] Defendants raise specific objections to the use of several of the experts' declarations. Most of these repeat one or more of the objections described in the text and are rejected for the reasons set forth in the general discussion. Defendants' objection to reliance on the declaration of Dr. V. Meenakshi stems from her litigation with the department and an asserted lack of objectivity demonstrated in her declaration. (Objections at 79.) Of course all facts bearing on potential bias should be weighed by the trier of fact. Having done so, it is not at all "plain" to this court that Dr. Meenakshi "intended" to describe "only the very worst instances of mental health care."

[21] In their closing brief, defendants qualify their various objections. There, they contend that "[t]he findings go too far when they give expert testimony conclusive weight without considering whether the testimony is supported by independent evidence in the record." (Defendants' Reply on Objections to Findings and Recommendations, filed November 7, 1994, at 25.) Defendants' assumption that the magistrate judge failed to consider the evidence of record is simply unsupported.

Defendants also contend that "the findings go too far when they credit experts' opinions on the quality of care in individual cases without any clinical evaluation or other reliable diagnostic information." (*Id.*) Defendants do not, however, identify any instance in which this type of opinion was purportedly offered or relied on.

Finally, they contend that "[t]he findings go too far when they accept experts' descriptions of the factual material that forms the bases for their opinions as proof that the underlying facts exist." (*Id.*) This objection is addressed in the text.

The evidentiary objections raise issues concerning the propriety of reliance on expert testimony in general, the reliability of the testimony in this case because of the sources of information used by the expert witnesses, and the propriety of the expert testimony addressing the prevalence of illness. The court turns to these issues seriatim.

Defendants contend that the expert declarations "are entitled to little weight in *1303 determining whether a particular condition constitutes cruel and unusual punishment." (Objections at 82.) They appear to premise this argument on the lack of personal examination of inmates, (*id.* at 84), and suggest the declarations are unreliable insofar as they are based on medical files "pre-selected" by plaintiffs' counsel. On this basis defendants contend the declarations are not evidence of inmate suffering or of the prevalence of mental illness in the CDC. (Objections at 79.)

Defendants' contentions concerning the use of expert opinion will not lie. The law contemplates expert testimony in the form of opinion when "specialized knowledge will assist the trier of fact . . .," *See* Fed.R.Evid. 702; *see also Daubert v. Merrell Dow Pharmaceuticals*, 509 U.S. 579, —, 113 S.Ct. 2786, 2795, 125 L.Ed.2d 469 (1993) (assistance to trier is "a condition [going] primarily to relevance"); *Jordan v. Gardner*, 986 F.2d 1521, 1526 (9th Cir.1993) (en banc) (expert opinion is competent evidence of harm likely to accrue to inmates as a result of particular conditions of confinement).

Defendants' deprecation of the sources relied on to formulate the opinion testimony offered in this case fares no better. Fed.R.Evid. 703 provides experts with "wide latitude to offer opinions, including those that are not based on first hand knowledge or observation." *Daubert*, 509 U.S. at —, 113 S.Ct. at 2796; *see also Cabrales v. County of Los Angeles*, 864 F.2d 1454, 1460 (9th Cir.1988), *vacated*, 490 U.S. 1087, 109 S.Ct. 2425, 104 L.Ed.2d 982 (1989), *original decision reinstated*, 886 F.2d 235 (9th Cir.1989) *cert. denied*, 494 U.S. 1091, 110 S.Ct. 1838, 108 L.Ed.2d 966 (1990). For the same reason their attack upon the files selected is without merit.[22] *Daubert*, 509 U.S. at —, 113 S.Ct. at 2796 (latitude permitted experts in reliance on nonadmissible sources is premised on the "assumption that the expert's opinion will have a reliable basis in the knowledge and experience of his discipline.")[23]

The clinical testimony of plaintiffs' experts is precisely the type of testimony contemplated by the Federal Rules of Evidence: testimony offered by three psychiatrists and one clinical psychologist concerning the condition of mentally ill inmates based on statements by inmates, review of medical records, personal observation, and interviews with custodial and clinical staff. *See* Fed.R.Evid. 703 (advisory committee's notes). This evidence, together with the testimony of inmate witnesses called at trial, plainly demonstrates the suffering of mentally ill inmates incarcerated in the California Department of Corrections.

Defendants also attack the sufficiency of the testimony concerning the prevalence of severe mental illness within the inmate population. Expert testimony concerning this issue was offered by way of oral testimony, expert declaration (including the declaration of defendants' expert, Dr. Dvoskin), and documentary evidence. Defendants' only specific objection concerning reliance on expert testimony for prevalence data centers on the use of Dr. Grassian's declaration. (Objections at 80.)[24]

Dr. Grassian averred that "[e]stimates of the number of mentally ill inmates at Pelican Bay vary" and that he did not know the precise number of mentally ill inmates at that institution. (*Id.*; Declaration of Stuart Grassian, filed February 25, 1993, at 45 RT at 5–193.) Defendants do not dispute that there were mentally ill inmates housed at *1304 Pelican Bay. The objection to the use of Dr. Grassian's declaration is without merit.[25]

The objection to the magistrate judge's use of the expert testimony appears to be of two types: first

---

[22] Plaintiffs argue that since this case is about adequacy of mental health care for mentally ill inmates, random selection of files from the general population would have been "nonsensical." Second, they contend that, at least for purposes of prison tours, plaintiffs' experts and defendants' experts used the same methods and worked in teams. (Plaintiffs' Response at 26-27.)

[23] Even if defendants' argument were better supported as a matter of the rules of evidence, they have pointed to nothing which suggests that a different but nonetheless sensible methodology for selecting files to review would have materially altered the evidence before this court.

[24] Defendants' objections to the magistrate judge's reliance on the Stirling Report and the Scarlett Carp report, both of which contained prevalence data, are of a different character and will be discussed *infra*.

[25] Defendants also raise a vague objection that reliance on Dr. Grassian's declaration is erroneous because the parties stipulated at trial that references to depositions or documents in that declaration were for foundational purposes only, not for the truth of the matters contained in those depositions or documents. (*See* RT at 5:201-203.) Plaintiffs' counsel, however, also explained that those depositions or documents would be offered into evidence separately. (RT

defendants contend that he used that testimony first to establish constitutional minima and second, as proof of deliberate indifference. The court examines each of these contentions in turn.

Defendants argue that Judge Moulds improperly relied on expert testimony to establish constitutional minima.[26] *See Rhodes v. Chapman*, 452 U.S. 337, 348 n. 13, 101 S.Ct. 2392, 2400 n. 13, 69 L.Ed.2d 59 (1981) (expert opinions as to desirable prison conditions while potentially helpful and relevant, are insufficient to establish constitutional minima). The argument is inapposite.

The constitutional standards that apply to this case are well established, *see* section IV *supra*. The task before this court is to determine from the evidence whether defendants have violated these constitutional requirements. In his findings and recommendations the magistrate judge articulated the appropriate standards; there is nothing to support the contention that he used expert testimony to establish constitutional norms.[27]

Defendants also argue that "the Findings and Recommendations are replete with examples of use by the magistrate judge of opinions of experts to conclude that 'defendants' must be 'deliberately indifferent' because 'they' have not similarly embraced the opinions without question." (Objections at 8.) The attack is without justification. The magistrate judge did not conclude that defendants are deliberately indifferent simply because they have failed to embrace expert opinion, nor because they failed to adopt the recommendations of any of the major studies undertaken to assess the state of the delivery of mental health services within the CDC.

The court discusses in detail below the issue of deliberate indifference and the relationship between the evidence adduced at trial and the applicable standard for determining deliberate indifference. *See* section V(D) [*infra*]. It suffices here to note that Judge Moulds concluded that defendants have known for years of the gross deficiencies in the provision of mental health care to inmates incarcerated in the CDC, and that they have failed to take reasonable steps to avert the obvious risk of harm to mentally ill inmates that flows from the failure to remedy those deficiencies. The evidence fully supports those conclusions.

5. *Standards for Compliance With Recommendations*

Defendants' last "fundamental" objection is to the purported absence of any standards in the findings and recommendations to guide defendants and court-appointed experts in the formulation of the remedial plans recommended by the magistrate judge. This objection is again without merit.

Having concluded that the delivery of health care to those suffering serious mental illness is constitutionally deficient, Judge Moulds recommended development of remedial plans to address that constitutional failure. Requiring development of remedial plans is the method most often employed by district courts faced with systemic constitutional deficiencies because it is an efficacious way to both "cure[] . . . constitutional deficiencies *1305 and minimize[ ] intrusion into prison management." *Madrid v. Gomez*, 889 F.Supp. 1146, 1280 (N.D.Cal.1995). That process seems to this court to represent both a sensible and legally appropriate way of proceeding if the findings are otherwise upheld.

C. *Specific Objections*

Defendants have raised numerous objections to specific factual findings by the magistrate judge. The court has reviewed *de novo* all of the findings to which objections have been raised and now disposes of those objections.[28]

---

at 5:202.) Defendants do not point to any place in the findings and recommendations where the magistrate judge relied on Dr. Grassian's testimony in a manner inconsistent with this stipulation and representation.

[26] This objection is not without irony given defendants' vigorous contentions that the findings and recommendations are defective for failing to establish constitutional minima.

[27] The magistrate judge did take note of the congruence between the expert testimony before the court concerning the elements necessary to an adequate mental health care delivery system in prison and the components of a minimally adequate system described in *Balla*. (Findings and Recommendations at 29.) That happy coincidence hardly undermines the mode of analysis adopted in the findings and recommendations.

[28] The court feels obliged to consider in detail each of the specific objections raised by the defendants. Such consideration, however, has a tendency to obscure the issues actually tendered by this litigation. What is at stake is the

1. *Screening*

The magistrate judge found that "[i]n order to provide necessary mental health care to prisoners with serious mental disorders, there must be a system in place to identify those individuals, both at the time they are admitted to the Department of Corrections and during their incarceration." (Findings and Recommendations at 31.) He further found that "the CDC lacks an adequate mechanism for screening for mental illness, either at the time of reception or during incarceration, and has lacked adequate screening since at least 1987." (*Id.*) Judge Moulds concluded that "only those inmates who self-report or present with medical records demonstrating a prior psychiatric history, those who exhibit bizarre behavior, or those who ask to be seen by a psychiatrist will be identified as needing psychiatric care." (*Id.* at 35.)

Defendants object to the factual finding that the CDC does not have adequate procedures for screening for mental illness. (Objections at 33.) Defendants also object to the legal conclusion that the Constitution requires defendants to do more to screen for mental illness than they presently do. (Objections at 87.) Those objections must be rejected.

The evidence cited by defendants depicts precisely the type of screening described by the magistrate judge. It is screening based on self-reporting, use of records of prior hospitalization and/or past or current use of psychotropic medications, exhibition of bizarre behavior, and requests for care. (*See e.g.,* RT at 18:38; RT at 19:8-9; RT at 19:10-11; RT at 19:13; RT at 19:14-15.) Certainly each of those means of identifying ill inmates is appropriate. The question, however, is whether the Eighth Amendment requires more.

Under the Eighth Amendment the defendants are required to maintain a system in which inmates are able to make their need for mental health care known to staff competent to provide such care before inmates suffer unnecessary and wanton infliction of pain. *Hoptowit*, 682 F.2d at 1253. The evidence demonstrates that some inmates with serious mental disorders are, by virtue of their condition, incapable of making their needs for mental health care known to staff. (Declaration of Craig Haney, Ph.D., filed February 25, 1993 (Haney Declaration), at 18; RT at 1:115-16; RT at 3:8; RT at 10:101.) *See also Madrid*, 889 F.Supp. at 1217; *Casey v. Lewis*, 834 F.Supp. 1477, 1550 (D.Ariz.1993). Delivery of adequate mental health care to such inmates requires their identification. For that reason it has been held that correctional systems are required by the Constitution to put in place a "systematic program for screening and evaluating inmates in order to identify those who require mental health treatment." *Balla*, 595 F.Supp. at 1577.

Defendants do not have a systematic program for screening and evaluating inmates for mental illness. (Defendants' Exhibit D1338 at 34 ("Screening and follow-up evaluations are not formalized and staffing for these functions is inconsistent among reception centers . . . ."); Plaintiffs' Exhibit 440 at 4 ("There is a lack of comprehensive, standardized screening for mental illness and suicidality" in the CDC)). The mechanisms on which they rely are either used haphazardly, ***1306** or depend for efficacy on incomplete or nonexistent medical records, self-reporting, or the observations of custodial staff inadequately trained in the signs and symptoms of mental illness. The evidence before the court plainly shows that thousands of inmates suffering from mental illness are either undetected, untreated, or both. (*See e.g.,* Plaintiff's Exhibit 1 at ii-9, ii-10; RT at 19:141 (testimony of John O'Shaughnessy); RT at 39:74-75 (testimony of James Gomez).)[29] The federal Constitution does not tolerate such a lack of medical care.

Magistrate Judge's ultimate conclusion of systemic deficiency in the delivery of medical treatment to members of the class. Focusing on the trees presents the danger of forgetting that what is being examined is the condition of the forest.

[29] Defendants contend that the magistrate judge's reliance on the Stirling Report's finding that there were thousands of undetected inmates suffering from serious mental disorders within the CDC is based on a "gross misunderstanding" of the terminology used in the Stirling Report. (Objections at 93.) It is defendants, however, who misread the terminology of the Stirling Report.

The Stirling Report was a study of, *inter alia*, the prevalence of serious mental disorders among inmates in the California Department of Corrections. The consultants divided inmates into two categories: the " 'unidentified' general population group," defined as "those offenders who had *not* been assigned psychiatric categories in the CDC inmate classification system" and the "identified" group, "drawn from the approximately 2,966 prisoners (in July 1987) who currently had specific psychiatric classifications and/or were located in specific psychiatric facilities used by CDC." (Plaintiffs' Exhibit 1 at ii-3.) (Emphasis in original.) *See also* RT at 11:43-47 (Testimony of Dr. Thomas Greenfield). The consultants specifically noted that "[s]ome of the 'Unidentified' sample had in fact received mental

2. *Staffing*

a. *Sufficiency of Staff*

In order to provide inmates with access to constitutionally adequate mental health care, defendants must employ mental health staff in "sufficient numbers to identify and treat in an individualized manner those treatable inmates suffering from serious mental disorders." *Balla*, 595 F.Supp. at 1577; *see also Madrid*, 889 F.Supp. at 1257 (citing cases).

The magistrate judge found that the California Department of Corrections is seriously and chronically understaffed in the area of mental health care. (Findings and Recommendations at 36.) A workload study undertaken by defendants almost a decade ago found that the need for psychiatric services far exceeded the available staffing resources, (*Id.* at 37), and the Stirling Report and the Scarlett Carp Report confirmed this finding.[30] (*Id.*)

Defendants' objections to these findings consist of arguments that (1) they do have staff who provide inmates with mental health care services; (2) the magistrate judge failed to specify what level of staffing is required by the Constitution;[31] and (3) the Scarlett Carp consultants "designed their plan to be well above constitutional minima."[32] (Objections at 94.)

Defendants' first objection is inapposite. The fact that defendants have some staff providing mental health services is not evidence that they have sufficient staff.

Defendants' third objection is based on the declarations of defendants' experts, Dr. Dvoskin and Dr. Koson. (*See* Dvoskin Declaration at 6, Koson Declaration at 18). As the court now explains, that criticism is unjustified. Moreover, as the court also explains, *1307 the Scarlett Carp report hardly stands alone.

The Scarlett Carp study did find the system was substantially understaffed. (Defendants' Exhibit D1338 at 34.) The Scarlett Carp delivery system and staffing recommendations were based on a goal of providing care based on a community model described as providing mentally ill persons with "reasonable access to necessary care," (Defendants' Exhibit D1338 at 41), considering, however, "a reasonable assessment of what is feasible . . . to meet constitutional obligations and the mental health needs of the inmate population, given budget constraints and public policy." (*Id.*) Elsewhere in the report, "reasonable access" is defined as "timely, responsible, and adequate care provided by qualified (and appropriately licensed) staff." (Defendants' Exhibit D1338 at xi.) These standards are not materially different from the constitutional requirement of ready access to competent medical staff. *Hoptowit*, 682 F.2d at 1253 ("The Eighth Amendment requires that prison officials provide a system of ready access to adequate medical care.").

The goals of the Scarlett Carp study and the design criteria incorporated to achieve those goals closely track the mandates of the federal Constitution. For that reason the assessment of staffing needs contained in the Scarlett Carp final report is significant evidence that the level of mental health care staffing is constitutionally inadequate. That evidence, however, does not stand alone.

Several major studies have been done regarding mental health care in the California Department of Corrections over the last decade. Each has concluded that the system is seriously understaffed. (*See e.g.,* Plaintiffs' Exhibit 456 at vi (1986 Workload Study concluded that "workload is clearly excessive with

---

health treatment while incarcerated without their classification yet having been updated." Plaintiffs' Exhibit 1 at ii-3. The consultants found that "[a] large number of *unidentified* individuals in the general population, were they to be screened, would be diagnosable with the same serious disorders and exhibit related symptoms. Given the size of the unidentified population (over 57,000 at the time of the survey), even the small base-rate of 7 percent for the four serious disorders amounts to over 4,000 *undetected* SMD individuals." (*Id.* at ii-9.) (Emphasis in original.)

[30] The magistrate judge noted that the Scarlett Carp consultants determined that 732 mental health staff positions would be necessary to adequately staff mental health care for an inmate population of 119,000, that the budget for fiscal year 1992/93 contained only 376.6 authorized mental health care positions to serve a population of 113,000 inmates, and that the CDC had a 25 percent vacancy rate in authorized mental health care positions for fiscal year 1991/92 with no evidence that the vacancy rate had changed significantly at the time of trial. (Findings and Recommendations at 37.)

[31] This objection is rejected for the reasons set forth in section V(B)(2), *supra*.

[32] Defendants also contend that they have not been deliberately indifferent to the staffing shortages. The question of deliberate indifference will be addressed in detail *infra*.

existing resources"); Plaintiffs' Exhibit 1 at ii-19, 20 (Stirling Report finding that 20% of budgeted positions were unfilled, resulting in, *inter alia*, fewer patients being treated and/or patients received reduced care); Plaintiffs' Exhibit 2 at iii (Stirling Report finding of need to "[s]et adequate staffing standards for all mental health professionals and . . . [d]etermine why recruitment and retention of professional mental health staff is a problem.")).[33]

Plaintiffs' experts testified to significant understaffing within the system. (*See e.g.,* Declaration of Dr. Edward Kaufman (Kaufman Declaration), filed February 5, 1994, at 16 ("Every CDC institution I evaluated had a shortage of psychiatrists, psychologists, psychiatric social workers, psychiatric nurses, and occupational and recreational therapists . . .. Given the large numbers of seriously disturbed inmates in these institutions, many more mental health staff should be present. Staff were stretched dangerously thin in all institutions."); Declaration of Dr. Russell C. Petrella (Petrella declaration), filed February 5, 1993, at 39-40 ("The most obvious and pervasive sign of the lack of adequate mental health care resources in the CDC system are [sic] the unacceptably long delays in access to every level of care. Inmates suffer long waits at every stage of the process. . .. These delays, which I saw at every institution I looked at, are a critical sign of understaffing.")).[34]

The overwhelming weight of the evidence before this court demonstrates that the California Department of Corrections is significantly and chronically understaffed in the area of mental health care services. The Department does not have sufficient staff to treat large numbers of mentally ill inmates in its custody. This conclusion demonstrates that plaintiffs have satisfied the objective ***1308** component of a showing of a violation of the federal Constitution.

b. *Competence of Staff*

Defendants object to the finding that they have no effective method for ensuring either the competence of their staff or that inmates have access to competent care. They also object to the magistrate judge's finding that this violates the plaintiff class members' Eighth Amendment right of access to adequate mental health care. Finally, they object to the suggestion that a remedial order require the development of a quality assurance system.

Once again analysis commences with the observation that state prisoners have a constitutional right of access to adequate mental health care. Both as a matter of law and common sense, in order to meet that requirement of the federal Constitution, defendants must provide inmates with access to a competent medical staff. *Hoptowit*, 682 F.2d at 1253 ("The medical staff must be competent to examine prisoners and diagnose illnesses . . . [and] must be able to treat medical problems or refer prisoners to others who can."); *see also Ortiz v. City of Imperial*, 884 F.2d 1312, 1314 (9th Cir.1989) (citing *Hoptowit*, 682 F.2d at 1253); *Cabrales*, 864 F.2d at 1461 (9th Cir.1988) ("Access to medical staff is meaningless unless the staff is competent and can render competent care.").

Defendants' expert, Dr. Dvoskin, testified that in his opinion "a large system such as the California Department of Corrections could probably not provide adequate mental health care without some sort of management information system and some form of quality assurance." (Dvoskin Declaration at 9.) Plaintiffs' expert, Dr. Petrella, concurred in that assessment. (Petrella Declaration at 21.)

In sum, defendants are not providing adequate mental health care to inmates, and they do not have any form of quality assurance that reaches all institutions covered by this class action.[35] Defendants' expert has testified that defendants cannot provide adequate mental health care without some form of

---

[33] The Stirling consultants focused primarily on the effect of vacancies in authorized positions on providing mental health care services. They pointed to recommendations of the 1986 workload study and a 1979 psychiatric staffing study concerning staffing standards and recommended numbers of positions, but did not independently endeavor to validate or replicate those studies, or to assess the adequacy of the number of budgeted positions. (Plaintiffs' Exhibit 2 at III-7.)

[34] The court notes in passing that defendants' experts did not dispute this testimony. (*See* Dvoskin Declaration, *passim*; Dvoskin Deposition Excerpts, Volume II, at 303:14–17; Koson Declaration, *passim*; Koson Deposition Excerpts, Volume II, 274:21–275:3, 275:5–11.)

[35] Defendants apparently have some form of quality assurance program at three of the twenty-nine institutions in the class. They are, however, required to provide all inmates in the plaintiff class with access to adequate mental health care and they are failing to do so.

quality assurance. Requiring development of a quality assurance program is an appropriate remedy for constitutional deficiencies in the delivery of prison health care. *See Grubbs v. Bradley*, 821 F.Supp. 496, 500 (M.D.Tenn.1993). Defendants' objections to this portion of the findings and recommendations is without merit.

3. *Care of Mentally Ill Inmates*

a. *Delays in Access to Care*

The magistrate judge found that "[t]here are significant and unacceptable delays" in inmate access to mental health care at each level of the mental health care delivery system as it exists in the CDC. (Findings and Recommendations at 43-44.) Defendants object to these findings insofar as they are based on the opinion testimony of experts and contradicted by "percipient witness caregivers." (Objections at 17, 52.) Defendants also argue that there was no finding by the magistrate judge that the delays caused harm to any individual inmate. (Objections at 99.) Finally, defendants argue that there was no finding by the magistrate judge as to whether the delays are a result of deliberate indifference by any defendant. (Objections at 101.)

The constitutional requirement that defendants provide inmates with "a system of ready access to adequate medical care," means simply either ready access to physicians at each prison or "reasonably speedy access" to outside physicians or facilities. *Hoptowit*, 682 F.2d at 1253. In addition, there must be an "adequate system for responding to emergencies." *Id.*

At the outset, the court notes that the previous findings with respect to the inadequacies in screening and staffing, standing alone, render inescapable the conclusion that mentally ill inmates' access to care within the CDC is unconstitutionally delayed. Additionally, the evidence before the court plainly demonstrates substantial delays in access to mental health care for inmates housed in the California Department of Corrections.

*1309 The Scarlett Carp Final Report highlighted delays in access to necessary care as a deficiency in the present mental health care system. (Defendants' Exhibit D1338 at 34.)[36] It identified a "major problem" with access to acute inpatient hospitalization, and a "backlog of cases awaiting transfer to Enhanced Outpatient Program due to the limited number of beds available in designated institutions." (*Id.* at 34-35.)

Beyond the 1993 report there was extensive testimony concerning delays in access to necessary care at every level. (*See e.g.,* RT at 3:13-18 (In February 1992, the waiting list to see a psychiatrist after initial screening was over 400 inmates at the reception center at Wasco State Prison; delays lasted up to three months and had "escalated to the point where inmates were cutting their wrists just to receive medication");[37] RT at 22:3–6 (In 1991 and again in 1992, there were backlogs of 300-400 inmates awaiting transfer to enhanced outpatient psychiatric programs at California Men's Colony or California Medical Facility);[38] Defendants' Exhibit D880 (CDC memo to David Tristan stating that "[t]he problem of the backlog of male inmates awaiting transfer to CMF and CMC for mental health services is approaching the crisis level for the Department"); Kaufman Declaration at 9 (delays of up to several months in transfers to Atascadero State Hospital for inpatient hospitalization).)

Defendants' objections to the magistrate judge's findings in this regard are without merit. Because the evidence demonstrates that there are delays everywhere within the system and that those delays result in exacerbation of illness and patient suffering, a violation of the objective facet of the test for violation of the Eighth Amendment has been demonstrated.

---

[36] "The current system seems to place a high degree of reliance on inpatient hospitalization and transfer to Enhanced Outpatient beds . . . .. The vast majority of available mental health beds and services provided by CDC staff are at [three institutions] which are geographically distant from many institutions. Therefore, inmates must be transported long distances to receive needed treatment . . . . The current system of classifying mentally ill inmates further hinders timely transfer of inmates considered stable, or assessed as not mentally ill, out of mental health beds . . . which further renders an already strained system inefficient."

[37] This backlog improved after the mental health staffing levels were improved. (RT at 3:19.)

[38] These inmates were awaiting transfer to be evaluated for placement in the enhanced outpatient program; following transfer they still had to be screened before they were either placed in the program or returned to the transferring institution. (RT at 22:5-6.)

b. *Medication*

The magistrate judge found constitutional violations arising from the failure of the system to properly address questions arising as to the proper medication of class members. They may generally be classified as issues relating to medication management, and issues relating to involuntary medication. I address the questions in turn.

1. *Medication Management*

The magistrate judge found that defendants' current practices with respect to medication management violate the Constitution. (Findings and Recommendations at 50.) Specifically, the magistrate judge found that "defendants' supervision of the use of medication is completely inadequate; prescriptions are not timely refilled, there is no adequate system to prevent hoarding of medication, there is no adequate system to ensure continuity of medication, inmates on psychotropic medication are not adequately monitored, and it appears that some very useful medications are not available because there is not enough staff to do necessary post-medication monitoring." (Findings and Recommendations at 50.)

In light of these findings Judge Moulds advanced a series of recommendations designed to remedy these deficiencies. (*Id.* at 79.) He also recommended that the preliminary injunction governing heat plans for management of inmates on psychotropic medication be made permanent for a period of two years. (*Id.* at 50-51.)

Defendants object to the factual findings and accompanying recommendations concerning medication management. Defendants also object to the recommendation that the preliminary injunction be made permanent.

*1310 Defendants' objections to the factual findings concerning medication management are based on (1) evidence that they have a computer tracking system in place at each institution to identify inmates on medication; (2) some evidence in the record that at some institutions prescriptions are timely refilled and medication ingestion is monitored to one degree or another at some institutions, that various factors "may affect the way an inmate receives his psychotropic medication,"; and (3) that there is a "special procedure" by which a CDC physician can obtain permission to prescribe medication not in the CDC formulary. (Objections at 57-61.)[39]

The computer tracking system is only available at individual institutions; it is not networked to any other institution. (*See e.g.,* RT at 21:86.) Thus, it provides no solution to the significant problems that occur when inmates on psychotropic medication are transferred from one institution to another.[40] In addition, the fact that at some places within the CDC some inmates are getting timely medication and/or appropriate monitoring does not address the systemic failure resulting in gross deficiencies at institutions throughout the CDC.

Finally, the evidence of record demonstrates that some medications that are very effective in the treatment of serious mental disorders are not available. (*See e.g.,* Defendants' Exhibit D1196.) In order to satisfy the Constitution, medical staff must have available to them the modalities to provide inmates with necessary care. *See Ramos v. Lamm*, 639 F.2d 559, 575 (10th Cir.1980), *cert. denied*, 450 U.S. 1041, 101 S.Ct. 1759, 68 L.Ed.2d 239 (1981).

---

[39] The court finds that some of defendants' arguments in this regard border on violation of Rule 11 of the Federal Rules of Civil Procedure. For example, defendants state that "the evidence shows that defendants employ reasonable medication tracking systems," citing to RT, April 13, 1993, at 21:52, 21:86-92, and 21:110-111. The cited pages are to the testimony of John O'Shaughnessy, Chief of Mental Health for the CDC. At the cited pages, Mr. O'Shaughnessy testified to a need for case management within the system. (RT at 21:52.) He testified that at present, correctional counselors at each institution are responsible for "case management." (*Id.*) He testified that those correctional counselors typically do not have access to an inmate's medical file, and that case managers do not in fact follow inmates throughout the system. (*Id.* at 21:90-91.) The only testimony in all of the cited pages concerning medication tracking is testimony that pharmacists at individual institutions keep information on a computer concerning inmates at the institution who are on psychotropic medication; Mr. O'Shaughnessy also testified that this information is not available except at the institution where it is generated. (*Id.* at 21:85-86.)

[40] Plaintiffs argue that this computer system was only put in place in any event because of the heat plan preliminary injunction entered in this action. (Plaintiffs' Response at 183.)

The magistrate judge's factual findings concerning the constitutional deficiencies in medication management are fully supported by the record and will be adopted by the court.[41]

Defendants object to the magistrate judge's recommendation that the preliminary injunction concerning heat plans for inmates on psychotropic medication be made permanent on the grounds that the findings made by the magistrate judge are insufficient to support imposition of a permanent injunction.

The magistrate judge found that "[t]he principal obstacle . . . was motivating defendants to develop the heat management plans that are the subject of that injunction; now that the plans are developed and in use, defendants have little reason to abandon them and good reasons to keep them in place." (Findings and Recommendations at 51.) The court agrees with defendants that *1311 the finding made by the magistrate judge does not support issuance of a permanent injunction. The court finds, however, that the record in this action does support such an injunction.

The standards for issuing a permanent injunction are substantially similar to those applied to requests for preliminary injunctive relief; however, in order to obtain a permanent injunction plaintiffs must actually succeed on the merits of their claims. *Sierra Club v. Penfold*, 857 F.2d 1307, 1318 (9th Cir.1988) (citing *Amoco Production Co. v. Village of Gambell*, 480 U.S. 531, 541, 546 n. 12, 107 S.Ct. 1396, 1401-02, 1404 n. 12, 94 L.Ed.2d 542 (1987)).

Plaintiffs originally sought a preliminary injunction in this action on August 1, 1991, following the heat and medication related deaths of three inmates on psychotropic medication. (Findings and Recommendations at 2.) That request for preliminary injunctive relief was denied on the basis of a memorandum submitted by defendants at the time of the hearing on the request for preliminary injunction and evidence of some steps being taken by defendants to address the problem. (*Id.* at 4.) Since the preliminary injunction was denied in the fall and trial was then set for early summer, the matter was not revisited until April 2, 1992, when plaintiffs renewed their motion for preliminary injunction. (*Id.* at 4.) In the interim, defendants had done almost nothing to have a permanent plan ready for the summer. (*Id.* (citing Declaration of Katherine Sher, filed April 2, 1992, at paragraph 17).) The matter was resolved on the eve of hearing by stipulated injunction, after settlement negotiations with the magistrate judge. (*Id.* at 4-5.)

Plaintiffs have succeeded on the merits of the claims raised before this court, including presenting ample proof that medication management practices within the CDC violate the Eighth Amendment. The history of defendants' response to this issue demonstrates a recalcitrant refusal to address the serious issues underlying the preliminary injunction until forced to do so under pressure of this litigation. Sadly, the response in that specific context echoes throughout the record. Defendants have been confronted repeatedly with plain evidence of real suffering caused by systemic deficiencies of a constitutional magnitude. Their responses have frequently occurred only under the pressure of this and other litigation. Given that history, the court not only has no confidence that defendants will continue to adequately monitor inmates on psychotropic medication for risks from heat exposure, it regretfully concludes that without an order defendants are likely not to do so. The preliminary injunction presently in place will be made permanent for a period of three years.

2. *Involuntary Medications*

Plaintiffs raise several contentions with respect to administration of involuntary medications to class members. They contend that defendants do not have "consistent and appropriate practices for involuntarily medicating class members." (Plaintiffs' Trial Brief and Proposed Findings of Fact, filed February 22, 1993, at 16.) They contend that involuntary medication is not available at some institutions, and that it is underutilized at California Men's Colony. (*Id.*) They also contend that involuntary medication, when used, is sometimes administered in inappropriate settings. (*Id.*) In addition, plaintiffs contend that prison

---

[41] Plaintiffs and defendants argue over the propriety of non-psychiatrist physicians prescribing psychotropic medications. The court need not resolve this debate. Defendants' constitutional obligation is to provide inmates with access to professionals who are competent to treat their serious mental disorders, and to provide for the administration of psychotropic medication only with appropriate supervision and periodic evaluation. *Balla*, 595 F.Supp. at 1577. As the magistrate judge noted, under California law, any licensed physician may prescribe medication. (Findings and Recommendations at 50 n. 40 (citing California Business & Professions Code § 2051). To the extent that physicians in the Department may be performing duties for which they are not qualified, that problem appears likely to be addressed by development of a quality assurance program. *See Grubbs v. Bradley*, 821 F.Supp. 496, 500.

doctors order administration of involuntary medication over the telephone without examining the inmate to be medicated, and that custody staff are inappropriately involved in the decision to administer involuntary medication. (*Id.* at 17.)

The magistrate judge found on the one hand (1) that some institutions do not have protocols for use of involuntary medication and (2) that involuntary medication is underutilized, which causes harm to inmates decompensating as a result of mental illness, which in turn, results in the de facto denial of the procedural safeguards to which mentally inmates are entitled. On the other hand he also found that (1) involuntary medication can be and is administered without examination of the inmate by a physician; (2) that custody staff "can and does play a significant role in recommending the use of involuntary medication," and that custody staff can veto a medical decision concerning the use of involuntary medication; and (3) that inmates are "often involuntarily medicated in inappropriate *1312 settings." (Findings and Recommendations at 58-60.)

The magistrate judge found these diverse deficiencies attributable in large measure to (1) the lack of an adequate screening program; (2) the lack of adequate training of custody staff in the signs and symptoms of mental illness; and (3) policies which permit custody staff to use involuntary medication "in the absence of consultation with, or against the considered advice of, medical and/or mental health professionals." (Findings and Recommendations at 61.)

Defendants' objection to this aspect of the findings and recommendations rests, essentially, on the fact that they are subject to the requirements of a permanent injunction issued in a state court case, *Keyhea v. Rushen*, Solano County Superior Court, No. 67432, and on the presence of a state regulation governing administration of involuntary medication, 15 C.C.R. § 3364.[42]

Both the injunction in *Keyhea* and the provisions of 15 C.C.R. § 3364 authorize administration of involuntary medication prior to any type of hearing. *Keyhea* governs procedures for "long-term" administration of involuntary medication; the injunction provides for procedures which apply when involuntary medication is necessary for more than 72 hours, for more than 10 days, and for more than 24 days. (*See* Plaintiffs' Exhibit 103.) Section 3364 provides for "emergency" administration of involuntary medication and provides procedures that essentially track the *Keyhea* decree for administration of such medication for longer than seventy-two hours. Defendants contend that the procedures they currently follow pursuant to *Keyhea* and the state regulatory scheme exceed federal constitutional minima.[43] Defendants also contend that state law prohibits them from administering involuntary medication until inmates are gravely disabled and incompetent and, therefore, that they cannot be found deliberately indifferent because inmates who refuse medication deteriorate to a significant degree.

The issues concerning the use of involuntary medication presented in this case raise difficult and troubling constitutional questions, implicating the potential conflict between the substantive and procedural rights protected by the due process provisions of the Fourteenth Amendment and the right to adequate medical care derived from the Eighth Amendment.

Plaintiffs' first set of contentions concerning the unavailability and underutilization of involuntary medication implicate the Eighth Amendment; these contentions are, in essence, that the defendants are not providing members of the plaintiff class with necessary medical treatment.

The evidence before the court suggests that in certain instances involuntary medication may be necessary medical treatment for gravely mentally ill inmates. (*See e.g.,* Grassian Declaration at 23; Kaufman Declaration at 142.) There is also evidence before the court that such treatment is not being provided to those inmates. (*See e.g.,* Grassian Declaration at 23; Meenakshi Declaration at 28.)[44]

Plaintiffs' second set of contentions implicate the substantive and procedural protection derived

---

[42] Defendants assert that this regulation was issued pursuant to a consent decree filed in a federal class action, *Whitaker v. Rushen*, U.S.D.C. No. C-3284 SAW (N.D.Cal. March 25, 1985).

[43] With respect to long-term use of involuntary medication, defendants' argument has persuasive force. *See Washington v. Harper*, 494 U.S. 210, 249-257, 110 S.Ct. 1028, 1051-55, 108 L.Ed.2d 178 (1990) (Stevens, J., concurring and dissenting) (requirement that decision to involuntarily medicate an inmate be reviewed by an "impartial person or tribunal" provides greater protection to inmates than procedure approved by majority opinion).

[44] Defendants are correct that they must wait until an inmate is "gravely disabled" before administering involuntary medication; that is a federal constitutional requirement as well as a requirement of state law. *See Washington*, 494 U.S. 210, 225, 110 S.Ct. 1028, 1038-39, 108 L.Ed.2d 178 (1990). That requirement does not address the evidence before the court that inmates who have deteriorated to that point are left to languish in that state for extended periods of time without any treatment. (*See, e.g.,* Meenakshi Declaration at 28; Grassian Declaration at 142.)

from of the Due Process Clause of the Fourteenth Amendment. Prison ***1313** inmates have a substantive liberty interest in avoiding the unwanted administration of involuntary medication. *Washington v. Harper*, 494 U.S. 210, 221, 110 S.Ct. 1028, 1036, 108 L.Ed.2d 178 (1990). That interest, however, may yield where a seriously mentally ill inmate "is dangerous to himself or others and the treatment is in the inmate's medical interest." *Id.* at 227, 110 S.Ct. at 1040. In those circumstances, the inmate's interest in freedom from involuntary medication is said to be outweighed by the state's obligations to, *inter alia*, (1) "provide prisoners with medical treatment consistent . . . with their . . . medical interests" and (2) take reasonable steps to ensure inmates' safety. *Id.* at 225, 110 S.Ct. at 1039.

Because of the inmate's liberty interest, the High Court has determined that the Fourteenth Amendment surrounds a determination to involuntarily medicate with protections containing both procedural and substantive components. Specifically, the decision to involuntarily medicate is a medical decision that must be made by medical staff and reviewed by independent medical decisionmakers. *Washington*, 494 U.S. at 232–233, 110 S.Ct. at 1042-43; *see also Bee v. Greaves*, 744 F.2d 1387, 1395-96 (10th Cir.1984), *cert. denied*, 469 U.S. 1214, 105 S.Ct. 1187, 84 L.Ed.2d 334 (1985) (even in an emergency, decision to administer involuntary medication is a medical decision). That review must take place at an administrative hearing prior to administration of the involuntary medication, and the inmate must be given notice of the hearing, the right to appear, and the right to present evidence and cross-examine witnesses. *Washington*, 494 U.S. at 235, 110 S.Ct. at 1043-44.

Defendants do not have any procedures to govern the administration of involuntary medication for periods less than 72 hours, nor are procedural protections available prior to commencement of involuntary medication in the first instance, or at all unless the involuntary medication will continue for more than 72 hours.

There is evidence that in some instances involuntary medication has been ordered over the telephone without the inmate to be medicated first being examined by a physician. (Kaufman Declaration at 142.) The evidence also demonstrates that at certain institutions, custody staff plays an inappropriate role in decisions concerning involuntary medication. (Meenakshi Declaration at 29.) These practices violate the class members substantive and procedural rights. *See Washington v. Harper*, supra.

Addressing the constitutional violations which the magistrate judge quite properly found, while resolving the potential conflict between rights protected by the Fourteenth Amendment and the Eighth Amendment, and at the same time recognizing the appropriate deference accorded to defendants' responsibilities as prison administrators, requires a careful consideration of the circumstances when involuntary medication is to be administered and the rules concerning appropriate review. These difficulties, however, cannot justify a failure to remediate the violations.

c. *Mechanical Restraints*

The magistrate judge found that "[t]here was uncontradicted evidence that mechanical restraints are necessary in some instances for proper management of a mentally ill inmate, but that such restraints should only be used when physical assault, by the mentally ill inmate against others or against him or herself, is imminent or has just occurred, and that such restraints should only be used in accordance with strict guidelines." (Findings and Recommendations at 56.) He further found that the restraints should only be used on mentally ill inmates "when a psychological emergency has occurred," and, therefore, that "it is necessary to provide follow-up psychiatric care to the mentally ill inmate after restraints have been used." (*Id.*) Finally, he found that "[p]rocedures for use of these restraints vary from institution to institution within the class, and there is no systemwide review in place to ensure appropriate use of such restraints." (*Id.* at 57.) Judge Moulds recommended that defendants be required to develop and implement protocols to govern the use of mechanical restraints which, *inter alia*, specifically ***1314** address coordination between mental health staff and custody staff. (*Id.* at 81.)

Defendants object to the magistrate judge's recommendation on the grounds that there is a regulation governing use of these restraints. Section 3280 of Title 15 of the California Code of Regulations governs the use of mechanical restraints. The regulation addresses all of the areas of concern cited by the magistrate judge except the need for follow-up psychiatric care after the use of mechanical restraints.

The court finds several of the other remedial measures designed to address the constitutional deficiencies in staffing, access to necessary care including inpatient hospitalization, and maintenance of medical records sufficient to address the inadequacy of follow-up care after use of mechanical restraints.

Accordingly, the court finds it unnecessary to order further specific relief with respect to the use of mechanical restraints.

4. *Medical Records*

The magistrate judge found that "[t]he medical records system within the California Department of Corrections is extremely deficient." (Findings and Recommendations at 61.) Specifically, he found that

> [a]t most of the prisons in the class there are serious deficiencies in medical recordkeeping, including disorganized, untimely and incomplete filing of medical records, insufficient charting, and incomplete or nonexistent treatment plans. To complicate the situation beyond all reason, inmates are typically transferred between prisons without even such medical records as might exist.

(Findings and Recommendations at 62.) The magistrate judge recommended that defendants be required to develop and implement a plan for use of transfer notes and transfer of inmate medical records within CDC institutions, to "develop a plan for obtaining medical records from county jails for inmates on their initial admission to the California Department of Corrections," and to develop protocols for the maintenance of adequate medical records. (Findings and Recommendations at 79-80, 82.)

Defendants' objections in this regard are limited. First, defendants point to some evidence that inmates sometimes arrive at some institutions with their medical records. The fragments of evidence cited by defendants to support this contention is outweighed by the significant evidence to the contrary described by the magistrate judge.

Defendants also contend that they are not responsible for the failure of county personnel to transfer medical records with inmates arriving at CDC reception centers from county jails.[45] That contention is inapposite.

Defendants have a constitutional obligation to provide inmates with adequate medical care. A necessary component of minimally adequate medical care is maintenance of complete and accurate medical records. Defendants have a constitutional obligation to take reasonable steps to obtain information necessary to the provision of adequate medical care. The evidence of record shows that some physicians on the CDC staff can and do take steps to obtain medical records from county jails when inmates arrive at the CDC without them. (*See e.g.,* RT at 33:19.) Such steps are not standard practice, however. (*See* Petrella Declaration at 135.)

The harm that flows to class members from inadequate or absent medical records is manifest. (*See e.g.,* Kaufman Declaration at 19-20.) Eighth Amendment liability in this regard is not predicated on the failure of counties to deliver medical records. It is predicated on the failure of defendants to take reasonable steps to implement policies that will aid in obtaining necessary medical information about class members when they are transferred from county jails to the CDC.

Defendants also take issue with the determination that they are deliberately indifferent to the need for adequate medical records. ***1315** The question of defendants' deliberate indifference will be addressed *infra*.[46]

The magistrate judge's findings and recommendations concerning the inadequacy of medical records will be adopted in full by the court.

5. *Suicide Prevention*

The magistrate judge found that "defendants have designed an adequate suicide prevention program and have taken many of the steps necessary to implement that program." (Findings and

---

[45] The problem with transfer of CDC medical records when inmates move from one CDC institution to another and when parolees return to custody is equally well-documented and is undisputed by defendants. (*See, e.g.,* Defendants' Exhibit D1338 at 35; RT at 21:64-72; RT, May 17, 1993, at 87.)

[46] Defendants also contend that "a treatment plan is not constitutionally mandated for every inmate who receives psychiatric care." (Objections at 22.) The magistrate judge did not find that it was, nor did he recommend that it be required.

Recommendations at 75.) He further found that the program "has not yet been fully implemented, and that some of the failure to fully implement the program is due to the severe understaffing in mental health care." (*Id.*) He therefore recommended that the special master be ordered to report to the court on the adequacy of suicide prevention in the CDC twelve months after the order of this court. (*Id.*) Defendants object to this recommendation on the grounds that "[t]here is no basis for the court to oversee implementation of any plan in an area that is not constitutionally deficient." (Objections at 23.)

The weight of the evidence before the court shows that there are several institutions where the suicide watch component of the program has been inadequately implemented. As the magistrate judge found, this failure is due in large measure to the severe understaffing that exists throughout the CDC. The record before the court demonstrates that the purported constitutional violation at issue here is the chronic understaffing already described. That primary constitutional violation must be remedied; the remedy of that constitutional violation should redress its derivative effects, including inadequate implementation of the CDC's suicide watch program. No separate remedy directed specifically at the Department's suicide prevention program will be ordered at this time.

6. *Summary*

Plaintiffs consist of a group of inmates who have serious mental disorders. It is undisputed that failure to provide treatment for these disorders "could result in further significant injury or the 'unnecessary and wanton infliction of pain.'" *McGuckin*, 974 F.2d at 1059 (citation omitted). As explained above, it is apparent that due to a systemic failure to provide adequate mental health care, thousands of class members suffer present injury and are threatened with great injury in the future. The court concludes that the record in this case demonstrates beyond reasonable debate the objective component of plaintiffs' Eighth Amendment claim.

D. *Deliberate Indifference*

The magistrate judge found that the defendants were deliberately indifferent within the meaning of Eighth Amendment jurisprudence.[47] Defendants challenge that finding.

The court acknowledges the caution which both the law and propriety enjoin upon an inquiry as to whether high officials of state government are deliberately indifferent to the rights of persons within their charge. With due regard for the defendants and the difficult task that is theirs, but with equal regard for the duty that is the court's by virtue of its office, the court turns to that *1316 task. In doing so, the court stresses that the issue is not whether as to some particular deficiency the defendants have exhibited deliberate indifference. Rather, given the overwhelming evidence of the systemic failure to deliver necessary care to mentally ill inmates, the issue is whether the defendants have demonstrated deliberate indifference to that condition.

In order to find that defendants have acted with deliberate indifference to the needs of the plaintiff class, the court must find (1) that defendants knew that inmates face a substantial risk of harm as a result of the systemic deficiencies noted above and (2) that defendants have disregarded that risk by "failing to take reasonable measures to abate it." *Farmer*, 511 U.S. at —, 114 S.Ct. at 1984.

Plaintiffs seek prospective injunctive relief. Under such circumstances, deliberate indifference is examined "in light of the prison authorities' current attitudes and conduct," *Helling*, 509 U.S. at —, 113

---

[47] He specifically found that the evidence bearing on the issue "was not seriously contested," and that "defendants have known [about and repeatedly acknowledged] the serious problem with understaffing at least since . . . 1985." He further found that "defendants have known that there were thousands of mentally ill inmates . . . who were not even identified as needing care, let alone being provided necessary care, at least since . . . July, 1989." Moreover he found that "[t]he inadequacies in the mental health care delivery system . . . remain today." In like manner he noted that "[d]efendants repeatedly acknowledged that . . . their medical record keeping system . . . was woefully outdated and inadequate, and that they did not have a mechanism in place for screening and identifying mentally ill inmates." He concluded that "the fact that defendants have known about these deficiencies for over eight years without taking any significant steps to correct them is additional evidence of deliberate indifference." (Findings and Recommendations at 75-76.)

S.Ct. at 2477, i.e. the defendants attitudes and conduct "at the time suit is brought and persisting thereafter." *Farmer*, 511 U.S. at —, 114 S.Ct. at 1983.[48]

The question of whether a defendant charged with violating rights protected by the Eighth Amendment has the requisite knowledge is "a question of fact subject to demonstration in the usual ways, including inference from circumstantial evidence [citation omitted], and a factfinder may conclude that a prison official knew of a substantial risk from the very fact that the risk was obvious." *Id.* at —, 114 S.Ct. at 1981. The inference of knowledge from an obvious risk has been described by the Supreme Court as a rebuttable presumption, and thus prison officials bear the burden of proving ignorance of an obvious risk. *Id.* at —, 114 S.Ct. at 1982. It is also established that defendants cannot escape liability by virtue of their having turned a blind eye to facts or inferences "strongly suspected to be true." *Id.* at — n. 8, 114 S.Ct. at 1982 n. 8, and that "[i]f . . . the evidence before the district court establishes that an inmate faces an objectively intolerable risk of serious injury, the defendants could not plausibly persist in claiming lack of awareness." *Id.* at — n. 9, 114 S.Ct. at 1984 n. 9.

As the court concluded above, the evidence demonstrates that seriously mentally ill inmates in the California Department of Corrections daily face an objectively intolerable risk of harm as a result of the gross systemic deficiencies that obtain throughout the Department. The evidence also demonstrates that inmates have in fact suffered significant harm as a result of those deficiencies; seriously mentally ill inmates have languished for months, or even years, without access to necessary care. They suffer from severe hallucinations, they decompensate into catatonic states, and they suffer the other sequela to untreated mental disease.

Defendants' knowledge of the risk of harm to these inmates is evident throughout this record. (*See e.g.,* Defendants' Exhibit D880.)[49] It is equally apparent that defendants have known about these gross deficiencies in their system for years. The risk of harm from these deficiencies is obvious to plaintiffs' experts, to defendants' experts, to defendants' consultants, to individual employees of the Department of Corrections in the field, and to this court. The actual harm suffered by mentally ill inmates incarcerated *1317 in the California Department of Corrections is also manifest in this record.

Defendants' objection to the finding of deliberate indifference rests on two arguments. On the one hand each asserts, for different reasons, that there is insufficient evidence of their personal indifference. The second objection rests on the notion that their response to the gross deficiencies in the delivery of mental health care to those seriously ill prisoners in their charge has been "reasonable." The court now turns to each issue.

Each defendant contends that there is insufficient evidence to support individual findings of deliberate indifference. These state officials, all sued in their official capacities, each have authority to make decisions that directly affect the rights of class members, and thus all are appropriate defendants in this action. *See Los Angeles County Bar Association v. Eu*, 979 F.2d 697, 704 (9th Cir.1992) (quoting *Ex parte Young*, 209 U.S. 123, 157, 28 S.Ct. 441, 452-53, 52 L.Ed. 714 (1908)). Their claims as to lack of the requisite mental state are not well taken.

Defendants Khoury and Zil argue that they have no power or authority to change any aspect of the delivery of mental health care to inmates in the California Department of Corrections. The argument will not lie for two reasons. First, even if true, the lack of power does not necessarily contraindicate scienter. Second, the sole cite in support of the proposition is evidence that neither Dr. Khoury nor Dr. Zil had any independent authority to hire additional medical or mental health personnel or to "implement the Stirling Report." (RT, June 21, 1993, at 39:82-83.) That evidence does not speak to the many other areas within the scope of these defendants' authority that affect the delivery of constitutionally adequate care to class members.

---

[48] *Farmer* addressed suit by an inmate seeking "injunctive relief to prevent a substantial risk of serious injury from ripening into actual harm." *Farmer v. Brennan*, 511 U.S. 825, —; 114 S.Ct. 1970, 1983; 128 L.Ed.2d 811 (1994). In the matter at bar members of the plaintiff class are not only facing substantial risks of serious injury, they are experiencing actual harm as a result of the systemic deficiencies identified in this order.

[49] The exhibit, an internal Department of Corrections memorandum, reads in pertinent part "[t]he need to assess [inmates backlogged awaiting transfer for mental health services] is urgent. Seriously mentally ill inmates who do not receive needed treatment can worsen severely, losing most or all of their ability to function. Such inmates can also become suicidal or can pose significant risks to others or to the safety of the institution. In addition, the litigation facing the Department in this area, especially the Department-wide *Coleman* case, puts the Department at extreme liability risk if these inmates go untreated."

Defendant Wilson argues that there is no evidence that he had knowledge of the systemic deficiencies that have obtained for years. Given his official responsibilities, the suggestion by his lawyers of the Governor's ignorance concerning information he was duty bound to be familiar with seems remarkable. Be that as it may, they have provided no evidence to support their assertion that he is unaware of the evidence received in this case, including the Stirling Report produced pursuant to a legislative mandate and the CDC commissioned Scarlett Carp Report. Moreover, after five years of litigating, the claimed lack of awareness is not plausible. *Farmer*, 511 U.S. at — n. 9, 114 S.Ct. at 1984 n. 9.

Defendant Gomez argues that during his tenure as Director of the Department of Corrections he has made many improvements in the delivery of mental care services. As I explain below, however, the circumstances relied on do not refute the finding of deliberate indifference required by this record.

Defendant Sandoval argues generally that he was "hardly mentioned" during the trial and that the arguments made on behalf of defendants Wilson and Gomez apply equally to him. Those arguments are rejected for the reasons stated.

As I noted above each of these defendants is responsible to a greater or lesser degree for the tragic state of affairs revealed by this record. Each to a greater or lesser degree can make significant contributions to its solution. After vigorously litigating these issues for almost five years, defendants cannot plausibly claim that they lack knowledge of the gross deficiencies in the delivery of mental health care to class members. Furthermore, defendants continue to vigorously dispute any liability for these deficiencies even in the face of overwhelming evidence to the contrary. Each defendant's claim to personal innocence cannot be credited. *See Jordan*, 986 F.2d at 1529.

Defendants' second claim, that their responses to the failure to provide adequate care to the mentally ill, has been reasonable must also be rejected. On examination, defendants' response has been to question the experts who provide information to them, to commission more studies, to make ineffective gestures toward the serious issues that pertain to the chronic problem of understaffing, and to initiate planning for a central administrative structure to manage a completely inadequate field delivery system. While defendants ***1318** do not contend, nor could they, that the risk of harm to these seriously ill inmates has been averted by the steps they have taken, they maintain that these responses absolve them from Eighth Amendment liability in this action. Each response is addressed in turn.

Defendants maintain that they are not required to accept uncritically the findings of experts hired to study the mental health care system and recommend remedial steps. The argument, while true, is unavailing. Defendants have offered no valid explanation for their rejection of the findings that have been repeatedly and consistently made over the last ten years. Defendant Gomez, for instance, testified that he had a "tremendous number of concerns" with the Stirling Report because "[i]t didn't reconcile with what I felt was going on in the institutions," (RT, May 17, 1993 at 52) and because his staff "was not capable of providing [him] the kind of answers [he] felt [he] needed." (Id. at 53-54.) The director does not claim, however, to "have the capacity to make [ ] judgments on who's mentally ill and who's not," (*Id.* at 52) nor can he claim medical expertise. His articulated reasons for rejecting the information provided by experts with those capacities are thus without a sufficient basis. Given the essential consistency of the Sterling Report with subsequent studies and the evidence in this trial, continued refusal to accept the obvious is simple obduracy.

Nor are repeated studies a reasonable response. Whatever variances exist between the various studies that have been made, they consistently find a woefully inadequate system of mental health care with all its tragic consequences.

Similarly, where, as here, the delivery of mental health services at the institutional level is constitutionally inadequate, planning to add administrators to central headquarters is an insufficient response. Despite acknowledgment that the provision of services at the institutional level is inadequate, defendants do not intend to spend any more resources in the field pending development and implementation of a central health care administration, (*see* RT, May 17, 1993, at 47-49), which will take will take three to four years. (*See* RT, May 17, 1993, at 47). Defendants are not free to disregard the constitutional rights of mentally ill inmates for three to four years.

Defendants devote several pages of their objections to arguments that they have taken steps to remedy the serious staffing shortages in the delivery of mental health care to class members, contending that these steps negate any possible finding of deliberate indifference. (Objections at 16, 43-50, 94- 97.) I cannot agree.

First, none of the steps that defendants have taken have come close to addressing the understaffing problem. According to the data from the Scarlett Carp Final Report, the Department is understaffed in the range of some three hundred members deemed necessary to deliver adequate care to mentally ill inmates; this number is higher when the vacancy rate in authorized positions is considered. *See infra* at n. 32.[50] Thus, the 1993/94 request for 21.25 new positions (RT at 14:67) is not reasonably designed to remedy the problem.[51]

Defendant Khoury acknowledged serious problems with recruitment and retention of psychiatrists and psychologists at institutions within the CDC. (*See e.g.,* RT at 14:141-143; 14-171.) He attributed this problem to noncompetitive salaries, undesirable geographical locations and clientele, and inadequate incentives. (RT at 14:141-143; 14:171.) Even in the face of these clearly identified factors, defendants have failed to take any ***1319** meaningful steps to improve staffing levels.[52]

Defendants' objections may be read as obliquely relying on arguments premised on budgetary constraints to refute the finding of deliberate indifference. (*See e.g.,* Defendants' Objections at 7). Prior to trial, however, defendants acknowledged that they would not rely on the argument that fiscal constraints permit them to violate the Eighth Amendment. (RT, April 16, 1992). Of course it is improper advocacy to raise issues in post trial argument specifically abjured before trial. Moreover defendants' pretrial position seems wholly appropriate. *See Wilson,* 501 U.S. at 301-302, 111 S.Ct. at 2325-26 ("[I]t is hard to understand how [a 'cost' defense] could control the meaning of 'cruel and unusual punishment' in the Eighth Amendment. An intent requirement is either implicit in the word 'punishment' or is not; it cannot be alternately required and ignored as policy considerations might dictate.").[53]

Given the nature and extent of the crisis and its duration, it is not possible to credit arguments that defendants entertain a good faith belief that such efforts were sufficient. "It is not enough to say that . . . prison authorities considered an issue carefully . . . .. Prison authorities are also required to afford sufficient weight to the constitutional rights of individuals. The failure to treat constitutional provisions with appropriate respect constitutes deliberate indifference to the rights [at stake]." *Jordan,* 986 F.2d at 1529. Put another way, patently ineffective gestures purportedly directed towards remedying objectively unconstitutional conditions do not prove a lack of deliberate indifference, they demonstrate it.

Yet other evidence supports the court's determination of deliberate indifference. After completing a *de novo* review of the record, this court has come to the reluctant conclusion that defendants are simply seeking to delay meeting their constitutional obligation to the mentally ill inmates who are their charges. The court has reviewed each objection, the evidence cited in support thereof, and the legal arguments tendered by defendants. Some of those objections are so seriously flawed that they raise questions of good faith. In certain instances the legal authority cited does not support the proposition for which it is tendered. In many instances the evidence cited by defendants not only does not support their contention, it supports the very finding of the magistrate judge to which the objection is being made.

Acting for the sole purpose of delay perpetuates the human suffering caused by the violations of the federal Constitution which the evidence in this case demonstrates. Deliberate indifference is nothing if it is not that.

The court repeats, the evidence of defendants' knowledge of the gross inadequacies in their system is overwhelming. The risk of harm from these deficiencies is obvious. The actual suffering experienced by mentally ill inmates is apparent. In the face of this reality, the court finds that defendants' conduct constitutes deliberate indifference to the serious medical needs of the plaintiff class.

---

[50] The court is not finding a magic number that will render the staffing levels constitutional; the court is taking note of the evidence in this regard to illustrate the ineffectual nature of defendants' actions.

[51] A systemwide request for 64.5 positions was made for fiscal year 1992-93; those positions were added the year before trial bringing the total number of authorized positions to the 376.6 level found by the magistrate judge. (RT at 14:96-97; Findings and Recommendations at 37.) The request for 21.25 positions was made for fiscal year 1993-94 and was turned down. (RT at 14:67-68.)

[52] It appears from the record that several options are available to defendants to overcome the harm to inmates that flows from understaffing. Once again, the court emphasizes that specific management decisions rest with the defendants as prison administrators. It is only where, as here, defendants have abdicated their responsibilities to members of the plaintiff class that they must be required to make decisions that take seriously the constitutional rights of class members. *See Jordan,* 986 F.2d at 1529.

[53] The notion of budgetary constraints is, of course, highly protean. The administrators appear to have funds for those projects which appeal to them, such as the development of a central administration for mental health services. Whether or not a central administration is desirable, the point is that while money is lavished on its development it is diverted from the identification and treatment of ill patients.

E. *Use of Disciplinary/Behavior Control Measures Against Mentally Ill Inmates*

Plaintiffs also sue relative to an issue intimately related to the systemic failure to provide adequate medical care to mentally ill inmates, but nonetheless analytically distinct from it. They assert the inappropriate use of disciplinary and behavioral control measures ***1320** directed towards the members of plaintiff class.

1. *Insufficient Training*

Judge Moulds found that "mentally ill inmates who act out are typically treated with punitive measures without regard to their mental status." (Findings and Recommendations at 51.) He further found that such treatment was the result of inadequate training of the custodial staff so that they are frequently unable to differentiate between inmates whose conduct is the result of mental illness and inmates whose conduct is unaffected by disease. Defendants object to the finding that the custodial staff lacks sufficient training in the identification of signs and symptoms of mental illness.

New correctional officers in the California Department of Corrections receive a three-hour course entitled "Unusual Inmate Behavior." (Declaration of Steve Cambra (Cambra Declaration) at 3.) In addition, custody staff may receive some additional in-service training at the institutional level. (*Id.* at 5.) The average length of the in-service classes is approximately one hour, although California Men's Colony offers a two-hour in-service course called "The Skillful Observer," which covers psychiatric disorders. (RT at 17:130.) The question is whether, on the record made before the magistrate judge, this training suffices under the Constitution.

There is substantial evidence in the record of seriously mentally ill inmates being treated with punitive measures by the custody staff to control the inmates' behavior without regard to the cause of the behavior, the efficacy of such measures, or the impact of those measures on the inmates' mental illnesses. One explanation for these incidents is that defendants have a policy or custom of intentionally inflicting severe harm on mentally ill inmates. The magistrate judge found a less invidious reason, that the custody staff is inadequately trained in the signs and symptoms of serious mental illness. The magistrate judge's generous inference is well supported in the record.[54]

2. *Administrative Segregation/Segregated Housing Units*

The magistrate judge found that "[d]efendants' use of administrative segregation and segregated housing at Pelican Bay SHU and statewide to house mentally ill inmates violates the Eighth Amendment because mentally ill inmates are placed in administrative segregation and segregated housing without any evaluation of their mental status, because such placement will cause further decompensation, and because inmates are denied access to necessary mental health care while they are housed in administrative segregation and/or segregated housing." (Findings and Recommendations at 54.) Defendants' principle objections to these findings are based on a state regulation; their evidentiary objections are based on the use of the declaration of Dr. Stuart Grassian. Those objections are overruled. The magistrate judge's findings in this regard are fully supported by the evidence.[55]

The court must specifically address one objection raised by defendants. The magistrate judge found that "[d]efendants and their employees recognize the danger to mentally ill inmates from housing in segregated housing units, particularly Pelican Bay SHU." (Findings and Recommendations at 53.) Defendants argue that some of the testimony cited by the magistrate judge "[t]aken in context, . . . shows

---

[54] Plaintiffs' expert, Dr. Kaufman, testified in his declaration that "[t]raining of custodial staff on issues relating to mental health care was sorely lacking" at all the institutions he reviewed.

[55] Section 3342 of Title 15 of the California Code of Regulations provides for case review and psychological assessment of inmates assigned to segregated housing units. The case review is conducted by correctional counselors. (RT at 17-78.) John O'Shaughnessy, the Chief of Mental Health for the CDC, testified at trial that correctional counselors "may well" have contact with a mental health clinician regarding an inmate's mental disorders, but that correctional counselors generally do not have access to an inmate's medical records. (RT at 21:90.) The evidence of acutely psychotic and otherwise seriously mentally ill inmates placed in administrative segregation and segregated housing units for significant periods of time demonstrates that the regulation has had little or no effect on practice.

that defendants' agents took pains to evaluate the possible risks of Pelican Bay SHU, and ultimately *1321 concluded that the potential danger never materialized." (Objections at 106 n. 10.)

Plaintiffs' expert, Dr. Grassian, a board certified psychiatrist, interviewed twenty-four inmates in the Pelican Bay SHU. (Grassian Declaration at 17.)[56] He found that

> [o]f these, at least seven were actively psychotic and urgently in need of acute hospital treatment. Nine others suffered serious psychopathological reactions to SHU confinement, including in several cases a history of periods of psychotic disorganization. Of the remaining eight, five gave a history of psychiatric problems not clearly exacerbated by SHU, two others appeared free of psychiatric difficulties, and in one a language barrier prevented adequate evaluation.

(*Id.*) Dr. Grassian's findings concerning the seven actively psychotic inmates and the nine others suffering serious psychopathological reactions to SHU confinement, and the response of CDC staff to those conditions, (*see id.* at 18-43), fully support the magistrate judge's findings. The descriptions tendered by another of plaintiffs' experts, Dr. Craig Haney, are equally disturbing. (Haney Declaration at 45-47.) Given this testimony, defendants' assertion that the concerns about possible psychological harm from confinement in the Pelican Bay SHU "never materialized" can only be viewed as evidence of defendants' deliberate indifference to the serious harm visited on class members.

For the reasons set forth by the magistrate judge, defendants' present policies and practices with respect to housing of class members in administrative segregation and in segregated housing units violate the Eighth Amendment rights of class members.

3. *Use of Tasers and 37mm Guns*

Judge Moulds found that "[i]nmates who act out are also subjected to the use of tasers and 37mm guns, without regard to whether their behavior was caused by a psychiatric condition and without regard to the impact of such measures on such a condition." (Findings and Recommendations at 54). Defendants raise two objections to this finding, one going to the applicable standard, the other to the evidence.

Defendants first argue that the use of tasers and 37mm guns against members of the plaintiff class must be analyzed under the standard applicable to excessive force claims under the Eighth Amendment, i.e. whether these weapons are used maliciously and sadistically for the purpose of causing harm, and not under the deliberate indifference standard.[57]

Second, they point to an administrative bulletin issued September 29, 1992, setting guidelines for the use of tasers on inmates taking psychotropic medication as evidence that they are not deliberately indifferent to the serious medical needs of the plaintiff class.

a. *Applicable Standard*

Defendants' first argument is focused on the subjective component of an Eighth Amendment claim under which the court is to assess whether the conduct at issue is "wanton." *Jordan*, 986 F.2d at 1527. "[W]antonness does not have a fixed meaning but must be determined with 'due regard for the differences in the kind of conduct against which an Eighth Amendment objection is lodged.' " *Wilson*, 501 U.S. at 302, 111 S.Ct. at 2326 (quoting *Whitley v. Albers*, 475 U.S. 312, 320, 106 S.Ct. 1078, 1084, 89 L.Ed.2d 251 (1986)). *Id.* The court turns to the question of what standard applies.

The "baseline" mental state for "wantonness" is "deliberate indifference." *Id.* As a general rule, the deliberate indifference standard applies where the claim is that conditions of confinement cause unnecessary suffering. *Id.* In contrast, the "malicious and sadistic" standard applies to claims *1322 arising out of the use of force to maintain order. *See Id.* Whether conduct is "wanton" "in a particular context

---

[56] As noted above, defendants raise several evidentiary objections to the use of Dr. Grassian's declaration. Those are overruled. In any event, Dr. Grassian's testimony concerning the condition of inmates confined in the SHU that he interviewed is plainly competent evidence. *See* Fed.R.Evid. 703.

[57] Defendants did not present this argument to the magistrate judge in either pre- or post-trial briefing.

'depends upon the constraints facing the official,'" not the effect of the conduct on the inmate. *LeMaire v. Maass*, 12 F.3d 1444, 1452 (9th Cir.1993) (quoting *Wilson*, 501 U.S. at 303, 111 S.Ct. at 2326 (citations omitted.)).

The gravamen of plaintiffs' claim here is that they suffer from medical conditions which are exacerbated by use of the weapons at issue, and that defendants' policy permitting use of these measures against class members constitutes deliberate indifference to their serious mental disorders. The only policy in place regulating the use of these weapons covers the use of tasers on inmates who are taking psychotropic medication.[58] Otherwise, defendants' policy permits the custody staff to use tasers and 37mm guns on mentally ill inmates without regard to the impact on their mental condition. (*See e.g.,* RT at 17:158.)

The policy regulating the use of tasers on inmates on psychotropic medication provides that tasers shall not be used until (1) custody staff notifies the chief medical officer (CMO) or designee that staff is considering using a taser on a particular inmate; (2) the name, CDC number, and location of the inmate are provided to medical staff; (3) the CMO or designee reviews the medical file to determine whether any medical conditions prohibit the use of the taser on the inmate; and (4) the CMO or designee notifies custody staff that there are no medical conditions which prohibit use of the taser on the particular inmate. (*Id.*) The medical conditions that trigger these requirements are defined as ". . . the inmate [having] received any psychotropic medication in the previous six weeks, is being treated for a cardiac arrhythmia, or if the inmate has a pacemaker." (*Id.*) The CMO or designee's findings are to be documented in the medical and psychiatric sections of the inmate's file, and administrative staff is to document compliance with the policy on the "Crime/Incident Report" submitted to the Institutions Division.

This policy makes plain that the use of tasers is not restricted to "exigent circumstances" that preclude reflection on the propriety of their use in a particular instance; to the contrary, reflection, in the form of communication between custody and medical staff and review of a medical and psychiatric record by medical staff, is required prior to use of a taser on any inmate.

It is also plain from the undisputed evidence before the court that use of either tasers or 37mm guns on members of the plaintiff class can cause, and has caused, serious and substantial harm to mentally ill inmates, whether or not the inmate is on psychotropic medication. (Findings and Recommendations at 54- 55.) This harm to the inmate can be both immediate and long lasting.[59] (*Id.*) Moreover, continuation of the present practices permitting these weapons to be used against inmates with serious mental disorders without regard to the impact on those disorders will cause serious harm to members of the plaintiff class so long as those practices remain in existence.

Given the fact that the policy permits, or rather requires, deliberation before use of tasers on a subclass of the plaintiff class, and given the lack of explicable distinction between the two groups, the court concludes that the deliberate indifference standard applies to plaintiffs' claim concerning use of tasers and 37mm guns against inmates with serious mental disorders. *See Jordan*, 986 F.2d at 1528 (challenge to policy authorizing cross-gender clothed body search analyzed under deliberate indifference standard because (1) claim did not involve "critique in hindsight [of] the exercise of judgment of a particular officer on a specific occasion but instead involved policy "developed over time, with ample opportunity for reflection"; and (2) policy did not inflict pain on a "one-time basis" but would "continue to inflict pain ***1323** upon the inmates indefinitely."); *cf. LeMaire*, 12 F.3d at 1452-53 (malicious and sadistic standard applied to claim involving "measured practices and sanctions either used in exigent circumstances or imposed with considerable due process.").[60]

b. *Deliberate Indifference*

Having determined that deliberate indifference is the appropriate standard, the court now turns to the question of whether defendants' policies and practices in this regard amount to deliberate indiffer-

---

[58] Use of tasers on inmates on psychotropic medication causes physical harm. (*See* Kaufman Declaration at 159.) Thus, the policy prohibiting such use is apparently aimed at preventing physical harm. This policy suggests that the administration is drawing some unaccountable distinction between mental patients being subjected to physical as contrasted with psychological injury.

[59] Defendants did not object to the magistrate judge's factual findings in this regard.

[60] The court wishes to be clear. Application of the deliberate indifference standard to this conditions of confinement case in no way precludes application of the malicious and sadistic standard in the context of suits brought by mentally ill inmates for physical or mental injuries sustained by virtue of the need to restore order in an emergency situation.

ence. The court does so again noting the serious nature of such an inquiry and the gravity of a finding that state officials are deliberately indifferent to the well-being of those within their charge.

There is no dispute over the serious harm that can be, and has been, caused to inmates with serious mental disorders when the weapons in question are used against them. There is also no dispute that at present the only policy limiting use of these weapons prohibits use of tasers on inmates with specified heart conditions or who have received any psychotropic medication in the six weeks preceding use of the taser. Finally there is nothing of record suggesting a penological justification for the distinction between inflicting physical as contrasted with mental injury. Thus, there is no dispute that these weapons are used on inmates with serious mental disorders without regard to the impact of those weapons on their psychiatric condition, and without penological justification. The court can only conclude that these facts command a finding that the Eighth Amendment rights of members of the plaintiff class have been violated. *See Jordan*, 986 F.2d at 1529 (citing *Redman v. County of San Diego*, 942 F.2d 1435, 1443 (9th Cir.1991) (en banc) *cert. denied*, 502 U.S. 1074, 112 S.Ct. 972, 117 L.Ed.2d 137 (1992)).

VI

REMEDY

A. *Forms, Protocols and Plans*

The magistrate judge recommended a series of steps designed to address the constitutional violations he found. Defendants object to the proposed remedies on the grounds that the time constraints are too short.[61]

The magistrate judge recommended development and implementation of a series of remedial plans within specified time constraints. Two of those were to be completed within thirty days: development and use of standardized screening forms and protocols, and development and implementation of medication protocols. One was to be completed within sixty days, and the remainder were to be completed within ninety days.

The court cannot accept defendants' argument concerning development and implementation of standardized screening forms and protocols. Requiring defendants to develop and implement standardized screening forms and protocols is narrowly tailored to address the constitutional violation at issue. Given that over a year ago defendant Gomez testified that development of standardized screening practices was necessary, (RT, May 17, 1993, at 49), it is to be expected that defendants have been working on the problem. Under the circumstances, the thirty-day period does not seem unreasonable.

The court will also adopt the remainder of the recommendations insofar as they describe areas which must be addressed. This court recognizes the urgency of attending to the serious constitutional deficiencies identified in this order. Nonetheless, it will be important to consider the views of the special master and court-appointed experts concerning the amount of time that will be necessary to accomplish the tasks at hand. ***1324** Accordingly, the court will not establish specific time frames for completion of those tasks in this order. Instead, the court will refer the matter back to the magistrate judge for nomination of a special master. See infra. After the special master is appointed, the court will make further orders concerning appointment of experts and establishment of time lines.[62]

B. *Appointment of Special Master*

The magistrate judge recognized that the court may appoint a special master in a non-jury case where " 'exceptional condition[s]' "require the appointment. (Findings and Recommendations at 77 (quoting Fed.R.Civ.P. 53(b))). Defendants object to the recommendation that the court appoint a special master to monitor compliance with court ordered injunctive relief on the grounds that the magistrate

---

[61] Of course defendants contend that remedial orders are inappropriate because they have not violated the constitution. For the reasons explained in the text, those arguments cannot prevail.

[62] Defendants also object to the recommended remedial steps on the grounds that they are "void for vagueness." The court has already considered and rejected defendants' arguments that the court must specify in greater detail the steps that are required to satisfy the mandates of the federal constitution.

judge made no findings of "exceptional circumstances" to justify the appointment, and that there are no such "circumstances."

Defendants' contention that there are no exceptional conditions which warrant such appointment is unavailing. The constitutional violation which has been found is the product of systemwide deficiencies in the delivery of mental health care. Monitoring compliance with the injunctive relief ordered herein will be a formidable task. The court will adopt the findings and recommendation of the magistrate judge and appoint a special master to monitor compliance with the court-ordered injunctive relief. *See Hoptowit,* 682 F.2d at 1263.[63]

C. *Stay Pending Appeal*

Defendants' request for a stay pending appeal is premature. It will be denied.

VII

ORDER

In accordance with the above, IT IS HEREBY ORDERED that:

***

2. Except as modified by this order, the Findings and Recommendations filed June 6, 1994 are adopted in full, said recommendations to be implemented by subsequent order of the court;

3. Defendants' motion for judgment pursuant to Federal Rule of Civil Procedure 52(c), made at the close of plaintiffs' case in chief, is denied;

4. This matter is referred back to the magistrate judge for nomination of a special master. Said nomination shall be accomplished within a time period recognizing the urgency of the problems to be remedied and with such consultation with the parties as the magistrate judge deems appropriate; and

5. Defendants' request for a stay pending appeal is denied.

---

[63] The court reiterates that it is fully cognizant of the deference owed to the decision-making authority of prison administrators. The special master will not be appointed to make those decisions for the defendants, nor will he be appointed to "rush[ ] to impose notions of reform on the prisons." (Objections at 6.) The special master's responsibility will be twofold: to provide expert advice to the defendants to aid in ensuring that their decisions regarding the provision of mental health care to class members conform to the requirements of the federal constitution, and to advise the court concerning issues relevant to assessing defendants' compliance with their Constitutional obligations.

Appendix C

Residential Treatment Unit (RTU) for Ohio Department of Rehabilitation and Correction

DEFINITION

The RTU is a housing unit within the prison for inmates with mental illness who do not then need inpatient treatment, but who do require the therapeutic milieu and the full range of services and variable security available in the RTU.

ADMISSION CRITERIA

1. Inmate has a *Serious Mental Illness:* a substantial disorder of thought or mood which significantly impairs judgment, behavior, capacity to recognize reality or cope with the ordinary demands of life within the prison environment and is manifested by substantial pain or disability. Serious mental illness requires a mental health diagnosis, prognosis and treatment, as appropriate by mental health staff.

And

2. *Mental illness causes impairment in behavior and/or functioning.*

This may have been manifested as a history of recurrent decompensation of the inmate when housed in the general population.

And

3. *Inmate's mental illness is unable to be stabilized in less restrictive setting (outpatient).*

Prioritization of Admissions

- Inmates in any segregation status
- Inmates in crisis beds

- Inmates returning from OCF upon discharge recommendation of the inpatient treatment team

- Inmates who are candidates for involuntary medication

- Inmates with history of decompensation when off medication housed in GP

Procedure

1. Outpatient, Crisis or OCF Treatment Team recommends RTU placement based on inmate's clinical condition and submits Referral Form to Cluster Clinical Director or designee.

2. Correctional Assessment Form completed by security staff.

3. Clinical Director reviews case and recommends RTU placement. Submits Referral Form and Correctional Assessment Form to RTU Director or designee if inmate is already part of cluster.

4. If Clinical Director believes RTU placement appropriate and inmate requires transfer to another cluster (due to security status of lack of bed space), then Clinical Director contacts other cluster Clinical Director or designee to arrange transfer.

5. Clinical Director of receiving cluster reviews case and submits paperwork to RTU Director or designee to arrange for acceptance of inmate.

6. Clinical Director(s) notify MHA(s) and security staff to initiate transfer and classification notification and approval procedures.

7. If at any point in this procedure a clinical dispute arises, all attempts to resolve it will be made at the local (cluster) level. In the event the dispute remains unresolved, cluster Clinical Director will refer the matter to Central Office, Bureau of Mental Health Services, for resolution.

DISCHARGE CRITERIA

1. If an inmate, at any level within the RTU, is determined by the Treatment Team not to have a serious mental illness and this determination is well documented in the mental health file of the inmate through behavioral observations and examinations, the inmate *must be discharged from the RTU* back to his/her parent institution within three (3) working days.

2. When an inmate with a serious mental illness has advanced through all four (4) levels in the RTU and has remained stable at level 4, functioning essentially as a general population inmate for a period of time determined on a case by case basis, but not

less than 30 days, he/she may be discharged to the general population with appropriate mental health services follow-up.

[See next page for RTU Level System Table.]

RTU Level System

Level	Behavioral Criteria	Housing	Medication
Level I	All inmates entering the RTU do so at this level. Assessment, evaluation and initial RTU treatment plan developed during this time frame—generally 2–14 days. Inmates at this level are generally demonstrating symptoms of acute psychosis or other mental illness and may present a risk of harm to self or others, or an inability to control impulses with difficulty adjusting, socializing, or functioning without close supervision.	Single cells that are most visible and accessible to staff. (Cells nearest officer's station or staff office.) Generally located on the first floor near the officer's station and equipped as Crisis or "Safe cells"—stainless steel toilet and sink, no exposed fixtures, screened windows, etc.	Psych/MR nurse offers medications to inmates at their cell door. **Involuntary (forced) medication may be initiated at this level.** No self-carry medications.
Level II	Inmates unable to participate in total program due to limited impulse control and/or cognitive impairment; have some difficulty following verbal direction.	Single celled—generally on first floor if in cell block containing all 4 levels.	Med pass to cell door. No self-carry medications.
Level III	Inmates with the following characteristics: 1. Cooperative to the extent that simple concrete instructions are followed; 2. Able to comprehend and comply with unit rules with support; 3. Able to maintain acceptable standards of personal hygiene with support; 4. Able to tolerate low stress activities in small group situations.	May be single or double celled based on clinical condition. Cells may be located on upper tier.	Pill call line on unit. Decision regarding self-carry medications made on case by case basis by treatment team.
Level IV	Highest level of functioning on the unit. Capable of limited independent involvement in general population activities at first, transitioning to increased involvement. May be capable of being discharged to general population from this level.	Single or double celled based on institution and general population norm. Cells may be located on the upper tier.	Participate in institutional pill call. May have self-carry medications unless treatment team determines otherwise.

RTU Level System

Level	Meals	Out-of-Cell Time	Activities	Property/Recreation
Level I	Meals in cell through cuff/meal port.	One (1) hour per day. Cuffs may be placed on inmate when out of cell.	Most restricted due to clinical condition. Mental health staff assessment, evaluation, treatment team. Brief individual counseling as tolerated. Daily psychiatric assessment.	Property restricted. Recreation on unit as tolerated.
Level II	Meals served on pod/unit small groups.	Two (2) to six (6) hours per day. ULTIMATE AIM = NO CUFFS but if choice is cuffs when out of cell or remaining in cell, opt for out-of-cell time.	Free time. Activity therapy. Individual counseling. Weekly psychiatric assessment. Small group counseling sessions weekly.	Property may be restricted due to clinical condition. Recreation on unit and in RTU yard, if available.
Level III	Escorted to institutional dining hall.	Six (6) to eight (8) hours per day. NO CUFFS.	Free time. JOB on unit. Activity therapy. Group therapy, 1 hour, twice weekly (minimum). Bi-weekly psychiatric assessment.	Property as per institution policy. Escorted to institutional recreational facilities in small groups at specially scheduled (reserved) times.
Level IV	Unescorted to institutional dining hall.	Greater than or equal to general population out of cell time at the same institution.	Free time. JOB on or off unit. Activity therapy. Individual and group therapy. Monthly psychiatric assessment.	General population recreation and property privileges.

Appendix D

Dunn v. Voinovich
Consent Decree

[Author's Note: In reproducing the bulk of the Consent Decree in the case of Dunn v. Voinovich, *my objective is to make available to readers a legal document not otherwise readily available. As the principal author of the Decree that follows, I do not represent it to be either entirely original or some sort of model.*

Much of the Decree is original or the origins became buried in memory and have not yet surfaced. The Decree may be used as a model where similar issues arise, there is a climate supportive of an amicable resolution, and the PLRA, discussed in this work, does not prove to be an insurmountable obstacle. If the PLRA prevails but the partners seek to enter into such a similar agreement, but one enforceable only in state court, then the outline for resolution may be distilled from the Dunn *decree.*

As this is written, the Decree is about three years old; its major objectives have been realized; and the non-adversary environment that generated the Decree continues. Counsel for the parties, the Governor, Director Reginald Wilkinson of ODRC, and the numerous front-line players all deserve kudos for their accomplishments in this matter.

The terms of the Decree surely may be borrowed, but it will be difficult to emulate the spirit of cooperation which has generated its operational success to this point.]

IN THE UNITED STATES DISTRICT COURT
FOR THE SOUTHERN DISTRICT OF OHIO
WESTERN DIVISION

Juan Dunn, et al.,	:	
	:	
Plaintiffs,	:	Case No. C1-93-0166
	:	
	:	Judge Spiegel
	:	
vs.	:	Magistrate Judge Steinberg
	:	
George V. Voinovich, et al.	:	
Defendants	:	

CONSENT DECREE

I. INTRODUCTION

a) This is a class action brought under 42 U.S.C. §1983 seeking declaratory and injunctive relief.

b) The Plaintiff class challenges the constitutional adequacy of the delivery of mental health services to seriously mentally ill adult inmates in the actual physical custody and control of the Department of Rehabilitation and Correction ("DRC").

c) This Court has jurisdiction over this class action pursuant to 28 U.S.C. §§1331 and 1343(a)(3).

***

III. GENERAL PROVISIONS

a) The Consent Decree resolves all issues between Plaintiff class and the Defendants, including the Defendants dismissed in Section IIc of this Consent Decree, arising out of the claims for declaratory and injunctive relief set forth in Plaintiffs' amended complaint.

b) The terms of this Consent Decree shall be applicable to and binding upon the Plaintiff class and the Defendants in their official capacities, and their officers, agents, employees, assigns and successors.

c) By entering into this Consent Decree, the Defendants, including the Defendants dismissed in Section IIc of this Consent Decree, do not admit to any liability regarding the allegations asserted in this action. Moreover, this Consent Decree may not be used as evidence of liability in any other legal proceeding.

IV. SCOPE OF THE CONSENT DECREE

a) This Consent Decree applies to adult male inmates in Ohio who are in the actual physical custody and control of DRC [and] *** [a]dult women inmates in Ohio who are in the actual physical control of DRC. *** This Consent decree applies to all of the [existing] facilities as well as any new facilities which perform the same functions and which become operational and confine inmates during the life of this Consent Decree.

b) Mental health services as defined and described throughout this Consent Decree are those services which are to be provided to those inmates in the actual physical custody and control of DRC during the time that they may experience "serious mental illness" as defined in Section VIIIa, *infra*.

***

VII. POLICY AND OBJECTIVES OF THE CONSENT DECREE

a) This Consent Decree is intended to resolve the declaratory and injunctive claims of the Plaintiff class by providing for a comprehensive system of constitutionally mandated mental health care for those male and female inmates described in Section IV.

b) The objectives in providing such mandated mental health care are:

   i)   to reduce the disabling effects of serious mental illness and enhance the inmate's ability to function within the prison environment;

   ii) to reduce or, when possible, eliminate the needless extremes of human suffering caused by serious mental illness; and

   iii) to maximize the safety of the prison environment for staff, inmates, volunteers, visitors, and any other persons lawfully on prison premises.

c) Mandated mental health services shall be provided to inmates in the least restrictive available environment and by the least intrusive measures available consistent with the professional judgment of the appropriate mental health professionals and the security of the institution.

d) Mental health services shall be provided within the framework of a community mental health model. The allocation of mental health staff; the designation and allocation of various mental health services, including bed space devoted to psychiatric care; and, the staff space needed to support such services will initially be distributed, and subsequently adjusted, to allow for the most economical, efficient and appropriate delivery of mental health services.

e) Pursuant to the community mental health model described above, inmates with serious mental illness will be distributed relatively evenly throughout the DRC system as encompassed by this Consent Decree and in accordance with the professional judgment of the appropriate staff.

f) Inmates with serious mental illness shall not be barred from participation in available prison programs solely because of their illness. Reasonable accommodation shall be made as necessary to achieve this end.

g) Mandated mental health services shall be adjusted upward or downward as the prison population of Ohio may increase or decrease.

h) Counsel for Plaintiffs shall be afforded the opportunity to review and comment upon all matters in this Consent Decree which require either the development of policy and procedure or the implementation of matters specified herein. To that end, the Defendants agree to provide counsel with the appropriate material sufficiently in advance of the various target dates established here to allow for study and comment but in no event less than thirty days before a specific target date.

i) In the development of the various policies and procedures agreed upon herein, the Defendants agree to articulate objectives that are as precise as the subject allows and which are subsequently susceptible to empirical validation.

VIII. DEFINITIONS

a) *Serious Mental Illness:* Serious mental illness means a substantial disorder of thought or mood which significantly impairs judgment, behavior, or the capacity to recognize reality or cope with the ordinary demands of life within the prison environment and is manifested by substantial pain or disability. Serious mental illness requires a mental health diagnosis, prognosis and treatment, as appropriate, by mental health staff.

It is expressly understood that this definition does not include inmates who are substance abusers, substance dependent, including alcoholics and narcotic addicts, or persons convicted of any sex offense, who are not otherwise diagnosed as seriously mentally ill.

b) *Initial Mental Health Screening:* A part of the normal reception and classification process, utilizing standard forms and procedures and designed broadly to identify those incoming inmates who may need further evaluation which, in turn, may lead to mental health services.

c) *Mental Health Evaluation:* A clinical assessment by a qualified mental health professional performed on those inmates who are referred from the initial intake screening or by various processes and individuals at any time thereafter. An evaluation is a more intensive and detailed procedure than intake screening.

d) *Crisis Intervention Services:* Timely and adequate response to any mental health emergency with access to the full range of mental health services, including psychotropic medication, available within the prison system.

e) *Crisis Beds:* Beds that are available within the prison for short-term, aggressive mental health intervention designed to reduce the acute, presenting symptoms and stabilize the inmate prior to transfer to a more or less intensive care setting.

f) *Residential Treatment Unit ("RTU"):* A housing unit within the prison for inmates with mental illness who do not then need inpatient treatment but who do require the therapeutic milieu and the full range of services and variable security available in the RTU.

g) *Outpatient Mental Health Services:* The provision of appropriate mental health care and supportive services for those inmates with mental illness who are able to be housed and function in the general prison population.

h) *Inpatient Services:* Intensive, inpatient hospitalization during the period of an inmate's acute psychosis and designed to return the inmate to a less intensive treatment environment at the earliest, clinically appropriate time.

i) *Mental Health Professional:* Those persons who by virtue of their training and experience are qualified to provide mental health care within the provisions of the state's licensure laws.

j) *Control Unit:* A special housing area within a prison with inmates placed there for disciplinary or administrative reasons.

IX. INITIAL (INTAKE) MENTAL HEALTH SERVICES

a) All inmates entering the Ohio DRC shall be the recipients of mental health screening upon admission to the prison system and within the shortest possible time. Absent an emergency which may dictate acting sooner, twenty-four (24) hours after admission shall be considered the norm for completion of such screening.

b) Such screening shall be performed by a staff member trained in screening and may include correctional officers, nurses, and mental health professionals.

c) Mental health screening shall be accomplished by the use of a standardized form which shall be completed for all inmates who enter the prison system.

d) The screening process shall maintain a low threshold for follow-up evaluation and should include review of pertinent records which accompany the inmate as well as questions designed to identify prior mental health treatment; suicidal tendencies; the signs of serious mental illness, including unusual, observable behavior; and severe thought disorganization.

e) Written policy and procedures shall provide for prompt referral for a mental health evaluation as appropriate.

f) The Defendants shall develop appropriate screening forms and procedures; conduct training for those who perform such screening; and develop criteria designed to achieve consistency in the evaluation of screening information and the occasions when mental health evaluations are appropriate.

X. MENTAL HEALTH EVALUATIONS

a) Mental health evaluations, or an appropriate alternative response, shall be provided in a timely fashion as dictated by the nature of the referral. In cases of emergency, provision shall be made for prompt evaluation upon receipt of the referral.

Referral may be made by:

i) staff involved in the initial mental health screening;

ii) security staff;

iii) mental health staff;

iv) self-referral; or

v) any other credible source.

b) The results of a mental health evaluation shall be recorded in writing and included as part of the mental health record.

c) Mental health evaluation or consultations shall be performed by appropriate mental health professionals.

XI. MENTAL HEALTH SERVICES ORIENTATION

Information regarding access to mental health care shall be incorporated as part of every inmate's initial reception and orientation to the DRC institutions encompassed by this Consent Decree. The basic objective of such orientation is to convey by the most effective oral and written means a description of the available mental health services and how an inmate may obtain access to such services.

The Defendants will develop and implement written policy and procedure concerning such orientation. Such policy and procedure also will encompass staff training, the utilization of written material and oral communications, and any other special issues of communication relating to any relevant disabilities possessed by inmates.

XII. SINGLE PROVIDER

Having decided that it is fiscally and administratively appropriate to do so, the Directors of DMH and DRC have decided that the care and treatment of seriously mentally ill persons encompassed by this Consent Decree shall be under the exclusive direction and control of the Ohio DRC. DRC will prepare and submit to the Ohio legislature proposed legislation to achieve implementation of such single provider system. DRC may enter into any arrangements it deems desirable on such matters as contracting for services encompassed by this Consent Decree; reconfiguring administrative positions; agreeing to the adoption of standards for mental health services and subsequent monitoring by another state agency or agencies, such monitoring to be in addition to the outside monitoring specifically provided for herein at Section XXVIII, *infra*; or any other matters related to the services encompassed by this Consent Decree.

XIII. ADDITIONAL MENTAL HEALTH STAFF

a) In order to provide constitutionally mandated mental health services, and subject to the terms and conditions which follow, the Defendants agree to hire and place in service such additional mental health staff as is required to reach a total of 246.5 FTE mental health staff based on a total DRC prison population of 40,253 inmates.

These positions shall be allocated solely to the provision of the mental health services mandated by this Consent Decree.

b) In addition to the 9.35 FTE psychiatrists presently employed by DRC and DMH providing mental health services to the seriously mentally ill, the Defendants agree to hire an additional 16.15 FTE psychiatrists as part of the overall total for new mental health positions. The remaining number of mental health professionals and activity therapists shall be hired and placed in service in such proportion as is dictated by the professional judgment of the appropriate DRC officials and subject to review by the monitor.

The Defendants agree to be guided by the staffing proposals offered in the "Final Report"[1] of August 1995 and by the "Policy and Objectives" set out in Section VII of this Consent Decree. However, it is imperative that the Defendants be able to maintain flexibility on the details of the allocation of staff at the outset of compliance and thereafter in light of the inevitability of changing circumstances.

c) The Defendants hereby undertake to hire and place the agreed upon mental health staff no later than three (3) years from the date of entry of this Consent Decree. The Defendants agree also that within six (6) months of the entry of this Consent Decree they will specify in writing annual targets for the hiring and placement of said staff, with such targets submitted to the monitor and Plaintiffs' counsel for initial review. Thereafter, the Defendants will submit quarterly reports on such hiring and placement as it relates to the achievement of the yearly targets.

The monitor shall review the Defendants' efforts to hire and place the agreed upon staff. And where a target may not have been met, the monitor will review the reasons therefor and work with the parties on techniques by which to achieve the annual and overall three (3) year targets.

In the event that the Defendants have acted in good faith to achieve compliance with said staffing targets but have not achieved a target, then after notice to counsel for Plaintiffs, any necessary time extensions shall be negotiated by the parties after notice to the monitor.

All such extensions shall require the written agreement of counsel for Plaintiffs.

The above provision is in addition to any mechanisms for dispute resolution as set out in Section XXIX, *infra*.

---

[1] The "Final Report" is the report of the expert team agreed to by the parties and which served as the basis for this Decree.

XIV. BED/TREATMENT SPACE FOR SERIOUSLY MENTALLY ILL INMATES

a) The Defendants agree to provide not less than 120 inpatient hospital beds for male inmates and 11 inpatient hospital beds for female inmates based on an overall prison population of 40,253 inmates.

b) The Defendants agree to provide 710 residential beds in addition to the above hospital beds, to be allocated among crisis beds and RTUs in accordance with the "Policy and Objectives" described in Section VII herein, and the study described, *infra* at c.

c) In order to determine precisely what bed space for mental health services is available, may be available through renovation, or made available through new construction, the Defendants hereby agree to undertake a study of these issues and report thereon to the monitor and Plaintiffs' counsel on or before September 30, 1995.

This detailed study will be conducted by a multi-disciplinary team appointed by the Director of DRC or his designee and shall include persons with expertise in mental health and security. Plaintffs' counsel will be invited to provide input into this study.

The study shall address the following issues and such other relevant issues as the multi-disciplinary team deems appropriate:

i)   the residential space required for crisis beds and RTUs.

ii) the space required for individual and group activities, dayrooms, programs related to mental health treatment, and the required office space and equipment needed for staff.

iii) the distribution, and timing thereof, of such space following the principles set out in Section VII, "Policy and Objectives" herein, and the general approach recommended by the Expert Team in their "Final Report."

iv) a detailed plan on precisely where such space is or may be located and whether such space may be available by renovation, construction, modular units, or in any other fashion.

v)   a detailed plan which addresses target dates for the implementation of all bed/treatment space which is the subject of the agreement and study referred to in this paragraph.

XV. ADJUSTMENTS TO MENTAL HEALTH STAFFING AND SPACE ALLOCATED TO MENTAL HEALTH SERVICES

a) Where specific agreements have been reached herein concerning additional staffing and bed/treatment space, the parties have utilized 40,253 as the base figure for the overall inmate population. The parties agree that wherever the Defendants have agreed to conduct studies and where prison population forms a basis for such studies, then the same number of inmates—40,253—shall be utilized as the base figure.

b) The parties agree that the number of staff, including mental health professionals, and the bed/treatment space devoted to mental health services for the seriously mentally ill, as encompassed by Sections XIII and XIV herein, shall be increased proportionately with certain increases in the inmate population and may be decreased proportionately on the same basis.

c) Within six (6) months of the entry of this Consent Decree, the parties shall agree on a precise formula by which to operationalize the above noted adjustments.

XVI. MEDICATION

The Defendants shall establish procedures for the administration of medications which achieve the following objectives:

i)   the timely administration or taking of the medication by the inmates;

ii) the regular charting of the efficacy of such medication;

iii) availability of sufficient and proper staff;

iv) blood tests are medically prescribed and blood samples taken in a timely fashion;

v) the timely performance of lab work; and

vi) inmates for whom psychotropic drugs as prescribed are provided with appropriate education and information about such drugs.

XVII. FORCED MEDICATION

The Defendants shall adopt a policy and procedure on the use of involuntary, psychotropic medication.

Said policy, and its implementing procedures, shall in all respects comply with *Washington v. Harper*, 494 U.S. 210 (1990), and within that constitutional framework:

i)   assure that any such forced medication shall occur only within the context of an ongoing treatment regimen and in a treatment setting (defined as a hospital, RTU, or an infirmary with "crisis beds" for the seriously mentally ill.);

ii) the medical record shall demonstrate the consideration and rejection of less intrusive alternatives along with the rationale for resorting to forced medication;

iii) include strict time limits on any judicial or administrative order permitting such forced medication; and

iv) in deciding to utilize forced medication it must be documented in the record that the gains anticipated from the medication outweigh any possible side effects.

XVIII. HOUSING ASSIGNMENTS

Cell assignments for seriously mentally ill inmates shall be based on the recommendations of the inmate's mental health treatment team unless appropriate security staff view such recommended housing as a serious threat to security.

In such a case, the security staff representative shall state in writing the factual basis for his or her opinion. The issue shall then be resolved by an interdisciplinary review team which includes both mental health and custody staff. When such review fails to resolve any such disagreement then final review of the decision shall be undertaken by the warden or the warden's designee and a decision rendered in writing within twenty-four (24) hours of the filing of the security staff report noted above.

XIX. SUICIDE PREVENTION

a) The Defendants shall develop a written policy, defined procedures, and a program for identifying and responding to suicidal inmates. The program components shall include: identification, training, assessment, monitoring, housing, referral, communication, intervention, notification, reporting, and review.

b) The overall objectives of such policy and procedures shall be to minimize the risk of inmate suicides and to minimize the harm when suicide attempts occur. This will be accomplished through the dissemination of information, techniques, and procedures which will aid in the identification of potential suicides.

XX. PHYSICAL RESTRAINTS

a) The Defendants shall develop a written policy and procedure on the use of physical restraints in dealing with the seriously mentally ill which shall encompass a definition for immobilizing restraints procedures for utilization thereof, including duration; who may authorize; required record keeping; criteria and procedure for release; areas authorized for use of such restraints; frequency of use; and staff responsibilities.

b) The written policy and procedure shall include as principles:

    i) physical restraints shall never be used for the purpose of punishment;

    ii) medical approval and monitoring shall be required;

    iii) detailed records shall be maintained.

XXI. CONTROL UNITS

a) Inmates with serious mental illness should not be placed in a control unit solely because of their illness unless there is no other setting immediately available and then only for the shortest period of time consistent with the need to protect the inmate from himself or herself, to protect others, or to prevent the destruction of property.

b) Inmates with serious mental illness may be placed in a control setting when such an inmate has been the subject of a Rules Infraction Board ("RIB") proceeding or found to be within the rules governing administrative and control status and placement (see Ohio Administrative Code, §5120-9-08, Disciplinary Control; §5120-9-11, Security Control; §5120-9-13, Administrative Control; and §5120-9-131, Local Control).

c) Regular on site mental health rounds shall be provide to all inmates in control units.

    Policy and procedure for such mental health rounds shall be developed and, inter alia, shall identify (by profession) the mental health professionals who will provide the rounds; distinguish the function of rounds and treatment; the frequency of such rounds; and provide detailed reference to the emergency-type placement described in Section XXIa.

d) The hearing officer shall indicate whether or not an inmate charged with an RIB infraction currently is on a mental health caseload. This shall be done simply by checking a box on the appropriate form indicating *"currently on a mental health caseload."*

e) When an inmate who may be seriously mentally ill is the subject of an RIB proceeding, then the RIB chairman shall consult with the inmate's mental health treatment provider on the inmate's mental competency to proceed, and, in addition, must take the inmate's mental condition at the time of the infraction into account in determining the appropriate sanction.

f) The RIB chairman shall note in the inmate's disciplinary record any mental health consultation of the sort described in Section XXIe, noting the date, the time, and name of the mental health provider. The mental health provider will enter a summary of the content of such consultation in the inmate's mental health file, including the date, the time, name of the RIB chairman and the opinion expressed concerning the competency to proceed and the relationship, if any, between the inmate's mental condition and the conduct leading to the present charge or charges.

XXII. MEDICAL RECORDS

    The Defendants agree to undertake a study of the feasibility of a computer system using desktop computers for centralized storage and access to inmates' health records. Any system of medical records, whether computerized or manual, shall move in the direction of standardized forms and a standardized chart order.

    Said study shall also address the issue of the appropriate content of a medical record file. This study shall be completed by December 31, 1995 and implemented in accordance with stated target dates.

XXIII. CONFIDENTIALITY

a) DRC shall develop a policy on confidentiality which promotes the exchange of records and mental health information between persons providing mental health services to inmates encompassed by this Consent Decree.

b) Mental health personnel shall be required to report to correctional personnel when an inmate is identified as:

i)   suicidal;

ii) homicidal;

iii) presenting a reasonably clear danger of injury to self or to others;

iv) presenting a reasonably clear risk of escape or the creation of internal disorder or riot;

v)   receiving psychotropic medication;

vi) requiring movement to a special unit for observation, evaluation, or treatment of acute episodes; or

vii) requiring transfer to a treatment facility outside the prison.

Such information when disclosed to correctional personnel shall be used only in furtherance of the security of the institution or the treatment of the inmate and shall not otherwise be disclosed.

c) Mental health professionals who have a treatment/counseling relationship with the inmate shall disclose the following to that inmate before proceeding: the professional's position and agency; the purpose of the meeting or interaction; and the uses to which information must or may be put. The mental health professional shall indicate a willingness to explain the potential risks associated with the inmate's disclosures.

XXIV. MENTAL HEALTH CLASSIFICATION POLICY

The existing DRC classification policy shall be modified to include standardized criteria and nomenclature by which to clarify the treatment and program needs of seriously mentally ill inmates. Such modification shall be made in the form of a modification of the appropriate regulations or policy and procedure governing this area.

XXV. DISCHARGE FROM CASELOAD

No inmate shall be discharged from active caseload status solely because of any failure to comply with treatment. Inmates shall not be punished for noncompliance by removing them from the caseload. Inmates who remain in custody and are discharged from the active caseload shall be reassessed between seventy (70) to one hundred (100) days after discharge in order to determine whether any follow-up care is required. A written reassessment shall be entered into the inmate's mental health record.

The Defendants shall develop policy and procedure on discharge and implementation thereof.

XXVI. STAFF TRAINING

a) All correctional officers and mental health services personnel shall receiving training and continuing education in programs regarding the recognition of mental and emotional disorders. Correctional officers whose assignment includes initial mental health screening or regular interaction with seriously mentally ill inmates, including but not limited to an RTU, shall receive more intensive training than other correctional officers. This training shall incorporate, but need not be limited to, the following areas:

i)   the recognition of signs and symptoms of mental and emotional disorders most frequently found in the inmate population;

ii) the recognition of signs of chemical dependency and the symptoms of narcotic and alcohol withdrawal;

iii) the recognition of adverse reactions to psychotropic medication;

iv) the recognition of signs of developmental disability, particularly mental retardation;

v)   types of potential mental health emergencies, and how to approach inmates to intervene in these crises;

vi)   identification and referral of medical problems of inmates receiving mental health care;

vii)   suicide prevention; and

viii) the appropriate channels for the immediate referral of an inmate to mental health services for further evaluation, and the procedures governing such referrals.

b) There shall be a written plan developed by DRC for the orientation, continuing education, and training of all mental health services staff. In-service training shall include regular individual supervision of staff and continuing education for part-time staff.

c) Within six (6) months of the entry of this Consent Decree, and in collaboration with the monitor, the Defendants shall develop, then implement, mechanisms by which to assess the effectiveness of staff training.

All staff training programs shall include a statement of objectives which, in turn, will serve as the criteria by which to assess the effectiveness of the training for each individual.

The parties recognize that there is no single preferred method by which to assess the effectiveness of training and that various methods may well be utilized to achieve the overall desired outcome of knowing whether or not specified training makes a difference in the trainee's knowledge base and job performance.

XXVII. TRANSFER OF SERIOUSLY MENTALLY ILL INMATES FROM PRISON-TO-PRISON

When a seriously mentally ill inmate who is receiving regular mental health services is to be transferred from one prison to another, then the sending institution, using the most expeditious means available, shall notify the receiving institution of such pending transfer. The Defendants agree to develop and implement policy and procedure designed to assure that the appropriate health records at the sending institution shall accompany the inmate so transferred in order to inform the mental health staff of the transferee's current mental health diagnosis, treatment plan, medication needs, and any other similar matters to assure the prompt and continuous delivery of mental health care.

XXVIII. MONITORING

a) Professor Fred Cohen, L.L.B., L.L.M., of the School of Criminal Justice, The University at Albany, Albany, New York, is hereby appointed as overall monitor of the provisions of this Consent Decree.

Professor Cohen may retain such appropriate staff, with the approval of the Defendants, including clinical and administrative experts, as is necessary to conduct the requisite monitoring. The Defendants agree to pay for all agreed upon costs associated with such monitoring.

The monitor agrees to submit to counsel for both parties the curriculum vitae of any proposed clinical and administrative experts and to seek their advice and consultation prior to their retention. The names and tasks proposed for the initial team of experts will be distributed prior to the actual entry of this Consent Decree.

Should the Defendants during the life of this Consent Decree deny to the monitor any request of his relating either to the budget or staff required for the monitoring, the Defendants shall notify the Plaintiffs' counsel in writing of such denial and provide a brief explanation of the reason for the denial.

b) The monitor and any experts or other staff, full- or part-time, who are retained hereunder in connection with the monitoring function shall contract for their services directly with the DRC and shall in all relevant respects be governing by existing DRC rules and regulations regarding such employment; and especially relating to compensation and expenses.

c) The general principles for such monitoring include:

i)   the reporting and on-site aspects of the monitoring shall be more intensive at the outset and likely decrease as compliance is achieved.

ii) monitoring shall consist of a combination of empirical data, written reports from the Defendants, on-site inspections, oral and written reports from the monitor, and appropriate consultation in aid of compliance;

iii) the monitor's role shall include the gathering of appropriate data and statistics and on-site inspections as well as the general duty of assuring that required policy and procedure are prepared in a timely fashion and meet the objectives of this Consent Decree; and where disputes between the parties occur or where there appears to be noncompliance, the monitor shall attempt to resolve such matters in the most expeditious and nonadversarial fashion as possible; and

iv) minimizing interference with the mission of DRC, or any other state agency involved, while at the same time having timely and complete access to all relevant files, reports, memoranda, or other relevant documents within the control of the Defendants or subject to access by the Defendants; having unobstructed access during announced and unannounced on-site tours and inspections to the institutions encompassed by this Consent Decree as well as any administrative offices; having unobstructed access to staff and inmates and other persons having information relevant to the implementation of this Consent Decree; and having the authority to engage in private conversation with any party hereto and their counsel.

d) A review of records by the monitor or his staff shall not constitute a waiver of DRC's or DMH's quality assurance privilege. Moreover, any such disclosures shall not constitute a waiver or serve as precedent for other legal proceedings with respect to the aforementioned quality assurance privilege. In addition, the monitor and his staff agree to keep said documentation confidential and not to disclose, publish or use for public consumption any of the records reviewed by the monitor or his staff.

e) In addition to the quality assurance privileges described above, other records or information whose disclosure is objected to by either party based on a claim of privilege, confidentiality, or relevance to the implementation of this Consent Decree shall not be disclosed by the monitor. Such material shall be made available for inspection by the Court, along with a precise statement of the objection or objections to disclosure prepared by the objecting party, and the Court shall render a decision on the matter.

f) Within three (3) months of the adoption of the policy and procedures referenced throughout this Consent Decree, the monitor shall prepare report forms for use by the institutions and central office which shall be submitted to counsel for the Plaintiffs and the Defendants for their prior approval before being put into use. Such report forms will require the submission of specified data relevant to this Consent Decree for evaluation by the monitor. DRC shall prepare the reports quarterly during the first two years of this Consent Decree, and twice a year thereafter, unless the monitor determines that the interim goals have not been met. The monitor will specify the precise dates for all such submissions on, or before, the approval of the forms described in this specific paragraph.

g) In addition to the quarterly and then biannual summary reports described above, the monitor shall submit an annual comprehensive report on overall compliance to the Court and the parties noted above.

h) In the event that Professor Fred Cohen is unable or unwilling to serve as the monitor, the parties agree to appoint another monitor.

i) The monitor shall not be subject to dismissal except upon good cause and the agreement of both parties or by the Court upon motion of one of the parties and a showing of good cause.

j) Monitoring shall continue for five (5) years following the entry of this Consent Decree unless sooner terminated on motion to the Court by the Defendants, with the concurrence of the monitor, that compliance has been achieved earlier.

XXIX. DISPUTE RESOLUTION

a) In the event a dispute arises as to whether Defendants have failed to substantially comply with the terms of this Consent Decree, counsel for the parties shall proceed as follows:

i) Counsel for the parties shall make a good faith effort to resolve any difference which may arise between them over matters of compliance utilizing the monitor initially in an effort to resolve such dispute. Prior to the initiation of any proceeding before the Court to enforce the provisions of this Consent Decree, Plaintiffs' counsel shall notify Defendants' counsel in writing of any claim that Defendants are in violation of any provision of this Consent Decree.

ii) Within thirty (30) business days of the receipt of this notice, counsel for Plaintiffs and Defendants shall meet in an attempt to arrive at an amicable resolution of the claim. Either party may request the attendance and involvement of the monitor at such meeting. If, after twenty (20) business days following such meeting, the matter has not been resolved, Defendants' counsel and the monitor shall be so informed by Plaintiffs' counsel, in writing, and Plaintiffs may then have due recourse to the Court.

b) Any complaints by inmates objecting to any provisions encompassed by this Consent Decree shall be addressed through institutional grievance procedures under Ohio Administrative Code, §5120-9-31. Exhaustion of such institutional grievance procedures through appeal to the chief inspector shall be a condition precedent to any legal action by an inmate. During the pendency of this Consent Decree, copies of any such complaints resulting in decisions by the chief inspector and related documents shall be provided to Plaintiffs' counsel and the monitor on a quarterly basis.

c) No legal action seeking equitable relief relating to the issues resolved herein, including a motion to enforce the terms of this Consent Decree, shall be filed on behalf of the Plaintiff class or by a member of the Plaintiff class without first resorting to the dispute resolution mechanisms set out in this Consent Decree advising Defendants of the issue and making a good faith effort to resolve said issue extrajudicially.

d) If legal action is pursued, it shall be brought in the form of a motion to enforce any terms of this Consent Decree.

XXX. COMPLIANCE

The Defendants shall be deemed to be in compliance with the terms of this Consent Decree when they have substantially complied with it. Individual incidents of non-compliance do not necessarily prevent a finding of substantial compliance. The initial determination of substantial compliance by the monitor shall take into account the extent to which exceptions to substantial compliance are sporadic or isolated in nature, are unintentional, are the temporary result of actions by members of the Plaintiff class, and are addressed by corrective action.

XXXI. EMERGENCIES

It may be necessary to temporarily suspend a provision of this Consent Decree in the event of an emergency. An emergency is an event which makes compliance with the terms of this Consent Decree impracticable, impossible or extraordinarily difficult, and is caused by riot, fire, weather events, natural disasters, warfare, strikes, labor disputes, or other similar events, not caused intentionally by the Defendants.

Counsel for Plaintiffs shall be notified of any such emergencies as soon as practicable.

XXXII. MODIFICATION

The parties recognize that the change of some conditions or practices may reduce the necessity of change or other conditions or practices. The parties also recognize that the Defendants are entitled to substantial deference in the decision on how to improve mental health services. Therefore, the parties agree that it may be appropriate that this Consent Decree be modified from time to time. After six (6) months of operation under this Consent Decree, the Defendants may ask the monitor to review a proposed modification to any portion of this Consent Decree.

The monitor will submit a written opinion on such proposal to both parties which will bind the parties should they agree and the Court is of the view that the modification will allow the constitutional rights of the class to remain protected.

Where either party disagrees with the opinion of the monitor and not sooner than thirty (30) days after the written expression of such disagreement to the monitor and the monitor's efforts to have the parties reach an accord, then appropriate relief may be sought from the Court in the form of a motion for modification.

XXXIII. CONTINUING COURT JURISDICTION OVER THE CONSENT DECREE

The principal action here is dismissed with prejudice because the underlying claims for declaratory and injunctive relief have been resolved by the parties.

The Court, however, retains jurisdiction over this Consent Decree for the purpose of its enforcement. The period of retention of jurisdiction is five (5) years following the entry of this Consent Decree unless sooner terminated by motion to the Court by the Defendants, with the concurrence of the monitor, that compliance with the terms of the Consent Decree has been achieved. No action shall be taken on a termination motion until notice and an opportunity to be heard has been extended to the Plaintiffs. If legal action is pursued to enforce the terms of this Consent Decree, it shall be brought in the form of a motion to reopen the case.

Table of Cases

[References are to paragraph numbers.]

Index

[References are to paragraph numbers or to Appendix page numbers.]

vs. resistance to treatment,
9.6[1]
in right to treatment claims, 7.1
suicide risk, 14.6[3]
Protection from harm
failure to provide, 4.3[5][b],
14.3[1]
mentally retarded inmates, 16.2
of staff/others, forcible medication
for pretrial detainees,
9.5[2]
suicide liability and, 14.3[1]
treatment severity and, 9.3[2]
Psychiatric care. *See* Medical care,
psychological
Psychiatrists
duty to warn identifiable third
party, 9.2[1]
part-time, 7.2[1]
qualified, 7.2[5][c]
records, ambiguous directives in,
10.2[1]
Psychological testing, 4.3[5]
pretrial detainee, 15.2[4]
transfers for, 17.3[4]
unavailable, 15.1[2]
Psychologists
duty to warn identifiable third
party, 9.2[1]
professional evasion by, 14.4[4]
Psychosis, administrative segregation,
7.2[1]
Psychosurgery, experimental, 9.4
Psychotherapists
child abuse reporting, 9.1[1]
defined, 9.1[3]
divided loyalties, 9.1[1]
duty to warn identifiable third
party, 9.2[1]
therapist-patient privilege rule,
2.15[1]
See also Privilege
Psychotic symptoms, as serious medical
need, 4.5[1]
Psychotropic medication, 7.2[1]
antipsychotic. *See* Antipsychotic
drugs
discontinuance, 7.4[3]

injection
forcible administration of, 9.4
over inmate's objection, 9.3[1],
9.3[2]
religious objection to, 9.4
situational coercion and, 9.3[1]
against will, 9.4
noncompliance, 9.2
side effects, 9.3[2]
succinylchloride (Anectine), inmate
refusal of, 9.4
Public entity
defined, 1.4
duty to warn of probabilities for
harm, 9.2[2]
Puerto Rico classification system,
constitutionally deficient, 5.3[4]
Punishment, 4.3
cruel and unusual, 2.1[2], 14.2[2]
aversive stimuli, 9.4
drug-induced vomiting, 9.4
failure to provide alcoholism
treatment, 8.2[2]
failure to treat alcoholic,
8.2[2]
ignoring request for medical
treatment, 4.3[6]
inmate rights, 15.1[1]
objective severity, 3.5[2]
overcrowding and, 8.4[3]
for uncontrollable conduct,
13.2
inadequate measures, 7.3[1]
interaction with treatment, 11.3
lack of fairness, 13.2[1]
of person incable of understanding
charge, 13.2
solitary confinement. *See*
Isolation

R
Reasonable accommodation
difficulties, 13.1
Ohio approach, 13.3[1]
at work, 13.3
Reasonable care duty, warning
identifiable third party, 9.2[1]
Reasonableness test, 3.3[1]